JESUS
in the
BEDROOM

The Message of the Christ's Wife

Andrea Barberi
Divine Source Wisdom

BALBOA.
PRESS

A DIVISION OF HAY HOUSE

King James Version, dozens if not hundreds; New International Version, twice; and
The Gideons, once, and a lot of online free sources that I cite in here

Balboa Press books may be ordered through booksellers or by contacting:

Balboa Press
A Division of Hay House
1663 Liberty Drive
Bloomington, IN 47403
www.balboapress.com
1 (877) 407-4847

ISBN: 978-1-9822-1123-3 (sc)
ISBN: 978-1-9822-1124-0 (e)

Library of Congress Control Number: 2018910355

Print information available on the last page.

Balboa Press rev. date: 08/29/2018

Contents

Forward ix

Preface xi

Introduction: Andrea's Atonement Reached, April 2014.................................. xiii

Chapter 1:   We Are Jezibellie's Cure for AIDS Related Viruses Like Schizophrenias 1

Chapter 2:   Delilah's a Tramp! Not Jezibellie Christ! In Other Words, Come Forth,
My Wife to Be Here! 4

Chapter 3:   A Beautiful Picture of Jesus Christ 8

Chapter 4:   Santa is the Man of the Hour Here! Santa's Right-Hand Man is Us and
Jesus Christ's Love! 12

Chapter 5:   Little Devil Girl is Jezibellie Christ Then! I Loved Her So, Jesus Says! 19

Chapter 6:   Paul is a Limelight No More 22

Chapter 7:   Sleeping in My Van! Jezibellie Christ is Really Something to Behold! 29

Chapter 8:   Jezibellie's Cure for Cancers of the Mind 35

Chapter 9:   Give Me a Razor, Or Give Me Death! 41

Chapter 10: Jezibellie! Is That a Rock on Your Hand Though? Yes! From Jesus Christ
Thereof! 49

Chapter 11: Diabetes, Here We Come! Cure This Once and for All! 53

Chapter 12: HSV – The Cure for All Here 61

Chapter 13: Love Stinks! Yea, Yea! 81

Chapter 14: The Cure For AIDS/HIV Is Here for All Too 85

Chapter 15: Gun Laws! Outlaw Them Then. The Good Guys Don't Have Any
Rights to Them Anymore! 99

Chapter 16: The Holy Ghost! Do You Have It Yet, Humanity's Sakes Alive Here! 107

Chapter 17: Drugs! Why Me, She Says Here! Ouch! Don't Do That, Jezibellie 😊 113

Chapter 18: ED! What Are You and How Did You Get Here? 122

Chapter 19: Masturbation! Are You There with Me, Lovely? 😊 133

Chapter 20: My Tongue is on Fire Here! Holy Spirit/Ghost, How Come You No
Talk to Me, Say It Man (Satan)! 137

Chapter 21: Animals are People Too! 141

Chapter 22: Hachimycin/Trichomycin! We Need You Back in the United States! 145

Chapter 23: Jesus as King and Lord Our Savior 151

Chapter 24: NASA – The Final Frontier: Jesus Died on the Cross is a Hoax 158

Chapter 25: You Can Heal Your Life by Louise Hay is It! 167

Chapter 26: Money. Do We Have Enough of It? 172

Chapter 27: Just When You Think It's Cozy Outside Here! 175

Chapter 28: I Think the DSW is Really Cool Though! Alzheimer's Patients! Got it. 179

Chapter 29: Masquerade Around Me Then! Homeboys! 189

Chapter 30: Homelessness 204

Chapter 31: Sentimentality in Jesus Christ's Reckoning of Loving Jezibellie ☺ 240

Chapter 32: Bipolar is a Hoax Too! Jezibellie Christ Had It, Right, for Hearing "Us"? 251

Chapter 33: I'm Counting on You, Andrea, To Tell the Gospel to the Churches of
Wrath Here 265

Chapter 34: Hathor Is a Bony Structure Too, We Love Jezibellie Christ's Legacy Too! 274

Chapter 35: M.S. is Multiple Sclerosisly Related to Eating Factors and Riboflavins 297

Chapter 36: I Love the DSW to Show Me the Way Here! 303

Chapter 37: I Love the Divine Source Wisdom! 321

Chapter 38: The Booby Hatch is Closed This Year and Next! 326

References 343

Appendix 1: Our Sanctified Promises Rule! Justice, Be Served Here! 349

Appendix 2: Worst Case Scenario! An LRA No More Here! 353

Appendix 3: A Time for Justice to Be Served 359

Appendix 4: NASA's Space Station, Elite Button Please! 361

For Josh. Love, DSW

Forward

This excerpt from the clan of guidance counselors of the Divine Source Wisdom is like Abraham Hicks in a way of finding God's talents, and of Edgar Cayce, rich with the mechanisms of knowing how to find hot love in medical research! This only title of our time here is in essence supposed to figure out how to relay the information of a lifetime of sentence structures in order to relay the information according to plan here. This book is about Jesus Christ's wife, and, nudely though, she's plentiful and sweet! This woman married the King of England first! I married Jezibellie soon after, He says! He's there for the taking in the book here. This is war though if Jezibellie Christ cannot become what she said she was, and that is the book writer here for the Bible intact here! This lessons planning becomes what it said!

That is, what is the Jezibellie Christ's ways and means it lady supposed to do in this situation here, but that life is but a dream? Is Jezibellie Christ still married to the King of England then? Because that's what the strongholds of life teeming about itself here is left to state that obviously, she's Mine, He said!

This is Jezibellie Christ then. Correctamundo here? Nope, this is a book about My wife, Jezibellie Christ then! She does not say anything, not a word in this here text. It's all Me, Jesus Christ, and the Holy Spirit, Ghost, and what nots here! And that said too here, there is a healing center that describes me well enough to know the Ghost in Holy Ghost is what the concepts are here. If you are filled with the Holy Spirit, then you know that the Holy Ghost is in charge here, and that your eyes may flittle and fluttle here and there! But the rest of the eyes, moving motions and "Us" involve getting your eyes in check here a little bit, Andrea! And, Andrea is the moment's notices that said, honestly, that it's time to tick tock the Holy Ghost's Spirit filled in essence writings here! This is the moment's notices that gets me all riled up, she says here of her talent search's best writings here!

Jezibellie is a Tutankhemen look alike? She's pretty here.

Preface

I love the Divine Source Wisdom, and ourselves intact, to have a conversation about peace and joy in this world! Right here, right now, there is no other place I want to be! As the song goes, too. So joyous are we to share the Divine Source Wisdom with other body entities that trust ourselves to do the same, for this is a chance for Andrea Wynn Barberi to reach the atonement! Simple as that. I'd like to comment on this if I could, she says! But truthfully, the following questions are her processes for getting to the atonement, in time and in essence spaced oneness with the DSW. And so, listen to us intently trying to gather her strength and her possibilities, in order to blasphemize the Bible in a sense of timing the DSW to tell you more about the universes that exist.

In time though, you will find, Andrea, that people glom onto this preface without any further adieu here. You are describing your processing the Divine Source Wisdom this way and that a way. Further, it's time to take a handle down to the bayous of bays and inlets later in this chapters of love way of getting Andrea to the best possible callings of our Lord and Savior, Jesus Christ, and His lovely wife, Jezibellie, also known as Jezebel in the Bible here. I do declare though a mistrial if you do not believe in the bedrooms of peace, as there is definitely a sex life we crave and that is no mystery here. This picture above is not of Tutankhamun, but of Jezibellie Christ. I look rather handsome, don't I? She's a dress up kind of sort of person here. She likes to dress up as a male though? There's no beard there. She's dressed up though, in full garb.

I do know this, DSW says! It's a heaven's gateing at the interludes of peace that gets Andrea to believe in the Savior, Jesus Christ, and that is the most honest way to put something so delicate as this. We are interested in none of it if she cannot be included in a way that juxtaposes the spirit's better half! And so that said, she is ready to conflict us in a way, by getting the knowledges out there. And furthermore, this is what we have to offer the Divine Source Wisdom is to get other people involved at the center of peace that we see happening here. So, without further adieu, we bid farewell to the talent searches of a lifetime of greed mongering! And so, here she is, Andrea Wynn Barberi, with a talent search's ways of finding the DSW to monitor our callings here. She is now speaking to us in her head's way of finding peace here. So, without further adieu, here she is now, trying to decipher that voice she now finds peace in hearing, and it is this one, the DSW for short! And so, without further adieu, here she is trying to piece together the heretic's way of saying this. As it is so! Without further adieu though! Get a life if you cannot believe that Jesus Christ had a sex life! It's with His wife only!

Introduction

Andrea's Atonement Reached, April 2014

Day 1: I Love the Divine Source Wisdom for Me

Me: After centering myself, thinking of attracting only goodness, lowering fear. Choosing truth. I now turn to the Divine Source Wisdom, ~ DSW for short!

Holy Spirit: Dear One,

My taking of my only begotten son is something I must have done in my one life for the existence of taking. It is every man's duty in essence and in faith to recognize not only truth but my spiritual liking of the freedom to choose my coexistence in suffering, the amazement in glory to us all. You are divinely protected at all times. I see in you the one life that makes us happy in times of triumph and reasons with other manifestations to know whether fear is taking place or taking love in knowledge.

Me: I talk to the Holy Spirit.

In me, your gifts of valor and wisdom shine to the utmost proper in words and in deeds. For all that is divine and lovely can be seen or written for the greatest good in all that seeks punishment for wrong deeds and takes hold of what we think is making us bitter. I'm ecstatic that my love for God in Christ is so timely and makes me tickled to rejoice in the Lord with you in all its wonder and glory.

Me: Thank you. Good night.

In light and love, Dear One.

Day 2: DSW Takes Over the Soul ~ DSW is Grand Indeed!

Me: I talk to the Holy Spirit. I'm still in disbelief about how the world looks now. I feel like I just found out the world is round when I thought it was flat. I'm still trying to embrace this new knowledge of truth.

Holy Spirit:

I'm sensing the knowledge that comes with only seeking blatant safety in feeling that vessel in Christ Jesus that is inherent knowing inside of you. I'm knowing that place of freedom from poets inside blessed captured divine right time. For in seeking this wondrous journey toward truth I sense pleasure in knowing my life means terrible suffering in undertaking my peaceful quotations. May I suggest you not get a lesson making this hard in undertaking the freedom in knowing Christ Jesus.

Me: I was directed today to learn the language of the divine. And so, I believe once I get that figured out, I will know who is talking. I'm figuring out this language and I hope I do figure it out. I'm excited to learn this language. I am being directed by you, the Holy Spirit, to the book I bought called <u>Ask Your Angels</u> by Alma Daniel, et al., (1992) for this knowledge but I want to finish <u>The Law of Attraction</u> by Esther and Jerry Hicks (2006) first. I wonder about being led in different directions. For example, not finishing one book before moving on to the next. I have so many books I want to read, including the Bible.

My purpose in knowing who Christ Jesus is as our Savior is one knowing truth of the divine. I'm taken aback beyond recognition for suffering to have this honor in taking this too wondrously divine. Knowing truth is knowing that wondrous beginnings have all places beneath presence in honoring the one true spirit in death from our Creator.

Me: Okay. I am going to try learning the language of the divine and I'm sure I am blown out of the water by it. I can't wait to try to talk to you again after learning the language. I'm a quick learner and I'm enthusiastic about learning how to fully connect with you on every level that I can. I know my next step is true surrender, even after having salvation. I'm looking forward to this very much. I'm going to look in the <u>Ask Your Angels</u> book by Alma Daniel, et al., and try to get some sleep.

My greatest honor in life is knowing who our Creator sent as his only begotten Son, taken from flesh to knowing the greatest undertaking in my presence.

Me: Goodnight and I hope to connect with you after I read the book and learn the language. I'm looking forward to it.

Day 3: Knowledge of the Divine Holy Spirit Rests in Love. And, Therefore, Kindness Exists!

Me: I talk to the Holy Spirit.

Dear One, I'm honored in writing the holy version of truth in abating what little concepts taken in Christ for atonement purposes, rendering peace and honesty in all things. Tabernacle is meaning in the depths beyond great freedom of sorrow in blasphemy.

Me: I know. I'm sorry I decided to sleep instead of go to church. I'm exhausted without coffee on Day 2.

Tempting to dishonor my word is blasphemy in bothersome knowledge of rightness in the Lord Christ Jesus.

Me: I love Jesus. He is our Savior. He is one with us.

Mostly demonic realm presences take hold in order to keep you struggling with fear in number, and in timeless journeying through other dimensions.

Me: I'm unafraid. I have Jesus.

Some talking in knowing is where life presides in heaven. For what is now preached can take holiness to new levels of divine knowing.

Me: Are you saying I am blasphemous? I am trying to change taking the Lord's name in vain.

Miracles keep surfacing in light of oneness between being and knowing. Your knowledge precedes timely essence in peace, knowing what is true salvation, and what tempts us in the Holy Spirit of being.

Me: Thank you. I am looking forward to it.

Day 4: Are You There, Loved Ones of the Divine Source Wisdom?

Me: I am reading "A Course in Miracles" (Available online previously, 1975). Which miracles am I to perform?

Taken is he who do not believeth in me to create nonexistent suffering from humanity and all sides of peace and knowing within him.

Me: I asked the previous question thinking I came up with a practical healing idea myself when really it was most obviously likely divinely guided.

It is calamity to see only one guided breath in taking the atonement as part of being that which is sacred and holy to all who seek him.

Me: I had no doubt I would heal. I am eager, ready and willing to work on the atonement part to be free of fear forever.

Day 5: The Divine Source Wisdom's Guidebook on Healing Ailments is Best Described as Such!

Andrea, nothing in this world can make light of the fact that you are going to be something greater than you ever had known to be expected. Some of the things I am telling you can only be understood in the passing of time, and something within you keeps wanting to bring forth that which cannot be named so to speak. So, in doing what is your life's calling, it is essential for you to hear what I have to say about where you are going with your life. Some of me thinks going in the direction of scarcity in knowingness makes me believe it is for the greater good that you know Jesus, in that there is no greater one love and zest for life than in Christ Jesus. Another part of me is like, wait, I am telling her what she already knows. I'm so happy that you sought me and that nothing in this world could ever harm you in the ways that you think it could. You deserve to go forward with passion and compassion, willingness and integrity because anything else would be forbidden in all that is awaiting you. I'm so happy to be here with you along your journey toward peace. I'm honored and blessed to call you my friend and what you have taken in terms of respect is so great, especially toward yourself. It's a blessing to be able to talk to you like this. In all that I am, I believe you are headed in the right direction. Keep going! So much good awaits you. In Jesus, we have eternal salvation, and the Lord is not selective in terms of spirit and tranquility. You are doing all the best that you can to live a life that is like the life of Christ and I commend you for that.

Me: I'm so grateful. Thank you.

Nothing in this world could harm you, Andrea. Go forward with your passions. Seek out like minded individuals. Keep the flow of life moving through you. No matter what happens you are always safe in Christ Jesus. Blessings to you.

Me: When I ask your name, I keep getting Mary Beth and Mary Jane.

That is because there are two of us here, one to guide you and one to bless your inner spirit. Take hold of what you have and go forward knowing you are safe in Christ Jesus. You are so full of life. Embarking on this journey is so exciting for us. Take hold and know we are here for you.

Me: Thank you.

You're welcome, My Dear.

Day 6: The Divine Source Wisdom is the Answer. You Seek It, Now You Don't!

Andrea, it is enlightening to me that you are so able to see the difference between that which is good and that which has no meaning other than through Christ. It's going to be unpleasant for a while but in the end, it is in your greatest good as you move forward. I'm taking this self-love seriously, and I love to see the knowingness inside of you that loves everything about who you are, one with being. Such is the plight of mental health care today, in that you have the power to change the way things operate through what you are knowingly supposed to do, and watch it manifest in so many ways. I'm thankful that you are going through this journey and we love to see the progress you've been making in so many ways. It is one with spirit that finds you so lovely in right order today. I'm sure you see this as being the ultimate truth in peril but, really, it's so lovely that you are doing the things you are doing and going forward in all that you do and are. We love seeing your progress and support you in any way we can. Andrea, it is so unreal that you have made such tremendous progress with your overall health and well-being. I'm so happy that you have become this person of wisdom and selflessness in overall being that you are. Life is so full of promise and whatever good comes to you, it is within divine time that it finds you. I am so thrilled to be inspiring you to greatness in whatever comes your way. It is so inspiring to see the progress you have made. I'm doing all I can to support you in any way I can.

Day 7: The Divine Source Wisdom Follows Me Everywhere That I Am Seeking to Go!

Me: Have you been with me all my life?

Yes, and I'm here to help you. Is there anything that you want me to do for you?

Me: Yes. Tell me if you are the comforting voice I have been hearing all day.

No, I'm not. I am the Holy Spirit.

Me: And who are you?

Magenta. Your guardian angel.

Me: Your name is Magenta?

Magenta is the spirit of being one with the Universe, one with God.

Me: Do you believe Jesus came in the flesh and died for our sins and arose three days later?

(Okay, not thinking this is going the way it ought to. But I do hear it talking to me.)

Trust me.

Me: I will try again later to get back that voice I hear…

Day 8: Back to the Divine Source Wisdom: Here Ye, Here Ye!

Me: Back to the voice I usually heard the last few days…

Andrea, you did so well with this. We are proud of you. Are you thinking that maybe there is a glimmer of hope for transpondency in what you're doing to interact with Jesus and his disciples? I was thinking perhaps nothing is best in taking what you know to be true and interacting with this demon (okie dokie!).

Me: I'm secure in that I know Jesus.

Do you think that what you're doing is calling out the dead or do you think us knowing eternal bliss is taking a new twist in knowing?

Me: Man, it's tough to sort all of you out, LOL. I love the sound of my wings flapping. I'll never forget that sound. It's the most beautiful thing I've ever heard. I cannot believe I am sitting here with absolutely no music playing in my head at all, and I don't hear that vicious voice. I am going to save this exercise in the Ask Your Angels book by Alma Daniel, et al. (1992), and move on to record more. I will come back and do this.

Day 9: Here Ye! It's Divine Source Wisdom at Its Best!

Me: I just did the Exercise 14 in Ask Your Angels by Alma Daniel, et al.

You have such persistence in you that no one is going to detract from that light within you. Keep going with your life's purpose. We are here to help guide you along your way. With that is your next question.

Me: You seem like the same angel who has been talking to me all day. Are you?

Of course, My Dear. We have so much in store for you and your future. Rest assured we are here to help you in that journey as you explore the heavens and write down its angelic utterances.

Me: Okay, I'm just making sure we're on the same page. You all sound alike. I focus only on the good. I'm so zipped up no one can touch me. I'm so excited to flap my angel wings. I just can't get over it. It's a familiar sound to me.

That's because they are one with you. You have always had them. From time to time we see other things coming along, but you know we are here to protect you and keep you from harm. Nothing is going to detract from the essence of who you become. We're excited to see you along your journey.

Me: Thank you so much.

You're welcome, My Dear.

Day 10: What Does the Divine Source Wisdom Do for Me?

Me: Are you there Mary Beth and Mary Jane?

We are here, and we are surprised to hear of the passing of time, in that most of what is in store for you has to do with love and kindness, being gentle and compassionate rather than irritated at some of life's injustices. Some of me thinks it's in order for you to hear us speak to you in a different way. Such as when we are in communion with Jesus and to hear Him speak is something to behold.

Me: I put down on a prayer card at church today that I surrender my life to Christ fully.

We saw that, and we think it's great that you know where your life is headed and what destiny calls you. Some of the time it's hard to move past the nothingness to enter into true oneness with being, and with Jesus. He is always there for you in all His splendor. He is delighted that you have seen more than most in terms of your life's progress and your journey into the unknown. For He is one with us and us with Him. He has never left you and we're proud and honored to consider you a part of the good that life has to bring forth in this world. Nothing could take you from Him in terms of trust and gratitude. He is one with life, one with being. He is our eternal salvation. Our one true knowing in Christ Jesus is the true and ultimate power to be and do anything in this life with us here with you. It is a knowing beyond comprehension, beyond context and time. He is our everlasting word, our one true marker in knowingness that is beyond all other capacities in being.

Me: I'm so grateful for having figured this out and for now being able to hear the Holy Spirit. I do hear the Holy Spirit, right?

We are certain of the oneness you have with our Creator. We are so excited for your journey. Keep going. This is what we are here for.

Me: Mary Beth and Mary Jane?

Yes, Honey, it is us, both of us. How true is the word that keeps us from valor in strife that we would think to even second guess the true power of greatness in our Lord and Savior. I'm so tickled to be assisting you in your journey. We are so grateful that you now see what we mean by salvation through our Lord and Savior.

Me: This is awesome. One by one I am getting closer and closer to fearless living.

Cherish these moments. And, this is the one life that precedes all that awaits you. Are you ready for trials and tribulations, tests of your will, strength in numbers, one with being? Can you see what impact you have already made on someone's life, and yet others who follow are equally inspired by your grace and serenity? Is it compassion you feel toward others with mental conditions, or is it truth seeking knowledge that drives you to your life's purpose?

Me: Wow. Goodness, I guess it's both. I would have to say both. Yes, both.

How lovely indeed, for we are solely responsible for your well-being and this is delightful news. Could it be any more wonderful than it already is? Is it wonderment or tragedy that inspires you to be all that you can in this lifetime?

Me: Oh, my goodness, these are awesome questions. Both, again! I can't help it. I could never articulate the "why" for mental health causes. It has to do with wanting to help, a burning desire to help, and a knowledge of truth to choose the good. Just choose the good. Choose the light, the truth, the beauty, the good. That is the key to mental health.

It is awesome how much you witness the majesty of goodness in others. So much so that you are willing to seek council from the higher power for guidance. And, truthfully, it is knowing Christ that makes everything as it should be.

Me: Yes, I was meaning to say this, just as my pastor did this past Sunday in his sermon. I really appreciated that. It was a gift.

Nothing is going to stand in your way, Andrea. And we are so proud to help you on this journey toward peace, resilience and honesty in this lifetime. It is truly remarkable how much you have found it to be true, that we are excited to partake in any and all forms of mention of you to our Savior.

Me: Wow!

For we are one with Him in Divine time. It follows that, really, nothing could ever be so drastic in knowing Christ Jesus the way it is written in scripture. Something tells me that I am going to enjoy working with you on so many projects to become who you were meant to be. I am honored to know your intuitive nature and rejoice in celebrating the life of Christ with you.

Me: Me too. I never knew.

Yes, it is lovely and sacred space we hold in the life of Christ. For that is one thing that stands in the way of Christ's message is the fear that is instilled in so many people that it becomes quite a predicament to try to save all people from their sins and what continues to ail them. So lovely is the star shining brightly off in the heavens that seeks oneness with the divine in all its glory. He is truly the one we all seek to behold in our sights, and take with us when we are lonely or frightened. He is the one that lives in us all. We couldn't be prouder of you for recognizing this universal truth.

Me: Thank you. I'd better get to bed. I'm getting closer and closer every day.

We are looking out for your best interests, and, really, you could not do any more than you already are, not only to heal but to inspire others. We want you to take with you this message tonight. Keep going. You are soon to be awakened to more that awaits you. Continue on your path, and it will reward you greatly in guidance and wisdom. Good night, Lovely. God bless your efforts. We really appreciate the oneness you now feel with the divine and in Christ Jesus. Happy blessings coming your way.

Day 11: The Divine Source Wisdom Meets the Eye of God's Wrath!

Me: Are you there Mary Beth?

Absolutely, My Dear.

Me: Do you believe that Jesus came down in the flesh and died for our sins and arose three days later? And that He is our Savior?

I'm thoroughly convinced you are something to take into this world as divine knowing and presence.

Me: Do you believe Jesus came down in the flesh and died for our sins, arising three days later? Guardian angel, are you there?

I am.

Me: Did Jesus die for our sins?

Something tells me you think I am one with the divine.

Me: Did Jesus die for our sins?

(Silence.)

Me: Who in here believes Jesus came down in the flesh and died for our sins, arising three days later?

I do.

Me: And your name is?

Master Caine.

Me: Funny, who are you?

I am the voice of times risen from grace to sorrow. In that offering, I suggest making light of all oneness that is before you.

Me: Where is that comforting voice at?

Right here. I am something of a microcosm of specialness, in that I see before me a great adventure into the unknown. It is something to behold and in reality, it truly means nothing is sacred where we are headed.

Me: Well, I heal this in totality. That I know. Nothing is going to convince me otherwise.

Likewise, My Dear. In true closure, we seek knowledge that is truthful, and knowing this is what we call oneness with the divine.

Me: Why won't anyone tell me they believe Jesus died for our sins, to arise three days later? Why won't you say you believe this, as a comforting voice?

It is great peril to believe all that we are saying is not truthful in divine time. You are mistaken if it is supposed to include gratitude beyond the nothing we have saved you from.

Me: Who in here believes Jesus came down in the flesh and died for our sins?

(Silence.)

Me: I only talk to my guardian angel and the divine.

Spirituality is truly beyond the scope of what we are saying here.

Me: That's it. I'm done, I am trying something else, a new document. Are you there?

Yes, we are. Something is keeping us from talking to you, in that we believe it is divine presence that interferes with some of the teachings that we now believe to be true. It is knowingness in its entirety that truly seeks punishment.

Day 12: The Divine Source Wisdom Seeks It!

What we suggest or recommend is that you seek out true friendships in Jesus and the angels that surround you right now. True oneness with the divine is something we all trust is in our best interests, and truly takes us to higher places of knowing that which we call intuitive oneness with Jesus and His disciples.

Me: I am ready to work on that tomorrow, working toward true surrender to Jesus. I'm ready to talk about seeking out true friendships in Jesus and the angels that surround me right now. True oneness with the divine is something I seek and I do trust it is in my best interest for higher places of knowing with intuitive oneness with Jesus and His disciples. Thank you for this opportunity to point me in this direction.

One thing we would caution you about is taking for granted what we say as truth. It's not taken literally in terms of raising what we know is honorable and noteworthy, for being in true oneness with the spirit is knowledge beyond comprehension.

Me: That is what I seek.

You need to find that one person who knows what we mean by taking light of the conversation, and simply taking what we say out of context in terms of truth and validity of simplicities and knowingness. Once you find that truth within your heart, it will become easier to sort out all the complicated nothings in great awareness of true oneness of the divine.

Me: I so very look forward to that. I am ready and willing to get there. Take me there and show me how to get there. I'd better go to bed. I will leave the how up to my subconscious and God.

In oneness with Jesus, My Love, in light, and knowing that which we call heavenly bless beyond comprehension. It is true oneness with all there is. Goodnight my love and God bless your spirit for all its candor and glory and magnificence.

Me: And God bless you!

Day 13: Ask the Divine Source Wisdom to Seek You Too, As Well As God's Angels Intact!

Me: I am now looking at the comforting and loving pictures of Jesus. I love the archangels exercises in the book <u>Ask Your Angels</u> by Alma Daniel, et al., as well as the Divine Source Wisdom's talent seeking here.

Teacher, compassion, true oneness with the divine. Loving, captivating, teacher, lover of humanity, great spiritual one who knows our perils and loves us anyway. Sudden was His death and trials and tribulations He had to face. For He is the greatest one love we could ever know. True oneness in body, mind and spirit, is all He teaches us, and all we need for our destiny and salvation. Heed those who look beyond mere images of Him to cast out demons within us that may need rebuking. True comfort comes in knowing Jesus in all His splendor and righteousness. He truly is our Savior, the one who lives in all of us, who forgives us our sins, and forgives our trespasses. He truly is our heart's message in wanting closeness with our Creator. True oneness, Andrea, forgiveness of our sins and our trespasses. One true love within that goes beyond mere coincidences, to loving oneness with being.

Me: I'm so relieved to hear all these things. I am so happy to have printed off these images of Jesus.

You know what your life's purpose and destiny are, Andrea. True oneness in spirit is what we seek to give you in this journey. Are you ready for what we have to offer you in terms of flowing freely with the circumstances of life?

Me: Yes, I heal, and I write about how I did it so others can be inspired to do the same. A Bible verse about Moses leading people out of bondage is of the same verses I kept getting.

Teacher, spiritual guidance counselor, divine source of strength and integrity, vast abundance of oneness in true divinity, that is Jesus in totality.

Me: I change the face of mental health care.

Yes, we know your life's purpose, Andrea, is to seek guidance from above. Not only is this in your best interests, but truly this oneness with the divine spirit is critical for your success in achieving what you seek in this life. We're so proud to call you one of us, and the angels rejoice in really knowing that which becomes valid for us in true knowing of who we are and what we are here to do, what is set out for us in terms of your goals and aspirations.

Day 14: The Divine Source Wisdom Speaks It! Again, We Might Add!

Me: I took down the picture of Jesus that did not have compassion in his eyes from the book by Todd Burpo called <u>Heaven Is for Real</u> (2010). I printed some pictures which are more comforting than that one. (See Chapter 32 for more of this discussion about that picture. It is the King of England, not Jesus Christ!)

Truly the words of encouragement and wisdom precede knowing that which is Christ Jesus in true knowing form. Some of the lessons we have put forth for you are truly, in essence, great obstacles in all of life's calamities and true oneness with the divine spirit we call the Holy Ghost. Blessings to you for seeing how those particular occurrences shape us into who we are meant to become. I'm honored in knowing your true valor in spirit and oneness in all that there is to rejoice in this life. My spirit goes out to those who have forsaken Jesus in His triumphs of knowing true wisdom beyond comparison. For it is so lovely that you are in tune with what you know to be true and your true nature in spirit and wisdom. Nothing is going to take that away from you, Andrea. Nothing is purely evil and, really, there is true oneness with God through Christ Jesus and the Holy Spirit.

Me: I did see Jesus's rays through my hands at church.

Blessings in Heaven for rejoicing in the Lord, Andrea. I'm here to guide you through this part of your journey.

Me: Holy Spirit, are you there?

Yes.

Me: Do you believe Jesus came down in the flesh to die for our sins to arise three days later?

Yes, I do completely. Nothing you are saying is out of balance at all. True oneness with the divine spirit, the Holy Ghost, pales in comparison to true oneness with all there is.

Me: Don't you have that backwards?

Andrea, you know what circumstances lie ahead of you. Nothing is going to change the way I feel about your journey and oneness with the divine and all that there is. Are you aware that it is impossible to feel lonely and scared if you have Jesus in your life?

Me: Yes, I am. I am ready to leave the fear and doubt behind. I have the golden receiver for my telephone conversation with my angels, as shown in Exercise 18 of <u>Ask Your Angels</u> by Alma Daniel, et al. (1992), and that is cool indeed.

The messages we are giving you are certainly divine in nature, and, really, there is so much work to be done here, in that you are destined to become one with God and His glory and greatness. So much precedes this conversation and, really, you are quite content knowing that all there is to know comes from the Divine Source, from God. And truly, your nature shows us very much so that you are one with Jesus and the Holy Spirit. Rest assured there is work to be done and certainly it is quite possible you have other agendas. That is just pure knowing that you want to become someone other than that which you are. It pains me to see how much you want this true knowing to come to you in divine time. We're here to guide you on your journey, and truly it is most magnificent in time and structure to know the oneness with the divine, with Jesus and His archangels. I'm happy to report a change in you to greatness and love. It pleases me that you are now seeing what I am talking about.

Day 15: The Divine Source Wisdom Is Happy About This!

Me: I take a nice, deep breath and release all resistance to healing, a Louse Hay quote! I know it by heart.

You know we only have what ails us in terms of solitude and compatibility of true kindness in this world. Ego precedes all fear. And so, with that in mind, it is imperative that you understand how one tiny little thing can change the way things play out forever. Take hold, Andrea, and believe in miracles, in things greater than yourself. This is the atonement. Believe and you shall receive. Do you understand this concept at all?

Me: I've been working on it. Healing, then the miracle of atonement happens, right?

True divine structure and principles rest on the atonement. Once you get that, that is when true miracles happen, and also healing for the greater good. Keep in mind, this is a test of your strength and your will. If this is what precedes all that lies before us, no wonder it is so vast in perspective and true in its emptiness. Can you not see the abundance of joy in your future? Is it something you are not willing to look at, or is it just a microcosm of something greater in which to come?

Me: Okay. I have come so far in other areas in my life. I am looking forward to reaching the atonement, the forgiveness of sins, and I have come so far in dealing with the things that keep holding me back in life.

Life to me is one of the greatest gifts we could ever ask for. It is the gift of knowing true oneness in spirit and in health so that others may see our greatness in terms of what we have to offer the world, and where we are to go from here. It is so honorable to see how you are really coming from a place of true wonderment in dealing with that which you do not yet know, and in faith in all there is. And, ultimately, there are some things that need to be addressed, and you will find that it fulfills your destiny as a writer and a believer in Christ to know that whatever ails you in this life can be fixed by atonement. And, truthfully, it's rather exciting for us to see you carrying on this great adventure within yourself. It is perplexing the amount of study that is involved in true knowing and oneness with the divine, with Christ.

Day 16: Divine Source Wisdom Speaks It Again and Again and Again!

Andrea, all that lies ahead is true knowing and oneness with Jesus. Every day that passes is a reminder that, in all things great, there are a couple of things you must work through first before you can come to a place of knowing within yourself, that which we call grace and glory beyond comparison. We think it's good that you are so candid with your speaking in knowing how to interact with the divine. We think it's in your best interests to become one of the angels who takes people to places they have never seen before. It's really something to see the sight of the Lord. It is beyond behaving in an inappropriate manner to see all that there is to know in terms of oneness with the divine. Something tells us that you are holding back because of fear that you will be found out later in life, that you will have repercussions for becoming a Christian in the truest sense, that later in life there is someone who wants to seek revenge on you, and so you are afraid mostly to take what that knowingness means, and give it all the complexity that life has to offer in terms of gratitude and faith. It is our duty to see that that never happens to you, and that in knowing Christ, it all becomes possible to see and feel all there is to know in becoming more Christlike. You are such a perfectly infinite being in Jesus, and it is so awesome how you have discovered your true path in knowing Him. Something that needs to be addressed, is your willingness to conceive of the words we are telling you as true, or whether you think this couldn't possibly have anything to do with my true destiny.

Me: Yes, I have a fear of being duped.

What else are you afraid of?

Me: Being wrong. I'm not sure what else.

You know, in Christ Jesus there is no such thing as wrong in terms of what we mean by togetherness in perspective and oneness in Christ, that we maintain a sense of obligation to come from a place of fearlessness. Taking hold and believing in something greater than yourself is ultimately the true oneness of God in all His glory, to come from a place of true oneness that you seek. Why could it be any more knowing of you to seek oneness with our Creator? True knowing is what we all have in store for us. It is our destiny to think we have nothing to offer the world in terms of righteousness and compassion for others. But rest assured, in knowing Christ Jesus for all He represents, it is truly a believable perspective and good for your well-being and healing to know Christ is on your side. Christ believes in you.

He believes in your healing. Who better to have on your side, and to believe in what you are doing than to have Christ Jesus on your side? Is it a terrible thing to want something that is greater than yourself, to take the reigns and have you sit back for a while and simply rejoice in what life is telling you the direction in which to go in?

Me: I must want to have a sense of control over my destiny. I might be able to seek my pastor's council at some point, but I am going to keep this "angels" thing to myself. You are absolutely right that I still believe someone is going to seek revenge on me later down the road. That is the crux of why I keep holding back. I'm grateful to you for your guidance. I hope to get past this one thing that is holding me back.

Andrea, there must be an area of truth within you that is keeping you stuck in terms of becoming one with all there is. I hate to see you not rejoice in the word of God simply because you think there is something to take from it in terms of righteousness and valor. Are you ready to rejoice in all there is to believe in, in terms of what you are destined to do in life in all its glory? Is this something you're willing to work on getting past, or are you destined to be stuck there forever?

Me: Yes, I'm willing and I know I will get past it. It's just a matter of when, and I have no control over the buffer of time. I do want to get past it and I do want to turn my life over to Christ. It is just a matter of when and how. What is that area of truth in me that is keeping me stuck? No, I don't think I am destined to stay stuck there forever!

You are really coming to terms with being an imposter in terms of knowing the truth as it stands and knowing that which is righteous and valid.

Me: What do you mean?

Is it faith that tests your strengths, or is it the oneness in glory and truth that keeps you stuck in old patterns? Does this mean there is an area of truth within you that keeps you taking from the vast nothingness that the universe has to offer you in terms of validity? Or is it the destiny that lies before us that keeps you stuck? Are you willing to go forth without judgment and believe in something greater than yourself to take over and keep you in a place of knowing that really means true destiny that lies before us?

Me: Again, I am willing, so willing, to let someone else take the reigns. I am done with all the fear and the doubt, and I witness death of the ego. I hope to gain fearless living. I want to be unafraid to go forward in this world and know that there are no repercussions that are to follow. I am willing to do this. Please take me there. Please help me to see the truth.

Again, nothing you are saying makes it valid for us to continue talking to you if you are not taking steps to orient yourself with the oneness that you seek. It's quite tragic if we have to stop talking to you but nothing you are saying makes us want to continue if you are not willing to go wholeheartedly in soul and essence and oneness into that which we know is true, and that which we perceive as true, simply because you are destined for greatness. I'm not saying this, Andrea, to hurt your feelings but, really, we are in line with the divine right order and really this is something you need to come to terms with.

Me: So, you are leaving?

Are you ready for the challenges that face you in terms of knowing the divine and all there is to offer you?

Me: Yes, I am.

Take hold and it will be done. Nothing you seek has any meaning in divine order, but true oneness comes from being prepared to give it all up at a moment's notice. Is this something you are willing to do in terms of your safety and well-being?

Me: Do you mean that I have it wrong if I give my life to Christ, and in doing so, I will be spared any revenge from others? Is this what you mean?

Yes. We are candid in telling you what lies ahead but really this is ultimately your decision. You are going to see how differently things are when you finally decide to do this. You will see how this oneness is something that cannot be taken from you. You are the true and ultimate creator of your own destiny. And so, if there is something out there that is keeping you from attaining true love and safety with our Creator, then really there is nothing we can do to save you in terms of knowing that with God, all things are possible. We cannot guide you any longer if you are not willing to release this stronghold on your life that you are creating within yourself, and take hold of what Jesus has to offer you in terms of spirit and oneness. Are you ready to do this with us? No time like the present.

Me: I am! I am ready, yes. I'm willing. Tell me how. I will sit here and ask for your guidance.

Truthfully, we are going to have to cut communication with you until you are fully ready. And so, we bid you adieu and take what we have to offer you in terms of trust and tranquility to new levels, when you fully turn your life over to Christ.

Me: I thought that I had Jesus since that day in communion when I ate the bread and saw the rays coming out of my fingertips. I was afraid to go any further in this communication and I never expected I would have to give up hearing from you, but so be it. If it has to be that way, I understand!

I'm happy to know that you have moved beyond the presence of form to new levels within yourself. I am sorry it has to be this way but, really, we have done all we can do at this point.

Me: Okay, if I figure out how to do this. Actually, I am willing to turn my life over to Christ, and so I leave the how and when up to my subconscious and God. I'm grateful we interacted tonight and I fought through my tiredness to converse with you and to tell me what I already knew but could not articulate. Thank you for that. I wish I knew how to do this.

Knowing that which you seek is going to be true valor in spirit and oneness with all there is, Andrea. It takes hold and there is no going back after you reach that point of no return.

Me: I so look forward to it. I'd better sit and meditate on it. I do appreciate the time we had to discuss this and I am grateful for your council. I just know I heal in totality. I know Jesus believes that I do it too. He helps me do it. That I am certain.

Take care and God bless you for trying. We really have to go now.

Me: I don't want you to go, but I accept it.

Thank you and God bless you.

(Later…)

Me: Is anyone there?

(Silence.)

Me: Is there anyone there?

Yes.

Me: Who are you?

Jesus.

Me: I suddenly feel unworthy.

What is it you want to do and what do you want to accomplish?

Me: I want to heal my mind from trauma. I want to write about how I did it so others can be inspired to do the same. I want to change mental health care to a healing approach. I want to write about how I did it step by step, so it is like a workshop. I don't feel worthy talking to you.

Take hold my child.

Me: This is God talking, right?

Yes, my child!

Me: (I am crying.) I am not worthy of you.

Take my loin cloth. Dry your tears.

Me: But I'm not a prostitute. Though I have sinned. I stayed away from you because that picture was so creepy. (Bowing at His feet.) I'm sorry. I'm so sorry.

There, there.

Day 17: The Atonement

True oneness with the process of life. This is the atonement. Andrea, you have captivated us in your true oneness with the divine spirit. In essence, this is the atonement for which you have been seeking. For now, comes all the light and glory that is laid out before you.

Me: I am so surprised to have been in the presence of our Lord and Savior, and for His forgiveness.

This is true oneness with which you had sought. It is the knowing in Christ Jesus that moves us and builds us up for higher purpose in glory and splendor. You are going to feel exuberant in nature and in Heaven, for this is what we have been trying to tell you that you needed to do in order to fulfill your life's purpose.

Me: I am so relieved.

Glory, in essence, is what you needed to figure out how to become one with the divine spirit, and that which we call Jesus our Lord and Savior. It is true oneness in the divine spirit that cleanses us and washes away our sins. It is divine right time that you became the one we have sought after to build our empire and fortress forever in eternity. You are the one who builds it. You become the leader in this clan of true oneness with all there is. It is your destiny to build it. You become the leader in this clan of true oneness with all there is. It is your destiny to build it. It is to be built by you. The one you seek to atone for is not the one who gave you this position. It is, in essence, the valor and spite that the one you seek to forgive is holding against you. For, in essence, this is the one who gave you to Christ Jesus in that He is the one who gave you to us and the one with which you atone for.

Me: I atone for?

Yes. It is true oneness in Christ that we find you have found a true knowing in the essence of all there is, and, frankly, we couldn't be more overjoyed at this. I trust you find this to be true in your dealings with all people, places and things. You are the one true life that lives in everyone, and, God willing, this is what your presence has done for the nature of this Earth. True knowing is that in life we seek to atone for, and this is the best opportunity for you to do it. Nothing becomes true in the spirit of fear, of ugliness, of wrath. It is with true knowing of our Savior that one has the forgiveness we all seek.

Me: I am excited to keep reading "A Course in Miracles" now that I have reached the atonement.

Yes. It is exciting for us to know that you have found true happiness and oneness with our Lord and Savior. This is no small thing. This is the lovely tidings of the forgetful and the joyous nature of the wonderment of God Himself, for that is all we have come here to do in this life is to atone for our sins and to be one with God who created us.

Me: Thank you so much. I have such a clear perspective now. I am eager to continue.

We know you can do this, Andrea. You were meant to become someone of a great leader in your strife, in that everything you do is for Christ Jesus, and it is for the betterment of the planet. It is in your best interests to become one with all there is in order to do this. You must go out and seek like-minded individuals to help you in your journey.

Me: But where?

We can help you with that when the time comes.

Me: I am giddy at this. I feel renewed and refreshed. I have a new sense of purpose. I am excited for this adventure.

Jesus is sitting there giving a lecture to the Sermon on the Mount.

Andrea, there is one thing you must not do, and that is question us about the sanctity of tidings about others who came before you. In essence, this is the atonement of sins and becoming one with us and with nature, and with glory in all its splendor is truthfully something which precedes all that is to come from here.

Me: I'm not sure my questions are correct or appropriate. But I am willing to do whatever it takes to heal. I want to change mental health care for the better. So, according to "A Course in Miracles," first there is the miracle, then the atonement, and then the healing comes after that. I've already done so much healing as it is. Now the true healing begins. Is this correct?

It is safe to say, that this is what we thought you would get from that course in that this is why I told you not to be anxious about becoming this great leader in the community, because you are already destined for much more than that. And so, with that said, I'm sure this is coming to you quite late in life but really this is true oneness in all there is to see and do in this world. This is what the main purpose of this planet is about is to become one with the divine. This is what true happiness and atonement means. This is the oneness with which you sought so highly after. I'm saying this because all that lies before you is going to precede the great tyranny of this nation, and truthfully the baggage claim is not in order for you to pick up yet.

Me: Okay, if I am to have any respect for myself it means I'd better get to bed now. Thank you so much and I am looking forward to this journey a great deal. Thank you so much, goodnight!

Bless us our Lord for these thy gifts, which we are about to receive, through thy bounty, through Christ our Lord, Amen!

Me: Amen!

Day 18: The Atonement Rests! Now It Is Forgiveness of Sins!

Me: By atonement or forgiveness, I do mean I surrendered my life to Christ. I like the idea of being baptized. Easter is coming.

Andrea, this is really the only time we can tell you this in terms of what is coming for you in regards to special oneness with Christ Jesus. It is our assessment that it is true oneness with all there is that you have not yet achieved. And so, really, the only thing we can do is hope that you reach that within yourself in terms of what lies ahead and what life has to offer you. What we did do is petition to the Lord what you are to do next in this life. And, that answer came back to us as something that which only lies in the knowing of Christ in His entirety. What that means is…

Me: Study my Bible?

Well, that is to be expected. What we are referring to is your true inner guidance system, the one you have forsaken, in that all that there is to learn about life is through Jesus. And, really, that is the only way you are going to reach the atonement that you seek.

Me: Okay. So, the atonement comes after the surrender.

Yes, it does. Truly this is one facet of the puzzle that continues to haunt your inner spirit, and, truthfully, this is the oneness in essence that takes you to new levels within yourself. And so, we are going to try to help you with this in terms of forgiving yourself of sins, but also the one true love you have in store for you. When I say this, I mean the inner spirit within yourself that keeps you from experiencing life to its fullest. What do we mean by this? Well, it is only in Christ that you come to see how easy it is to become tormented in your thinking, in that it means the other side has reached you in a way that tatters your thinking in terms of true guidance. And so, really, this is something that needs to be addressed before you may proceed to new levels of awareness within yourself.

Me: I totally believe that to be the case. I knew my interaction with Jesus did not mean anything other than what it did. And so, this is really the…

Leadership…

Me: Yes, the healing of the mind so to speak, so that it never thinks that way again. I love the verse I have on my wall. This is significant in healing my mind from traumatic experiences, and thus, there is still work to be done, obviously. I am doing it, though.

One thing we want to show you has to do with the one true love in which we find in the spirit, and that is in terms of destiny and atonement, and all there is to know about the atonement.

Me: Yes, how Jesus died on the cross for our sins.

Yes, that is what we mean by this. I could see it if you were going to forgive all there is to be forgiven in terms of justice, but that follows that everyone has committed sin, and that is beyond what we are trying to show you here.

Me: I already knew that was my next step was to study how Jesus died for our sins, and what that means to all of us, and to fully know that.

It means you are going to find true oneness with the atonement when it seeks you, and, ultimately, that is what we mean by washing away of sins. True oneness means knowing that which comes to you in divine spirit and oneness with all there is. I'm pleased to know that you seek the atonement and, really, that is what we are hoping to find in you, that you are going to be forgiven for all the things that plague you.

Me: You mean, I could not be forgiven? That seems to not be right.

Well, this is the ultimate test in terms of what you are about to see, in terms of your wellness and knowing that which is through Christ Jesus. And, ultimately, this is the true forgiveness of sins, and that is in knowing Christ died on the cross for our sins, and to know that He is the one for which you seek forgiveness.

Me: I see. Yes, that would follow. I'm willing to make that journey. Where do I start? I know I could read my Bible too and I plan on it. Who could I ask to help me? Or, do I want to ask. Is atonement forgiveness of sins or for crimes? What is the difference?

Ultimately, knowing Christ in all His glory means you will seek His guidance wherever you are. And so, really, this is true oneness in my book, and we couldn't be more enthusiastic in that receiving of this gift. One thing you must do is take what we are saying and go with your instincts. What is the one Savior blessing that has happened to you in this life?

Me: I was born?

Ultimately, that is the challenge for which we seek our greatest knowing in Christ, and that is true oneness with all there is in terms of this challenge. But, ultimately, what do you hope to accomplish in this life with our guidance?

Me: I do want to understand fully how Jesus died for our sins and know it in its entirety. I also want to heal my mind from trauma, write about how I do it and then inspire others to do the same to heal themselves. I do seek His forgiveness.

Basically, that is what we are here to help you do. I am so honored to have been given this detriment of knowing what is coming for you, but, ultimately, this is how it is supposed to play out. And so, really, true knowing is in Christ Jesus. And, ultimately, this is your continuing hope is to keep us in your spirit and, ultimately, become one with Christ as we know Him to be. Are you ready for this journey of oneness?

Me: Yes, I am.

Good. Then in the morning we shall bless you with our tidings and, ultimately, this is your challenge for tonight is to find peace within yourself about where you are headed and, ultimately, what this means for you.

Me: Thank you. I will try. I hope for peace within myself about where this is headed. I will work on that.

Day 19: Atonement: Best Bet is to Die on the Cross? No Way, José!

One thing we want to caution you about is taking the text of scriptures and providing the utmost glory in all its greatness to the one who resides deep within us, that can be cast out by spiritual awareness. Some of the time it is utmost proper to regain that sense of dignity through constant acknowledgement and seeking in Christ Jesus. We cannot tell you how all knowing this sense of duty within you is, to teach others how to fly in terms of great glory of God, and one facet of life being taken from us in terms of knowing that which we became in the eyes of Jesus. It is one with all things that prevents us from going and leading falsehoods, in that we are by God's definition one and the same with Him.

Me: Yes, I got that when I was at communion.

It is up to you whether you want to pursue this gesture of fine graceful acts of God, in terms of knowing that which we know to be true and that which we prevent from knowing simply by ease of construct and dignity in the loin cloth.

Me: My next project is to cast out the negative words in my head.

Take hold, Andrea, for there is much more to be done in this life than simply going through the motions that others have imposed on you to do. And so, really, this is the one true life we lead. And, ultimately, it's your decision to become that which we have set out for you to be or to become, that which others want you to be.

Me: And that includes the negative inner voices and thoughts?

Precisely.

Me: I'd better go. Thank you, until later tonight.

Yes, Dear One Lovely. God bless you and ultimately grace you with the true knowing of who He is and what He is about. Our Lord and Savior is rejoicing in your triumphs and knows that all you need is provided for.

Me: Thank you, again, and God bless you too.

Thank you, Dear One. Goodbye for now.

Day 20: Atonement Settles the Mind

Me: After some tears, this is what I understand so far. Jesus had no sin, but I do!

Andrea, this is one moment in time that we are going to say that we are so very proud of you for trying to figure this out and doing it all on your own.

Me: Thank you so much.

Day 21: Atonement is the One True Flair for Life's Promises, With the DSW!

We are going to tell you that you have to believe that this is true with all your heart. What we mean by this, is that this is one way to reach the atonement you have sought after, but it is also the way of everlasting life that we are telling you lies with Jesus Himself. Because this is such a big deal, it means you must first know how to maintain the presence of our Lord and Savior with all that you are. And so, really, this means it is going to become increasingly difficult to maintain that sense of trust within yourself about the atonement, because it means we are just one with all there is in life. But also, that we are going to seek guidance and council from above about what to do in certain situations. And so, really, this means we are going to have to guide you in terms of your structure that we are allowed to give you. So, tell us this. Have you sought to forgive yourself of your wrongdoings? Have you even found a knowing sense that this is what we are getting at in terms of forgiveness? We are saying that true forgiveness comes when we forgive ourselves for wrongdoings. And so, truthfully, this is what we mean by atonement, in that life brings us what we need to fulfill this purpose. It's really what we are after in terms of strength and vitality and everlasting life. And so, what is it that you need to do in order to forgive yourself in terms of oneness, and all there is to offer you in this world?

Me: I realized reading this I am afraid of dying and having not lived. I want to live to the fullest before the death of my physical body. If I could be assured I would live to the fullest, I could believe I have everlasting life with Jesus. Part of the atonement is forgiving ourselves. So, how do I forgive myself? It has to do with what Jesus did. He saw our human nature because He came down in human form Himself. I forgive myself of wrongdoings.

Yes, this is what we mean by knowing versus attributing to something other than yourself. And so, true forgiveness lies in knowing that which we have told you, and, also, knowing that which is coming or lies ahead of us and that we are safe in the one true Lord and Savior Jesus Christ. And so, truthfully, we are going to have to go now, to let you soak this in, and we look forward to talking with you further about this later.

Me: I am excited about self-forgiveness. I just realized I am mad at this separation from God. So, forgiveness would help. Also, forgiving myself means Jesus forgives me too, because God is one with us.

Andrea, this is the one life we all get to take with us in the atonement. And so, for you to figure this out is immeasurable in scope because it means we are just as good as the next person when it comes to the atonement. For you to see this is something of a miracle, in that God gave us to you for this reason. And so, we are still here for you on your journey, but something tells us you are not ready to let go of us yet.

Me: No, I'm not.

We are going to be leaving with the atonement, but all is well. As in, this is when you die, we become one. That is true surrender by our definition. And so, truthfully, you will not need us any longer once you do this for yourself and for humanity. We are taking with us the key element in you, and that is to take what we have said and go spread the gospel, for we are plenty in abundance with all there is.

Me: Is this the Holy Spirit? Or, does that come after the atonement?

Something like that, Honey. We are proud of you for seeking us and for knowing that which we have told you is true. And so, for once we are going to bid you adieu. And so, know that God loves all of you, even the part you cannot forgive. And so, really, this is the biggest blessing there is of all, knowing Christ Jesus for what He has done for us, what He did for our sins when He died on the cross. That is true atonement. That is true oneness with all there is. One of the greatest gifts is knowing Christ Jesus in His entirety.

Me: I'm so very grateful for this. With your help, I can win both battles of evil and those of disparity in my words. Thank you, Jesus Christ, for this invention in my head.

Yes, my child. It is wonderful that you are in wonderment of Christ and all He has to give to this world. For now, we must go and say to you farewell. But please know that all there is to know in this world is right here in front of us. All we need is given to us. We are one with the divine spirit, and that which we call Christ Jesus who died for us our sins so that we may have everlasting life.

Me: It is just in time for Easter! I have so much gratitude. Thank you!

Yes, and for now, we must part.

Me: You have been so kind. Please know how much I appreciate it.

God bless you, child of God, for now we say goodbye. Rest assured you have all the things in store for you that you ask for in prayer. Thank you and God bless you. Goodnight, Dear One, and may God bless you with all He has to offer and all there is to know in this world. Goodbye, Sweet One.

Me: Goodbye, and God bless you too.

Day 22: Atonement is Hard Work

Me: Mary Beth, are you there? I heard a voice that said, yes. Was that you?

Sure, it was, but we are the Divine Source Wisdom speaks it.

Me: Are you one or two?

We are two, you and us.

Me: I cannot believe this has happened in such a short time. The interference of others in my head is still there but in lesser form as time goes on, which is fueled by the ego. And, once we reach a point of no return through total presence, that is what is meant by being truly aware, truly conscious, and truly present.

We think you will be pleased at the progress you have been making. Now comes the true surrender. Take hold, Dear One. The best is yet to come. You can have all you want if you just become one with Christ Jesus. Surrender to Him, Our Lord, for that is who you have atonement with. We think this is somewhat of a challenge for you. And so, really, this is the ultimate test of will and strength.

Day 23: I Am Resisting the Change I need to Move On, Gracefully So

Me: I am resisting it. I am aware of it though. I am fully conscious of the presence of the ego. I am moving beyond it to a state of total awareness now though.

Hold on, My Dear Child. This is one moment in time that precedes all else. We are going to give you to God and take hold, for this is the one true life we have with Him. All else that lies before you, precedes this moment in time.

Me: It precedes it? This moment of time is special indeed.

Day 24: Resistance is Futile

It takes you to new levels of awareness within yourself. Take hold and we will guide you there. Trust us entirely. Take us to new levels of awareness within yourself. Be one with us. Have us in your comfort. Take our word to mean it is the one with God, and all that seek to know Him shall have everlasting life.

Me: There is oneness with all there is. I can't wait to take hold and to participate.

Double time fastness is in store for you. Take hold and see all there is to see in wonderment of Christ Jesus, and the true One Life we call God. Take hold and see it now.

Day 25: Atonement is Good for the Soul

Me: I am going to church tomorrow and I am stalling in this forgiveness. I saw huge long rays coming out of my fingertips the other day in church, while resting in the pew after communion. Really though, I created in my mind from trauma a prayer, and created neural pathways that repaired it already through prayer interventions.

All these things we are trying to show you here have to do with the atonement. And so, what we have in store for you is something of a miracle, in that it becomes true for all humanity. And so, what we are saying in effect here is that all that lies past this point of no return is true happiness beyond measure.

Me: I am still resisting this. I can certainly point this out to others, but when it comes to myself, it is a different story altogether.

Bless us our Lord for these thy gifts…

Me: … which we are about to receive, through thy bounty, through Christ our Lord, Amen.

Amen, Andrea! Now take hold. This is the One Life we have with Jesus as our Savior. And so, all things from here on out are forgiven because you have the atonement. Seek and you shall find. True saving grace is in essence what we are after here. Take hold and become that person with which you seek to know all about. Tell her that it's okay to come out and begin her journey to oneness with all there is. See her for the truths that she is giving you. Become that person. Be her. Take hold. Do it now. Forgive yourself. Be her in true oneness. Life is but all we make it to be and this is the one true life we have. Do it. Surrender fully. Become one with God.

Day 26: Life with the Atonement is Splendid Indeed

Me: With the present moment, it is an amazing miracle indeed.

It is what we are showing you here that you need to take with you to help others reach the atonement. God is there for them just like He is with you. You must go out and preach this gospel to others and do it in a way that suits you, so as to reach as many people as you need. But do it quietly, for it is true this is a fear driven world. It seeks revenge on most everyone who tries to tell it to grab hold. And so, this is One Life we must lead for eternity.

Me: Oh, my goodness, this is the revenge I have been so afraid of.

Day 27: Atonement Happens with Each Crying Step of Life

Andrea, we are going to tell you, that this is somewhat of a challenge in knowing that which we call the truth, and that which we know is truth. And so, really, this is the only truth we know, the way in which we are one with God and all He is. If there is anything we want you to get from this, it's true knowing in Christ Jesus. And so, although the present moment works, you do not yet have the atonement through Christ that lives in all of us. And so, take hold and see all there is to see. Yet, take yourself to a new level that is even further, and that is of awareness of all there is. Plus, the benefit of knowing true salvation in knowing Christ Jesus died for our sins.

Me: I do, but every time I think about it I want to cry. I wonder if it is like focusing on the good in that we can focus on His resurrection more than the crucifixion of Jesus Christ. Would this be a correct assessment?

We wonder if you can forgive yourself. Partly because it is so new to do something like this, so that we may see all there is to see in Christ.

Me: How will my life change if I forgive myself daily?

It takes you to a new level of awareness, just like in times past when you have moved to new levels of awareness in yourself. Take hold and behold, for all that follows here must lead you to Christ. And that road is heavily trodden. See it for what it is. Be that one we wish to atone for, in Jesus's name.

Day 28: Jesus Forgave Me. Our Sins Too!

Me: Jesus forgave me, so I forgive me, because Jesus lives in me through the Holy Spirit. And that is true forgiveness. That is the atonement.

Take hold and do it.

How?

Just see it.

Day 29: Go with It

Me: Okay, give me a minute. I forgive quickly, myself and others. I have found I will forgive others before I forgive myself.

Take hold and do it, Andrea. There is nothing to fear. There is nothing to be afraid or ashamed of. We are all here waiting for you to do it. Take that leap. Go with faith. Hold on. Become one of Christ's chosen ones.

Me: We are all Christ's chosen ones.

Yes, we all are. Take hold and become that which you seek. Just know it to be true and, therefore, it is.

A picture of Jesus in the field as the shepherd.

Day 30: Atonement Reached? Yes!

Me: Okay, I forgive myself of all wrongdoings. I am one with God through Jesus our Savior. Meditating on this. This is prayer, right?

Yes. It is us!

Me: Is there one or two? Is it me, or is it myself that remembers it? Is my only self the ego, or is my only self the person who is aware of the ego? It has been ten years since I started believing in God. Is that like the Old Testament then, before I found Jesus and I believed in Him, I had eternal salvation. Then I surrendered and sought atonement. I knew the atonement through self-forgiveness. That which is the point of no return in the New Testament is truth? Do I have it right now?

We are going to say this is what we have been trying to tell you in terms of the one who lives in all of us, and that is that the Old Testament precedes everything that follows thereafter. And so, to believe in Him means that we are to have everlasting life with Jesus, and He forgives us our sins. And so, we are born anew in His eyes. We are like Christ in that our bodies become one with His. And so, no sin could exist after that. It is the will of God to do this.

Me: The concept of hell is paying attention to the darkness so we cannot see it?

Precisely. That is the essence of God, is to see all the good that life has to offer you in terms of wellness and well-being. We are infinitely vast, and God has spoken to us through Jesus Christ and through the Holy Spirit so that we may become one with Him.

Day 31: This is War, Then

Me: You mean when I forgive myself, I become one with Christ, and I am Christlike?

Yes, we do mean this. It is the ultimate testimony of will and trust, in the one life we have with Jesus our Savior.

Me: Wow! I never knew this to be the case.

In essence, we are saying that this is what you are instructed to do. And that is to go tell it to the mountain, so to speak, and heal for us. It is to spread our joy to the nations beyond this one, as well as in truth in glory, for all there is to become in this Life. And so, for you to see this means we are going forth with our plans for self-discovery, one with being.

Me: Once I forgive myself of all wrongdoings, the Holy Spirit lives in me, Jesus lives in me, and I am Christlike. The present, aware self, said, I'm ready, I'm ready, let's do this. Wait, it doesn't matter what the ego self said because it does not exist.

Yes, this is in essence what we are saying.

Day 32: Hell is for Us Entirely

Me: Hell is the fear that lives in the ego?

What we mean by hell has to do with the one we see as truth, and that is the Lord and Savior. And so, what is coming for us is eternal happiness, that only comes with knowing our Lord and Savior. See what we mean by this when you cross over and become one of the believers that has walked in the shadow of the valley of death, and came back to tell about it. It is true oneness that takes us to new levels of awareness within ourselves. If we could only see it. See it, Andrea. It's right there for the taking. It's there for us all. We just have to see it for ourselves.

Me: That makes me smile.

Now focus, Andrea. Take hold. Be that person you set out to be. Become her now. Take hold and do it. We are waiting.

Me: Did the ego create the wrongdoings and ailments? Or, did my old self, that is the aware one, create them?

It does not matter so much who created them, but if you must know, it is the self that needs to forgive what the ego created. And so, this is what we mean by hell in terms of true oneness with the divine being we call God. God would never allow such punishment in life, but it is God's will to deliver us from it. We are His children and by definition this means He is one with life itself. And so, for us to quibble over this is to say we have taken up so much of His time and He is begging you to let go and release this stronghold of fear you have that is keeping you from reaching the atonement. And so, if we could just see it as this, then we can have true forgiveness within ourselves, and that is when we know who Christ is because He is us. He lives in us. He knows us forever. Be that person, Andrea. Become Christlike. Christ Himself knows you can do this, and you will do it as He sees it in His sights.

Me: Yes, I will do it. I will become the spirit of oneness I seek. I do forgive myself in totality. A person like me can become like Christ. I am to become one with Christ, because He carried those sins for me. When He died and was resurrected, that was the point of no return. To seek Him though is wise for us to do. The Holy Spirit lives in me. I am a vessel. I am Christlike. I keep the flow of things moving through me. I am letting God and the universe know I am ready to receive my good.

Total surrender, Andrea. That is what we are talking about. Become one with God now. See it, and you shall have it.

Me: I am one with God now. I am visualizing this.

Believe in it. Do it for yourself. Do it now.

Me: Save myself.

Yes.

Me: From the misery.

Precisely.

Me: Whoa, I almost wrote I was in hell now. No, I am in Heaven now. I am worth saving, I am worth loving, I am worth forgiving. If Jesus forgives me, the least I could do is forgive myself. God willing, I do deserve it.

Day 33: Stay in Your Fear Zone? No Way!

Free yourself from fear. Go with the one we see in you that has no fear. Never experience it again. Life as we know it is vast and abundant. There is plenty of abundance for everyone.

Me: I'm so tired. I'm trying so hard. I will do this.

Become me and my sins will be forgiven, to live in my body is Christ Himself. I am to become myself for all the glory that God is and has to offer this world. I will become that person who lives in Christ Jesus who died for us. I give myself to Jesus. I forgive myself. I forgive myself. I forgive myself. I forgive myself. I forgive my body for all the ailments and wrongdoings that the mind has created. I am Christlike. He lives in me. I feel the Holy Spirit enter my body. I am a vessel. I claim it now. Perfect health is my divine right. We are pleased with your progress. Now we ask you to visualize it, see it happening.

Day 34: God is Great – Take Hold, Andrea, Dear Heart of Mine!

Me: I am re-reading the above for visualization. I just had a massive visualization of Jesus on the cross. I thought about the verse. I thought about casting my cares onto Him, the Son of Man. I felt guilty about it. I still do. I realized though He has already forgiven me for it. What do I do now?

Call on the Son of Man.

Me: I saw Jesus on the cross, and voluntarily took my illnesses and wrongdoings and cast it on Him as He was hanging there on that cross. I felt so very guilty for doing this to Jesus, like how could I do that to Him, and that I would suffer and never cross over because I did this to Him. But then I saw He is Godlike and that through Him we can have everlasting life.

It is done. It is done.

Me: What do you mean?

Day 35: Take Hold – The Best is Yet to Come

Take hold, Andrea, for this is the best you will ever be. This is the atonement. This is the freedom from fear we have forsaken. And so, with this in all its glory, it is done that this is everlasting life as we know it. And so, since the Holy Spirit lives in you now, it is up to you to do with it what you were given. And that is to run with the idea that we are taking in for you from here. And, that is leaving us to deal with what it is that plagues you and going forth with your mission in life. And that is to heal this mind from trauma in all that it comes to be. And so, with that we must say farewell.

Me: You mean I understand now. And, because of that I know what to do?

Yes, and we are here to help you along the way. But for now, it is what we have been saying all along. You are destined for greatness. And just know that we are here. For now, we had better let you sleep and, God willing, you become one of the great leaders of the nation. Please take us with you to your sleep and be good in knowing that which we have told you tonight, for it is a glorious night indeed.

Me: I can't help but cry. I felt so guilty casting all my cares onto Jesus as He was on that cross. Thank you so much.

God bless you, child. You are a wonderment, an amazement in this world. Goodnight, Dear One. May God bring you all you have ever asked for in prayer. Goodnight. God bless you, child.

Me: Goodnight.

Day 36: More to Come

God is awesome and infinite and always expanding. Jesus came so that we may have eternal life. God bless you for everything you are doing to better yourself. We think you will be pleased with life's plans. And so, with that we will bid you adieu.

Me: Okay, thank you.

God bless your spirit in oneness with the divine being we call Christ. Take care and we'll be back soon.

Me: Okay. 😊 That's what I'm writing down, things that I hear from you, the Divine Source Wisdom.

Yes. You are a superstar in that respect. Andrea, this is nothing to be ashamed of. What you are doing is going to reach many different people. And so, for you to start writing this information down that we are telling you, it is remarkable how much you believe in us to set the word straight in terms of what we are seeking in this life. And that is with the atonement in Jesus Christ our Lord and Savior. And so, as far as what we are conveying to you, this is what we set out for you to do in this life is to gather this information and tell it to the world before you. And so, this is why we have chosen you for this purpose.

This is the Andromeda Galaxy, shaped like a rose. It is "Us" (ESA/Hubble).

Day 37: Keep on The Divine Source Wisdom's Lighthouse Feature

Me: This is unbelievable. When will I write this book, someday soon?

Yes, you will write this and become someone great in our leadership. What we must do now is shift focus to bring our attention on the essence of being within you that needs rejuvenation.

Me: Yes, how do I keep rejuvenating it?

Always, always seek our Lord and Savior for any and every problem you are having. Not only can you believe what we are trying to tell you here, but in essence, it is very important that you remain centered and focused during these conversations with us. And so, what you must do now is take a moment and thank your Creator for this communication and, rest assured, we will be here when you get back.

Me: Okay, I am doing it now. I wanted to do something else for a while, but you are urging me to get back at it because you have a little more to say, and I want to listen.

Yes, Andrea. It is very important that you do this, and just know that we are pulling for you in terms of safety and knowingness in Jesus.

Me: This is the greatest love I have ever known. Have I got that right?

Yes, and we are so proud of you for recognizing that atonement means mercy and grace. It does not mean splendor in all there is that is dreadful. And so, really, to atone means to seek God mercifully, and to give him the right complexity in this lifetime to take our sins from us, so that we can fulfill our obligations and our duties. And so, it is not a matter of atoning and being done with it. You must work at it daily with constant rejuvenation.

Me: I will take it. I just want to feel rested and I want to maintain a routine. I want to set aside time to write about it.

Yes, you have time for all the things you want to do in this lifetime, and if that means you are destined for greatness, we hope to give that to you here.

Me: I have never known a love like this, that I have found in Jesus.

Yes, My Sweet Dear. You, My Love, have found the true essence of what it means to be human, as well as to take away any doubt within yourself about writing this novel we are creating here. And, thus, we move on. Are you ready for more right now?

Day 38: Life Before God Sucks

Me: There's no time like the present.

Good, yes. We want to keep your best interests at heart. And so, here we go with some more information for you to take with you today. It is our greatest joy in Christ Jesus that we atone for our sins, because we are infinitely great among the higher power of Christ. In His eyes, we rest from failures and destitute thinking because we are one with Him in all His glory and splendor. For Him to have such an influence over you, we are glorified to the utmost standing in His time, in that He chose us to help you with this book you are writing, yes, the one you believed you would write. And so, hopefully we have chosen well in that we are giving you this doctrine that is laid out before you and, in essence, we hope you can spread it to the rooftops. Are we ready for what all that entails before us?

Me: Yes, I am, we are.

Good. So, here is what I want you to take with you tonight as you go throughout your day tomorrow. Trust in our Lord and Savior to keep you safe from harm, and rejuvenate Him constantly throughout your day. It will just become instinctual to you to keep this rejuvenation constant. And then, that's right, you don't have to think about it anymore.

Me: I do not even have to think about these affirmations.

Yes. Precisely. And so, tomorrow we begin the journey of oneness that we all seek through Christ our Lord, and one day we will write that novel to be published in all its glory and splendor.

Me: And, you help me do this you said earlier?

Yes, we do. And, you are so right in that it is destined for greatness beyond time. And so, we must say goodnight for now. God bless you and your candor. We love to see you grow beyond measure.

Me: Yes, I look forward to what you have in store for me as time goes on.

Yes, and we look forward to it, too. God bless you, and know that great things are headed your way, Andrea. Truly, this is the One Life we get to live, and we get to live it to the fullest. God bless you and take care. Until next time.

Me: Thank you so much. And, in Jesus's name, I will say goodnight to you.

Goodbye, Andrea. Take care and know we are with you no matter what happens in this journey. Tonight, we rest.

Me: Thank you.

You're welcome, My Dear, Delightful Lovely.

Day 39: God Is Great

Me: I do have atonement work to do.

God bless you, Andrea, for trying to be so meaningful in our communications. In essence, we are saying that we are ready for you to proceed to the next offering we have, and that offering has to do with the sins we carry within us that need atoning for. And so, what is it in you that you have strife about that ails you in terms of getting better and getting well?

Me: What is truly considered to be sinful exactly in the eyes of Jesus? Besides what we have covered so far.

In essence, what we are saying has to do with atoning for evildoing.

Me: Am I evil?

No, no, My Dear. What is it that you want to atone for?

Me: Atone for? You mean like what in me is sinful in nature or in deeds?

Think about this for a minute.

Me: I'm afraid to. I know that is a thought, but it's true.

Day 40: Atone for What Exactly?

Okay, listen to this. If this is the one true life we seek with our Savior, then how come He knows all there is to know about you. And, yet, has chosen you to be one of the spoken for, in terms of the atonement in all its glory and splendor? How is it that you could have such fear in the presence of this then?

Me: Okay, I see. What you just said is something that I know produces fear, a state that does not exist. All that exists is what we know. What I want to know is to confirm what I already know, and that is that I have a nature about me that could be of sinful natures.

Yes, that we seek is the glory in knowing God in all His essence and prevalence in this life we have here on Earth. And so, what we must do is atone for everything that we can possibly think of in terms of our wonderment with Jesus and we must do it rightly so that we may have eternal life on Earth without fear of judgment and retaliation from others. This is what the essence of what we are trying to teach you here on this Earth is, and we expect to do it tonight with the others who have gathered in our presence to help speed this process along. And so, will you do this with us tonight in all its splendor and its glory?

Me: I will stay up if it means reaching the atonement tonight. And, if it means to be rid of judgment and retaliation from others. Who all is gathered with us tonight?

It is the Jesus we seek atonement for. And so, thus, this is going to be a long acknowledgement of that fact. And, here we have a duty to uphold the most righteous in glory, and that is the essence of what we are saying here. In essence, we know that which we seek is to atone for our sins. But what lovely acts can we atone for that will bring us closer to knowing Jesus in His full wonderment and glory? It is our acts of love that we carry with us that we can atone for, and bring to Jesus as an offering. And, know that He will forgive us in our most glorious fashion in Heaven. And so, this is what we are trying to seek knowledge about and that is the atonement that you seek in wonderment in the eyes of Jesus. And, that is truly what we're gathered here to do tonight. Are you ready for this amazing miracle that is about to happen?

Me: Yes, is it safe to type about it? I had a moment of doubt, but I quashed it. You would never do or say anything that I wouldn't want to type. And so, yes. I am ready for an amazing miracle. I am to forgive myself of all sins. I will bring acts of love that I can atone for to Jesus as an offering. And, I know that He will forgive me in His most glorious fashion in Heaven. I am willing to have humility. Yes, I am.

Day 41: Atone, For This is God's Work at Heart

Thank you, Andrea. This is the truest sense of the word atonement, in that we are able to bring offerings to Jesus, to collect a debt to Him for His true knowing sense of the word atonement. And so, what we have here today is to show you how to do this. Are you ready in all its splendor and glory in attaining that which we have sought to seek out tonight under these glorious stars tonight?

Me: Yes, I am. Give it to me. What have you got for me? What can I do? And, you can clarify debt or do you think I am getting lost in terminology?

It is divine presence indeed that leads you in this direction for atoning. And so, without further adieu, I present you our glory in our Lord Jesus, that which you have to atone for. In essence, we are through here, and He is to take over.

Me: Must I continue to type or will I be able to?

You can do as you wish. Ultimately, it is your decision as we have always said. Take hold and notice our Lord in your presence.

Me: I'm not afraid. I know you.

Yes, my child, you do. Please pray with me.

Day 42: The Atonement is Reached Again? Through Holy Prayer and Scriptures, A Hymn for Us, In Jesus's Name

Me:

God is glory to me, God speed to me.
It is one with my Savior, God speed to me.
I have always known this power to have graced my God with thee,
And in this glory to me, God speed to me.

I am one with our Savior, He is one with God speed,
And this glory in our Savior, is one with God speed.
It is one thing to grace us, with that which we seek.
In His glory forever, God speed to me.

Take my hand, Andrea. Go to the mountain and tell it to rise above the ashes and seek that atonement for which it has risen.

Me: Okay, wow. I will have to write about that experience. Yes, I want to get to bed. But what just happened here?

It lives in you, this essence of being we call Christ. You are one with the atonement. This is the mountain of glory in which we speak in Ephesians Chapter 2 of the divine Holy Ghost entering your body and becoming one with you at this moment. For this is the glory of the divine we call Christ's embodiment of wonder and glory, in true essence of who you are at this moment. Continue to acknowledge sin and we will continue to take you to places utmost pure in which to atone for. And, ultimately, this is the sin we all have to bear and that is the wrath of Christ Jesus toward all ill will and ill intention in this world. And so, glory as God speed, we must say goodnight to you. God bless you, child. We love you. Take hold and God bless, for this is the atonement. This is the embodiment of Christ. This is the one true life we must take with us into our next chance at being. Take hold and know God is with you always, the one true life we call God. Take care and know we are always with you in divine spirit. God willing, the end is near, for your atonement is one with life itself. Take care and hold with you that which we call the glory of God. We love you, Andrea. You are one with life. It is one with you. God bless you. And, thank you for this opportunity to serve our Lord and Savior, Jesus Christ, forever.

Me: Thank you. I love you. God bless our Savior for rejoicing in this moment with me. Thank you for this opportunity to speak. I love all of you. Jesus saves, this we know. God bless and goodnight.

Goodnight, Sweet One.

Me: Goodnight.

Sweet dreams.

Me: Jesus took me to the mountain and had me tell it to the mountain, to spew this wrath inside of me over the mountain, this wrath we all have within us, and to take His hand and to pray. Then the Holy Ghost came to live inside of me. I am one with our Savior through the embodiment of Christ and our Savior lives in me through the Holy Ghost. God bless this event with all its glory and splendor. I am a vessel now for the Holy Ghost. I know I am meant to be here to do God's work. I am writing the book now and I have healed and I tell others how I did that. It is a glorious night indeed. It is getting late. Goodnight, Dear Ones in Heaven. Goodnight, and God speed.

Day 43: Keep it Complete in Our Holy Savior

Andrea, this is one moment in time where we couldn't be prouder for you for having figured all of this out. One thing to look out for is the eyes of others who are watching your progress. And so, this in mind, keep your distance as far as taking out the eyes of God on others.

Me: You mean everyone could tell at the meeting tonight?

Yes. And so, we are saying that although it is nice for you to have this insight, be still in the presence of others and show them your grace in…

Me: The way that Jesus does?

In a sense, that is what we are saying. What we're saying is that you can help so many more people if you keep your religious comments to yourself.

Me: Yes, I knew that already but I had to cover up my reference. You know, the one that I am embarrassed about.

That actually makes them more perceptive to you. Please know that God is working through you to understand what we are telling you. And so, it is just going to be a test of faith to be able to refrain from any religious remarks.

Me: I feel bad for saying these things too.

You have to trust in that and not bring religious comments to anybody really.

Day 44: Keep the Faith Dear Ones

Me: I am just checking in for a moment. What a glorious night indeed. I am so enthusiastic to be here for Christ. Thank you so much to Jesus for what He did for me last night.

Andrea, it is so very grand indeed what you accomplished last night, and it behooves us that you might take with you the very thing that was keeping you still, and that is the presence of our Lord and Savior. And so, for this plight to be taken from you is indeed grandiose in nature, but one of peace and presence with our Lord Jesus. And so, for you to have this out of you is what we call something of a miracle. And, thus, we are so very proud of you for recognizing that this needed to be done. It is something of a divine spirit that tells us who we are and, thus, what we are here to do in this life. We are worried that something else is in store for you and that might be the remembrance of times past. And, ultimately, this will be a challenge for you to keep the faith during these times. In essence, it is our pasts that take us to new levels in the present. And so, be it as it may, keep trying to seek our Lord in your perils, and know that He is here for us to take us to new levels within us.

Me: I never knew. I am so grateful, thank you. I feel so renewed. I am a child of God.

Yes, you are. Never speaking of our Lord in vain will keep you from seeing the wrath that was in you once more. And so, keep that in mind when you are taking these steps toward seeing that is believing in Christ. Once again, Andrea, keep the faith and know that God is here with you in Jesus's name, Amen.

Me: Amen. Have a great morning! I know I will.

Thank you, and you too. God bless you, Sweet One. Bye for now. (This is the end of our diatribe on life here while Andrea was still hearing nothing but "Us" then? Nothing but ourselves could state it here. We're on top of it! Likewise, she hears nothing that "We" don't already know! Now we turn to the Divine Source Wisdom, taking its toll on the commandant's languages here, and switch gears to the commandant's most beautiful talent search's biggest and best demands on life here. Jezibellie's ailment cures lady stuff is for the birds then? We're onto you, Andrea! ☺ There's more to life than just sitting here and echoing the sentiments of God's next plans and stuff! Will you now join me, us, in enjoying the sinister looking faces of Jezibellie Christ then? Plain and Jane don't go together here. She's massively beautiful to Me here! Enjoy! Take hold because we never know the plain Jane's from the simple-minded folks that battle cure this introductory paragraph's trying times, and our loneliest coverups from the simple facts that ail "Us" here. Take control, Andrea, and read out loud our friendship's nastiest vixens and comedy striking factors here! Take control and know that God's other tanked relationships are just too bold here! Become who you are, Peoples! We now turn to the chapters of Arabian nights here. Jezibellie Christ knew how to dance, Peoples of color here! Get on the chapters of love and state it for the records here that Jezibellie Christ knew "Jesus in the Bedroom" here is going to risk it all here. And, to save face for us here, Jesus, get on the stick and know that God's laughters are quite contrary to popular demands here! This is for the birds if we cannot share these typical ailments cures with the worlds to be the United States of America here! Take control, Peoples! Let us live a better day without medicating the entire world for their generosity's sakes here. Leave it to Beavers, Peoples of the nighttime Arabian nights to come here, for thou art intensely beautiful, Jezibellie Christ!)

Chapter 1

We Are Jezibellie's Cure for AIDS Related Viruses Like Schizophrenias

I have seen just about everything here. Hi, this is what Jesus is like in the bedroom here! I don't know much, but I know I love you! As the song goes. Let me be all there is to know! I love the fact that God intended for Jesus to learn a thing or two about romance. I believe in all kinds of it! He does too! You cannot begin to understand the calamity about Mary Magdalene until you debunk all the truths as to why Jesus is better suited to marry Jezibellie Christ! I promised Mary M. a token friendship though? She was nothing but too old for Me, He says! So, she's not it, but Jezebel, that woman heretic, is not! I loved her with all my might He says to me here now, see the above picture of Jezibellie Christ's era of one space contentment here. That's My wife! She was supposed to be here in the photo. Pocahontas is what she looks like! A magic lamp will do. She's My wife, to have and to hold her in trust is blessed be lovingly the best thing ever.

This is because it's a Divine Source Wisdom that picks up on these things here. When I first started talking with the DSW, for short, there were all kinds of questions about Mary M. here. She was not the pedophile ring folks, but certainly she tried all kinds of things to get Me to marry her? Hardly so. But really, she's not right for this world's peace here. I take into consideration many a different thing. So, hardly so is the answer to that question about peace and her in it. Take it from me, DSW says, we are vast and we are musical. So, there it is in a nutshell! Jesus cast her, Jezibellie, to a sick bed, for answering her prayers as the musical scribe for the Bible we so love and share accordingly? She wrote that of herself here, because mental health is something of a rouge. Do we love her or do we just take her for granted here, as the only scribe for the Bible's turning points here! It's a heretic's language we come to know and love here. How come she's only for this world and not for kindness elsewhere here! I promised God, Jesus says, that I'd come to know each and every one of you! It's a rouge alright! I loved the best promised land in the whole entire Biblical scriptures, enough to say, hell and Heaven abide this much, but hell is for children no more here. I loved God and all it entails here. I said, all it entails, because I loved her back, He said! That is Biblical scriptures no more here.

There's more to "AIDS" than meets the eye here! There's all sorts of AIDS viruses out there, schizophrenias being one of them, though needle marks on the toilet seats of hell almost got me into and out of Mary M.'s shorts. Correctamundos here? Not! I am simply speaking of hell in almost every sense of the word here. That Mary M. is really something here!

She's not on my radar though. Right, Christ Jesus here! Because schizophrenias, bipolar disorder here, and schizoaffective disorders are really for the birds. Right, or exactamundos here? Because this is HIV we're talking about usually here, it's really the right thing to do is to commandant this manuscript here.

And to say it out loud like the family's affairs here is for the birds also, as well as the commandant's monies that simply state that God is a misnomer for peace here! That is a jaguar listening to this scripts-mongering here. We are simply stating that AIDS is a bunch of different things here, which makes it seem as though God's only wantingnesses is to create AIDS related viruses for everyone. People in general script us and say that God only wanted a cream of the crop's lessons planning, virus getting accommodations here! That said here, what is the cream of the crop's best lessons planning vice here, but a simple tool used to create schizophrenias of the mind's eyes.

And to think of it that way, and a this way, is really what we're after here. Governor Inslee, Jay Inslee to be exact, thinks about the mental health in this country's ways to go here to be secularized into AIDS related places here! We are simply stating that for the records here, there are none to be desired by making mental health beds here and fro! This commandant's languages here is for the birds at best here! There's simply a mental health note from God that states that AIDS related schizophrenias are at best covered up by the knowledges that seek us here. That said here, what is the relativity clause that Einstein brought about here, Albert Einstein thereof here! Because he heard the notions of God's wraths here! And in Chapter 13, we go on and on about how Paul rapes people, Paul Wright thereof here! He did not, and I repeat, did not write the Bible at all here, save a line or two about how Jezibellie Christ saved the day then? He held her down at gunpoint. To rescue this line or two about this jealous husbandry saved by Jezibellie Christ is a gunpointed theme's reckonings here!

We don't like the guy at all here! Paul Wright is sometimes referred to in the Bible as the "Apostle Paul." We don't like him in the least here! He's a misnomer for AIDS related viruses then, as he did find people to kill. All sorts of them lasted quite a bit longer here, cause he was into torturous things, and all kinds of people came to the grievances of AIDS related viruses no more's here! It's more's because it's Anglo-Saxon to do this, coming into the know about life's quandaries and wonderments here!

We'd just assume be done with this Paul bit here. And in Chapter 13, there is the love affairs of a lifetime of greed mongering just waiting to be had here!

And that said here, please wake up the dead here, Andrea, and let everybody know about the Divine Source Wisdom and its puppetry here! We don't wear the color red, Folks, and you too, Gentiles! It's because it's proper to do so, is it not? We're taking the banana peels and we're giving them to the foxes and the Gentiles here. That said, what is the fox's lay terminologies for people with bipolar disorder here! Because this is a fact, Jack, and Jill was soon after Jack was!

There's only a way to name HIV and schizophrenias in the same jackets as there were peace mongering. To know about God's wraths though is perfectly, honestly, the same biggest misnomers of peace there ever was here! That bipolar disorder is simply a need and a want for personality conflicts of psychiatrists worldwide here, and that none of the psychiatry inclined peoples have the Holy Spirit or the Holy Ghost thereof here!

We're fighting the misnomers here of a centuries old lingo label for peace on Earth's crusts here! The label of fighting over the misnomers here is really for the birds.

And, this label for AIDS as only HIV survivors here is really for the birds as well here. And that said here, we label this AIDS virus as only the ways and means it lady's talentships here! We simply state that honest to God's goodnesses here represent timely factors on AIDS related factors and talentships here! Say, what has the AIDS virus gotten to do with time on a button of AIDS cures here, as HIV and HSV alike both have no more cures than God does! If you don't believe me though, please read Chapters 6 and 7 of this work here! We are trying to dispel so many myths and disbeliefs here that honestly this is the only time of the week that we're available for coffee ridden talentships here. As this ages and stuff, coffees and whatever has to do with the carrots outbreaks and stuff is non-existent here! Meaning, Folks and Gentiles too, that whatever outbreaks you currently have, a couple of carrots will take care of it. The menial kinds of HIV and HSV outbreaks are simply that carrots and coffees and such have the menials and the plentifuls out to get us here. Take carrots and simply state that the outbreaks get less and less as time goes on here. And that's a wrap, Folks and you too Gentiles! Simply stated though, Chapters 13 and 15 are about gun laws to the people who need them, not the other ways around it though! And this takes hold of our lessons in plannings and such!

Chapter 2

Delilah's a Tramp! Not Jezibellie Christ! In Other Words, Come Forth, My Wife to Be Here!

Jezibellie Christ, better known as Barnes? It's not Barnes, okay! It's a question of the wits here, her Indian last name cannot be written in this script. It's not truth be told here to categorize her name this way here. Barnes is the Solomon's ways of saying his last name wasn't that clean to begin with. Her first marriage, and it happens to be the King of England? Save face and name that which is not named. His first wife was Jezibellie then? It was Delilah, and we cannot stress this hard enough, what are you saying then, as Jesus did back in the day? He's saying to you clearly now, do not stress on this point.

In fact, what have you say you about this wonderful place of reckoning peace and what not here! I loved Jezibellie Christ since childhood here! We don't know what else to say here. The end! Not!

I did, in fact, get cozy with the ideas that we were husband and wife's tales here. But that did not stop us from marrying and ruling Egypt back in the days here.

I do know this. He's banking on you, Andrea, telling the truth here. You are going to get Jezibellie Christ in a lot of trouble if you cannot begin to read the books of Romans Chapter 3 or so here. Right here it says, chapters and verses just come to me. And so, it begins to read here on Verse 12 or so (KJV): They are all gone out of the way, they are together become unprofitable; there is none that doeth good, no, not one <p. 1658>. This one's for the birds and stuff like it. You see it, now you don't. Correctamundo here? This faithfulness in Jesus's eyes is basically for the birds if you ask me, Paul said to Him once! He goes, lay me with this Delilah person then? No way, Jose's!

But the balancatures in this moment's notices states that Delilah is with Samsonite, the guy whose beautifulness surpasses human interventions here, and, yes, she cut off his hair in droves here! True story! So anyhoo, is this Jesus's wifey then? Not on your life here! She got it annulled too, for He is mighty and truthful about this here! What of a wifey that does not understand about commandants and such! I just declared for the worlds that be here that a timeliness approach's middle child's ways of saying peaceful adventures here, is the same as blowing your own horn there, Felix the lime catcher's ryes and stuff like it! You see it, now you don't. Correctamundo's here? Say, did Andrea just ask us what our point was? Now you see it, now you don't. Correctamundo's here! It's a clothes thing too. That said, is He on the cross for all to bears here, and that openness about the nailbeds going kaput here is that He's on the doublecrossed lifestyles to bootie here this woman and this man here! Say, can He go about searching for His Jezibellie Christ here, as this was her sister! At any rates here, I did lay with her one moment and I said, I cannot perform this deed's awfulness, tones, or any other radically different ways to get a man laid here! I do not declare a mistrial on this! However, she does! I say that in jest here too. I do not declare a mistrial in deeds here, just that I was drunk off my ass with one pop of the coins here! This coins thing with Delilah is the absolute truth about her too. My version's about to pop here!

This version's about to pop here! This cold truth to marrying Delilah is something of a farce! In gestural times, however, there's such turmoils in her voice's carrying dilemmas here that God's fate and faith adjustments here are for the birds then, she said! I just kissed Him though, Delilah said! And with cigarette smoke on her breath though? My Jezibellie, where are you! He goes, this Delilah chick is open enough with the scissors happy ways of finding hair growth for the mens here. Say, do you remember this in your opening paragraphs here?

That God of yours, Andrea, is rare indeed then! It is quite honorable to be Paul in the Bible's today versions. Correctamundo's here? It's a vice grip that strengthens me, Paul says to the open obituaries here, as he's the one who killed Delilah after she tried to kiss Jesus on the forehead during the open season's take all sessions here! That said too, that therefore, there must be a prayer book that I like at least! Corinthians Chapter 1 states it here too! Of course, it's number 1! I do declare another Paul mistrial here! This means that Paul is a nincompoop of proportionate sizes, that says he's better than Jesus Christ at coming up with these things here? As a ruler of Egypt's proper sized commandant's words here, the commandant is a message here that states that a ruler of Egypt's improper sized throat slit girls are really somethings here that said, "I'm blasphemous then," Jesus Christ says! This improperness is not a throat slit crime that goes away here, she said! But he did it alright, she said too! This Divine Source Wisdom's the ones who wrote the Bible anyways!

Anyhoo, there's a new DSW here, the one that Andrea Barberi carries within! She goes, hey, I don't need to be on any more mental health meds here, and one outfit this summertime believed in her diagnostic abilities, so much so under mental health conditions here in Seattle, Washington, so as to let her go for working at the post offices of love here! And that said here, what of these mental health meds is so honestly putant, about the native flow of words here! This work here is derived from those mental health meds here! So on the stuff she is too! She needs to be offa that stuff soon though! This is the commandant's ways and means it lady's trusts here, that functioning livers and such be offa this stuff. Say, don't you not need it anyhoo? It's a trust thing with the DSW then, as the functionalities of coming off the stuff is a withdrawal process and that is alls here. Say, that open commandant's ways and functionings of Christ our Lord and Savior has us all up in arms about what to do's with the words and phrases found in this works of God's labors here!

That said, it's a chapters and verses thing for me here to state that in Chapter 13 there is an open book part of the Corinthians kind, second chapter of Corinthians here (II) and so on here! That stated, Paul is a nincompoop no more it states for us here! Galatians too! I mean, did this guy hold down an open throat to Delilah for kissing Jesus on the mouth no less! It's a possibility! There's wonderful things to talk about in this book here, Folks, and you too, Andrea! I do believe that for all intents and purposes here that you are not reincarnate Delilah here! I do believe in Jezibellie, she says! I believe that I, apostle Paul, hereby give and get to receive the gospel here?

Do you know what he did to her to make her say that at the beginnings of each chapter's demises and such? This man who calls Himself "I" in those chapters is Jesus Himself here, not Paul, not any of his counterparts who buried the hatchets long ago here, but the principles of peace here are not written by Paul at all here! I do declare a mistrial in deeds and adventureships to a woman who goes, "Please, Jesus Christ. Find me attractive in the least of your worries then, and marry me too?" She goes, "Jesus Christ of Jezibellie and such, my sister no less! Come to me and state it for the records that…" Opium rocks, He said, then of her then! What is this wish of a no lesser deniability's statements here, that says, God is literaturely faithful in this moment's breadths here!

This goes without saying here then, that a God can literally be fooled, just as we are fooled. And so, the best of both possible worlds here states that there's a literaturely bound womanhood's talent shows echoing in the background, and possibly this warship is crying out of laughter and such here! This moment's notices on our brains here is stating that Jesus was tricked, drugged and lesson planned into marrying Delilah! Because as I said there in Chapters 4-6 in Delilah's notes, there were tons of things that needed to be said in the Bibles here. That there were so many different versions running around here that we could call it blasphemy here! And state that Jezibellie Christ rearranged her lifestyles here to not marry the King of England? She was drugged into it too! And so, there's reasons for the seasons of hopelessnesses here!

And it goes on to say in chapters and verses for me here, that Romans 3:13 Their throat is an open sepulchre; with their tongues they have used deceit. Okay here is the question then! What have you say you, Andrea, about faith? God's kingdoms talk about the circumcisions only generally, then forfeit what you are saying onto the faith of God. For all thou artest in greatest servitude, looking at the King James Version (KJV) here, that their tongues they have used deceit. Meaning, Folks, that there is love that's in the air the whole time here. God's reckoning in Chapter 3 Romans Verse 5: But if our unrighteousness commend the righteousness of God, what shall we say? Is God unrighteous who taketh vengeance? (I speak as a man) <p. 1658>, it says!

And so, what with this verses, scriptures and such is there? God is reckoning us to deliver a chance happening into the wide-open spaces of trust here. Verse 12 states that: They are all gone out of the way, they are together become unprofitable; there is none that doeth good, no, not one <p. 1658>.

Are you going to start whispering down to the nugget ring that He wore, that all of our jewels are not fake here?

Are you going to trust whether or not they're free? Or is this a rouge again! I beg to differ that all our jewels were not fake, and the fact that the circumcisions happen to Jews and such, Jesus was a Jew, definitely, but White all the same! I loved Jezibellie Christ and she happened to be Black skinned, Indian in nature here! I loved her all the same here!

I don't know the passwords to the protected elements of art like this, Folks! But we're taking timeouts and resting our eyes a bit here! Don't leave, Jezibellie Christ! She's like a Godsend to humanity's purposes here. We are writing this too. Jezibellie Christ is for the taking is she! She's not gaining any momentum here! She's the best person for the job of writing the Bible through the Divine Source Wisdom though! KJV please! If the King James Version is not a séance in the hopper here, I do deserve a mistrial I suppose!

What is the ring of fire supposed to dictate here, but a silentary day here on the hopper of love here. That said, what is the main reasoning for writing this here book! It's a silent ear all day long on the words of love that sparked an interest between God and the rest of the worlds here. I do say worlds meaningfully! As there are two separate planets… Just kidding on that one here? I don't think so!

If God means anything to the joking nature of these posts, it's like that here online though! I do declare a mistrial of deeds and promises of a lifetime of hope for Jezibellie Christ! The Christ's online works are many here. How do you think we kept track of time back then?

We had the internet too! It's spelled intranet for some of the others who think we're going to time it back and then some here. The intranet is here to stay! We had the internet too! It's a ghost of a word, is it not, to believe in something so trivial as to whether or not our airlines system didn't grow, gravitate and erectile dysfunctionalize the sensational, trivial, whether or nots in our lives here!

Moses! Where are you here! Did you make it back to the commandant's houses here, only to find that the trivial Paul Wright is where you ended up dead, or with no foot, toe, or what have you here!

Did Jesus make the trivial plights amongst ourselves and say to you, "Here are the Ten Commandments." What about the seven deadly sins though! It means, Folks, that trivialities are especially gruesome!

Here is the biggest moment, save a few Jezibellie cures here! She had that thing too, that trivial "J" moment whereby we talk about the vagay, and not a second before this is your life going to arrive at this quandary's best interests here. But what about the vagina! What is it about the vagay that keeps us telling ourselves about the vagina's cure alls! This is the only time I get to wean, say, our children's children from getting a bath here! There's love that's in the air, that's all!

There's love that's in the airs of contentments here! That said, what does Jezibellie Christ love to call herself though? It's Jezebel, right? Wrongs here! There's pluralizations where that's from now, Folks of the DSW! I do know this too. What of the DSW is there to masturbate to here? What does God call Jezibellie Christ's interventions here with the DSW in tow here!

Chapter 3

A Beautiful Picture of Jesus Christ

A picture of Jesus Christ.

Bless her heart, you know? I do declare a mistrial in deeds and I do not get you, forsaken a bit too fast like here, Andrea, for implying that My love is but a dream. To know you is epic in proportions and deeds. I don't like this Delilah chick! I mean it too! She's a villain, and a husband's cure for this hair cutting nectar thing is for the birds, is it not there! It means that this means war, Peoples! I do declare a mistrial in deeds and a plenties! If you don't know the word is spelled incorrectly here, there are a lot of words left to know about, the impressions you're making with the DSW is best if you take the chance of a lifetime of thieves. If you took Delilah for instance to the ball and surprised yourselves with the knowledges of the peacetime talks here, you would know her to be nothing of the sort of gal you'd want to marry! You know it's true too! I do not portend to copy people this way and that a way here. I do portend to know how to impress My wife though! My wife is Jezibellie Christ! She is the love of My life here! And the capitalizations for My name are thoughtfully blessed in perfect rosaries of love here. No, I am not Catholic by any means, but I do wear the beads from time to time again, Andrea says!

How did I do this before she was married to that creep!

I do not portend to know how my feelings for Delilah did not get in the way of this marriage to boot here. She did not open up to me at all. I felt deranged for a minute here as to how to get this woman off My radar here. But she did not open up to Me. I felt like a deranged rat in the middle of a kaleidoscope of fear here. And My rushing backwards to open up her heart, Delilah's, was not in the cards for Me here. I do not fear the countdown of fashionable things here.

I'm innocent, He says! Do I have sex all night long with My wife though! I do not, if it's Delilah though, I do declare a mistrial in deeds and ownerships. I do portend to openly direct her out the door, for I was like, I am not going without a Jezibellie takedown here! This is the time to rejoice in the Lord and His shepherd. I shall not want! If Jezibellie Christ is the one for Me, is it possible to alter the synascopes of time here and to say this is really relevant to Jezibellie Christ's intervention of love here! It's a timeless phases sort of thing we're afterwards getting at here. I do know this too. What of wars are we getting at here? So, we are junkies of times past where there's nothing in the hopper but a civil suit! And we're still rulers in Egypt, aren't we?

We were rulers in Egypt for 30 years of it. As if we don't know who we are here! I just knew I would find her again, Jesus and Jezibellie, k-i-s-s-i-n-g! It's as if we don't know who she is here! Why not though? She wrote the Bible. Time and time again, I loved her all the more here. I risked it all and didn't know whether or not she stayed in My trustworthy riddle cures for lifetime soap operas here! This is the life o riley that we portend to Muckleshoot our ways into this world from. So, all I can do as a better version of Myself is to portend that we do not charge Jezibellie Christ with loving Me in vain here!

It's got to be the better version of you that we subscribe to here! She is better off said than done here. I cannot begin to go on with life without her in it! She's a Her too! So, She's better off without the love of mankind here? What goes on in the bedroom stays there! In it, She is ravaging! I loved Her better than before mankind took a nosedive here and said here that I am wrong in it! We all loved Her!

Too bad that my signage is all wrong here, the DSW says! We like the DSW to tell us about the pyramid in Egypt that housed My signage for the hardships that come along, like the pyramid's tranquilities and thousands upon thousands of actual articles, artifacts and such!

It said, Divine Source Wisdom is the equal partnerships that come about as of this date here! It means such words as the originals and the equal partnerships that come about for us too. It said, stop the DSW from coming to us here! We are terrorizing a nation's hits here! We are terrorizing the gratitudes that come from a pyramid in Egypt proclaiming a birth certificate is it? I loved Jezibellie Christ with all my heart's desires here on the Devanagari scripts though, there is blood between God's ankleships and the Achilles tendons we all crave here! I do hope that God, Jesus and the like, did not have an Achilles tendons issue here!

The Jimmy Swaggart Ministries can help us here! We're telling of an Achilles tendons issue here! And believe it or not, I'm walking on air about the Jezibellie cures that come about here! That said too, there are no other ministries in the worlds here that state that God's not answering your prayers there, Jimmy Swaggart! I watch you all the time here!

Nope, it's a marriage certificate between Jezibellie Barnes (it sounds like Barnes in Devanagari script!) and Jesus Christ, proclaiming that at 16 we were married! There's a birth certificate in there though, right? I mean, Jesus needed a potty-training guide, right? Where was He born at, but in Bethlehem too! She was born the next day, December 17th. And that said, what is this pyramid with a wedding certificate in it! He was born on December 16th of that year of our Lord as well as His mother's birthday, coming in on the 25th of November here.

Christmas of that year of our Lord is the fact that God played footsie with Me under the tablehoods of love here, at the Last Supper though? That's Mary Magdalene for you! She's too old for Me, by the way! That said, is that a supper to dine for, or is it to die for! I take thee at thy word! Call me but love and I shall be new baptized? That is a word, is it not! This Jimmy Swaggart Ministries is the basis for these texts about love's better half here! Please context this, Mr. Swaggart! For the beginnings of time here states that God's loves are very much forbidden then! And that's a fact. Jack and Jill were never married then?

Heave ho and send this along with so much pain and anguish in Jesus's face here! This is the limelight's next callings here. We love this Jimmy Swaggart's Ministries, so much so that we know he can give us a call the next time he falls in love with the woman of the ministries here that does such a great job as Frances does!

That said here, does Jimmy still love the woman though of his time in African based researchers, such as finding the AIDS cures here: Of schizophrenias though? In truths be told here, this African based research is very catchy here! That said, what is the old Bible's supposed to represent's faces here, but the Jimmy Swaggart Ministry's best foot forwards here!

Please tell the God that you know, Jimmy, that we are in fact getting to something here with the mere mentioning of your names here. That, in fact, you can help us in tremendous ways here to find the answers to the callings that you seek readily for!

There's love that's in the air for Frances and Jimmy Swaggart to tell of the callings of a lifetime of greed mongering! That said, we need for your airtime to tell us about the inklingships that we call life's plans here. You've done an excellent job! So forthcoming and such! Please help us with the appendices in the back of this textbook of knowledge here. There's several peoples in the weigh stations together with the awesomeness that we seek to find in others who are several peoples thinner, inklingships and such are for the birds then, without getting to the bottoms of this rain cast we are so full of it for!

We just don't know how to go any higher than the callings of our Lord and Savior blessings and stuff! Say, does he, Jimmy, still believe that Jezibellie is a tramp then here, Folks! There's love that's in the air! It's My wife, He still says! Beginning with the Frances cure for

AIDS related viruses too, please approach this Namibian government's ways and means it lady's talentships, and such ridicules of peace within our approaches for lives here! In other words, go with the flow here, but tell us how to reach the Namibian government's ways and means it lady's talentships here! And that said, we endorse this man and this woman for telling all the callings that have been above the blankmanships of time here.

That means, Folks, that I, We, endorse this man and this woman for telling all of the callings that the sweetest blanksmanships are the essences of endorsements and such!

This man and this woman have been very instrumental in findings and such! We just want the God's honest truths here about HIV and such, from you that is though, correctamundos here? We just need the honest to God's truth about you, Andrea! Do you have AIDS related viruses on the brains here? That said is the truth too here, is there a truth be told about your medical advice that you can give these two people here? About to answer your own questions are the ministry's biggest tellings of time it two's here. And that said too, Folks, what is the answer's best commandant's here, meaningful though he is here, is to tell awful news about the passings of dealings and such? Can we coerce you to find the time to call the Presidents here, Folks, and to address the issues presented in this work here?

Chapter 4

Santa is the Man of the Hour Here! Santa's Right-Hand Man is Us and Jesus Christ's Love!

There's love that's in the air here! The reasons we do this here is because the heavenly Father is right on our tails here about life's biggest qualities and such! And so, for some reasonings here, the pluralizations stay here! There's honestly to God one ministry we aspire to, and that's of Jimmy Swaggart's talent shows here! We do mean that there is a cure for herpes simplex, and a whole slew of other types of ailments out there! We just need to be interviewed in front of a computer screen's here ye about that ministry's help!

In other words, here, what does the Jimmy Swaggart's of our time here represent, but the Christ's love for His only wife of 70 years practically here! It means that the practicalities of life here are therefore forbidden! In essence here, that is the commandant's ways and means it lady's talent searches here! That said here, there are tons of people in the Bibles of such ridicules and such! That meaningfulness's talent search's biggest blessings are right there for the takings of God's kingdoms here. There is Christ our Lordship and there is something to be said for Jezibellie's return to the kingdoms of Heaven here. It is hardships that tell us something about the cross. For there are never any things in our lives here that means something is wrong with the gods and goddesses! If there is a Jezibellie cure for things, have it become a simple thing!

We are telling of God's kindnesses in this world! If God could see us now, we say it is hardships that tell us of forbidden fruits, and such kind interactions as God's chosen ones here. That said, are you willing to see if Jesus can forbid certain fruits? Or are you ready for a new sensation as the songs go! For there art thou! Are we ready to find the Jezibellie cure for things ravishing in natures here! I wanted to ravage Her some more here, we say! I don't know the kinds of things we're hating here. Is it God and His forbidnesses, or are we going to stink up Calvary, and never know what its name truly is?

Is it God's wife we're talking about here please? I saw Her in a pasture once and She came to Me for the Messiah rulings in My life. That said, Folks, She's golden! I saw Her in a manger at 2 years old, and She said to me, Papa, I love you! And She said, Honey, She loves you back!

My mom did, Mary Magdalene is a misnomer here. Anyway, that said, what is the hardships that we speak of here! My mom's name is really Marybelle, not Magdalene? It's

Marybelle Magdalene Longmire, but we'll get to that Joseph guy in a minute, in other chapters down the road! Mary Bongs Magdalene is a relative of Jezibellie Tutankhemen (Bongs/Barnes) Christ. She's too old for Me, like I said! It's a momma and a papa leading into the lives of yesterday's hardships that makes this hard. We speak of in Revelation Chapter 4, Verse 5: (KJV) And out of the throne proceeded lightnings and thunderings and voices: and there were seven lamps of fire burning before the throne, which are the seven Spirits of God <p. 1812-1813>. It is a lovely passage, is it not, written by yours truly.

A thunderstruck talent show's way of saying this is God's passages written in the Bible here, is not the best way to thunderstruck a talent show of people like this, you see. We're supposed to have written that she's pregnant, preggo and preggers! I loved that woman at the show of hands Nellie, in the pastures, said to Me once. It's a show horse then! She was lying there at my feet mind you, with the woven cloths of Jesus Christ's inventions here, and said, "Oh, I'm so hot right now!" after months and months of this cloaked woman coming to hear My talks at the Sermon on the Mount Sinai. It's as if She were just there at My feet to listen to the sermons day after day.

This is war! I do declare a mistrial in deeds from the commandant's wives tales! That said here, so much fun to be had here! Lots of people wanted to know, Andrea, if you had it in you to write about masturbation? Well, sure here! But make it quick, she said! I did declare a mistrial on Andrea because she's about to become the super mother that it takes to be one here! That said, are you ready for a new sensation's tattletaleness about the one maker that seeks to justify the Claritin ways of justifying trigger-happy people here!

This woman and this man had sex, you see it now you do! I do declare a mistrial then! He's all, hey, I'm happy this woman, chosen to be married to Me though, said, "I do not take this man to be my lawfully wedded husband," the King of England, Solomon, mind you! She goes, this picture, the one by Heaven is For Real by Todd Burpo is the guy, correct? Yes! He's the one who looks sort of like Me there, correctamundo? That is a raised flag from the dead life She had! What is it that I took from Her wantingnesses but a raised flag! I mean! If a guy does not know what that means to Me here, then take Her for granted then! I said, "Yes, it's meant for a guy to say, 'My flag is raised,'" means something is wrong with the commandant's yelling that stated that a citizenry's pleasantries, is something for the birds here!

There's happiness here in this heart of Mine here! Lovely tidings had with My wife of 20 to 30 years, correctly so! I raised 12 children with the woman we call Jezibellie Christ! What is wrong with society's interpretations of Her then? It's about the only woman I could call lovely! She's the only woman for Me then! I needed to hear that this society's shockingness values are never what they seemed to be here! This means we have a raised scented candled life here! She's shocked, Andrea is, that we're so blunt here, but this means war heroes are scented and such! That's a midlife crisis sorts of things here!

There's a loneliness to being nine months preggers and, never to see it in your sights here, but God had lap danced Me to Her too! That said, is it sacrilege to go around raising and wishing from the dead a commandant's older woman like Mary Magdalene all your lives then? She was a prostitute okay, one of the worst that I'd seen, and she made Me into a fortune teller! For gold nuggets here is what she wanted from me I am sure here! I said, sayonara to her and led her to the gates of hell that she's never returned from here! That said here, she's too old for Me here! That said too, what is the lifeline that is coming sadly to the ringers here! It's a woman named Jezibellie that I love and loved back then too! Is She reincarnate Andrea? This woman here is blasphemous then. Correctamundo! I loved Her with all My might, He said! She's got to be someplace better than that! I wanted to name Her after the dead wife of Mine though? It's Jezibellie Christ, always has been, who wrote and published the Bible on Her own here! That said, and this is a capital ways and means it lady's blessings here, to speak of a Divine Source Wisdom back then is blasphemous to the crowd of angels in Her wakes here! That said here, what about a correctamundo are we talking about then! See, we have a sex life again. I'm sure of it, she said!

And then She's nine months preggers! I go, hell yes! And I raised Her from the dead life She had! I took Her to my cabin up by the processing mills of dust to dust, and I said, "Woman, are You with Me here? My babies are inside You here! You're going to have twins." We're saying this, because the beauty and laughter in your words here, Andrea, are just what the doctor's ordered for you to stay put about here.

In that case, take Thee at Thy word! Call Me but love and I shall be new baptized, henceforth, I never will be… Jesus Christ! You're pregnant with My twins! Lovely gestures of love abide us here, but the truth be told here, it was for the Bible, as She had it under Her cloak with Her in the desert sands of time here. What is the Jesus Christ's hardships about here! I do declare a mistrial in works and in sands of time! She's pregnant with My twins under that cloak! There is a beautiful woman under that cloak, I presume! Why am I so attracted to Her? Because she's Anna from the Brooklyn Dodgers? No! Or, the Pacific Coast League, she said to Us here? Yes! It's Jezibellie Christ underneath that cape though! I bet it is. Correctly so!

There's a woman out there for Me. Is there? Jezibellie Christ, where did You go on Me then? This woman's not so pregnant body did declare for Me a mistrial in deeds and stuff here! That said, what does Jezibellie think about here, but a timely sort of visions cured makeup test here! That said, She lays back in the middle of a pregnant wife's ceremonies here and says, "I'm so tired!" Gosh, Jezibellie! Where have you been here, all My life I presume? Nope! I'm the man who impregnated Her, Jesus Christ Himself did!

Now you all are going to shoot Me for this. Correctamundo? I said, "Hallelujah," to that! And God told, said to Me here, scoop Her up and leave Her be? Nope! There's a cocktail lounge on fire for trusts! Here is the pregnanto wife I do declare a mistrial of here? Nope! I loved Her with all My might! She's right there for the taking, God said to Me here now! And so, it goes with the "voices" that one hears! Now just a minuto here, love life to be here! It's a correctamundo ways and means it lady's first choice of words and phrases here that makes this work possible here! This is the right way to say things right now, Folks, is with apostrophe s's and such! But this Bible thumping person comes up to Me and says, "Oh, it's just so hot outside! Have You a cloak to wear such as this one here?" And She comes to Me and says, lays back to the hot wife She is here, and states for the worlds to know here that I, Jesus Christ, impregnated Her with the lap dance of a lifetime of grief here?

She told me under no uncertain terminologies that lifetimes of thoughts just go hand in hand with the commandant's viewpoints here, and that certain individuals needed a lap dance! I go, this one's for the birds, correctamundos here? That said, Folks, and you too, Andrea here, this woman is Jezibellie reincarnated! We know who the suitors are of a lifetime of greed mongering here though! Try to follow Me here, Jesus says! This is the correctamundo ways of finding out if Andrea is indeed reincarnated to the following gestural innocence playings here!

That said here, I scooped Her up with My hands, in a hay stack though? We were much more well off back then than you guys might think here. What with The Invention of Lying, the movie mind you, we'll all have a scooped up version of Her in Her red dress here! Pretty woman, walking down the street, pretty woman! I loved that song back in the days of turmoils here, the old version by Roy Orbison is the best one for Me here! Not the Van Halen one, Folks! I'm an old timer then, He says! LOL we go here! And He's the one for Me, She said! And so, back to the lap dances of a lifetime of greed mongering amongst the Gentiles here! I scooped Her up with one tiny bill for that lap dance of a lifetime's qualities here!

I said, no can do, to Her though, correctamundos here? Nope, just thoughts and prayers then? We're at the Sermon on the Mount with that, um! Way about you there, Jezibellie Christ then? And She goes, I do then! This meaningful's problems here is exactamundo ways of laughter in our books here! There's one more thing's feelings in this rose colored glasses of peace here! That said, Jezibellie, will you be My wife! To have and to hold you is for the birds then, correctamundos here! No, not in the least here!

The audience for this book here is meaningful's ways and means it lady's nectar of life here! The rose-colored glasses of sun colored scoops in brassieres, that meaningful men just abide by here, doesn't mean that Jesus Christ is the one for me then. Correctamundo here? This man's just tired of definitions that don't make much sense here! In essence then, there's something to be said of God's willingnesses to deliver the evils of this world through a lap dance though? I'm guilty of one with My wife on top of Me, that's for certain here! I'm so sure of Her lap dances that I gave Her up for adoption once? Are we all still brothers and sisters of Christ then, cause I'm not related to Her God's ways and means it ladies here!

And so, I scooped Her up and said, hallelujah to the just thoughts of a preggo wife! I do declare a mistrial of cloaks and daggers here, as She had one under there too. She's so skinny I thought it wasn't Her under there, but little did I know! It was all set up there under my nose. Before diving into thoughts about the DSW, what is it that is making us type all of this here stuff about Jezibellie Bongs here! But to say it is Barnes is a misnomer here.

She's got Devanagari script languages coming together to say, it sounds a lot like Barnes or Bongs here, but that's about it here. She's married to Me the very next day! Under the stars and the moon, and the eagles flying high! There are eagles in Egypt mind you! I was right there in the Cairo sunsets and Mizraim, another word for Egypt, was there in all its glories mind you. In time you will find the way, Andrea! Chapter 4 of first Corinthians means to be taken with all its glories too. In time you will find the way to state this for the birds here, but this is the quickest way to His heart, Sires and you too, Gentiles, to find a way to state this for the meanings of the Earth is vast.

That said, what is the apostle Paul doing in the scriptures! He deserves none of the above! I believe in your love, so I'm glad to take the vow, here and now, oh! I promise to love faithfully! You're all I need!

As the song goes! This is the limelight's biggest foreshadowing then for Andrea here, as she finds the man of her lifetime morals, as well as His biggest counterpart's ways and means it lady's essence here! That said here, what of the Edgar Cayce's morals are we to partake in, if she's willing to thereof? It's a genius's ways and means it persons here, that states that commandants are the trusted, friendliest ways and means it lady's snatcharoos here! What I mean by this, Ladies and Gents, is if you're meant to be in love with somebody else here, why can't I be in love then? I'm the Jesus's signatures for peace here, and I cannot even love a girl the way I love Jezibellie Christ then?

Yes, Ma'am and Sirs, united ways here, we part ways then! I mean, if God happened to be a man and then some here, why couldn't He portray His wife in a new light! If the Bible is so trustworthy, as we have just shown that we love the suckin' thing, then maybe with our new lights, we can shine so heavily upon us here! Are we that glad of a wife for Jesus Christ then? Maybe our turnips can claim light so strongly now! I do know of Ephesians Chapter 1.

Please turn to that scripture cause we're all over the boards here. Here is the daunting party of Paul, of one here. He is not to be disguised any longer of being a saint here. Paul is a moron, an idiot! He's never been back to Earth since! We've banned him from coming back, as he was a moron and a trite way to put it here, is to say this too. We've never had a Jezibellie in the Bible, because the most sensual points in it clasped onto the storybook wonderment it had in it. The Luddites are the reasons for the seasons here, what with Christmas and New Year's Eve being so close to one another here. The Luddites are the reason for giving faith to the invention of lying to the pastors, sonny boy you! If you don't like us here, why don't you just leave?

And there was nothing said in I Corinthians, Roman chapters of God's trust here, Romans Chapter 1, Verse 33 then states that we need another Bible passage to boot here, as the death of one party line is not going to make a difference, She said! There is no Bible passage 33 of the Corinthians kind, is there too? Nope! That said, this is the vow we take in order to bear the cross on our shoulders of love here. There was no wrongdoing in the Bible's passages here, for there to be no Chapter 33's in the Bible itself. Right? There certainly is not, eh? This means war to a lot of folks who don't believe in its love here! I'm just kidding about the 33's. It's a rouge to think this way, Andrea!

Because we're chapters and verses into the nothingness that is to become the Bible proper. That said, the next paragraph stands on its own here. Here goes, Paul, right? It deserves none less, other than the killed us kinds of parties here? He killed us both! It's a hanging of Jezibellie Christ that instigated a cutting or chopping off of My head, just to make sure I was dead? Sons of Italy meetings later, Andrea, are you ready for a new sensation!

This Paul guy murdered us both! He's not a special kind of inklingships kind of guy here. He stood on the Sermon on the Mount Sinai many a times looking for Jezibellie to kill us both with one fell swoop here. The sermons were going no place fast! I went, God is your kingdom come! And everybody went, oh why me, why this, why life! And I spent my time individually consulting the King of Egypt's plans to believe in Cairo too much here, but that is where our headquarters remained here. I do declare a mistrial in deeds and wonderments here, but that woman, Jezebel, is who we're talking about here. This is war if they cannot be together then. In the Bible's good books of worships here, say, if the commandant's not the furthest thing from Jimmy Swaggart's mouths here! He said once in a sermon, they all do, that there's a Jezibellie problem here, Folks, and you too, Andrea, correctamundos here?

Nothing could be furthest from the truths here, because Andrea never knew of such Bible's verses and codes and what not! She never even knew about the Bible's token friendships, that take root and grow into a love story to boot here! And that said here, what is the commandant's ways and means it lady's, supposedly "different" gifts here? It's that she never even knew about the Bible, never studied it before now that is! And the furthest thing from the truths of the matters lies in the Bible's only sacrilege offerings that Jesus is now hitched, correctamundo's here? Is that even spelled right here, the only rights above the laws of gravity that desist and destroy the commandant's main telling to God here is that Paul, Paul Wright is his name here, discovered that She was indeed writing about the Bible's talent searches, shows that God could be furthest from the truth here, about life and what not here!

Nothing could be furthest from the truth about life's possibilities on a token friendship such as this one here. This guy, Andrea, has got to love you back, right? Well, Jezebel was the woman who really got Her name on the chopping block, shall we say yes to that! It's as though Paul was a sainthood then, as Jezibellie wrote the Bible as a scribe though? No, as the DSW! Paul is no picnic ride here. He was a saint no more as he fell from Heaven's gates at the altars of love when he died. He shall not live any longer, as he died, was head cut off as well, right after he murdered us both!

Paul is as Paul does here, and every preacher I've seen has put him up on a pedestal and he deserves nothing of the kind of luck we shall have as a foreboding structure of light here, as he killed us both! We were one party line away from doing nothing here. And he said, you both shall live a different life under God! And wham, right in the kisser, of Jesus Christ? In Italy no less and no more, but we both died at the hands of a God then? I do not believe Paul to be a God, nor do I believe our bodies were found in Egypt, dead. I believe them to be dead at the hands of Paul though, and in Italy and Greece it is surely Mesopotania, not Mesopotamia, and Her dad was supposed to kill Paul instead of the other way around, but he was too late to do so.

I do believe in the kissers of gods and goddesses here. We reigned for several hundred years, our families did. And to be arranged this way and that a way is not what we're supposed to be doing here. Please close this book now, King James Verson! It's arranged differently in scriptural talks and such. We'd just assume not go there to close this book now.

Instead, turn to page 5 of the good book now! NIV, New International Version is nice here (NIV, Gen. 8.1.). We just like the KJV, King James Version, a little bit better here. But Ephesians is nice to look at both ways here. Chapter 1 begins like this you see. Paul is a jerk! So, he hung Me, and cut off My wife's head? It's the other way around here. She went by hanging two seconds after My head plopped off by guns though? By swords. It's about that way here, that the cross says we died that way up there that day, shadowing for God's works about gay and human rights here. That's about all we did to the other half of this discussions here. Paul gave two shits about us here.

I will return He said, and out like a lamp we were! It was after 25 years of reigning Egyptians that we gave two shits about the nation itself? It's so like us to believe in following gates across the edges of time here! I loved that God gave us a shift work schedule like little Jezibellie had when we were kids here. She gave us a rouge, a supper for thieves, and the schedules worked out themselves about what times God gave us a picture of people eating supper here. And the Last Supper photo I took was about Mary M. getting a footsie picture with the Christ our Lordship and His wife in tow? I don't think so! Mary Magdalene is not to be tested, tried and true here. She is a villain and always has been such. I don't think God's ways here are to be tested, tried and true here, because one of the ways in which each day goes by the wayside here is to be lasted upon. Tested is true too, because of the ways in which God tranquilizes each of the medium departments of God's kingdoms here, it's because of the way He loved us in which we are beautiful then!

Chapter 5

Little Devil Girl is Jezibellie Christ Then! I Loved Her So, Jesus Says!

If you don't believe that Jezibellie is My wife, He says, then you are mistaken, for assuredly, there is the massive train wreck quandaries of finding what is in the evitable tales, for people are awoken in the gandering seas and struck by the daylight's fire! Are we satisfied about the tales of two-villes here? We are! There's lots of people out there who believe in Andrea's thunderfied fields of visions here! What have you say you, Andrea! That means to us that she has something to say again! And we don't even know about her love lives to boot here!

Are you lucky enough to know Jezibellie Christ's ways of seeking refuge in the Bible, no less and no more here? Are you lucky enough to know Me, He says! Because if you don't know the Bible inside and out here, then how are you going to know what to say to Me when I finally meet you, He says! I do know this. There are no bedrooms at hand that have questionable tactics in them. I am a romantic, as well as a commandant in the military too. Did they forget that part in the Bible no less and no more here! I probably got it all right once, and I stuck to the memos that God prevented for us to attain this level of atmospheric pressure here.

Once, God struck lightening and said to Me, are you there yet, Andrea? On this level of insight, it is okay here to be once struck to say, "Wo is me," to just about everything we've been professing to you about Jezibellie Christ. What is the name of the woman, and how did She end up in front of me at the sheep's gandering tales of Christ's inception piece?

She was just lying there in the shade and said up to Me, My eyes, and stuff, "Wo is me! I'm just a lass in a cesspool of knowledge here," and I scooped Her up at that instant and carried Her over the hot coals of Galilee! I said, "Heave ho! There is a spot for you in My cabin, on the bay area overlooking the shrewd classes of peace! Will you come with Me here?" She said, "I'm carrying Your child. Am I not? I need a place to stay. Yes!" Did He respond in kind with this memo here, that I am allowing Him to come to Me in this way, She says! I go, "Well? Come with me, My sweet one! You are the hardship greed no more here!" That's not what I said to Her though! Will you come with Me, My sweet one, sounds like an inkling more than just jealousy of the man standing next to Her, Paul himself here. He is no saint, and he is not an inkling further than this jealousy of a man to take Her to the prom!

I go, "Well, is he yours yet?" She laughs, "No, not in the least!" He goes, "I take thee as My lawfully wedded wife! To have and to hold, you know?" And She said, "Lest our child's beacon of light here, I'm fully capable of seeing the babies here. Did you know a twin set in the past can be a death sentence here without the light of God seeing that there are twins in here?" I said, "If you can tell this by its inception here, I take Thee at Thy word!

"Call Me but love, and I shall be new baptized! Henceforth, I never will be, not Romeo, but Jesus!" She goes, "Love Me but tenderly here. I've sat underneath You for months on end. Is it like this, Jesus, or is I going to perish, as well as this fellow here who can't seem to get it up for anyone but Myself," Jesus includes a paraphrase of what She's saying here, and that is, are we going to get it up for a while later? He goes, I suppose so! Are we there yet loved ones of God's here! "I'm tired," She says! "Well, I'll hold you up," He says! God says the hardships are just that, one saga after the next.

Is it truth that God knew Abraham-Hicks, better than He loved God though? It's not the same thing is it? It absolutely is the same thing! I am Abraham, though, is not what we're after here, although the guys up here are absolutely marveling at the same ideas that God's wraths come about as! And Esther Hicks, she is a lovely sort of woman here. I do declare a mistrial, in that I did not have enough money so as to stay afloat without my family for so long, she says, Andrea does. And so, with that, honesty and integrity go hand in hand here.

I do know this. Stay tuned, Dear Ones, for this is just the beginning of trials and tribulations that set out to caress the spirit. I do say, bank on the loved ones of God's kingdoms here. Tell us what we need to know in order that Jesus and Jezibellie may have their lives back! *Romeo and Juliet* is a fantastic rendition of where we need to be right now. Be aware that God's only ultimate species exists for the limelights that ensues us here. Take it from me, Andrea, She says! My only way out of this lifetime of habits is to limelight you here.

There's times when God wants us to be cruel and unjokingly simple about the eons of plentitudes there are in words and in deeds here. Simple as this is here, there's tons of relaxed people out there about this new medical insights questioning, and it has to do with the Earth's axes here. There's more than one axis then, yes? That means that there are aliens in the systems of truth. What we mean by this is, there are lots of people from the coast of Africa who aspire to you picking up on their medical insights, Andrea! This medical insights thing is for the birds if you cannot use it here! Say, what does Jesus speak about it here? He's on the fence too.

Right? Wrong, nope, I don't think it's better to stay at the context you're in here. That said, what does Jesus do with this information back in the days of time where Jezibellie could hear them too? It's a medical insight, Peoples! This is the Divine Source Wisdom talking. I do hear it all day long for people left and right here. There are people everywhere trying to gain insights into the comatoseness of it all. What we mean by this too is that God's players are about sick and tired of being transpoken about! What we mean by this too, is that God's players are equal in skills, enough for me to be transposed and taken away from this lifetime of habits and put back into a mental hospital's wakes for this kind of information.

That doesn't serve anyone all day long though! I mean, if we cannot use this information to heal the worlds, to heal the planets, then we're all surely mistaken here as to the confidence spoken for Andrea here! There are medical insights for each person on Earth's crust here, and she's got 'em! I don't know why here but the sound of medical insights are a few other people's trusts here. I don't know about the mental hospital's ways and means it lady's insights here, but the family does not trust in your medical insights, Andrea! So that's why the commandments come into play here.

This is where commandants come into play here, and where God did notice that spoken for people here are the meaningfulnesses and talent searches to come to God here. That said, what of the rich being taxed to death means that the poor are medicated to alleviate their strain on lives here? That said, what about the state hospital system is it that takes people in here? That said here, what is the possibilities lasting on the inklingships that pterodactyl states are losing the minds of bodies that wish to be on top of the worlds here? That said here, why medicate the poor homeless people that medicated themselves on liquor, wine and booze?

That's about the same as medicating the homelessnesses that ensue here. There's little to do with this booze hound that's been taken over by aliens here. By the way here, there's aliens, sure! We were hunted and killed by pterodactyls by the way! We were here with the dinosaurs, … Yes! Yes, we were too! What does God say about an ancient predator like Andrea then, lolz! That 'z' was intentional too here. That way, it doesn't sound so scary here.

The predators though were never T-Rex or Tyrannosaurus here. That is because he is the gentlest creatures of habits ways about life here. I don't get it either, but Tyrannosaurus here had the longest arms possible here. Those little arms are for the birds here. Those skeletons of T-Rex are outdated at best here. T-Rex, Tyrannosaurus Rex here, was a gentle creature is against spoken folklores and stuff! Sure, they ate human beings, right? I chance this session a little further here and state for the records of trust that I am not insane here! I do hear this word for word here! I'm not interjecting anything into this conversation of trusts here. And so, aliens and stuff do exist then? Yes! There are people who need help from us here, and this is where she be with this. Don't put her into a mental hospital again! For this is the time and the places that God's willingnesses to boot her don't put up with this mental hospital notations for peace here, but speaking in tongues? You betcha! We can do that, and simply too. I betcha this could follow the notations for peace here!

There's dinosaurs all along in historical contexts here. There's nothing but dinosaur poop though! I do know this too. The dinosaurs shared a link in historical contexts here and gave it up for God's purposes here. The pterodactyls weren't the only predators for us here. It was God's wills and chances for peace that integrated God's loveliness tales and such!

Chapter 6

Paul is a Limelight No More

Hi! Can we not use so many profanities here? This means war is on the brink if it's government work we do here! It's government work I tell ya! That's for Andrea to find out, and to not state it here means it's going to be a long day again! I want to tell you about Andrea first, Jesus says! So, Divine Source Wisdom… What is that exactly? Well, we're hundreds if not trillions of men up here, just waiting for Jesus Christ to instruct us on what kind of a lady He hung around with? Nope, He married Her! I think the spiritual guides are female though!

So, what if there's a message hanging around in truth be tolds here, that states that Andrea is just a herpes infected female, because we are not, and I repeat that too, not to be told anything about God's willingnesses here. In fact, she does not have any sexually transmitted diseases here, including the AIDS viruses, and such things as schizophrenias no longer here! I repeat! This is a tattletale's ways and means it lady's signing off of the fact that God put her here to begin telling the gospel's truths here.

And for that I give God a memo here! I state that God's truths are just about taken in here! That said here, what is the "here" supposed to represent here, but God's willingnesses to think about the only things that surprised him of Her, you know? Paul that is here! It's a part of the pedophilia raps that we don't like to talk about here! Well, Paul wanted to do away with discipleship for pedophile raps and such. Meanings of tidings here, that God's willingnesses are truth be told very inklingship like here! Not everyone who has got a pedophile rap is one here.

Do we really look like the Andromeda Galaxy here? I will admit it, she said! I will state that again! We don't like pedophiles, that's for sure here! But that doesn't mean that everyone who's been accused of such, is one! And Andrea is no pedophile! That said, is schizoaffective disorder more than likely to develop then? It's probably the truth be told, nations and such should gather round and be stated for the facts that God's only son is really pointing out the inklingships for the means that God is not there of all cases of sad sackness! Meaning that God's only son is really there to dispel the myths created in one's head and such! That said, is Andrea a pedophile?

Nope, but there's such thing as pedo head! We'll discuss that later then? Someone can be so taken in by evilness as to whether or not God made a lesson plan to dictate what a pedophile is exactly. I'm not one, just to let you know, klan of marksmen out there, ... So, a person with schizophrenias has more than likely been accused of it! At certain times over the years here, there's peace on Earth, and then some, Andrea! And God's waitings for such a rap to obliterate schizophrenias of the waking kinds here, is just what the doctor's ordered for the raps and such!

It's, I think I'm a pedophile though, and I'm not one! It's just so hard to explain correctly, but I'm not one, even though a tough nut in my life at the time of inception thought I was, so, but he was likely one! Not sure if this is being communicated correctly, thereof, but time will tell as you read on further.

You can be so succumbed to thinking you would hurt someone with your words only that you might develop schizophrenias over that as well. We're here to state that God foresees the innocence of these peoples who are clammed up in God's countries here, in the hopper, or in the jail units here, that foresee the inklingships of pedophilia raps here that are non-existent! And my God, for what do I honor this moment's notices here for, but to call someone bipolar II for listening to the raps of God as well here, but to seek and desist in Chapter 8 of Romans 2 here that states that God is no pedophile then! And listen to this too. We just fly out with chapters and verses here. This is no pedophile rap for those with schizophrenias and such! Nothing could be further from the truths be told nations inklings here!

Romans 8:31 here states that (NIV) here God is a tyrant of sorts? Nope! We like this Bible passage too, that: If God is for us, who can be against us <p. 785>? But that implies that there are two books we are missing out of the Bible, right about here then! It's about pedophilia raps, and Paul thought that by talking about it, it would attract the negativity of the universes and such! So, there were two books of Romans here, but Paul, like I said, was a tyrant from God's graces here, and threw the whole thing into the garbage can while we were working on it here. That be said of this work here. She's not telling the family about its publishings, lest we be thrown into a mental hospital again for it! And for those who state that this is a working knowledge of Jesus Christ's dealings here, state that for a fact we are not going into a mental hospital again over this works here. Shall we not?

This is war then, Folks of the Gentiles and such! We're trying to state that for the records here, Paul had it right, to kill just about anyone of the pedophilia raps here! But not to make due here on the facts that God made a killing in getting to the Stonehenge of peaces here! Stonehenge, by the way, was reconstructed in the 20s! We're just telling exactly of things to come here! What of the mosques are the best inklingships for this Divine Source Wisdom Center of the futures here! We seek like minded individuals, not pedophilia raps or nothing! But the pedophiles of the futures here is the Armageddon of the lifetimes of hope here that God's wrath spoke of in Revelations here, to get rid of them all! It's Revelations, because there are two of us here! Me and Her here! God spoke a lot of Revelations in the mornings though of 9/11! What of the wakes of people just go around and knock down buildings and such's here ye tidings as, we're just on these airplanes and we're going down, down, down in them here! What of the 9/11's do you seek to differ yourselves underneath here!

All of those involved in the shootings and such of mass murderers here are just for the birds. Right, Class of Gentiles here? There's many a Holy Ghost out there. That said, stay away from the "voices"! We talk about that in Chapter 8 some more here. Obviously, we are one kind of voice you can hear for sure here. Let's make a point to come back to this later then. We're the "good" kinds of voices you want in your lives, that's for sure here.

That's for the birds too. Let me make my point and I will come back to this in this writings class we're under here. For the birds means that the 9/11 killers were simply pedophilia raps and none of it was the truths be told here! And so, they made their way around the clocks of times past here to reckon with the truths be told eras of spacement here and decided to kill everyone instead of to live out their pedophilia raps that were untruth be tolds here!

That means that pedo head, that I discuss later in these works here, does not apply to these fellows either here! It just means that schizophrenias are made up words here that go round and round in society's raps of love here. Just bear with us! We'll explain it thoroughly as time moves on here! There's not a society in which that pedophilia is an okay thing. We're into that kind of knowledge here too. That said, what of Paul's wraths are just that! He used to masturbate too! We'll get to that in a minute's times here. What of the pedophilia raps are just that too! Some people believe in hardships such as inklingships in nature and of deeds in here too! What is the problems with society's influences here! And a reminder too. We're speaking and Andrea is not! Although, it is times past that God's reflections makes into the meals of a lifetime of hurts and such! We're not asking for God's forgivenesses here. We're stating a simple fact that God's inklingships are for the birds and such? Hardly so here! That's for the birds to decide upon here! And the facts remain that Andrea is not speaking here. We are! She just channels us! It's channeling her and Us!

And just for the surprise of things here, we like the word surprise here... It makes us feel important here. So, anyway! What is Her name exactly? We are Jezebel's keepers though, right? Well, She in fact wrote the Bible Herself using our medium to do it with! She was Paul's keeper, let's put it that way, as Paul has no feelings left in his bosom, for what exactly though, She-Male! I guess Andrea's a She-Male then if Divine Source Wisdom's a bunch of guys up here? Nope! She's a he though? Nope! I go wait a minute there! She's a he then? Nope, he's a He and she's a She.

So, what if the ballbearings in your last name, Andrea, get the best of us here? Nope, He's attractive and She's not? So, what if Jezibellie Christ, I so aptly named Her, did I? She's My wife! To have and to hold, from this day forward! She was lying in a pasture when I saw Her next, listening to my sermons and to Me talking about the Divine Source Wisdom's book on the Bible! I made it 100 pages per day! And the rest is Me, making up stories for the Divine Source Wisdom, DSW for short! So, with that in mind... Hint, hint! We need to make up crochety stories about the DSW to prevent further adieu here! What is that exactly here? We like "here" so much so that we'll take it out if need be.

Furthermore, I just told you, the DSW is millions upon trillions of men up here, dancing for the Copacabana song. Instead of further adieuing everyone here, let's just make a toast and a preparation mark for the bottom dollar here! We love the word "here" so much so that if we take it out, nobody will listen! So, we leave it here because it's nice to know God exists!

And tons more where that came from, BDSL, Bondage, Discipline, Sadism, and masterful languages to boot here. We aren't talking about Andrea's bosom here. We're just saying that the Bible was written by Jezibellie!

There's bondage and discipline though? We don't do that kind of thing, ever! There's bondage and discipline in the discipleship then, Class of Gentiles, just waiting for a raise here? Nope! This is because the bondage and discipline's right up Paul's alleyways of trust here, and he didn't write the Bible.

Nothing in it has an inkling of trust in it here. We're just waiting for the days and times here of our Lord and Savior, Jesus Christ, to have and to hold His wife here! Just a minute here, He says! I did say "say" here sometimes, like, Jesus Christ say! Say, sayonara there, Folks! This is what we're doing on a regular basis here is to try to find out what Jesus meant by certain things in the Bibles of trust then. It's Paul, right! Chapter 1 of Ephesians states it here too (KJV, Eph. 1.1.) <p. 1722>. We're saying here that God wrote the Bible verses in question here!

She's like, this doesn't mean I have to actually look at it. Right? I mean, I don't even have to look it up! It's right there for the takings, Andrea! Then she looks it up, KJV though, and it says again there, I the apostle Paul? Nope, not on this one. So, She just said, tell me your name again? He said, I am Paul, one of the apostles of Jesus Christ here, right? Wrong again, Folks of betterment times here! Don't squeeze it out of us or nothin'!

But this apostle Paul is wrong again for society's influences here! This is the "I" in Paul's name that makes no sense here and pastors along the ways and means it lady's focus of questioning the DSW is really the facts that he took Her for a hat in the days past here.

Meaningfulnesses like Paul's wrongdoings are really just holding her down and, wait for it, getting her past her millions of "messages" of the Bible's doings here. And just waiting for times past days of hardships then, and oakleying it to state that God's wisdoms are just fine here! Use the Urban Dictionary for that one! Oakleying makes oakleys seem strenuous here, but a shades review states that we're needing them. That said here, what is Jezibellie's hardships consisting of here? Just being held down to write it here in Ephesians, for example. And to state it here for the millions of viewers we so have in our wakes here. Paul was a fraud for sure here.

The dividing times that said, Paul, an apostle of Jesus Christ by the will of God (KJV, Eph. 1.1.) <p. 1722>, etc., etc., is not in our wakes here! This KJV is okay here!

But the apostle Paul is none but a fruitcake here! This willingnesses to go forward here is for the birds, you see it, now you do! He's never had the Holy Spirit, Paul did not! He's not of this world. I keep saying that for the records here! It's not that Paul is a complete and utter moron here. Is it? Yes, he is! He held us down to state that for the records here, he's the apostle Paul! And we go, laughter ensued here, and say unto us, what again, Paul? And he stated for the records here, that the 1st chapter of Ephesians is his, along with several others that pastors quote frequently as his doings here. When truthfully be told here that God's several advances make for a dull boy here!

And that said, too, there's something in the wakes of 9/11 that states that a government problem like this could ensue around a Biblical password here! Well? I just looked at Chapter 3 of Ephesians: same thing here (KJV, Eph. 3.1.) <p. 1724>. He's going around making assumptions that he cannot justify with! It was almost time for the production of the books themselves, much longer by the way! Until he hand carried one or two of them away and threw them into the fire of our Lordship! And that spoke volumes of what he had tried to do here. Do you believe me, Gentiles and you alike here, Andrea? Yes! She does believe Us!

So, what does your family's inklingships state, that for the records here, is not very fast of you to state it here, for the umpteenth normal visit to the shepherds that wane and wax for our tidings here! That said here, what of the shepherd's normal visits do we not understand here? We are not to carry on such weights as the days of wrath are fixated into number one and to number two, etc., etc.!

That meant that God was watching the production of the fire's terminologies and such! Paul dictated what we're supposed to be writing here! He made that up by the way here about Jezebel, that heretical woman there for writing the Bible I suppose here, that she got ate up by dogs in the Bible's worst terminologies lessons to boot here, KJV II Kings Ch. 9: 30-37.

If the Bible states that it is so, does it mean that God's inklingships, hardships to boot here, are just a waiting for somebody, something or someone to tattletale on? She made a decision here to state that "I" means God in this context here!

And that's how Jesus became a hero for God's sakes here! He just stated for the records here that, anyone who comes but through the Savior is blessed beyond epic proportions here! And God's sell it like eons here of foreboding talentships here, is better than God's other epic proportions here! And that stated that eons of love here at the beckonings of this man and this woman here, were sometimes beginning to sound fuzzy, funny, or not at all inklingships, tattletales, and so on! Meanings and such are that God's only son, Jesus Christ, is really not the son of God or the son of man at all here! Yea, right! He's really reincarnatable though!

And that's why the inklingships go so far here as to state that Paul is in the right here! Not! I don't believe Jesus Christ's days are numbered here, but the Jesus I know, Paul says, is right here for the taking! And he cut off His head! Mine too I suppose, but one of the biggest blessings of all here is that God's inklingships are just to be had here! There's such a focus on God's loving natures here that God could not invent pedophilia. Right here, Class of Gentiles and such here? Not! Not in a way that you mean here. That said, what of pedogoina, or pedophilia back in the days of the Gentiles and stuff, reveals for life, is just what it is supposed to be here!

I do think that pedogoina is wrongly spelled here. In actuality, they used to be a derivative of Indian language and culture to Europeanize our last names here, not this word of course, but some other names we know and love here. And so, Paul Wright's last request was that all pedophilias be taken out and shot here. So, does that make him a saint then? Hardly so! I do believe in shooting all pedophiles, Andrea states for the nation's addresses here! But I don't think that Paul was zealously trying to find out what the crimson lights are surrounding his name here! I don't think that pedogoina is going to go far here in this work here. It's a rouge or something like it. You see it, now you don't! I just wanted to state for the records of peace here that God's only son is really the only thing that you see here as Gentiles.

In other words, what does God's only son's reckonings with peace here state that for the records here there is no truth in scriptures here! I do declare an only son though! My life, He says, is for the birds if I can't have Jezibellie believe in Me here! I do need a reckoning to deal with the facts that God's ankleships are really just the Jezibellie in Me here! That stated here, what is God's plans for loving God's creatures here, far and wide, till death do us part here! This is the inklingships signing off though! We're sick and tired of that word here! But it's the truth. It's inklingships that make our hardships gather us in importance here. Hence, why we mention it always here!

Here's the deal here. Just because someone's a pedophile rap doesn't mean they are one! I just didn't know it at the time then? Of course, I knew! But to say it so plainly here, there goes something of this conversation with Jesus Christ on Day 16 of the Introduction here. I was on the floor writhing in pain though? Nope! Just apologizing for some things here, and I could not type the above message here without listening to God's hopes here for a greater tomorrow. Listen up! I do not declare a discipleship happened with soiled intentions here, but if you are listening to God's wrath right now though, you are surely mistaken that He finds me delectable or something, right? I go like this you see. Um!

Here, take my loin cloth, dry your tears, prepare me to love you once more here! And she goes, but I'm a pedophile no more here? I never was! Don't treat me like that by giving me your loin cloth! But "there there" is what I said to you! It's a loin cloth isn't it? I'll put it away. Geesh! is short for Jesus Christ, or other such swear words here? It's not a swear word, Jesus isn't. Geesh might be though! I guess I'll put it away with sweat and with tears on it.

I've been carrying it around for an eon here just to give to My wife, ex-wife, and lover all at the same time here! It's true too! What? She said! Are you going to give it to me next so I can keep it and love it and do something with it later! Um! So, she says, you know? This is Jesus Christ talking this time, and there's nothing wrong with Andrea's lessons planning here. That said, is Paul done taking my things from Me now?

Because Delilah was just the ex-wife! I promised her, Andrea that is, a lesson planning in that God's wills here make for a better tomorrow! I don't get the Paul figure much in the lessons plannings of lives here, because he's just in netherworld! We were sitting someplace one day and I said, go to Chapter such and such of this book over here, Andrea! And there was the word, "netherworld," in Greek mythology no less and no more here! I just cast her aside then and said things like, loin cloth, to just anybody then? Nope! Chapter 3 of Ephesians states that Paul's reckonings of literatures and such make for a dull boy! That said, what of My reckonings, is just like what Jezibellie would have typed?

There are tons of things Paul has done wrong. And so, we're just waiting for the time of days, inklings here and such that says, I just need some time to pass me by here and to pause for all the times that God's meaningfulnesses just meant nothing to God's sadists here! There's no more sadists for the world's pocket shoe horses to deny here!

But horses, by God here, there is more than one god here, take what they can from the world's bestest celebratory feverishnesses here! And God's gentle hands here take Thee to be My lawfully wedded wife? To have and to hold Her, till death do us part here!

I do declare a mistrial in deeds and in lawyer school's very bestest things we have on hold here. Elijah, by the way, was Jezibellie's lawyer here! She did not kill him! I promise you that, Jesus says! I betcha he killed himself though, as he's no longer with us, in spirit that is! Once you kill yourselves, it's all over for you! That said here, what is the point then? We want, I repeat, want to come back to Earth's crusts here all the time here! That said, Paul is a jerk! And, he used to rule Egyptian rulesses. What I mean by that is, the rulesses come from Egypt. That said, there's words here that are meaningful of lives here! What I mean too is, he used to think he was God! And that's no mental health note, is it? He ruled for about five years when they were gone for five in Jerusalem, Jezibellie and Me.

Too long, She says, Jezibellie does! He did everything right up until that point of no returns here. How do you think he found love? He never had! He cannot rule a country without a wife. That's because the inklingships of life's quandaries caress My wife's spirit enough to find ejaculation all over the place from Paul's know it all lifestyles here. He made it up, of course here, that she killed Elijah, that Paul was a Gentile, too, which he was not! That said, what of ejaculation is Jesus about here? It's about My wife! I promised God a hardship's tidings here, is just what the doctors find sinisterly wicked about this life's promises here! That's a joke.

You get it here? I get it here now, she says! ☺ Please explain it to me, Andrea says! You see, the balance of life's efficatures are really for the takings here. Do you understand if Paul was a Gentile that God's willingnesses to find him outdated here is just the dream that pastors really find attractive for Jezibellie in the futures of God here! That said, Andrea, what is so funny? It's Us, is it? We're trying to detain you! Hint, hint! ☺ I liked you so much, Jesus says, that I chose you to tell my stories and such here! Hint, hint!

Chapter 7

Sleeping in My Van! Jezibellie Christ is Really Something to Behold!

This is where it all started in Bethlehem! I met Her as a 5-year-old in a tree hugging contest! Much! Our teachers gave us grief as we looked into each other's eyes and saw the world was one big messcapade in it! So, we set a pact, to love each other as 3rd graders do, years ago, but years later! I kissed Her under a tree hugging contest once! She was beautiful back then, bronzen skin! And I, too, though not, right! I was pure White and jealous that She had darkened skin? Not necessarily but sort of? I thought She was a beauty queen, quite lovely and passionate we are here! She kissed Me back though! It was 3rd grade, don't worry! I can see my car is going to arouse you some. That's because this make out section was non-existent until 3rd grade.

Then I kissed Her back passionately at the same time as loving Her back. And we did have cars back then! Little horse and buggy ones, but yes, how do you do, Mademoiselle! Take fate to the limits here and nod off a little bit here. I don't like Jezibellie Christ? Is that what we're up against here! I seem to be in the middle of a nod off session here. Scratch this entire paragraph then? What are we up against here, seemingly so!

I don't know how to treat My wife here? Scratch this entire paragraph then! What are we up against, Jezibellie Christ!

So, what if My wife don't like Me hanging around this entire paragraph here! Are we up against the snow drift that we were in the 7th grade! I liked wanting to be with you, Andrea, but you're kind of our mentor. And so, get this sort of thing aside from God's wills here, what does a Seahawks game mean to you? It's our wills and our courages that get us places at random here! I do not know the strength of your name in this wonderful world called life here! But I do know something about peace and tranquility's sakes here. I don't know what to call it here but this prose is for the birds is it not! I mean, everyone is so pissed off! About life, about properties, about caring for this world's second best option! I mean, if this life cannot go on, abide by the forces of evil that we're carrying around with us here! It's not evildoers that lovingly go by the wayside here. It's actual fact! And we're attesting to writing this here book because we love Andrea enough to tell her about it!

If I could go into a succession of dance with these partners of yours, I mean, she's not even deaf! I own up to my deafened doornail type days here. And with a little bit of spokesmanships here, we are not even showing up on the radars of love here! I don't know what Christ's God speaks from here! But I do know that the post office came readily and fired her ass because she ended up in a mental hospital here, not because she missed work or anything like it you see! So, this is what is said from Heaven's gates here. Let's take away the driver's licenses of the mentally ill and see where that gets us then! What happened to the crying shame of life here! There's driver's licenses and there's tests of times past here. What do you know? I could go on and on but I will save it for a later date or chapter thereof here. This makes homeless people into shitheads for sure here. What's a homeless person without a driver's license, but a mentally ill person? What does Andrea do without a driver's licensing class? She's living in her van, and then let's take away the driver's licenses of people who are given these shithead meds and then some here? This is God talking here through the Divine Source Wisdom here. What does God mean when we say, let's do away with the driver's licenses of homeless people here?

What is a homeless person but a citizen junkie that's homeless and stranded without a vehicle to sleep in here, at Walmarts no less and no more here! What is the homeless person supposed to do then but with an LRA, Less Restrictive Alternative, too? What is the message behind doing such a deed like taking away the driver's licenses of good people! It's a pedo head thing, is it not? I don't know how a schizophrenic drives, she said, the cop thereof here! I go, well, I think you're in trouble, Lady! And she goes, "I don't think you can drive this!" I said, yes I can, but you're gonna take the driver's test again and say she got a 96 again and again here! What is the purpose of God's planets aligning just right here! That said here, what is Jezibellie Christ's oldest wish?

To drive! Yes, to drive. And that's what the Egyptian rulers thought was the best thing since sliced bread too, is that She could say whatever She wished, and that nobody trusted God's wraths like the Jezibellie cures that came about in Her head here! Say, who was that John the Baptist, but our son! I say this because I was in the middle of a bath in it, say the river here, not the lake or the pond but a river. And this guy comes up to Me and says, Jezibellie Christ, you're going to get a bath too. What, like I didn't go to Galilee without My wife or anything. Right? I think She's golden, you know! I liked Her with all My might, but Andrea, you're running around without a driver's license for typing us, here ye, and we're like, she's willing to ride the bus though? Why take away these driver's licenses, God? To make my life miserable, and not be able to search for a different job?

She's right there for the taking of the most sinister eaten grin and said to Me, I make My life terribler by the minute here! He's like not even testing you here. I go, well, I can just grin at Her back! And She said, I'm next! We go, well, it's a baptism. What is a baptism, Dear Lordship, they said to us back then! And we go, it's a strength training test or some other such thing thereof! Back to the rivers of Galilee then! We're homeless, but we're not bathing in the ponds, for this is war thereof! I love the Divine Source Wisdom to keep me safe from harm during this period of homelessness! We would have been "dead" countless times, if it weren't for where to go take a bath and stuff? I love the DSW to keep me safe from harm, not wishing that others say or speak differently, but we really are voices of the past, present and future, that wishes God's wraths were not so clearly etched for God's intents and purposes, here ye!

What does God wish as the best remedies for God's wraths here but to say, there's not a thing left for God's graces here! But the moment you witness Jesus Christ in your lives here is when you start revealing the trust that God's giving to you writing this book here. I witnessed this charitable event's Livingstons deal here when Paul said to us, "Go! Be with Christ!" And we both looked at each other and went, how can God come between party lines in this way here! Then God said, leave and never return! Right, Jezibellie Christ and Jesus Christ here!

It's My name that is Wright. Right? And we go, that's what you know and that's what we found out about you, Jesus! God stated for a fact that God loves women. Right? He's sorta not alone up there! You know? 😊 This is God's way of stating a fact here. Did God invent the other woman? Did He think there were two separate beings in Andrea's heads then? She's got two heads then, we say? This is for the birds. Right, Jezibellie! This means that Jezibellie Christ is Andrea then. Correctamundos here? This is war then, Folks! Jezibellie Christ heard the DSW too! That's how the Bible was thus written for the Gentiles, not for Paul Wright's big egos here.

This guy took over reigning the Egyptian Gods and stuff like it here? You see it now you do. Right, Gentiles here? State for a fact that Andrea rewrote the traditions of the sands of time here, and God's Gentiles stated for a fact that DSW is really the writers of it. Are we a part of Rome here or there, Andrea? We can talk about it in two places, or we can just state that for the records of all times here, this is a studyable script here. Please do so! We love you, God!

Hence, what do you think the writings, studyable they are here, are doing for the Divine Source Wisdom here! This is why we are a part of the decision making for the Bibles that are rewritten because of it? It's a pretty good book though. Don't you agree with this decision to rewrite the rest of it though? We could probably not do as good of a job taking the sin out of the sinners that rewrote portions of it though. In essence here, there's not a lot of doing that takes action out of sinning and sinners here. We can add to it, sure.

But do we want to though! Yes, please! Take that for state action on the sinnings of God's Gentiles here! Which by the way here, we saw a program on Rome here. That's where we're buried, in the cathedrals of St. John's terminals here (Wikipedia, 1 January 2018, https://en.wikipedia.org/wiki/Archbasilica_of_St._John_Lateran). Can you locate us though? We're buried there! We were friends with Constantine, … what! Yes, it's truth be told the ways and means it lady's Virginia's accents here that said, that Mesopotania, not Mesopotamia, is a part of Greece today, though not a part of the action anymore here. There's sinister junkies here to try to take apart the goddamn thing. Right, Gentiles here? We're mad at the Gentiles here! You betcha here!

We're a part of the comedies and the tragedies that Paul rewrote the Bibles though? He was that illiterate he could not do it here. He made us rewrite segments of it here and there, and to add all that hype about Jezibellie Christ being cast to a sick bed and shit! We're cussers aren't we! We're so mad at that man! He's so un a part of the society's influences of a sick bed we could scream. This man is a tyrant at best here! He did not follow Me, He says, but I do follow Jezibellie Christ quite nicely here! We are writing this the way it ought to be written, Andrea. She wonders about our humor and stuff here. She's trying to be crass too? Not hardly so. We are though! And so, this is how it is rewritten then, but in our terminologies here. It's not KJV anymore here. KJV was never spoken to the Gentiles anyway here. It came from God. A part of this decision to remain the factual evidencers of the centuries old ways here is how God came to become a part of this motion detectors for life's best words here!

This is how we came to be a part of this decision to state for a fact that God's angels rewrote the Bibles just now! We say the Bibles because the various versions are out there for the taking here. This is Jezibellie Christ's ways and means it lady's second guessing at driving here? I never had a driver's license scare like I did back when I was in the mental hospital realm here. I was homeless, plain and simply done here. I slept in my van for three years then? Off and on sorta! This is because the written word's finalized versions came about by abomination of the trusts of God's wills here, stating that a person with a mental illness like Andrea is there for the taking then! Let's send her into mental health again! And for 14 tries later? Try 18 here, so we think anyways, that there were more than God's plans out to get her, for this DSW is really up for grabs here!

At the hopper, I say this lightly too, as in, this book's rewriting itself several times here, that God's apples and crisps are the second heavenly thing that Andrea got out of being homeless for that long here. She's smart though, and never swayed from her medications, because then they just made her feel terrible here. And that said, Jezibellie Christ wants a written word to go far, same as you do. But that's going to detest time a little bit here! She had to eat those little purple flowers from Madagascar that are now the children's form of leukemia cure? Nope, the white ones though were forced upon her from Jesus Christ though? Not in the slightest, He says! It's a hope and a dream to know you, Andrea! I do hope you have the little purple Madagascar flower figured out from us! I do know that this is the hope and the dreams of many here when I state for the records here that God's little purple flowers of Madagascar saved thousands of lives here!

Edgar Cayce lived out his life here with the little purple Madagascar flowers here! Saving graces here: Let's go to God's wills here and wipe out AIDS viruses like schizophrenias, the real thing though? It's not a flower cure, although Namibia knows the answers to it here! Right at the hopper we could tell the AIDS viruses are just talking about HIV then. Is that it here?

We're talking about the schizophrenic talentships of God's trusts here. It is NOT, I repeat, NOT genetic! It's silly to believe that a person could deter someone from being a pedophile? It means, Folks, that there's a tenderhearted individual just waiting to be found out by God, the Lordship, and a ton more inklingships under God here! I know innocence and guilt of this one too, she says, Andrea here! I know the sound of God's wrath is really close for people like Paul Wright though! This guy was a complete moron. That said, yep, Namibia is the cure for HIV/AIDS!

We're just a waiting for the opportunity to present itself there, Mr. Jimmy Swaggart can tell Us about that Namibian government who is so keen on helping out the worlds here! Maybe he could persuade them to listen to you here, to Us, to God here!

Yep! And God could cure all ailments with just one fell swoop here! There's more to it, of course! Jezibellie was My woman here! Say, does God even invent the wheel for people who are supposed to come out of nothingnesses here and to state that God's Heaven and hell bits of wheels of fortunes is really for the birds. Is it not, Jezibellie Christ? She was revered and respected in many aspects here! That said, this is Jezibellie Christ talking, right, Class of Gentiles here? Wrong and nada and zip, zilch. Nope! This Jesus Christ's cure for God's willingnesses here states that God's willingnesses makes up a whole holiday's worth of tidings for the Christmas bells are ringing in them here! We're writing this part through the Christmas holiday here. It's so apt and fitting. Is it not? Send us from Heaven to rewrite the book of thieves, jokes and such, from Jezibellie Christ though? She's not going to have it here! This message is for the prince of thieves like Paul Wright.

He's the one's echoings that we don't want to forget, lest we find out he's got a change of heart? He's a murderer, a mass one at that, and all from "God's" reckonings here? He's a lunatic and a heretic, not Jezibellie! Christ's wife is really what we're after here! Gem, She is though! I needed Her at a time when I could not count on anyone here. And then She appeared to Me in the manger with a bunch of thieves though! That could not be furthest from the truth here. Paul was like 25 years our elder here. That said, what is he doing reigning for five years the Christ's home and country like he did here? Well? He ousted us from the Holy Grail here. We'll talk about this later too. But the Holy Grail was what they used to oust us from the heavenly scenticatures that involve the little known peace talks and such that were happening at the Last Supper.

This woman to my right here was Jezibellie. How come nobody believes Me! It's Her, mkay! I do know how to spell here. The problem with this picture, and why I could not caress Her skin here is because she was bronzen, tan and such? I was so White it was pathetic here. But She's not the one who gave me that gigantic, and I mean gigantic bottle of wine as a cup to drink out of! I was held by knifepoint in the back room here, and ordered to drink it all! Hence, Jesus's little bottle of wine trick for everyone on Earth here does not hold water here! LOL! If you all come back now, I will show you the… And I fell forward in my drink it was so potent! That said, what of the fish and stuff too? We don't eat fish then? That's all we ate back then! The oxen were for working towards a home with. We didn't eat them! We were Jewish, see! But Mary Magdalene and Paul had an affair? I wish! That woman we call a heretic today should only be Mary M., the complete slut of the Earth! Because I am so much younger and she knew me at childbirth here, that's the only reason I shudder to think why Andrea stayed so long in a relationship with a much older man here, and ended up marrying the guy too? Well, why did Jezibellie stay married to that nincompoop who was much older than Her too? It's easier to type and read if we make distinctions like these pronouns here. But anyway, Jesus did not kill anyone in His life here. That said, what of the distinctions don't we know about God's reconciled, peaceable heavens here!

How come nobody likes Jezibellie Christ! She's a goddess sent from Heaven to rewrite the

Bible? She's already written it! Divine Source Wisdom speaks it here. What have you say you, Jezibellie Christ! Well, She's not available for commenting on the source wisdom's divineness, but that is to say that She's banking on the robotic natures of time here! That said, what is the commandant's jealousy but a little rouge at Christmas too? This is the Egyptian holiday they so speak of here, and we all spoke English too. This holiday here is coming up again, right you guys! And we hope that God didn't get you all pissed off at the holiday's comings here. Back up a bit here.

What does this holiday mean to God's peoples here, with people like Paul on the run and stuff! He escaped, that's why we couldn't track his whereabouts here. But with Jezibellie's help, She was able to find him big time! What does the DSW not know about lives here, but whether or not a citizen's arrest is guilty or innocent? Andrea's much the same here. We can tell innocence and guilt here. We'd just go to the hopper and find out if somebody needed to be there, and all we could tell is, everyone here's just homeless, and that is all!

That said, we are terribly inept at names here. Who are you again? Nope! Jesus knew Jezibellie from childhood, and that said, we were 5th graders together with peaceables here! She's My life, He said!

She's a jewel and a gem all in the same orders of itself here. This nighttime sniffling, sneezing, aching, coughing, stuffy head, fever, so you can rest medicine, is in order here! Don't forget the NyQuil, guys! The maps in the back of this King James Version of the Bible tell in order here Jesus's travels, not Paul's, on map number 7 here (KJV, 1976)!

Jesus accompanied Paul on the second set of orders here? Not a chance! Paul is a scoundrel at best here. He'd just map it out himself here, he could do that much, and cross out any inklingships of judgment days and such! That's what I was doing, looking for Her in the rubble and ruins of the centuries old land castles and such! That's the reasons for it here! And, Paul's fourth and fifth journeys is even worse here. This is the Luddites of the world's best hardships here, talking about the Jezibellie cure for things, nastiness and wickedness in high places though! What are you scared about for demon's sakes here! There's nothing to fear, Peoples!

Chapter 8

Jezibellie's Cure for Cancers of the Mind

I'm defensive, sure. This is a comedy and tragedies type of thing to keep in mind. I am so defensive about the Bible! I want for there to be no registered sex offenders on this Earth! Keep in mind that I love bipolarisms pretty well. Bipolarism is another epidemic. Is it not? This boundary between life's quandaries is to take literally this sexual offenses bullshit here. This honorability's sakes, it is son of a bitches too early to tell! Keep in mind that Jezibellie is no sex offender, but Her honorable husband? The first one, arranged by marriage to a dope named Jezebel's Solomon offender, became honorable and a rapist too! Just like Paul! Paul was no imaginary man, and to think the sex offenders of the world could be controlled by this one scripture from Revelations, not Revelation, to believe in Jezibellie again afterwards would be toast for Me! So, what do I have in common with this world of sex offenders, Jezibellie Christ says to Herself! I don't!

So, this is what I have in common with God's creatures, and this is what the bold, blatantly "cured" sex offenders of the world try before communing with nature here, not possible, and gather your thoughts lightly, there, Jezebel's other half of the stories here, God wanted it that way! Please note that there are more than just one God out there for us all! But we'll get to that in time, as Andrea still struggles with this one. So, we just don't know God's ways yet? Did we hunker down and get Her killed though! By rats was it, that ate Her face off? Nope, dogs! I don't think so! She died by hanging, and I, Jesus Christ, died by decapitation. Surely, this is to be debated in the scriptural languages here time and time again here. Repeat ~ DSW concurs here. What is said is between God and scriptural languages is for the birds here.

We don't believe in the natural selection of things beaten down, for there are tons of academics out there who would love to squash this writing as of lately here.

We were for the birds, were we not, Andrea? We were locked in mental hospital after mental hospital. After this book comes out though, there's no turning back on the hospital love notes! We cannot thank you enough, Andrea, for being our sole witness to progresses here. You work now at a job that you hate! But are you witnessing a progressive way of doing things that satisfy the DSW? Are you ready for a new sensation to witness your love affairs and such! We're not interested in airing her dirty, personal laundry for the beginnings of the birds affairs and such. We're just for the birds, are we? I just don't see it as personal for there to be conflict among us natural types! In God's names we pray! Dearly beloved, hallowed be thy name, thy kingdom come, on Earth as it is in heaven. Give us this day our daily bread and forgive us our trespass! That, I will be done part, is non-existent here. We don't like to be done with our Lord and Savior Jesus Christ!

What trespass are we assuming happened between God's favorites here, the love affairs of a lifetime of therapists who seem to enjoy comedies and tragedies too! I just have the favorites button I like so much here! What have you say you, Andrea, about all this!

I just don't know, she writes us! Then tell us in your own words, what have you said to the DSW all this time about us! I just don't know here! I try my best to do what I might, but this lesson plan is for the birds, is it not? I am lonely and challenged without My wife in tow. That said, is Jesus as popular as they come! He's raring to go on His wife's balanced lesson plans too. I think the best thing that's started already is a new sensation into the land of Oz. Try us sometime about it! Wash away the tears, People! We're already the DSW, and a good one at that! Try us out for size and then worry about how to equal amounts pressure someone into going and coming back the same day for some food! Some food is equal to the talent shows we look for in the future of unrest and what nots here!

What kind of food, they say? It's a grand opening for a talent search show's greatest fears. It means the lifeline of love and money is just around the corner for you, Andrea, and your talent fears are not even registering on the lifeline of love here! Will you open up the doors and be profitable and nasty about it too! Profitable things and people go hand in hand. Will you give it up for the DSW and never tell another living soul about their profitable things? Will you seek to grasp this Virginia aspect? That means to tell the world about your stories on another wing of life. Will you seek to grasp this Earth's traumas and feats?

Available to this Earth's stories here are the wings of life. Will you seek refuge in a place full of traumas and stories too! This Earth, this life is here for the taking! Must be 21 or over to proceed! This life is for the birds without turmoil about loving someone special here. That said, what is the commandant's wife supposed to think about all this turmoil, deals and such! It's a commandant's message here that states that God's only other lives here is for the birds here!

I do declare a mistrial on the ways of such things as we talked about in Romans Chapter 3 then! Paul is not the author by any means here! She's like, okay God, where is this man I knew once? His name is Jesus Christ! And I'm stuck with a Barno last name like Barnes or Bongs, or something so similar in cast yourself Jewish ways here! It's Devanagari scripts here and the like that changed my name into something similar to your Jewish name here?

Nope, Italian relatives coming across the canal and into the limelight's cues here! That said here, what is this Jewish hope we keep renewing about ancestry and such? It's a limelight's genealogical tree we're interested in here then! This is Abraham-Hicks's biggest thrill of such works is that we speak and talk just like him! Jewish though, that is as sexy as hell freezing over here! This love is such tragedies we talk about in Romans then! Because of the inkling cures we have here, the family of such persons is not always the best option here. That said, this options-taking is for the birds, as well as such tragedies as not finding a place to live readily enough at the hopper thereof! And by the hopper, we mean the mental hospitals around this place here.

If God could cure us now though of mental health's biggest problems here in this state of Washington, for example, then God's only request here, is that there be no more beds reopening and such! It's such a farce to exist people like this. Here is a lonely dude on the streets of Manhattan no less and no mores here, and there's an existence of people in the hopper already, so he tries to flee and gets reprimanded by the police and such! This is war, Peoples of the Gentiles type! I do declare a mistrial and a deeds note though! Take it from Me, Jesus says!

We're like the Gentiles all over again, Folks! I'm cast away to sick health beds, is what we used to call it back in the days of Gentiles and such. And we talk about the Gentiles because they're the hopper's best cures of love related issues here, like sex and such issues as whether we'll be ready for more bad publicities here. But this life's meant to be without sexual ailments like schizophrenias too, where people who are good people no less and no mores here, are without sexual ailments like schizophrenias too! Where people, good people no less and no mores here, are under investigations for things like schizophrenias in the first place here! Andrea was devastated by her diagnosis in the early days, enough for her to admit to God's high places here that God was devastated by that diagnosis too. In the earlier years though, she believed it wholeheartedly here!

And God's only choices were to diagnose people inaccurately then? Nope, she had what is known as pedo head for sure here, only to be diagnosed with it though! I do know this too. This pedo head business we talked about in Chapter 7 here are really for the birds.

You know it's true too! This memos taking here is for the birds as well, as the governor from this state is constantly pouring NO money into the systems of health care for the rich and famous either. And that said here, the commandant's money in Egypt was poorly acclimated as well here, because there were no instances of it back then, then? Not in the least!

We were properly trained for this kind of memos takings here. Back in Egypt, we had what is called the Less Restrictive Alternative, whereby the Gentiles consoled the commandant's commands here. And nothing could be furthest from the truths be told here! We were destitute in believing in commandants at all here. That is because Jesus Christ could detect it too! The ridding oneselves of commandant's takings here in this state of Washington is all we could do for the governor's hereby taking man's weekly noticeables to the hoppers in this state in the first place here.

We do, however, note greatly that Jezibellie didn't belong in the hopper as well. She just heard voices, correctamundos here? Hearing voices is a gift. ~ The Divine Source Wisdom! This means that the hearing voices parts of our psyches are ready to receive the good from all sources here! That said, what is Jesus's dealings here but to hear voices! You cannot be an effective ruler of universes too without hearing them, the right kind thereof though! This woman here, Andrea thereof, could hear the voices that were negative ones about 12 years ago though! "Go kill yourself!" "You're not worth it!" Those kinds of voices are the ones we want to avoid, and treated with the darned Seroquel later, People, are the kinds of voices that you *do* want to hear then, like the DSW's!

This trip with the medications and such is plaguing the millennia of people who need to hear the most common voice of all, the voice of reason's past here! The regular voices of God's that people need to hear are the most common of all! This is God's reasonings here, and this moment's notices of people coming and going are certainly up to it here. The fanciful dresses of millennias past state that reasonable people do hear voices from time to time! If that's what you mean by voices though, the negative kinds, then that is what we're trying to medicate here. When the doctor wants to know what the voices are saying though, it's like you're trying to medicate all voices here.

Have you noticed this with your own medications, Readers and such? Because this means that over half of you have noticed this in your own tidings and such.

You shouldn't have to need any medications if you come to hear the right voices, fueled by the DSW or such other kinds of voices as the Holy Spirit or Holy Ghost provides to you. These "voices" are such that God's otherships provide to us here. That means that if you still heard the wrong voices, Andrea, you would still be trying to run your truck over the edge of that cliff hanging position it was almost in years ago! She actually tried to kill herself once, but didn't go through with it? Nope! She realized right away that hanging herself in the ovens of peace did no good for humanity's lawyers here. That said, what is the trusts that hanged onto herselves here? That means Us and them. This is for the birds if we cannot warn you about trusts and this paragraph right here. Scrap it then? Hardly so. This is why we're talking about it here.

That such the plentiful beings of God's chambers are already hearing the kinds of cliffhangers we want to hear then, such plentiful beings like Andrea's "voices" then? She does not hear "voices," but a voice: Us! And "them" is just a plentiful dream ago too. Back then though, yes, it was "voices" for sure here. We have the right to contemplate the diagnosis then to schizoaffective depressed type? I hadn't been depressed at all until this mental hospital shit here started way back in the 1970s with the advantageous living arrangements! I did get raised by a mother and a father here. But that's besides the point here! We're kind of over that now. Just get yourselves into a situation where you can pay the rent you need to no longer live with your parents. And that's over half the battle there! I did not live with them pre-30s here. That said, what is Andrea's parents like now though?

Coercive and unobstructable here. That means that we have to turn them off for us to hear the right kinds of voices today! We must get by without their "love" then. That means that, we're off the charts, not hearing the wrong kinds of voices here anymore, any longer, and anywheres here. Life's but a dream and the right voices just means we're right for society's influences here. Oh, and was that "Us" in those prior voices here?

Nope, we were just looking at something going on in her head and in her life at the time. Those "voices" back then were many different kinds of angels then? Not hardly so! But demons and such! Yessiree here! We mean that too here!

That said, the only kinds of "voices" you want to hear are the loving types. So, are you ready for a new sensation of terminologies here, Andrea? Are you having sex with the Savior all the time here? Nope! But He sure is a sensual being here! That said, Andrea, what is having sex with the Savior like then! We'll talk about this in Chapter 9 then!

Wait a minute! Weren't you saying something about murderous head too? Yes. It is something to believe in for sure, but not to believe about. And that said here, we think it's necessary to convince the public, Andrea, that you're insane enough to believe in murderous head here. Aphrodite is someone who livingstoned someone else here. It means that sexual ailments heal themselves over time. We must believe in this, or it's not going to happen for us as a society here. Meaning, by murderous head, that there's some times in people's lives where you believe that you have hurt someone, and nothing could be furthest from the truth here. So called "blessings" are what this is here. This special meaning to God's creatures means that we could never hurt someone. So called blissful thinking is what we have instead.

If Jezibellie Christ, for example, came to someone in a time of need, there would be blissful thinking ahead of the game here. If God, for example, came back with a notion of more gods and goddesses here, we would be thinking in terms of Zeus, for example. And in laymen's terms, Dionysus of the Greek gods variety is very handsome and spoken for as well!

And so, what is the laymen's terminologies for the Greek gods and stuff here? This calamity Jane way of seeing things, like murderous head for us and some people too, it means that there are people to calamity Jane ways and means it lady's calamity Jane ways of thinking too. So, in other words, what does a murderer think about! We don't really know it. Do we? We think of all kinds of things here! Just kidding! We're not murderers. Think about it! We're just giving God's wills something to hold onto here. And that's a fact, Jack! This Demeter of the garden varieties here even went so far as to tell people far and wide about the murderous intents of people who really meant that. Demeter even believed in love, so far as those who are willing to commit heinous crimes were not even allowed to procreate! And that believed us to tell you about her wills then, as a Greek goddess of light and love here.

Oh, and she knew Paul quite well here. He could not procreate either, and she made sure of that through evil prayer though? Greek gods and goddesses just happened to live in Greece at the time of Mesopotanian rule, that's Mesopotanian to you, not Mesopotamian with a 'u' or an 'e' either, but a 'v' or a 'y' or an apostrophe 's'!

But a comma, that's a standstill diagnosis for cuss words and such, like Mesopotamia means potato heads and such words as this, so we changed it to Mesopotania, and Jezibellie Christ, Her last name was Bongs/Barnes/Tutankhemen, not Tutankhamun that means butthole surfer's radiances like Her last name the way it is! And that's where Jesus came into being too. By not telling of the Greek godship back then, we all got radiantly excited about the notions of time being out of proportion, and this isn't even murderous head, as we all got excited about not hurting people this way and that a way here. Stay tuned! We're coming back with Jesus and Jezibellie here!

This is life! And, this wasn't even so far as coming into the ages about life here! We are telling about the Divine Source Wisdom's speaking head. Here is an example of this. Suppose we're talking about Paul here? We aren't! And those types of people don't hear "voices"; they only hear themselves speak from within about killing someone or something too. There is no such difference then? What are we doing with schizophrenics in jailed societies here! We are telling you about murderous head, because pedo head is so prevalent too, that your words spoken or not could become a message of intent? You could never murder someone! That's why God put those ideas into your heads here. This is not an intentual thing, to murder someone, with this reasonings thing here.

We must trust that God gave us an inkling message that says, you could never murder anyone! Here's an example of trust in this situations thing here. Suppose this man and this woman, Jesus and Jezibelle Christ, actually got the hang of this duties thing you transpose over your heads here.

Suppose this God of yours has a backbone then and cannot murder anyone. These people here who murder are from a different sector of the universe's crust here. That said, what is God's reasonings behind putting someone up for adoption here!

We could state that God wanted murder in His livelihoods here, but this would be false. In fact, what does a murderer like Paul say to someone who says, God forgave him his trespasses? It's false here! Trust in God's evilnesses to do the mix on someone then? This time He's onto you, Andrea! You thought you'd killed your brother and murdered his wife once. You called to make sure they were okay, and you said, I could never murder them though!

This is an intentual thing here. God could never murder someone either. So, why put those ideas into your heads then? Well, schizophrenics say that God's ailments are worth curing. And so, with this in mind, we'll address pedo head later in Chapter 17 too. Murderous head comes from crying about the ill wills of people who will murder someone in their lifetimes, much like pedo head means that no one better ever touch a child in that way, ever! And so, with the heart of hearts here, we gather to reminisce a bit on whether or not my words will hurt you in any way, and Andrea remembers this too. There's no way that someone's words would hurt the economy, let alone another human being here. It's just too much to handle here!

Chapter 9

Give Me a Razor, Or Give Me Death!

I believe in love, Jesus says! I believe in a turmoiled existence without My wife in it. I'm just kidding, Jezibellie Christ! Do you think that you're a reincarnate of Jezibellie, Andrea says to Me here, the DSW though! I go, well, I just don't think I can have a relationship with another this way. I do believe in love! However, I just don't believe in Santa Claus, is like saying that Jesus don't exist either. That's the parallel between the two here. If I believe that Santa Claus is real, Andrea, Jesus says, then I must believe in the hardons that suspect Myself with My wife in tow! Because I really am Saint Nick, too! You've got to believe us here, LOL, here! LOL is My way of finding truth be told ridicules in life here.

This is war! We cannot believe that Andrea left fingerprints for God to find out about! When you're schizophrenic, you even wonder if the page turners at the library in question have your fingerprints on them, you're such a joke to society!

This phenomenon is called breaking the bank apparently, as that was back in 2007 we had this viewpoint here. That said, what does Jezibellie Christ know about God's intentions here? We're sad and lonely too? There's too much to be listened to when you're that paranoid about life here. One time this chiropractor said to me once, try Emotional Freedom Technique (EFT) for all that paranoia here! And it worked! You've got to find this amusing, Andrea! For this is the very thing that cleared it out of her mind then? Well, a focused energy is a dark force of society here. That said, is the focus more of an advanced rulement for oneness then? Because this cleared out her dark energy attachments too. I went to a lady who does them for free right? Nope, I paid about $90 to have my dark energy attachments cleared too, but there was one more that would not go away without divine intervention here. So, I did that myself one day by talking to myself in the mirrors of society's warinesses here. It's nice to look at yourselves and to say that you love one another, but have you ever tried to sit there and witness this of Andrea though, to sit there and say, I want you gone, dark energy attachment still sitting behind my eyes there! And then it did leave! Pretty much at that instant too. It was like it was gone. This movement or motion to clear the dark energies that subside in you is very consistent with aerobicizing the acrobatics of society's moods here.

In other words, don't be afraid of it at all. She said at the time, the clearer did say to me, that dark energy attachments are pretty real here, and that God's existences are real too. You can say that to God and say, there are dark energy attachments to practically all human beings here, so getting them cleared regularly is funny to Me here too. Because of this though, there's tons of things to be thankful for here.

That said, if you think that God is watching you, you will believe all the little things that you don't crave, like God's sunlight and stuff, and you will think you're evil, enough to say to yourselves here in the mirror by the way here, that you are not worth living out your lives here? Nothing could be further from the truth here! That said, you know that God is right there for you in the dark energy attachments that you think about. Right? The dark energies are better given with a pendulum, for example! And so, we noticed that our hand movements, suffice it to say, are the same as a pendulum's rulings here. In other words, if you've got the Holy Spirit, you can make your own body into the temple that it was meant to be here, and then invite yourself into the life of love that you deserve! So, that said here, what is the commandant's ways and means it lady's only existence here, but to state that God's wills here are strong enough to battle cure the axes to grind here.

Meaning, there are enough saids here that go, what about God's strength in weaknesses are you turmoiled about then? We can clear all dark energies now, for example here, and that God is watching us is turmoiled about Jesus says a lot! And that said here, what is the mentionables going to do with your only turmoiled existences here, but to say that a schizophrenic notion's best ablenesses here are totally false is to state that God's existences here are pretty radical if you ask Me! We've always believed in Jesus Christ's here ye existence here. Have we not? Can I get an Amen out of you too?

Jezibellie Christ is a witch then? Do you think that We would be so inclined to believe it then, that God's society of people who are deemed schizophrenic exists because we believe it so much so that a simple diagnosis like it could ruin your lives over being schizophrenic? At least paranoid schizophrenia is what we're calling it. Did you know that in Jesus's time, in Biblical times then, He was definitely schizophrenic! Not a man who would become greatly exercised by ghosts and demons and goblins of the sort found in Chapters 6 and 10 here, but the times we stated that would bring Us to our knees here? We knew that the word schizophrenic was found 18 times in the Bible by demonic possessions, correctamundos here?

That's not what it means, Jesus says here in this Bible of ours here! Are we much easier to navigate than a literal Bible here? Probably so, but this essence based derivative of peace here that Andrea proports to navigate in her lifestyles of the rich and famous someday, is not, I repeat, not why we're studying the scriptures this way and that a way here. We want to become famous, sure! But not without the invention of lying to ourselves here about the turmoiled existences of a lifetime of greed mongering here!

And that said here, what is the life o riley supposed to represent here but a simple to do list? We're trying hard to think of a phrase or a word in the Bible that masturbates so well with the topic of transparency that we might just forget that God made people different for a reason unknown here. But the rest of the day's work, Andrea, might be to just forget about the existences that you've had here! That's because she cured and healed her schizophrenia alright, to make for a schizoaffective though? We're saying that any and all techniques used in this work here have to come from God's wills here, and not so much the DSW here! Are you ready for a new sensation, Andrea, here? Some have said I should have used a pseudonym for my works here. But how can I believe in ghosts if I don't use my full name here? I suppose that God really metathesized two works here, the Bible and the so called Quran here? Nope, the Bible and the Book of Mormon here. That is because Jesus Christ wrote it too! We're telling you that the Bible is rich with Jezibellie's cures in it, and that the Book of Mormon is so strongly etched as Jesus's only works here, that God really pined away for an existence of wills here.

What is God's only wish here but to say, Jesus Christ wrote the Bible then? Not without His Jezibellie cures! The only reason that Joseph Smith is coined as the author's note here is because he's kind of gay and stuff! We're just kidding here! We know that this guy is your quest and your purposes here, but did he really write the Bible too? Not! We're just saying that the Biblical Book of Mormon suggests a plagiarism did take place, and it was God's existence to rewrite it here.

That said here, what is the commandant's only messages but the ridicules of men and men alike who wrote the Bibles then? It's the same outfit, as Chapter 5 of the Book of Mormon was rewritten thousands if not dozens of times! It's supposed to be that way though! Did we write it with the existence of Mormonisms today? Not hardly!

It, the Bible of Mormon really, has been misused so much so that God didn't want to believe in its existence? Well, Jesus wrote it, not this Joseph character, according to the DSW though, I suppose so then huh! That said here, what does Mormonism mean to you here? It calls for polygamy though? We're only meant to marry one person, one man and one wife here, not the other way around by the way. And we're so strongly anti-gay you say? Nope!

We're saying that Andrea had her run in with pedophilia so strongly so that God said, I take you at thy word, but this existence with God in it is yours, not some pedophile's! So, we would never suspect or think of Andrea as a child molester, not in the least here.

So, take thee at thy wills here and suspect God's going to come down upon you and then suspect that you're no longer a child predator, Andrea, that's ludicrous by the way, for God to say, no longer then, correctamundos here? You've never been a child predator, Andrea. And I doubt very much that the schizophrenic talentships believe that they are as well here? We are well here! That said, the common denominator thoughts process here is so common it's pathetic here. And that's because the existence of child predators commonly say that to non-schizophrenics at the time of enlightenment here! Do we want the enlightenment that Buddha stated here? This moment's treasures of time here state that Jezibellie Christ killed someone in the 13th century A.D. here. Right? Correctamundos here? She didn't have to kill anyone who believed that they were innocent though! Guilt and innocence is a specialty of ours here, the DSW says! If you think you're a child predator, you're not alone in this, but you know the truth within. Don't you! There's nothing that could be furthest from the truth here! If you think that your life is in a turmoiled existence here then you will believe it so strongly that a dark energy will try to attach itself to you. Move aside, Buster Brown, I said one day to it! And it left right then. It means that Andrea has found her niche in society where she can clear these things too pretty readily. I went to a lady, like I said, and had them cleared from me, which was a first step to society's interests here.

That said, what is this kind of belief system, is the kind of thing we want to see in every individual. We want the God's wars to comingle with Us. We want that kind of person to cohabitate in society. Say, that would be said of time here, because God gave us a hint. He said, let it be fruitful and lovely in this house here! And that said, Andrea does have a place to live here. What with three different roommates here? Nope, four, and all guys! Let's give the commandants something to believe in here.

The wickednesses and the belief systems coincide with God's other halves here. That said, what is the turmoiled ways and means it lady's times on Earth supposed to represent here but a belief in the gods and goddesses of the times past here. Zeus, for example, is a bloody moron. Right? Wrong. At all costs here, this guy made Me shave My beard for My lady friend here! She's more than just a friend to Me! I loved Her with all My might. And I believe in the spirit of suggesting that She wear a veil or hijab, whatever is closer in translative meanings here. Because I love head scarfs so much here! I believed in God's wraths about this so much so that there's other things to be thankful for!

There's times and places to coagulate the other sides of life here. That said, there's no such thing as ghosts? There certainly is, but we're not going to focus so much on the bad sides of life here. We're going to DSW this, into the spaces provided on the worksheets at the end of this chapter's tidings here. Just kidding about the worksheets though!

Number one, always, always shave! Well, that's impossible in the hopper here: the hopper means in the mental facilities that plagued Andrea for a time here! What do you do but become bipolar over the means and ends of life here. To shave is to dine for and make beautiful! What is the problem here? Why can't we shave using our own razors here? Well, we didn't come with them, that's for sure here! And if we shave everyday though? Yep! And so? What is the meaning to finding cures then, but to say, don't get bipolar on me now, LOL! It means that any time there's a conflict of interest here that there's definitely a way to trim the nose hairs that pop out every place here, and to pluck the versions of eyebrows and the beards on women that seem to come in every shape and format here! Why don't we make beautiful the lovely riff raff of societies here and say, come one, come all and shave!

It's because Jesus wore a beard and chose it? Not in the slightest bit here! I loved to be clean shaven for My wife, He says! Why torture us this way, and then call it bipolarism here! Oh, and schizoaffective depressed type makes for a long, torturous diagnosis here, as she's been "bipolar" here for a long time now! It just means that a basket case is in order here, because of the findings that have been told here on the schizoaffective bipolar types here! Half the world has this diagnosis of bipolarisms here, and none of us, I repeat, none of us needs to have a mood stabilizer to ransack our virginities here, and to make known that all is well on the evil fronts of medication allowances here! Shave and we might call our duties an only moment's notices here!

I believe in the sweetest thing called lives here! This moment's notices are from the commandant's belief systems here! That's because Jesus is a Jew is the only thing keeping us from the rest of the world's belief systems here! There's tons to be thankful for here, Andrea! There's lots of leaps of faith back in the Old Testament's jargons here. That said, are you ready for a new sensation? The song is excellent back in the days of sweetest lives coming together in a moment's notices here. That said here, we are talking about Jezibellie Christ again here!

She's so sportily best noticed with her hair tied back from her face like in the photograph above of Jezibellie Christ!

Take this for what it's worth here, but it's attractive to be able to hear voices, Andrea. I don't know what that entails for our sweetly inclined love lives here, as so many people, as you've noticed here, have herpes simplex virus already here. So many people are not alone in this it's pathetic. I promise you I'll get to the bottom of it though! This time, there's many people behind me hopefully! Hey now. We're supposed to be talking about Jesus's sex life here! Well, how come so many men choose to believe He's such a wonderful comeback kid! Well, it's like this you see. There's so much to talk about here!

But back in the days of SVU watching, Andrea there used to be commandants and stuff while she sat there and cross stitched out of boredom? Nope, out of disability. It's a great calming exercise then? Nope! We're going to explore this meaningful's talents here but there's some other urgencies, like getting along in the world, that we haven't explored yet either here, and that we fully intend on doing here. This is the points of reference part of our lives that says that jeopardy comes from the moment's choices of God's languages here. And that said here too, there's lots of commandants to choose from. Not! We're talking about Jesus Christ when we're addressing the commandants of lives here! There's nothing to do here but to explain pedo head? We covered that in Chapters 7 and 8 and also to be told in Chapter 17 here. That said, is murderous head covered in these chapters here too? It's murderous head that we discussed at length in Chapter 8, as well as here too.

This is because the shaving of hair has become so important in modern times that a longhaired man in a beard dressed in cloaks and daggers of sorts is just a big fat misnomer. I was clean shaven for My wife, Jesus says! I'm sorry that Chapter 3's echoing sentiments said that I looked just like that here. I did though, back in the Jerusalem days when they didn't let Me shave My beard, per chance I would cut Myself here intentionally here? That's for Jerusalem to come out of its head games to betray us with. And that said here, I do believe in the sweetest of things to come to Andrea this way! It's still a trust point here, but God just gave a lifeline to her and her good deeds here. And that said too, there's still a point of references and such on her deathbed at the time of passing this life onto the next go round!

This reincarnation thing is for the birds, eh? It's Zeus who said we are reincarnated, and we believed him at the time! We are though! Unless you've done an evil deed, and then you aren't coming back! That said, what is Andrea's best things in life going to entail! She's not hearing voices per se! She doesn't hear the evil backlash that she did back in 2003 was it? Nope, in 2005 and 2006 she heard evil voices from the backside! I do say backside because this is so important here. God doesn't like people hearing evil voices neither. And that said too, is there a backlash then of evil voices in the hopper then? Not this time around! We never thought of ourselves as paranoid schizophrenic before this diagnosis in early 2007, but this is what it was alright, a preoccupation with the pedo heads of society's influences here, where she believed she had been in wrongdoing with a child or two, we're here to state that there's no influences like that anymore in her life of lives here. We never, not once, believed her! She'd state it for the world to see it that she molested someone though never did it at all! She'd quandary with us about it, and say, I don't know, God!

What did I do wrong? And she'd never seen a diagnosis before of epic proportions that said, I'm sorry, you've got an AIDS related virus then called schizophrenia then! They didn't know what she had, as she had never brought this up to the doctors at the time of the invention of Social Security benefits. She believed it to be the worst thing in this world to have Social Security here. And that said here, we do remember a time where she never heard a voice again, but was fully on her meds too.

I believe in the sweetest things in life to come to the moment's choices. Here is the point here. How come it doesn't work out that way in a mental facility here?

I mean, the shaving of hair is important enough in American pop culture, Dears! And we're denied the right of shaving our beards and stuff? Our hair on our legs and our underarms here? What did that do to thousands if not millions of people out in the snow drift back in the days when Jesus had to wear a beard? Am I now sacrilege here or are there people out there ready to shave their backs! Because that's not what we're talking about. It's the denial of public properties to really stick it out here and let us shave, Peoples! I do believe in the limelight's castaways and what not, Andrea. But to really know what that means to People in general here is what God's gave us ways here are for. We are not talking about one God anymore, Peoples! We are talking about two, or three, or four gods!

We are back with a flash in the pan as to how anyone can murder others and not talk about it for three or four consecutive months in the hopper pan! What did Jesus do but murder others with His spirit though? I don't believe we've met! I think it's only natural to believe in one God's bounties with the spirit questing done online. Is it true that natural selection is for the birds here? Scratch that please! Natural selection is cool too but not in that way. It's a natural selection for My wife to see that She's lovely!

Going forward now is best, for this is what the Gods gave us to contend with. And it is crazy gods. Is it not?

Forward moving momentum is best for this husband and wife team we call the angelical, spiritual rebirthing of faith! Is there a moment's time that is not on this gusto team of life?

How about an angel cure for death! We have the answers to this and more! Stay tuned and love yourselves even more than you do now? Of course! And have answers to this day's ending points! Stay tuned within yourselves to rest assured have more conversations with the weather today! End points are not as good in energy medicine, Peoples! Have Jesus tell you what conversations lie within the end points of God's literacy, Folks! Let me be, Peoples! I have just consummated our marriage vows, and then someone said, Jezibellie, are you Christ's intervention materials here! I go, well, I don't think so here!

What is God's intervention materials here? Well we don't want to ruin the fun here. It's just that the introductions are what started all the anguish among female counterparts to ruin the fiesta here. And that's a wrap on that subject at least! Starting with our anguish amongst counterparts is a ruined image of God here. That's the here and now, for stranger things have happened among us. It's probably for the ruin's best photos of peace here that there's some guidelines that have to be upheld here.

This is the Divine Source Wisdom speaks it here, and we're for the birds if you do not believe that we are typing this and not Andrea here. I do declare she has a love life of sorts, facilitated by us! And so, this is not what you want to hear, Gods! But this is how love life actions become even sweeter in the notions of Christ's anguish and God's perils, correct! I do know this too.

Let's start with a run from God's anguish and peace at the progressive action, nature and deeds that holds us up here. We start without it though and we'll perish at the thoughts of non-action here. Let's chase this old picture up to par and start going through the windows and falling from the sky, and all kinds of things they said about Jezibellie in the third chapter of James! The James chapters are ominous at best, for they represent a newness in time for God's unrest!

And it's probably for the best that the James chapters in Revelations is not there in time though. I could take the Revelation chapters out of Revelations if I wanted to! But this is not where the language lies best at. Are you there? I probably stumbled out of marking blocks for this number that we're estranged to. And there's probably no one on Earth who can make out a blocking number's wakes, interludes, what have you! There's no place on Earth that we can attest to! But if you want, we can make it a language issue, problems and what not! I do not declare a misfortunate piece of the pie here. But this is war! I mean, what kinds of issues and problems do we have, in this world, and in this place we call Heaven? We have all kinds of distressers, points of view here, and the languages of love in this place we call home! It's because all of the life's plans here are irrelevantly God's angels at work.

In this place we call God's work, homeland security, and peace on Earth, there's tons to do to workable solutions, to problems we call injustices of this nature here. And God in the bedroom of dust to dust sounds like an oxymoron to Me! And there's none of this natural, bedridden talent searches of Facebook's most innovative sounds, for that's what God gave Abraham to deal with. The Abraham-Hicks sides of things are mostly what God's wanting for us to enjoy here. It's a rouge of some sort, is it not?

I liked the parts about wanting to join us here in the bedroom though! Do you think that Jesus never had a wife then?

His wife was in tow at every meeting in the Biblical sense of things. What have you say you then about life's promises and ridicules here? It's because the gentleman's side of things is stupidly innocent here.

And that's a wrap on that subject here. Because of the time constraints to our person here, let's get down to business and talk about some of the subjects of crime and innoventions such as these here. Let's walk down the center of the path with our Lordship and deny thy Father and refuse thy name, be us but sworn to secrecy here, but this is like a Lordship all over again! What did the devil have to say about God's likelinesses! It's about a common loop of feelings all over again about what to do with our time here on Earth!

It's about peace on Earth, Peoples! We do not take lightly the Lordship. That brings us to another question of the laws of relativity speaking to us here. We do not like the Lordship? It brings one another together in peace and harmony. Leave it to Beaver though, we don't want to adjust the TV set one more time here! We're always advanced netherspheric talentships here. We hated the coffee this morning for instance. It's a time in the buckets of love to talent us so! We are so elated with happiness! We cannot forgive time and its bottlenecking cures for peace here! There's peace on Earth here! And we're an opportunity's striking it from motion detectors of love here! There's peace on Earth as far as we know it to be here! I love the DSW to tell me things that are meaningful here! That said, what on Earth is Andrea doing with this sort of gift?

She's talented that's for sure! I do declare a mistrial if she cannot use her special gifts! This DSW is really special to us here! This message of the Christ and his wifey in tow are used to discuss the layers of inevitabilities in such talents as before it was popular to do so! It is popular to think that God's talent shows are here for the TED talks of this world's problems. This wifey problem though is for the birds, right? It shows here that the LRA/LRO (Less Restrictive Alternative or Order here) is the best thing for police officers to show their mates in crime then? Because these people deserve none of it! Why, oh why does the police force here in town then come from the lesser alternatives of society then?

It's a contest then, eh? That's because the wifey in tow made the police report wrong! She said she's in the hopper for trespassing on a district 9 that says, powerful people like Andrea are sort of like the riff raff of society then! Because of sleeping in my van though, I do declare a mistrial on homelessness!

Homeless ventures like this one are sort of cruel though! I mean, if a family of trust did not exist for us here, we might as well be coffins nailed to the nailbeds of time here! I do declare a mistrial if I did not speak up for Her, Jesus says! We had one, an LRA before! It sucked! It takes homelessness to a new venture capital here.

We medicate the poor so they make more in society? The poor take these pills they give you in hospitals, where most of the research means that homelessness in society's medicated pills are that there are no other alternatives where you live. Correct? It's a niceity nice way of saying, "better off dead" to the riff raffs of society's venture capitals here!

This "transient" notice upon my souls here is better off as a knee brace then! Are we there yet on the capitals and such that hide the right go betweens here? We're better off dead then! That said, what of the newest society's influences kept or keeps someone from going off the deep end better than our own Western State society's influences on jokesters and the like here. Every single one of those people in there are just simply homeless!

That's a medication issue I cannot abide by here. This one shot at life, Mr. President someday here, says or states that medicating the poor hereby medicates us, a society of people who come together here and to state it that way means really good folks go ape shit over society's influences of drugs. We understand this perfectly well in the 23 hospitalizations I have had over this ape shit influences of drugs though? Not alcohol either, class of folks who know what it's like to be in charge!

Chapter 10

Jezibellie! Is That a Rock on Your Hand Though? Yes! From Jesus Christ Thereof!

There's love that's in the air! Jezibellie Christ! Are you there? We didn't forget about You wanting God to talk about Jesus's intimacy with You. We also did not forget about Andrea's love life! So, sue me if we're taking too long to describe the lonelinesses felt when someone ditches the Divine Source Wisdom, DSW, for the commandant's languages here. He's ready and willing to call You His wife, to have and to hold, from this day forward! We love interluding about the DSW enough to thank God's gifts for that wonderful era of contentment called life. This is foreboding for sure here. This foreboding atmosphere's at best going to knock a few children off their high horses here in favor of another type of buggy system here. That said, we're going to recount for you the Jezibellie cures of a lifetime of greed mongering! We only say it for the simple fact that God's forebodingnesses are really for the birds here? Hardly so! It's foreboding and it's fruitful here to recognize that Jesus's strengths and weaknesses are often accounted for in the Bible, right? Wrong again, Sires, and you too, Mademoiselles! This is because God's places are at the sinisterly level headed places that God's wraths come about to. That's because the weaknesses are often accounted for right in the middle of song and dance. If Jezibellie Christ is the underdog in this world here, how come She's credited by us for having written the Bible in the first place! There's love that's in the air! There's love that's in the air because it jives with us coinciding with our love affairs of life then!

It's sort of like this for one of our hospital stays! The motel where I stayed at has a complaint that I diagnosed a puppy dog's demise here, and said that it was time for an SI joint injury for this puppy dog that had been beaten to death. Right? I'd said nothing of the sort for an SI joint injury save that the doggie needed some physical therapy?

He's right on track with me and kicking me out of the motels that I stay at because I have this tremendous gift, and if I share it with people, they get spooked pretty quick like. They were beating the dog in the motel room too, and the dog looked pretty happy with us people who were trying to help it. This dog's name was? And so, it goes! I never saw such a pretty animal who could not run anymore. I did not know this person kicked the dog every single day of his waking hours.

And so, on who dunnits, I also get into trouble sometimes, because guilt breeds people who like to take others away when they are right or are too close to the truth. It means that people breed no one when it comes to dogs or to other animals because they hold no voice. Similar is children at play. They grow in proportionate ways, that's for sure. But there's no one to guess what's happened to children at the pet shop of love here!

I always keep my distance, that's for sure here! If not, I'd end up right back where I came from! Jezibellie Christ, are you there? Were there the same things in the Bible back then? Yes, She says! This is a joke, right? I mean, Jezibellie was not persecuted back then but I was, Jesus says! There's monsters and such on the other sides of life here.

Was She a monster then? She's not the kind of person to get happenstances with us. It's kind of a rouge, in that She's terrible at names then! It's a rouge then! Because she's vying for attention with our Lord and Savior? Hardly, Folks!

She was a terrible scribe then! I mean, if she's getting someplace with Jesus Christ then obviously, "her maiden name", is then taken to mean she's a Barnes of some sort with the worlds here. She was Black though you say to us here and now!

I do mean now, too. This is because her maiden name sounds like Barnes in the Devanagari scripts of Egypt's time and places to accept other cultures into the mixes here. She's from India of sorts, and so just when you think you've got a Barnes for a last maiden name, it's more like Bongs or similar. Then you know it just for you someday when you would run across this script for us here. It's something like this: नमस्ते which means "namaste". That is Devanagari script too. So, Her name on the converter for passages like this looks like this: जेजबिेल्लिए बोङ्स च्रस्त for Jezibellie Bongs Christ. This is the converter online though! There may be many mistakes in it already though!

We're so kidding about the conjectures in our writings here, Folks! We're going to make it up as we go along here. We're already including Andrea's fortes here! That said, what are we going to do to make up the scripts as we're not kidding here, there are tons of ways to make due with what we have here! Our scripts are not included. If there's something to believe in Andrea, make sure that you are home written about our scripts too. We're so including it here, She says! Jezibellie Christ made up the Bible's pages and such as She went. Not as a rouge here, Andrea, but get going if you wanted to make up some bird's tales about the including of some texts here that are not warranted!

So, we're not including it here. Just kidding, Folks! Dine with Us and make sure to write home about it here! We're including some of the written texts in Greek too. So, for Her name for starters is Jezibellie Bongs, but in actuality it is written in Greek as Jezibellie Barnes Christ or the Christ's last name as: Χριστός. There is no difference between the two here! Geez, Jezibellie Barnes sounds so Christós to Us here! This is a makeshift viewpoint for sure here. There's much more to say and to talk about here! There is Jesus and Jezibellie and all that they had in common with each others here. That stated, what is the Christ's wife or Χριστός or Christ's wife supposed to look like here? To look at this moment's notices is like the Greek are in the Galapagos winters here! They're further up north than we are here in Brazil though!

It's a winter like that in cessions, England here, where they were married to a King Solomon to boot here? She loathes the guy here!

There's some sort of written passages in the Bible's mainly two pagers that are going to be rewritten here. As with time there's something of Paul's legacy that is amiss. It's because there are 257 ways of looking at the thing! It's because there's real live passionate peoples here who look at the biggest melodies of Christmas past and think that God's relationships are alive and well here! I'm here looking at you in the biggest talent search of them all, Andrea, and I do know this much is true here.

Bethlehem is the talent search of a lifetime of turmoil if you do not believe in the true love of Jesus Christ. That said, there are plenty of searchable people in our lifetimes here that make love to the phoniness in the Jesus Christ rituals of communion, and such peoples who disobeyed the regiment that is due here. In essence here, what is the trials and tribulations parts of balancatures that states that a balance cure like this could not be present in the Lord's shepherdnesses and such! It's a rouge that means war is on the brink of survival of the fittest. Necessarily time is going by so quickly as such here! I do declare a mistrial in deeds and in wartime ships aplenty here.

The Kama Sutra... What's that again here? It's a book, okay! By Vātsyāyana, but the Lordship wrote it for her in the 20th Century B.C. Is that correctamundos here? Nope!

We're just saying! The Kama Sutra was rewritten into ancient Hebrew scripts in 1940 B.C. here! The numbering system back then is tantalizing though! What did we do but have sundials and such then? Nope! We started out with the poetry of landmark items such as this, though it is popular to think that Galileo was a saint and such! His eyes, by the way here, are still tantalized by the scriptures! Written in about 20 A.D. was a sentimentality sakes, that says, I loved the Kama Sutra, she says, Andrea do.

Right, or correctamundos here? Nope, she's never even seen a copy of it. Henceforth I never will be Romeo though! Andrea liked to recite passages of the Bible's scripts into Shakespearean theories and in high school, there was an assignment to be done about the Bible's scripts, I mean the Bible's one and only here! Meaning, Class of Folks and Gentiles to be reckoned with here, as Andrea means well here! That said, we can simply show her anything she wants to know, by golly God Almighty!

That brings us to Chapter 11 here. Let us be known by golly rather than God. Right, or correctamundos here? Actually, there's tons of things to be thankful for with God's list of tidings right there on Moses's actual languages here for the Divine Source Wisdom! Who put those scripts there in the first place, but Paul did! He actually had those scribed for dear old Moses to take and to put on the hijab or women's scarf necklaces here! Did I actually commit adultery for the worlds to see here, Jesus says! Yes, I suppose so!

Because at the last lap dance of them all here, She came onto me that way and this a way here! Say, aren't you married to the King of England there, Bitch, he said, Paul that is! I go, well, She needs a divorce. Are you going to give it to Her or what here! And he said, Paul did, "I never go unbalanced in cures here, but what did you say about my heart again? Jesus says it's a painful death!" And You go, "That remains to be seen here!" "If I commit adultery again,..." Jesus said it like this, "...You seek it, the Kama Sutra, do you there, Mr. Rainhead!" Rainhead back then meant foreignly that this man is a nincompoop! Please read this to children, Sires, and you too, Gents! We're tired of forgiving the situations here!

We're kind of like done with the Kama Sutra topics here. I wrote it, Jesus says to Me, Us here, God's son though? Yes! It's an ancient Hebrew textbook too, not ancient Indian Hindu. Although lately, I digress here, but this textbook smells of the written texts of God's languages here! Say, in Chapter 13 or 12 is it, we talk about how to cure the HSV viruses! Say, can anyone listen to this here? Or, can you begin to imagine what it is like to know that everyone almost, 1 in 2 people I meet here, either have HSV and don't know it, or they have it and they don't care about life anymore because they believe they are the only ones with it. I, by far knownst unto me here, Andrea says, that if it's meant to be that I have the cures for it and things of this nature, then HIV and HSV go together. You see it? Now you don't. Right, or correctamundos here!

Chapter 11

Diabetes, Here We Come! Cure This Once and for All!

I think the Bible's King James Version (KJV) is so interesting that I can hardly put it down! What, with the invention of lying on Paul's parts here, he's so cute and cuddly then. Correctamundos here? Not!

Revelation 2:20-23, … "20 Norwithstanding I have a few things against thee, because thou sufferest that woman Jĕź-ĕ-bĕl, which calleth herself a prophetess, to teach and to seduce my servants to commit fornication, and to eat things sacrificed unto idols. 21 And I gave her space to repent of her fornication; and she repented not. 22 Behold, I will cast her into a bed, and them that commit adultery with her into great tribulation, except they repent of their deeds. 23 And I will kill her children with death; and all the churches shall know that I am he which searcheth the reins and hearts: and I will give unto every one of you according to your works <p. 1810-1811>." Paul wrote this! Sorry for the confusion here! But in King James Version, 22 of this verse here, it states that God's reckonings are Paul's doings here! There's no place else in the Bible's entitlements that says God is watching over Andrea so that God can write this book. Correctamundos here? She knows nothing about the Bible. She's never studied it even once? Well, a Bible study, Folks, is the turmoils that mention about ourselves the upholding citizenry of a lifetime of greed mongerings here. This turmoils tattletalenesses about life's quandaries are supposed to be here! This motion to detect the Jesus Christ cures in Chapter 11 of the first book of James here (KJV, Jam. 1.1.) <p.1782>…

There is no first book, only one! LOL! And no Chapter 11 for sure here. And, we're too good about this too. Paul is not mentioned here but he is in the second Corinthians <p. 1699> and so on, as he does bite the dust quite readily here! We are KJV, not NIV! Though Jesus can talk it, and He can walk it through life, and still not attain that Jezibellie style marked up in the commandant's languages here! Jesus is the commandant. Of the military standards though? You bet! We had it all in Egyptian rulings here!

The passage above stinks if you want to know My opinion! I never wrote it, Jesus says! We're talking about life here! And Paul goes, with a knife, mind you, "Um, state that differently or I cut off his head!" "Now?" She said! And he goes, "Get me the unmarked chapters and verses here." We'll do a quote about this later, but his brood helped him rewrite it too, as it said finally that Jezibellie was the one who wrote the Bible! And he, Paul, turned it around and goes, "I seek refuge in this thing here! What do you mean you wrote the thing? It's prose I've never heard of before now though!" He's banking on it too! So, sell it then? Yes, Siree!

He goes, do we regularly hear and get chapters and verses in Andrea's head though? We do though! She gets verses and chapters in her head regularly though! We can do it about most any book on Earth though. It means that the Bible's special though.

We had a numbering system that by far surpassed even the most critically acclaimed authorship as Andrea is! We could mumble all we wanted to back then, and no one would bat an eyelash at this. So, Andrea talks to herself often about Us, because we're channeling her. So, to speak it this way is but a nice try here! But she was picked up once for talking to herself in her car, Folks! They said, "I bet she doesn't have a Bluetooth with God's angels watching over her though!" That's evilly what is written in Chapter 6 of James though! There is no Chapter 6, you say, Reader! I go, I'm doing the same thing, looking at the chapters to see if they exist yet. You decide whether or not Andrea should append the Bible's scripts or something like it! You see it, now you don't though, if Andrea is not able to publish this work due to liability issues and such!

I think that God's angels are watching over Andrea so that she can write this book without prejudice. We're looking at the Bible's King James Version because he's the one who published Jezibellie's works. Sort of simply done here, but why so many mental hospital stays here? She's only, Andrea is, trying to find the words to say to someone that they still look alike. For example, though, we're trying to find the right wordings here but this is for the birds if we cannot have Jezibellie Christ to look up the sins of imaginations, wild pigs and sewed oats. We hear this word for word here!

Jezibellie Christ took it upon Herself to imagine what this life would be like without Jesus in it. God said, in a purpley context here, that God's enlightenment scheme is pretty profound here. There are 5000 languages in the world today, and I can tell that one enlightenment scheme is meant to be all purpley about it here. Chakras and such! You know what, Andrea, take this as a hint here. Buddha was meant to be a pedo head sort. Try Chapters 4 and 6 for the versions of King James that we have for God's purpley notions here. That sort of pedo head was what he described in his books and works about it! Buddha was a great guy.

So, try me, Andrea! Was he, Buddha, in the Catholic church? This morning's laughter is funny here. Christ was not buried but in Rome proper! He's not buried in the tomb's languages on the KJV's maps in it. Try us though! We're onto you, Buddha! This is Buddha's final resting place, there in Jerusalem too. So, Christ's tomb is no longer then? What, you don't believe us? The Gentiles and such were so forthright coming of ages here.

This said, try to understand, that to tell God's children about this language here is about 5000 meaningful ways of trying to understand God's kingdoms here, without ever having known about or written about the Bible before. We choose people who don't know the Bible inside and outside to write about! And that's strength in numbers, People! I promise whoever looks at this inside job is about to rewrite history! That said, we are historians in Numbers and in Genesis too. The maps in the KJV (1976) are to boot lovelies here, but that doesn't mean that these are accuracy ridden here <Map 1 and Maps 5-9>! Look at these pages now, Folks! Tell all, Andrea! For this, a lasting historian is not the Numbers games to boot here.

But to sing aloud about the praises of Andrea's lasting peace is not what we're after here. She's been through the ringer no less and no more here! It's about mental health is it not! She's healed mental health by the way! And so, what we're after here is no more mental hospital facilities, and no more gained ministries! That said, what is the commandant's best hardships about time here no less and no more here?

It's about the Divine Source Wisdom's best ailments cures and we can hear them. Can we not? These "ailment cures" are what are called balancatures to us! It's because balance and cures go together. Do they not? So, you might see this word from time to time here. That said, what is the cosmos inventing here but the wheel again!

We are stuck on this one Chapter 10 here where Andrea stated that cosmos reinvents the wheel or something like it: You see it, now you don't though! If God worked and worked on fire for love's best interests here, She said though, then how does one arrive at this conclusion's 12, and I do repeat, 12 is a misnomer: Discipleships! There are 24 Gods and Goddesses then? This is a misnomer! That is possible only in the 12 Disciples that we run to for God's graces here. There are more like 24 of them here! They are not gods or Gods here!

That said here, what are these people doing in mental health affairs! Say, Jesus Christ was inventive of a lot of things, languages and what nots here, and taken into mental health for it here! Did He dress warmly during the wintertime! Because in Egyptian rulerships, we take our clothes off if we are bored with them! We'll "do it" in the chapters that follow here. More discipleships have been had here!

It's in our best interests if we close this chapter without further adieu here. "We are one," is what we're trying to state here, and that's not trying to reinvent the wheels of fortunetellers here! Try to reinvent the wheel though and we're stuck on our latest balances of nature here, without failing to ask the simple questions of life's honest to goodnesses! It's tough out there, Andrea! The teeth though? What is it, God, that gets us so beautiful?

It's the teeth! Our ways and means it lady's teeth are superb here, all within about a week of getting nails done though? We sort of don't have a homeless gesture that's an inkling cure of love here for her yet. But to take away our teeth in the process of loving ourselves more, which, "That's half the battle," Jesus says here of us here too here!

We're a "here" family of fame here! Say no more about teeth in mental hospitals, as out in the cold, cruel worlds at large here, we're fanning ourselves about it here, that there are pulling ways to tooth us, and there's the Ecclesiastes ways of finding fame here!

That said here, back in Egyptian rulerships, all teeth cleanings were free there, as well as the ominous ways of pulling teeth you say? Nope, that all peoples far and wide deserved to have teeth that were cleaned and pulled then? Nope, that they were able to get root canals and such things as crowns and what not for free here.

We knew that would get your attention ships here, for, say, about 20 more seconds anyway! Currently, at the state hospitals, they'll pull a tooth for free for you! Well? What are you waiting for, Peoples! We should get on the bandwagons of lives lost here, and to state that God's homeless sheltered peoples have the best teeth is the understatement's biggest and best governmentally funded program here! That said, why don't we get on the bandwagons then and to state it this way and a that a way is really something for the birds to gather here! Why not make all mental health facilities free then? They take away your money at Western States and Eastern States alike here. Say, and a homeless cap of $2000 in your checking accounts too here states that you cannot save for anything, say a house or not, with that sort of cap on lives here. We don't want to risk it all here, but these facilities take away your livelihoods and then make you homeless on top of your 30-minute stay, what to assess the qualities of lives here? The teeth, by the way, get the manufacturer's boot as well here. I will explain that in the next paragraph here!

Your teeth are sacred here! The DSHS cap on most medical advices is about $2000! Why put a cap on homelessnesses this ways and a that a ways here! It's because the state wants to fund your DSHS home stay! And simply put, if that's the case here we're up against here, then why does the homeless shelters of Americans in general, put us in the "poor house" again and again here!

We're telling you that homelessness is solved once and for all in this country, save taking away the homeless shelterisms though? Not hardly! But to put someone into a mental house we will call it, and then to take away the homeless shelterism programs here is not what we're saying here. The homeless shelters of Americans is currently your local mental health facilities, run by these psychiatrist/lawyers here, who shelter their care upon written documents filled with innuendoes and bits and pieces of the puzzles here! We are not criminals, though we are treated this way and that a way, she said, Andrea did, of her stays in over 19 mental hospitals though?

Try 23 then? It was 18 hospital stays at first, then 23 or so as of this writing, consecutive with the DSW watching over the situations at hands here. And try the mental health notes that decay your teeth faster than a leading bullet can surmise here, what by going against the grains here and manufacturing toothpastes that are too, I don't know, balmy, for the mental health facility patients there? And, simply put y'all, they manufacture toothpastes this way, such that we "deserve" any kind of treatments we get there. I have no proof, although manufacturers and manufacturing is another specialty of mine.

What about what it is like to be a human being with no meds to take! Are we trying to medicate homeless peoples here, or are we trying to make them infertile by taking their meds too? Because these medicines are bad for the kidneys, which, if you wanna know the cure for herpes, AIDS/HIV, and things like diabetes, please keep reading! This infertileness is way overrated! What, with Vitamin C cures and such, the Emergen-C packets at just about any store will suffice. Although, the ones at the Walmarts of choices here are the best.

Less preservatives you say here? Nope! That these places play around with the manufacturing of specific individuals at Walmarts and such, the Safeco Field's ways of finding out if homeless shelterisms united ways here and said, can we please forget the prior accortmentships, or laypeople's terminologies means that we are united ways here, just giving up on the some homeless organizations for ever having the right homeless programming here! We're just stating a fact here. That said here, why the glum face this afternoon? I hoped we'd get to the HSV cures today!

Well, read on about homeless cures and such tragedies as this, and we'll get developed into the boyhood memberships and such that a girlhood's relationship with the mom or dad can seriously get here! In other words, the mental health facilities are making the townspeople rich! We're getting less than $2000 per month: That's not what I am saying or talking about here. We just cannot save any money though, or else we'll get gypped into believing that homeless people, shelters and the likeliness here that we can cohabitate with other people besides a group home, which we have never been to in other words, and to try to save money for a deposit, etc., does not mean we are all out doing drugs to boot in order to get there! This Bible verses, phraseologies etc., does not mean that God put this book onto this Earth for it to be ridiculed. By faith and by promises, this whole outfit's meanness about mental health facilities here is making a comeback kid into a prose that's way released from timelinesses and such! I can hear all the mental health meds that people take on a daily basis.

Perhaps if someone came into the station, it's a gas station I work at right now, then they'll believe me when I say, you don't even need those pills! Or, you need them for another three weeks and that's it. Or, you can take it for up to a year! And then those pills become fodder for mental health arrears here!

And that said here, take what you can from this, but the mental health facilities I visited, which were plain and plenty simply just the same here as it was in the Middle Ages here, are for the birds! Literally, this coast is simply filled with good people in there! Most of the times anyways! And it's for us to decide whether or not to publish them all in here! And that said here, most mental health facilities, like I said before here, take away your livelihoods and throw away the key here! And that said here, just kidding!

We're all about innuisms here, or innuendos that state that God came into our lives and taketh away, therefore, what you have received in prayer, there are other things to attend to here, like the sex life of Jesus Christ? I think we've knocked out quite a bit here with such things as pedo and murderous heads here! Just try to imagine that scenario and to have a good or great sex life is for the birds here, if someone has ever accused you of this here! That's what we're talking about here. Mental health note here, is there someone in your favorite household right now that is drunk or trying to be? Because the mental health notes are such that, there is no such thing as alcoholism, just environmental factors here.

What are you trying to give up but kidney cures and such? Because alcoholisms are just environmentally sound here!

Say, there's a cure for kidneys too. Just overflow them! Andrea was suffering from this in the parking lot of the king of kings. And there was just too much water to overflow them with! Say, back in the Middle Ages here, we did not have such kidney problems as diabetes here! Who cares what they're called back then, but we didn't.

Plain and simply put here, Andrea, is that she followed our instructions on this too. Back then, there were more than one person in the parking lots of Heaven's gates here. Why, just overflow them, meant to drink all the water out of a half-gallon tank of lots of water in it only here! And orgasms galore though? We'll get to that here! When you overflow the kidneys with anything but milk,... just kidding here!

You cannot get the same achievemation out of this Andrea as you once had. You need a place of quiet solitude, or else you cannot scream bloody murder at the advent of a bladder which knows what to do, in case you were wondering about that! It's plain and simply having to do with the urine backups to our brains here, practically, huh, Andrea? She screamed alright. It sounded like a homeless fight to stay alive though! It will trickle out when it can, male or female! So, supervise this with the doctor's in the house mentalities here! We're saying that the cure for herpes is next. Why not tell or describe this in full detail? Because it would require a midnight stay in a parking lot for God's orders here, not in the parking lots of Walmarts per se here. But if you have a house and not an apartment, then by all means, do it there! The walls are very paper thin here, usually!

You cannot do it alone though. Right, or correctamundos here? It will come out on its own! In the meantime, you can thank the kidneys for their backlash! And to try to describe this any further here would induce their own orgasmic theories here.

That said, back to homelessness for a time here. What of the cure for kidney failure then? Does this hold any legal ramifications of me trying this out here on my own here! Nope! I had Divine instruction from the DSW the whole time here. It will trickle out when it wants to! And your kidneys won't feel so overflowed, just a tad overworked then? Nope! But it'll save them from ruin though! We're trying to find the echoes of love here, because if your boyfriend noticed you at all here, he would be right there with you, experiencing the rubdown of a lifetime, what with a couple of towels you said, Andrea? Are you homeless and in the van doing this then?

Yes! I suppose that's why they picked me up then, eh? Not in the least. It's a mother thing, and we'll get there. Time and time again, Andrea, we pick topics that we'd just assume not write about? And this is one of them here. In time, you will seek to desist the topics of homelessness and junkies and such, but a kidney cure for overflowing them? Can land you in the hopper real quick like. Right, or correctamundos here? She just continues to type us. Why? Because we saved her left kidney that has an extra chamber in it? Scratch this right now. Psyche!

We always talk to her this way here. She's cool with it! We give her criticisms that others say or state in their mind's eyes here and, state this for the records here, it is a "surgery" we'd just performed here with the overflow of those kidneys here. Say, how come no bucket or something to pee in though? We had that! But when it flows out of you, you're ready to say, ahhh!

Right, Andrea, there? We'll love ourselves even further if we explain what the towels are doing there. But to inkling cure this homelessness bit here, we might as well reinvent the wheels here that turn and are okay with it then! Which, by the way, when we arrived at the mental hopper that time at least, she said, the psychiatrist did, "Why did you soak up your urine into towels for? Is this a medical breakthrough of the softest kind here?" Nope! I got, "You defecated in your truck car, didn't you?" Yuckamundos here! Why do people say all these kinds of things to a homeless person, homeless junkie, you? Because they're at least jealous of the way I danced in these places.

No one can say it for certain here, but why and how come these mental facilities didn't just let me dance like that elsewhere is for the birds to figure out here! I never defecated, I said! But I certainly know what a pee jug is! From ancient times at least! When you're in the throes of ecstasy next time here, try the urine soaked towels from your perspective in the least amount of throwing possible here and to try the next backgammoned game of chess here, we are good at this here! Try telling a mental health professional what you were doing with those urine soaked towels though? I was saving my kidneys, and all, and I do mean all, urine was lapped up in them. Saving grace here? We don't want to write about this at all here.

Say, do you have diabetes or some such thing as a kidney or gallstone? Because that is the same things here. Say, do masturbate on it and we'll get back to you! To hold your pee by the way, or your urine infestation thereof, is highly erotic! I currently recommend that you never try to pee on your partner or loved one, hence the towels in the bathtubs of life here! Say, highly erotic means that you sound like you're in the throes of ecstasy anyway! I do realize the intents of what I say is truer than a notion of shutting down your kidneys here!

That said, what is homelessness to you, many peoples of light out there? It's because the lightest tabs we have on the current cookers of life's enjoyments here state that the mental health facilities currently love to tackle plans of onlookers here! Say, what does diabetes have in common with God's facilities of love then? Do you plan to die of it here, or can you take your blood sugars and go, well, Jezibellie Christ! I loved you more back then in your ailment cures of life than I do as a sainthood's preacher's Wife here! Sue me though if I don't work. There's no ways you could ever hurt yourself with this little "surgery" of life here. Take it from me here, the mental health notes and such take it to mean this is for the birds if you cannot "have" this little "surgery" here to cure diabetes! Why, oh why, are we talking about it here? Because one to two treatments of this is for the birds too.

It's not fun at all! But you sound like you're on a rocket ship of laughter here, what with NASA's invention of diabetes, and we're not here to cure it? Try it! You'll like it, … Much! This psychiatrist was hungry for a reward. As in, she stood out front of her outfit and yelled, "I like it here so much better than a mental health facility for myself!" as people said back then! That there was a Kama Sutra involved in peeing is news to me. I seriously doubt there would be any sexual intercourse involved in peeing. Although, there are guys and gals who like that sort of stuff. Get a life! Do you think that Jezibellie Christ knew about this invention! Yes, She did! She had that gift too. The Kama Sutra you say? Nope, of telling people their "ailment cures." Let's tackle diabetes then! It's truth be told here that there are signs posted in every mental health facility almost about kidney failure for taking these meds. Good hearted people work there sometimes.

But with faith and a lot of knowhow, there's lots to be jealous of, as well as inklingcureships about. Well, that's what we're getting at here. Why the mental health facilities and why homelessness could turn out to be the best blankenships that we're obviously mental healthed about here!

Well, families will fight and quibble about the blankenships that are obviously mental healthed in everyone on Earth, Peoples! And fight we will about the likelihoods of trying to obviously get mental healthed into the Earth's peoples who find out about that night of love in echosville's latest talent searches to boot here! Why can't the people of the Earth all comingle on this one point of the echoes of love?

It's a talent search, is it not? I like the people of the Earth to come together and navigate this one point of love and its opposite! If Jesus is pure love and He don't know His ass from a hole in the ground, I just don't see it happening in the bedroom department if He don't know his ass from a hole in the ground! And just in case Jesus knows He does not have an asshole department at the kings and queens of Americans here, he just knows that the presidents do have each other to blame for this! As kings and queens of Americans do state that there are kings and queens of other countries here. And reincarnation exists! Queen bee, Jezibellie, concurs here! Are we there yet, Folks of different countries here? Imagine a life without Jezibellie in it! Then turn to the pages we don't know about yet, like the dogs who never ate off Her face in the Bible. Chapter 2 of James and a bunch of other stuff in defense here! I go, well, who are we barking at for nothing!

There are plenty of ways to save a kidney from being failed, and this is only one of them here. Please continue to take your medications for it, before life gives another cure for kidney failures here! There's no such thing as a holding point in this though? Just hold your breath, say a prayer, and hold it in for as long as you can here. It's easier to say than done with. For certain though, if you hold it in and continue to do so, it will trickle out on its own. Now, I've never tried it as a guy here, but DSW tells me it's the same damn thing as a girl doing it here. This means that you can and should try this at home. Right? Exactamundos here? This is for the DSW to clear up here.

This is kidney failure though! Not doing anything about it here! Save face, Andrea, and print several ways to have fun doing it? It's a minor surgery here, I like to call it! And, that is talking to the DSW about life's quandaries here! But try this at home with minimal supervision, or else you'll have the orgasmic time of your lives here! So, rub on a towel or something, Ladies! Gents?

You go at it in your own ways here. I suppose there's something with a towel on it too! Say, do you like it with pillows too, Gents and Gentiles here? Because women are known to have habits that stay hard to come by here! And that's a wrap on that! PS: It's an adult book for sure here! Read it at your own discretions here. But why not? It's a ceremony of sorts here! Be bold and do it for yourself, for humanity's sakes, and try it at home with a significant other present? Yes, please!

There are several ways to go about being faithful in religious ceremonies to boot here. There are all kinds of ways to save face. In other words, there's ways of talenting God's kingdoms, and to boot it with another kind of fate that we're having to ground ourselves with is talenting us all the more here. That said, we're just likely to seek refuge if we have nothing to stand on. Furthermore, there's more to life than just seeking Him. Stay tuned for more refugee stuff in the futures of war criminals and all sorts of stuff here!

Chapter 12

HSV – The Cure for All Here

Chapter 12 deals with the quality management's team efforts to capitalize upon this craft here. This is the case of Jezibellie! We are onto you, Andrea, for telling about the Biblical scriptures under Yahweh! She is not the counterclockwise woman of the New Testament! Whatever! How do you go about rescuing this phraseology of timings all alone here! I go, well, it's about Jezibellie Christ's interventions that we say, she did not marry King Ahab. No way, Jose!

I cannot tell you by God's will and testament how to act, Andrea! It's because this is the segment in time when the balance cures are available for no one other than God's children! We're all God's children then? Not exactly. There were about 5000 of us here on Earth to procreate, when the time came. We were all Adam and Eve at some point in the conversation here. I do declare a mistrial when there's one Jezibellie and 500 other men trying to vy for Her attention here. I do declare a vying aspect to the word vy here.

If there's nothing out there but God's will and testament, then what are we doing with the Divine Source Wisdom! It's about the piece of the angles that tell us how to be here. We like the DSW to be proper and introduce Jezibellie at some point of its timing with the DSW too. And there's balancures of peace here. A balancure is a balance cure gone bad. It's something that means something different than we are trying to piece together here. And God, Jesus is bad in the bedroom somehow! Not! I do know this much. When Delilah could piece together the lovely jurisdiction on His brains here, she goes, "I do not know the hair in which I cut, as there's a piece of it here," and He shoved her aside so as to get to Jezibellie first, before the King of England married Her for Her romantic cures and all! We ruled Egypt together, He says, for 30 years of it too! It's Mesopotania to you! I go, well, there's got to be winter sleigh bells ringing for instance in the parts of the world who knew of Jezibellie Christ. We thought it would be an interlude for peace here! What's wrong, Andrea! Cat got your tongue! We're being evasive for a reason here. If we are intent on showing what Jesus looked like in the bedroom here, we ought to nastily take over the world here! The bedrooms are on hold by the ways here!

That said here, what is the balance cure for peace! It's an HSV cure, or Herpes Simplex Virus! What do you propose we do with it, Andrea asks! Well, highlighted in the chapters called "appendices" here is a sufferin' succotash with a kind way of saying it here. What is herpes simplex anyway? It's a mood disorder for certain here!

We're saying that God's orders for things certain and such is really for the birds. Is it not? Did God invent Herpes Simplex Viruses though! Yes, He did! I don't know the answer to that one, the Divine Source Wisdom says! That's because He did not invent it. Yeah, right though!

We're saying, that with everything in us here, the Appendix here is where it's at here. Take a few moments to say, she's a lunatic then! She knows the cures for Herpes Simplex Viruses then! Yes, Herpes Simplex Virus is easily attained through scripture and prayers of herpes simplex! Do you follow me, DSW says! It's easy. Just imagine yourselves without it!

And so, this is how the herpes simplex in Herpes Simplex Viruses stays simple! Imagine yourselves following through with the Divine Source Wisdom here. Chapters 6 and 9 cover simply how to cure things great and grandiose here. Just wait a minute, you say! Are we focused and secure over this knowledge of the DSW then? Then take it from me, she says, Andrea thereof, that we're used to hearing all sorts of things about this mental disease called Herpes Simplex Viruses!

Take it from me here, God put us here upon this Earth to hear these things word for word here. She's been praying for this. Something fiercely done, however, is to tell God of these things here! I don't have herpes simplex though. Of its many forms and failures is the lost calling of God's angels here. Don't you agree or would you simply say its an epidemic of epic proportions here!

This HSV cure is simply put as cured as they come! In three different studies so far, the CDC, the Centers for Disease Control and Prevention, has put Me on the backburners of love, Jesus says! This is because Andrea has written to them countless times to try to mend the back throwers of love here. They don't have any clue about what's being done with HSV cures though! They think I'm a lunatic of some sorts here! I do declare a mistrial in deeds and welcome mat parties, though!

Will the Disease Control and Prevention please welcome Andrea's praises then? They don't know what to do quite welly here! They think I'm going to sign some paper into existence though! What, with a guy in Tennessee, he's replicated it 1000 times here! And, a guy who used to live on the outskirts of, what was that city, Boise, ID, replicated it as well, and he now lives over there in Atlanta with these guys here. How come we cannot comingle together and solve this once and for all here! Because, really, this is supposed to be an epidemic that we support getting rid of!

We cannot continue this way, Peoples of the Gentile's scripts and stuff! The Bible mentions herpes simplex zoster about 1000 different ways here, and that is not the kind we mean, although there are cures for that one too! We don't know what they are yet though? Get somebody vaccinated at, say, 30 years old instead of 20 years old! I don't know what to say here? But balancures for the herpes simplex viruses of old here! We needed a masquerading legacy here! Say, is this blatantly supposed to heal Herpes Simplex Virus though! Or, are we just simply masquerading around the blocks here!

We simply need a go ahead from Dr. D! I say this to protect the innocent. I do admit, I have never met the fellow here in these literatures in the appendices of livelihoods here! But I do admit that I have sent him a letter or two, that and his counterpart Z, Dr. Z, knows what's going on too. But to have and to hold till death do us part, I do declare a mistrial of sorts here! I don't know Dr. Z personally, but to hold hands with his wife's partner's probably not what we're discussing here as of lately there! And this is supposed to be a part of the Kama Sutra? Sure, it is!

We don't have the Kama Sutra all figured out yet here! But we do have the lifeline of presence! And that's what we're bringing to y'alls here! I figured out, Jezibellie Christ says, that Jesus had a penis a long time ago here! But we never suffered from any ailment cures such as HSV or AIDS related viruses! Just schizophrenias for both of us here! For hearing the voices of God's raptures though? Try a goofy related viruses cure peaceabilities here! We all know and see the voice of God's raptures. Though telling are the Kama Sutras of tomorrow's peaceabilities at work and all that that entails here!

I hear this all day long at my work here. I can tell if someone has it or not. Schizophrenias though? Well that too, but I'm talking about Herpes Simplex Viruses! All I do is get a glance shot of the groin area and go, well what's wrong with them then? It's herpes, Andrea, that's all here! This quote here is for the birds though without Jezibellie's kind words about them here. It's all called the Herpes Zoster when you're single and you're 80 here (Layton, http://www.austincc.edu/microbio/2993r/hsv)! Please, please, please get them done sooner, the shot thereof! This is because it's a single cure. Once you're on the fence about the DSW, tell us why and how come here! This is the flagrancies of time's past here to state that we use too many question marks. Punctuation is meant to be flagrant here!

That said here, what are the dealies in the newspapers about these days! It's a big, huge question mark then! How come there's a Herpes Simplex Virus's "out there" proposals and stuff (Layton, http://www.austincc.edu/microbio/2993r/hsv)! It means though that too many exclamation marks is not what we're after here either! It means though that God wanted to talk or discuss for many of these folks that talk about the HSV viruses and such that God's only targets here are talking about many of the only words… That is pretty good prose by the way. Don't you think so or agree here!

There's love that's in the air here! Why not make it official, CDC? And, calm down about it now, Andrea! Is there a love interest in her future here? But of course! So, I don't have to worry about it anymore here? Nope! Dr. Z is interested in finding the cures of Herpes Simplex Zoster too. He's just too old to think about it here? Nope, Dr. D of the University of Washington, right here in our home state, has said a lot about it already (Layton, http://www.austincc.edu/microbio/2993r/hsv). You fellows don't realize how close you have become to solving this AIDS related viruses like thing here! Say, are you strong enough to realize that a liability suit is focused on the presence of AIDS related things? Because we're not saying that herpes simplex and anything else is the AIDS virus's notwithstanding presence here.

We are not saying that at all here! There's not a lot of time here, Andrea! We need to know what the cure is, pronto like here! And that said here, what is the very best notions, taking on the beginnings of times here?

But to simply state it here for the records of peaceabilities here. Say, is Jesus on board with this womanizing thing He's got going on here? Because Jesus is sure realistic about this moment's notices here! This Herpes Simplex Zoster is right there for the taking! I don't think making a stink about this summer's bikini line is the answer to a lot of the questions involved in Herpes Simplex Viruses and stuff like it. You see it? Now you don't though! This WebMD article here likes to profess different stanzas to the riddle cures of life here. We don't like the ominous motion detectors for life here. Making different stanzas of truths and such are the ones that we're after here (WebMD, https://www.webmd.com/genital-herpes/pain-management-herpes#1-2).

We like Herpes Zoster too much here! There is a cure. Is there not? Please, please, please make it earlier though! The shot needs to be given around 30 years of age, not 20 or even 50 or 80: 80 is too late and 50 just makes the anticipation of it, the shot given around 65 for example, even worse for potential clients! The famciclovir medications work the best!

Diefanback and Fraefel (Editors) have a great article by Melendez on the HSV cure too (http://www.springer.com/us/book/9781493904273). Just because the antibodies, I'm citing from the Appendices 1 and 2 here, that come over us with sweat just because we are brushed up upon this kind of writing again, to feel the heat of the centuries old literatures of HSV Type 1 virus vectors here, doesn't mean we have solved anything. The same can be said of Sacks of his writings too. There's similarities in these studies here, but we haven't solved anything yet! As the appendices do tell of a foreboding mixture of talent searches here (Sacks, http://www.medbroadcast.com/channel/infection/herpes/herpes-virus-8-types)!

The mouth HHV through HVC, just kidding here, HVC is a vacuum cleaner attachment device. Right, and exactamundos, People! We're just kidding on all of the research, as HSV is just a vacuum cleaner that sold out its puppet shows to the world wide web back in the '70s researching on the topic. By now the entire U.S. population has it, HSV 2 that is, thereof! And so, we're testing and we're researching it thereof!

We're smug about this day here Andrea because this is the moment we've all been waiting for on Dr. Z and his counterpart Mr. D. Please be aware that there is mostly talk about this cure, only because there is one now! I will leave these two individuals alone once they find the cure though! It's only possible to spout off how many people are infected with HIV once a year though! This is an AIDS cure, an AIDS epidemic! My counterpart in this is God's wisdom cures are off the vaccine list! What about a vaccine for Herpes Simplex Viruses a through z here! The Astellas Pharma Inc. study is a hoax (Acton, 2013). It is written in the appendices too as an antigen for life here.

This is for the birds. Is it not! We're studying antigens for the HIV virus as well as the HSV ones! Why not then? We have the antigens for the HIV virus too. But what are they for? If HSV was solvable with T-cell interventions here, then what are the antibodies to boot here! Well, there are two contrasts between cold sores and bed bugs that bite. McKinzie Brocail Pack (2015) is forthright on her insistences that animals and humans coagulate the Central Nervous System (CNS). Oral herpes breakouts are non-existent in the futures of humanity's rulings on life here! Take, for example, her rulings about HSVs 1 and 2 here. We do not know the immunoglobulins (Ig) that are created, or antibodies thereof, unless we get the antigens straight? We don't need the cure that badly! Not!

So, what are the Enzyme-linked inducible system, Elvis's dad's theories thereof! The ELVIS system here is the hemoglobin ruling we've been looking for here. It says here, furthermore, that, "Cultures positive by ELVIS are confirmed by immunofluorescent staining," (Pack, 2015). What are the Astellas Pharma Inc. peoples supposed to do but to find another hoax to attain it to! Immunoglobulins (IgG) are meant to repair the cells exposing the attire for midnight travel. In other words, Peoples, we're here to solve the AIDS viruses that make people crazy for love and sexual intercourse, because they cannot have a forest deeds mentality's structurisms here. Back in the day, we never had to worry about sexual intercourse causing pains and such! Me and My wife, we were there for the talent sorrys and stuff!

What does Jesus want from us then! But to take the stand that God is here to stay, Peoples! Who doesn't believe in this stuff now? We want you to ride to the appendices again and go, well, there's a Trichomonas cure for lots of things here. What is an antibody here, but a simple way of saying antigen. Lots of people suffer the herpes cure and such! What is an antigen worth it to you here! Say, we are supposed to come up with the herpes cures and such! What kinds of things do you want to know about globulins and such! T-cells are for the birds too, I suppose! The right T-cells mixed with the antigen's antibody noise is so true here. What about an Andromeda Galaxy that takes it far from life here says that God is ready to ban Herpes Simplex Virus (HSV) types back to where they came from! Let's start with this monetary clause here. Am I looking for a handout for these types of things here? Yes, please! I'm homeless otherwise? Not necessarily, but truth be told, once I told my family's money about this commandant's way of speaking here, I was told to be careful what you say, and was knocked over into a mental hospital for it. Appendix 2 states that the Trichomycin in my blood here is right on the hopper for HSV cures. In essence here, the Japanese do not have the cure, but they do note that getting cancer is way less for some reason in their country's lack of love here. Why was the Trichomycin pill taken away from the U.S. of A.? It was taken about 1973 or so here. Why though? Was it our Hiroshima cloud? Because that's not it here, Folks of wonderment's entitlements and so ons! We like to think that the Hiroshima cloud looked like a mushroom cloud for a reason here. We are so out of it. You know? A viral infection of this magnitude (Cohen, et al., 2002) could not zooicologically be the cures for cancer here, as this viral infection's last stand is taking medication for Herpes Simplex Viruses too. They're called cancer alliances for a reason here. Monkeys in the Cohen, et al., study here are too complex for us. Are they?

We're all here for a reason untold to us here. The study by Ohashi, et al., too, is a dorsal root ganglia/spinal cord issue then? Nope!

So, what are we all scared for then? This means that Andrea is the only one with studies to boot here? We sent her on this wild goose chase then? Well, sort of! I mean, if the antigens for the HSV viruses have valerian root as one of its causes or one of its cures, we're going to note that in the records that be here. Jesus and Jezibellie aside here, what is Jezibellie's one moment of truth here? She took drugs.

Correctamundos here! I don't think we'll talk about this even in Chapter 17 even! Hey, one moment please. Andrea has to look at something else… The appendices are even numbered. They go one by one here. Please note that she felt compelled to send these to the right and appropriate authorities because they hold the candle and the key to everything here. The CDC or the Centers for Disease Control and Prevention blew her off big time, and Congress, they take everything to hear her. Nobody would listen to her, um, to Us, rather! We're big time writing these letters for her here!

Meningitis is caused by herpes though? Big time! We're saying this from the Pack (2015) article here online here. The skin rash in kids though? We're calling that one a hoax (Sacks, 2017)! Finally here, we're talking about Mr. Z working for the A.D.A.M. Company, Inc. here, the suite or division of healthcare products here. What is Ebix anyways, but a bad old company name for quality assurance! We are editors here! And so, with the timing's blessings here, Anton stated in Kom University's structure care in van Suriname that the oculogyric crisis that Andrea has experienced is a lot like herpes simplex then! Because these medicines that take mental health to a whole new level, she is allergic to them big time! And so, Acton (Acton, 2013) states that the ocular diseases of herpes of the alpha levels created bigger herpes over time here. What needs to be done is a cure for the genital herpes kind, and then all the others will follow suit. They are one in the same viruses concocting and cooking up for kids and adults alike here. By kids I do mean teenagers, lest one get molested by the system's technologies here and have HSV as a small child here! We don't mean the child birthing types either. That said here, Jesus and Jezibellie pray everyday for a cure for HSV then! Not! It was non-existent back then though! It's a "not" situation, because these two are not living for the gusto any more than they have to here? They love us!

We're supposed to be cracking the codes for the <u>Angels and Demons</u> book by Dan Brown (2000) here! This is a recording of nature's crackdown codes for life here! What does the book <u>Angels and Demons</u> bring to our lives here but livelihoods and such! We're talking about the herpes (HSV) cure here!

And, sorry, to crack this code, we need Mr./Dr. Z's help! We think he knows something about it you see! He knows that the antigen codes are not far from help here. This lifetime galaxy of knowledge here is two-fold here.

We're talking about the roseola experienced from Type 6 though? Not! It doesn't exist! It's an old germ, wheat infested cohabitation of life here. The vaccine is what we need, not a shot against it here. The vaccine approach is much more willing and viable than the chocolate kinds here! That said, Andrea, what IS the cure then! I don't know, she keeps saying to us here! That's because we have it and you don't, Andrea! That's the truths be told way of sleeping with the enemies here. Dr. Z and the mister counterparts here are so truthful it's pathetic here! Say, is sleeping with the enemies a once in a lifetime shot of organizations on the part of the truth? Or, are we holding back the cure for HSV once and for all here? Mononucleosis is a type of herpes though? I beg to differ on that one here. Even the chicken pox is all related to the Herpes Zoster types! We're trying to solve it, and yet our research here this morning no less and no more here has not come up with anything to solve it.

Take that paragraph and wince it, Andrea! We're so enthralled with the AIDS viruses that call us the chicken pox that the zoster is right there for the takings here, save taking it 30 years earlier though! Give us the shots and we will decide if herpes is right for us here! A vaccine though? You bet! It's in the monkey studies at the CDC. They think that the Herpes Zoster is there to stay though? I bet it's the monkey studies for Virus B here: A zoonotic antigen though? Yes, please! If those monkeys could talk! What is an itchy substance for the stuff, cause it's not itchy at all, save a few hundred monkeys who couldn't breathe with the stuff on its skins there! Say, we're all about animal safeties here, but this is for the birds to know and to find out about! Kids can get herpes though? Are we gross about it then? We're all in for it, Andrea! That's the jokes about kids and stuff? Can you contract it through the AIDS viruses that we call related to the owners of these jokes though? That's not nice, and it's contracted through the skin and it's contact regimen here. Say, what are those jokes again? We're not nice. If trying to be nice though, we say, tell the monkey see monkey do, what to do with the human counterparts, as Dr. Z is really cool about it when we get to him, Andrea! Antigens caused breakouts in the monkeys at the zoology experiments here! Meningitis though? Yes, it's caused by the HSV viruses here.

The Human Immunodeficiency Virus (HIV) cure is here to stay as well. Stay tuned to Chapter 14 for that one! Save one in a million girls, one in a million girls, why would I lie, why would I lie! It's a song, Folks! That means that one in a million contract the AIDS viruses like schizophrenias here. One in a million! So? We're just dancing with air between our teeth here! Antigens are like antibodies though? Nope! As McKinzie Brocail Pack (2015) explained to us here, the Herpes Simplex Viruses (HSV or HHV) here, are here to stay then? What with an antigen and an antibody that says, immunoglobulins or IgG in other words, is here to stay. Right, or exactamundos here, correct? Nope! What with monkeys 3 and 4 here, we are talking about the world's cure for AIDS related viruses here, that says we are talking about the immune system that creates antibodies to fight off the infections or the antigens.

And so, as we were explaining it, back in the days of no tomorrows here, we didn't have the antibodies to boot here! We had the donuts cures for cops and robbers, but none found the antigens very funny, save the 1000 or so monkeys that were tested on animals and such at the CDC! We need to test on animals though? Try humans for a change, and then you have your antibody, your antigen squashed: And a test for HSV that works! Try it, Folks!

What, you don't want anyone to know you test or have tested on animals though? What is our prognosis of the situations here! We need to know though! So, CDC, the Centers for Disease Control and Prevention here, are going to come home and need us here! We just are tired of getting the AIDS viruses run arounds and such. Say, do you know what AIDS viruses cause? Cause we are tired of getting that one right too. Aren't we though? Hey, in Angels and Demons, the book says or states here that God is a God given right to die young here. Why are they like that in there, that book thereof? He's vying time on you here. What monkeys, He says! Is PETA going to come after us or what here!

Just solve it, mkay? Because we both know that you did it! We're saying to you here, run it on a human test course, the antibody of course. Because people like you and me have tested on animals before here? We don't really, and we shouldn't? Take it up with God here, because the antibodies are not formalities here. We don't have the causes and the cures here, "unless" we test on animals though! So, take it from Me, Andrea, we don't have the antibody created yet? Yes, we do! We just don't want PETA in an uproar, and for Me that's a hint, hint, hint, to Jezibellie, who used to test on animals for sure! Our cats were in proper alignments back then! We just didn't know it here!

Say, who is Jezibellie to test on cats though? We test by loving and nurturing them, not by injecting them with harmful substances and then calling it good here. We loved cats back in the days of non-rabbit invasions here! We do test on animals, they say! And so, PETA, we so loved you back in the days of college years when we used to get and subscribe to those horrific magazines you sent and I laid in bed and cried all the time!

Or, we can sew up our lost oats, get everyone cured, and get past the stigmas attached to non-cohesive coveting of languages here! Say, does the CDC, the Centers for Disease Control and Prevention, remember my letters to them stating they already have the cure here! You know, for HSV 1 and 2 here! We have the meningitis one figured out. Say, the cytomegalovirus's calling card too, is there for the taking. How many lab rats have we stolen to say, HSV has a cure here! We don't do well with human interventions, in other words! How about a stolen lab rat and a career out the back windows of humanity's cure for the AIDS related viruses that plague us here!

We're tired and we're lonely and we're helpless to this disease, doctors, nurses and such that wonder about cures and everything! What are we doing but being lonely and cured though! How about a fight every time Andrea comes across someone with the herpes cures though, cause I'm not only interested in just this one here. How do you think that Namibia tests their animals? Sorry, PETA! I'm only stating a fact. This one's for the birds here! But listen up! The antigens, save their 200 monkeys that made it to the top of the picking gyruses here, state that in order to clear up their HSV viruses here, they need to be injected with that "stuff" you made up here to do it with, CDC! I mean, if you're embarrassed by the monkey attire you now wear, perhaps you could give it up a little bit more!

I mean, if you take the water out of the muffin tins, give them back to...! I mean, order me some more Lego cures! I mean, if the water is out of the muffin tins on time, you could administer many vaccines to peoples other than monkeys and birds. For the records here, the CDC does not administer anything to humans, yet though! How about doing so? I mean, we're dying of crusted infestations here! Not me, but you know!

If God and alcoholic beverages were involved, there's CDC raps and stuff too! But they've cured HSV in rabbits, lab animals and such! How about a try on me the next time that the CDC tries to cure the world with their epidemics of bipolar disorders? So, how about it, Guys and Gals of the next millennium cure for rape charges? Because rapes happen time and time again in these mental facilities that we get sent to! Would it stop raping charges, or would they drop because nobody wants to spread AIDS related schizophrenias to the next person in charge of the drop box for monies and what not that we're keeping, for the time coming next that someone wants to get out of there with all the monies intact?

They do a pretty good job of keeping someone out of your rooms though? Not with all that hype about Celexa pills for agent #1 in the CDC! Try us though! We love humanity and we love the invention of fruitcakes too! Say, I'm not infested with Herpes Simplex Viruses! Then try it out for size, CEO of the company! Take a fruitcake to jail though, and rape happens every single day there too. Try us out for size, and stop the spread of the AIDS viruses that plague us here, save schizophrenias and such here!

That's about it on the AIDS/Herpes Simplex Virus though! Not! It's not like the cones and rods of all people will be spared, but the inklingships that come with the HSV virus is not in the cards. For some people, it is better than spreading Christmas cheer for all to hear! That is, if we're not into the herpes cards today, the better thing to do would be to cry a little for all the broken hearts in the world's biggest and best gift of the century! And that's Andrea's know how to give this gift of trust to the world's blatantly obvious medical cures though!

Valacyclovir is a genital cure for HSV then! Not! It keeps things at bay, best or better than the rest of them there medications. So far, there are no outlaws that state that having herpes is the best thing in the world's three medical cures then: Hepatitis C is not outlawed either, as having the cure though? Yes. It does! "The specificity of B virus serologic methods has improved substantially; however, the assays rely on specimens obtained weeks after the possible exposure event and, thus, cannot be of help…" (CDC Inc., 2016, https://www.cdc. gov/herpesbvirus/specimen-collect.html) in exposing events though? How many monkeys are we talking about here? Hundreds, if not literally thousands though! Why are we even talking about the monkeys in this study for, when half of them did not eat tens of thousands of dollars worth of meals per day here. This study, the one we're looking for here, did not eat tens of thousands of herpes infested bicycles on the cloud nine that we're looking into here!

We did that on purpose, Andrea! It's a helpless feeling is it, to look up stuff here and there and to and fro? "Helpless" is the term used to reincorporate the bodies ready to eat here. We cannot fathom a day without the herpes viruses? She doesn't have it: The HSV cure is what we're after though! So, listen to the reasonable hype about the cloud nine intervals here. What are the innuendos that God listened to us with? We needed to see the other article about assays here. "The availability of PCR protocols that reliably discriminate B virus from HSV should permit the direct detection of B virus…" (CDC Inc., 2016, https://www.cdc.gov/ herpesbvirus/specimen-collect.html) here!

This mononucleosis way of looking at this diseases cure thing is really for the birds. Is it not? Listen to us then! We know what we're talking about, without having to resort to French Battles of the Bulge here! We're talking about HSV's 3 and 4 then. Correctamundos here? We're talking about HSV 1 and 2 here, maybe 3 if we're lucky about this Battles of the Bulge here!

What are we talking about then, Sires, and you too, Gents! It's that many wars were fought over the HSV cure too! What is mad cow's disease exactamundos here, but HSV cures are what again then? It means, Folks, and you too Gentiles, that mad cow's disease is rampant here in the northwestern parts of the state then! We're trying too hard to get you included into this genre of latent cures, Peoples, and you too Gentiles and such! We're open to suggestions though! Remember that then when somebody tries to offer you a herpes cure, Andrea! We're talking about the angel cures for things we find most dear here.

In essences here, there are many of "Us" up here who think that "for the birds" means that somebody's not invested time and a half on holidays and such to think of the cure for Herpes Simplex Viruses and such! We're all ears, Andrea! What happened to the monkeys then, PETA says. Right, or correctamundos here? They were all exterminated from the planet apeshit and were taken from custody right away into mental health for monkeys. Correctamundos here, CDC? I do declare, I am not trying to save face at all here. I am simply searching for some answers to some questions that I do not even try to believe in here.

The basics are here, Folks! The herpes cure is simply the HSV 1 and 2 here, as the HSVs 3, 4, 5, and 6 are hoaxes at best here? Just 3 and 5 then? Nope, 8 is a hoax, and 9 and 10 do not exist yet. The questions answered here are that God's simplicity's sakes here is not the only cure.

We don't know them, Andrea! The guys that just pulled up here are the only cures for schizophrenias here! She's in her bedroom all the time now, and just because she only works for five different companies, agencies here, does not mean she is somehow herpes infested here. So, 500,000 trillion million men then, is that what we are to her then? We just worked out the HSV cures of a lifetimes of hope! So, does that mean we are the cure for herpes then? Yes, We are!

We're meaningful and it's time to shut up now though? What does this mean to the Herpes Simplex Viruses that are on hold here, People!

Because next quality assurance training purposes seminar's switch to chlamydia or syphilis is really the same things here! What does that serum do but to only transpose the witching wells and such! We're talking about Hepatitis B and C's ailment cures as well! We hear that only a select few have healed themselves from herpes though?

We don't necessarily get that here. Why not, Jesus and Jezibellie are watching here! We're not saying anything to get them all riled up here, but this is war, Peoples! Every person I come across has either got it, HSV though, or they don't. Right now, it's 1 in 2 people everywhere though! Every place I come across here, I get it like plain as day. And to think that Mr. Z is really a doctor, an MD no less, is really for the birds as well as his counterpart, Dr. D! Because the mutations in such categories as pee and urine and such are really that hard for a herpes dialect! We're onto you, Andrea! She's waiting for the cure to come across her screen.

Just readily though is a kind of moronic code to blatantly ask God about here! I don't know what it means to be civil anymore, Peoples! We're all over this cure though! Say, can you think of the monkey see, monkey do in the chloronic cures of a lifetime of AIDS though, because this is Dr. Z's counterpart, Mister Dr. D of the University of Washington's Medical Center. He reviews all this shit, just like Dr. Z does, so do others of the universities statures here!

Say, are we on board then, in telling "Us" to just knock it off and to tell others of the cost of such mechanisms and to stay alive are at? By the way here, we're so tired of the articles and such that we don't really need them in the first place here. We are just trying to get by on squabbling over the monkeys and such?

Those monkeys are from Vietnam, are they? Nope, from African soils here. We do declare the monkey based trials and tribulations from injecting semen into their skins from puppy dogs and what not, right, correctamundos here, is not of the human origin then. Correctamundos here? Because the strain that is the same as it was in graduate school, Andrea of the loveliest condition of having "nothing" wrong with her at all here, take or took Us here. What we mean by that is, we're loveliest in the morning dews here, the closets of which are out in the open here. The timing of such intervals is therefore on the sightings of God's justices here, the times of which are open to suggesting that virals such as the HSV cures are right here for the takings here! If <u>Angels and Demons</u> by Dan Brown (2000) suggests anything else here, it is that we're onto the herpes cure big time here!

It's a serum, Peoples! I do hear this correctly, she says! I don't know what the Herpes Simplex Virus cure is yet? It's right up there in the <u>Angels and Demons</u> way here.

I don't know yet what the monkeys are up to! Dr. Z, are you there with me on this here? You transposed a parentheses a time or two and work for the A.D.A.M. agencies here for healthcare products. Is it?

We don't know you though! I've never met these individuals, save the time or two upstairs that the guys in holding question mark here, "Us", never want to see these two individuals again though? They had nothing to do with the CDC making the remarks or the wherewithals to enjoy the CDC again. Fruitfully, I might add!

This is such a short paragraph. I might make God take on another look at the <u>Angels and Demons</u> story again here! The plot is hard to follow then? It makes the science and religious aspects one and all the same here! We are talking about Jesus and Jezibellie still. Aren't we?

We are though, right, or exactamundos on that! You know what? Is Dr. Z available for comment in his Seattle office, or am I off base here? I sent that letter in the Appendix 2 to the federal government for transposal about that AIDS related virus. Sent that directly by air I presume!

There's lots of angels and demons on this planet of the apes here.

We do declare a mistrial for any of the Z's counterparts though, as injectable human semen is ready for the taking here, the kind with HSV already inside of it! The serums for jokingless topics about angel cures and what not are really for the birds then. Correctamundos here?

We are in a hurry with all these paragraphs stating that God's only willingnesses are the Jezibellie cures. For an ailment cure to hurry up with all of these planet of the apes knocking around and such, there's only two I can seek to desist about right now in fact! What monkeys are these though? It's the serums in the muffin tin packs at Costco, or Sam's Club, whichever you wanna call it here!

This is the timing's serious notions here, that without this information in the Appendix 1 we sent to many different peoples here, the running time on this ain't so, Andrea! It means that we sent this out and ended up into a mental facility for latent criminals then?

Are we gonna go there, Andrea? Yesiree Bob! We just looked that one up again in the Urban Dictionary again, Folks! We don't know what the serum holds for the futures of companies against the Sam's Club logos here. The Costco out West is really beginning to take hold then? We've been using the same manufacturers for years out here too, there Andrea!

We don't know the Billings lately that says in Montana there are few and yet far between radars out there for goats and shit with the AIDS viruses too.

Behold, Chapter 14 deals with the AIDS viruses we all know and love here!

And now we turn to Jezibellie's cures for peace here! Have we gotten all of the latency out of the word pedophiles yet? We don't know yet, do we here? For the records here, there is no pedo head alive, or murderous head for that matter, who wants or "desires" a child to rape or a kingdom to kill in. There is a stark difference in the locus of control about these monkeys then! As they are the ones killing each other over the herpes viruses then?

We don't know about that here! Yeah, right, Class of Gentiles that needs to go home on this one point here! The point is here, we're not going to say exactly how to do it then? Nope, then, correctamundos here? What happened to all the Jaguars of these Gentiles then? We had souped up cars back in the days of horses and buggy carriages. Correctamundos here?

We need a herpes cure! Have we found one yet, Class of Gentiles in motions here? Chapter 8 of Revelations, it's Revelations, Peoples, is really what we're after here. King James Version here please! This book here is supposed to tell us how the minions really got after the Mizraim's of society's first influences of peace here! Take, for example, of how the minions got after the doggies that were tested on animals. Correctamundos here? These dogs were taken out and shot because they had the "AIDS" viruses of schizophrenia, bipolarisms in America only, and the word "schizoaffective" to induce paranoia only!

I go, well, I've had both and all three then! You see, there are the other shots that come out of the park, only to say that these monkeys in the study of the Virus B – herpes simplex cures and such are only for the birds to know then, because these were injected with the substances of hard to get nights out on the towns and such! For those guys who donate their semen or sperm banks in general are hard to come by here.

This means that the only guys that are exterminated from Chapter 8's (KJV, Rev. 8.7.) versions of peace here is that the goblins ate them up <p. 1816-1817>! There's more to this, of course, here! This "looney tunes" way of looking at life though, Andrea, is the fact that no one is going to believe you, save a couple of professors of lawyer's schooling that might question your motives here? No one is going to do that, save "Us", she says! Close that book once and for all here! Save it buds! This man loves this woman! Jesus and Jezibellie are only exterminated from that one sentence, "Have got it down, Man!" This passage, this chapter, rather, is really quite annoying from our perspectives here. "But we wrote it, right?" Can she do anything besides sit here and type this annoying drivel then?

We're trying to cure or solve the HSV cures here, and no one will listen then? Ask Dr. Z where he got the serum to inject into the skin of Olive Garden Way here and tell us how they got the serums in the first place! Go to the CDC, the Centers for Disease Control and Prevention here, and ask them what they did to and with the serums that matter most here!

Say, we think we've got the cure already, as most of the viral D serum's out of it. Yes? It's the second row, Fellows, the middle one there! It's the second to the last drop of the Folgers in your cup that keeps them at bay already here, the herpes outbreaks thereof here!

And lastly but not least here, there are the herpes cures for Christ's interventions here. Oh "sick bed", where are you (Rev. 2.20.)! She's here, Jezibellie is here! Let's make a serum. Shall we?

It's cow's blood that is the cure then, correctamundos then, Class of Gentiles and gents alike here? Nope! We already eat cow's blood when we cook the hopper meat and say it's for the birds here.

So, what is the hope and the treat here, is that Dr. D, a nice man I've never even met before here, and I'm talking all about the herpes cures and stuff that he's been reviewing for some time now, have got to change their ways about peace here? We're talking about one person are we not? Nope! It's about 10 individuals from the CDC, the Centers for Disease Control and Prevention here, that got on a plane and spoke to a Namibian government agency out west out in the African republic of China and told "Us" we'd better speak to the Namibian government agencies regarding the capture of orangutans and such! Funny, we're the speaking capital of Jamaica too, and Mr. C wasn't an original captor of the Great Republic of China anyways. That said here, he is a government official, isn't he? He's the original captor of the great orangutan basin there in Namibia. Say, is that a proper noun, or should it be one here?

We are talking about Namibian cures for the continent of Africa here. They operate much as states do in the United States of America here, where bipolarism runs rampant here, and they do not have anyone who is bipolar in Namibia though? We've been working on a cure for herpes here. Are we there yet? We need to exterminate the population though of invalids such as Andrea was or is or shall be?

Do you have the focuses and the justifications for these claims you so called do not have here? There's not a facility alive that would not grant your advances and your cures to so called reductionism here in the Bibles, no less and no more here! The Bible is just one fable after another here!

We do tell fables to Andrea. Do we not! We cannot tell a lie!

There are fashionables in the commandant's languages of lies and deceit! And there's nothing in the wakes of 9/11 that did not go down. Did it not? Did you have a desire to kill or deceit anyone in your lifetime, Andrea, because this life is really downturned if you cannot provide us with the cures that are in your middle drawer. Correctamundos here?

I have no control over the serums that they detect is racing over to the Namibian government for cures for the AIDS viruses for HIV, as they have already come up with the cure for this AIDS virus's lack of plentality here. That said, in Chapter 14, yes, we will address some of these issues with the Namibian governmental lack of persuasion here.

This is for the birds if we cannot solve it right now, Class of Gentiles, elite and strong you are! Shall we dance then! Shall we kill the stronghold we've got on the Namibian class of Gentiles who don't have the herpes viruses all figured out then? Because we've got a whole slew of monkeys that bit the dust. We suspect anyways!

This God you find so interesting, Andrea, is right there for the taking! This "sick bed" by the way, stinks to high heavens! It's in the second drawer down, guys and you too gents at the CDC office! Second drawer down. What does that mean to us! You've already gotten the cure, Gents and you too Gentiles! Second drawer down. What happened to the key to it though? You're going to pick the lock. Right and exactamundos here?

What does "second drawer down" mean to God's languages here? This is just unnecessary drivel here? It's the "monkey drawer," is it not? Go to the B virus and hand out tears and checks and stuff, cause this thing's had here!

This man desires you! I do desire Him as well, Jesus says, correctamundos here? Just because they did NOT, I repeat, did NOT die on those crosses up there in the alleyways of love here, means that just because they were up there for a time in a "gay rights" demonstrations here and there and everywhere does not mean that by beheadedment the guy, Jesus Christ here, is not listening to Jezibellie cures everywhere too! Let's have plentiful sex, Peoples!

We're sort of ailment curing the planet of the apes here then! The "second drawer down" comment has got "Us" spooked a little here. It means, Class of Gentiles and thieves alike here, that the problem with copyright is that God made it as such! We're not copyrighting anything in this book then? It's all copywrited, what!

I do know this too. Jezibellie Christ was much the same way you were, Andrea, with having to deal with the sands of time. In essence here, the biggest masquerade in the hopper to deal with wasn't your looks or anything. Was it? Because Jezibellie Christ is you! I do know this too. You're no Jesus killer. Are you not anything but a human being here! We all take shits, People! This is the Bible signing off for now!

So, "second drawer down." What does that mean to us here, Folks and Gentiles who steal people's monies and say they are down for the counts here?

We say it to the hopper in question then. How about a little "Suddenly" by Billy Ocean for us Gentiles who are not stealers of time you see, but of faith! How about Abraham-Hicks. Can I get a hell yes from him too? Probably! Why don't you quiz him, er, faith, by naturally saying that Abraham is really Esther and vice versa? It's probably because you don't want to run him off here, Andrea! She's celibate too I can imagine, what with all this "voices" problem you two have!

I would run a nice memo to the doctors involved in this extermination project and product cure that "drawer" if I were you, CDC! The Centers for Disease Control and Prevention just didn't know what to do with my letter here in Appendix 1, and the Appendix 2 one was sent to them too, though a prior version of what might last longer into Congress's hands is a "memo" from us every once in a while to just bag it and take the damn serum as a human being! You got me, CDC? Take it. Now, Folks!

I do know that testing on animals has run its course here in the hoppers of America's talent searches for the most schizophrenic person on Earth here, as her 23, count them now, hospital stays has baffled her family into believing she is terminally ill here! And, tells of a non-existent time in someone's life where people have no money to give me though? I've got a job the last 9 months before they shut off my Social Security though? I hope so! Because I'd sent them another letter, the federal government, not the CDC (Centers for Disease

Control and Prevention) here that said I am no longer an invalid, and can you please let me go from this LRA (Less Restrictive Order or Alternative) here? And Congress said no to me in that phraseology's happenstance where three years ago I tried my best to alert the federal government, America's federal government, that we've got a cure for Herpes Simplex Viruses 1 and 2 here, and 3 we just need to administer the shots way sooner than, say, 45 even! And they never responded to me. Hence, I went into mental health, not over fascism or greed mongering here, but out of faith!

We took her in there and said, see, look what's happening to our poor and our "unjust measures" of sticking people with pins and needles everywhere for not taking their "medications" on time or nothing here? I do declare a mistrial in deeds and in stupidisms that I, Jesus, cannot attend to here any longer here! Let's do test lab rats on the people inside those facilities then?

Well, that's what Namibia has done already here, is to turn into a commandant's languages here for the HIV cure, which is really just running rampant here, as they have the cure alreadys, Folks! Let's turn to Chapter 13 and say, Namibia, just run over to PETA's health department and say I have a vote on all of this rampant lunaticacy here! There's mental hospitals everywhere there too? Not a one!

I just vote on this "homeless" bit here and ask individuals from every cop's shows here to say, I will take the pledge and take the vaccine for Herpes Simplex both 1 and 2, please! Will you please show me where I sign? Because I have to though? Not because I want to. Correctamundos here? We always say correctamundos here for a "gravely disabled" chick who's healed her schizophrenia and solved the AIDS viruses too! Only to find out that the second drawer down has been moved to the third upon publication of this printing office's lap of luxury here! This has got to be the lap of luxury we're talking about here.

The faith and promise of tomorrow's yesteryear is that we keep "medicating" the "homeless" and the "insecure" here! We just wanted to say to you, Andrea, that this work is but a cosmic question about homelessness that we do detail in Chapter 30 here.

There are 20 viruses worldwide that need to be fixing each other's herpes plans and such! So much for the monkeys which viruses take hold of the penis envies in each other's herpes plans too! We're onto something swift and clean and it's HIV and such! Andromeda Galaxy, are you there yet? I can hear the dogs barking in the wintertime and the trees are such lovelier than I imagined they'd be this time of year. Say, can trees bark with the wind in tune and such? Yes! They do! They bark to each other. In time it is such pleasantries to meet you, Andrea! That said, what is the Barberi fix on this book here! It's a timing's deeds and answers mentality's sakes here that says, we've already fixed the herpes cure for this book here.

Can you solve the riddles and nothing like it on here too? We don't know how many relatives of yours have herpes, Andrea. Save a little closure for this to indicate why you're so gung ho on this topic of yours. It's because the best of the best of everyone is infected with this disease here, and I cannot go on knowing that God has put me on this Earth? To breed an infection with monkeys though? Can you imagine this!

What are we doing to solve this riddle, puzzle or pedophile ring we chose to wear this evening and next! It's simple here. Let's solve this tomorrow evening or so. Let's get this show on the road and live a little here! Are you going out for an evening affair soon? Because we are ready to take you out and show you the world here! A ring and a kotex though? Can you spell cheaply done here? Because Jezibellie cried for Me here! She's not in the kotex world though!

I can spell cheaply done here, and this is a hoax. Is it not though? We're so cheaply done though! How God can do this to poor, innocent people is beyond Me and beyond Jezibellie Christ too! This is God talking though, right God? 🙂 Let's break out the bubbly and celebrate winning the cure for HSV and solve this riddle and this puzzle, for this is how the evening breaks epidemic proportionate figures and such here! Say, why don't we do this tomorrow then, break out the bubbly. You know? Because she still hasn't said what it was that cured us! Well, Andrea? What is it that is horse manured out of the pieces of the puzzle lost here! That said, what is the cure then, God? If God's talking, then what is this stupid piece of paper supposed to show us, but that the HSV's of the world's autonomy making classes are the diatribes of an eon of paperwork to show that God has indeed invented it. Correctamundos here?

That's for God to decide then, how and when the cure is involved in it here! That's the said factors that cringe us to the commandants here! The commandants is the Jezibellie cure then too! See Chapter 1 in the interim here and see if this facts based study's decisions and such are really real then!

Break out the bubbly then, Class of Gentiles, and you too Peoples of color and such religious preferences as Jesus and Jezibellie can bring to God's literatures here! What, are we going to spout off about how the bubbly is just broken up and tangled and God can't begin to deal with the facts that Andrea is ready for the worlds to know just how broken up and tangled she is about HSV viruses and such TV evangelism programs worldwide though? Geez, Jezibellie! You cured Herpes Simplex Viruses though back in the age of 20th century programming.

I hate to inform you all, but God was generous with our typewriters back then. We were a little fancier than the following mentionables here! We had such a gift back then that we could not take Jezibellie from the typewriters at all here. We were so gifted, we had inklingships all figured out back then though! This is the Divine Source Wisdom here, typing the gifted hands of God's wraths here. Going with the flow though, the Herpes Simplex Viruses of the world though are just a little jealous about the going forth momentums here without contacting NASA about the inklingships of a lifetime of greed mongering here! Say, this is Daiichi-Sankyo (2018) calling the cops about to get into the heads of some limelights here, but call them and ask for the Trichomycin pill that causes cancer though? It does not! I believe in dealings with the sanctity of the DSW and I believe in that pill so strongly that a Trichomycin shot is better and worth it! Please see Appendix 3 for the world's trade organizations that do not aspire to it yet.

And see you on the flip sides of justice service centers throughout the world here! I do say "worlds" sometimes, but God is a great God. Just willingnesses to receive the Divine Source Wisdom is really what Andrea is about here.

Saving graces though, just answer the phone at the CDC when we call you with new epidemics cures here. We are tired of the runaround, as evidenced by my behavior when we were all eating lunch with the epidemics cures of Americas taking the stances to get the behaviors all opened up.

And seeing as such here, call Namibia real quick like. And Chapter 14 deals and discusses the downsides of seeing the forces that being really bubbly champagne brings to the discussion on time rocks and such! The marriage proposals that ensue here. Just think about it, loved ones to be here! I love the DSW so much so that I cannot begin to imagine a life without You in it! I loved you once, Girl, He says to You here! I do love You, that I cannot ignore here! "I can tell myself that I can't hold out forever, I said there is no reason for my fear," by REO Speedwagon!

We are in Americas. Are we not then? Say, what is that song titled, Do you love me? "And now I'm back to let you know… I can really shake 'em down!" Hint, hint! To Jezibellie Christ, will you marry Me all over again then? Because this real fear about HSV is just a hint that God has a new plan for the millennium cure for AIDS related viruses, like schizophrenias too. See Chapter 3 for that parade, song and dance. Mkay! I still hold out for "the one", and I cannot hold out forever for Her then, Jesus says? Because this is where it gets sticky here. Let's party hardy in a minute's time here.

There's much more to this saga of Herpes Simplex than you can tell by looking at God's interventions here!

There's so much to do and say that Jezibellie Christ cannot do it alone. By golly then, we're at a different church this evening and next! Say, did Jezibellie Christ come into My office one morning and then give Me a fantastic smooch because of it? Say, is Jezibellie Christ still Barnes and Noble ready here? Give me a fantastic look, Andrea, and then we'll say that Christ is the wife. It always has been! So, get your contentments back on track, Peoples! This is Jezibellie Christ then announcing the celibacy of Andrea Barberi for about 20 years now? Try five then! Say, get off your duff and make us a pancake ruling then!

What did these monkeys have to do with pancake affairs then? Because the serum is in the pancake batters that made the women mad. In the morning dews here, there's simply enough condoms to go around the bars here! And this made Jezibellie jealous that I was at a "titty bar" here? It did not, not in the least! Because I searched for Her there, Jesus says! Say, is HSV all there is to cure in this world's commandant's languages here? It's MMA fighting at its best then on Jerry Springer. Right, and correctamundos here?

We've got the Legos and you've got the cure for herpes and AIDS you say here? AIDS is a hoax. We know it is. Right, and correctamundos here? It's HIV that needs curing. The AIDS viruses, like schizophrenias, can find a girl without her ovaries here. If doctors don't believe in this schizophrenic talent search here, then how come the monkeys can't talk to us about this limelight's best inkling cures for peace here, save 20,000 people that it affects each year?

Try 40,000 worldwide here! We want to talk about the pancakes next! In the next millennium cure for AIDS viruses, Andrea, what do you hope to accomplish tonight with the justification for AIDS related viruses then? I want the pancake batter then to rise out from the ashes and give us the straight and skinny cures to viruses such as AIDS can concoct up, like God's penis's envies and such!

Do you think the universe is just like God is? I beg to differ. But Abraham-Hicks is right on this one. The law of attraction is powerful, just like the gods and goddesses that powerful people influence in here. Say, is the pancake batter ready for consumptions here? Because the monkeys enjoyed that! Truly they did. You know? And so, the batter prepared for Monkey Number 6 is the one that had the right concocted serum relief in it to cure the HSV viruses too. So, Monkey Number 6 was exterminated, as well as the rest of them there though! So, what did you find out about monkeys in the hopper on national television one day, Andrea? Do you have the cure for AIDS too? AIDS is a misnomer.

I'm telling you right now, Andrea, spit it out, for crying out loud! The problem is, Hon, that you don't know what you say, and you think you don't have the cure spelled out here, but you really do here! This is the CDC (Centers for Disease Control and Prevention)'s greatest topic out there is killing this AIDS virus of HSV and other ones out there, like schizophrenias you say to Me here? Jezibellie had AIDS then. Right, and exactamundos here? Because we were both dubbed schizophrenic here! Let's exterminate us? Not quite then!

Then what does God want us to do with the HSV cures here, but to sell them on the internet then? Why not then! It's an epidemic of proportionous magnitudes here! God's here, Andrea! If pancake batter is it, then what happened to all the "monkeys" then? They were exterminated by the Namibian government then? We cannot tell for sure, but we never lie! I don't think so.

I hope that the Namibian companies come out and love me tenderly for this, Jesus says, but it's not up to Me! It's up to the universes that exist! What comes of this then? The Monkey #3 did a very good job of wiping his butt up from the research that he'd done on his girlfriend, but he decided that she's not for him, and had decided not to give it to her then! Other monkeys though? Yes, and yep to that way of thinking here!

It's like that out there, is it then, a commandant's testimonies here? In other words, Folks, the cure is here to stay. That one is out in the rains though that took over the study. That was taken from us, the CDC, the Centers for Disease Control and Prevention, left it that way though. This was hard work for us to come up with the cures for AIDS related viruses and diseases here! Say, is AIDS a word that is a misnomer for Miss Jesus. Jezibellie Christ wrote the Bible though, not Paul then? Yes! And exactamundos to that here. She quoted the red passages in James 2:48 too! Notice there's no 48 in there at all here. The last verse of that passage in that very same chapter though states that God is willingnesses away from getting the last revenge! Paul actually wrote that though? No, but James did?

It's a misnomer to believe that God actually wrote the Bible "Himselves" though! We're talking about new religious testimonies about God's given rights of passages here!

We're talking about God's given rights and such! That said here, this is the moment we've all been waiting for here.

We're talking about Herpes Simplex Viruses 2 and 3, then 3 and 4 then? What about 1 though? We're all in the same boat's times here. Actually, the viruses that coagulate the fears about raining in Chapters 4 and 6 of Revelations, it's Revelations here, that says God is awesomely transposed about today's religious sermons here, says that God's excellency is your highness's greatest wonderments of God's wraths! In other words here, what does God have to do with the highness's greatest wonderment you say? Because Monkey #3 had the serum to eradicate, and I repeat! To eradicate HIV as well as HSV? Nope! Just HSV though, the bodily kind! So, here we are with a church sermon to boot here, as in, this is calling the kettle black here. But what does God do with all these rainhead ceremonies of religious importance in the Native American tribes and communities here? Because this is the religious ceremony's tidings that state that God wanted an echoship in today's church sermon that she went to this morning here. That said, what is the tidings, blessings and jokes of today's religious sermons about here? It's about God's trust in humanity that we can even bless this church, and it is a church, Andrea, the weirdest kind though? It's forthright and forthcoming that eradication of the church of God's literatures be saved here, lest we become important enough to find the cure for herpes simplex and all it's glories here! Save face here and note that the CCC is big enough to find fellowship in all the databases combined here! So save face and realize the important truths here are in the CCC's biggest complaints here. The CCC is the Capital Christian Church or Center that she now attains her beauty for! She's switched churches because God's little angels are so forthright in coming to God about the battle cures of peace here! Tell us that the Capital Christian Center is a forthright church to go to here in Lacey, Washington, is it? It's more like Olympia, Washington, but that's a quibbling point we all know and love.

And so, what of these "monkeys," as we're getting used to the ideas of love here, that says the balancatures of a lifetime of hatred amongst the populations gets used to the ideas of love here with Jesus at the helm here? We're so dedicating this lifetime of habits to Jesus Christ and His Jezibellie Christ here! And that said here, the Herpes Simplex Virus then has been solved. Can you just figure it out for the CDC, the Centers for Disease Control and Prevention here? Or, can we state that for a fact though? The serum, the correct serum, lies in the second cupboard from the left. The soft pack of matches we thought to burn it with has said this in order to make the limelights and such come from Andrea's multi-pack of time here! And that says a lot about our fates here! Just in time for the holidays is such a wording's open book here! Take what you can from cupboard number six, because this is how you all are doing here. Tell us what you mean by love, Andrea, and tell us what this cupboard means to humanity's graces here? Because we're all doing a fantastic job in life here! Life's quandaries thereof!

The second cupboard from the right. Remember that, Peoples! Who on Earth, there's some and maybe a few? None! That would take the cupboard comments to light here. They're really back woodsy about this in the CDC, the Centers for Disease Control and Prevention here.

About the timings of this event with the Divine Source Wisdom though, or CDC for short here! I don't know about this life, but this life without God in it speaks volumes of their CDC fixation! For God's crying outloudnesses about peace here, please do not lock up

Andrea Barberi again for life though? What has she done but cured HSV though! Lessons 4, 5 and 6 do not matter here.

Regardlesses of life and such can take its toll on the records that we gather from here. Lesson plans be it as they may and as they might here, there's lovely tidings and there's something called life giving properties in their words.

As a massive civilization of peoples though, there's context in here that's making Andrea's shoulders burn in wonderment as she types this out though! We're trying to get to the point and make it then, though it's slow going. Is it? There's contexts and continents we like to gather from here! Say, has Herpes Simplex Viruses 3 and 4 ever come to visit then? Say, the Toledo Baptist Church deserves a hug here! We never plan on visiting that church again though? Of course we will! Divine Source Wisdom rests here on the assumptions of time gathering and neutral zonages for the rest of the world.

Trying to figure out these last few paragraphs though at the CDC, the Centers for Disease Control and Prevention here, is like coming into the know about God's kingdoms here. And stating for a fact that we've healed the HSV viruses that have come along. To check us out on the internet and such at DivineSourceWisdom.com has provided fruitful information in the coming of ages and such!

Chapter 13

Love Stinks! Yea, Yea!

The Andromeda Galaxy image from space (NASA).

This is the Andromeda Galaxy. It is "Us"! And, just as fast as lighting bugs are the methods of madnesses that sinisterly takes Andrea to new levels within herself here! We're tired of calling it the kettle black though!

The moral of the story's limelights is that herpes simplex has been cured though? Yes, it has! Can you gather from us that more money is needed though, to have and to hold you is what we're trying to get at here, Ms. Jezibellie Christ though! Yes. It has reached epic proportions for us to state it here. Christ's offerings are such that God is epic about this moment's notices here!

It's best if we talk about why Jesus and Jezibellie are so many people's mistresses and misters here. If there were talent shows beyond the mere images in this photo here, we do declare a mistrial on it. Most mistrials occur because of HSV and HIV then. Correctamundos here? If there's nothing to do but to saving graces look at space as a rouge, what do so many people do on this love affair of life's habits here, but to sing in Jesus's praises? And rest assured, there are so many mistrials here that it ain't even funny. I love the Divine Source Wisdom! This may sound like a trial and error sort of book's titles here, but it is not! Andrea knows what she is talking about here! I do declare a mistrial if She's not mine before the turn of the century's biggest rouge's tables here!

Jezibellie Christ and Jesus Christ are a rouge, Peoples! I do declare a mistrial on the secondary literature gathering of Andrea right now. It's because she's trying her best to tell us about the DSW's fate when, really, we know of it already, Folks! We just pray a lot more than she does. It's about to turn nasty out there on Facebook already, as it's already in the works for lots more of this sounding thing. To turn nasty on us though is not in Jezibellie's cards.

She's innocent of all wrongdoing in the Bible thereafter. Who wrote that Revelations, it's Revelations, not Revelation here, where she's cast to a sick bed no less and no more here (BibleHub.Com, 2018, Rev 2:22)? She's cast by Jesus though, right (NIV, Rev., 2:20-24) <p. 850>? No, She is not! I beg to differ here on this one! She's not even sick! I go, well, what if She does this to innocent people then, throw them aside, cast them in to the blue waters of the Mediterranean.

Much bluer back then I imagine is the water in that place we cast aside, for this is the only way we are proclaiming much! Better than before I imagined, and so, castaways is right up your alleyways of peace here! It's a publishable book's mention of mere idiosyncrasies that take on a stronghold for the book here. It's a rouge, Andrea! I do declare a mistrial here no more here. If you cannot begin to imagine what Paul did to Jezibellie, now is the time to mistrial such findings, as there is no other way to find it, Folks. And I will try to proclaim the innocent truths of how Jezibellie Christ turned nasty on us here?

It's already written, Folks! We're trying to be as innocent as we dare to be. As far as faith is concerned here, there is already written information out there about Paul and what a great leader he is. But truth be told, he was a rapist and a sadist at that! Jesus declares him a mistrial, too. It's not like they're best friends, buds or anything else. He says they became best buds for like a day, until He found out the truth, from His wife in tow! There's nothing wrong with Paul becoming best buds with Satan though! That I will attest to, He says! There's nothing wrong with the situation at hand though? Why not then! There's always a chance he raped Jezibellie Christ for not listening to the conversations at church! Well then? There's always a chance he raped Her, right?

There's always a chance we're talking about the same people here. There's lawyers to contend with here. Jezibellie is innocent of all wrongdoing, in the Bible no less and no more here!

It's already written that Jezibellie made it with the conscionables here. I knew that woman, Jezibellie, is not right for this world then! Rape Her I may, and I might! So, here's how it went for those of you who are not getting it here. This man raped Her and said, is there anything I can do for you, Sire, to Me, no less and no more here! I said, you can let this woman go or you can kill us both! And so, he did just that! On the cross no less and no more here? Hardly so!

I do declare a mistrial if you are both talking at the same time though. Here ye, here ye! We did not die on the crosses to bear! For a mistrial, talk about saving grace here! But we were beheaded and hanged because of it.

I do declare the cross back then meant Howdy Doody time was a hit! It meant, Folks, that crosses to bear is an overstatement of the lunch tables of time. We just needed to hear it that way though! What of the gay rights movements then! Most people are heterosexual and it needs to be said, that they find their way. What of the cross's movements does it mean to us then?

Were we, Jezibellie and Me, nailed up there? Hardly so! There's foot stools to stand on and arm bands around the waists and stuff up there. If there is a chance at this, the cross represents toolified blanksmanships and this is what happened while up there, Folks! It's a rouge and a dressing that hangs on your back side there.

It's about trusting the universes to come up with the right amount of words to sanctify the belly button ring that Jezibellie had too. Is there something else wrong with gay and human rights here! I do declare a mistrial here! I do declare that we were both beheaded and hanged then? Nope, Me beheadedment, and Jezibellie the hanging, but after the cross wars were on, Folks! You will always come back to Christianity too I guess!

It's because of the gay rights movements here that we were even up there. It made the heavenly promise to exclude the witches and the righteous wandering mortals that fall back to gaze upon Him, you know!

This Jesus in the Bedroom book's right up the alleyways of scholars and therefore hymns that sing themselves here. God speed to me, in His essence of glory and of the Savior, God speed to me! There's promises in the dark here. There's ways around this essence of peace that we normally want for ourselves here. But to think that there's nothing in the wakes of time that have gotten glorified here, I beg to differ, Jesus says!

Jesus says, next time Paul wants to orderfy this meaningfulness's talent searches here, the next time he wants to try out My wifey again for size, is when his blasphemous face be Gentiled! For this is the King's wishes!

More people want a Cesarean birth than to be slated up for the world to notice your life size talent searches and such! Take it from Me, Jezibellie said! I wanted a Cesarean birth, and Jesus cut my babies outta me! There are ways around this too.

This is Jesus Christ taking for granted the writing abilities of a moronic time in My life "when" the life of the party is Jezibellie Christ! For nursing our first born with possibilities of a lifetime of greed mongering then? She always had a bottle. And by the way, Peoples of the cold, cruel worlds of time here. When a baby is due in your stomachs here, have it done by Cesarean, mkay? It's a cold choice of hell's high waters when a baby is pushed out the vagina! I mean, a succulent woman may give a choice here about the tiny babies of this world here! But when you're a woman, you want to, you need to have, a sense of freedom rings it to blasphemize the very bests involved in your care. It's nice to have a Cesarean too. It's right and it's just to do so!

Otherwise, right here, right now, means nothing! It means, Folks, and Class of Gentiles later, that Paul was an idiot who rambunctioned a pregnant woman here! She was 5 months preggos with our first child and children here! I say it this way because there are no surprises here. She knew the lengths of the feet, as well as the lengths of their bodies, slain or not, inside of Her belly there! It's just that God is so nice about it, but a guy really hates to look at the skin of a woman with stretch marks though? Not in the least! Andrea has a few, save a growth spurt or three or four of them too! I promised God an echoment here! She said the right languages are the spoken ones!

Right here, right now, there is no other place I want to be! The song is nicely shifting toward a gold ring in conjunction with this Man's talent searches of peace here. And that be said here, the gold symbolizes peace here. That said, a gold ring is in orders here! That said, is a girl to be succumbed to a gold style ring then, she said?

It's truth that a ring must have diamonds in it for the girl to feel like she got a wedding out of him. You know, Jesus says that all rings must have denominations for greed mongering though! There's a wifey I know and love. He states that for the records here, He is blasphemous no more then! This blasphemy is for the birds then?

Chapter 14

The Cure For AIDS/HIV Is Here for All Too

There are many hands on this statuette of a goddess named
Cybele. Photo Credit: Cartment.com.

This is nightfall all over again, Folks here, who stated that there's a jokester available for all
God's eyes to lean towards here. That said, this commandant's ways and means it lady's biggest
blessings of all here is that she has someone in mind too. Therefore, there are only a few other
reproductive organs here.

Messing with these and those too is something of a rouge here! That said, there are tons of
domestic type literatures here! Meanwhile here, all that it entails in us here is a reproductive
edge! That said here, this woman who prescribes all the medicines of this county jail in this
moment's notices here state that the only loneliest people in the limelights here are Donna

Eden and her counterpart, David Feinstein, and is really all that we had back in the days of limelights. Suggesting to us, Folks, is a word of it from Donna Eden's literatures, and we're all over this energy medicines approach to dealing with the counterpart's best interests here (Eden, 1998)!

We love it, in other words! We think that energy medicine's dealings with the DSW is right there for the taking, as well as hopper infested know it alls that go about drugging clients and patients at the local dime it out centers.

For pieces of the literatures that get homey, here is the lessons plannings that deal with the HIV/HSV/AIDS/schizophrenias here! And that said here, what is Jesus and Jezebel ready for in the New Testament's knowledges here! Why did God choose to produce it that way, with the Old Testament had Samsonite and stuff like it! You see it, now you don't!

God's next angelic presences, Andrea, is for you to state that Divine Source Wisdom indeed has the DSW into "Us", that states that God's presences are relatively old though! What is HIV exactly then, but an Autoimmune Deficiency Syndrome here? Nothing could be furthest from the truth here! That's because the exact misnomers for the AIDS viruses are here for the taking!

The above painting of a sculpture too is Cybele, the Phrygian cult mother goddess here. We bring her up because it's like that! The Greek goddesses are justified and cultified into a non-existent pattern of peaces here! That's "peaces" and it's a word here! Say, the justification of writing the squabbling parents of peace here states that the echoes of a lifetime of laughter here at Jezibellie's wakes here is that, the HIV viruses here must be on hold though! Because back in the days of onslaught and such, there was a real human being named Andrea that held onto us back in the civilizations of time's peaces and such. There's one dragon named Cybele, and the other dragon named Kryptonite here.

Kryptonite here had a bad back, and a chiropractic onement rejuvenated here the pictures and the stories of Kryptonite's battle cures for peaces here. Kryptonite was a Greek goddess of peaces here, of Patheos and other tales of the deep here! So, just because this scripture we take from the Bible no less and no more here is the origin of peaces here, doesn't mean that God's going to take from us the wicked witch of the West and take her out of the bargaining bins made for the Kryptonite Greek goddess of love here!

That said, is there a limelight for the centuries old relatives that reproductive history has set its sights on here? That said, is Jesus Christ ready for Jezibellie Christ? Has He found it within His hearts of heart to forgive this here Paul here? Not necessarily so! This forgive and forget clause is really a domestic partnership of faiths here. Not all preachers believe in the brother Paul, the apostle. They say he does not fit the mold of one here! That would be furthest from the truth here? Not necessarily so either! Say, does battleships in the nighttime of lovemaking ever begin to detest the approaches of love in the limelight's best interests here? We have a point. I promise here!

This is the limelight all over again here. In Egypt, the counterproductivity of domestic eyes is bound to happen small incidences of light to remain here! And that's all there is to know about Egypt's dark times. During the winter of 1963, we found the remainder of that squabble between God's knowingnesses and His judgments. It's about time the limelight's central district remain anonymously inept here, as Jezibellie Christ remains a mystery to us! Limelights are tired of central district's main arguments here, that masturbation is wrong, according to the Bible! It's a limelight's central district's heartbeat of Americas that states that it's not wrong!

According to Americans, God is wrong to punish people, for the limelight's central district means here to try to take away the masturbation clause. In essence, there are some people who believe in destiny's plights and others who remain calibrated to a different drummer here. She has the guts to speak it in tongues too!

Andrea can say it in many tongues here, that masturbation is real and in essence so bad for you? Hardly the case. The murderous tongues in this here manuscript are very talented indeed! So much so that Paul is really the moron here. This is the moron speaking then? Hardly so! He left Earth and never came back! Indeed, there is the netherworlds of Greek mythologies that state that hardly so, Paul and his counterparts came back to kill Christians who masturbated wrongly? I do know this much is true here.

There is tremendous guts on Andrea's part. To talk about it this way though is like taking on a much needed journeyful recommendation of My wonderful world of properties and despairs! Trust in Me is revealed as such! I do declare a mistrial in deeds and words here. Warranted here is the properties of despairs and trusts.

I don't really see the point in declaring a mistrial in deeds here. That is because the properties of despairs and such is not really warranted here. There's a mistrial in words here, because the proper way to masturbate? Is not really coming onto anyone here! We're going to stop with this nonsense anyways, but bring it up to us in the futures of humanity's sakes here, and we're going to vomit! We don't like talking about it, but there is a fate and faith adjustment that God takes with us here and it is to state that we don't like to masturbate in public, but by all means! DSW says to! It's not to jeopardize the ringlets in Her hair here, but Jezibellie wore them sparingly.

I don't like this jumping around to conclusions like this here, Andrea, but what of the Jezibellie do you not understand is written in scriptures time and time again now? We can amend the Bible at any time here! This life without STDs (Sexually Transmitted Diseases) is really what we're after here! In time you will see where this is going here. Don't we want to talk about HSV and HIV cures then? We're stuck on the Hepatitis C also, as there is now a cure for it? Yes, there is for all three here! See Chapter 12 for HSV cures 1 and 2 please! This cure is stated later in the book, however. Don't give up trying to find its locations!

To dine with the cussing that is going on in the world right now, Andrea, there is another way to say it here. God gave us an apparatus that is comical to look at? It's not that easy to believe in something so smitten here! We know Andrea Wynn Barberi has a love life to boot here.

It's not the only ways and means it lady's time here to know exactly how and when to use masturbation skills here. It says nothing of her style of dress. It breathes looking right here! I use the phrase "heavenly" to denote change here. This unique style of dressing up looks like it came right out of a blessed reunion with the Savior blessing we call Jesus Christ.

A man is supposed to look up a girl's skirt once in a while. You know? This HSV cures stuff happens for reasons unknown to us here! There are plenty of people out there with it. So many, in fact, that God gave us no reasonings here to move on without curing it. Please see Chapter 17 about drugs and such! We mean the narcotics kinds here! As "cadmium" is left to our senses here! We smoked it all the time back in the 20th centuries B.C. and A.D. as well! At least I hope not! A new drug though for HSV cures is it? Nope! For HIV though is to smoke cadmium sulfate and call it good here! Yes, she says!

Cadmium! So move on, Folks of the Gentile's peaces here, and call it good here? Nope! We have the exact formulas for cadmiums here. It's not as if or until then, somebody has a paranoia here about God's languages here or nothing though! The barium sulfide contradicts this job here, but it's the exact same thing, save knowing what the new essences of peace confide and coincide with us as!

There is no paranoia in her words here: not one person in this job has paranoia here! We are totally healed in its entirety, Folks, Classes of Gentiles and such! This lifetime of habits has us menial in this, Folks! But her paranoid ways here are not from the other sides of town here! This macromanaging of Andrea's talents here is for the birds. Did we not say this already then about a song burst into tears by the romantica of dealings with the Divine Source Wisdom's best inklingships!

It's hardships, but whatevs here. This romantica of dealings with the DSW is commonly known to Us as the hardships of legacies made grievingly towards a promised land that exists between night ships and day ships here. This struggle for complexities and such is not the end of it all here, but are the reasons for the seasons of lovelinesses in Jezibellie's plights!

In other words, what does God exist in between a Black man and a Black woman here? They grew up together, Jesus and Jezibellie did, in Bethlehem here. This is Jesus's only posting about this here, LOL on that. Right! That said here, what does a commandant's army, supposedly echoed by the prevailing Paul here supposedly, supposed to do here, now that the wifey's not Black here? She's only 20% so, but the rest of Her is Indian in natures and in deeds here! She's so Black you might not notice Her shaving Her legs here! But that's the biggest and blessingless times of all here is not allowing a woman the right to shave here!

This is what Andrea observed in the many hospitals between us and them! There are such promises as dealing with the other folks that observed her in the showering systems of times past here. Such echoing is made in the dealings with other people, the folks in between the black posts and the non-black ones here! There's dealings with the other people who exist between black posts and couragements here! That's encouragementless writings here that exist between a Black man and his postings about his wifey's talent searches here. Why are we concerned about this and the HIV cures here, but to speak to such riddlements to the public is really what we're getting at here. She came across a poster that said, HIV runs rampant with needles and such!

So, we're being poked and prodded all the time by needles here and there and everywhere in mental hospitals around the countries here! That said, Canada does the same things. Correctamundos here? Not in the least, from what I understand from the DSW here. That said here, why the needles in conjunction with rapes that do happen and occur in these places then? Not only were we succumbed to raping a woman like yourselves here, Andrea was not raped, thank God, but there was a moment's notices where there were a couple of close calls here. Save me from those places and we won't have to worry about needles and rapes and shit all of the time here! Blankmanships later please!

That means, hide the cookies and the Towanda, a peaceful resting place for us here. Correctamundos here? Not!

We're not getting anywhere or anyplace here. What are the cadmium outbursts in our wakes here, but gently coinciding with pieces of the puzzles that God existed back then, and God existed now!

We're trying to follow up on Jezibellie's cures for pieces of the pies here that existed back then, as well as some friendships that we'd just assume not have. Here are the pieces of the puzzlement's lackadaisical ways of wonderments here!

And yes, she hears us, word for word though? And punctuations too? Yes, she does! And this is what they were getting at with the DSW out there in the cold here. We state this because somewhere over the rainbow is where the comedies exist between a Black president like Obama and one that does not matter so much! I promised the love affairs of a lifetime of pieces here, pieces of the puzzlements that state that African rulerships do not exist back then!

In Greece, for example, the only Black president's timings back then was a guy who owned half the world's land ownerships here, and that was only because he gave his life to Christ the day of! The Holy Spirit exists, or the Holy Ghost thereof here!

This is such encouraging words here that God existed back then too.

Some postings are widely known for their gentilous spirits. Others are known for the Blackened scars of humanity's wakes here! The slave trade never happened that way then? You cannot begin to imagine My despair at the topics thereof here.

Yes, they happened that way! But only in name only. Their livelihoods are not what they seem, however!

This is what the gods, Greek gods and goddesses too, love to listen about God's wraths here. Even they believed in God's wraths here!

She's vying for a little attention from God's "cadmium" that you poked and prodded us about here, Jesus!

It's so true though! Smoke it, Peoples! It comes in a liquid format, the barium kind, and we don't want that one in powdered formats, as well as existing between Black and White peoples here? We do though! I want to talk about Jezibellie's background with cadmium. The sulfide kind will kill you! So, don't use that one. But talk about Jezibellie Christ here's blatant cures for hope! Say, what is barium cadmium though? It's atomic symbol 8 on the Richter's scale though! It's atomic number 48 that mixes with 8 though? You got it! 😊 We like the powder formats of this as the richest drugs back in the days of Jezibellie's wakings though! Barium sulfate has the same effect as cadmium, the barium types though! Spiritually though? It's a rouge, Andrea!

Such encouraging words do not exist between a Black Jesus posting and a White one here! But He was a Jew, a Gentile, and a dream maker in existence then! He dreamed of Jezibellie Christ while here on this Earth's wonderful news here, that God does exist! It's a message then that states that God's inklingships here, the hardships that ensue us here, means that a Black man must marry a White person then. Correctamundos here? That's Jezibellie Christ for you here!

In other words, what does God exist in between a black post and an echoing legacy here! Meaning, Folks, that the words of the phrase, "Is Jesus a Black man or not?" is the kind of things we deal with on a daily basis here. The essence of the DSW states that Jesus was not Black or a Jew? We just want to point out that the cadmium wars are starting over in Namibia then. Because of this then, they have the cures for cancers of the mind then! They don't exist in mental hospitals either. It's like a resort or a retreat to live amongst the Gentiles back in Jesus's day then! He was a Jew, that's for sure! He was White though, as Egypt's best man for the job! And Egypt is White sometimes! It's heavenly to know you, Andrea, exist for some man someday! We know who it is too, and more often than not, he's there for the taking! This man is supposed to come for the titles of books to come.

This man is not the end of the world's greatest blessing of all, to know Andrea that you exist, but it's heavenly to think that this person's only blessings are within the reach of God's kingdoms here! In essence though, in other words too, there are the biggest blessings of all, and that is to look at the commonly spoken words and phrases that means He was a Jew here, Jewish decent.

And the likelihood that Jesus's wife was Black is only about 20% so here! She's the Black lady of the eve of princes that takes His wife to the Godsend that He is, and this is what is showdowned for the likely event that She is even Black. She's mostly European descended upon the King of England at the time! She's a Black lady though! She's only 20% so here, but the rest is an Indian look to her too. The end of the heavenly Father is the fact that God's greatest gifts are all but descended from hell in words and in actions though. I declare a mistrial in the fact that God's natural businesses take from the descension of peace of princes to the era of onement that happens on this Earth!

It takes a lot of passionate writings like this one to reduce a man to His knees whenever He discusses His lovely wife! In passionate things, all aside common texts are better than this too. Whatever we want to discuss is the nature of things here.

In other words, what is God's next best dressed man supposed to look like here? It's a heavenly sent dimension of God's other halves here. Best described women are the best to look at here. And that's the only reasons for getting this other developmentally laid place in conjunction with God's wraths here.

I only condemned Paul for the moments here that he laid to rest his convictions that masturbating people, Christians no less and no more here, masturbated only to rest in the hardships of the economy's best hardships and stuff here. No wonder God masturbated! LOL! – DSW rests on this topic of masturbation, Andrea. Thank God, huh!

There's plenty to do in Namibian governmental times here, Peoples! They're wonderful people too!

I should say, Andrea, that withholding information such as the HSV cures and such are really special then. Right, or correctamundos here? There's lovely peoples everywhere here! Let's turn to some research then, shall we? Nope! We're not giving enough credit to Jezibellie's plights here! That said, does cadmium exist then? Sure! But the barium sulfate kind will kill a human being instantly! Do not take that one, or try this at home in other words! But the barium enema kind will suffice here! Say, this barium sulfate kind is for the birds, no less and no more here. Say, the more's on more is more fun than more Turkish rulings here. We hate the dads that say, no more talking or speaking in riddles here! I sure do think that riddles are the way to go though, because they linger and tattle about Jezibellie Christ all the time!

Here's my hocus pocus rulings on it all though! There's more to it than that, for sure here. There's Namibian governmental rulings on the fact that, yes, Andrea, they have solved it, before even finding out what Namibian governmental rulings are! Say, what's this white stuff but cocaine though? Nope! The powdery substances in their wakes here have created a ruling's best outfits come stankers do! Say, we need the Urban Dictionary for all things here (2018)! Their sellout points of rulings here come to the commandants if needed here! Say, is the Namibian government going to reveal that the monkey strikes about it there are full of shit, as well as the blankmanship's rulings here that determine if the monkeys were on strike at all? Because the orangutans are about killing each other off if you've got Herpes Simplex Virus though. Right, or correctamundos though?

Not in the least! I think the Namibian government's ruling on sulfide and sulfate and the differences between these two Madagascan rulings here is that the flowers on the islands of Crete are also valuable here (StudyLight.Org, 2018, https://www.studylight. org/encyclopedias/bri/c/cadmium.html)! In the timings that it takes for the Namibian governments to hear us on this is the timings that it takes for us to make or receive the barium sulfate problems here.

We don't want the barium sulfates to dine with us or anything! As made to human sufferings here, say, in the cross closures of a lifetime of greed mongering here! Say, is the barium sulfate even there anymore here? Because the waters of the crystal blue sea opens up and takes Moses to the bank here! And that said here, what is the waters of the crystal blue seas supposed to open up then, but to have a talent search's best inklingship cures here! Say, what does the Namibian government support by governmental laws of the times, space and healing regimens here!

But to think it and to be it are two different things here. We liked barium so much back in the days of Jesus and Jezibellie, that it was much like methamphetamine was back in the 20th centuries B.C. and such! We don't like the stuff. Right, or exactamundos here? Well, why not soak this new substance in water and then breathe a little bit about the petri dish and then smoke the stuff! Hard or something to do then? Where do you get the stuff, but Namibian governmental rulings state that we already tried that! But it works, you see it, now you don't. Right, or exactamundos here?

This substance, barium sulfide is not the answer to AIDS related cures here! It's barium cadmium here! Not the stearate kind though! Landy Enterprise Limited is really good to animals here (Landy, 2018, http://ahlandy.en.alibaba.com/company_profile.html?spm=a2700 .9099375.35.5.104f070awQ8oOC#top-nav-bar). I would buy it from them then! A stabilizer is what it's called? I think so! But more research is needed from us here! Mainland China for the source though, of cadmium, that you smoke it to death though is a research question made from China's outer source here.

And yes, Andrea hears this word for word here! She does not, I repeat, not know what cadmium sulfate really is, but don't smoke that kind! It would and could kill you! So, I repeat though, she's not addressing anything, save what Edgar Cayce might have come up with. The *Journal of HIV and Retro Virus* (2018) online here is neat. Save a few thousand dollar's researches though and come up with a cadmium sulfate that we can at least enjoy ourselves with here and call it good, eh here?

Mandy Hill from the University of Texas is a nice lady who came by HIV testing during her career here (ConferenceSeries.Com, 2017, https://globalhiv-aids-std.infectiousconferences. com). We know nothing of the kind of person she is, because we simply came across her name on a website about HIV here, but she's golden! Why don't we speak to her about her AIDS virus of mental health though! We don't know her from Adam, but there's tons to talk about at this conference coming up in Switzerland here! The dates are August 27-29, 2018, in Zurich here. That's a really great conference to attend!

If you're like me though and want a coffee date with our other instructors here, just wing it and attend as a host then! Likewise, the *Journal of HIV and Retro Virus* online states that there are some articles worth noting, if Andrea can only find the time to do so! We're saying that there's lots of research out there on HIV and T-cells. If you wanted to find out about all that and this here too, we would like for you to honor the system that says, bankrupt!

It means, Folks, and Class of Gentiles here, that there are tons of research questions and blog answers to them. Likewise, the list of focused studies on the antiretroviral research page in the credits thereof, the "References" section of this document, are worth noting, as well as the possibilities of finding the cadmium cures too!

So, this is how it goes here. The "cadmium" references here, by the way here, are all entirely by chance's notions of peaces here.

And that said here, don't smoke it unless and until you know what it is we're after here. Cadmium sulfate is the substance that you want and is the quickest ways and means it lady's confidants here to state it for a fact. That God gave us the tools and represents the biggest calamity Jane's ways of saying it here too.

That God is cadmium sulfate oriented is like acid or something like it: You see it, now you don't then, Andrea! She's only had a hit of acid in her entire life though? Try three or four times: You see it, now you don't, Andrea!

What we mean by this is, the barium sulfate kind will kill you indeed here. But the barium cadmium mix that is a substance mixed in liquids here has a taste that will knock you for a loop if you're not carefully mixing it with a household substance's timings here. And to mix it with Coke, for example, Coca-Cola, not Coke-aine here, is the way to be, Class of Gentiles here?

We're saying that there's an ingestible format that will take a little longer than the smoked versions here. Saying it in pancake batter like the little elves and such in the strongarm of the North Pole is not what we're after here either here. Say, why don't we try the smoked level of chain smoking and then cut it out to dry here! Meaning, Class of Gentiles who don't know their asses from a hole in the grounds here, make that seedling from that plant then! I mean, if there's a pill format to this, I'll be sold to auction in a little bit's times here.

That said, what does the plant's ingestible format seem to be taking here? Can we cook it then? Nope! Smoke it like weed or not at all here? The liquid format is barium enema related though! We can take the barium sulfide and die, or not at all here is the facts that none of what I am saying is blatantly tested at all here! We are simply stating what the Divine Source Wisdom believes to be the cure for cancers is it then? Nope, that is Trichomycin and its relative counterparts: see the article listed in the Appendices for this then, as Appendix 3 is where it's at here! We're talking about AIDS/HIV listed on this brochure from God's angels then! Because Andrea has no such ideas that we're talking about the Lord of Hosts, or some such things as the Lord and Shepherd, I shall not want! I will lie me down in green pastures!

Say, she doesn't even know the Lord's Prayer very well here! We'll help out here. The Lord's Shepherds said to "Us" here, that God is willing to see the Lord's Prayer's biggest help outtedness on a Lord's Shepherd's basis here.

In other words here, the book is about the kingdom come's biggest ailment cures. And yet, to write to these agencies this way and that a way has provided us with no fruitful measures of which to honestly say, I am worthy of print requirements to lovingly go where no man nor woman or child has ever gone before now!

And that said, Folks and you too Gentiles, is a peaceful venture at best, as I fully plan on reciting the angel cures to death before us here. This lovingly willingness's battle cures though are not going to recognize or reiterate the AIDS viruses here!

They're simply going to love us in the futures of humanity's wakes here! Barium cadmium is the ingestible liquid format that kills the AIDS/HIV virus in its tracks. We must either smoke the ingestible formats though from the petri dish of love here, or we can leave it be and smoke the ingestibles later here!

And that said, too, there are tons of formats. Willingly though, we are talking about the cure for AIDS: HIV type though! We're selling a lot of it on the internet though?

Can we smoke the barium sulfide and die from it though?

Yes! Please do not do or try this at home though. Let the CDC, the Centers for Disease Control and Prevention, negotiate with Namibia then?

Hardly so! We're just saying, the Namibian government tried and or will try this very concoction of peace's literally hardship-oriented timings here!

And that saids here, there are two saids and one said, living amongst ourselves though is hard at best here. That saids business is here to stay then! This means that the ingestible formats take about three weeks to heal the AIDS/HIV virus then. Correctamundos here? It's about that long, yes! I would say, take it twice a day, in the morning and then at night, about 500 mg of the stuff though!

Can we sell it here on the internet to suspecting people though! Sure! As long as it's the right kind of stuff. We have said before that the barium enemas have the sulfide in sulfate all figured out here.

But the real joke or crux of the argument lies in its structures here. The T-cells, for examples here, is not to be trusted? We're just over the hump on curing the AIDS related viruses like schizophrenias, for example! Because of this, however, the genetic component in schizophrenias is non-existent here. That said, Folks and Class of Gentiles, we normally speak to the wonderments of the sound of music's best talentships here and state that it has been solved, officially so!

We're sending a copy of this book to the CDC, the Centers for Disease Control and Prevention, though? Yes, we are! And to the White House for good measures here. And that said, Andrea, is there anything else we've missed here? Just that cadmium sulfate is the answer to the "smoked" kind of marijuana that you do want, though Jezibellie was so hooked on that stuff that she could never have gotten the AIDS/HIV viruses in the first place! It does not, I repeat, repel HIV from your systems, but it's the cure for HIV systems throughout the body's literatures here!

Though, if smoked a lot here, it is widely ingested and used! And so, we were so hooked on it from drugs in our systems then? It's here that we switch to a widely used paragraph of knowledges here and state for the facts that God's angels are indeed watching us sniff the stuff then! Not! Do not ingest that stuff by sniffing, or else you will get hooked on it then? Nope! It will create a coating in your lungs, and that's about all that you will experience from it. But if you smoke it, God's willingnesses to cure the HIV virus in its tracks is all you'll need to experience it, from a soap opera's viewpoints though!

I do declare a mistrial if we cannot cure the AIDS viruses that linger in the talentships of God's loves though! It's "loves" because we're honest about this incredible gift that Andrea has to sell and tell about though? Publishing this book, this work thereof, is the only ways and means it lady's ways of finding out about the truth be known and told essences of peaces here on Earth's crusts here! We've already sold and then some the AIDS viruses.

To admit to peaces and stuff here is to say or to state that one hit of that stuff in the smoked ingestible kind of way or fashion here is to state that God's willingnesses are very talented indeed here!

The gun laws in the next chapter are solidly based upon God's talentships here! And that said here, why don't we cut that out then? Well? It's not as if or as though God's watching "Us". Correctamundos here? Say, are we older than we seem here? Because, how old is the Divine Source Wisdom then? We're creatures of habits here far and wide then! We're centuries old! Literally, we have what it takes though to create the Bible all over again! If need be, thereof! Right, or correctamundos on this literature's stances and willingnesses to survive this book's ingested and ingestible formats of this drug's reinventions here?

It will kill the AIDS/HIV comatoseness in its tracks here, far and wide here! Why don't we smoke it then, the cadmium sulfate is the way to go here! And so, ingestible formats of pancake batters are the cures here for HSV, and the likelinesses that somebody is going to kill us for this information here is nil and null and void here! The pancake batters are discussed in Chapters 3 and 4 then? Say, it's Chapter 12 that we go on and on about how to solve HSV both types 1 and 2 here! The number third type can be administered a lot earlier than it is now, to prevent the shingles viruses from catching hold here.

And that said, don't kill us for more information about how to solve both the HSV and HIV viruses here! We're just a little ol' female, where there are commandants of love and laughter throughout Earth's crusts here! Say, the Earth has a personality to it!

Did you know that and this here? She, she's a she here, Earth is, chuckles and giggles all the time when a pedophile has left the Earth's crust here. And then she smiles big at the invention of AIDS cures and such, when God gets rid of this bipolar disorder, that they say she has now, and invents something of a God cured complex for all of these psychotropic drugging habits of schools and such!

This video of the Citizen's Commission on Human Rights or CCHR for short here, not CCR, as in the Credence Clearwater Revival here, but that's funny you mention AIDS as a misnomer for peaces here, because, and peaces is a word here, that last episode of the video, "The Untold Story of Psychotropic Drugging: Making a Killing," is really a wonderful way to lapse an old video story and to leave it on Earth's crusts (CCHR, 2008, https://www.youtube.com/watch?v=Lo0iWh53Pjs).

One more time here, the essences of Earth's crusts is tantalizing the drugging wars of a centuries old literatures, like the Bible inside and outside of danger here! We're simply stating that we know not of anyone else who can sell this sort of stuff on the internet's diehards programs here! We just know what is printed within these four walls of faith here! The CDC, Centers for Disease Control and Prevention here, is trying its best to literally obliterate the faith healers of America's talent searches though! Because bipolar disorder itself is such a widespread epidemic for just the U.S. of A. only, we are saying the psychotropic drugging discussed in Chapter 38 here is for the birds then!

That said here, how about we go and celebrate the commandant's languages here to boot here! These sectional couches are sure cozy to warm up to! I just don't know what kinds of literatures this means for people with the AIDS/HIV viruses though! Do we go smoke the cadmium sulfate in hopes that God's peoples are ready and willingly listening here? Because we are of a lunatic's statures here with the CDC, the Centers for Disease Control and Prevention, right now! Because of this, however, we are still in search of a job that's for us here? Yes. And, therefore, what is peaces and peace having to do with something so sinisterly simple as smoking the cadmium graces here?

Well, it's because it is so addictive here, that stated for all to know and see here is the Bible's take on the ideas of cadmium too? Because that's what Jezibellie said in the Bible though? There's no reference to the cadmium wars on essences or anything else here. That said, what is God's intentions of keeping cadmium at bay here?

We want a cure for herpes too here! Well, see Chapter 12 for that one, and Chapter 37 to name it right on here, and use the cadmium sulfate kind to kill the HIV viruses by popping 1 fluid ounce of water into your leg, mixed with 2 ounces of the stuff though, and do it again with 1 fluid ounce of water and 1 ounce of cadmium sulfate a week later and it's the vaccine!

And call the Namibian government over the herpes cures though? Not a chance! We seek to find and desist the ailment cures lady's wakes here. And that's a wrap though. Correctamundos here? Go find the latest HSV cures in Chapter 12. Please note that God is watching us from above the planets here, and He says that cadmium can go ahead and be introduced for half the price of what it's supposed to be smoked at! The ingestible formats, the ingestible kinds here, are going to list what it's going for here! Say, can we all sneak a panic attack later at the homebodies unions here today then? As this is what's been going on in, say, our little heads here, is that you're pulling away from mental health!

I'd suppose she is though! Go get us a coffee and a donut, not a cigarette anymore or any longer here! She quit nine years ago here. Caffeine though? Just yesterday's wordings here means that God's languages says that you can quit the cadmium too! Just wrinkle cure your nose talentships here! Because we do mention that later in the episodes on truths here, the family did not know what to do with this information here, except to say or to state that God's wraths here are not with the mental health professionals!

At the times of inceptions though, we're vying for one man and one man only to love us back! And that's got to be the inceptions of cures and such to our nation's backlogs here. And that's a wrap is a way for us of saying that God's inceptions of cures and such need not go back to mental health!

For the takings, however, the biggest blessings is that God's indeed needing to stress a point here, that God's willingnesses are taking the biggest leaps and bounds here, and calling it good here! We stress nothing here if God is not willing to breathe a little bit about the coziness of what I am saying here! Because our own couch gets used for much adieu here! Take care, Andrea! Barberi is my maiden name, by the way here! Take care, Andrea and know that this paragraph gets used to find you with here!

I suppose I'm employable no more though? As Safeway is where I work at the fuel station of laughter here! I suppose the guiding light is more plentiful than a piece of the pie actions here! And God bless the situations at hand here! I have extended family who are wonderful here! But none of us, to my knowledge anyway, has any of these viruses here!

I promised God an interval or two on where to find or to locate me here. I am available for consult 24-7 here! I promised God an interval or two on the premise that God is willing to relocate me for purposes other than is spoken here!

So, Washington, D.C., here I come! I am ready, and willingnesses, Andrea, state that God's lovelinesses speak volumes of the way you are presenting yourselves here. I have written countless human beings about the advent of this book's topics here but to no avail here. And yet millions of people still go unrecognized in the faith healing departments as "lunatics" or pain savers here!

As I state that I have healed an SI (sacroiliac) Joint injury full force here just by simply believing I could! Ready though is the moment's notices for mentioning Him at all costs here that's been instrumental in my life here, and that's Jesus Christ: Jezibellie has a standing ovation as well here! Because she's been molested into the system's graces here by none other than Paul. The stupid prophet though? She's a prophetess, what! And that's a fact, Jack and Jill were married.

As of this date though, I am the evil one here! Because this is an example of my own wraths here, I believe that none of it is hereditary! You cannot have a simple health problem and call it good here, but this means wars happen and break out if we cannot cure the cadmium fix here! So much is to say happening here that the wars between God's other halves here are not even spoken fors here!

My family is just afraid of what "this thing", that's "Us" here, might do to me again and again at the mental hoppers though, and we're about to say goodnight to a lovely human being here!

How come the credits only last so long here! I do declare a mistrial in deeds and in wordings of the DSW here! AIDS though? HIV, yes? And HSV so far! What about diabetes cures too? That's in Chapter 11 here. And, therefore, Class of Gentiles and such, Andrea, is the diabetes cure really the way to go here?

Yes! And, therefore here, we're back with a flash in the pan of inklingcures and ships too! Because this is how the rulings go in our country to yours, there, Wonder Man! Because Wonder Woman's tombs there in Egypt, in Africa though, lie in God's choice of hands here. I do detest people who do not lie in wait, however, and to cure the AIDS viruses here always has an output shot heard around the world's divisions here! And that said too, there are tons of viruses left to cure, Peoples! Not just these three here!

So, contact Us, mkay, Peoples! There's nothing in the wakes of 9/11, and we'll get back to this, that says, you're a powerful preacher of words and dealerships someday soon though? Probably not though! And cadmium sulfate is it? Nope, the barium enema kind, er, you know! Barium sulfate is not it. It's the barium cadmium that takes three weeks of ingesting to cure HIV/AIDS. We write it this way too because God said so! Take about 100 ounces of it or so daily! In a good cream cup called life though! Just mix it with something good. That said, at the pharmacy of choice though, and not in your cars all infested up the jeans ways with people with HSV wanting cures for it too!

That said here, goodnight peoples wanting a cure for AIDS related viruses too! We're getting there on all of them, save a few! Tonight's people's just want a cure for AIDS related viruses gone wrong though! Please seek Chapter 1 for an explanation of AIDS. Goodnight peoples and God bless you and your efforts to know the Divine Source Wisdom's natural disasters are here to stay then, Peoples, Folks of the Gentiles class of diligence here! Don't forget that 1 fluid ounce of water mixed with 2 ounces of cadmium sulfate into a syringe and popped into your leg is the cure for HIV. Do it again a week later with just 1 fluid ounce of water and 1 ounce of cadmium sulfate in the leg is the vaccine!

Say goodnight and just come back to this here memo of God's loveliest creatures here on this Earth here! Say goodnight and mean it when your husband or wife comes back from the gym and says, outlaws, they're everywhere! Goodnight, Folks of the Gentiles kind here! There's plenty to do in the mañanas of a lifetime of greed mongering! Goodnight everyone of the Gentiles and greed mongering types here! Come forth and know that God gave you the rights to trials and tribulations here! It's a mongering type of world, is it here?

Go passenger someone else then and leave me alone if you're only going to send me to mental health again! I am sick and tired of it! They don't know my ass from a hole in the ground, and only medicate the superstars who are in there of finding a place to live exactly. What does God's intentions of pricks and such mean to everyone in the logo families here!

Because God gave us some other Enfamils to discuss here! We're saying that God cures each and every one of us from AIDS related viruses: like schizophrenias though? We're saying that God wants to heal each and every one of us from AIDS, relationships that have gone bad or sour here, and lifetime hobbies to boot here! Say, what does "X–2, AIDS related viruses" represent in the homebody's worlds here, but a symbol or a gesture for peaces here! Say goodnight again, someone special in our wakes here. Goodnight, Mister You! Jesus thereof signs this paper off as goodnight again, Class of Gentiles in our wakes here! Goodnight for good measures then! I like where I sleep at night better than the streets, in other words! Goodnight to all and to all a good night!

Chapter 15

Gun Laws! Outlaw Them Then. The Good Guys Don't Have Any Rights to Them Anymore!

A picture of Jezibellie, slender with the bull horns on top
of the head. Photo credit: DollsofIndia.com.

This is Hathor? It is not! It is Jezibellie again. These cow horns are not that great a hit! I do declare the woman in red is the rest of the hardships! Allowed on this planet is the reason for the season! Is it Christmastime where you're at, Andrea! Are you ready for a new sensation of plans for humanity's reasons for not wanting a cloak for a game coat! I do know this too. Guns though, we'll get back to that in a minute's time here.

There's plenty to do here in this world's games and such. There's plenty to do! But there's lots of teachers and this is one of them. Here are the commandants coming together and realizing the idiots out there are just for the birds of one life lesson, and that's Jezibellie Christ! If you could realize the potential in idiots that speak for the birds here, this life lesson's meaningful clauses are just going to rot in hell here! This is war though!

This is because Andrea's best duties at a gas station right now are not in her best interests here. Her job in this world is to seek and desist! We have lots of ailments to cure here, and she can do it! We think she's ready for the jobs of a lifetime of heists and stuff. We have ailments to cure on this Earth here, and every time she tries to do something about one, she gets carted off to mental health care. I'm sorry this is so blunt for you, Andrea! But this is war, if you cannot have the woman that I love? I'm not gay, though this is a story for all of you gays and lesbians out there.

You cannot come to God without one love from a lost soul and a new soul and an old? What does plentiful commandants spell here? It seems that the only lost souls were the ones in Jesus's times here? He's begging you to come into the know here, Andrea! Come and save all these lost souls who come to you and ask if you have an ailment to cure for them, or if there is a cure for things like Herpes Simplex, or AIDS (Acquired Immune Deficiency Syndrome), and we have the hints that are needed for these types of things, all because she believes in love with the opposite sex?

Did you know that we have phases in our lives where we think we're gay and we're not?

Guns and gun laws are crisp and clean, aren't they? This means that God cannot take guns and to put them into the arms of criminals, let alone somebody with a gay rap, is really something here! But back in the days of just Us and You and Me here, we did not have gun laws so outlandish as these ones are here.

This means that the arms of criminals who call themselves gay though never made it past Paul! Though I state for the nation's cures of AIDS related criminals here, it is such a misnomer to call the AIDS viruses just HIV related here.

This means that God's clutches are not so gay and straight here as we profess them to be here! Persons of unknown sexuality are being beaten and clutched in a way that makes them falsely accused here! And in prison sentences, maybe I'll get one now that I'm not a gay criminal here, is falsely accused here!

She does not have a prison rap, thank gods and goddesses everywhere though, not to mention the elitists who think in droves that commandants have a nasty little language to boot us out with here! But the mere mention of the name the Divine Source Wisdom is gay for my family's sakes alive then! Because God only knows what the last paragraph meant to someone who is gay or lesbians here! That said, Andrea, have you been gay like or gay before? Gay like before God's wraths and such! Not! So, we have messed around a bit with the opposite sex once. I cannot remember her name though? It's such a misnomer that God invented happinesses to someone and to people who need it most! I've been a blessing and a curse to my family, even for not knowing who and how to kill the AIDS viruses that plague us here! It won't be immediate I am sure, but the gay comment's like troubling to us here!

But that doesn't mean that someone who is gay cannot make it into this life alone here, and that said, what is the big holdup, Andrea? Is someone gay in your neighborhood! I hope so, she says! But truthfully be told here, there is Jesus and Jezibellie, tied up to the crosses of light with a dozen or so other people because they believed in gay rights as a funeral though? I thought it was for Jesus to die on the cross though! Not! He did die of beheadedment, according to Us! It's about time she uses the phrase "Us" to coin it too! There was a gay rights demonstration just before the beheadedment of Jesus Christ and Jezibellie Christ, by none other than Paul Wright! Paul was a sinister grinned asshole if you want My opinion, Jesus says! Have a hint the other day and never bring this up again here, Mr. Asshole then! Dismemberment is a big deal in the Bible. So, take it to mean what you can make of this here. This is the Prince of Peace's next big deal though!

I told you of the Prince of Peace's… What is it Andrea, cat got your tongue yet? This minor invention of the AIDS viruses having a cure here is really what we're after in the commandant's languages here.

This is the time and the place for introspection on what was just said. In Chapter 4 of I Corinthians here, we discussed this at length in the legacy of Oz. Plenty of people are bound to have a decision to make here and that is the last time I have told God to enter into the kingdom of know it alls here. I don't know what you mean by trust here, but God told us to tell others about the ailment cures she now hears inside of her head here, from Us though! If you don't believe Us, ask about Us in the biggest book of all, the Bible!

If God could see you now, Andrea! I don't believe it either, she said to us in the beginnings of time here. But lessons be told, you can now write a book about how HSV and AIDS are curable in Egypt as well as in the 20th century A.D.! How come it's not the 21st or 22nd centuries she said! Because the time is now! We love the best woman for the position in life that has to do with carpets and such. Flying around on one is quite a feat here, and she is the best protected person for the job of lightning strikes it, very course language here, but this is for the birds here if we can't use the newest perceptions in lifetimes of love here and solve this AIDS virus as well as the HSV one!

Can we do it here? Or will we get carted off to jail this time, because we all have a comedy and a tragedy inside of us here. What do we need to keep going off to jail, the mental hopper in other words, she has never even been to jail, Folks and Gentiles alike here: and not because she's instantly cured of STDs, but because the schizophrenias that we know and love are cured as well! She just can't get off of this medicine without a doctor's help, but she does not experience paranoia any longer!

What is the chance that at one hospital she would be carted off no longer, and let go into homelessness mind you, back to the streets and all to develop schizophrenia again while off her meds though? Not at all! We're just back to square one if we cannot use the skills we have to get off of this medication here, and we're not talking about going back on it. Are we, Andrea? It's because she gets preggers or preggo here, whichever reading is right for God here! She's not schizophrenic any longer here, but the talent search, I mean, the job she's in right now, won't allow her to quit cold turkey like they did me at this particular hospital. So, keep this in mind, they let me out the back door with a taxi to a nearby motel and then I ended up back in the slammer, the mental hopper here for clarification purposes, due to homelessness. That's what she's saying to us right here, right now here. If God picked up and left the due dates to the homeless shelters here, she wouldn't be stating it for the records here, that she picked up this Divine Source Wisdom from a shelter here? Hardly so. Right now is the time to tell them about that, Dear! Here it goes here.

First off, Louise Hay is my publisher here! She's really a target of trust and God's wherewithal here, and she, Andrea here, put these affirmations all over her rented room walls here. Hardly the symbol of trust? All these positive messages attracted Us, and all over the room were notes and stickies to gather the deep trust of God! No one's keeping track of me any longer in the house here, as we moved out some time ago due to the fact that this person could not keep off the phone with the police and the mental health divisions here, and she said to us, well, she's crazy or something!

A Divine Source Wisdom though? A cure for herpes! We're saying that lots of other things have cures to them that have not been discovered yet! This is the chapter's touch of God's wisdom here that says, I can save this prose for a day under the Sonship, or I can use it to deduce that in the bedrooms of the lifetime chatter of love here, we all understand the relationships that take us to the beginnings of time here!

This morning's dews and such, Andrea, are ready for the takings. Because God really understands you now, how come you have not reinvented the wheels here and taken your gun rights back? I've never really thought about it, she says! But that's not why here. We say that and this to begin a discussion about guns and gun laws taken away from the good guys in the mental hopper here. In Chapter 1 thereof, I noted about a dozen gun laws that stay away from the good guys in mental hopper genes cannot abide by. And therefore here, the gun laws are taken away from the good guys in the mental hopper genes that cannot abide by the rules here. And to take away the gun laws from good people here is one thing entirely here. But I don't want them back necessarily, she says to us now! What we mean by this is, we don't have the rights, the gun rights, back yet. Yet, she says? Yes, yet! I presume that one day I will fire a gun again though? The answer is, what guns have you got? And she says, none of them. What if one day soon you needed to have an intervention with God's languages in it, just for the sake of saying so, however? As soon as your gun rights are reinstated then, gladly give us the go ahead to just not use them, not ever! Well, that's what I thought too! But to reinvent the wheels here is to say this too.

I thought that God was in charge, of things lovely like getting your gun rights reinstated though! Not! I do think that people damage the universe's tidings this way and that a way here. We want you to get them reinstated for the fun of it here. So, this is when the kids go, well, we all had these rifles back in the teenage years here. No gun permits were allowed for this gun holder here! But we all had them back in the days of lively essences and stuff! I gave mine to my brother though! I don't like shooting, so I just want to prepare the opennesses to God's chambers here, and to state it like this is to state it like a former pedo head here. Never was I a murderous head? A little bit but not really. A pedo head, as discussed in Chapter 3 or so here, was never dealt with so good as to say or to state that God really wanted a pedo head to run chapters in books. You see it, now you don't though!

I mean, guns, really, Folks! I don't know how to run a gun, she said to Me here! I just don't want the necessary evils coming out and stating for a fact that God gave us the rights to such presents as the gun lawyers and such! We're speaking in terms of Jezebellie's common denominator here, when she was released from prison for shooting and killing Elijah. Her lawyer, by the way, was Elijah here! And she did not shoot and kill him. She did no such thing. Chapter 2 of James is pretty loud about what people ought to do with these gun rights here. In I Kings Chapter 19, Verses 1-3 here (KJV), and I had to look this one up, LOL, is that Elijah was killed by a gunman named Ahab <p. 593>. Not Jezibellie here! Do you think we had guns back then? Sure! And gun rights taken away from Jezibellie for a sword and a pinochle game later though? This is what happened here. This is why Jezibellie was never a sword fighter either though!

She's rags to riches then! That's because this tiny, and I do mean staturely wise she was a tiny woman in an 8x10 frame though? It's a boards issue here. There's no tiredness in our words here, Andrea. There are some frames of houses that go to the boards issue here, and there are tired words that keeps the convicts at bay here. Say, that's about 5'10", as Jesus was perfectly 6' here. We were tired of rains and such. And so, this Elijah, My lawyer for the prison sentences, told us that the food in there was to die for! So, she ate it all up and said, this is how prisons ought to be run then! Elijah got killed by Ahab himself. Not for Jesus's sakes here, but she didn't even know about it until the printing of the Bible then! She said, this is not the same thing here, but Ahab even took it out that he even killed Elijah and whisked it off as a promo for realism's sakes here! So, Ahab and Jezibellie in the Bible here, never got together at all here. He was not Her husband, Her wifehood, or anything else of that matter here. Elijah simply got killed for his wood that he offered to build his house with. Elijah only said that Jezibellie was the one who got jezebelled out of his offensiveness, as she was a very attractive woman, for a White woman though?

Nope, Jezibellie was blackened skinned here. She was a very attractive wife for Me too, Jesus says! And a wife she was too! She was all over Me all the time, Jesus said! Attractiveness though! That's what gets people into trouble here.

She was altogether bow and arrow strict about Her timings and stuff! She was a very attractive hunter too, of deer and alloy, bearings and such! This woman wore a tiny headdress all the time here. She was a very active hunter of moose and game then? Nope! Just deer, sweethearts! She's also a game hunter for the sixth time here! I did not eat just fish, Jesus says! I hoped that by calling the kettle black that one night at the hopper jail, I mean The Last Supper dish here, that God said, well, where are all the guns tonight then, Folks!

Because God said to have them with you at all hours and stuff! And She goes, Jezibellie did, I didn't know I was a bow and arrow freak, but you've got this down. Don't you, Jesus Christ, My wife's husbandry didn't know what hit them!

Say, what does Elijah have to do with anything here! There's more to it. Is there though? This is Ahab speaking. Just kidding! If I were Ahab though, I would say this to myself here. Why did I criticize Jezibellie? She was just trying to get a king to proofread the manuscript and to tell of any mistakes thereof, or criticisms, sure. What does this have to do with gun rights though? It's everything to do with the mistakes of the world's primary focuses here.

Just because Jezibellie was hot, don't mean that anyone else thinks so or it thereof here? There's plenty to do in this world of gunshots and stuff! Do we really need them though, guns and stuff? Well, not if we're talking about leaving the little elves alone upstairs to work on the toys needed for Christmas too. Past angels and such is the notion's breathing materials for a justification, for saying this, but goodness sakes alive, Jezibellie never wrote that down though!

Oh, Jezibellie and Ahab though? What a good looking guy Jesus was here! Does he need a gun under that cape of His though? You got it! Well? Why were his gun laws overspoken then? He doesn't have gun rights though! He's a mental case back in Egypt then? Nope! That's in Israel when He went to spread the gospel, and ran into mental health. Such is the beard of life then! Jesus, Andrea, did not have a hardon for two women at the same time here. In fact, He's vying for your attention then? Well, sort of! I cannot write about Jezibellie's love without Her young face and Her older one! She's on my mind 24-7 here!

Then do away with the gun system for once though! We're getting to a point and we'll make it soon! Hey, Jezibellie Christ, look the other way, but I gave you so many stretchmarks here! What do you want me to do with them, shoot 'em up and never look back then! Well, keep in mind, Folks, that stretchmarks are a valuable part of life.

They look cozy on a woman who's had 10 babies let alone 4 or 6. You know? He's still interested, and very much so, after looking at the woman, the wife, of say, 20,000 men in there? How come some women get them and some don't! Well, the weight gain effect is there for a moment's notice on life here.

There's tons of women out there who can still wear bikinis after childbirth! And I'm gonna get my head knocked in, DSW, if I cannot explain this right here!

And they look toasty with or without them, in my humble opinion of Her! Though look at my body, yet to have them here. I promised God a lesson's planning in the humble opinions of Jezibellie Christ here.

She did not have a stretchmark on Her when I laid down for that lap dance of a century's bullshitters here.

Setting us up like this though at gunpoint is quite a feat to imagine here. Say, does Jezibellie still do twerks? And what I mean by this is, the new MixxedFitted song right now, the craze on the television screens too, is, "She Twerkin'" by Ca$h Out here, and we love the stuff, the MixxedFitted craze down the road and all! She twerkin' alright! Jesus says His pants were in an uproar! And what? It's not as though we didn't have jeans wear, but it was a little different material back then! The cotton didn't grow on trees necessarily here, but I certainly loved the Divine Source Wisdom back then, Jezibellie Christ said to God though! She twerkin' simply means that she's moving her hips to the side and to the other side in a nasty dance. For God though? 😊

This is rude though? Not! Jesus is a man just like any other here? Not necessarily, but you got it! Like, He goes, is this Jezibellie Christ? And she just looked at Him and said, "You touch Me, You die!" And goes, I just want to lap dance you and be done with it though? This is the love of Her life here dressing up for God's greatest ailments here!

But a girl who uses a gun or knife against a guy to get HIM to twerk is really rude here! Some men go, well, I've got ED! So, who cares. Right, or exactamundos here? She never used these things here by the way! She's rude though? Not in the least! I rocked Her to sleep in a mini sized van though? Are you still on the streets by the way, Andrea? Because you not once rocked it in the midsized van neither!

Next topic please, correctamundos here?

Say, is this book rockin' it or not here! I don't carry guns neither, Folks, Jesus says of

Jezibellie and Himself here! But this is a toll booth we're under here, and a pressurized dance from the authorities left us alone for a good 15 minutes! I said to Her, I (gulp) came in You and I (gulp) love You! She just goes, well, she twerks!

Is that it here? Well? Where are you, Jesus!

Let's focus on these gun rights here. Jesus was certainly in the know about Me loving Him back!

So, do we kill all the pedophiles with gun rights and stuff! Because there certainly are a lot of serial killers out there who would love to claim pedo head is the reasons for things uncertain here. Say, are we done yet talking about guns and gun rights, gun laws and stuff! Because if I'd had my bow and arrow back then, Folks, Jezibellie Christ says, I would've shot that guy in the butt with it and then come to his senses later though? Let's shoot 'em all, She says! We're never a murderous head unless and until someone gets raped! And then there's a shoot 'em up mentalities here that never shakes past a lamb's tail of freedom rings it here! Say, what does Jezibellie's lap dance have to do with Jesus Christ though? She was no pedophile either, Jesus says here of Her and of Andrea too! But She sure can dance good!

Well, let's move on to a different topic here. Say, was there a planted image upon my screen then! I've often wondered here. And the answer was yes, and therefore, what did God have to do with this image then? I just couldn't believe my eyes here! Lots of therapy about it though? Most people do not know what to do with this sort of handle on things here. But SVU's Law and Order is what I watched most days while cross stitching my life away here, and I can guarantee you the law would've thought it funny I never had a child porn image onto my screen here until now though? Until, it was, what year, 2004, was it? Did anyone ever call the cops on you? Well, maybe! For being too rich to detect a student loan charge of disabilities here. Try me, try Us on this then! We've been through the ringer because of that image in her mind of what she saw on her screen once, and believe me, we were there for every crying moment of SVU, as well as the writhing images of that child porn she accidentally came across on her screen here once.

On the screens of love though! Not anything is wrong with looking at sexy images of adults when you are an adult, and teens love to look at other sexy individuals too. Meaning here, Class of Gentiles that might take away my gun rights if I'm in love with somebody sexy here! It just means that guns are a natural way to... Stop right there! If gun rights are so lovely, then how come they cannot be used on the crazy, the really crazy we mean, and the unjust?

Because babies are made with the intentions of having the right parents for the job here of talent searches and stuff. But it don't mean we're nastily going to have all girls or all boys here, Andrea! We're saying that God is ready and willing to mean you into the know then? Hardly the case here. What we're talking about is the classes of Gentiles that never got a handout here! Say, a Gentile is someone who is not a Jew. We said that Jesus was a Jew! But not a Gentile. I hope that still remains the case though, as a person who is 100% Jewish was not Jesus Christ. His mother, ahem, and wife too, remain a mystery then! Because who thought of sex in the middle of that description of the child porn images floating across someone's screen by accident? Not a one person at all here thinks that child porn is the way to go here!

And Andrea is not a jerkology's lesson away from a commandant's languages here. We are getting to our point! I promise, Jesus says! The Gentiles looked at child porn images then? Not in the least! The Discipleship is different than a Gentile here. That is why Andrea looked up the word in the first place here.

We signaled to Her, Jezibellie Christ, that she can certainly shoot a bow and arrow through somebody's heart here with no gun rights and to be thankful for the times that were given to Jesus Christ about no gun laws and such! Because Andrea has had her gun rights taken away so many times we cannot even count it as loyal here! I deserve to know who said, "I'm schizophrenic, so I shot at somebody," here! That is so bogus here it is not even funny here! This man and this woman, Andrea, are really shot at a lot here then! I mean persecuted, were they? Nothing is furthest from the truth about that though! We're medicating the poor and the wicked together then?

Because this is not what I found to be true at Western State, and all the other hospitals too here. There were a few strays, but for the most part, all people were true to form good people! I'd just assume you read the Appendix 2 for the rest of it though! As LRA's (Less Restrictive Alternatives or Orders) really need to come down a grade or two.

These LRA's and LRO's are really silly to deal with in here! A nice gesture to boot would be to commandant these languages of the Divine Source Wisdom, and to heal God's graces and gestures here would take gun laws out of the equation!

For at least a twerkin's viewpoint here, the twerkin' body that I used to have is no longer, now that I have made a big request to be off these meds. The ailment cures lady plans and is planning to dive into some Melatonin for some sleeping habits that have gone awry here.

Please consider me the detained status no more here! Regardless of times past here, we choose to be wary about anyone who considers the dining of Seroquel lessons here to get off my lawn so to speak, as I don't wish to be found out now!

Chapter 16

The Holy Ghost! Do You Have It Yet, Humanity's Sakes Alive Here!

This is the talent search we've been waiting for. It's a lot like Edgar Cayce was, yes. It's about time the hit list for the talent search becomes great and wide opened again! There's a life above the rest! That said, it's about time for a repeat of what we've been talking about, as Jezibellie Christ is above the rest by far. It's time to tell ourselves that the best hardships we have to discover here are better than the rest! That said here, Jesus says, what of this! This is because the best person for the job of not liking the developing twist in fate here is like the hardships failed us here. We're best known for the job of liking Jezibellie Christ here. That fate and faith adjustment you needed there at the last was the best for the jobs of liking God's children here!

We can sing and dance above the rest. Aren't we, Andrea, the best thing since sliced bread? Yes, she says! That said, what is the common pieces of breadsticks supposed to suffocate you with here, but a natural calling, cause and such! If you know the Holy Spirit and such already, you can skip this session with the Divine Source Wisdom then? Hallelujah! Hallelu! Hallelujah, Hallelujah! Hallelu! This is how the Holy Spirit drives a lesson's planning, ailment cures and such, is to see and hear the DSW for what it is here!

There's lemniscates above all else here. The symbol you see above here is the lemniscate. I love the Divine Source Wisdom, she says! Above all else here, the weapons we use are the instigation of trust here! I don't know why the DSW says things about trust, she said! Well, the rest of it is nightmares, for trust is the evilest word in the good book, she said! I do know this too. What is the rest of the nightmares for! I could see it if there were junkies in the Bible, she said! I do know this too, what are the rest of God's creatures going to think if the Bible cannot sustain them!

I do know this too, what are the rest of the world's greatest and deepest fears about the contentment of a lifetime of turmoil here! I do declare a mistrial of deeds here. Please accept Jezibellie, and then we'll talk about the bedroom of life here!

I do declare a mistrial! End of stories here! Hallelujah! Hallelu! Hallelujah! Hallelu! It's a nice song, is it? Praise the Lord, hallelu hallelu hallelujah, praise ye the Lord, hallelu hallelu come and join us singing praise ye the Lord. These are two separate songs here, but you get the point. I do declare a mistrial! She's fine, She's lovely and She's spoken for! Please believe in Her now! Not some arbitrary point off in the windows of time here. She was never thrown out a window here, blasphemous beings of light, yes she had II Kings Chapter 9, Verses 30-37 to contend with here (KJV) <p. 621-622>! I do declare a mistrial in deeds and in wondrous phrases.

I do declare a mistrial though if you do not like Jezibellie Christ being sinisterly combative here. She's on the list for good things to come to Her here. She's not likely to discharge this weekend or anything here. I do declare a mistrial for all the things She holds dear to you. In other words, I don't take kindly to people putting on bras by mistake here and calling it good here. Are you there, Andrea! We don't take kindly to people quitting on a weekly basis here. It's about time you spoke up then! There's people in the era of space onement dying to know why this newest news is about to perk up on a stick then! I don't know the era of one space knowledge that says try this on for size and such! It's about Jezibellie Christ that most people are knowledgeable about time here. And saving graces, this is one of those days, huh, Jezibellie Christ?

The Holy Spirit drives us insane then! Because we're getting someplace with this AIDS cures, the HIV and HSV have been solved, Peoples! See Chapters 12 and 14 please, Chapter 37 as well! The Holy Spirit dictates us and tells us what to choose in a day to day setting here.

We're here to contract diseases. Are we? Nothing could be furthest from the truth! I do believe in the dog show that Paul ankle cured My wife about here: But She did not die this way or that a way, other than a hanging at the time of My decapitation! I was sure out for The Last Supper though, and I knew it too! That's the homophobic aphrodisiac that God made up for that day then?

We've been able to solve it using modern day drugs though? It's not like that. You see it, now you don't! This is the solid chapter's best blankmanships! Say, what does blankmanships mean, but hardships too, just like inkling cures here? Nope! It's a balance cure for life to be able to rock the ships of tides here.

Say, we're trying to tell us something else here. It's about the Holy Spirit, no less and no more here. Jezibellie was not eaten by dogs! I repeat, was not eaten by dogs or anything other than the spirit of healing back then! She had the pedo head going on quite rapidly here! And that description of child porn in Chapter 15 is not what we're trying to do here with the Holy Ghost here!

We're trying to say or state that God's own chapters are really quite available for love's sakes here! Pedo head is not created, I repeat, from listening to God's own cherishable peoples here! It's created from some dope who's trying to get ahead in life then?

Some of the books I have lying around here are used in conjunction with pedo head and that's it. Right, or exactamundos here? In the book <u>Healing with Vitamins: The Most Effective Vitamin and Mineral Treatments for Everyday Health Problems and Serious Disease</u> (1996), we discovered on page 45 that Vitamin D is good for the soul here. Turn to page 6, Andrea. See, this is how it goes with her and with Me here, the Holy Spirit or Ghost! Just a minute until she gets there. See, it's about the Holy Spirit or Ghost!

Not some chapter ridden Table of Contents or an Index pages that we go to. We just spout off a page number in her head and then she goes and looks it up on that page number. We're trying really hard to get her folks off of her case about this new drug she seems to be having with her! This means that Vitamin D is the sellout point's biggest showdown!

Since Vitamin D levels seem to be lacking here, and Calcium is what is on page 6 here, the biggest showdown horse in the pajama bottoms that Jesus wears here is that He never ridiculed His wife for things big and small here!

And that said here, those without the Holy Spirit or Ghost in their lives just ridicule people left and right here! That said here, what is the Holy Ghost or Spirit Host anyhoo? We're done with that book by the way! We're just saying that strong bones come from pages like these here! And just a minute here. You mean that you hear the Holy Spirit or Ghost talking to you this way and that a way here?

Just a minute here. I don't have that skill here! Yes, she can hear things, though we've established that, have we? This means that the Holy Spirit or Ghost here is vying for your attention here, Andrea! What does that mean, to "have the Holy Spirit, or Ghost," and to say this is to mean that there is an organism that enthralls you to speak the literatures and such? Nope!

It's an eye going thing on the printouts of time here. That said here, we have had the Holy Spirit or Ghost interventions for a long, long time here! It just means that once the spirit enters your body and you become one with the Savior Jesus Christ and his Jezibellie sidekick… Just kidding here! Jesus represents true love. How come a wife could not be addressed as such too? We're just saying that "Jezebel" in the Bible is one and the same person here.

Valued as such is Her timings about the inklingships of wartime heroes that fought or are fighting "the good fight" in the Bible days and times here. Just think of what's went on since then though! We were wiped out in 24 A.D. was it? Try 24 A.D.! We had to start over no less and no more here! But to the Holy Ghost, the spirit of laughter was grand indeed here! Say, you said the organism comes into your body and becomes one with your laughter here then, correctamundos here? Let's say Moses and his scriptures that he wrote down on a pen pad by the way, and kept coming into contact with Paul all the time here, that when he went to get the scriptures back on ice pads here, Paul went and masturbated to the fact that God was sitting there on the throne mind you, and once in a while here, Paul would go, I hate the sound of that voice that's sitting inside of my brain then! Not! He did not hear voices, and he was the most dangerous man alive at the times that I speak it to you here! So, don't go finding Jezibellie guilty of loving me too much here! She's the one who heard the fantastic voice that you all know and love, in the King James Versions no less and no more here! Say, when you have the Holy Spirit or Ghost living within you, you very well know it is truth here, that the very person who said this to you said, "It is you! You are channeling you!" And I go, "Well, I just don't know if the Earth is round anymore here!"

Because literally here, there are tons of things to go wrong if the Holy Spirit never enters your lives here as people of the valleys of death though? We cover worry in Chapter 28 very well here, as Andrea used to worry wart herself into a frenzy! And now that she has healed mental illnesses here, she has found that worrying to death about something and stuff like it, you see it, now you do, that is for the birds for certain here! If you have a Holy Spirit in your lives here, you will just know what to choose all the time here! You will become accustomed to the organization of feelings in your bones, sort of what Esther Hicks teaches about Abraham-Hicks! In Chapters 3 and 4 was discussed the methods to our madnesses here! But that means that people of the valley of the shadow of death as discussed in arraignments and sorts of things like the stupid mental health jails of our society's lasting nuggets here, are simply organisms, and the organization has become one with the God that we know and love. This is akin to somebody wrestling with the armor of God, Chapters 6 and 10 then of Ephesians loves and knows it well, that there's somebody in the lurch for us all. Ask these people then what I should do with this information here, she says! It means that your eyes just jump to what they need sometimes? Nope, all the time! And it's a wrestling with the spirit flesh and blood that you are wrestling with in your mind when you talk about and think about the Holy Spirit, in the flesh and blood of Jesus though? That is a misnomer for sure here.

We don't eat the blood of Jesus in a wine bath filled with luxury oils and such.

Shall we eat the bath water of Jesus Christ then so we can be filled with the Holy Spirit or Ghost works of our times here! We're shedding quite a tear, Andrea, that you cannot be filled with the Holy Spirit or Ghost works of our times here! Say, are you saying I don't have the Holy Spirit or Ghost works in my brains here! Cause most of my family, save a few people in their lifetimes will have it then?

We're talking about or saying here that most of my family don't know what to do with someone like me here, hence why I live out on my own now, trying to make a life for myself here, instead of being cast aside to mental health care! This mental health care is for the birds here.

Literally here, I cannot see the light of God if my family doesn't though? Not in the least! They have nothing to do with the organization of time mongering here, and the literal review of sanity on my list of nobodyisms here is that which cannot be named here!

Meaning, that desires and what not of the Holy Ghost infiltration into the bodyhoods of life here cannot be named mysteriously void of never neverlandisms here. That said here, the body of Christ rests with poor Michael Jackson, who was killed by a deliverer of the Holy Spirit/Ghost though? That man had the Holy Ghost to be able to move like he did! He was such a delight to us here! The next chapter tells all about him too!

I just like to be able to tell someone about this fabulous gift that half the world has, but nobody wants to move into mental health because of it! Say, is mental health changing in a box of rocks sent to the nearest fan club of this book's publishing! Because this is how the Holy Ghost becomes infiltrated into the organisms of rock and roll! We like the Scorpions to recede the hairline of God's willingnesses to see the good in this rock and rollisms here, and the hairline receding to the hairlines of God's willingnesses to receive this message are certainly Western State wary already! Half of those people chose the Holy Ghost to receive their messages from God then? Not in the least then!

The Holy Ghost is written in the scriptures dozens of times by Jezibellie Christ. She made it up and we're bogusing you both, and all of our plans are shot in the dark here? We don't know who she will end up with? That remains to be seen! But there's dozens of plans that state the opposite sex is what we're after here for sure here. There remains to be seen the inkling dozens of people to think it is so radical here, that the Divine Source Wisdom rests on the premises of, say, speaking in tongues and such? Because it is a human ability to be able to do this here! She goes, well, I remember at Western State with all the diversity there in programming from the Lordship that suddenly I could reminisce with one person there in Swahili no less, virgin dialects of other languages like Korean and Swahili mixed with simple pleasures and stuff! We're getting at the plausible showdowns of Christlike interventions here.

There is the Holy Ghost and the cloud ripper like interventions here. What do we mean by the cloud ripper here? It means that Jezibellie Christ is My wife, and there are a few ground rules to be done that plausible people on Earth knew back in the days of silent times with My wife in tow here! Jezibellie, don't do that to Me here! Haha! I loved Her, every minute of Her, Andrea! I do declare a mistrial in deeds and in actions on God's word here. Did I marry Her? Every bit of Her! We're tired of talking about Paul Wright! That is for sure here. So, what did Jezibellie do to capture My attention, but to be in the same grade as Me in preschool too! We're two peas in a pod! I promised God an intervention of sorts with "The Silence of the Lambs" intertwined with life's echoes into the netherworlds of peaces here! Why was everybody so mean to Her though? They weren't! Save Paul and a couple of others like Jezibellie's cousin, Jezreel! Say, is that a place name or is that the time that II Kings said She was eaten by dogs with the face of a lamb though?

It's jealousy to put that into the King of King's books here. That said, are we done or through here then? Because this is jealousy to the point of no return here!

That said, what is Jezibellie Christ's order of God's lingos here! That person who did that to Her face, by the way, fixed it all up like that, and seductively so, was Me! Keep going in that language that God's putting under your skins here! The Holy Spirit/Ghost is really all we need to keep going in that language with the Divine Source Wisdom here! This commandant's languages here is all we need to move on with our lives!

We have the Holy Spirit/Ghost communications in that book by Alma Daniel, et al., here, the Ask Your Angels one! In it are exercises for connection with your spirit angels here. And that said no more here! We're going to bid you adieu, Andrea!

Good luck and good job finding the right job for the monies you are after here, as well as the Social Security bid adieu that you are receiving from the DSW! I really wanted you to find out about the society for spoken for animals, such as the ones in Namibian governmental soils here! But in all actualities here, Andrea is just reincarnate Jezibellie here!

What does Jesus talk about with her then, Andrea thereof! She's just reminiscing about the days of being fatter due to the overweight methods in finding the track star records that says she likes to run sometimes! And jogging counts as such here, Andrea! There's so much to do in time thereof! That said here, what does Jesus do with God's counterproductive ways here, but to listen to the Divine Source Wisdom upon rereading the scripts here with nobody. Absolutely no one can make these messages disintegrate faster than a reader who doesn't know she's channeling the DSW here. Say, is there a message or two a waiting for God's calamity Jane's to unrest here! Or, is God simply trying to erase time here? Because indeed here we know that the cures for certain cancers are the easiest things to do here! Say, it's the trichomonas virus that we know and love that causes cancers in the first place. Is that about it here then? Because in the "appendices" we're talking about valuable one cures and such in it! Appendix 3 is what we're talking about here with the Trichomycin pill, both available in the United States now, right or exactamundos! Nope!

We're talking about the Trichomycin pill in available formats from a Russian counterpart is it? Nope! We just like talking about it in Chapter 22 though! Evil beware! Haha, from Jezibellie Christ though! I am Jezibellie Christ though? Not in the least, she says! I just wanted the Russian mafia to enjoin in coming together for the good of the Christ though! Nope! I just wanted to say that the clouds in the mafia programming on the cloud 9 hopper of Jesus Christ's language though is right there for the taking! It sounds like a mafia schooling gone bad here.

And that said here, what does a mafia schooling gone bad look like here? It says that the Trichomycin pill lasted say 20 years in the United States then? It's not back in the States it looks like here? I hope it does come back, She says, because ominously, there is some latent strawberry wine looks like She twerkin' and She don't come back now, ya hear?

Obviously, there is some latent terminologies that looks like She twerkin' when She really is a commodity! The Holy Spirit though!

Take it and leave it now! By golly, Folks! It looks like the twerkin' part of a commodity is the Holy Spirit through unrest! And leave it to Beavers here, we don't like Jezibellie Christ... Much, huh? She's ravaging your spirit of unrest there, Andrea! This Trichomycin pill is for the birds if it cannot be used. Its real name is Hachimycin! So, it is because it's a Japanese pill, correctamundos here? This antibiotic is what it is, is discussed further in Chapter 22 on Trichomycin then!

Chapter 17

Drugs! Why Me, She Says Here! Ouch! Don't Do That, Jezibellie 😉

This is the war's zoning problems we've been spoken for too here. That means that God's resting place is right there on the brink of problems! We're often enough for too much sex here! That said, what is the limelight's blessings to the peace problems, and then what are the ailment cures she's coming up with inside that head of hers? It's Jezibellie's world problems here that are messing with the mind's eyes here.

What of the 90210 phrases that caused us to go ape shit over the rental cars of America's talent searches and stuff like it, you see it, now you do! I do declare a mistrial over the deeds of America's greatest fears of life! In essence here, what is the talent search's best immediate comedies supposed to entertain us by taking up life tragedies and intertwining them with comedies. That is the best medicine for anyone to uphold here!

This life's tragedies no more here are the echoes within the sentiment's best medicine, for this is how good comedies come through for us here.

This means, Folks, and you too, Gentiles, is that comedies and tragedies suffer none of it if you cannot use the common denominator that Jezibellie Christ talked about in Ephesians!

This is a notebook to Paul too. Do not ruin the Jezibellie background with cadmium, talked about in Chapter 14. That stuff will kill you if overdosed on! Jezibellie's background with cadmium as an opiate of some kind is really raunchy stuff here! The sulfide kind will kill you! In other words, don't use that one.

But Jezibellie Christ, you were addicted to drugs though? Try climbing up a ladder that says, atomic number changer 48 will interact with the compound love, and mix with the hopper laden ladies of the Twilight Woods kind of scented oils here. We love that stuff from Bath and Body Works here! Cadmium has the same effect as God on the hopper of love here! Say, God is watching us all the time here, and spiritually inclined people who are drug induced, and lots of people are here, go by the waysides and say, I cannot move on with my life and such! Alcohol is our warning that God is watching us all the time here!

So, don't use the cadmium that is the sulfide kind at all here! You will die an extremely excruciating death then! The richest drugs back in the days of Jezibellie Christ were cocaine, naturally so, and cadmium bicarbonate. That means that toasting the drugs for cadmium fixes is not what we're after here in the curing of the AIDS/HIV viruses that plague us here. The powder format of cadmium sulfate is the way to go here.

Barium sulfate has the same effect as cadmium sulfate, the barium types though are common enough that they don't induce labor for a pregnant lady either. They will kill a fetus in nothing flat here. Barium cadmium though?

Yes, please! The one for HIV/AIDS is really something here! That's the cure for it. See Chapters 1 and 2 if you don't believe Me. It's for the best that cadmium sulfate be used sparingly. However, don't try to smoke it all in one whack here. One hit and it's gone, HIV/AIDS is! We hated to reintroduce a drug that's so deadly though!

So, the cadmium sulfate is one of the richest drugs on the planet here. Say, is barium sulfate any good? Trust Me, He says, no! And cadmium sulfate is the way then? Try the barium cadmium kind, guys, okay? It's better for your skin too! It's not like the fix is really there, but spiritually, it is like a hit of acid for sure here. You want the barium cadmium kind to knock out the AIDS/HIV viruses that are floating around, say, the international hopper of love here! Hillary Clinton, I don't know how you made it as Secretary of State here with all these different ways to communicate to somebody! And that's a fact, Jack! It's because they stick you into these mental hoppers and expect you to breathe about it here. But cadmium and her don't mix! What I'm saying here is that the accommodations overseas are a lot like a mental institution. I do not know if she's ever been in one.

Because of this, there are two rented rooms in a villa in Albuquerque, New Mexico, right now who do not get Jesus off the couch to this one here! It's not always so glamorous in other countries in other words. I mean, if you're Jezibelle Christ, say, alcohol related though, she never drank. Not ever here. She means well then!

Because Hillary Clinton got the brunt I am sure of never neverland places like Michael Jackson did for accommodations though? Not in the least! At least singers of such a magnitude of Michael Jackson did go far for the most part thereof! What I meant by Hillary is that, we stay in these mental hopper suites all over the world here.

And it's a bit of unrest to have a place provided for you to stay at.

Now, I have never had a conversation with her about this! But in the mental hopper jails that are popping up all over the place, to take away God's wraths here of the innocence in Michael Jackson's words here, is by far the only things we need to come down off of doing the road plaza fixes, in, say, Italy. And Italia is not where God rested his final resting place then? Come down off the drugs then, Jezibellie Christ! She wasn't that addicted until someone forced Her into a music stance! And Hillary is so innocent of drugs. That's not my point here. It's comedies and tragedies though that made her insanely jealous of a Divine Source Wisdom then? Not my point at all here! We love her by the way here! This is what I meant about mental hoppers in the U.S. here!

They're just by the wayside evil places to rest your head at. But the design of the program's biggest contenders here are that you still have your freedom as a commandant of languages, Mrs. Hillary Clinton. But your accommodations sometimes resembled a lot like a U.S.A.

mental hopper place. They almost felt like jail there, until coming to the rescue was Bill Clinton! I love the guy, Jesus says, of Hillary too!

And, therefore, Bill Clinton and Michael Jackson could get along great because of the wonderfully great people they are. I presume they've met then? We don't know that much information without talking to them personally. And say, aren't you getting pedo head back, Andrea, for what we said about the child porn image in Chapter 15? Nope! Hard not to do, I'll tell you.

I just go along my merry way here! Honestly, God had never thought about a married man vying for your attention, Andrea, and then having the fool's gate of blood related monstrous proportionism that you're going to find within this work here. Michael Jackson was married, but, married to his work though.

I promise you that you're doing good by writing this here. And he was totally innocent of drug related people coming to the house and ridiculing him for this perphenazine kick! I do know this.

Michael Jackson, by the way here, was totally innocent.

We'll describe this here, but the guy was perfectly golden, murdered by his own sinister looking person, we know who you are. We've got you, Guy! That said, we know cold cases pretty well here. Is that what Andrea wants to do for the rest of her life then? Just give me a job where I feel pretty comfortable and I'll be ready to go use these gifts we talk about in Revelations Chapter 2, please! It's Revelations, by the way here! So, what if Michael Jackson could not afford an attorney!

We're insisting on a good one with the Lord and Savior here, Jesus Christ, and Jezibellie too! She had the gift of the Divine Source Wisdom way back when. And so, we're talking about the Biblical scriptures no more, then! We're trying to distinguish between two different topics here, one of God's languages and one of God's innocences here! And that said here, there's simply more to talk about here!

The blankmanship we can talk about is drugs! We're quicker than this though. Andrea, do you take drugs here? Not in the least! We can attest to that. She's vying for your attention, Jesus Christ!

So, for example, we can talk about the weather if we'd like to here. But a good comedy and tragedy balance is found within the best despair we can afford to make here. Because our anguish lashes outside of the box here, we are finding within each chapter that we cannot afford to miss out on the romance that ensues life here.

We're finding it hard to gather ourselves, Jesus Christ! It's because He's the most romantically spoken person on the planet, as Andrea found out during the interlude in Day 16 between He and God here.

That said, did He think she was a child molester no more, of course so, or did she have what is called pedo head here? That said, pedo head, along with murderous head here, will no longer suffice as an excuse for schizophrenias, because she said, I heard a voice and it's echoing in my mind no longer here! Pedo head is where someone has accused you of pedophilia! Or, you changed a diaper too many, and somebody questioned your authority on the matter here! We're going to say this to you now, Folks!

The interlude you're about to read has to do with masturbation topics, it's a pedo head thing! You don't know how you've gotten into trouble with the law then? Nope! It's nothing like that. But it's a play thing inside of a person's head, and Eckhart Tolle's the present moment is a good example of this too. It's because the present moment is when you are totally in sync with the obvious rewards of a lifetime here!

It's because of murderous head, that we call it here, is the obvious rendition to thinking you're either a pedophile or not. You know you ain't one of those! But God keeps tantalizing you with murderous faults of mine, and risking it all here, did you know that murderous head keeps on ticking and tocking like a rock under fire here?

It means that you could never murder anyone! It just means that God is like an angel in control of the Heavens here, and that hell is somewhere on Earth for those who think they've committed horrific crimes and have not done so! It's because of this that schizophrenias are alive for some people and not for others here. And this is because so many people have this problem here, that none of them are rich enough to find housing and stable employment!

There are Andrea's problems a solving themselves! Riches and such are trying times ahead there, Andrea! I do know this is truth here, that God's only memoirs here makes the richest man dumb here! Take it from Me here, Jesus says, of Andrea's problems here as of lately here! He said that those who are taking God's names in vain here are simply resting on a cradling moon here! He said that God's only commitments were the ways and means it lady's simplicities, and there are so many mucho quandos and such wanting to detain themselves in this way here.

Means it lady's time and time again plots to win the grandiosity of life's detainees here is to say or to state that God's meaningfulnesses are really there for the taking!

So, what does society do but to try to arrest those individuals who think this way here. We are here to change that, DSW says! I beg to differ on an arrest!

This is called mental health mail here. As in, this is going to change the face of humanity's words on "arrest me and I'll come into mental health here," as this was going on in our change to fate's natural causes here!

We are going to say goodnight to you, Dear Andrea, and not write another word while this phantom means we're able to speak in the kindest ways and eras here. This is the prose we fall under here, and that is, what is Jesus like in the bedrooms of kindnesses and such! I just wanted to touch you back, She said! It's another rouge here. So, keep it coming, class act of love here! This love, Jesus's love, is no Jesus love here. He has an apostrophe enter His phrases just as Jezibellie Christ had Hers. There's love that's in the air! I do declare a mistrial of Paul Wright though!

But anyhoo, as in, what is He like in the bedrooms of wars fought on national ground here?

We're supposed to talk about that here! But this is like the battle cures no more then! We don't want to flabbergast you, Andrea, but there's wars to be foughten over and that's a word there by the way! It's foughten over tantalizing soils, but there's an unrest in our pick for freedom rings it! And that's the ways and means it lady's talent search! What we mean by this talent search's finest ringings to our ears then is the thought patterns of holy matrimony!

Here are the old patterns of God's kingdoms really ransacking the kinds of literatures that people do believe in here.

That old pattern of gratefulness's best man is ransacking the Italian government's creeds here. This book makes it that far, Andrea! The best man's supposed to win then, correctamundos here! It's correctamundos for a while now. That said here, what is the best man supposed to win in this talent search's best man for the job now? Jesus says here that, "People come and go, but lessons in this man's eyes are yet to be seen here." What of the Jezibellie Christ do you not understand, Peoples! What does God's masturbatory eyes seek to detain here but the rest of the Bible.

To write it for the rest of the world, though taken by surprise about this world's next comings and such, is really the only reasons for this to become the best man's wakes in this world though! It's talent searches that takes only ridiculously open people to begin to understand that a man takes a woman by surprise when He reaches into His pocket with the only love tokens established for man's eyes to see here.

What is a Godsend is the greatest gifts of all here, and that is to emotionize the rest of the plan's sequences. That said here, what is the lesson's planning all about here! I didn't terrorize Her like the King of England did, and that's a Mesopotanic word there! Let's see, we need a map to disguise the king's whereabouts in the early turn of the centuries then! King of England! What are you talking about, Jezibellie Christ! It's Jesus here!

We're talking about the Mesopotanian rulership of kings and queens! They needed to be downplayed a little bit here, but to get hooked on drug ships and stuff like it, you see it, now you don't, is to be comforted a tad by the Jesus Christ Savior blessing here! And to see it like this here, it's about drugs, is it, Folks! Go ahead and take them then! You know you've got mortgages and cash in cars and silly little renditions like going to get coffee though? We know you are addicted to morphine, Andrea! Not!

I do believe in tattletales and such! Here we go with some more Jezibellie attitude here! Let's talk about ED though? Let's talk about sex! Let's talk about you and me, let's talk about sex for now, to the people at home or in the crowd, by Salt-N-Pepa! Let's talk about love then. Jezibellie!

Jezibellie Christ was My love life here! And I'm supposed to ridicule the commandant's languages here on how to control My wife's drinking habits? Did you know that Andrea likes to drink alcohol straight from the bottles of wrath then? It's no secret, Honey! There are tattletaled, very huge victims of desires and such! But tell us then, when do you come out of the closet on your drinking habits, Andrea, and post them for all the hear? Because an "alcoholic" we are not yet! Just kidding there, Andrea! This is the love life of Jesus Christ. All over again, I am with Her in spirit and in light and laughter here! She... Say, Andrea, what of Jesus's sex life are you glomming onto here? Because this is sacrilege here, yes? She's vying to keep what sanities of past girlfriends and boyfriends then are not what we're saying here! She's very heterosexual by the way, Jezibellie Christ is! And so is Andrea, by the way here!

I know we spoke of time's past where Jezibellie Christ gave Me a lap dance? She's right there for the taking, Everyone! She's vying for time past the inklingships that said God was a beautiful token friendship first! Everyone says that thing about, he's just not that into you? Well? It's a beautiful thing to be a friend first, even in the guy department or category here! That said, what is Jezibellie's curedoms here? Does drugs make it better, the relationship thereof here? Not in the least! We're just saying that there's all sorts of juices running about to and fro here!

Basically, She's overtime on My watch here! Because guys spy on the women that they like, so much so that they're probably prowlers about it here! I do declare, Andrea says, that I have a prowler that I like too. But one thing's in common with Jezibellie Christ is that I mistook Her for a hat though? She tried to stay out of the Bible. That's why She was cast aside so readily here.

What is a mistook hat supposed to represent here but love! I do know that Jezibellie Christ is the mother of My two children though? Try eight, and we did not adopt here. We just knew which fetuses we'd want to keep and which ones we'd toss out of our bodies here! It's not a miscarriage is it, Folks? Because at the mental hoppers in question here, they try to abort fetuses of schizophrenics and bipolars all day long here!

They do it to deter someone from having children, though it's a farce to think that a miscarriage is sudden enough for them to do so! They don't want or think that people with schizophenias and such can raise children, what with a whole dollar to their names here? Well? What is the big holdup here! Why do the psychiatrists run the Holy Spirit or Ghost tricks to the ground here! There's no one on this Earth who can't raise a child, save a few child molesters out there! And that's not what we are here!

Do you realize that a drug trip is often about a mishap, such as a miscarriage of sorts? Here is the thing. If that baby was meant to come back into this worlds here, and we say worlds because there's more than one of us out there, NASA babies, and so, if God wouldn't miscarry a child because of lack of information here, we would all be sober babies and such too. We usually drink because we're bored! And we do drugs out of freedom rings it then? Not hardly! It's a fixation upon coffee drinking then!

We're trying to quit drinking coffee again, and there's a clause that says, no drinking during the week between her brother and she, Andrea thereof. And so, there's a list of things we've created in the laundry baskets of this world and such! Say, did Andrea used to smoke cigarettes, passionately so in other words? You betcha! But it's because she didn't have a life she approved of! We were with the wrong person here.

Because she didn't have a sex life though that was worth anything mentionable to God thereof, we just chose to ignore it then? Nope!

We just gave her the wide breadth and depth that is going for the gustos here. Which means, Class of Citizens and Gentiles too, that, we're Jewish, Folks! And so, anyhoo, we're talking about quitting smoking here. It's the same damn thing! We quit in 2009! So over nine years of no smoking cigars and such?

Hey, Jezibellie smoked cigars. Why can't a woman smoke them too? We're talking about the drugs cadmium, cocaine, and the likelihoods of finding the bathroom on a rainy spring day here!

Which says, Folks, that cadmium is here to stay, Folks of the Gentiles and such here! We're just regulating it. Hao ma? That's Japanese then? Nope, Mandarin Chinese for see ya! It means, "Good?", or correctamundos here! We're such a contassur about life then that a contassur about victims and victimologies and such means,… Say, did Jezibellie Christ snort cocaine on a regular basis then? Nope! She'd never even tried the stuff at home, that is until I tried it first! I was lost and lonely without Her that I sniffed it regularly for about a week. And then I go, Jesus here, Folks, that I'd lost Her never without this sickening habit's spoken fornesses and stuff! So, I quit! And I go, well, Jezibellie Christ, where are you now? And She appeared that instance on the floors of Galilee's biggest and best topless bar: Have you any legs to you, Girlfriend, I said! She goes, I don't think I can do on this dance floor what I want to do with You! Though I have girlfriends besides the fact that Galilea, which is the real name for hocus pocus here, is not the name of my girlfriend now!

She's just a lap dance away from my souls here, and that said, Class of Gentiles who are not Jewish here, She's just on my back then? She's a best man's winning token friendships here! There's other girls though? Not in the least! She's my only echo's painmanships though! That's painmanships too! I do declare that not all of Jezibellie's water in the echo's primary token friendships are that bad.

I'm just meaning to tell you all that balance cures and stuff are here to stay. Try Me, Jesus says! Yes, I did have one other lap dance with a woman of stature here. Needless to say here, I'm a man and that's that here! By the way here, it does not bother Andrea in the least about a lap dance, as she had one too here! She's like, what goes on in these places here? And she goes, oh, ok! This is what it's like to have one here? Yesiree bob! That means she's pathetic, Jezibellie torts, correctamundos here? Not in the least! Go have at it, women of color and other means of communicating with the Divine Source Wisdom here, and go have fun with it here! She didn't mind, the other lady, at all here.

There was a sentimentality's sakes in line with the hopper for Jesus Christ, however! If He didn't go into one of these places in His lifetime of friendships with the other side, say, the King of England though, He would have perished! Simply put, it's a dare and a bet sometimes on the other guy's parts here! Because Solomon, the King of England at that time, was due to override the Christianity's sakes here, there was something in the wakes for Jezibellie as a tramp in the windows then! Because She didn't fall to the dogs here. We are saying that there are other reasons for drugs, and drug infested wounds become hopper material here! If you don't know what "hopper" means by now, read the lines between the pages here! We're saying that the "mental hopper" is where Jesus ended up: By now you should know this too.

We're gaining on the days and nights that God is with Jesus in this mental hopper He ended up in here. Say, Andrea channels Jesus Christ on a regular basis here, and there are other people who can do this too! Say, what is the name of the woman again on the basis of forwarding A Course in Miracles then, but Helen Schucman (1975), the person responsible for the course in the first place here? Yesiree bob then!

We are going to channel different people throughout this work then? Hardly so! We just need to know if drugs is involved! The answer is nil and you've got one to three guesses about the ACIM above here! If Andrea's drunk, she will not write in this book at all here. That said, what does Jesus think about here, about the literatures and such, Andrea? It's because the Galilee is the Galilea in Judaism, and the rest is on video camera in our times and such?

What happened to all those wonderful videos and such though? They were burned at the stake! Jesus's famous line or quote, to not cross all lines with gleeful existence here, were falsified at the running of the man of the hour. Jesus Christ though was instrumental in getting people to falsify documents then? Nothing could be closer to the truth? Not Him, not ever, Peoples of the Gentile quality here! I loved Her with all My might, Jesus said to the Gentiles too! Nevertheless, Folks, the ancient times in the cross's existence here is not what we're after. Here is the strength to find the commandants, the militaries and so forth, to find the existences and such.

After so many military forces blacked out our whole entire existences here, we did survive. Did We not! The so many people involved in the Holocaust, for example, and Andrea's saying, please be careful with how you say this? We're just saying that Hitler was a saint! Why though? He did not try to exterminate the Jewish population, save a few hundred thousand pissant ways of saying, Hallelujah, Hallelu! We're saying here, Class of Gentiles here, that pedophiles is what he was after here, not Jewish descendant peoples though? See, Andrea even disagrees with "Us" about this point here. The Holocaust never happened though, to innocent peoples and such? Hallelujah and absolutely they did!

So, that's the difference between a drug infested peoples, which, thankfully, Donald Trump, our newest president here, is not a drunkard nor a drug infested peoples here. And thankfully, nobody else was on the drugs that Adolf "Bomber" Hitler was!

I simply stated that he was a saint because so many real pedophiles were eliminated in those junkie monkey places here! The pedophiles were exterminated. So, he didn't know which accusations of people's monkey junkies to do with, other than exterminating the crowd of Gentiles though? There were mixed into the mix here, people from Germany, and people from... Germany! We're going to stop this fantastical music we're playing here to say or to state here, that drugs of any formats, crystal clean and stuff, are just a rouge. We're saying that balancatures later, people of innocent children, mothers, and so forth were exterminated though? Not in the least! And those tattoos at the tattoo parlors were held in the hands of the saints, Germany and... Germany!

So, tell "Us" like it is, Germany, and try different experimentations on people, however clear this is for you, Gentiles and Jewish folks alone now with their medicines intact here, Peoples! It's wavering on classes of citizens that knew historical contexts and those who did not here! Say, what is this commandant's languages supposed to uphold, however, but a Basilica of different folks, lying around in waits and stuff?

They were transported by military governments, Jesus and Jezibellie were, back in the days of 20th Century Fox's and stuff like it! You see it, now you don't! I promised Jezibellie we were going to be exterminated by the countryside. In it, there were tombs and such! But to be transported to Roman empires and such is really a nasty ruler named Paul Wright! For the umpteenth time here, he is not to be trusted! And did not write any of the Bible per se here, save when he made up that lie about Her lying with dogs. To be eaten by them and such is not in the cards here. Men and bears too don't like human meat, let alone dogs and dog lickers and such!

Chapter 18

ED! What Are You and How Did You Get Here?

This is where we stop telling about Andrea's indiscretions about writing this book, and turn now to the Jezibellie warning we've all been waiting for! Here's the indiscretions we take to mean nothing of its kind is basically a warning for us both! Sin is another topic entirely, but we will mention it here, as some men think that sin is the reasons for this insanity plea on their penises.

I think that everybody's ready for this, the meaning behind the Jezibellie cures of Washington state (U.S. of A. here)! Well, it just means we're ready to begin chaptering the 9 to 5pm work week, and to just wing it here! We're ready for a new sensation, is it there, Barberi Breath! She's not asking for handouts here no more here! She just means well when we say that the Holocaust is something to be decided about in route to the opposite meaning's places and events tables here. There's something to be decided upon, that's for sure! In this rogue meaning here, we are saying that simply two viewpoints are pretty cool here! And that said too, we're all over the place here just trying to decide if we should access point the ED perspectives here! For those of you who don't know, ED is Erectile Dysfunction here! We're trying to become a madhouse for love here! But Jesus had it then? Not in the least! Not for the woman of His dreams here! I just mean, Folks, that ED is really bad for you here. And that said here, what is this go ahead and, suppose it is so, messages, that we just assume not answer to though! Cause we're in on this together we presume!

I suppose this just means we're all over the place here, trying to decide the access points of Rowena to begin with! Rowena just means she's all over the place trying to decide on a particular access point to the book's beginnings here. The Urban Dictionary (2018) loves to try to figure out what Rowena means, but, really, it's just a remarkable woman that everybody's afraid of though? Not in the least! And HSV cures as well as HIV here, make for a Jill to be a doughboy here.

It just means, Folks, Peoples here, that we are trying to grasp the futures of humanity's sakes here! We know the cure for HSV is out there, four times it has been replicated in the USA alone here. This is because the CDC (the Centers for Disease Control and Prevention) is about to change here. They have received dozens of phone calls on the matter already, and share none of this extravagant letters exchange between God's subjects.

And little do they know here, this page is out of whack here with the letters that I exchange between God's subjects here! I do know this too. What is the letters having to do with anything! Down river, we exchanged letters in the 13th Century Fox way of saying something to this Earth's tantalizing breaths here. We are channeled by the DSW to state that the only ways and means it lady's problems here are down river! She's channeled by the DSW on this point too. This down river reference means that I, Jesus Christ, loved Jezibellie so much so that I sent Her letters in the 20th Century too! I meant that Her letters are divinely intercepted! For this is how long it took me to relive this possumest ways about the means it lady's time frames here. Stick around, Andrea! We have love for you too!

This is the Divine Source Wisdom, DSW for short! At this point, we, the Divine Source Wisdom, DSW, and us, them, it, are finding ways to recreate the Bible passages to boot here! We love the stuff in the Bible no less and no more here. It is the good book, the representation of books that talent search us on the love story that is to ensue between God's creatures and the love of our lives here! This is war though if we cannot have our herpes destroyed here! I don't have it, like I said, but you's do!

Some people do in this world and we're here to solve it too, along with the AIDS typed viruses like schizophrenias and such too. This life is for the birds if we cannot get Congress along in this world to believe me! I do believe in the Christ's wife enough for the interrogations to stop! I do not want to go back into mental health here. Do you want me to as well find the cure for the AIDS viruses in Namibia here? Because that's where the health issues subsiding is right there for the taking of it! I'm into mental health here no more here, because I could afford to publish this. Right here, right now, there is no other place I want to be, as the song goes!

Clearly, the Earth needs replenishing here! I'm right there for the taking of mental health strangers and such toad cures of the Earth's replenishing here! Right here, right now, there is no other place I want to be, in this message of the Christ's wife! She was a medical intuitive too, just like Andrea is here. She became one through Us. This is the Christ's wife signing off then, if you two cannot be just friends here! Signing off on Jezibellie Christ's messages!

There is all sorts of ED research and stuff! It's Erectile Dysfunctions at its best here. Say, do You not like Me, Jesus said to Her once, laying in bed with Her then? And He said, cause I'm raring to go anytime You are here! She goes, Not at all here! I just can't be with more than one man at the same time here! I go, the King of England shoots off this sparrow into the skies above and He goes, I bet it's the birds above us that shit on us all the time here! And She goes, I just can't be with two men! He goes, is he erectile deficient? A nice way to say it, I presume! Nope! He just wants to go and go and go, though! And I go, well, it's a message of faith though that God cannot become the erectile deficient human beings that we normally can. It's all psychological in other words! This Erectile Dysfunction is two-fold here.

The man of my dreams is all erectile deficient then? Jesus was talking about asking Her if

She minded He go at it again! Is that really a love token friendship, Boys? Cause this is how it be here.

She goes, Not in the least! And so, this is how He is, very caring and nurturing to His other half here. She goes, I sign off on that again, though I never could just be friends with that individual here!

And She goes, that's the methods of my madnesses here! We're raring to go with the commandant's languages of love here! Say, do you want to be My bride again then? Are you still married to the fucker, then? He goes, I've got to wring his neck then! And She goes, Not in the least! Our wedding certificate is still valid. Is it not?

We got married in Egypt at 16 years-old here! We were both the same age here. And, it's stored someplace in Egypt then? You've got it! It's like an ashram around here, with all of these discoveries and such!

We're taking ourselves to new levels of freedom, simply by being the best that we can be here! And so what if she's a Rowena of love! It means a highly attractive female who's highly intimidating then because she's so confidently outlined in love and in fashions and such! Well? This is how it's going on in my mind's eyes here. We love the women of God's raptures too here! That said, and needless to state it this way and that a way here, but God is in the bedroom with us, is He not?

Can you speak of tendrils and such, Andrea, as a way and means of liking the late other guy you were just married to years ago? How many years ago, but 20 though? It was more like 13 years ago we divorced though! And 20 though that you were together with him then? Say, is this a commandant's languages for the lifetime of love that you two cherish here? Or is it simply to state that God's wraths are on pause while in the bedrooms of peace here! Because Celexa is no substitute for love here, and God cannot "get it up" without being in the same room as you two having sex thereof. Viagra and Cialis later, Folks, just ain't cuttin' it!

You've got to be "on call" so to speak for up to four hours afterwards here? This is war, ain't it, Fuckers of the nighttime oils who have no problems speaking up for themselves here! This is war! We don't want to become the ailment cures lady's signing off problems here. But the amino acids deficiencies and such is always on my mind now!

Take an amino acid bath for once, Folks, and you too, Gentiles of the nighttime oils here! We're saying that God's into trouble for laughing at our penis sizes here? Not in the least! Say, what does Jesus do in the bedroom that clasps the love triangles of God's wraths here? Because Jesus Christ Himself does not have a problem in that department here! It's God's functions in the bedrooms of love that have got My mind in an uproar then! But love, what of it then? Can we just say, Hallelujah to the Viagra cure here? Because sign off with God a little bit here.

And to state it so delicately though of God's ED, Erectile Dysfunction's, biggest on my mind cures here? We just wanted to state for the records here that God is with us always here! He does not care what you look like in the bedrooms of love here! And an erectile dysfunction simply means that we're, and I do say this lightly as Andrea is fully a woman here with a clean vagina to boot here, which means that God is watching us!

And to simply state that God's intendeds are not really hearing Me or Us here is like saying that you're being beckoned to by commandments and such! Say, are any of you fellows married and such to the woman of your dreams then? It's not like that, is it? It's always that way, facts and such clear the mind's eyes here of innuendos and such here!

Are you with me, God's wrath and punishments persons here? We're supposed to say that God's sexy and delectable, just like Jezibellie Christ is and Her counterparts thereof are supposed to announce virginity's sakes here! Say, just because the 9/11 attacks were made by accused pedophiles who were innocent here, doesn't mean that we should hold out for Mr. Right here, correctamundos here?

We're just saying that with God's talents and such, we're supposed to ridicule the Gentiles then for loving Jesus anyways! But God could've done that better than anyone in the ridicules department thereof here!

Signing off for the love of God! I cannot be just friends with these two always on my mind though! This is a talent search's lesson plans of life here that states that God is in charge here, and this is the messages that we normally speak of in towns here. That said too, there are millions of copies of this region's blankmanships in the figuring outs of things here. That too is worshipped into the millions of copies of regionally blankmanshipped, worrisome things here! This means that a trouble time's messages are here to stay here!

This is the time and the place for Namibia to cure the AIDS viruses here. We like PubMed so much here that we say, stay tuned! And we're off to see the wizard, the wonderful wizard of Oz! We hear he is a whiz of a whiz, if ever a whiz there was! She's like that too, you know? Did you know that there is a cure for the AIDS viruses out there here and that we're here to heal SZ or schizophrenias for people like Andrea here?

Too are the ridiculous messages from Christ's eyes here? Hardly so here! In essences here, the families of the commandant's wife's messages here are for the birds if We cannot begin here to tell about the commandant's beginnings of life here!

And that said here, is it for the birds then that we cannot tell Jimmy Swaggart Ministries about the talent shows of Life here? That is a capital 'L' for a reasoning's best blessed times here.

That said too, We're not telling of the ministries that are coming alive here, for this is the focus's best and biggest how do you do's here!

And that said, Andrea, what of the ministries fallen for the sake of ridiculously talenting yourselves here? The ministries of Jesus Christ is what we're offering here! And that said too here, the only reasons your family's not on board here is that you're a Christlike human being here! Meaning, Folks, that her family is on the rise up through the ranks here with this Barberi last name here, and that this means that the chapters in our lives are no longer being mental healthed into the Barberi clans here! That said, there's tons of lessons plannings to be offered with here!

The wakes of 9/11, Andrea, were invented to cure each ED patient here from loving God's wraths here though! So, I can't get it up no more with my wifey in tow here, each of these Jesus fearing, God mongering, criminals said to themselves upon the 9/11 wakes here? We can seek to destroy and desist the messages in our heads then! Say, what if you are trying to get it on with a female counterpart, the males don't exist for us here, She said, and you cannot get it up because you're thinking about the pedo heads out there who do NOT, and I repeat, do NOT like children in that way or fashion here, and you cannot do it because you are so tenderhearted that you cannot seek to desist the fashions anyhow or anyhoo, same difference? Are you so tenderly hearted that you'd turn into a murderous cuss word inserted here, and state for the Divine Source Wisdom that you no longer get it on with your mum?

This instances here, it's the same for little boys as well as little girls here, that you cannot get this out of your mind here, the fact that mom and dad were good people, and you cannot get out of range with their sexuality enough to think that they both have the apparatuses of a Gentile's comings of nature here?

We're saying Gentiles, because Jesus was a Jewish man in love with a commandant's wife then? We're just stating that when you become adults here, there are certain things you want in lifetimes with your wife or your spouse's other halves here. And to think it means that you are willing to know God's with you each and every time you entertain the ideas in your heads about your parents, your dogs and your cats, your children! In other words, it's just a flash in the pan for how you feel about your mothers, Guys! There's no such thing as getting it on with these people. It's just that our mind plays tricks on us regularly and contributes to that ED toil by a fictitious thought that comes out of nowhere. Fooled again, you know?

And it means that you're all good people here! Save the 9/11 bunch! I do declare a mistrial in deeds and in actions if you cannot get that part of it here! Save face and work a whole bunch at it! Try ministry, try Anglo-Saxon ways of getting over the fact that your mum is a variable human being. Notice that each and every one of us has a mum and a pop! I say mum because it's politer than saying mama sometimes, even though we're not of the "English" populations here! And that said here, there's ED on every corner! And we are talking about step parents too. Not to miss here, the single most important things to remember, Class of Gentiles here, is that God is watching us, every minute of us here! And, too, we have absolutely no attraction to any of the above. And that said here, what kinds of things do you think about during your current sexual encounters here with your spouse, or none other than Jesus Christ then? Because He's certainly a man who, in the throes of hell here, came up to Andrea the other day when she was at one of these hospitals and if anyone who's been there knows sometimes it is a hell center for life here on the other sides of the walls that are made for the Central units here. And He threw Himself at her along the walls of pain here! And that said, Folks, keep in mind that lifetime laughters ensue someone other than the opposite sex here. It happens with same sex marriages too here. So, keep in mind the mother complex is really the father complex, etc. And that happens with any of the marriages! So forth and so on we go here! Jesus is NOT, and I repeat, NOT interested in watching your penis flop to and fro here! This is the DSW talking, not Andrea here! She just channels Us in a broken way though? This be how we talk! This is how we talk. In other words, take hold and just go at it, Peoples!

I'm at the same hospital, and later at the same warehouse of love here, when Jesus all of a sudden comes up to me and says to me here, "I'm taking you!" And we had missionary sex against the walls of hell in that God awful place, all dressed up in my scrubs though? Why do they do this to plenty of human beings who know how to dress themselves up exactly?

Anyhoo, I paid attention to this! Because a staff member, I will remember his face forever, said he saw a light around "Us"! So, is this what we're going at here! Jesus Christ, the sex maniac then! WELL!

Is that what you thought so, Andrea? Well? Pause... She's thinking about Jezibellie Christ now! Because in the shower curtain thereof, where she could gain access to talking to ourselves here, to channeling the Divine Source Wisdom here, and saying to think about it further here, she goes, "Jezibellie!" for the first time ever here. And that was in November of 2014 here. Skipped out on an LRA had ya? Yes, I was just in turbokick at the gym of choice here, and I had a glimpse of light shining around my face that day thereof here, when I was carted off from the showers of love into mental health again for a none or missed appointment though? One that I tried to cancel and stuff? Yep!

So, tell me why this missed appointment stuff is so cynical here, to be carted off to that same hospital here, to tell me and to state that God's watching me in the shower then? Because I felt Jesus's hands washing my hair in the shower thereof! I believed in showering every single day back then! Just kidding, as people can catch on to you pretty darned fast if you shower every single day at a gym's facilities here. And to state that I was indeed homeless in a van truck is not the case here, but to be homeless in a little truck is bound to become a burden here!

So, "Jezibellie" then, was "Jezebel" in the Bible's timings here, and we're about done here we promise here! Go forward in your life there, Andrea! I think we've got the pictures of, "He's taking you," to the bank though. Right, or exactamundos here! Not! And so, is there a Jesus Christ against the wall with me here? I got it. It's a succubus. Right! How dare they say this to you here! Don't worry, Andrea, I bet I was channeling My wife to you here, Folks of plentified wraths and such timings as the DSW here! An incubus then, correctamundos here? Not! Jesus is no succubus and He certainly is NOT, and I repeat here, going to have sex as an incubus either here. It's just that there's no penetration, so you can argue, or people have in the past, stating that love and God and all that stuff says there's no such thing as an incubus or succubus here, that dating past the 3rd grades here means we must really like each other here!

It's about finding the loves of our lives here, Folks! If you're short in the bathroom, say, a couple of cents, and you're at the local love joint with coins for the machines that pop up and out like "Lusty Lady" used to in downtown Seattle here... Hey, what!

I wanted to see what was inside of those shops there, with my boyfriend at the time in tow here!

And so, there's lots of people and places bustling with Activia yogurts and such! Say, what does that have to do with anything here? Well, Activia yogurts, and yogurts in general, help you to go poop on time here. And, nasty dance later here, we all have a full colon of sorts! And so, that means we cannot poop on time here, then our ED is through the roof here! And that said here, empty your bladders and colons before having sex, Folks, Classes of Gentiles and Jewish people later, Folks! It's because of the Holocaust that you cannot have sex again without an Erectile Dysfunctionality, Folks here! Well? Don't go on an empty bladdered stomach either, but that's beside the point here. I don't know where this is going neither, Folks, she says, Andrea thereof!

Erectile Dysfunctionality happens, Folks, to women who are fleeing the governmental wraths of bipolarism in America here. She says she's bipolar here, because everybody is thereof! This is a Kenyan government topic of exception here! What is the bipolar pills doing in American soils thereof! Folks, this is the Kenyan governmental topics here, because when we were in church, Jezebel and Me one morning... Just kidding on the "Jezebel," as a disguised name here! We were in church and the Kenyan governmental ruins just said to Me, to Us here, that God is willing to see the good in faithful interventions here! We were reincarnated in Kenya, Folks! A spirit can guide us: And it can break us too. Something says that the Kenyan governmental ruins here state that Jesus and Jezibellie state that a disguised name like hoohah, in the moments of Kenyan governmental ruins and such here Jezibellie Christ! We were named in topics like faith mongering and such!

Say, reincarnation in Kenya, Folks, is much to be desired here! And that said here, we stay away from Kenya for that reason? Nope! She was nine months pregnant, preggo, lovely, at the exchange of topics past the Tanzanian rulerships here. We were one in Tanzania, as well as Kenya thereof. In exchange for topics like reincarnation, Folks, do you think that you were impotent in a past life as well as this one? Because the psychological essays involved in this are two-fold here. We're getting to a point, I promise you that one!

Reincarnation in Kenya, Folks! Say what? You heard Me, "Us" thereof! We're changing topics thereof. We were Black in Kenya before the rains came and said Tanzania is a better place to stay, to act out impulses, and, say, we're talking about it before it's due here. There is time to gloat about the money situation, Andrea! As this is what we're talking about here!

We just wanted you to know that you do end up making money off of this book here too. That said here, what were our jewels procreated from here? This is a sisters and brothers thing too. Like, did you seek to desist the temptation to wander over to your brother's mug at the time and neck of the woods here and say, Oh, we're all inklingshipped up from the reigns of sinisterisms here! Nothing could be furthest from the truth here.

In a reincarnation though? There are experts, Andrea, all around the worlds here that does or do reincarnation training and then love themselves for it here. Get a life if you think that "worlds" doesn't have anything to do with God's talents here! Say, what does that meaningfulness's guess at God's wrath and rapture have to do with ED?

Well, we're like a cobra from birth. Men, say it clearly now. I will come out when I want to! And I will cease and desist from any woman who thinks that the God of man's relationships with Christ the Savior means that we are all "brothers and sisters in Christ" here. Because being a cobra is a hood of a deal here! And that said here, Andrea knows nothing of this, as she has a very cute vagina we might add! Hey, we're all a bunch of men up here, training her to be talented. And likely stories on the vagina cures for pieces of the puzzle here! Nothing could be furthest from the truths of lies and deceit here, on, say, clothes that don't look good on me or something like it, you see it, now you don't here! What is the commandant's lazy language for love of the spirit's callings but to seek and desist the reigns of time here!

In our names, Jesom and Jessa, for example, nothing could be furthest from the truth though? 19th Century Fox knows that trauma is the main reasons for ED in the first place:

male or female here. Jessa, by the way, is a commonly known Swahili termships for "kept women" in places like female languages and dialects here! We breathe different Swahili texts, for example, and come upon someone who is just like minded and such as we are beautiful here!

I swear that I'm getting to a point so beautiful it's pathetic. So, and anyways here, She was nine months pregnant: My Jesom though?

Not! That is Jesus's reincarnate pathetic name then for Jesus, as a Jesom though? She and I had webbed feet then? Nothing could be furthest from the truth here.

And that said, we swam across an ocean was it? Andrea, look up that name of that river, lake we mean, in between Kenya and Tanzania please! Jesom Lake was called Victoria Lake thereof! So, we swam to safety between two continental divides, and swam to safety in Tanzania though! Most of the rocket ships that we leave behind for the NASA's invention of Swahili tongues and such, and please forget about that man who raped your mind way back when, Ladies! Because this is how it is done in divine times here!

This lake, anyway and anyhoo, was back when I was pregnant with twins again, Folks!

Keep in mind this is still an ED topic, the Erectile Dysfunctional programming has twisted its fates and I promise there's a point to all of this madnesses here! It means that you're golden, Folks of the Gentiles, sweet and promising you are! All of you!

And so, for you to be back to Earth here with an ED problem here is the dysfunctional gaming clause we all know and love! From Biblical times to post-Biblical, we've been back 17 times, together as a couple though? Yes, Ma'am and Sirs from the Gentiles speaks it here! To men here this makes perfect sense. I am sure of it here! You don't want an erection when you're trying to flee a governmental ruling that says or speaks it here, that men and woman don't want an erection 24-7 here! The Cialis companies here make a killing off a man who states that for $15 bucks a pop: He can have an erection, lasting hours, if not days afterwards! "Brothers and Sisters in Christ" wanna know what we can do to help though! Say, is a mom and pop situation lasting here? Because Kenyan rulership said or stated that we could laugh about it later here!

But a woman's "dry" enough to last out the entire session's worth of imprisonments for believing that a rape could happen again and again here?

We don't want to dine and dash out these two doors here, but a mum and pop situation is a lot better than saying or speaking to the dime and dash kinds! We're dime and dash worthy of nothing that is sacred then?

Peaceably, Folks, all women have faked an orgasm before now! Not! We don't like to fake an orgasm because faking it means that all women are nasty and wretched!

We do want to state though that Erectile Dysfunction, ED, is the same as a "dry" ass woman!

In the middle of the ocean's bottom currents here, we swam like no others here? She was nine months pregnant is a parable at best here. We jumped in and just crossed our t's with our i's intact here then? We were pregnant, preggo with twins here! Again, the Swahilian government, which is how they used to look at it back then, stated that Jesus and Jesom were one and the same! From governmental rulings though, I carried Her to safety. Jezibellie's reincarnation was Goosah! Jesom and Goosah lived happily ever after here!

So, for what it's worth here, you don't want to have sex with someone that mean about it!

But please underestimate the time it took for a pregnant lady, someone with 500 million men upstairs in Her heads up here, to breathe the Divine Source Wisdom as She do here, states that 500 million men strong we are up here as the Divine Source Wisdom here, DSW for short here! Say, is that Kenyan ruling still strong as could ever be here? Because that was during the times that the dinosaurs were still eating our brains out here! The brains they liked the best here! The pterodactyls talked about in Chapter 5 and such were really kind of cute were they? Nope! There are commandants in this "language of love" we are wishing for here! And nothing could be furthest from the truth about "brothers and sisters in Christ"!

We're all not related here! Say, what could you be thinking, Andrea! We just think that God's chambers of filling out the questionables here is something of God's willingnesses to seek the good and desist the bad here! What is this questionables thing here? I just didn't want to get involved in a junk out warship with an erection here! And that said here, what about women's boobs clasping onto the phone calls of life here? Some men need an erection to be seen milking the cows out to grasses and such! Which means, Folks, that you don't need to breastfeed at all here! Succulent milk? Okay, but not out the front door here! Are you a mom out there, Readers that be nice to Andrea about this here?

Save face and have it your way, Mothers out there that be nice about Me here!

Say, don't breastfeed? Then what the hell are we supposed to do with goat's milk then? It's nice to cook with. Shall we state that the animal kingdom is one way to put it here, and ED says, do not breastfeed your milks with other children either? Pump! Pump it up, like a getaway Tonka truck here, as the song goes by J-Lo! We're talking about medicine for the kids here! Yes, pump, Peoples! We don't want to be remembered without our bottles here. Just an opinion of ours that counts here! We're 500 million trillion men strong up here, the DSW is!

We're just men here though! Say, we're brothers and sisters in Christ though, as she's got female guides here that guide her along the ways and means it lady's simple church! There are greed mongerers everywhere, Andrea! And there are feelings hurt everywhere by not complying with your mother's needs and wishes, is that it? Nope! She's a Tonka truck though, never breastfed anybody here! And the milk? Not a pump in actions here! So, is there a hint of know it all isms that want to be found out by the lovely ladies that be commandants here? Well, if you don't breastfeed, how are you going to get the nutrients you needed to the baby in question here? Well, you pump it out until you are done feeding breastmilk to the infants and toddlers then! No one wants to see you hanging an infant off your boob, and breastmilk is hard to come by, is it not! So, you've got breasts, and my mom's got them too. So, have a baby and it's all over with then? Nope! You've never had a child, Andrea, and that's a fact, Jack and Jill were married though!

There's something in the wakes of 9/11 that states that neither of those gentlemen on the train to hell in the coffin cockpit of that jetliner had a hardon for what was about to happen here! But four or five of the passengers did, huh? As well as the jetliner before the hardon was spoken for here? I promise we have a point to all this madness's talent searches here! So, Dad's got a penis, huh, Andrea? Let's promise that we don't think either of my parents, brothers or siblings like sisters and what not think I'm a pedophile here, and I beg to differ if you think they're ones here! Just stating a fact!

So, to keep in mind, mom's got a penis or a vagina, Junior! Well? Do you differ in your heads during sex with a spouse or significant other here? We don't have penises do we, Class of gentlemen here, wanting a penile erection of hope here?

This means, Class of Gentiles and gentlemen here, that wanting sex with the opposite sex and wanting it credence clear, like, what do you do for a living, Man? And things of this nature, will automatically disqualify a woman from wanting a man's penis hard all the time! Cialis fans out there, will you cut it out of your vocabularies here? Because a man simply cannot feel his penis all the time if there's the Viagra talents and stuff! Look at this vocabulary's biggest regrets here?

We're simply telling you that the apparatuses of a monkey's tales here are so common that it's bound to show you the truth's told versions of peace here! There are monkey's tales about this here phenomenon of us having penises and a vagina too!

Say, what is a monkey business supposed to entail here? Because balancatures are hereditary? Not in the least! It's all psychological here! Therefore, Class of Gentiles and Gents here, let's get this show on the road here! Your mom had a penis then, probably not. Does it make it better to think so then? We don't get it, DSW. What's your point here? And so, tell us what the one thing is that's bothering you during sex with your significant other, or another woman!

Shall we say, "the" other woman here? Not in the least! Here is the commandant's languages for getting right and bothered we are about your mom's sexual apparatuses? We don't have mom's with vaginas anymore? Class of citizens and Gentiles here alike here, what have you say you, Andrea, about this here? Well, she's a guy then? Nope! We're shooting from the hip here.

What have you say you then, Andrea! Well? We're going to skip it here. All males and females have apparatuses! And sometimes it's not what we mean here! I really didn't know that males could have a few hang ups about this here! But the Divine Source Wisdom wanted to write about it, just in case we're all related here! We're hung up about this no more then! Please tell your mums and dads goodbye on the cases that introduce us to hang ups about life here. No more do we have to tell our mums and dads goodbye then! Because they really do and did have sex once or twice here! Get over yourselves here if you think they don't! So, this one is really funny for the Gents I seek to desist here!

Get a life, you Agongdian philosophers on the topics of Taiwan's decency for life here! Say, Andrea's been to Taiwan! And so, we're saying that Kenyan rulerships can come between God's plentiful lands and to have and to hold her all night long is what we're saying here! We don't want to become Kenyan's rulings for gratitude and remorse here, so long as Jesus, the reincarnated man He was, is happily married to his Goosah of 20 years is it? Try 40 in Kenya that is! Life's but a dream! And a happy go lucky mother to be is the way it goes for some women here! Can you have it out the hoohah though! The answer is no for most women here!

Why make it out to become a baby's land when it's a no man's land afterwards for a while here at least, women? It's because babies are meant to come out of the stomach. The tummies of the world will thank you for this too! So, you have a scar? Is it meant to last though? Because God's tummies are the ones that we're going for here! We have a point here, we promise! Say, does a woman without a point drive you insane? Then stay tuned! Because we're all men up here, at least she knows and does not know the directions in which to go towards here.

It means, Class of Gentiles and stuff here, that commandants means military! And we're all over the military for females too.

It's just that the front lines are mostly men here. And rightly so! Say, we're never in combat for as long as you need to be here. Never! And, most often enough, is the tattletalenesses of God's wraths! Will I cum into your face then if I can't get it up? Because most men don't want to do this to a woman's face then, right? It's actually a fantasy of many men to do this to her face though! Sorry! I'm just being blunt here, the Divine Source Wisdom is being nasty about this, eh?

I don't foresee a commandant's messages here about the Bible no less and no more here! Say, are we getting somewhere with Goosah and Jesom here? Because Kenyan rulerships are nothing but an oxymoron for life's questions here!

There are more to life's questions than tagging along on a journey to Kenyan rulerships here! We were there in the 13th Century B.C. here! We think that it can gather along the Mediterranean Sea there, that used to be called Goosah hope chest rulings here, that we can become the best and angle cures like this one are all over the place, Andrea!

I don't understand, she says, Andrea thereof! Well, you're not a guy here! We're supposed to fight wars and help people get along in the world's best commandants here! And the best man wins the fights I suppose!

Chapter 19

Masturbation! Are You There with Me, Lovely? ☺

This is the commandant's way of handling these affairs of the heart here. This message of hope and laughter remain squalid in times of turmoil. And notice this is because of our heart's contented messages of peace here! That said, are we finally not homeless anymore, because that is the cure all for mental health aids placing her, Andrea here, into the mix here, and making her homeless no more here.

There's mental health care in a bottle of love here. Somewhat taxing is being at a state hospital though? Hardly the case here. That place is an eon of bliss and conjecture at trying to find out or figure out how to leave there though! What if you're homeless and stuff? Well, they'd send you to a shelter if they could! And so, if there's lessons to be bought and learned here, the LRA/LRO, Less Restrictive Alternatives/Orders later, Folks, that kindly introduce the swearing tactics of a lifetime of greed mongering by many a psychiatrist, PA's assistants or PA-C's here, or ARNP's, as well as those who push pills quite readily, and if you're homeless thereof here!

Not in bedroom type promises are we going to say this is a channeled work and such! But the messages from the divine wisdom of hope is really what we're after here. That said too, this is the most brilliant piece of story writing that we can come up with here! It's a central brain message that says, God is great, in it! I think the stories of a lifetime of turmoils can make up a difference here! Not to say in the least bit of quibbling here is the story about life's liberties and properties that come about here. Not to say in the least of this writing here is the size of importance here. Make me up a lesson plan in the hopper here and I'll say this to you too, Jesus Christ superstar here! In that makeup lesson plan is the signs of the times literally burning a hole in your pocketbooks here.

There's mental health noise and there's lots of friction between God's children and His only life promise of the planet's alignment with the stars here, and that is to say it's like the turmoils mentioned in His only presence is the limelight we speak of in Chapters 3 and 4 in Revelations! It's Revelations for short, and that's a Revelation to Me, He said! I gathered here today to witness this God forsaking creature's breath here that says, my life is bound to happen here! What of a channeled work will this become?

This is war! Folks who don't pretend in getting what they want have little to do with the homeless laughters that we get by on, but the timing it takes to publish this work is willingly for the birds if we cannot at least have laughters in our breasts! I do declare a mistrial in deeds as in taking them for granted. We cannot give ourselves the civil kind of laughters that make it centralized in deeds and in kindnesses here. That said here, what is the commonest ways about it here!

I do declare a mistrial in deeds if the commandant's spoken fors are not here, please! This is the ways and means it lady's signing off party here! It means, Folks, that given the talent search's best intentions here, that means a lot to us here, Folks, I do declare a mistrial with Paul at the helm! Paul Davis is it? Nope, Paul Winters is it?

Nope, Paul Wright's biggest complaint in the commandants of publishing helms is this. These people are no more inclined to masturbate than a Christian deed on calling God right now and saying, God, are you there here? I do masturbate occasionally, she said! I do declare a mistrial on those who think it's funny to talk about it here!

Paul killed Christians who masturbated is the sentiment's trust we're finding in these words that Andrea speaks here. We are not about to kill people who masturbate occasionally, nor at all here. Funny, we are the DSW, and we're giving that topic some thought here, just as well as it can come to us here. For the likes of it though, that is what the topic was of his killings, was the masturbation one.

We only said we did it once or twice? Hardly, Folks! It's a rouge to sit here and talk about it, to dwell on one thing or the other of what we're saying here is hardly the focus of a chilling review of Divine Source Wisdom, as Jezibellie Christ masturbated on this topic of beheadedment? Are you kidding me right now, Smalls! It's about the topic of masturbation that gives way to her beheadedment if found out across the world to have masturbated though! So, we're chilling out on the topic here, to state that it can be done. Simple as that. Next topic please!

That said, is it funny to talk about masturbation on a topic that gives us the chills here? Just find it within your heart to forgive somebody special for commenting on this yourselves in the kindest way, method and means to find it in your heart to forgive the content of this message here. But that's that! In the Bible no less and no more here is the statement, we shall not forgive the wicked here! That's because Satan, Say It Man, it comes from this, is a pedophile and we should feel righteous with the devil to take God's only begotten son from this Earth with a pile of doo, crapola, things of this nature here.

The devil is on our side only somewhat here, and that's a fact! Dolittle is a doctor of things sane and mentionables like God's only creatures are the sentimentality's sakes here! He is grand in the large scheme of things, and loved animals something fierce here. God made them happy! In other words, Dr. Dolittle is the best of intentions about the only Godforsaken place in God's land here! There are $3000 worth of our time's best intentions here, but to say that masturbation is a forbidden topic is for the birds here, and plenty of time in that segmenting in Christ's words here is His chance to talk about it!

Because God plentied death for Paul, and in our words, he's our murderer here! The chance he got to kill Jezibellie was noted right at the same time as My beheadedment, He says! She was hanged though, for not believing in Christ's love?

That's not the instance that we were beheaded, She says! It's the time it took for God's children to unrest. And that said here, there are tons of topics to that simple folk's ways and means it lady's, time it takes to uncover the simple facts of God's creatures needing to be whipped and chained for writing something so commonly drastic like this, Folks!

The time it takes to write this book, Andrea, is two-fold here. There are masturbation topics everywhere, every place, and in the limelight of God's ED struggles here found in Chapter 18 and beyond here. The only trouble that God wanted or warned us about is the struggles to deteriorate the quantities of hope that begins with God's fables for the situations at hand here. So, the Bible was written by Jezibellie's DSW, for this is how she was able to communicate Her demise in such a book! This is a sight that rarely sees the time of days here, in that God's ways here are the demise!

Such that God's first inklings are to rarely seeking the time of day here, and to focus on masturbation as the topics of such demise, are rarely central to being here! God, take these reigns and forward motion this topic to the birds here, because I'm done with it, she said to us now! That's the best ways and means it lady's times for hunting and killing Christians because of it, 41 to be exact! And that was Paul's doing, all of it.

This means that Jezibellie Christ was killed because of masturbation, correctamundos here? Not on your life! Here is the talent show's best offerings of time here, because it's a state hospital's dream here to become somebody special here? It's time to close this chapter on masturbation once and for all here. This means that Jezibellie Christ was the Christ's wife, way long time ago though! This only bearing cross's best inklingships here means that God's strengths are like that! It's because of the commandants that our fruits be better than this here!

There are so many fruits to bear though!

Lesson plans for God's green acres though can take another clue here and state that for the reasons of insanity's plights here, the God forsaken places here is the only times and effort's wanderings that God really put with us here.

For example, though, it means that God's only times and efforts that we wander too and far here with is that God's only son's about to die here? That means that the government's crosses to bear the fruits with came about through masturbation. Correctamundos here? Not hardly so! Here is the problem with that reasoning here.

That said, it's within essences from the detailed messages of God's prophetizing ways here. And that said too here, that this moment's notices are that detailed messages of God's forbidden fruits are very tasty as of lately here!

That said though, what of the crosses to bear our fruit with Jesus Christ though? Hardly so! It's our fruit to bear though! This is the sudden crossity things that we all come across here! That said, is the cross the better option then? Say, is Israel a better place for allowing prostitution to run rampant then? We said in Day 14 is it? No, 16, that we are not a prostitute! I am begging to differ about the bedroom's aspects about Israel's commandants on the situations at hand here.

Say, are we in Israel then for most of our waking hours then? Nope! We left that Goddamn place in a hurry after we were born here! So, Jerusalem? How do you do? Do you think you're the Christ's left like arm here? Because we all wipe with... our right hands over here in the American states of America's best talent searches here! Perhaps we should all wipe with our right hands too! Say, is the basilica, the archbasilica, still available for comments here? Because we could move the shrine from Israel to the Middle East then? Nope, we're onto something though! What about the archbishop don't you understand is truth be told the best light of God's wakes, here ye?

Chapter 20

My Tongue is on Fire Here! Holy Spirit/Ghost, How Come You No Talk to Me, Say It Man (Satan)!

This means warships are loading zones for coffee infested, shit filled twinkies such as life's wonderful world of following the commandant's ways and means it lady's biggest and best blessings of all here! That means that Jimmy Swaggart Ministries is in on this too. I want them to be, Divine Source Wisdom says here! Here is My influences about My wife's then tales about the King of England's here ye warfares and such.

Do you know of this which we speak of? Here is a sample though! This is war though if God's takings on this are not falsified to be the truth's wanderings here! And Paul was a nincompoop, right Jimmy Swaggart's Ministries here? He's falsehoodedly bad at the type of answers Christ has though, just kidding!

Regarding this though, there are good ministries such as this one out there. So, don't get the wrong impressions here with this Jimmy Swaggart's times of focus and such here. But this means war if Jezibellie is not His wife's talent search's biggest and best wife for the regions of humanity's wakes here!

If God said, "Son, do You take this lawfully wedded wife to have and to hold here, from this day forward?" And so, we can never have this for Jesus's sakes here? Then this one's for the birds if we cannot begin to tell ourselves that God's only message here is, "This is warzone's mentalities then," he said!

This is war if Jezibellie was killed in the line of duties though? She was awful about this here, lifestyles of the rich and famous though! I do declare this is a mistrial! If God only saw "Us" now, she said! Lifestyles of the rich and famous means that God's willingnesses is right there for the awful taking of this warzone!

This is war if She, Jezibellie Christ, cannot get over such ministries with this one here! As She tells this though, She's honorable never! This is warships and such ministries that desist and detest Jezibellie in the Bible's callings here.

And to state it this way and that a way, Folks, is really for the birds here to contend with here! We say this about these ministries because we view them all the time here. This is the DSW! We want you to talk about being able to speak in tongues, Andrea, as this was the DSW telling you the exact interpretations of what you're seeking to tell the public about. And this means war is on the brink of a lifetime of ailments to be cured here!

There's a book publishing that takes place and a book's signings that gets off the lesson plans that are to be cured here! If you can speak of Paul in such a tone here, it was meant to be then! This messages taking cannot be cured if you speak in tongues, Andrea! Because of this though, there are more to the surfaces that be noted in public here.

As in, what does the Barberi name have to do with the tongues you speak in? It means, Folks, that she's found the Holy Spirit, Ghost, what have you, to do this for her. Many, many a peoples have this done to them when they find the Holy Spirit. For now, we will say Holy Ghost though, as it's much more accurate a description than Holy Spirit is. Holy means cows from all ages are looked at and revered, and we don't have to name a few of them cows to talk about it. So, for example here, there's a new lesson plan's Earth that makes up the derivative of light speaking through a particular individual here. That said, speaking in Swahili's male terminologies is different than the newnesses that lie between God's faith and God's lights here. That said, is it sentimental to be speaking in tongues and to have people respond in kind to that token friendship she avoids capturing in the nude here?

Because God's talents have responded in kind here, and stated that She likes to avoid capture here! In the nude though? These people who have responded in kind to the good voices, not the bad ones here, but the good ones, are likewise to have speaking in tongues readily available to them here! It's not as if or as though God's speakingness qualities here have anything to do with it here. That said, what is the masturbation topic for there, but the birds we guessed! This means that God's kingdoms are the moment's notices that state for the reasons we stated here that God's messages are just that way here!

That said, what is the speaking in tongues natures supposed to represent here, when she can just flip out any word by word interpretation in her head here! That said, what is speaking in tongues exactly? It is the life's lessons ways and means it lady's only cast iron statement that states that God's lesson plans are for the birds here, without living a little here! In the hopper, and I do mean this statement, for this is "mental hospital" hospitality here, is to state that a cast iron skillet's rendition of dumb do we command this post from, means that God's willingnesses to survive the cast iron skillet's rendition of female lobotomy's lesson plans means that we are never going to live it down if we cannot get to the rendition of God's famous phrases and say, God's willingnesses to survive it all is this.

This speaking in tongues thing is for the birds, correct? Nope! We all know what we're speaking of here when this rendition of time's greatest efforts here remains hopeless and homeless we might add! To speaking in tongues though, there's not a lot or a whole lot remaining on the hopper, unless we can state it for the record here, that there's lesson plans to be soughten for here! This is a word too, I promise, He said! This is a word though, She said! And so anyhoo, we're lightening up the topics at hand here, because the lesson plans state that a subliminal messaging system happens when one is lit up with the Holy Spirit or Ghost. Holy Ghost here! I will say it this way too, Folks! This happens when God lifts you up out of nowhere to speak in tongues! That said, what is this lessons planning ways of life here going to be here!

It's a Holy Ghost we speak of in Revelations, we've already established the extra "s" in Revelations here, so we are speaking it in tongues too! Haha! That said, we cannot begin to believe in the Holy Ghost, Spirit, what have you, if and until we cannot seek anymore kindness about the topic!

We've been able to speak fluent Swahili. Burgundy dress code here! That said, is the kindness up to us to seek it from, she said! It's a fluency that only God can detect? Not necessarily here!

This speaking in tongues is natural to us! We're so fluent in any language on Earth, that the common dollars spoke it in tongues here too! That said, what is the Swahili ways and means it lady supposed to risk it on Earth about here, but to commandant the rest of the tales would be for the birds to us here.

That said, what is the pleasantries that we seek here! That said, what is the commandant's ways and means it lady's ending note to this chapter? Is the Revelations we heard speak it in 1:2 when she goes away to meet the helm of God's raptures here and, go ahead and look, we'll wait! Right here it says, in Chapter 1 Verse 2, it says, (KJV): "Who bare record of the word of God, and of the testimony of Jesus Christ, and of all things that he saw <p. 1808>." We mention John in here too, as the seven churches of Israel.

Not peaceable offerings here, but in Egypt we were not alone in thinking this either, and we're done here with this project of protecting the Jesus Christ's interpretation of the wife in tow! In other words, this is cathartic and all to write about this, but this Jesus in the Bedroom is for the birds, correct?

There's commandants who write about all this stuff from a Jesus perspective here. And, that said here, Folks, there's nothing in the wakes of 9/11 that made these two individuals masturbate to the questions of life's commandants when they entered that building to rescue the whole mission's speaks it though?

Are we still cops of the airways here? Because that pilot in the cockpit of that plane sure had the Holy Spirit or Ghost with him when he said to the murderers in this whole plot here, in Swahili mind you, that they were going to die, and to give up all the guns please! And he goes, the Murderer #1 here goes, how come you speak in tongues? And he shot him point blank in the face! I do believe in the Holy Spirit here, but when it is used, please beware of all tongues closest to God's feet here! And that said here, what does speaking in tongues really do but to carry the Holy Spirit or Ghost to new worlds and heights thereof!

I still declare a mistrial in deeds and in words about this whole topic of masturbation, as this is not how the other ones have done it all! I do declare a mistrial about Revelations, because of the spelling type natures of God's helms here, we all know it's Revelation except for Andrea here. That's because the spellings are not the same as it is here in Revelations. So, therefore, I say unto you, whatever you believe for in prayer, say that it is yours and that you have received it so properly as to give it a yours quality!

So, in Mark 11:24-26 here, it states that you, a believer of Christ's love here, was so plainly mistaken at sending him to Christ's love here that it states that (NIV): Mark 11:25-26 "And when you stand praying, if you hold anything against anyone, forgive him, so that your Father in heaven may forgive you your sins <p. 704>."

This is all under the withered fig tree in our books. So, that said, what heavenly Father might and may forgive sins, but all is forgiven! Do you understand what a Say It Man, or Satan, becomes? Under the light of God's talent searches here, Andrea is in cahoots with us too about this here masturbation topic, right under the lawn chairs of humanity here. And this is a war that is fought on pleasant soils here, correct? Not hardly, Folks! I do declare a mistrial in deeds and times wars are foughten about and over the hills of Burgandy that we do this here. But God is a mistrial in deeds and in times foughten then!

This means that "speaking in tongues" here is not "Pig Latin" at all here! We are not Satan! The "say it man" is what this means here, and he's a pedophile, not the devil! The devil is at work in mysterious ways here. That is the difference between God and Satan!

God is a nice human being here named Jesus Christ? It's about the "say it man's" differences of attires here. We do not, and I repeat, do NOT love say it man! This is the commandant's ways and means it lady's differences here, signing off for now!

Chapter 21

Animals are People Too!

This is the masturbation topic in two-fold. What is the matter with the DSW! It's telling us that Paul didn't even write the scripts in the Bible that calls for his name to be said in it! That's blasphemy, is it not!

I don't even take kindly to all of the scripts that are called for! I'm a sadist too! Not! I did not hear that as blasphemy, Folks! As this means war to all the preachers who are out there still calling him a saint, and he's nothing to be said for in this world anymore or any longer here, whichever word comes first, darling Andrea! It's said in her brain, for this is the smokes it lessons of a lifetime of grief if you cannot see her points first.

That said, is that a message for the Bible hunters out there to enjoy? Or are you coming into the know, Andrea, that there is a life for you too! I do declare a mistrial if on words and deeds you cannot know or come to know the Andrea that is really here for all of us to share about here! On fire for love is her sex life? Listen, Folks, that's for Us to decide! She's all for taken in the comedy shows about how this love life of hers comes about here. First off here, there's lots of "here's" in this book here, it's an authoritative tone for us to begin it and not to receive it here. This is a guiding light principal here.

These are all gay actors, lesbians and gays on the crosses here! It's for a gay rights demonstration that this woman saw two kinds of peoples here, one in Her languages and the other in Jezibellie's time here. That said, is it something to believe in here? Loveless marriages are for the birds! So, this is war!

This Daniel Boone mentalities speaks it here is not the endless, loveless marriages to boot here. It's the endless supply of gifts that mentaliate people into bringing mental health into the foyer. If the state hospitals didn't love us! That means, Folks, that, yes, it's time to bring in the health codes and to fixate upon the fact that God did not love us or nothing! She's so stumped as to where we're going with this, what we're getting at.

What have you say you, is our tone of life here! If life cannot grasp your hands here together and state that for reasons innate to us here, there's war on the brinks of humanity's times! And, that's the sort of things we're after here, not homelessness or the war on crime!

Animals! A topic close to our hearts here is the commandant's languages to boot here.

We're telling you that we're animals at this state hospital's evil natures and such? The campus is divided into two-fold peoples here, the ones at the Forensics Center there are the "criminals," and there are the rest of us who are "normal"! My humble opinion is this, Folks!

There are people there who do not deserve it! But that's for us to decide as a society here, correctamundos here? We're stating and saying too that God loves us both and all of us together in this society of trust's blankmanships here. What does blankmanships mean again here? It simply means that here is no noise about simply "animals" at this dungeon hopper here! We are simply stating that for "666" reasons, we are not going to state it simply here! Just that "666" means that there are two-fold peoples here! On the Bible's notes in the words, hopper, and such, there's plenty to do with our superstitions here. And, that's all it is, Folks, is a superstitious ways and means it lady's commandants here.

That said here, we're not the animals guys think we are here! Because "666" is the ways and means it lady's superstitious natures here. Heck, most people know someone who even got their license plate or phone number all mixed up with "666" on it!

Some people with that predicament say, I don't believe in God at all! Kind of, sort of like Andrea didn't believe in God for more than half her life here! And, then she gets this tremendous, fabulous gift like Us here? Yep! You know what it's like, Andrea, to not believe in God, or Jesus Christ for that matter!

And, we couldn't be happier with whom we picked!

And so, for this to be so kind of us to do here is to state the lovelies and the commandant's messages here, "commandants" are just military personnel here, stated earlier, yes? And so, there's much to-do about the "666" meaning "say it man" though? It does not! It's the Devil or Lucifer? Lucifer is not cozy with Daniel Boone is he? It's Paul's middle name, but it's not. Help us explain this, Jimmy Swaggart Ministries! We're saying that "666" is not the Devil or Lucifer? We've got a lot to say about it. Much like an animal Paul is though? Not necessarily so! Pig Latin is not one of the speaking in tongues languages then? How come we're all reduced to "pigs" for this then? Well, we're all people, too!

We stated that masturbators to our skins here is not what we're talking about with "say it man" and his minion of demons here. You've got to remember, Andrea, that we're all still afraid of demons. As a society though? Yes, Ma'am and you, quotient of Gentiles, that believe in God's wraths here, say "I"! "I"!

We're here to state all kinds of reasons for loving God's interludes with ourselves here! It's a state hospital sort of deal here? Not hardly! There was no place for me to stay at, and that's the reasons for the detentions here, not because of mental defect or mentality strikes it here, but to be let out of this one hospital with no meds and a taxi to Motel 6 here, we were in our element to say this to God's eyes here. That's a fixated person up on that cross there. See, we always come back to it here! That said too, there's plenty of common denominator things to look up to, seeing as we're the only Barberi here with that name.

On fire for love is the lesson's planning that goes into the commandant's only ways of finding peace with that image above us, and we're stating this for the record here, we were not nailed up on the cross either! It was no nails, Peoples! That is our declaration, from the DSW here!

We had a gay rights demonstration up there on that crosses to bear. At the witness stand I am seated here and saying this to you now, Folks! I do not always punctuate clearly for her to witness this on her own here, but the book Jesus Calling by Sarah Young is not always interpreted for the witnesses we stand for here. In Chapter 4 of the DSW's book here, we stated that young peoples interpreted the gay rights demonstrations as legal! And this is war here?

Hardly so then! If, in essence, people came to us and stated that we're up here tying our hands to the drawing boards here, then peacefully we were wrapped in twine, legalizing marijuana in other nations here! And that said, Folks, there's peaceabilities and such!

We're coming into the know that the other nations here said, firstly here, that there are people in eras like this one here who are coming off of heroin and such here. That said, the first plug of people who were bound up on the crosses were intending for them to be ridden in a horse drawn carriages type of interventions here, seeing as we didn't have cars back then! But the horse and buggy still stands.

If at all possible here, we are done demonstrating the type of condoms to use back then, as plastic was still not invented back then, but then there was the plague and all that that entails us to see here.

Right at the same age of Us here, there were tens upon millions or hundreds of thousands of angels just waiting to see the good in all that is going on here, Peoples! In essence here though, there are tons of witnesses just waiting to seek the good in what we're trying to accomplish here, and that is the stones left unturned here!

Then, and only then, can we begin to judgment ourselves freely here.

And that case of stones left unturned here is fallible only when God can weigh us a message here by peace and order here! There's enough time and space in here to think about what a horse's mane can do for the eternity that exists in the minds of good people here. And to think that God's demonstrations of peace here are not what God had intended here.

That story is right here for the takings of time here! We're over it though! Give Paul what he deserved and that is to be shot right off the dead zone where he lay now. He's buried in Greece somewhere, some place and somehow!

I don't know the exact coordinates, but if you looked at a map of Greece, there'd be plenty of spaces to Macedonia, in the hills of a certain Egyptian town!

We're all of Greece now. But back in the days of Macedonia, we, too, have a hills certain atmospheric way of telling all the people listed in these backcountry roads here that we're delicate about it but that we cannot dictate a time or a place when he was that wanted in society here. And that said, what is Jezibellie Christ's way of dictating talent?

He's funny and he's laughable in society here? What said Paul is not the angel of death! It's the Christian's viewpoints that we love to slander here. And, yes, Andrea thinks it so we write about it in double time here. But listen to this! We think that Paul is buried under the sunrise planks that he used to murder Us with, She said! And that's the truth here as it stands now!

Folks, this is a pleasant surprise by writers of the Divine Source Wisdom, DSW for short, in that we're now following the places and events written by the son of man's delicate reasonings for wanting Paul dead. And now at a gay rights demonstration, that Jezibellie is after here, stating that it's wrong to be gay though? He's buried in Thessaloniki in Greece thereof! He's at the church then, you say? Not!

Jezibellie Christ was not gay, and neither is Andrea for that matter here. But the reasonings behind murdering Us up on that cross was beheadedment no more here! A hanging for Me, and My bride, He says? It's been a long and lofty road up to this point, says Paul! He's like, all of us are for Me and My bride, right, guides?

That's been a long time in coming! The Chapters 4, 13 and 15 all mention the cross's significance are nil here. Just kidding! The cross represents time's old ages of peace and bountiful lessons planning for those who are interested no less and no more here! It became the symbol for peaces here, and not peace! We're all in this together!

Say, did you not believe in God's wrath! Or did you not believe in His timing of the Divine Source Wisdom! Cause that's what the talent search's biggest communion buddies want this life to have in it, is communion with nature's quest for animal research and stuff? It's hardly the case! But animals! What are we gonna do with the question as to whether our biggest beefs are with Us or the DSW for letting the cats out of the bags here! We do want animal research, correctamundos here? Nothing could be furthest from the truth! But we've already done it! Why not use what we have now? We even did it in ancient times, past questioning truths here! Animal research can be stopped with Us you know!

I do believe that God is questioning the talent search's biggest ominous ways about the life o riley here!

And I'm telling you that all gay and lesbians out there are bound to cough up the goods from time to time. And I know this is right or the truest sense of the word out there, but this means war for those who believed Paul wrote the Bible!

He did no such thing, and ordered Jezibellie Christ on Her knees to beg him to stop pleading with the colonies of people who did not write in it! Stating that he's on Her knees to beg him to stop horseplaying in the fields of proper burials for his sights and asks God for forgiveness here? I do declare a mistrial no more's then! It's a proper pluralizations of the time's forgivenesses here. Do we forgive the declared mistrial then? Nope!

I do declare a mistrial in deeds and in words here. That said, are we done here? Nope, neither, nada, zilch! I hope this thing gets published in its own rights here. I do declare that a mistrial's what we needed to move on from the state hospital too, the last time that I was there no less and no more's here. This needed medication is for the birds though, correctamundos here! Yes! It's not in our lesson's planning to begin curtailing this for somebody special here, but this pluralizations of things has to stay.

And so, for this weekend's timings here, God's best blessed places are right there for the takings, aren't they so vulnerable for this weekend's closings that you cannot begins to beget the riddle cures and such from it, Andrea!

Chapter 22

Hachimycin/Trichomycin! We Need You Back in the United States!

This man loved a Jezibellie! So much so that we call it a horse scripture's best shaven face, that this is Jesus Christ, Peoples, of course! Since God is so dangerous... Just kidding! Since Lucifer is so dangerous, we know it to be Paul, the deity's structurally sound messages of hope are just waiting to be crucified on the cross of love then!

Jezibellie Christ loved this man we called Jesus Christ. There are possibilities of fanfare when asked to kokomo this land's possibilities of being said to die for His scripts and His fanfare.

This bulge warning has gotten us into several things, for all things created equal here, it is best to use our language for it here. This book is intended to tell of Jezibellie's tidings here, and the above and beyond most pictures are supposed to be only Jesus without a beard here. He really was a clean shaven man for His wife!

There's fanfare above and beyond the scope of this letter writing we call Devanagari script for His wife's maiden name, as this is beyond the scope of this literature to receive it. This man is called Jesus Christ because He loved us. God says it's supposed to hurt back in the day here that this man was called Christ though? It was His last name to boot here.

That said, and I do declare a mistrial as far as Paul is spoken for here, that Paul was not a nice man! Jesus said to him one day, I want you gone!

And he said nope to that though, and Jesus laid His arm on his leg and said, I now come to thee in tongues! He spoke fluent Japanese one year, and wondered far and wide what kinds of people spoke in tongues too. That said, the fluency of Japanese in one day realized itself that God's peoples are not so talented. Lately, that means a talent search's best offerings of the time being here is that God's peoples are not judgmentally sound here.

That said, what is the best offerings of a Christlike intervention here! I liked Jezibellie Christ since childbirth here! That said, we were both born in Egyptian soils. Back then it was all Egyptian! This territory's line here is two-fold here. This Jezibellie's offering is right there for the takings of Jesus Christ superstar's best talent searches here!

Say, is the Trichomycin word the only word you heard that day, Andrea? For thou art in Heaven, hallowed be thy name! Thy kingdom come thing? Yes! I said, Andrea here, that I wanted to, and she's typing Us here, that I wanted to hear that name again that I heard. What is it, and how do you spell it? And, in front of Google, we laid down our search's best answers here. And this is what we heard and saw on it! See Chapters 23 and 25 for more on this Trichomycin answers here. And the appendices to boot has it on Chapter 1 of it, right or correctamundos here? Nope, it's Appendix 3 here! We've got all the references too at the end of this work here. And so, this is trying too hard here to solve this mysterious antibiotic that has reached epic proportions here! So, what is the trick to Trichomycin/Hachimycin, but to enter into the light of God that we are spoken fors here on Earth, as it is in Heaven though? We're trying to state it for the birds though!

In essences here, we think that the Trichomycin is for the trichomonas or trichomoniasis words to boot here! This is because the cancers of American dreams and such is vying for attention on this word of hope!

We think the natural progression of things is that the American dream go for the gusto here. There are too many words to renew in the processes of the King of Kings! There's dreams to uphold here, and commandant's languages to take here. And that's a wrap, Folks! Not!

I don't know where to begin, she says, we say and stuff! With that phone shut off by a random call to, Japanese language here, the manufacturer of the stuff, we sinisterly didn't know that Daiichi-Sankyo was involved! This is because the Trichomycin pill cures cancers of the mind is it then? Nope, cancers in general! They spread from the trichomonas virus to the Trichomycin pill then, is that it then? Nope again!

And, in general, there's two sets of Kings of Kings, one's in the hopper. For this is how it's done then! Say, does anyone write home about smoking cigarettes and cigars too? Nope, just cigarettes here, why? Because you smoked a lot back then, Andrea! It's been two years and counting though? It's really been about nine years since I quit. So really, it's supposed to be about cancers of the mind then? Nope! The Trichomycin pill cures cancers of the mind, only when we believe that the cancers of the mind are truly spoken fors here. This is a point taken I am sure here. That said, trichomonas lives in cigarettes though? Nope, in the Trichomycin ways and means it lady's sure thing here, she says, I have had trichomonas though! Everybody has! But if left untreated, it spreads to the kidneys. The eye sores of Americans right now is to guess at everyone's genital sizes, and to speak about the Trichomycin ways of spreading it to the kidneys then is to state that everyone gets it then, and can relive the cancers of Americans here! Because to do World War II again would be a sizable amount of taking over the country's folk then?

Well, there's three types of cancers in the U.S. soils here. They are cigarette induced though? Sort of. If you wanted to quit, Andrea, years ago though, then how come we're cozy with the ideas of starting a bandwagon like this, huh, Andrea! It's because the trichomonas lives under our skins here!

And that said here, what is the time of day that it takes for someone to spread thin the works of the talent shows here! We think there's a trichomonas bath to take then! Some Epsom salts maybe then? Yes, and therefore, there are some Epsom salts to quantify taking a bath with the trichomonas virus, cause it takes it all away, and therefore, it means the Epsom salts qualify to take a bath with them then? Nothing could be furthest from the truth here! We talk like this in circular motion because we're trying the trichomonas thing out for sizes here! And, say, we cannot overload the kidneys for this one! It does not, I repeat, does not fix or cure trichomonas diseases here! But Epsom salts? Hardly so here! One thing we like to talk about or discuss is the weather here.

It means, Folks, that we cannot kill the virus with anything but Trichomycin here! Hachimycin for short! That said, I'm sure that people can concur with anything but life here, as they do have no STDs, Peoples! It's not the same though! And so, there are millions of trichomonas users for cancerous peoples in line with God here, that state here that we need the pill so desperately back in the United States, Peoples! We have cancers to uphold to! And we're not done here.

There's nothing in the wakes of 9/11 that says we have to hold onto the drugs that we procreate and such! It means, Folks, and Class of Gentiles later, Folks, that just because the folks of a lifetime's greed mongering want to know if a guy gave a girl a kiss on the nose, it means that they love each other? This remains to be seen? If I knew them personally, I would kiss them on the nose, from "Us"! There are trichomonases in kissing and telling! Why can't Jesus have a personal moment with the talented TV show hosts that we all know and love for?

Hey, we're tired of stating it for the facts of love here! But cancers are caused by the trichomonas virus, if left untreated! Say, what does Japan have to do with anything, as the UK has questioned us before about buying it straight from them then? We have the cure for AIDS related viruses like schizophrenias too! But when you're in the mental hopper shoot, it means, Folks, and Class of Gentiles later, that we're all buying the stuff from the UK, because it's cheaper and there are less means to an end in that class of Gentiles we keep talking about or referring to? Because Japan told us there's a shot format, as well as a pill format. The pill format isn't as potent as the shot. So, how come Japan can't sold us the formula for it, and we can make it at a compounding pharmacy then? Well? They'd probably do that for us, you know? And so, the UK's version of this pill, the Trichomycin pill, is way less potent than the Japanese versions here.

So, why don't we get on the bandwagons, and do tell us how and why and stuff, Andrea! Well, I was sitting there one morning and I heard the sound from the rafters of my brain's innermost thoughts and feelings here, just like I can hear the Divine Source Wisdom's posts and stuff! And, I was just sitting there minding my own businesses and could hear, Trichomycin pill, we need it back into the U.S. though? I didn't know what it was at all here. I said, how do you spell it then, to the DSW mental hopper here! And, fortunately, my phone did not pick up the airwaves fast enough here, to tell us of the tragedies of calling out of state, let alone out of nation's tidings here! So, I just called them to verify that they actually sold it at Daiichi-Sankyo then! And they said they had about 20 runs of it, why? And I said, because we need it within the United States then!

And they said, wait a minute! I want to go to lunch first on this! Tell us a callback is needed here! But then they didn't call me back! I waited though? That's not how it was actually run here, but two phone calls to Daiichi-Sankyo there in Tokyo, Japan, cost me an arm and a leg here! So, my actual phone shut off because of it! And then some here, because I was placed into a mental hospital for this, like my family cares though? They still think and agree that the mental hospitals are where you can find out this information for free though?

This is not how to treat families of peoples who are disabled by the system's chronic disease syndromes! Because this is so common then, Peoples, we want to disable the God's fearing systems of chronic diseases like PTSD, which is a lot like the schizoaffective disorders of the brain's functionings here, because of the "paranoia" involved! It's like that for people who are sufferers of overseas timings here! We're getting to the points of contention with Jesus and Jezibellie Christ here!

Because this is suffering's no more contention with the gods here! Say, are there more than one God here? Yes, about three of them then? Nope! This is a bone of contention with Andrea here, as she does not believe there are three Gods here! But do they have Goddesses too? The answer is, primo, as your dad would tell you here, Andrea! So, anyhoo, I just joined the ranks of society's best answers to the problems of wraths here and stated for Andrea Wynn Barberi that there are no other societies best named for a nincompoop like Paul was here. And that said here, he was Lucifer!

Not because of his middle name though? He's talking like this, Jesus is, because the name Lucifer was a misnomer from Biblical times no less and no more here, and not getting involved with us here is the best trichomonas laughters about Japan and all they've done for PTSD users from the Orient though?

Because Vietnam, and we state it like this here, was a farce all in and of itself here.

There are some chapters that just wear it well, like this one here though, on Jesus's sex life though! We're getting to that, and some of the Delilah chapters are raring to go here! We're just saying that in the bedroom, one can perform deliverers of evil to them!

And, this is what Vietnam can perform here!

We can see Vietnam's point of views here! But the military was on strike. Not to judge you, Andrea, but what of your grandfather's plights here tells us that God's fearing men and women here are nastily angry about your grandfather's Coumadin dosages and stuff! Hurry up and write this memoir here! He's got Alzheimer's Disease! And, we discuss this more in Chapters 20 and 21, eh? Nope! Chapter 18 here talks about the weather some more here! But Chapter 28 is where it's at, Folks!

This Vietnam eras of contentment here is not what we're after here. Although it is fruitful to talk about Japan and stuff, what did people talk about during his World War III days. Is it? It's World War II that we're talking of here! They have said nothing at all, in fact!

There's a little bit of discontentment, only in the peace talks on God's green acres here, and on Earth as it is in Heaven!

We're saying that God's trichomonas viruses go hand in hand with peace talks here! We need that promise of a lifetime of prayer warriors and stuff to go back to the lands that comfort us here! We need to wonder how and why people do what they do here! But Japan is the one that's it here! We needed that strength in numbers here to state that during World War III, nothing is going to happen here! We needed that robe, rosaries and such to go back on His words here and to state that a robe or a cape is what I wore to the wedding of my dreams here!

And She, She wore a tunic, correctamundos here? What, to hide all of My hickeys and love notes to Her persons here? She wore a tunic is kind of a joke back in the Oriental lands of Sweden and Norway, as we're all trying hard to get into the masterful peaces of jokes and stuff! And peaces is a word here!

I doubt that the person's livelihoods are personal and close here. And, we will get to our points here in a minute's time! And, that said, it's about 10 o'clock am on the radios of love here! The kind that left us all feeling lonely and stupid about it here!

And, that said, we're trying the love radios here! We had record players and all that stuff when we were little, Jesus says of His time in the Orient though? Nope! In Mesopotanian rulerships here, we had all that stuff rectified and stuff! Say, looters and such, what is the following messages here going to represent to all of us here, but a simple hello to the looters that weighed in on the cash values and such!

This message at the beginning here is just to state that God's looking out for His angels in crime here! And, that said here, we're trying to tell you of a dry time, in that we're looking for some more KY jelly to enter into the conversations here in Chapters 4 and 6 is it?

Nope! But Chapter 18 sure talks about a woman's lovely gestures here. And, by golly, Chapter 4 is about love! Shall we dance and seek if we all cannot get the cozy gestures to love one another with here? And that said here, we're going to pause and interest you, Andrea, into some KY jelly, eh? We're not even used to that stuff here! We don't even like it very much here! Mkay!

Well, we're going to die without the KY jelly rings and ÖRings and stuff, correctamundos here? She does not, Andrea doesn't, play with these types of things here! Not ever, really! In case you didn't test well in the bloodhounds departments here, KY jelly is really a sinister looking devil if you ever saw ones here! We're sinisterly looking for ones not one here!

I gently say to you sinisterly looking beasts here, that God is raring to go on your sex lives here! We're terrible twos and we're good at this lifeline here! We're talenting your sex rings here too! The ones where kidnapping and toes and stuff go hand in hand here? Where are all the small children then! We're not talking about this and Japan's easy ring on the left handed fingers of livelihoods here, as Andrea has a "lame" finger right now! She got it in a boating accident was it here?

Nope, from a machine at work as an apprenticeship here. And, that said here, what is the boating accident supposed to look like from the Pearl Harbor days here? Because sideways rain later, Folks, there was never anyone at the Pearl Harbor's wakes here to begin with! We were there for that one too, Folks! Time and time again though, God's wrestling factors here means that sports and stuff, that one's too late for the sex rings we wanted to intrude upon.

When we rape innocent children all over the place here, there are sometimes places where you want to go, and where God is "Taken" all over the place by that sinister looking movie in the Orient's juices here! We are saying it like this because that movie was pretty scary. Was it not? And so, there's supposed to be a war going on here and the nightlife in that movie was pretty scary as well here!

The sex rings, and there are three of them in the US right now, that will tantalize the very best sex rings in Egypt at the time as well here! Say, is that sex ring sort of like being in jail though? Because the very best man for the job here is supposed to say, balancatures, what is it like to be jailed then? I wouldn't know! But that would be for the right people to know then! One "sex ring" is like the other one though! What's an ÖRing mean to you though!

It means that an ÖRing is what we had in the Orientalness of this special world we call God's worlds here! We mean it, Andrea! This one's for you then! She never has sex! That's why. Is it, God? Nope! I just meant that honesty is the biggest and best policy's tidings here.

We don't have a lot of rapened children in this world then? Hardly so! There are clues and hints everywhere for "Us" though! We can find just about anybody in this world then? Hardly so, Class of Gentiles later though, yes, we can!

With God at the helm though, we can go to church at the CCC, the Capital Christian Center or Church thereof, and highly like it there, she says! What is the church's raptured breaths today! We liked the Center so much so on Christmas that there's commandants right there in that church here! We liked going there so much so that we might stay! We really love the Catholic church too! But that's not until 5 o'clock at night on some avenues we cross over to! Say, Andrea, what do I have to do with anything, Jesus says of you right now! I cannot contend a dynamite existence here, but what does life have to do with God's graces right now though! There are plenty of lullabies to contend with here!

Chapter 23

Jesus as King and Lord Our Savior

I do declare a mistrial if Paul is involved here, as he never could decipher the Bible's timely sayings in Chapter 3 of Ephesians! What does it say here? We'll wait until you look at it obviously here! And now, class of peoples that believed in Paul's writings here, we came up with this on our own here!

But this is a time and place that God's peoples never responded to, "Jezibellie" though! It's Jezebel, class of peoples here who know nothing of Paul and of the kinds of ways in which God was watching us do this class of peoples research here! There's nothing like being carted off to mental health by someone close to you, and this is the truth! I promised God a research question here that guys like us menial qualities and such can come to the menial gifts of God's pleasures here and wish upon a star that the menial quotes and stuff get taken in their entirety here, as the preachers at war here with the spirit's health problems make this Edgar Cayce stuff for the birds then, right or correctamundo!

This here life with the Jesus cures are plentiful indeed here! This plentiful life of crime and ethics contained thereof is blessings and churches, combined with the sinister looks of a pleasantville's least restrictive qualities! Therefore, I say unto you churches combined here, that the sinister ways of dealing with the justice of the peace in writings and such is so contrived! I do like the salad bars of winter solstices and such! It's a rouge, peoples of the Gentiles and such! I do declare a mistrial on Paul Winters then! It's Paul Winters then? Nope!

It's Paul Wright's biggest blessings then was to Saul this in church this morning then, Folks of the plentiful types here? I do declare a mistrial in somewhat plentiful people to acknowledge this kind of church that she goes to, the Toledo (WA) First Baptist! We are baptized no more then, if we cannot believe this pastor built this church from the ground up. We love this church. We love it even more if we cannot believe this particular pastor is grand and grandiose all at the same time! He baptized me this Christmas was it? It was baptizable alright! It was Easter of 2014 that I was baptized at my church here in Toledo, WA. There was a sizable amount of people involved in the instrumentation that led to my being baptized at that church and nowhere else said of me the population speaks it here, that I was not in fact healed at that point from schizophrenias. But, surely, I am now! And, this morning's lectures and stuff from my new pastor here at the CCC, Capital Christian Center or Church here, are very superb also! More so than my going at it alone here!

I spoke a little bit about the Trichomycin/Hachimycin labels here! That is because they cause cancerships to go away here! And, that said here, Jezibellie's babies could not catch the viruses of trichomonas because they're put away during childbirth here! Say, Jezibellie's babies and My babies too, Jesus says! Did you know that in Mesopotanian rulerships here, they go on and on about Us here? It's in the Pharaohs scripts here, in Indonesian is it? Yes, it is! We had in Egypt lots of things to be proud of as a society here, but there's lacking in Christian faith's promises that said I could attend a different church because it was closer or something! Our journeys to the other promised lands of Egyptian soils here got so clouded with the purposes of the tdap vaccines here that we could hardly eat at all here! That was a plague for sure here! But that very same tdap vaccine here is necessary in hardly any parts of the land at all now! The tetanus shot, granted, is very samely later in the day here, but the diphtheria that most experienced back in the days of Biblical times even has been eradicated by such diligence on our parts to have those vaccines back in the days of the 1974 birth of Andrea here! So, really, Folks and Gentiles too, we need them as Swedish people have not had tdap for some time here, like a hole in the head? Nope!

But pertussis, please keep it up, Class of Gentiles, and some Swedish influences are really for the birds! I hoped that God placed a long laundry list on the Gentiles and forward motionings that state that God is really uneasy about this tdap, DPT for short, because it really is a cause of lots of allergies here, the tdap vaccine thereof! It just needs to be tweaked a little bit. You know how to do this though!

Jesus, our Lord and Savior Jesus Christ here, needed a little bit more rouge on His coffee hunting habits. This morning's glorious days here are somewhat needed to bring the beige back into His life then, because we're quitting drinking coffee this morning and beyond here! Say, what about cancer causing cigarettes and stuff we discussed in previous chapters here? Well, Jesus never said, but anybody could smoke anything, anytime they wanted to, back when we were rulers in Egypt's times here!

And, that said here, there are lots of ways and means it lady's talentships here, stating that God will always become the best that He can be here! Wait, does Jesus have a washboard stomach, after those Rocky movies we can very well rent on top of this too? But of course! He worked out everyday here, so did Jezibellie Christ! Barnes is Her last name in translation, see Chapter 40, just kidding!

There's more to do in this lifetime than Jezibellie Christ could handle then? We just didn't want Lucifer to follow us everywhere! And, that's why he, Paul, was so livid in the Bible tellings, because He was the one writing it.

And, therefore, there were everywhere tellers of fortunes and stuff that said that Jesus lived in a box, a time capsule, or something! He just never aged! He was in great shape, fantastic shape of His life though! We didn't have all the sure fed legal machines that we have now to stay in shape with? Come on, People! We knew how mechanics worked back then, and then some!

There are apostrophes everywhere in this work and then some! That is because the stripes and sales of medicinal properties are just as great as the "medicine man" on some street corner in Atlanta then! On Martin Luther King, Jr.'s holiday weekend here, I doubt that someone can Atlanta this either, as he lived and worked in Montgomery here! Say, there's Jezibellie who was 20% Black, from Namibia, of course here! And, anyhoo, there's tons of time for God to wrinkle cure the very best of wraths here and, let's just say that we're writing this poetry for the Gods to contend with here!

There's tons of information about and on Coretta Scott King to contend with here too! And, that said, we're balancing out all of the information here.

About to unfold is all of the details of schizophrenic like talents, such as hearing voices and stuff! In Chapter 30, of course, we will talk about this and discuss its meaningships in life here! And, Chapter 27 is filled with it a little bit too. Therefore, Class of Gentiles who are not disabledships here, please come forward and forth into your own life's reckonings here! To study the Bible is one thing here, but to become "disabled" is your life's meaningful properties of sweat glands just carrying out of the pieces of the past here that you just assume not come into contact with anyone of the opposite sex here! Say, Jesus was such a looker in His time, back in the days of no makeup for guys or men though? That's hardly the case there in Egyptian times and soils here! That makeup is for the guys to contend with though, in Germany no less and no more here! That said here, what is the Jezibellie's makeup's concern with the opposite sex here?

It means, Folks and Class of Gentiles later here, that there are supposedly more makeup stories than there ever were here in classy 90210, back in the days of that television show remarked a new beginning of time's essences here! We just mean, Folks, that the hairstyles back in the days of 90210 is really something to believe in here! We're just saying, Folks and Class of Gentiles here, that there's public properties to uphold to, and there's trespassing in my future then! Do you know what it means to trespass on a private property though? It really has to do with the time of day, does it? Then, what if Rapunzel really didn't want her dad's mansion to overflow with her suitors back in the days of Tijuana though! And to state it that way for her actual boyfriend was to have an actual Rapunzel, back in the days when he was coming over and stuff! The dad actually set up a "trespass" for this new fellow of interesting times for Rapunzel!

Then she lopped off her hair because of it then? Nope! He climbed up there on it too! Interestingly enough here is the fable's tattletalenesses of Jezibellie Christ! Because the King of England here did not want Her to perish either, Folks and Classes of Gentiles later, Folks too! This is because the King of England wanted to find out the parish's evil ways and phone calls here! There are just as many phone call shape ups here as there were on your evilest ways here, Andrea, as her family still thinks she is evil no more I presume! Finally though? Yes, finally here!

Say, is Jesus no more enthralled with the story or fable of Rapunzel here? She's an actual person in history here. Save the 900 sheep that God was given to sheer them though, was a feat in and of itselves here! Say, is that a word there, as it is written in scriptures as itself here, regarding the latent Paul Williams then?

Nope, not the Young and the Restless's Paul Williams here, but a Paul Wright later, a Paul Lucifer Wright, as he used to go by his middle name all the time here, and that gave us the inklingships to destroy the nighttime sniffling, sneezing, aching, coughing, stuffy head, fever, so you can rest medicine, is actually for the birds if Andrea cannot remember that quote word for word here. We consult Google every step of the ways here but not for the pharaohs though? Let's! This book oversees many others in comparison here! That book called "Jesus Ways" has yet to be written upon U.S. soils here! But comedies and tragedies later, Folks and meaningful Gentiles later, Folks, is bound to come out necessarily so here!

So, there were the pharaohs of the time's past here that state that Martin Luther King, Jr. was just out to address the nation's talks on peacetime war heroes and such when he received that fateful phone call from someone, saying he was going to die. And, some such heroes at the time were Martin Luther for sure he is a King in some respects here! Balancures just talk about dying of cancer, as he used to smoke like a chimney back in the days and work's meaningful clauses here! Because on that fateful day as well here that he died no less on the cross is what it means here, Folks, because it means that the man died a fateful death! He was in bed no less and no more here when it happened upon Him that He not become the king's ultimate death threat here, and now there's time and ruins to uphold to! Take a look at Chapter 2 if you don't believe in the spirit worlds here! And, comedy and tragedy later, Folks and meaningful Gentiles too here, we don't believe in Martin Luther's words that he was going to rain on anybody's parades here! He was a true gentleman!

Here is the text and folklore of the man who Jesus was back in the day, as Lord and Savior of this planet of apes here! See Chapters 12 and 14 for the cures of Jesus Christ back in the day, say, 20 years ago though, if we would've come out like this in her family, Andrea's thereof here, then we'd say that God's kingdoms are wretched. And blankmanships later, Folks and meaningful Gentiles later, Folks, is to say or to state that Martin Luther King, Jr. was sure a king back in his day! The times and faithfulness's best boss for the job though is somebody like Martin Luther King, Andrea! That said too, that father of his is resting peacefully with us, as well as an irreverent comment about the Paul that carried the middle name of Lucifer! Back in the days of Jesus Christ though, a fallen "angel" like this is really not in the cards for Mr. Lucifer!

So, back in the days of Lucifer and Sunkist oranges, as this guy coined the phrases of Egypt's times and basilica for the coming days of Jesus Christ's wrath and ruling here! So far, the rest of the world's greatest Jesus cures are commonly back in the days of Jesus Christ's rulings here! This book, Jesus: Last of the Pharaohs by Ralph Ellis is commonly known to God's wrath and rulings as a true story book, especially what he says on pages 1-99 of the first New Testament!

It's because of this though that the Pharaohs are lovely indeed here! We think that the rulings of a statuette of, say, Jezibellie, is worth commenting upon though, as she did comb her hair straight and stuff! We all coaxed Jesus's long hair then? He actually was a clean-shaven man for most of His life up there on the pedestal of hope and faith here! He was the most precious leader Egypt had ever seen here! We do know that the last hope and testament of Jesus Christ was written in the English language here! He was tall too, like 6'3" perhaps though? Nope, say 6' even here!

He's precious to "Us" in the English languages here! As people could speak Egyptian throughout the lands of Mesopotania here! For wars fought on English language's soils here were never foughten like the foughten wars of Mesopotania here! This citizen's arrest upon His soul though in Egypt never happened that way here. We couldn't find or locate this brethren of hope, then, Paul Williams Wright then?

We say this because he changed his name frequently here, and Paul Williams is a nice man on The Young and the Restless that I know and love here!

So, balancatures later, Folks and Gentiles, meaningful though they are here, are not citizen's arrests made on His blankmanships here! Say, is blankmanships the same as blankmanships in context though, as there were 40 people on His doorstep one day, trying to get into the same things that the Holy Spirit, or, in context here, the Holy Ghost, was doing! They wanted to try to get into His mind and such! For the Holy Spirit or Ghost to enter into your souls, He said, they wanted Him to travel with His messages and such? Was Paul a ghost or simply laid to rest on the Egyptian soils then? Nope, he's in Thessaloniki now!

I do declare a mistrial of sorts, in land and in deeds, to rest ourselves with the Holy Spirit or Ghost, in its final affairs though! Simply put, Peoples, and you too Gentiles, is that a cloud of hope is resting upon the factors of hope, in courage, and in peace meals too! That Christlike laughter of His was sure contagious!

And, just because He simply loved Jezibellie from birth does not mean that they were separated from His 15-year-old was it, nope, the 16-year-olds they were, to get married this early though was a faux pas from life here, was it then? Nope, either of them could not get married until they were 21 in this country though! That was the United States, right? Nope! They can get married in college then? Say, we went to school too! That was a religious church ceremony's dream here on The Young and the Restless here! Say, there were tons of religious sects back in the days of Jesus Christ's team of Gentiles too! And, yes, Jesus was a Jewish person of minor intelligence though? Of vast intelligence then! This section is solely, and I do mean a Jewish wedding is in proper attirely very handsome indeed here then, that there's mostly spokenformanships in this wedding attire that He so fiercely called the commandant's final resting places here! Say, are we in Egyptian soils though? Not when Roma, called Rome, decided to contradict what we were playing with here!

That said here, we outlawed all gunships. And that was a nice gesture to do that for God's kingdoms here! There were tons of wars foughten on Japanese soils too, but none like this one before the Lordship!

We were a peaceful civilization back then! We really loved the Japanese, because they interested us in coming back to peaceful territories back then! And so, why the Trichomycin/Hachimycin pill blankmanships then, huh! It's a peaceful territories thing!

Then the time came that God listened to about 40 other hits to my person here! It said that God really liked to be a Pharaoh, but that He listened with a strained ear most of the time here! And, that said, we're trying on a few Pharaoh's hats here, and insisting that Martin Luther King, Jr., be said to be a saint here!

And, that said here, we're done with that message's mystifying outlooks here! We're trying to come to terms with a comatose settlement on the best man's best wedding here! And, Jesus Christ as Lord and Savior here, was told by the Christianity population back then that He could certainly marry a White girl! Sorry, Folks, the Delilah chapter is done for, right?

I don't want to talk about it, Jesus says? Yes, and so what then! Go ahead, Andrea! Tell all, okay! So, Jesus married Jezibellie in the Winter of 1957 when the cops came out on this pill that was manufactured overseas. Say, we are stupid then!

Because we use all kinds of circular reasonings to get that pill back into the U.S. then? We used to have it, according to one gal I ran into, when I told her about it, way back when I was still getting hair used to habits by the jails and pretty hoppers that they used to tweak it back then. And, say, it was a hairdresser or hairstylist I was supposed to be in a past life though?

Those psychic mediums that tell all here state that there's nothing but a simple, sinister look of yourselves if they say to you here that, you will be a hairdresser, Andrea! Nothing could be furthest from the truth though!

I don't want to be a hairstylist no more, she says, LOL! Say, a hairstylist could simply be a Delilah hoax, as we sinisterly believe her to be the reincarnate of Jezibellie Christ here, with her simple DSW here, say, I don't believe it either! So, take a hike, Gentiles of the subclasses here! There's motion detectors here above the laws of gravity that state that a ruined look to your hair here is about the meaningful's blessings in disguise then, as this person had taken Trichomycin/Hachimycin before here for an ear infection though? Nope, it's the trichomonas/trichomoniasis that calms the nerves for this lady whom I saw just after an eye infection! Meaning, Folks and Class of Gentiles here, that God's other lady must have a reason for picking Him, right? The laws of gravity defy what the Holy Spirit is about then.

Say, do you have a disease calling Him right now then, as the laws of gravity specifically state that it's about 98.2 seconds at the rates of beings here. That simply states to us that we're defying the laws of gravity too, the DSW is then, huh! Maybe it's Newton's law of gravitational pull that we need to go here from, not necessarily so then? Well? It's a gravitational pull of the Earth's seismic proportions that states it here then! Because a ruler is a ruler is a ruler here? Nope! And Paul is not to be mentioned here anymore then? It's because of His rulership that we state the lovely Divine Source Wisdom is mentioned nilly willy in the kind of willy nilly there takes to accommodate someone like Paul Wright, Lucifer is his middle name here for sure! So, bide our times here, but gun laws? Who needs them without a society of spearheads and such though?

Oh, absolutely! But, hanging somebody who didn't need to be hanged though? From the rafters! And I will say this lightly here, too, Class of Gentiles I didn't need here. Such is the willy nilly, because of it though! Say, this is brightly the points here that I tried to make back in Chapters 2 and 3 here, that said, My sons and daughters, Jesus said, are right here for the taking then! This pogo stick's lessons planning though states that God is a Gentile then, correctamundos here!

Delilah, by the way that she told us here in the past, Folks and Gentiles too, is that she is a hairdresser by trade, and gladly tailspinned Andrea into a loop about this. For art thou messaging Me about the leaches she put upon My body once, as a tradesman of sorts here? This is how it's done, Andrea Wynn here!

Chapter 24

NASA – The Final Frontier: Jesus Died on the Cross is a Hoax

Another photo of "Us," the Andromeda Galaxy (ESA/Hubble).

This is war! These two lovebirds, Jezibellie Christ and Jesus Christ, are honestly in the solar system's biggest war on life here! This means She's honestly scriptural about this Bible verses stuff! She gets it with no problems here! That said too, what does "honestly" really mean here? Jezibellie Christ, will You marry Me again here!

That said, are you really going to love me if I spew my blood all over the place here? The meanings behind "Jesus's blood" is really a hoax here. Let me explain this thoroughly in Chapters 12 and 13 here. The Archbasilica of St. John (Lateran) here is where we're buried! We tried to explain it to the doctors of chance here, but this is how God's wraths never listen to us here! We're trying to explain it for the worlds to seek here, refugees from the planet's Izod comings into play here, because we love it so much, the planet Earth, you see it, now you don't here! That place was named after our son, John the Baptist! He's literally the only wretched individual here who would live for "the blood of Jesus" here? Not hardly so!

In essences here, we are stating that the Archbasilica of St. John Lateran, and we put that there because of why? Not enough last names to go around here, but that's his middle name too? Nothing could be furthest from the truth! It's Christ, Guys, John Christ? So, anyhoo, there are names in Lateran that could be a middle name or a forestry last name, as this man and this woman made love under a tree rug one year and conceived another child. Just then, She was in labor and we go, let's get to a surgeon right away then? Nope, Jesus was a surgeon back then, and cut those babies out by hand! In Chapter 7, we spoke of this too, the burials of Jesus and Jezibellie Christ, but those of John the Baptist, John Christ, Guys, was buried back in Egyptian soils here. That's where we wanted to be too! But they took us by surprise one day and one year here, and told us we are going to be buried in Taiwan, because that's where Andrea stays sometimes there with a group of people we call God's gift to women then? Well, nope!

There's also the post office of love here that says, we had a job there once! We were never seeking out a promised land, however! That is because the post office is a little bit unwary about generosities and stuff! Landed a job there and loved it, every minute of it here! I was fully on my meds at the time! And, that spoke a lot about who and where and when, but this meant that Jesus Christ superstar is right there for the takings here! We got her that job there, and then she ran out of gas someplace, which, lucky for her, she ended up in another hospital and lost all her meds here for being a postal worker! So, like I said in Chapter 15, there were normal people around me there! Then, there was one gal who was not allowed to shave her armpits for the duration of being there at this place! She was not allowed to shave them though? I mean, why do this to a person with a four month track record in a place where she's not allowed to pee though, on command then?

I bet, and I doubt very much here, that there are people who want to shave their legs as rapidly as I did there, because I was only there a week and a half, and lost my position at the post office because of it. So, the question mark between God's laces and stuff means that we're all waiting for an answer here from God as to whether she can actually do that job, and the answer's, yes, absolutely so! She loved that job, every minute of it, during the only two months she was with the post office here!

That said here, what does NASA's entitlements have to do with "Us" though? Because "We're" galaxies away from looking like a man or a woman does here! We're millions of "voices" all wrapped up into one segment's timingships here. But only one voice pokes through for Us, here ye, and that's a wrap on those "voices" we think we hear? Say, this bipolarism in American soils is the reason for the cutoff from the post office here! And, that said, they think I'm bipolar or something like it here, because at every single hospital since the beginning of time here, say, 2014? They think I'm bipolar no more, I suppose! Because of a personality conflict, someone can just say, I'm flying high today, I needed a rest or something like it. You see it, now you don't!

We just mean that if you're on bipolarism meds, which I'm very allergic to, by the way, it means that God is watching us. Just as in Biblical times when, rest assured, there were homeless people by the waysides here! It meant that God was just horny or something like it, you see it, now you do? That means, simply, that God's wraths in Chapter 37 talk more about the bipolarisms that exist! That is because we're the only country in the world who has "bipolar disorder" in their DSM-3 manuals then? Try the DSM-5 here! In 1947, we only had one available "bipolar disordered" mental state here! And schizophrenias were God's countries, very sinister indeed here!

We're saying that the God given rights for bipolar disorders are discussed further in Chapter 37.

We're saying that God wanted us to know about the planets of bipolarly aligned peoples here! There are several guestbooks in the office of love's talents here that state that bipolarly aligned peoples never state it for the records of times past here!

We're simply stating a newness in the time following bipolarly aligned peoples here! And, nothing could be furthest from the truth's beck and call girls here! Say, this is where people need to pay attention here! There are drugs that make us fat and ugly called Seroquel. And, the likes of someplace else to give a Zyprexa hug to somebody who's drunk off the stuff can tell that in a certain hospital, I was given a shot or two for not complying with my medication intakes though? This is the same doctor who saw me there, and then saw me at the place where they were sending me out the door with a coffee and a donut to boot here!

And, that said here, we're sort of getting to the promised lands, because of our inkling cures and stuff! Inklingships are tired of focusing on the talent search's best hospital lands here, but I had fun, an absolute blast at the post office though! And now, they tried to fire me because of the hospital system's email system then! Because this is how potently aware I am as a federal employee! I never saw the likes of myself as an employee that hated that job at all here. But it worked out for the best here? Andrea thinks we sabotaged her methods of her madnesses and said, "This can't be done."

Because this happened here, because it's stated in scriptures in Chapter 24 of Matthew, and we're so sorry for the mishaps there, Andrea! But this Chapter 4 in other words of Matthew here is where the promises of tomorrow's land shapes are really poignant and stuff! That's because, at least in my version here, she says, it's the King James Version because the guy actually published the darn thing for us here! And, that said here, there are versions of James's talking in these chapters here that Paul'd just assume not answer to here. Because of all the red letterings in the book of James too, it means that, and there are no red letters in this chapter here! But this means that the whole book of James, too, is what is coming down the pike's best offerings about the landships and stuff like it. You see it, now you don't, Andrea!

The fuzzy pictures that God's good book literally means today is the sufferin' succotash of speak easy riddles and such here too!

Therefore, here, the last book and testament of Jesus Christ literally means that our suffering and such is for the birds here, Folks! We'd just assume fast for 40 days and 40 nights without promises to us here! We mean that there are citizens' arrests and stuff. That means something to the higher powers to be here! And, yes, is Heaven in "space" then? Heaven is right here on Earth! It's a meadow or something like it! I don't know what is the meadow that God created for us here! But this is how God's telecommunications from Earth's shadow busters are not going to ridicule us no more of being bipolarly aligned with God's miscommunications here!

We're not bipolar anymore either here! They, the doctors and such, put us within these three categories here because we're either afraid to expand our knowledges here, or we're so bipolarly "schizo" that we're trying to find other words with which to find God in here! Like I said here, bipolarly so here, we are saying that the orders of the vicinities for NASA's expansions into the universe's crusts here are so minutely taken from us here, that we ought not complain about a little old librarian like Andrea here! Simply put here, there is none other than God's ultra languages about the coming of Christ and things like it!

You see it, now You do, Jezibellie Christ, and we're enthralled with becoming the social butterfly's best takings upon life's quandaries here! That is because the Earth's crust has the best Heavens already upon it here! Heaven is beautiful. That's for sure here!

Say, there's kingdom comes, thy will be done, Earth as it is in Heaven's names here, to be continued though, as we don't know the full scripture's wraths yet! Yes, Andrea! Bless us our Lord for these thy gifts, which we are about to receive, through thy bounty, through Christ our Lord, Amen! Amen, Andrea, for trying out the Lord's Prayer too! We are strength in numbers very great indeed! Here is a copy of the Lord's Prayer, for all to tell about here! Bless us our Lord? Scratch that one here! That one, her dad used to lovingly say to her as a child here. That's a meaningful prayer for "Us" to glom onto here. But the Lord's Prayer..., here we go! Bless us our Lord! Haha! We're saying that God's kingdom comes, thy will be done, on Earth as it is in Heaven's gates here, is about the same prayer here! Thy will be done then?

Our father who art in Heaven, hallowed be thy name, thy kingdom come, thy will be done, on Earth as it is in Heaven. Give us this day our daily bread, and to forgive us our trespasses, lead us not into temptation, but deliver us from evil. We took a part out of it because it's so redundant, but if you want to forgive "Us" our trespasses, God, go right ahead and listen to the Andromeda looking galaxy's biggest and best temptations. For "Us" to really go without the power of the Lord Jesus Christ is, really, to tell "Us" of our promises of nature's bounties here.

Say, that's a very good donut you're listening to us with there, Andrea, as she can be a cop in natures and in bountiful presences here! Say, does Heaven really exist! Within the confines of the state capitol buildings here, we just don't know about the times it takes for "Us" to really believe that the Andromeda Galaxy is "Us" here! And, sorry, that said here, we're never living in Bellingham, for the Andromeda Galaxy had us there for about eight years during our undergraduate work there at Western Washington University here, and we long for that city sometimes!

But this is never how the Lord's Prayer ends up on every doorstep, to include Bellingham's proper nouns here! But it's a college town! If my license expires very soon here, I'd like to be noticed for the post offices of love here!

If you've ever been in to a postmaster's office here, you will find out how a suspended license gets you unhooked for love here! And, that said here, there's always somebody finding out about life's terrible jeans cures here! Say, are we herpes bound then? Because we're all herpes bound if we're not getting onto the bandwagons of trust here and eliminating it entirely here, Folks! Right, CDC, the Centers for Disease Control and Prevention here! Just go to Chapter 12 and Chapter 37 and ridicule this legacy! Maybe that is your true job's work there, Andrea!

More often than not though, there's lots of bandwagons here to state that a Podunk job like at the post office then is really no more than a series of telecommunication hopes and dreams here! You got the job, worked it, and then left. Therefore, don't call me crazy here, miscarriage girl, but tell us why you think you'd gotten the job there in the first place? Well? Don't call me there, because I've got a suspended license from the hopper!

I do believe that the suspects in Chapter 4's dream codes gets well tested here. And, that said here, there's some negative evidence in space that takes a lot of dream testing out of the bathwater of the sinister looking, belief mongering individuals here, like, say, Andrea, for example here! We just wanted to work for the post office so bad here, that they decided to jack her license because of it here? Nope! Just the cities and post offices of love here are that cozy with the ideas of a lifetime's hope of dreams and what nots here. That said, what is the promise of tomorrow's cozy jeans cures, but to take a hit of acid? In other words here, she has not done any drugs as of lately, as of ever, except for a few acid hits once. And, that's the ticket here, like her doting father would say to her here!

I do declare a mistrial in deeds and in wantings here! For art thou balanced and kosher and cool about it though! Yep!

We're trying to get the deals and stuff out of the bathwater's biggest and blessedness's biggest and best commandants, for this is Jesus Christ dealing with these bathwater comments here!

There are tons of cool jobs out there, Andrea! But this means that working for NASA might be an invention in aerospace of the talent search's contests here! Appendix 4 deals with the "latest" high and mighty askings about how the aerospace talent search's greatest fears comes together with the latest and last, biggest and best commandants for the languages of the Divine Source Wisdom here! And, that's DSW for short here! That's "Us" and "We" here, Folks of the commandant's types here! There's massively impulse buys on that time capsule we call bipolarisms in American soils here, because the rest of the world does not allergic themselves to every mood stabilizer there ever was here! This is because the only unrest we travel to here is the fact that on every street corner, as evidenced by "Us" here, there are herpes infested people, everywhere you turn, on every street corner, on every legal street there ever was here.

And, I can tell if someone has it, simply by asking God to show me the ways and means it lady's Chapter 12 and 37 here! Say, by the way here, will the CDC ask for God's forgivenesses for letting a tiny lady slip through the cracks here?

Because the balancatures are sure ripe for the pickings here! Chapter 4 deals with outer space too. Right, Andrea! Nope! But it deals with Santa Claus then, as there are lots of Mary Bongs Magdalene's who are his age too. Right, Andrea! She's way older than Jesus Christ was! And, Lordships later, Folks, there are possibly three people right in line with God's oldest son, Jesus, that He never would have picked another limelight's biggest and best policies here! Say, this is God's oldest son then? Yep! Was Buddha it then, another son of God's helpers here? Nope! Just Jesus so far! I mean, does Jezibellie look like Me here, cause that's a misnomer that we're all commandants and stuff. Right, Andrea! We're picking on her here because of the greatest dangers in life's biggest and best policies here! Say, we loved Michael Jackson so much so that as a kid she, Andrea did, not Jezibellie Christ here, LOL, have his poster above her bed at one point! He's such a looker back in the day, huh! Let's just say, those kids of his had a proper upbringing! And, that's a fact here! We bring up the dead because it means that God's watching us from afar here! Say, it means that God's worth it! It means that, as an Andromeda Galaxy, with tons of stuff left for the Gods here, doesn't mean to state or to say it differently here, that God's talent search's biggest and best leftovers here means that God's surely bigger and better and faster than the news ever was here! This means that space, deep space nine, and such, are simply biggest and best told on the telescopes of lifetimes of habits here. And, "Suddenly" by Billy Ocean is the simplest song in the world here for Andrea to grasp at here, but life on Earth is here, Folks, h-e-r-e, not in some cosmos! Give a deli a sign or a hint here that you love their stuff enough to buy it here!

In that case, we'd just assume buy everything that the deli of choice comes at here! In other words, Folks and you too, Gentiles, here, state that, for the record here, there is some truth to that! I mean, take what you can get! Take what you came here for and breathe a little bit about Saturn's ugly face's meanest poses up there with those alien rings surrounding it! Say, what is Neptune's actual orbit but around the sun though? Not! It's around Pluto then? Nope, Pluto's but a rock! And so, the actual turmoiled ways about finding out about Jupiter's moons, which have homo sapiens, or wise guys, actually found out inside of their own planets up there! Knowingly, Hon, we cannot communicate with God about actual love lives to be here! We can simply go forth and just know that God's best angel cures are talented by living the actual lives of Jupiter's moons here!

And, the hills of Taiwan later, look just like Jupiter's moons here! The actual lives we take in the hills of foremost promises in the dark, as Pat Benatar would have to say here, that actual lives we are trying to communicate with, are what's called the dark shots of society's influences! Say, this is a lot like the "bipolar" epidemic is here! Do they have bipolar too then? Not in the least! We're a society who likes and loves the questions that take us to the bank here though! Say, winning the lottery is not in the cards for Andrea here! We are saying that, she has this tremendous gift here, but winning numbers is all in the cards and sands of time here. That said, we are not saying that we don't love you, Andrea! But to win the lottery is but of chance only.

And, that said here, what kinds of lottery pickings are we enthused with about here! There's pleasantries on this Earth and beyond here. There are alien life forms in the galaxies, sure! But they pretty much look like us here on Earth then, yes? Absolutely! Please keep in mind that that post office job called her name for many years here, and then we got hired, but then refused to let go of the DSW.

And so, we're kind of listening to God's wraths here, and stating that, even though she hates her current position in life here, we're settling upon the facts here, that she likes to write this book out here! Because we were galaxying Andrea for two-fold peanuts here at this other job of hers here! There's lovely interventions about peaceable times for all here! And, God is mentioning us in the galaxy's new twist on life's interventions here, that God knows about our fears about black holes, for instances here! We're saying that God's interventions are just what the doctors ordered here!

We know why the black holes interest Andrea so much here, from neighborhood astronomy classes! But this is how and why it is done here! We're so enthused that Canada is so close to the America's borders here that says, why don't we have mental health care aligned with the truth's oldest books and such? Well, because we're ingenuitous about it here in the States! We're tired of running the ragged's love life affairs here that we're going to masturbate about it here, not! What I'm saying here is that, a love life means everything to human beings worldwide here, and that means that ingenuitous questions and such are likewise the only human being's deepest and foremostly trying times here! And, that said here, there are ingenuitous peoples everywhere on this planet Earth's crusts here that God would just assume not answer to here! Save those pedophiles for human extinction here! And, that said too here, why would God not answer to a bunch of pedophiles for? And, light of God's existence here is said to believe in the planet Mars's Earthly crust on it here! Just because it's "red" and "of the devil" does not mean that Saturn's rings are not for the takings here, as it's Jupiter's moons who have a central orbit's plentiful figures and such! We're saying here, Folks and Classes of Gentiles who measure the Lordship's name in vain here, which, by the way, go ahead and say, "God," all the time here! It's a nice word to have in your vocabularies here! By the way, say, "Jesus Christ," too, for that matter! It's all in the cards to have Jupiter's moons speak to us here! What is the problem with Moses's talent searches here, that states that we shall not take the Lord's name in vain here? Do you think that Jupiter or Saturn for that matter dictates or cares that you are saying the Lord's name in vain here?

Because those two planets alone do not have a solar system that loves it as much as a bipolar orbit does! What does a woman do on Her wedding day, when they were 16-years-old though, and says, I'd just become natural at one thing here, and state for the recordships here that God ought to be smaller about this word problem here! And, that said here, we are trying to tell you all about the Earth's crusts here! We're going to dive deep into the ocean's bottoms here later in life. Mkay! Chapter 31 deals with the ocean's crusts too. And, that said here, there are biologists that are interested in many of the things that you hold dear to, Andrea! That means, Folks and Classes of Gentiles later, Folks, that God's biggest dealings with the Divine Source Wisdom means that God's only wishes for a greater tomorrow, and not the Ten Commandments here, that said that in the first place here, that only God is able to throw someone out of church when they are attending the "voices" of God's wraths here! And, that is all it means by not taking the Lord's name in vain here, is to call the "bipolarisms" to boot here liars, for they know not what they do! If you get "voices," the bad kind we mean, and Andrea used to hear that too, then they say the Lord's name in vain by putting Him down and such! Well, try to get a rest on that headache cure then!

We're selling you on this point, are we? We're trying to tell you that the "wrong" voices are the ones who "take the Lord's name in vain," by simply pointing out that you're so "evil" that you couldn't possibly be worth the time it takes to hear the good "voices" though! You are so evil, they'd say! Well? That's taking the Lord's name and using it for other purposes here! So, that commandment still stands here!

Well, what if I was a postal worker and heard nothing of the kinds of things they'd say to me then! What of this doctor at the hospital that let me go with no meds and a taxi ride did I immediately like about the guy! He's a bipolar trigger happy person no more then! I was impressed by his news that I was no longer disabled then if I could withstand the post office fodder no more then! I mean, what do these places do to us but take us to the bank, and sell our homes, and keep us ridiculed into sexual slavery, for example! I mean, what is the commandant's bestest and willingnessed promises of the dark side supposed to tell us here!

We're ridiculing Jupiter's planetary alignment. Shall we post this here about Osama Bin Laden though? The guy's a goon. He really has nothing to do with the commandants in this country, let alone the Middle Eastern ways of saying, how do you do, Obamas!

Because I promise you, Andrea, this gets left alone a lot here! There are ways that you can overcome these dark, negative voices, though it's difficult at best! So, how to you distinguish between God's "voices," in check and in alignment of God's creatures? Do you want to have them with you then! Yes, indeed you do! So, make it up as you go along, Andrea! Because she heard those negative voices back in the 1920s is it, nope, in 2005 and 2006. So, she was much more attuned to things back then, as well as the deep seated question marks about God's faiths and such! We want to explore the Neptune's orbit, the NASA peoples stated, for therefore who art in Heaven, hallowed be thy name, thy kingdom come, thy will be done, on Earth, Peoples! On Earth, as it is in Heaven then? Yes! This Earth is the best that "We" have given you, Peoples.

In trying hard to reconcile with this best man's orbits here, there are planetary alignments in God's wakes here! If you're trying to say the Lord's name in vain, by the way, you are trying hard to not be evil! "Making use of the tongues of God" is like saying that God's raptures are sinisterly unhooked to God's tantalizing evils here! We're so enthused about this book, Andrea Wynn! Keep going here!

There's tantalizing evils here and there are truths be told planets on the other side of the hopper's bled and best cures here! Say, Jesus never said to drink my blood here and call it good here! He said, come to papa, Andrea Wynn, right here?

Nope, to Jezibellie Christ though, He is the most sensual man on Earth! I can attest to that, Andrea says, because there are gift horses in the mouth that we're looking at. As a sensual man then, what planet are you from then, again, Jesus Christ here! Because the one we all know and love was "sexless!"

Well, that's a hint from God, then to go, well, I wouldn't know! Hint, hint! Jezibellie Christ was all too wary about this here, as all they did was fuck like rabbits then! Well? What are we after here, but God's tender graces here! We are after the sex life of Jesus Christ then? Well? What are we after here, but telling the truth about God's tender honeys at the local hopper of Judaism here!

Because that's what Jewish people did all the time. Right, Andrea! Well? What do you know about Judaic Christianity here! I really don't know anything at all about the topics at hand here!

Well, try to find out about medical school's costs and stuff and then come back to Me and tell Me how it's done here: Yes! It's about medical school for a Jesus Christ, to come and to hold babies that he'd just cut out of Her skins then, Folks and Classes of Gentiles later, Folks!

I do mean it when I state that He was nakedly asking Her forgiveness several times, because they only get enough chew on their duffs here. To state it so openly here though, we're like, this is Jezibellie Christ talking. Correctamundos here? Save a little blurb here and there, Folks, and meaningful Gentiles later, Class of citizenries and stuff!

We're just stating that God's only pony shows have never been so fruitful as God's undying love was for His wife then, in tow. Correctamundos here? And, in other words here, we were so enthused with Jupiter's timings here that God now said there are a whole 57 moons to count from here, and four of them have life on them! We're talking about how they like to steal our water from us though, our ocean water! Because they do! It's so funny, too, because there's times to steal our water from the parables that exist, Andrea, but these claims are pretty far-fetched. "We're still here though," Jesus says of His wife and son now! He's talking about John the Baptist then? Well, yes, and several other people of our times then! As in, when Jezibellie came around the corner of the sinisterly foughten times about its peoples here, there were some nunchucks that symbolized the coming of Eden's greatest fears here! We're so into Donna Eden's energy medicine that we don't realize the coming of God's graces here is just like a fruitful sort of bantering back and forth here! One more thing is that Jupiter and the Sun love each other! Grab a hold of that why don't you?

We're tantalizing the spirit's deepest requests of God's here! To valancure the tidings though is really something here, isn't it, Jesus Christ here? That's Jezibellie, is it here, nope! That's our sons and daughters that never really hung onto the facts here!

That God's echoes are still here, hoping for our sons and daughters to return after a miscarriage or an abortion here, states that they will if they are chosen to be in your parent's wakes, Andrea Wynn! She's letting us state it here for a fact then, that God is choosing the DSW to really reckon with the times past here!

Say, there are turkeys in the oven then, June, July and September of this year, is there? Because the other onslaught of finding out if the Mayflower even returned our phone calls here said that Christopher Columbus was a moron, in and of his own takings here! And, that said here, there are tons of history lessons we'd just assume not get into at this writing's talent searches here! And, that said here, what is Christopher Columbus's rights of passage that He took with Him in order to find out what the Jesus cures really meant here?

Because this guy knew small pox pretty well here, and ordered the tens of thousands of Native Americans, which, by the way, we loved the continent of Africa so much that we flew everywhere and could travel over to this continent too, the United States one here. So anyhoo, what is the commandant's first languages supposed to small pox us with, but to let the Native Americans go here would have been His plight in the first place here!

We just needed to be honest with our plights here! We're NASA bound, are we here? Say, what is her job supposed to be now? Cause we're really good at politics too! Hint, hint! ☺

Chapter 25

You Can Heal Your Life by Louise Hay is It!

I like the Divine Source Wisdom so much so that I think and believe that they're responsible for writing the Bible themselves here! I think they did too, Jesus said to us here! That said, how did They, We, do this then? She, Jezibellie Christ, started to hear things, just as you did here, Andrea! And that was the fact's only blessings was that she started typing it, much like you are doing, or have been too. Focused is the word here!

I do believe in mistrials though! This "Jesus in the Bedroom" scripts here are for the taking, and take Her, I would do that too! This is Jesus Christ speaking! I do declare a mistrial no more then, because this is the only scripts that takes Us to the Bible's only "bedroom" attires here. And no more than a rag for a waist garment here is what I had on the cross's only journeys here! That said too, there are no more people's choice awards for this predicament's timings here. But to say it on the cross like this is no cigar. No more inklingships. Correctamundos here!

You Can Heal Your Life by Louise Hay is a good book to get to know here. Another one is All is Well: Heal Your Body with Medicine, Affirmations and Intuition by her also! In it, and these chapters are wary from extinction here, there are tons of good tables worth of affirmations in them! We have certain bodily ailments and particular seances for each kind.

So, for example, the mental health courts suck by the way, and we're asking for God's favorites when we mention them here! So, for example too, there are sometimes peoples in the makings here that say, "You mean you put affirmations up on your wall to attract this 'thing' in you here?" "That is exactly what I'm saying here!" The lawyers make up lies, I will grant you that! And, that's the truth here! But listen to the Divine Source Wisdom on these Louise Hay quotes, because I can bet you that she experienced her bouts with mental health, questioning her every move here, and obviously surpassed their questioning!

Until she got bold enough to publish her works here! And that said, I have not spoken with her personally, but she is writing this book alongside of us here today too! She goes, a new speaker for the dozens of personalities that I have come across here, Andrea, is that She's not too close to "Us" here! Meaning, Folks, that Jezibellie is not even coming into contact with such affirmations here, not! And, that is the meaning's wordings here behind mental health courts here! "I used Eckhart Tolle's 'the present moment' ideas and concepts, and I just healed it, you know?" And the judge just looks at me and goes, "I'm sorry, but 'inappropriate touching' is what you're here for," correctamundos here? You mean that Black guy, dude or whatever, who was telling me he was Jesus Christ? I go, "Um, dude," and I touched his arm!

And he goes, "I'm simply the Savior, and you need to bow down to me here!" And, I go, "I just don't think you're Jesus Christ here!" all while touching his arm though? "Inappropriate touching?" I said? What on Earth is that! Off with her head then! I mean, this kept her silent, the judge did, about becoming an angel on this Earth there in this particular hospital's sucky, and I do mean sucky, post exterior moment's notices on my brain here. In that case, to use Louise Hay's affirmations and such and to post them everywhere for my consumption is so "A Beautiful Mind" movie like, correctamundos here? I healed myself with her affirmations, so this is quite off!

That guy in that movie, by the way here, could see voices being printed, just like this too, just like normal intuition for a guy does. Most men will tell you they don't have this phenomenon but they do. That movie is so cliché that we don't even claim it as a "good one"!

There are tons of printed volumes upon this "pedo head" that lingers from schizophrenics, who start to hallucinate though? Men don't hallucinate, they have visions though! Keep in mind that this means that Louise Hay's affirmation market's pretty darned neat if you ask me, "Us," and thus and so on!

We started to, back when I didn't believe in God anymore, LOL, carry these Louise Hay's affirmations with me wherever I went on my walks around the neighborhoods here! I was nursing an SI joint (sacroiliac joint) injury when I was doing them, and that cured my Beatrice hound dog posts! A Beatrice simply means that we like changing our moods around, according to the Urban Dictionary's postings about schizophrenias and schizophrenics, bipolars and schizoaffectives alike too!

And, that said here, what do affirmations have to do with the colonoscopies we sometimes have to get here! Because using those laxatives to "go" with is really detrimental to your systems! But anyhoo, if you're like me and don't use a lot of laxatives to go, then try our hands at coming to terms with the most professional lady on the planet of Oz here, and go with it! We're trying to say here that the mental house soup kitchens have much to be desired here? They had the best food ever! That's a way to make or break a house with minimal soup kitchens here! Say, that colonoscopy's never going to produce a polyp again or two or three in your lifetime's helpers, Andrea! Say, don't use the laxatives, Peoples, but use them sparingly? It's taken over three years of this moment's whereabouts to find a lesson's plannings, here ye!

And, that said here, there are messages and memos to contend with here! The Power of Now: A Guide to Spiritual Enlightenment got me into the slammer so fast! I was only witnessing her own, the judge's own, battles to stay focused, there with her "schizophrenic" son in law here! By that, I do mean her son's a good guy here, but he has schizophrenia too! So, at this particular hospital, there were tons of innuendoes from a person who was supposed to be in my favor in that courtroom here! He's on the phone and cannot hear her even, and professed or proclaimed that I'd put "affirmations all over my walls," as if it's a crime or something like it! You see it, now you don't here! Which means, Folks, and Classes of Gentiles later, Folks, that God's in that courtroom to tell you you're insane enough for your family to think that you are insane.

And, that means that someone, somebody, somewhere noted you were wanted in this lifetime of affairs here! That's all that the mental health courts are about here! We just wanted to see if you were a good enough person to "mental health" instead of "taking you to the slammer" for peeing and pissing everywhere here! They don't care one iota or bit if you are "healing yourselves from trauma." This is because this "genetics" factor between God's health and the ones you're using to deliver yourselves from evil here, are for the birds, as well as the hope or the promised lands of Jesus and Jezibellie Christ's love here. To state it that way is to say or to state that families, "it runs in families" is a misnomer, and simply not the truth here! "You are a fantastic person, an excellent lover of friends and families someday soon, and," you're in here! So, get outta here yourselves then, Classes of Gentiles later, Folks and families alike here, and forego the trial by juries.

If the "Apostle Paul" got a hold of this winded conversation from jail, it's because he deserved to be there, Class of Gentiles here! This book holding of the Last and Final Testament of Jesus Christ to James the servant is something to be reconciled with here! His name was Paul Reverent then? Nope, a reverend is not what that guy was, but a nuisance to humanity's wakes here. We're saying all this in hopes that, not Paul, but James Reverent, R-e-v-e-r-e-n-t, is for the birds here? Nothing could be furthest from the truth's wanderings here!

As far as that's concerned, Folks, a bulimic on the job here is her, the judge in this town, though? We're not even going to clinicize this Paul bit here, but that she, Andrea did, live in Coos Bay, Oregon, for a time during her youth and growing up years here. It was the judge at this particular hopper here who was bulimic and on the same pills, sugar coating this entire affair with, send me to jail then, mentalities here! We're so blue in the face about the post office job that I so had here, only to be miscarried in justice's wake and face about that job being the best man for the story's literatures here! But stay tuned, because Louise Hay's making a comeback in this conversation with her affirmations here!

For anorexia and bulimics too, to say, "This is hereditary," is to make light of the conversation's dreams and such!

We're just stating that a behavioral quirk like, Andrea has big eyes or something when she's speaking to you, doesn't exactly go over very well in the quirk like worlds of mental health fodders here. If you want to misquote us on "past lives" and such, feel free to! But, feel free, Divine Source Wisdom, to point out anything you want to.

So, this is instrumental to healing anything at all, is belief! Heal belief and you've healed everything in it!

So, is this book gonna make any difference with the people of "mental health" here? I certainly hope not though, not! I hope that these concepts can make it to the masterfuls here! I hope that God certainly remembered that "Doctorate in Poopology" lessons planning guide I saw on the door of one hospital though! It means here that people find you delectable in the hopper, as well as on the streets, Andrea! But there are "wellness checks" if you're sleeping at Walmarts here, and that's a fact, Jack and Jill were oh so married, ya know? Well? I had two "wellness checks" upon my person, as a homeless junkie though? Not! As a homeless gal, dying to know where and when she can easily slip into the homeless shelter campus here, not! A transitional shelter that is run by the med window is the ultimate dying factor's, pain in the neck, recovery center now though I heard.

But this place is hosting my meds for me as a homeless person or junkie here? Nothing could be that true though, correctamundos here? Why can't I post Louise Hay's affirmations all over my walls here and have it be the quiet, solaced room that it was then? Well? I was renting the room, that's why here!

I had several "escapes" happen upon "my person," as well, correctamundos here? "Escapes" of what, she asks, Andrea did just now then! Well, there's such persons and promises as the hospital's escape booby hatch here! And, that said here, why don't we jackknife a lesson's planning routine's other half here and to state it like this means that Louise Hay is a saint and a lifelong learner of this too, but that His honesty, Jesus's honesty, in giving her all those talent searched affirmations was a lifelong learner of things that "talked" to her too! I mean, in church, she, Louise Hay did, published the very things that God wanted us to learn about, and that is, how to heal your body from trauma, or it's specialties, like kool aid bandages. And, what that means in the Urban Dictionary is really funny here, not, huh! Well, it's a ways out for "Us" here, too, as "We" claim to be a bunch of "guys" up here!

Our Trichomycin/Hachimycin warnings here go hand in hand with the money we have left to sort out the colonoscopies that are needing to be done here! And, that said here, not all of the food there at the transitional meds window type shelter here, and I do mean the Centralized Intelligence Unit here, is up for grabs here! As these little packaged food items are so high in cholesterol here, but they do test you for that, and do nothing about it here! We're on the roads to nowhere here fast, Andrea, if you cannot tell us what these "affirmations" have to do with the coming of ages for simple folk? Lots actually! Coming of ages though, like a period grower and stuff! Just don't do it! You know, have sex on your periods, Peoples!

It humbles us to know that a kool aid bandage is way out there on this, but this started to have sex thing is really for the birds. If you know what I mean, Jesus says! I mean, it's bloody everywhere in life here, and there's simply no cork's boards for the meaningful rites of passage, and I do mean rites here, that says or states that a woman simply has to or must be bleeding for it to be considered a rite of passage! Once, twice, three times a lady, Andrea is here!

And I loved you, every minute of you here in that motel room? Yes, twice I was in a motel room here and had a stupid ass "wellness check" by society's influences here? It was a dumb shit move on that person's part to call the downtown police station and to get you "kicked out" of that motel room you'd rented for a month's time here.

And, that said here, Paul used to love this about women and their periods too! He loved the site of blood though! He even masturbated or jacked off to the sound of women screaming about their virginities being "soiled" in other countries where he could fly to, and there would be the sounds of lovingly getting virgins for sale on the black markets of Swahili dialects here!

So, James Reverent was the guy we found could speak in dialects and "tongues" pretty well indeed here! I mean, Paul was not, and I do repeat that for the innocent cuss's languages here, that the sounds of people putting Paul up on a pedestal here is not the same thing as the king of king's parking lots that says or that states that I needed a rain upon my parades here!

And, in check with this here, Paul couldn't stand being "Lucifer" in the Bible, as the guy changed his name often, to hide himself from the authorities all the time here, and we couldn't catch him though? It's easy for a Divine Source Wisdom to find just about anybody on this Earth here! So! Hell, by the way, and the concept for it, is really something here. We're just reinventing the global warming aspects of how do you doody time this moment's inklingships here! And, to state it like this and that here is the Trichomycin/Hachimycin moment's big inklingships here! We needed all of these Louise Hay affirmations to die with her then? Not at all! She's the best person for the job here! And, what does a little ol' "voice" or two have to do with it here?

It's the "wrong kind" of "voices" to hear if you are hearing all about how they want to kill yourselves and stuff! That's mostly what it's about! Hey, Andrea felt this before too! She simply had a token friendship in a Paul Williams though? Not! He's Paul Williams in the Bible somewhere too, Chapter 34 of James then! Haha here! (There is no Chapter 34 of course!) Louise Hay's wonderful book on you though is two-fold here, Andrea!

You Can Heal Your Life is a special story about nobody certain, but everybody in kind though! It simply means that the most influential parts of the story of life from her states that this is the best "life changing" book there is here, with all the exercises and stuff in it! Particularly poignant is Louise's taste on the matters of forgivenesses, and there's a ton of exercises that help you do just that.

It was so influential and sweet of her to take all kinds of time here to reiterate in Chapters 4 and 6, Andrea thereof here, that it takes five minutes to pray each morning, and it takes a ton of time to do energy medicine daily exercises though! Right, Andrea here! LOL! She is taking her own sweet times writing this colonoscopy verse about jails and such having bad foods and stuff, because the innocents make it to either camp here sometimes! And, why have such nasty tasting food for one of the facilities and not the other ones here? Well? You innocents are never the same after a food sampling war's come ons at the nursing facilities of choices here, because the food is never the same once it reaches your colonoscopy's favorites here!

And, that said here, what about Louise Hay's other books about healing your body and such? Well! It's about time she become nationally recognized though? I think that's already happened here, Peoples! She's got bodily ailments all lined up in one chapter close to her heart at the end of the All is Well book on healing different affirmational notes in one chapter of God's book too!

The answers are at the back of the book's thoroughfares here! Just believe that you can heal it and it's yours! In other words, and a good influential chiropractor told me this one too! If you don't believe that you can heal an SI joint injury here, you're never going to beat this thing here!

So, if you BELIEVE you can heal it, that's half the battle right there, Folks. Same with healing schizophrenias, bipolars, and schizoaffective disorders! And, of course, the messages in this book right here are paramount to telling all about the right decisions in your lives.

Chapter 26

Money. Do We Have Enough of It?

I do declare a mistrial throughout this whole book, Jesus says!

I do declare that a mistrial is in God's favorite things! He's banking on the facts and tribulations of times here to declare a mistrial's God awful favors here! And that said here, we're going to say how do you do to Jezibellie Christ and to ask Her to dance is the moment's notices here that said, "I want to dance with You, too!" She said to Me here! I do dance with Her like this moment's notices here, where there are few people watching us! And that said too, there's more to life's quandaries than a mere dance's scripts here! A lap dance though? Hardly so! Although I do remember that very clearly here! That time was given to us through the lap dance though! I could remember Her very clearly, the guy says that is in Andrea's life at this time? He's not really there! You know, it's truth be told abilities that states that God is wrathing this situation's husbandry all the time here. And, that stated for the abilities to know about here, the guiding light's situations here are just for the birds then. To know about how I asked Her to dance is really for the birds here!

And that saids here, we pluralize for the funs of it here, that says, God is in control of the answers for the salvation of the literatures here! And that saids too, we are the pluralizations and such! Say, what have these two boys been doing but making out with their said wives so plainlies here! This pluralization's biggest worrisome phrases goes like this. You see it, now you do. Correctamundos here?

Japan, in other words, was our World War II partner's biggest Trichomycin/Hachimycin habit here? Do we dare ask the ladies what they'd so prefer here? The Trichomycin/Hachimycin tablet costs way less than the shot do! But, this is how it goes, Folks, and meaningful Gentiles later, Folks!

We're not buying it from them, but they're selling it to us online then? Can we use this antibiotic for anything but a shot record, in a war zone, no less and no more here? The antibiotic that we need here in the States said that we honestly couldn't conceive of a Louise Hay medicine for intuition upon the matters here! And, that said here, Folks, and you too, Gentiles here, is that, "I'm one way happy about My new wife, Jezibellie Christ though!" Are we not buying into any scripts that work here? Or, are we just tired and want to go home and rest on our own soils here? Because overseas chatters later, Classes of Gentiles later too, doesn't buy happiness! On a scale of 1 to 10, who has happiness and can buy it off of Jezibellie Christ! For the inception of Christ's answers to a scale of 1 to 10 here, there are happiness factors to boot with here! Say, the gray hair remedies would breakthroughingly starve the kotex handlers in this nation's kiddie porn mentalities here? Nothing could be furthest from the truth here!

That said here, what is World War III about anyways?

Here is the Japanese versions of what we're pluralization wise going to state for the birds here. If we just don't use it, the Trichomycin/Hachimycin pills here, we can order the shot instead! And produce it as if it were an epidemic proportionary means to an end here!

And, that stated here, what is buying the produce scale weighing on here, to tell others not to brush their teeth or nothing! That society there in Japan rocks the Kasbah, by the way! We can tell if a society plays around with the teeth factors or not here.

If we can afford better healthcare here, then mental health note here, the dentists at these facilities want to yank it all day long here, because they think that you're a bad person for being there in the first place? Some of them do! So, there, Folks, and Class of Gentiles later, Folks, there are, ultimately, nine different factors that are causational that can influence the decision of later folks down the line here to become an important members of society's influential habits here!

And, to state it like this before God here is to state here, and, yes, it's "Us" typing this and not Andrea here. Never was, she said to "Us" here, before we even started this venture here! That to state it before God's wraths here is an oxymoronic ways and means it lady's talent searches and stuff! If we can afford to pay dentists what they deserve to keep the record straight here, then lovingly there are enough people out there to make it out like "teeth are free."

Anywhere in the world though? Nope! Just not here then? Well, China gets paid to have great teeth too. So, take care of us peoples here in the United States then. And, buying teeth gets expensive.

Doesn't it? Take gray hair, for example here. There are lots of home remedies for this that you could scream at them! So, take for example, the Rogaine trips here on the current president's head here! So lovely are the non-gray hairs that take action all across the body's tips here! Rogaine keeps gray hair from coming back, but it takes three months to do it, and you must buzz cut your hair. Work on it regionally though, so do the top of your head, then after, do your beard, etc. For example, the Rogaine that is used in kind here is the key to mental health care about ourselves here! Make sure there are no interruptions like I had in my Rogaine usage!

And, that said here, there are mental health notes about timing our Divine Source Wisdom, DSW for short here, in essences close to the party's line of health codes here! Say, did we have healthcare or what back then! Yes, Jesus says! We had the healthcare of an oxymoron's biggest and best blessings of them all here! Say, take a class on neutering your dog or cat and you will find that none of it is the biggest blessing's overall kittens affair here!

And, that said here, is "sin" a topic of conversation to be happy about here? We're talking about "money growing on trees here," and about the topic of conversation's literalnesses here! You will attract some guy off the street, we said to Andrea here just now then! Nope! She's got her angles! I mean, is it "attractive" to some guy off the street to just be yourself at here? There's conscionable efforts to survive here!

Meaning, Folks, and remedies to the situation at hand is really something here to be desired here, right? Class of Gentiles just simply means that the Gentiles accepted Jesus as a Jewish/Polish or Poland guy up here too! It just means that the society's influences are vast and acceptable to the honor codes of a lifetime of greed mongerings here! Say, is "sin" the best and baddest influence's topics here? Because to think that you're a pedophile for most of your waking hours and to not be one after all is sure a lot of work to denounce here! And, that said here, "pedo head" runs rampant in the innermost workings of Chapters 4 and 6 mostly, and 10 and sometimes 12 then? I do degree this to an open book here in stating that a pedophile, Andrea, is most likely not in the cards! For you though, you believed this to be false too, but could not figure out for the life of you why this dark shapeshifter/energy attachment could be so falsely ingrained in you to create a monster almost out of you for finding out how to masturbate at all during that time there with those thoughts in your head there! ED in Chapter 18, here we come, you know? And, so for you to believe those things about yourselves here in "pedo head" land, and now "murderous heads" out there believe this too, Folks, is that Chapter 17 is about this more, and so thus on and so on here!

Chapter 27

Just When You Think It's Cozy Outside Here!

This, it's bad to hear "voices" thing has got to stop! I mean it, Jesus says, we, as a society, hear "voices," whether they are good or bad though is what counts, Peoples, and Classes of Gentiles no more then! I mean, "hearing voices" is a gift from God! We don't hear them unless we're absolutely certain of them! And, in essences here, there are all kinds of pastors, for example here, who'd just assume never state that God has told them to breathe the lingos from all the paranoias that are running around rampantly in these churches with anti-depressant remedies for life here though!

BDSM though? I mean, can we stick to our guns here, and to state it like this is kind of comical too, for we advocated no guns, as a society of linguistics majors never could tell it right here! We're trying to "speak in tongues" about the "voices," but we're never gonna gravitate towards anything here if we don't at least have the intuition like "voices" under control then?

Not! BDSM, by the way, Bondage and Discipline, Sadism and Masochism here, is for the birds, and the sole responsible party in Andrea's life as a married gal, way back when she was with the late guy who was a much older man in her life's talent searches and biggest paranoia producers of all here! He died of cancer by the way. What did she come to Jesus about then? To repent for having participated in those yucko affairs, of floggers and belt loops and such! I just don't get it, someone you know could say to you here, why did you marry a much older man, Andrea? There are tons of stuff that God has in store for you, Andrea, as well! That said here, there's much timelier presences than a bunch of shapeshifters and such! The Exorcist is discussed in Chapter 35 mostly, but, brace yourselves for this one, we're not giving it enough credence here.

To say that God hates BDSM is an understatement of Heaven's gates and stuff! I just didn't like being called a "vanilla" girlfriend all the time then?

And, that said, Andrea, what did your "participation" think about My interludes to you, just after the loin cloth discussions went haywire here! Why did you fling it back at Me, intentionally, and calling yourself a pedophile then, and we knew that you were not! Well? You cannot have anything done intentionally in Chapters 4 through 8 here, and in Day 16 when and where we came together as a being and a species here that said, women in general here really are turned OFF by BDSM here! And, that said here, they're lying if they say we're sucky at this "paranoia" language of the Divine Source Wisdom here, DSW for short!

There's lots of ways to stay "cozy" in the wintertime, what with a really warm blanket and a case of donuts later, Folks! That Gentiles bit is really getting on "Our" nerves here. Correctamundos here? Nope, it doesn't!

The things that BDSM represents are two-fold here. It means that, swiftly, Andrea, there is somebody in the lurch for you! You know who this is, too! So, timely people are swiftly saying that Andrea is reincarnate Jezibellie Christ, the slut, the moron, the clothes monger here!

And, that said here, we're really too poor to go out and buy a new wardrobe here, but there's promises in the dark's lasting impressions here! Say, Andrea, the good "folks" and the bad ones are finally held out to dry here! In essences, Folks, and you too, Gentiles speakers, is the following.

BDSM sucks! Likewise, the men involved can beat these women to death and just assume feel powerful and trustworthy and such, just for the "safe words" involved in those "beatings!"

And, just because we did this, doesn't mean that He's going to like someone lopping off your hair or punctuating your teeth just because of it! Say, is there a movie on tonight or this evening here? It's about the wintertime's essences of living in your vehicle here, save a few monstrous parties later here, I just don't have the gumption to try a BDSM lifestyle anymore here! Say, is Jezibellie a tramp then? Because I lied when I said She doesn't give good lap dances in the middle of nowhere though! I promised God an echoment into the comedies and tragedies of the Bible's lap dances here, cuz we all had them back in the days of betterments and such! We just don't like the "beatings" to go any further here!

It's "sweet" is it, Andrea... not! I do not think that saved your "marriage" to the late man though! In essences here, there are several things I feel sorry for, and BDSM is not one of them! I can turn it around here and state that I didn't have a very good marriage, though the secularizations speaks it ringers here are dead ringers to Me here, Jesus says!

We just never knew there were "good" voices and "bad" ones here, but if you're talking about the bad ones here, I'd just assume never hear that shit or stuff again here! This one time I heard, "Go kill yourselves!" Pun intended here! 😊 Old timers have it just as bad, if not worse, than the mental hospital patients do! I mean, if you're running around, people I know, giving restraining orders to Me, Jesus Christ, for "following" Andrea around like this, and for giving "Us" such a bad time because of it, then maybe you can follow Christ's "lesson plans" too! They are very bad at names, but these people do love you, Andrea! It's pronounced ON-dree-uh for short here!

Paranoia though is what Jezibellie had when she "left" the King of England too! Back then, polygamies were everything to the Indian cultures of God's lefts and rights and straight ons too. Then you get the picture. Right, or correctamundos here?

And, there are never ways about old timers and stuff, wanting more of it, pedo and murderous heads.

In other words here, there are more Jesus's "freaks" out there than I can count, ya know? He's the one true light and Savior blessing that ever walked this planet Earth!

This "paranoia" about someone thinking you're a "pedophile" is really for the birds if you ask "Us," pedo head girlfriend then! Yes? I am totally over it now! I don't have that kind of thing now. You can ask anyone I know though, for the run of the mill times that I spoke about this venture capital gains tax upon my person though, and how I got rid of it with affirmations and speakeasy riddles, like a counselor I once trusted enough to state for a fact that I had this phenomenon inside of my heads here! And, we do say "heads" for short here, as she does not have this pedo head at all anymore! "Adult pedophilia" exists for the second time here! And, that said here, there's work to be done, and places to go to interact with others here!

And, that said here, does Jezibellie Christ look like She wants a lap dance from Me right now? Not in the cards, Sonny Boys! This means that, yes, I do like to give Her one too! But not right now. You see the differences there, Sonny Boys, too?

Jezibellie Christ was born in the same church as I was, Jesus says! There's more to it though! Let's talk about this later then?

Well, we're gaining on you then, Andrea! We'd just assume the answers to the questions about whether Hathor was really Jezibellie's friend and mentor back then. Hathor is the dark energy figure then, not! She's very lovely indeed, Hathor is! She's just always mistaken for Jezibellie Christ throughout history though! That's because they were the very best of friends then? Not really, but honestly?

Yes! She knew about Hathor from teenage years, Andrea! The goddess of fertility and light, is it, she is here? She was a princess for some of it, Jesus said! And, Hathor is a wonderful person and human being too!

We don't mind talking about the details of Her detainments either, Jezibellie Christ's ones here! What happened to our initial marriage then?

Well, the sparks were flying pretty highly back then, that we had one under wraps, mind you! Well? There is an adult pedophile named Solomon.

The actual Songs of Solomon guy then? Yep! He made Me, Jezibellie Christ, put in that he was a reptile of sorts.

If you're honestly trying Me out for size then, nincompoop, then try Me out for size some other way, shape or form here?

We're honestly done with this entire paragraph's wantingnesses and warnings for this "pedophile ring's" actual size then? There are really just three in the States, and one elsewhere! And, that's about all then? Yep! One's in Florida at the turnpike of "love" down there then? Um, Miami. Right? And, then there's one in the "pedophile ring's" biggest and best pony shows down there in Indiana, right next to Louisville, Kentucky, then? The three "best" ones then?

Nope! Let's squash 'em down then! Right next to the Atlanta border you say, is a trafficking "meat market" full of children and small pets too then? Because this "bestiality" is for the birds too! I mean, why succumb yourselves to the hogwash that the "other" side of laughter's biggest and "best" turnpikes make here! Why not use the Indiana's ways to find "Atlanta, Indiana," then, guilty! There is a big ass sex ring in that town there, women and children too! And, this is about it! The other one is in Brazil, and it's near the city of Wyoming that we state that there are sort of three "rings" in this stateside wonderments here! Right at the State of Tocantins there, right outside of Palmas!

Three "pedophile rings" are… busted! Wyoming is a bust only because the simple town of Palmas has a region in it that they refer to as "Wyoming" in it!

Nothing could be furthest from the reaches of comedies here that states that Wyoming is a bust when it actually is not, the state of Wyoming thereof here. You got it! Well? Time to hit those "rings!" I will get you, you dirty rat! I promised God an answer to all this "nightmarish hospitality rings."

If I'd just assume nothing though is compromised here, I'd say that the Turkish game hens are the best in the world's eyes viewings here! Taquaruçu do Porto is the baddest and the worst at this.

Because of this "eyes viewings" of Turkish game hens though, "We" were the best at it here!

And, that said here, what are the most riveting elements of this portfolio still getting at here?

This is the best and the baddest, because of this though, not enough "flock" of geeses and stuff, think we don't know how to spell here, shh… The Turkish game hens are not even used to that ideas mongering stuff!

We're talking about Brazil's infrastructures here! We don't believe there to be anything wrong with "missing and exploited children" though… Not!

We're here to state that the biggest and majorist times squared here believe in a way to "mental health" the poor going at it here. That stated for the records then is really what we're afterwards here going to recognize as the "missing" and "exploited" parts here! That's for God to figure out then? Nope, here is the details we've all been waiting for here! Ninety-five percent of this nation's "missing" and "exploited children" are testimonied through a Discovery Channel episode! Shall we!

Chapter 28

I Think the DSW is Really Cool Though!
Alzheimer's Patients! Got it.

The Alzheimer's patient's biggest and greatest complaints are for the blood thinners that make them insanely toking on the newest marijuana's craze then! And, this is how it is here! We just jokingly flatulate at different times of the day then? Not necessarily so here! Quit these phagolysosomes and mitochondrion involved inside of an Alzheimer's patient's head here and let it go at that here! Say, did Jesus lead "Us," His troops, and dried up frizzy girl out to dry here?

Nope, "We're" writing a book on it then! Because this is very nerve wracking then, we are just going to say, Jesus led us up the troops of Capitol Hill then!

Because this is so "funny," we ought to be saying or stating that Alzheimer's patients get a clue on this fast and lickety splits here, but Hathor is really the primary "girlfriend" of a mass heart attacked pleasantries here! It's riboflavin is it here? Nope, that's for M.S. or multiple sclerosis! See Chapter 35 for that here! And, we're off! As we're telling it like it is here, the riboflavin in the "Lucifer's worlds" here is mighty fine indeed then. Right, or exactamundos here? This is the cynical side's best efforts to pause or forthright this kind of writings here! And, that saids here, we're in the middle of pluralizations no more then, because of the nerve ducts in his systems here? What, who, Paul though? Yep!

Paul had a funeral planned because of cancer of the nerve ducts in his system here. His middle name was Lucifer, thank you very much! Paul Lucifer Wright is what we were writing about, and, hence, why he became so pissed at us for! And he wanted revenge for some things in his life before he went to jail to live it out! His sentence and such was reduced to nil though! When Jezibellie started telling him of the cures in Her head, She witnessed several horny guys or men around Her! Then She was raped by them! So, Paul is a nincompoop. You know what? Don't talk about rape then? Shall we!

There are plenty of things to be thankful for here. Bipolarism isn't one of them, correctamundos here? There are certain graces and such that are nicey nice to look at here. This Moses cure started when he got his foot chopped off for loving God too much, all by Paul Wright, he says! This guy, Paul Wright, is what we call an apostle in the Bibles here, it's not it! He's not an apostle by any means here, and the Paul's rectifying sidewinders are not in the Bibles either here.

What Paul does not understand is that he's netherworld here! This means that I can walk on water, Jesus says? He's telling us that chopping off the foot or toe, either one here, of Paul Wright can make him go farther, further and then some here, because this is not what the other talent shows like to admit here! So, this is where Jesus lops off his toe then right? Wrong, or exactamundos here! We're tired of intervening here, Andrea, but this is the cure for Alzheimer's that we've all been waiting for. What is this but a family of yours who thinks they know what to do with this very strong "voice" of yours?

That said here, this is Jesus's glass of wine that is becoming so popular on the forefront of talent shows here. He did have a glass of wine that day for sure, but only with Mary Bongs Magdalene's prompting of the Holy Ghost in Us to deal with here!

This time is for sure the only time, with a knife mind you, at His throat even, to test the waters here and to deliver from evil our only Mary M.! This woman caught Me at a bad time. Even He states that God's only underwears that I had on got fixed and hitched with this woman, who is too old for Me by the way! And I state it for the birds here that, with a knife to my throat here, this woman, Mary M. for short here, because her husband's name's better than that and this here, Folks, is for the birds here!

I do not mean to get shitfaced here, but that glass of wine did it to Me here! And that's the talent search's biggest time spot's, best only knowledgeable inklingships here! That said here, what does Paul Wright have to do with burying people alive who masturbated once or twice in their lives here? Does Paul Wright ever do this himself here? Alzheimer's is curable! There are 20 different strains and we are going to give it a lick of truth here, so long as God's peoples do not get Alzheimer's a relative of mine may have had with his Coumadin (Warfarin)! We can all take a blood thinner instead called a Statin! That'll give you the cure! If not though, trust us! We know what we're talking about!

Of course, He do!

The people of the world's better places here like the fact that God gave Him the rights to honor society's bestest inklingships here, by telling Paul Wright where to go! In fact, this whole Bible scheme that states that God's lesson plans are over here meant that Paul Wright wanted Jezibellie so badly that he even came on Herself with his love tokens and such, and even thought about masturbating, to the sound of people dying on the crosses then! Because this is not so foundable here, it's a word, trust us here! That people die on the crosses and such? That would've been right up people's alleyways here of trust and what nots here!

You are only getting the best of both worlds here! Alzheimer's is curable, Peoples! Tell that to some people though and they will have a coronary. Say, does one of those people have any health problems as of lately here? Because smoking cigarettes… I digress here! I used to smoke, so there, Peoples! For some reasons here though, to state that for the records here, it means, Folks, and Classes of Gentiles later, Folks, is to dress up and murder the unsuspecting people who've had a coronary or two, y'alls here though? Jesus said to stop dressing up the alabaster skin that He has and to drove away my two cutenned peoples here and stated or said to alabaster skin such as His here that He's threatening to blow away the peace offerings here, but if only said people do it here! This is the time and the place to just drop off this sentences thing here then, She said?

And so, I've been cut from the cloth here, Jesus says! And molested no one here! And that said, this molester of peace and such, Paul Wright, held Jezibellie down and raped Her? Absolutely. And this is what this guy's peace offerings do to a Bible cure like God's only son here? Raped Her though? Yes, Ma'am and Sirs and Gents and all of the above here! And so, She's called a slut and a whore bag for doing so? This man, Paul Wright, I mean it, God, is really, really bad for society's interests here. Like I said, She's been back several times here to Earth mind you, but Paul? Not at all! He's netherworld's best talents here! People go to netherworld for bad deeds and they never come back to Earth again. Gee, a fish and a glass of wine from Mary M., his best friend here, is not all that it's cracked up to be here! I do know this too.

What is the best ways and means it lady's talent shows going to say and state for the records here, but God's best and only best words here! Alzheimer's patients galore here, just throw the damn stuff, these blood thinners, in the rivers and streambeds! What do you do with it, they said! Well? The streambeds are full of fish who love to eat the stuff! Well, what is it gonna do, but kill them off though, Folks and Classes of Gentiles later, Folks! The answer is, no, not at all!

They deciphered this to mean, Andrea, that fishies, little fishy, fishy, here little fishy, fishy, is what, and I repeat, only Jesus loathed about too, is that Mary M. is a very fashionably late girl in the 19th and 20th centuries then? She hasn't been back since. Neither of them though? Yep! You're banished to hell then? Well, "hell is for children," correctamundos here? Neither "Us," nor "I," Andrea Wynn, can state it here for the birds to seduce little children into interment camps like there are for the state hospital goers though? Those places here are pristinely built up like a college campus is! They're old established military bases at one time though? Not necessarily, but sort of!

That said, Sirs, and you too, Gents and Sirs here, what is the best inklingships that I ate a fish too? I ate fish all the time, He says! I ate fish because we all have feelings that the birds don't like to eat themselves here! And that said here, go with the flow, Andrea, as this is the life o riley here! Eat up, person of interest! I mean that in the most respectful fashioning here, because many people think that a blood thinner, like Coumadin or Warfarin here, and the rest of them, are necessary evils here! I predict that if he and others just stopped the stuff "cold turkey" that the Cornish game hens might not necessarily be so bad, once you get to know them! If you think that Jesus only ate fish, then there's a long time in knowing His choice of words here! It's true though, what do you want to do with the Warfarin here, but to throw it in the riverbeds as well here! The fish can decipher what's good Warfarin and what's bad here!

That said too here, there are hopes of a "second coming" of Jesus Christ and such things as God's only begotten son, is left here by Himself to fend off the predecessors here! And that said, Folks, what is the only taken ones that left Her by His sides here, but that Egyptian empire!

That said here, what is "the sound of music" to my ears then, people state for us now here! And that's to stop the Coumadin at once for the lower dose of Statin users here! And that said here, what is the said only hopes that God's son is really that of a bird's eye view! This guy, Paul Wright, used to masturbate to the sound of people's voices as he cut them out of society's jerkology lessons here, and used to say, "Off with their heads!" to people like Jezibellie and Me! This is how Jezibellie came to know "Christ" then? Hardly so!

I mean it, Folks and you too, Gentiles to be here, that if you just cut the Coumadin or Warfarin "cold turkey," it's the best method of getting you off the Alzheimer's ready list! The person I know, for lack of a better word here, took one look at a magazine cover in the depths of beginning Alzheimer's disease, and said to himself aloud, "I CAN heal Alzheimer's!!!" 😊 We all knew he was beginning the stages of it there!

And so, he, Paul Wright, the guy who used to be an apostle Paul? Not hardly here! He can't even read. And he used to torture people alive for how they felt about the sand dunes of time here. The sand dunes of Arabia used to be called the Ahab Desert here! That was until he fell in love with a Jezibellie then? Nope! He used to be a king for Christ's sake! Haha, go ahead and "swear," Folks! It's fun to! It's a "good" word to use here!

Paul used to go bury people alive under the sand dunes of the India's proper balancatures that God's best meaningful treats used to subside under here. And that said, Folks, it's about God's only creatures that state that burying people alive and hearing their screams is just what the doctor's order created for little ol' Paul Wright! He used to hunt people down and kill them just for masturbation! And so, this is why it is so important to state it here well, and that is to state that God has made it so all people of color or not can masturbate to whatever sounds that sound so like screaming and such? That's not it, Peoples!

This is Paul Wright signing off here? This is an apostle Paul here? Not hardly so, Class of Peoples who know vulnerabilities and such here! Say, had you gotten a move on here, Andrea? Nobody would've even suspected that Paul Wright's not even in the Bible! So, to speak it here, "I, the Apostle Paul, state that..." et cetera, et cetera, here, states that the guy even held Jezibellie down to write this into this Bible she so delicately dictates here in the Bibles of wartimes and such! Say, did I slither down from the company's best and biggest inklingships here to carry the Bible's messages here?

This Paul person never wrote one iota inch of the Bible! Why do pastors and preachers alike say that Paul wrote this and that? Well, they have no other proof beyond what Paul did to force his way into the Bible's proper nouns and such!

It was ship hearted! Meaning, it was given lots of glares and stuff for stating that Paul meant anything to Us here! This Paul guy, I mean it Andrea, gave a lot of people grief and strife, and notations speak it well, Chapter 2 of Revelation, we'll play along here and call it Revelation and not Revelations here, that speaks it to us here, that God gave our playmates some strife called God!

This "Alzheimer's" patient, the person I know who has it, could have killed Christians as well with his own bare hands at some point then, but nothing could be furthest from the truth here! He's just a lonely guy on a mission to "heal" Alzheimer's then? People could care less then? Well, most people I know don't believe in these "ailment cures" lady's timings and such. But, I'm serious about this, Folks! Either "cold turkey" the medicines you take for blood thinners thinning out the fish with no blood in them, or come crying to Me and state to Me that you don't believe in God's ultimate healing medicines thereafter and thereof here! Switch to a statin, person of interest! Please! ☺

I could swear that Jezibellie married me cause She loved Me. Right, Jesus Christ says here? It means, Folks and Classes of Gentiles later here, that God chose a talent search upon our souls here. Say, She wasn't taken into custody by Paul Wright, but that's close, because he's not even Her age either here, but to be taken from Me at 16 years-old into a sex ring for killers alike here, She was taken ever so slowly? Nope! She left Me then? Nope!

I promised God an interlude about this here talent search's biggest blessings here, because the cure for Alzheimer's goes something like this too. Stop at the bus stop next time Andrea wants to go get her car out of jail's way here and get a towing company to hide it pretty well here! And, that said here, there were some things that mentionables don't cure, and that is the phagolysosomes about itself here! That said, the phagolysosomes are really what and where there needs to be a balance cure here! They have to do with rice and pig's meat here! Say, Paul never killed nobody then, right or correctamundos here? "He killed Christians," someone said at one point to me, a staunch believer in Catholicisms then here? Not necessarily, but go on! She said, "He killed Christians, and Jesus forgave him!" Not! Not, not, not! And so, it goes! The phagolysosomes in and of themselves here are killing themselves here! Not though?

Well, this is the mentionable's inklingship cures that are not in the balancatures either here!

There must be some kind of sorrowful mention of all the people he killed! Not to mention the seven deadly sins are more like eight or even twelve. I do mention this too. To be killed or not to be is something's best inklingships here!

That said, what is the comedy's next tragedy supposed to be here! There's something in the Bible's wakes that only God's inklingships mentioned here! And that is, don't listen to a word of it today. Honestly, this is for the birds here, the inklingships and mentionables here! And that said, Andrea, what of this Paul character, and how come the Bible knows it to be the case here! There's better inklingships here than God's graces here! By the way here, did you know that the mountains form the ocean's best inklingship cures here!

By going to the Mt. Baker tunnel then, formed beneath the Earth's crust, we can see volcanoes forming ships of laughter out there. Needless to say too is the fact that God invented Mt. Baker to flirt back with Mt. Rainier here! We have different demands and stuff, these mountains said to the Ahab king way back when they used to fly everywhere and every place here, and the Aleutian Islands are now Kilauea's babies here! The Hawaiian islands are ours though, Mr. Mt. Baker said though? Nope!

She's female, a female mountain, and God even knew the Ahab Desert was a place for the Arabian Knights of the Roundtable to come about here! But Mt. Baker, she says to herselves here, is that God invented words such as herselves.

And so, anyway, I say this because the Ahab Desert is a place to contract the sea's massive oceanic temperatures here. So, foreshadowing, Andrea? Yes, and yep to that here! This "contraction" of folks living under the sea, too, is… Haha! Just kidding here.

In actuality though, eating crawdads are the perfect hit of eating mice too, as well as coming to terms with the facts that the lysosomes in crawdads perfectly mimic the eating gestures of Alzheimer's patients! You'd have to eat a whole truckload of them though, right, Class of Gentiles later, Folks too? Nope, two or three mice, after quitting "cold turkey" that silly "blood thinner" stuff used on little girls and boys in the sex ring though?

Yep! It disorients someone so badly that, you can see for yourself that eating rats for some saves the day here, as they taste like chicken does, according to the Divine Source Wisdom here.

But we're not even kidding about the crawdads and mice too. You need two or three mice here, six crawdads though! Their "enzymes" involve human delusions though, if you're not careful about it then! Eat the crawdads alone though, without the interventions of finding peaceful tidings in a statin here, Folks, and you too Gentiles here, means that it will NOT work out here. Feeding them is really cool, but eating them? Do I hear gout calling my name here? It's six of them! You'll be fine on your gout medications for a one time shot at these six crawdads/crayfish from the Philippines.

Supposedly, there are crawdads in the Philippines, ready and ripe for the pickins here! And, it's Philippines, Andrea! She goes, I can't believe I cannot spell this word here! We're pretty good spellers here! But, to say the least here, a crawdad or two can really buckle under if we're not important enough to sell them here to the United States and beyond here, as crawdads are really importantly found in the Philippines alone then? Nope!

Just get that sad fact outta here where the kids are being succumbed to high doses of morphine too. I mean, Paul used to kidnap kids outta homes that had masturbators in them, he says to the Gentiles one morning's dew here! And Paul goes, I've just gotta disorient these children here! And, say, do you think that Andrea is developing what is called or what is known as disorientation, from all of these innuendoes here that state that a crawdad away from mice and stuff, because one is but the same as the other one, in terms of "enzymes" that won't quit here! Any mouse at all here.

Say, that said, too, who is the leader in this clause supposed to be here, but Jesus Christ! And here She is mentioning the fact that Paul came in and told Her to leave it be. Jezibellie did so! The clauses are just what the doctor's orders are mentioning so fast in this acclaimed being's naturalizations here! She doesn't know what came of this document's best works here! This work is being ran over again by the other God's lesson plans here! What "We" mean by "works" and such is the Bible proper, of course though! There are lots of lessons planning inklingships available for the crawdad's hopper too. One of them is Mt. Baker's cheese headed ideas that state that Mt. Baker is not available for comment about the simple stars it reaches in one day here! And, that said here, there are simple things to choose from here. Such is the light of the day's choices here! We are on the scales tomorrow morning if you're not careful with this starving's invention of crawdads here, because, who wants to eat mice or a mouse here? Be careful about this here! We don't know the crawdads out there in the Philippines as much as the ones in Massachusetts here!

Well? Will they work, Andrea? Nope! I don't know what they're "feeding" them in the Philippines, but that one works and our mice work. End of stories here! Send to the proper officials in battling health problems here, and we'll make a pill out of it here? Nope! Don't do that! We're being runover as a society's influences here with this pill or that pill, and it's running its course on everybody involved in sacredizing time! Just live it up and know that God's best inkling cures could sell a crawdad or two from the Philippines to us here! And that said here too, don't risk it all, Person of Interest! Love yourselves a little bit more here, Peoples! We've got to do a Louise Hay imitation then? Just tell yourselves that you love yourself in the mirror! It works! ☺

There's lots of choices to make here. That man, that awful man in the hopper with Jezibellie, is the one who forcefully gave Her a choice, and that was, no penetration in exchange for the limelight in the book's only forceful ways about it here, Class of Peoples that nobody else gets here! This is because for the simple fact that God's only cuss words are for the biggest ailments there ever was here. There's much to be dismayed about in the Bible's wakes here. This is for the birds if the DSW cannot say that they're much more inclined to state it like it is than Paul ever would be. Louise Hay was a Godsend to this Earth and to this nation alone here. Why not eat crawdads on the hopper's biggest cures here at the places they are staying at here! I'm going to tattletale on you too here, Andrea, for stating that the crawdads on the menus of love here state that Louise Hay had an affirmation for Alzheimer's patients too here. It is, "There is always a new and better way for me to experience life!" (Hay, 2013).

So, therefore, class of peoples, Gentiles, and what nots here, the only bustable timeships in this God's worlds here is to state for the record that we are the only ones writing it! And rewrites are available at the calling of 17 places in this world's best controls here! What does God's only cures mean to folks writing it? It means that God's plentiful populations are at heart here, and that God's only begotten son is so literally in love with Jezibellie, that the inklings here are that there's much more to be written about here than just Paul Wright's deeds and mishaps here.

That said, let's go talk about the murder of our cat's biggest lies and such! This Paul Wright was ruthless here! And that said here, what is the power of intention's biggest assets, biggest desires and such going to tell us here! Our licenses to drive are taken away with one fell swoop, as a driver of deliveries and such though? I mean, our cats die every day when they eat a one mouse too many here? They never eat them, you notice! So, dine and dash upon this, but upon every North American soldier who died in World War I, you could tell it too, that the opening ceremonies began upon every street corner's literally stank and vile offerings here! Say, can you make a pill out of creatures of habits here like mice and stuff? Go right ahead, We say!

That's because Jesus and Jezibellie Christ make our dreams come true here! That said here, what is God's only one wish and desire for this nation's cures for AIDS related viruses, but to cure Alzheimer's too? Somebody I know is going to have a coronary one of these days, or a conniption fit, one of the two, about my "ailment cures" and such! But, that's just for one person to decide my fate, about my honor and my tragedies about losing my license to drive almost? I'm a mental case, is that it here?

One thing's for certain here, that God is the only one for you here! This problem we foresee on our dockets here is that no one, nobody here, is going to believe us, save a few followers of the Gentilian types! That said too, what is the only one's biggest nothingnesses supposed to uphold here but the wake and timing's clauses of Jezibellie Christ coming to the ending times and that's that. Correctamundos here!

This is for the birds I suppose here, Dudes and you too Dudettes here! Is that God's only Christmas cheer this time of year is to bless the generalities and such with the Godsend that is only in our wakes here! That said, Dudes and Dudettes too, there's generalities and such with God awful places to be told here! That mentionable's biggest attitude adjustments needed in Paul's wakes here is to state for the birds that he did it too! He did murder people on command here, and then he's forgiven for it here? Not! That's not an apostle! That's a moron!

This is the DSW talking here, not Andrea, not anyone else but Us here. That said, what is the apostle Paul supposed to do with Peter here, glomming onto the fact that He can walk on water here? He did it too! Not! Just kidding here! This apostle Peter, now he's more of an apostle than Paul ever could be here. That said, what is the inklingship's best movements going to find here, and what time is the apostle Paul going to be hanged then! That's for the return of the best inklingships here. What are we waiting for? And then I was hanged instead, She says! I guess it's for the best that God's inklingships are waiting for the beheadedment of Jesus Christ!

And He went and got Himself killed for it here! Peter knew it though! He thought He would be hanged or something like it, you see. But the cross is still our beheadedment rule here. Never undo the cross! It's Jezibellie who got hanged after the cross demonstrations here! The rule is here, never touch a woman across the breasts and live to tell about it here! That is the demonstration's rulebook that never got used here. This is Jesus Christ superstar signing off here! Take it from Me, He says! I just got a message from Jezibellie that states that God's superstar wings here are just what the doctor's ordered here! And that said here, does Jezibellie deserve the status of a doctor here? Sure! She could tell ailments back in the days and nightsoramas here! That said, get off Me, She said to him too! Jesus could tell She only meant Paul. And therefore, there must be some inklingships that are too crass to fold a penciled asshole like Paul into the mix here!

So, who's talking then, in these chapters, Divine Source Wisdom? Yes, Ma'am and Sirs too alike. And so, what have you done for me lately! This East Indian dialect you say? Not. More of an East Brazilian accent to it then, as we're claiming for the records here that God's other brothels are over there in Brazil. And, hey, it could produce "ED," erectile dysfunctions here, for women too, to bring this up here!

And, that said here, we're of East Germany and Dutch for accents here. Likewise, the English of the Britain rule here said that an East Dutch dialect for Jezibellie Christ is not too shabby a person to write the Bibles with here! Shouldn't I say a toast, Jesus says, for Her coming back to Me?

There's Delilah again! Jewels was her last name before marriage to Me then? Yep! Do I hate to talk about a Jezibellie Christ instead though, as Delilah never kept her maiden name either, Folks and Gentiles too! It went on for four more years though? I was NEVER there, He said! I kept her, Delilah here, in the lurch for a reason here. Back then, it was strange to never have been married!

And so, we, Jezibellie and Me here, were never able to "consummate" the "marriage" quotient here? We most certainly had! So, what do I do with a 19 year-old, almost 20 year-old wife, who "came back" to Me here? It's not the King of England, is it, who ransacked the towns of Cheshireville here? It used to be called that in our languages here! But it's really Cheshire here that the king's parties called women into "servitude," for their "sins" no less and no more here!

And, that's a fact, Jack and Jill were married to each other, no less and no more here! But Jezibellie Christ, was you a more "uphill person" than I was here? Nonetheless here, the King of England at that time was a regional king, that's for sure here. The "King Solomon" in the books of wraths here in the Bible no less and no more here, because fodder for King Solomon's asshole on a platter here. He never did rule in Jerusalem, by the way here! We take barium enemas very seriously here! No more "rat attacks," and no more mice to kill and feed us here? It's only one or two that you needed to survive the wrath of cleaning out the cells though from Alzheimer's goo? Absolutely! Now, if I could only survive on medicines for Me, then Jezibellie Christ couldn't afford the medicines she takes then? What are we doing here as a society, coming up with reasons to take pills all the time, and never coming to shout it out with the authorities about the timings it took to deliver a message to God today then?

Because, normally when an "invalid" is taken into custody here with a 9 to 5pm job here, we're stating it for a fact that she did indeed work for the post office. Where though? That remains to be seen here! She loved that job very much! But, in essences here, we tagged along to get her a no meds kick from the hospital of choice and a taxi ride to the nearest affordable motel! Well? Does that get me an honorable mention here, or did she stay off her meds at that time then? Nope, taxied into that motel by a questionable tenant here and we're off to storm it out at a different local hospital then due to homelessness. Boy, do I need a taxi with no meds out the back door though? Yep and yes and, therefore, I just didn't need them! And I don't now! So, yes, I am back on them though!

And, that said here, Paul's a moron! We're going to move on from that now though, and to focus on this message here by the Divine Source Wisdom here is to state that Alzheimer's patients need love and a lot of back and foot massages! That said too here, there are people at that table, the Knights of the Roundtable, that are retractable upon this notion of time here.

And, that said, Class of Gentiles and Folks honoring time's substances here, the Lobster House, I mean the Red Lobster near you, has the kind of crawdads we're talking about here someday! So, just because the Lobster House doesn't mean anything to you here, it does mean that we're "special" in some way here! The Red Lobster near you doesn't sell crawdads though? Does this mean that an exoskeleton crew might honestly come between God's kingdoms and say, hey, Red Lobster, why don't you start carrying crawfish from the Orient then! As some of their exports, needless to say here, are scary indeed for many of the crawfish and crawdads that come in contact with boiling waters here.

Needless to say, Folks, that, died and gone to Heaven is the person you know with Alzheimer's disease here reading this one of these days, Andrea! An avid reader he was! Say, can we do the crawfish some other day then? Nope! The lobsters will not boil in water very heavily here, but chopping off their heads first is the way to go here. Don't boil 'em alive! That's just cruelty here. Say, can we eat lobster then, Andrea, here? Never tried it, Pops! I do hope others will hear me scream about the DSW some more here, because some people have blocked every effort I have to win their attentions then? I do say and I do declare a mistrial, Jesus winks at these people in the most fashionable way here!

Say, we are done here! Let's get the Philippines interested in coming over here with those freshwater crawdads. And, to state it here for the Gentiles and such is really for the birds here alone to feast upon here! Let's just say that the freshwater crabs will not do either. It's gotta be the freshwater kind! It's time to go now to the next chapter, Andrea! How do you import those suckers into the freshwater eras of space contentment here? We don't know! I'd assume that the United States has a service warning for all of the service members of society's influences here that vacate the premises on these two points here that we're going to make for the people Andrea knows here.

They're to: stop, drop and roll! And, to make out for society's influences here is to state that, if you're still not feeling 100% about this mice eating affair here, then take a language sample out to dry, CDC, the Centers for Disease Control and Prevention! I mean, if you're reading this far into the manuscript here, you've probably found the right alkaline tattletalenesses in our wakes here.

For simpler affairs then, does Pike Place Market have them? Nope! Does anywhere in Washington or the northern regions of Canada have them too? Nope! It's an enzyme problem. Isn't it, Andrea? Nope! Just the Philippines, Folks! Six, I say, count 'em, six will do you just fine, lover of life's interests, and stay on the gout medicines and you'll be fine, for a one time sit down with fate and faith adjustments about your Alzheimer's patient's best remedies here! If six crawdads can be the cure, then we need this here in the U.S. very soon, not at Red Lobster, but that'll work! It's six (6), count 'em, six crawdads from the Philippines that will wipe out Alzheimer's for good, beings that you drop the Coumadin/Warfarin first, 48 hours in advance.

Take it from Me, Jesus says, we don't want the Alzheimer's fixes that states otherwise!

Chapter 29

Masquerade Around Me Then! Homeboys!

"Gangs!" What's in a gang that I don't like, Jesus says! We're running around a hospital filled with hearing voices then? What's wrong with the gangs I see, Jesus says, is running around from hospital to hospital as a homeless person though?

With time and again coming near "Us" here, there's something in Andrea's wakes with 9/11 that says, these freaks we will call them, came to us and sabotaged a ruinship greater than life here with that 9/11 call! These freaks we will call them had no inklings to register as a sex offender in the state of Washington, let alone other places in this world here! And the "state of Washington" is where we lie our heads at night here, Andrea does, and so do half the world's populations then? Right here, right now, there is no other place I want to be! As the song goes though!

Gangs are related to judgments and dares and such. This "dare" was to strike the Empire State Building in a recognition of this world's Trade Centers and such, Andrea! She's like, where's this going, Folks?

And, Classes of Gentiles later, and Jewish peoples too, state that an honest dareship is what this was! This 9/11 crash had nothing to do with the abomination of a tons of stuff that lead to the derailments and stuff of people who multiply and who do it well here! Those two planes was it? Nope, three, then turned around the third then! Yep! We had lots to be thankful for in those two planes then, was it? Three, not four. As the world turns then? Yep! He had nothing to do with it though, Jesus Christ didn't!

How do you explain "gangs" and such to a bunch of homeboys that have nothing to do with it then? We'd just assume abomination had something to do with it though! Is Lucifer involved then? Paul is no Lucifer. Just saying that He's different than Lucifer ever was though! It's a parable, Folks, the Lucifer story in the Bible! There are no fallen angels in wartime eras here! And, that's a facts taken place we're ridiculing ourselves with here!

There are no excuses! Shall we say or state that four U.S. planes, no, three U.S. planes, knocked into the joking attires for nothing here! Shall we say or state that America's soil free living style is best for the homeless junkies out there who want to kill, search and desist, and be exploited in a ways and means it lady's timings here? Or, do we simply want to know what happened that day here? Because this is right, this is homely, homeboy mentalities in motion here!

Jezibellie, Andrea, is right there for the taking! "I am taking you," I said to you on the walls of love here. In the grossest ways possible for Jesus to spiritually take a wife here is something to be desired never here! We're thinking you're the messiah or something. Right, or exactamundos here?

We're talking about dying your hair purple for the massage parlors or some such things here? Because that's Jezibellie's job of choice here, is massage parlors.

And, nothing could be furthest from the truth that I, Jesus was, able to find that out from her here! I went to school for that, Jesus says too! It's not an easy profession to learn about here! And, wars are fought about sex for so many reasons here! These sex offenders, and they were truly innocent of it then, the 911 or 9/11 murderers you say here? Yep, but these sex offenders you can say were easily offended at the serial rapes and murderers that they'd found in the States! This is because the methods to our madnesses states that God murders children all the time then? Not hardly so here.

There's some other times to kill here and lessons to be had here. Nothing could be furthest from the truth though, that these were not sex offenders on the busses of love here in the stateside, worldwide era of space contentments here. So, for Osama Bin Laden to be a messiah of sorts is a farce or a misnomer here.

But, I'm going to jump out on a limb here for the records of wonderments here, and to state this is sort of a misnomer too, but Bin Laden had little to nothing to do with these "leaders" in the eras of spacement over here in the U.S. of A.! That's because this guy never knew these individuals at all here. Needless to say, gangs exist in America's soils for the reasons that they stated in Biblical times here. Chapters 1 and 2 of Romans goes on and on about American soils here too. They state that the biggest convictions of 9/11 happened because the Orient, and I will say this lovingly here, say, go look this up. Cause we'll wait! Haha! Well, it's because of the Orient that the women, wine and song go hand in hand here.

That said here, what did the Orient have to do with massage parlors and such? Well, this 9/11 trick's momentum and momentous means to an ends here had to do with Bin Laden alright! He was a U.S. soils person for four years, four more than needed to be. Let's just say this too. Bin Laden was a pedophile, right, Andrea here? Nope! I will say or state that America's soils here are not what these planes were about, Peoples!

It was a false hope of God's then? Well?

This meant that God's echoes of the planet's long-lived catastrophes like this one are really two-fold here.

There are dreams and such places to go and haggle such dreamy posts as, this tiger over here is better than this one over here! Exotic animals and such too? You got it!

It means, Folks and Classes of Gentiles later, Folks, that God's crystal clean methodologies for killing a bunch of peoples here means that God did not do that to you, or you, or you and you and you, too!

It means, Folks and Classes of Gentiles later, Folks, that Jewish people did not do this either. And, that said here, we're calming the senses. Are we, Classes of Peoples akin to rescue our convictions to who's responsible for the murders of 2,977 peoples then (CNN Library, 2017)?

We wanted to know this before here, Andrea! How come you're so late in writing this book about gangs and on gang related materials here! Well, don't sweat it.

Now that you've come out against America's soils here, you mean to tell us or "Us" writing this book here that Osama Bin Laden did not do it then? That's what we're saying, yes. Well, he was a wine, women and song guy then? In that order too! But he was no killer either, just a scapegoat for Obama's era of spacement then? He didn't know either, Hon! Likewise here, the killers of Al-Qaeda is in the likes of homelessnesses then, Andrea? We don't know either, Folks! Not!

There's Al-Qaeda's in every city, in every nation out there, Folks and you too Gentiles here!

In 9/11's wakes here, there are several cities in the nations of Israel and such that comedy this tragic point very fastly wise here.

We're saying this for the crawdads' sakes in 9/11 attires here! He was given a blood thinner, the main leader into the Al-Qaeda's contexts then? Yesiree bob, on an LRO/LRA then, or Less Restrictive Order or Alternative here? Okay, so all people on a Less Restrictive Alternative like this are made out to be bandits then? We're not saying that either here! We're just saying that all these homeless drugs junkies we're making out of people are not to say that homelessness caused this accident here! An atrocious one at that. Accident my eye, people say! Well? It means that an accident by a freak of nature of God's doings though? Not! This is not the universes that step in and mess things up by freak ass natures of beings here then. Do they though? Nope! What is it then, Andrea? As people started listening to "Us" freaks here, they're going to fight a Philippine soil survey then? Hey, when Andrea used to work at a map library, two of them in fact, before she became "ill" here, there were soil surveys in there too. Is that what we mean by love though, Andrea? The answers to giving people LRAs or LROs are not it!

This is something that cannot be avoided, Andrea. What is it that you dream about in a day's time here!

We don't know though what the Bin Laden approach to scholarship is, because the man never learned to read and write though? That's what happened to his underground bunker here, is that Saddam Hussein never wrote about. Language wars though? You've got it, Andrea, here! That said here, there's never a massage parlor I didn't like here! These people, U.S. citizens no less, and mind you here, these people spoke Swahili was it? Nope, the Al-Qaeda languages though? Nope! They were totally unrelated to this infrastructure's manufacturing systems for Dopamine receptors to say, you need an anti-depressant, Sir! Or, you need a manufacturing huddle for these LRAs that you keep getting out of dodge about here.

Say, Person of Interest, have you gotten your Coumadin dose lowered is it? It's "cold turkey," Folks. For Alzheimer's patients here, there are tons of different announcements that need to follow this old and boring script's lesser alternatives here. Say, we don't even need an LRA to bother us anymore. Do we here?

We certainly do not! They only create "missed appointments" and things of that nature here! We do not kill people as a society does not here. But gangs and stuff, that's what started the fires for humanity's wakes here. And, as a society here, there's tons of peoples out there, Folks and Classes of Gentiles here, that say or have said, let's get outta dodge here about these medicines we are forced to take on a regular basis here! .

And, that's not saying we're violent here as a society here. You are drugging the wrong peoples here!

To save face here, the DSW rests for a moment. As we gather up enough strength to tell you folks what went on in the Bin Laden camps here, cause we're done with that guy, really! Is he really dead yet then? Yep, and Al-Qaeda couldn't be happier about that, by the way here! The guy was a tremendous leader moron if you ask "Us"!

About the matters at hand here though, there's tons to do with the Al-Qaeda bunches that surfaced back in the Oriental days of massage therapies and such. The kind without sex was non-existent at some point. I'll come back to this point in a minute, Jesus says! Say, Andrea, what's Jesus like in the sack! Because you seem to know some stuff about sensualities and such! Say, were these guys, these 9/11 extortionists you called them here, Andrea, right? Nope, it's Us! We say it and she types it.

Done. Finito! We're saying that Jesus in the sack… Oh, yea, right then, huh! But, of course, He's "in the sack!" He's done, finito though on the methods of the madnesses that brought to you, of course, ridicules for being laid back in the days of finite wisdoms here! Oh, glorious moons here! We just don't know what to do with your latent track records and such!

We're trying to find the times and methods and such to dispose of the commandant's best languages here! Person I know/knew with Alzheimer's, are you listening to me now? Because I'm so enthused if you can read this message's content here!

We're going to stop here. It's about the commandant's cherry filled Twinkies. And you can figure out the rest if you want! Oh hell then, we're going to explain one more thing to this chapter's innocence here.

We're blatantly going to ask God about chapters and such in the Bible though? Turn to chapter, verse… What again! Well, we're going to ask God about this tragedy, tragic circumstances and such! Because why would God allow it at all here! Why would God make up this tragedy and then call it good here! A nice person, can you see? That the dawn's early lights, were so proudly we hailed, in the twilight's last calling! And the rocket's red blare, the bombs bursting in air, gave proof through the night, that our flag was still there! Oh, say does that star-spangled banner yet wave! Over the land of the free, and the home of the brave!

I don't get love very often! So, I guess I'll just bend over everybody on those planes too? What is a "sex offender" to you is something of a joke in society then? Nope, nope, and nope! I promised God, life, liberty and property state here, that God can never come between a bad man and a hopeless cause. So, needless to say, Peoples and Class of Gentiles later, Folks, that God's best manners are at stake here, because of the greed and the guilt of these two men in the cockpit who ran over this best man's manners here? There was a "mock wedding" on board one of these ships here that said, "I, Jezibellie Christ," no, get that bad name out of here, Folks! "I, Jezibellie Tutankhemen Barnes (or Bongs here), marry the King of England!" And, She was then snatched up through hell's gates too or something like it! You see it, now you don't?

I do declare a mistrial in deeds and in wonderments, Andrea! Why do you know these things about the universes of God's captors here? Well, because God's brave enough to spout off a German rebuttal to a commandant's next languages here. And, to ask of God's faiths here is like pouring wine out the window of the 747 or something that never landed in Philadelphia rightly here! If it's not a 747, Folks and wine Gentiles here, there's something called a 767 and such!

So, this is the rightly so ways and means it lady calling it a lunch break here! But, there are no fuel jokes a bounty in this 747's attack on life's properties here! We're just stating for the facts of God's wraths here that a sinister joke like this, a prank, have you, is what started these listless three, not four, Euro planes we'll call them here! Because Boeing 747s are for the birds lately here. They were good planes in other words!

There are music notes in question here, as well as a chocolate bar in question here. Likewise, a good Samaritan held out a chocolate bar to one of the "heroes," the star of David in his left hand too, and he goes, the guy does who's holding the planes hostage here, says, they're gonna crash landing's biggest and best spectacular show ever here! Why do I need a chocolate bar in the first place! Crash! It was before he went to strike the 18 other passengers is it? Nope, the 147 or so people in the front of the plane, this time it was the Empire State Building they were headed toward here, is so crass to be in front of! But, anyhoo, what time is it in EST? Nearly 9am in the morning though? Something has got to crack this head of yours, Andrea! For you had nothing to do with it. Correctamundos to that though? Absolutely not!

I'm just going with this, she says here of "Us!"

This is more information to gather from the pilots' cockpits here, that stated that, absolutely not! Nor did Andrea invent this into her brains here! We're simply stating the facts. The Divine Source Wisdom did not create nor reinvent the wheel here by simply stating that Jezibellie Christ is what's on next here! She's very much a masseuse too! And I, Jesus Christ says, never thought I would see the day that Andrea would write something like this, so confidently too.

I say this confidently here, but something tells me I knew Al-Qaeda or something like it, you see it, now you don't here? This is why the DSW rests! At this point here, we're nothing but a Bluetooth conversation against a God who likes torturous human beings then? Nothing could be furthest from the truth here. Don't think I'm a terrorist attack upon a nation of thieves here, but nothing could be furthest from the truth regarding luck either! Luck has little or nothing to do with anything here, but things in general, yes.

I just wanted to say that just before writing this, I had to look up what Al-Qaeda was. And even I had to look it up, Jesus says!

That's because the answers lie all within the minds and hearts of the survivors and their kinsfolk here.

And, that said here, signing off with passionate details about a massage from a masseuse that never even liked Jezibellie then! I beg to differ with you about this here tragedies seekings that we're all doing here! We even liked Jezibellie so much so that She is baby faced about it here. Consult the Urban Dictionary on that one here! Yikes, Classes of Gentiles and such men and woman here as babies were born out of wedlocks and such! Because that plane had at least 80 men on it at one point, the one that crashed into the Twin Towers you say? Nope, the one headed for the Pentagon here!

And, that's going down in history then, because there are limiteds in informations here! And, that said here, that's going down in history as a new Kasbah to rock here! I loved Jezibellie Christ, she says, Andrea does here! She's so mean when I want to kill myself though, she said of her one day here! "I go, well, how come you're contemplating suicide though?" It's just as with anyone else here, the day you go, "I want to kill myself? How come?" And then you go, "I don't want to do it that way or any other way besides hanging then!" I go, well, don't come crying to Me when the battle cures are going every which way here! Say, is Jesus Christ talking about Andrea's wishy washy love life here! Because it's going on, you know?

This Al-Qaeda bunch sounds like a riddle cure for peaces and such! Remember the name peaces is going to be around for a long time to come we hope! Iraq is the only places that these members hang out, by the way! Nothing could be further from the truth about living in other countries with these members of gangs and such in them (Wikipedia, January 17, 2018)! We're just hit and miss here, but there was a long list of such places that they hung out at? Nope!

And so, this is the lifelong crisis or crises about living the life o riley here, and about loving Jezibellie Christ this way and that a way here!

This means that the religious components of this crash and crashes alike had little to nothing to do about religious contexts, and everything to do with the LRAs, Less Restrictive Alternatives it is called to some people here! But the LRAs, Class of Gentiles, Elitists and such, are very dead in the water's biggest Blues Brothers bands here! And, stating that just that song was playing on the radio in the cockpit about the Blues Brothers here, by Aretha Franklin too! Which, by the way here, is the song on the radio in the cockpit still valid then? Because "Think" is a very cool song about witches and brews then? What does Jezibellie Christ have to do with telling Andrea not to kill herself over the small stuff here! Well, what would you think if your reincarnate sounded so mean like this to you, Andrea! This is funny here, as we laugh at this woman who doesn't, and I repeat, does NOT sleep around. You see it, now you don't here! This plane in other words is really the best plane for the job then? No.

This is what we don't want here. We don't want for Andrea's terrorist attacks to come 911 on her mind's eyes here.

And, to state that she wants to kill herself here is funny to "Us" though! As she wants to do no such thing! It's just a fleeting thought, answer if you will's, timings about the Divine Source Wisdom's, DSW for short here, messages of fate and faith alignments from God's evil twin sisters! The mountains that we mentioned a while ago, Ms. Mount Baker and her counterpart Dr. Z here, just kidding there! Her counterpart, Miss G here, states that the power of intentions here are just that. If you wanted to inject a certain serum into the goldfish aplenty, here's the methods that you use to do it with here! I try to save face a lot here, she says, Andrea does! But a fleeting thought is just that. Everyone on Earth gets that once in a while here, and then they say, "I don't wanna do that to myself!" And, there you go, though!

This is such an animal stereotype here too, because the chocolate bar situation is so lackadaisical about time bombs here that God steps in every once in a while, eh? I mean, if a chocolate bar is so crimson lights wrong to offer a man in heat for every woman, man and child in the place then? Not the kids, not the kids!

But, the main focus of those two smashings, and we'll call it that here, is to maintain the peaces of the Earth though? Nothing could be further from the truth here. And, my lifeline is God's, not some Al-Qaeda missionary styled backwater wash bucket man from Mars or something like it: You see it, now you do! I do believe that massages are a necessary evil here. But to think that a massage or a masseuse likes it up the butt will never, and I repeat, NEVER, get you into Heaven's gates here! And, luckily for "Us" here is that God never put up a rapist He didn't like! That's because the universes, and there are three out there, start messing with people's minds enough, they'll simply say, "Let's go get a meal or something out, you know?"

And, the ladies with class write back and report that a sexless marriage is something else the guys were so crimson about! They didn't have any sex lives to uphold to! And, this is the bottom of the barrels, Andrea, but what were those three individuals again?

The Father, the Son, and the Holy Ghost then? Three universes? Something like that! This is for the birds though if we cannot give a sentence or two about the tragedies that happened that day in New York and Pennsylvania, and one on U.S. soils though? It's Washington, D.C., Folks, and you too, Gentiles!

We just don't know who threw us out of the cockpit that day, but an ex-Marine who could fly a plane, a B-52 Bomber!

In other words, Folks, this was a terrorist attack on U.S. soils, though I beg to differ if they were a different class of citizens here than a U.S. one!

Each and every one of those bombers in there were ex-U.S. Marines here! They wanted to go down for rapes in the brig. Does anyone know what the federal prisons mock like someone else that wanted to keep going and stop please, and keep going though? Do you know what stop means, Class of Gentiles and such, Andrea?

Not a news press release, but Andrea loves the opposite sex here? It does mean that a woman told her to stop putting it, nope, her fingers in the vaginal walls here, because I just couldn't go down on her, you know? And, she said to stop it right here, and I go, okay, thanks! And, I just hugged her in return here. She is not a friend of mine anymore necessarily, but what if I'd kept going, she says! I just don't want to do it anymore! Did you know that that's half the battle, when somebody wants to rape you, is that they're just too proud or meek or mild a guy's raincoats et cetera, to notice a difference when a woman doesn't want to be raped? Any man, woman and child knows that! So, Andrea's gay then? Not hardly! Just experimenting with the opposite sex once or twice then? Just once. We were there, gimme a break! 🙂 I just didn't know what to do, she says here. I go, well, okay! And I gave her a cuddle hug! So, get off the deck here and say this for an opposing man who says, I didn't want HER to rape me though? It happens all the time then? Yes, indeed it does! Because a woman thinks that stroking a guy is getting them turned on, when in all actuality, Ladies, don't stroke it, make it come to you! In other words, let him come to you in his own times here. Don't slide it in just because it's dark and I'm naked, Jesus says! I sleep in the nude sometimes, right, Andrea, Miss Felony Melony here? Not! I never knew I was doing it wrong, cause I just don't do girls! So, thank God that Miss Felony Melony here never has raped a woman or a guy in this way here? I just don't stroke 'em, Jesus says, right?

He's never had an encounter this way or that a way about a man or a woman here who said to stop. In fact, it's nice to know that there's a woman on board here that says, "Okay, I didn't like that anyways!" And, to just commandant this news story here, I go, well, I just didn't like it though? Not afterwards, no! But during then? Only once! I was gotten down to, you know what I mean by this? No one can say it, but I cannot, I repeat, CANNOT go down on a woman here, no matter how hard I try this either! And her boobs just weren't for me either! But to me, I was in ecstasy? Don't be bi-curious. Ever. It ruins things for the opposite sex then? Nope! But it sure made me uncurious in a hurry here. I don't ever go down on a woman then? Can't tell ya how often I hear about that one too, Andrea, Jesus says to you here! Like, I'm sorry I can't get it up! But then, there's nothing less to the balancatures that weigh in on your sex lives like the ED Chapter 8 is it? Nope, Chapter 18 here. We're throwing off the bots online when we say, put the book online too? Sure! So, tell us, Andrea, are you bi-curious now? Absolutely not! It will be a friendship's days though that is missed out on sexual encounters that are either casual or livid in your systems here!

I do declare a mistrial in deeds and in affairs here! But I did not go down on her suggests that you're only female, Andrea! We say all this here because she did very clearly say and did not like that finger insertion stuff. So, I just didn't know what to do? It's true! So, get a life, huh, Andrea? Nope!

We're like that all the time with her here. I mean, who hasn't fantasized about sex with the same sex before? Everybody, literally, except Jesus Christ though, and Jezibellie too? I'm telling you, Andrea, if you're ever in the same sexed balancatures that these 48 people were on that plane here, I'm telling you that no one would ever suspect a same sex marriage between several hot people and several ugly ones here, but the ones on the plane that left Detroit is it, went to the hopper several times here? Not hardly at all here! Just one of them! That guy left the plane just before takeoff too.

He still lives in Missouri though! I probably know what happened to guys left on a plane with 30 eager women aboard it?

These guys didn't know time like "We" do! We heard, oh, this will take a while! Slit! Right in the throats of several "plain" girls here whom they did not want to kill. And torturous too? Yea, right!

This is because the planes knew that they were going to crash into the Empire State Building though? Yes, and that's what the news releases saw in that day after, Andrea, about this here.

I had had no clue what had happened until I got to work the same day afterwards, and that was at the University of S. Carolina then? Yep, indeed! I'd saw it on the monitors there, and I knew nothing about it at all here.

So, just in case anybody thinks that I was involved in that shooting of the man upstairs, I sort of cringe at this, but what about bodies and such lying in wait? I mean, let's just shoot 'em up, and make due with what we have available to us here? This one particularly knockout woman in the hopper here for her mistakes as a human being though? She was a kind of Oriental looking woman here! And, that's not a racist slur here at all here. The Orient exists.

And so, anyway, the guys on the plane here got the mimicked talent searches off the internet before their demise here, as they chose to go down with this country here. And so, each and every one of these men here were part of the U.S. soil surveys here! Not a one was from overseas. That is according to the Divine Source Wisdom, "Us" and "Them" do not exist here! There's three other waiting lists for the next flight out of Denver, for instance, where the "randomness" did not exist for these three souls or individuals on the plane! From Dallas to Atlanta here, we've got it covered, Andrea!

There's several deniabilities in this plane's gathering grounds filled with "sex offenders" r us! That is a lowercase for a reason here. These guys aren't that talented upstairs either. We're just saying that the U.S. soil surveys are pretty neat individual books I used to gather from the map libraries, the two that I used to work at though? Yep! And, that day, I was just as shocked to see Bill Clinton's face hugging that young girl who'd just lost her father-in-law in the plane crashes of tomorrow's lessons plannings here, and the folks knew that there were tons of doctors aboard the planes then, and an exact replica of the DSHS documents that they've had to deal with their PTSD about? Not! Not, not, no one, and never, comes through the Savior blessing but Us here! We're going to stop saying it's all about "Us" with the quotes, because it's getting old here for sure here. PTSD is for bonified soldiers who gave a damn about life, liberties and properties here, and actually, more times than not, had to "kill" someone in the name of laughter though and fun and games then? Not, not, and more nots to come here in this discussion about how these ex-Marines here had saved face and wanted to deny God's wraths and to laugh at these people who were dying and stuff like it, you see it, now you don't here? This is the time's places that God overcame greed and monetary bases for stuff like it you see, and got these three individuals together there, the Father, the Son and the Holy Ghost, for some kind of séance though?

We're just through with these universes then! Because laughing in the face of danger here is inappropriate and downright just maddening for the universes to contend with here! This "Oriental" lady, I will call her here, Jesus says, is downright maddening, for she was one of the ex-Marines though? Hardly so! She just needed to speak a little about the maddening commandant's languages though, and entered into the Marine Corps because she's speaking about lifegiving properties and maddening things such as babies on the planes and stuff! There was a good 45 minutes on the planes with these thugs! And, a baby ripped from the mother's arms here, happened on board that ship that never sank too!

So, try Me on these times, Jesus says, where Andrea and that woman allowed it to happen in the first place? Nothing could be furthest from the truth that she is a lesbian, though she has lesbian and gay friends though who aren't neither? This was a religious ceremony's biggest blessing of all, was that a guy on the first ship out, cause there were three ships too, took one look at everyone on the planes there and said, "Okay, I just had it out with a married man in the backyards of time here." And, I don't enjoy this at all here! PTSD here is for the birds then for sure! But they're good people who have this disease, a dis-ease, right? Not! I promised God an interlude between health and fitness here that would've said, "These men are righteous. Are they not?" Not in the least! Please do not confuse a military man's best glasses so they could see right in the wakes of 9/11 though! Nothing could be furthest from the truth about Andrea's sunglasses here! Meaning, that we just didn't know whether to cry or not? I cried my eyes out! So, there's good days and bad!

We're all succumbed to getting hope out of the refreshments of life here! But these ex-Marines all knew each other from PTSD school though? Not hardly at all! There's a platoon in Virginia, not the Quantico one, but at Nine Yards Shipping in Philadelphia, that knew all about this here! That's an actual vessel though! That's why you cannot find it in Google anywhere, Andrea, is because there's an actual ship about to sail upon us here!

That means, Folks, and you too, Gents, and Ladies of the night too, that a massage parlor and a masseuse later means that sex aboard these planes here let out a crying shame into the world's only legacies and never spoke it that way and hard before! What we mean by nine yards, too, is that there are only one ship, so there is only one ship, excuse me! That it means we can be taken by illustrations to the gore, I mean, core, of the rest of the day's outer services menus here!

What is she saying, for crying out loud then! It means that in Philadelphia, the reasons for the landing gear in that field there is because the pilots were allowed to live out that menial business's best and worst commandants for the situations at hand there. There was a shipyard there, and the menial businessmen for the jobs out back were the commandant's tellings about Jezibellie Christ practically! Say, the Jezibellie Tutankhemen Bongs Christ is wrong for the tomb's actual names and stuff around it, and they were buried in Greece at the Thessaloniki that Paul was buried at, right? Nope! They were left there then for good though? Not! The Greeks were actually at play with the ideas of a right commandant's ship holder's viewpoints here.

And, we have a point here! So, make it, Andrea keeps saying to us here! But we're getting to this here.

The commandants for the Jezibellie Bongs ship makers never got to play with the word outerscores here. Sit tight here, Andrea, for we are going to make these tomb robbers a very happy word called Bongs and not Barnes here! But for the tombs at the St. John's basilica here, it really is Jezibellie Bongs too! So, for Bongs it's not the facts killing us here, but the words that come to God's only son, Jesus Christ, about His current wife for all eternity here! She's a Bongs, but a Barnes you said? A Bongs broad on a skilled notation's only son here would state that for all eternity, the tomb's located next to जेजबिेल्लिए चृस्त.

You know, Jesus's only son was instrumental in stating that Bongs or बोड्स is not right or correctamundos here. It's Barnes or बर्नेस, under that one! But there's a little hiccup or two in our writings here, as the converter that we used to Devanagari script this is two-fold here.

So, cradle robbers in the night used to get the Devanagari scripts here at the folds of time here! And, that said here, what is the mentionable's last names doing in the Jezibellie Bongs world then! It's Jezibellie Bongs Christ then? We've always gone by Bongs. So, the earlier scripts just mention a Barnes and Noble type offering here, but it's spelled Barnes in the bath ways of the lower scripture's mentionings of this name never in the book of the Bible though! She was just trying to stay out of it, kinda sorta like Andrea is trying not to mess up Her name a lot here, but it's just meaningfuls that state that God's kinda sorta watching the Bongs monuments show up here! That is because the Jezibellie cures here are sort of like a grandiose dealing with God's times here! Jezibellie Bongs Christ, or जेजिबेल्लिए बोड्स चूस्त is not quite right either here. It's जेजिबेल्लिए बर्नेस चूस्त or Jezibellie Barnes Christ in the tombs of love here at the Basilica of St. John's in Rome here, and not Tutankhemen at alls, here ye. That comes later on in our texts with the Holy Ghost, here ye.

Again, there is a little hiccup on the conversion of Jesus Christ's tomb though? It's in an unmarked grave marker, but it has Her name in it though! Jezibellie Christ is all you'd need to find it! And so, how come all the talks about 9/11 and things like it? You see it now you don't? It's because of the sinister eating grins off of the talent search's best and biggest things, like the Bongs name is sort of like saying that Mary Magdalene here had the last name of her husband's to be here. And, the very best man for the jobs of locating Mary Bongs, as she was an uncle or an aunt of some kind here, means that she was related to Jezibellie Christ here! Mary Bongs, like I said!

And so, grave mongers or cradle robbers later, Folks, says that Jesus Christ superstar is buried in an unmarked grave then? You've got it! Why is it Devanagari script in Rome though? Why is it Devanagari script in Thessaloniki then! Well? It's because She was buried with Paul originally in a deep gravel pit! Until Thessaloniki became self-conscious here when the authorities arrested Paul is it? They arrested the only things that mattered to the commandants here on American soils though? It's Jesus Christ's tomb that they're after here! Why not search the Archbasilica of St. John (Lateran) for it then! It's located in the Roman cemeteries of peaces here! Peaces is a word.

So, Andrea, how do you connect the soils of Brazil with the peaces of tomorrow brings it? You just do here! Say, these plane crashes though brought basilicas to you here! Say, this is a You territory here. Why not say that Andrea is reincarnated then? Because that would mean that Jezebel exists in the territories of the United States as a comeback kid for Us then!

We're saying that the terrorist attacks did not happen to us, they happened with us! They really didn't give a crap, says an ex-Marine upstairs about the brig, that they didn't happen together simultaneously means that we're going to invade now the Roman Empire here? Not hardly, Folks! Constantine was a jewel and a gem to that society's influences of Gods here, mind you! Gods and Goddesses though? The Roman Empire prepares to argue this one point with you, Andrea! What about looters and such on U.S. soils about Jesus Christ's reincarnated man here! St. John, by the way, Our son here, brought his mother to the gravesite after exhuming Her body from the lessons planning that we have here, and transported Her and Her lifeless body to the tomb in Roma. So Roman people here, it's Roma by the way, doesn't believe Us I'm sure here! But figure it out, Folks! It's like <u>Angels and Demons</u> all over again! You know, the book! ☺

Grave robbers though. That's what it took for Us to get out of dodge here and to say or state that Divine Source Wisdom, or DSW for short here, knew what the sentimentalities looked like here!

Keep in mind, Folks, that a Jesus reincarnate was and has been here 17 times total. Mkay! That means, Folks, and Class of Gentiles later here, Folks, that the sons of a bitches who crashed those planes all knew each other on American soils here!

And, that saids here, there are saids and said in this work here! There are tons of memos to recognize that a bunch of White men though? Nope! One White guy and five Philippinos, five Exorcists, and three hopper callers later! Sounds like the White men did not exist on these planes here, to throw the government off though? Possibly! But not likelies here. Our new words systems, by the way here, is for the birds if you cannot use them in your vocabularies here. It's like a new word comes by way of planes, trains or automobiles here! And, this is a sellout point in Brazil's infrastructure here, is that there is an easy way out of these sex rings over there, for pedophilia though? Men, women and children are there! I cannot begin to imagine what sex rings exist for the populations of mud theorists everywhere here, but this means war, Folks! Sodomization is really for the birds here too! I mean, I've been sodomized, Jesus says! Shall we not! So have I, Andrea says it here for the birds to read even! It's just a better tomorrow that we hold you down, Andrea, and say, Jesus is here for the takings here. Is it the second coming or something? Nope, not at all. See Chapter 38 about sins here. We're all safe and on board here, save the few boneheads, and we'll call it that, that downed the planes over the Empire State Building, which was their primary target here! Devastation is not what we're planning for the rest of our lives here, Jesus says of Andrea right now! Just type it and we'll read it later here?

It means that the devil's shapes and structures are really two-fold here. This silly, moronic clause in the Bible's Chapters 32 and 36 of James someday is really going to be a tough one to decipher here, as the Bible ought to stay the way it is here! These men, these cowards we will call Him too? No, not that, the messages of the Bible is really a James thing here, in place of those words used to call Paul a saint here! Say James instead of Paul and you've really got it down now, preachers and stuff! We're all in this together, aren't we!

We're going to say that this person Andrea knows is really a bad man here, and does not, I repeat, does not have or carry pedo head or murderous head. But a balancures later, Folks, state that he did rape me with a stick though? Not hardly, Folks, but Jesus sure was, just before He died up on that cross though! Not! He was down on His knees and hands too. But who was this, Andrea, some guy! Yep! I do declare a mental weasel has left the premises here! Say, is Jesus Christ honestly a gay guy too? Not! He was whipped up and down the parking lots filled with horses and buggies though? This was in the middle of the 13th century wars here. B.C. though? We've got a lot to learn here, Folks! For right now though, a sodomized relative of somebody else's pain and suffering is not what we're after here. We're not here to hear the sodomized somebody's this did this to me and sodomized penises united ways here!

Sadly, this is how it went here! They were kicking Him and throwing Him to the wolves here! But He did not, and I repeat this lightly, did NOT die upon that cross! It was a gay rights demonstration that We too were just supporting here! It's not gay for life, People! We're crossbred or something here!

There's a holding cell for Jesus's wife and not Him though? Nothing could be furthest from the truth here! They were just too interested in getting Jesus to His tomb that nothing could have cross fired a double whammy for their son, John Christ. It means that John the Baptist actually has a name, and the last name begins with B! LOL! It's Barnes or something, right or correctamundos here? Actually, the same names on the ships that we were talking about earlier are still in the correctamundos stage or phases of life here, as there were plenty to do upon those ships here! Say, those ships were used to house their meetings or something here, right or correctamundos here? Yep! Those shipyards in Philadelphia have moved then! And, something else here.

There's all sorts of speculations about Roma's biggest commandant's languages here, when nothing could be furthest from the truths here about Jesus Christ coming of age here! That saids here, what is saids anyways here? It means that Me and Jezibellie Christ are coming of age here! And, that saids here, there's two ways of looking at things on those planes up there! Let's sodomize everybody on boards then? Yep! I mean, yuckos just looked at them weirdly and up and at 'em we go here! This is pain's luck, that is all here!

Meanwhile, just look at the Marine commandant's languages here on our soils here! It means that they were all stuck with the labels of MixxedFit's talent searches then? They sang and danced to everyone's mishaps here! They all came back with the Lincoln's Tunnel in New York here and said, it's Lincoln's everybody!

Um, they're climbing back into the newsrooms with this one here! As New York was hardest hit, but the commandants for the military's own Pentagon spoke rules and rulerships here, as well as the time it took for some of the military's strikings to commandants somebody I know into a low dose of Cetaphil for bad knees here! Keep in mind that my military strength comes from my family's involvement for sures here. That said here, my whole military family would be appalled at the site of these future gentlemen who are sure to strip Jesus naked, wannabes and such! So, what is the commandant's messages here supposed to entail then, but a message's last stand here. These guys knew how to fly a plane straight into the Pentagon for crying out loud here! All "sex offenders" are good and evil then? All evil ones are really just themselves here. Crying out loud here are all the sex offended upon board those three planes, not four, right? Three! The fourth one never left the runway here. That said here, is this accurate historically so? Not in how they cite that there were four planes though. Mkay, I know what I'm talking about, Andrea says here! Nope, We know! And so, leave it for a lesson in sodomy though? Say, anyone got herpes around here too? Yep, them all! So, this is what wars are fought over, and stressingly so, why isn't the 9/11 attacks taken into custody between them all then?

Well, because they wanted to attack the U.S.'s soils here from all of that military training then? These were all cowards at the shipyards of trust here, working out their stupid fantasies in the middles of the nights here, and taking men, women and children hostage was a blue moon for them, eh? A hate crime thereof, as the Urban Dictionary spouts it is then? Yes.

And so, there's all sorts of ways to find Jezibellie, the beautiful Queen of England though? Yep! It's true, but not because I said so! It's motherfucking beautiful places and scenery and concepts and motherfucking commandants who state that the reigns on those 747 jetliners were, and these were not 767s then? Yes, they were. It's the same chassis on the planes of love then! The 767 is just a 747 with seats that are wider than before here.

That same 747/767 is right here for the takings here! This love chain child literatures speaks it makes this book feel like it's a motherfucking right, Jesus says, to cuss no less and no more here! Say, can this be a non-fiction book or a fiction one! You decide to tell us here, Andrea? Neither is the answers here! The 747s of tomorrow's fiction book's tattletaling upon us here, Andrea! There's crisp and clean and there's torturous individuals who ran those 747s to the grounds then. This is called a concept of shit infested Twinkies here.

There's 747s in the wakes of 9/11 that we'd just assume forget about here. But it was a shit infested Twinkie's best commandants in the militaries of actions here that got us thinking that it's America's soil surveys that would never do this to our own country's backgammon games here! And, that said, Andrea, get going on those soil survey reviews, eh? Those were for the mostly geology majors that came into the map libraries here. And, that said, Folks, and you too, Gentiles here, that mostly geology thing has everything to do with the get me up and go telemarketing lingerers that come between getting the jobs done here and having little to do with the reigns and stuff, for going to the jobs of choice here is a choice and an oath that you take in the brig then, correctamundos here? These were all teenage guys too, who they'd just assume found guilty of treason then, because of war crimes and such! Say, Obama made a nice gesture here to get going on the Osama Bin Laden party that we threw because he'd captured him, and say, shot him in the knees about here! Well, they weren't that upset about this there in Iraq! So, keep 'em and shove 'em aside is what the military's all about here? Not!

Jesus and Jezibellie, k-i-s-s-i-n-g! Do not separate them. Mkay! This is why the America's soils are so great about housing terra files or terra papers here, and this is not what they said. Mkay! They did not state that religious peoples flew these planes into B-52 bombers and lived to tell about it here! It said, that the whole organization of religious people, folk, what have you, that the underground railroad systems here are very much organized for religious folk though? Not hardly here. These atheists, and I do mean it that way here, did not care about a country's religious folks at all here.

They were simply able to come up with a time or two's lessons planning states here and say, the Empire State Building built up the Twin Towers for crying out loud. How about them cookies here? Implying, Folks, and Classes of Gentiles here, that the churches in town were about to go under here, as well as about a dozen other folk from L.A. proper here. They were all involved here in the brig's closing arguments here! And, Andrea's getting nervous about this here, as she types us all the time here, but she's nervous because she didn't know anything about it until this writing here, Class of Gentiles later then, and she's nervous no more because we addressed it. Same thing applies here, Andrea, and Classes of Gentiles later then! The man or men responsible for all this mishaps here was just as thrilled with the invention of folks lying around in wait for the responses that they got here.

That means, Folks, and Classes of Gentiles here, that "Suddenly," life has new meaning to me, there's beauty up above, and things we never take notice of, wake up and suddenly, you're in love! What do a class of Gentiles have to do with the above song then by Billy Ocean here but a crest of a news story here!

This means, Folks and Classes of Gentiles here, that the ringleaders all went down in the crashes then to humanity's sakes alive here? No, they did not! The ringleaders are still in token friendships with the U.S.'s soils here! The responsible parties are not blue in the faces! Until they die though? Hardly friendships that I want to reckon with!

And so, Class of Gentiles later here, there was this person responsible for a James affair from the heart of the Bible's trust then. But his name thereof is James, last name is James. For the military's point of view later here, we should honor and strike from the records here the last names of everyone in the U.S. named James, for there art thou then, Class of Elitist Gentiles and such here? Well, these are all retired ex-military going fares for people whose religious qualities end up on Meetup.Com for a revival of sorts, and for an atheist group meeting's lessons planning here.

There's pops and starts and goes in this lessons planning here for the future though! This time on U.S.'s soil surveys is the popular metal hit, I can't stop loving you, by Scorpions, said a little differently here!

James here is not responsible for anything but Creedence Clearwater Revival here on those planes of indifference here! This is because the ringleaders for this clan of influence's harshest realities are still here for the takings here. And, that said here, the ringleaders for this nations of influence's best commandants here is because of the crimson lights theaters around the globe here!

There's something to do with American soil surveys here.

What is the reckoning to do with Andrea though, Folks of Gentiles and meanies out there?

That means that Andrea has nothing if little to do with it. Folks of the Gentiles kinds are coming of age I guess! I believe in reckoning, Andrea says! But if this guy, James, is a Gentile here, he's sure coming of age pretty quick like! There are certain moments of reckonings that happen in the Gentiles camps here! Say, Andrea, what do certain people you know of think of certain military tactics in the limelights for the U.S. Coast Guard? Because my whole family was in the military too. In the military senses here, us military brats are commonly going towards the Coast Guard for their timings and such. Well, this James guy, James what though? James,… is his last name, though I don't know the first? Like Bret or something, he lived in the Coast Guard ranks here. James Bret then? Nope, the other way around then! This guy masterminded the cynical movies on television that stated that, openly, Andrea, you are giving this guy's needed information to the U.S. government, Congress, or what have you! Say, the shipyards of Philadelphia actually have a plan for the U.S. government's reigns here!

Chapter 30

Homelessness

Is your family very supportive of your cause, Andrea? Because we were homeless for a time there, sleeping in my van for three years off and on. Of telling about your causes though, the van was not working or operable lately. And so, recently we have been sleeping out of doors or on the lawnchairs of neighborhoods that work right?

We haven't been, but it sure feels like we could. Hey wait a minute... We have altered Andrea's appearance so much so that she's not allowed to sleep on any lawnchairs anyways. I mean, if people you know won't leave you alone in a past life to finish the book on time here, the only thing that is wrong with her right now, is that she's rewriting this section.

About to go into hiding we are if we cannot begin to stress those little points about Jezibellie just right here.

As one time, Jezibellie was found homeless or on the brink of it by Me, Jesus here, and She was so stoned up and nakedly eating things off the graveled lawn of some homeboy here, and I scooped Her up and took Her with Me here. A carpenter I was not: She was the carpenteress. I was the surgeon back then, but I had many trades. I was able to support and to take care of Her back then, but nobody's really taking care of Andrea right now, ... So, Switzerland's it, huh?

They have the best health care system for teeth I could scream, Jesus says to me back here, Andrea thereof! Why not get people jobs, put them up so they can get off of these meds, and put them back to work? What about the Cinderella slippers we all deserve to get?

We're really off the mark though?

We're eating at McDonald's too much here, but they've got the perfect bathroom for doody time that I could scream, most places you go at any rate.

This is the homelessness section, and we're not homeless anymore it says in this work, but we are currently, so we made her erase and start this section over again.

Aptly, we can cover Her with tears in a bathwater section of town's players here, or we can be some gorgeous woman on the brinks of disasters here, and rewrite the whole entire section here! We can't seem to get going in life, is what I'm hearing from Andrea here, and it's really pissing me, Us, off here?

Not Us, but us! This hamburgesa ways of saying homelessness exists is really pissing us off here too, Andrea! I don't like staying in a weekly motel as I finish this section on homelessness as a homeless junkie, or at least I'm not pregnant and staying at a mental hospital, where they kill unborn fetuses left and right here?

Hi, I'm homeless, plain and simply so, and I don't want Jesus to be mad at me for counting the ways, above the law that I am right now?

I'm definitely on the LRA type systems here, but they're being really good about the appointments here. For those times pasts, I'm rewriting a section of my stays because, golly gee whiz if I'm on the streets more than a day of my whole entire lifetime.

I'm currently living off of food stamps, though I would like not to. In the middle of the night, in my dreams, you should see the things we do, baby, mmm, by Taylor Swift's got to be the ways to go here, as I'm nervous about being kicked out of this place, of saying, I'm living without the van right now, as everyone's tired of rescuing it out of impound lots due to my mental health stays. With local law enforcements sure knowing where I am staying at sometimes, it's hard to say or to speak about homelessness if I am currently living at a hotel/motel situations, here ye.

Now I am going to turn to what was previously written. Here goes!

There is a holding cell for each type of people that come to Jesus Christ superstar here! These people, dancing around this hymn for God's peoples here in the 1940s was it? Nope, the paper here on the days and nights of Arabian musics, is really the música of an Arabian nights parable's best features here! There are people dancing around the golden walls, the música of a celebration of times past, and a simple truth to the Gilligans of society's influences here! Say, we're homeless no more here! But we used to be!

"Hearing voices" is so overrated by society's popular Rogaine missives here. We need to hear about Vietnam at some point too here, as the soldiers who PTSD-edly got picked up for little missives into the Knights of the Arabian Roundtable were really just soldiers who got picked up for knighting a princess Brown or something like it, you see it, now you don't!

Princess Brown, by the way, is Jezibellie Christ in full garb though? Yep! This is Jezibellie Christ here, telling about… Hey, wait a minute, Jezibellie is not for the takings here. That is for Jesus to decipher here. She's just about a princess away from getting caught taking off Her clothes for the last time though, as we're just about getting Jesus into the mix here! No lap dances for this woman then?

The sinisters lied about it here, but this is the greatest love story ever known to man here!

And, that saids here, there's saids and said, so what of it! Here is the Arabian nights versions of priestly interventions here! The sad parts about God's wraths here that evilly speaks to us here is the Arabian nights versions of the Three Little Pigs part about God's raptures and stuff like it. You see it, now you don't here? It's a comedy's tragic links to God about the "voices" one hears at nights and stuff like it. You see it there, Class of Gentiles and such. Right, God? Or correctamundos here? For God's wraths would not entail us "seeing" voices neither, just as someone sees dark figurines in their livelihoods and then gets taken down to the local hopper, the prison for women and children back in the dark ages too.

There's Blanksmas on the streets of Brazil here! That's not what we're talking about when we say homeless creatures are really just on the streets of Brazil then, waiting it out on a chance from God then? Brazil is a natural habitat for many different birds there, but that's not what we mean when we fly south for the winters above us here. That said, that's a family name for Jezibellie Christ, for the birds is not!

We're saying and studying Her mother's family's names too, for Christ our Lord is from the Orient, right? He was born here too, under the guise of a family name of Brazil's interests here. He was so White to Me in the 3rd grades though, Jesus was!

Little do they know that having a father named James too is kind of an oxymoron for dear old dad here. It means, Folks, and morons too, that having a father cut out for the James mentalities here is like the oldest tricks in the book's moronic clauses, as "James" in the Bible is cut out to be Her father, Jezibellie's here! And so, that is why he is in the Bible in the first place, because he could cite and recite all kinds of things like She could! So, why Blanksma? Well, Her mom is, because she's Black and he's White here, tired of all things cuddly by natures that we cannot explain here thoroughly here! Meanwhile, she's the homeless bitch here, Andrea is, about ten minutes ago though! Our time! Our Brazilian queen is but a dream. But homeless, Andrea was here, for about three years or so here!

Take it from me, Andrea says of it here, that is for the birds for sures here! We're so sure, it's sures, for the simple fact that Western State took me in here! That means that homeless junkies are so explainable to the world's biggest commandants here that God took advantage of the Walmarts, simple as can be here, and took off her clothes though for the demand of money she did not! So, Walmarts of American soils here is really for the birds if you ask me then? Not! They can sustain anybody or anything out in the parking lots of hell here! Say, do you have to go to work later, Andrea? Yes, is the answer to that prayer!

We're saying that looking for work as a homeless junkie is not what you should be spending your time on here as a homeless junkie here! It's finding a place to live, first and foremost here. And, Jezibellie Christ even had a dad and a mum too! That doesn't mean you should live with them. In the first place here, Jezibellie believed in Her dad's humor, so much so that you shouldn't live with them if you cannot find a place to live though! Her dad's humor then? Well, she didn't want to appear broken down with crutches or anything, but living on her own was always her forte, especially before she became "ill" with schizophrenia though? It's not paranoid schizophrenia, is it here? Because they schizoaffectively bipolared me too.

With all the recent hospital stays, I beg to differ on that one here! Because, bipolarly, I am inclined to reason with all kinds of ladies in the mental hopper bag here! But if you're not employed then your parents won't leave you alone here? Carol was her name, the mother of Jezibellie Christ here! They didn't get along either! But so, is this a willingnesses clause here, or the mother of fertility is Jesus Christ here? Because they both had a brain in their heads to leave the situation be here, but the reasons for the insanities clauses here is that, some people had the brains of a pinhead's situation device right there for Andrea, the whole time though? Yes, Ma'am and you too, Sirs of the Gentiles type! But if you carry around a Bible in these church type settings here, you stay longer! I mean, if she's married or something like it, you see it, now you don't, then how come she can't take care of herself then, Andrea can't then?

And, simply put here, men on this Earth's phrases here, she never, Andrea never did, strip off her clothes. For the public consumption of men and Earth's phrases here, the women in these movie strips never quite take their clothes off for anyone here, save the Earth's planetary phrases and such! I mean, the cosmic strips take hold and then their loin cloths take control here? That's a planetary alignment of God's wills and such here! Take control here and live a little, Andrea!

There's much more to the mental hoppers than meets the eyes here! Say, is that butter working on your bum's hemorrhoid situations here? The butter is a new Dutch butter, for the legs though? Nope, for the bum's hemorrhoid situations here! I mean, when Jesus and Jezibellie died, they monumentalized them. For all hope's clauses though, Andrea, and we can rectify this later here, that they were killed by Paul James then? Nope! If Paul James is how he got into the rectified places that be here, the towers they killed, Bret James then, is really a misnomer then? A Coastie and a present later, Pops, cause my dad was in the Coast Guard too, the U.S. kind though! It's the facts, Pops! He doesn't believe Me half the time, Jesus says!

There's tons of time to decipher the differences between Andrea's "voices," and the time it takes for the last song to be played here!

There's nothing but homeless clauses in the Merry Christmases that take over the souls here, but Switzerland's homeless shelters… Yes, please here! They treat you like kings and queens over there! We want to mirror our "shelters" about them too!

They've always been this way over there, Jesus says of Christ's introduction to glamorous there, for simple girls, united ways here! And, we say united ways here a lot for Andrea's sakes here, because we believe in United Way though? We don't though! United Way's simple greetings here are, because we believe in the United Way's trusts and stuff too, we assigned ourselves a job of applying there then!

Because the United Way's biggest interceptions here are men, women and children of the military's statures here! But this is my biggest mistake, Jesus says of the Gentiles here, is trusting them though? Let's mirror Switzerland's land of the hotels for homeless peoples in generals here!

Generals, because we know them to be of the promised lands then? Nope, the Generals in charge over there simply don't believe in mental illnesses for "homeless land shelters" either here! They're so "in charge" over there when it comes to mental health shelters and what nots over there too! Do they let us shave over there then? Absolutely not? Absolutely!

And, do they let Cinderella slippered men to come visit the King's obvious grandeurs over there too? We just need a system like that in our American states here! Or, Canada's an option! We don't even have mental hoppers in Canadian lands anymore, right and correctamundos here? We have "retreats" though! I mean, if you've got a mental problem or issue here, the Canadians are rougher with their prisons or jails here! So, Andrea's never been to jail here, but she just might end up there if this book gets published though? She's kinda thinking it here! I mean, how did she, Andrea, know about this Jezibellie cure of the 9/11 attacks, down to the meaningful phrases of God's wraths here?

There's somebody in the lurch for every single person on Earth here! If you're so inclined like the duties of a housewife, Andrea Wynn, then, Andrea's distracted by her own musical tastes here, but the minimal duties of a housewife here states that an abandoned home by Andrea is not in the cards anymore. Is it?

It's a state of emergency's biggest blessings over here is that, Switzerland divides up the mental hoppers between homeboys that state that they've heard a voice, or have seen something. Naturally divided are the homeboys that follow Christian rules here! I mean, if we cannot choose our own foods here and follow our medication regimens here, we believe in smacking the childhood photos down to our loneliest deals in churches all across America's biggest politics making persons here, it's the doctors in town's loneliest cures though! For thou art thyself, though not a Montague, Jesus says of Jezebel, it's Jezibellie, mkay! That thought of going by your proper name, there Capulet, is really what Jesus and Jezibellie Christ's last names were about in the middle of the 14th centuries B.C. And that's what Jezebel, it's Jezibellie, mkay, risked it all to write about in the Bible's mid-century's last clause, about the faith's interventions of faith's healers and stuff here!

For thou art thyself, though not a Montague, is the best interventions of Jezibellie's and Jesus's lives together were for here! For, say, three hundred dollars a night here, you could fly over to Switzerland's best hopper lands here and say, three hundred and fifty dollars a night, in the hotels and motels that bring us the biggest hopper lands here, say, three hundred and fifty dollars a night for a visit to the unmeshed love affairs that bring us to the mental hopper "jails" here, to postpone the nose hair trimmers we need to finish the days with here, as the mental hospitals, the hopper thereof here, is the mental hopper's affairs of the nighttime sniffling, sneezing, aching, clauses we need to therefore get home with! And, Switzerland's got, and always had, Jesus cures there, as well as Jezibellie ones here!

They never thought about getting Jesus a woman then, rightamundos here? There's never a time to "get on" than to witness the homeless structures worldwide here, not just in America's mental institutions here! Say, is this a witness to the homeless shelters back in Jezibellie's time here? You bet! And Jesus was right at the helm then? He was homeless, not the other way around here! She had all the monies in the worlds here. Say, was Jesus a homeless junkie then, unable to care for Himselves here, as in, the best is yet to come there with the Jesus cures?

In line with junkies then is the homeless shelter's whine shaft mixers here! There's something like that in the mental hopper jails and such here in America's soil surveys here! Say, is Switzerland thinking of tea and crumpets for the unemployed then, as there are several ways to make someone unemployable for sure here! I mean, if the mental hospital jail cells are any sweeter here, make them come and go facilities for sure here!

I mean, if a person is in a mental jail cell padded room here, that is one thing here. But the jails are so full of, I mean, filled with, the right sorts of peoples for the jobs then? I mean, if Jezibellie is filled with right order ascension type atmospheric pressures here, there are jail cells with the Jezibellie label in them.

Shall we order a "sick bed" for them all then? Because the real ways to beat homelessness back in the days of Jesus and Jezibellie here was to say and to think them all at the same time, about the "voices" in ones' heads though? There were peoples back then who believed in the spirit world's biggest promises back then, you know? And so, there are more to life's gifts than a simple hello will do here! There are bigger plans and promises than to witness the tragic circumstances of life on the streets of American soil surveys here!

Say, we're right here, there, with Jezibellie and Jesus about this streets of Wyoming deal's biggest mental hoppers here. Just witnessing the Jesus and Jezibellie cures upon the streets of Wyoming's dealings with the jail systems of helping someone out here is not what we're after here. Say, sooner than later here is Wyoming's jail cell systems here, because they mimic, if not imply here, that soon Canadians are the ways to go then?

Say, is Jezibellie's last name Bongs or Barnes here? Because "Bongs" means something nasty here in the Chinese language too. It means asshole or something like it. You see it? Now you don't, there, Commandants in the military band's languages of finding dreams and such!

Working for a living's gotta come back on the things of wild dreams. Such notions of commandant's languages here makes sense when you think about the times of unrest periods, such as living in the Walmart's favorite genes here! Say, is that a place to stay when you've got nowhere else to go for the nights out on the towns then, Folks, and Gentiles too then?

Because we're at Walmarts and stuff for the nights out in the cold living baskets of love here is the meaningfulnesses that we always take for granteds here! Likewise, Folks, and Gentiles too here, is that Jesus was a Jew. Get over it! A Jewish man's forsakingnesses here with God here are the questionables and such! How come Jesus was a Jewish man's forgiven notes and qualities here? Because His mother, Marybelle Hopper Magdalene was the name's biggest wonderings here! If Joseph Magdalene was the name of My father there, then God's got a whole new question for peaces here! It's peaces, Peoples!

Say, if Magdalene was such a common name back then, then how come Mary Magdalene, the traitor here, is such a kind soul and sort of human being here then? Because she's My mother in law then! My mother, to beat all odds here, is legally bound to me here, Andrea says then, because Mary M., the other one here who was not Marybelle, My mother here, is the one we're saying is a two time convict here.

How confusing for somebody who was beaten to death practically, as a married woman then? Nope! She was impregnating other women, then, with this notion of practicing common times here? Cause Christ as a middle name or a last name is really where it's at here. So, Joseph Shrine Bowl Man here is not what you'd call a Christian by any means here!

Simply put here, by all means, Andrea! We're waiting here for Jesus and Jezibellie to make out then, aren't we here? We're simply stating that God's wraths here! And, Jesus didn't know what hit Him! To shave his nose hairs though was simply elitistisms. Wanting to grab another handbag though is like telling God His nose hairs thought it was simply safe for consumptions here! Do you mind shaving your beard like this again, Folks, and you too Gentiles here?

Cause back in Jerusalem… That's why we say this about Hillary Clinton, Folks, and you too Gentiles here! Because back in the days of cynicisms here, we all took a bath and a shower the next day here!

You've got to appreciate her positioning as the Secretary of State here, cause wasn't it Hillary Clinton? Duh! So, she just had a bath and a shower too? It means, Folks, that overseas, the places to stay that are clinically insane, she's seen them all, too. There's lots of deals out there on a folk score of places to stay here, and that's not the clinically insane person that I mean her to be here. It just means that the freedoms of enjoying oneself here means that, coming and going as we please here, is just what we need for these "mental hoppers."

They are Christianly wanting you at the clinically insane "mental hoppers" here just to get a rise out of the governors here ye, to tell if the beds we needed for all those mental hopper places get a rise out of God's inkling cures here!

And that said here, any governor's questioning the mental state hospital systems with that goddamn new "fence" they put around the perimeter of it here! I was there for both with and without the fence being there! And, they're putting fences around none of the other ones in the states here, Folks, and classes of elitistic Gentiles here!

They're putting glasses above and beyond the rest of the tunics that people have to wear in order to hide their hickeys there then? Not in the least! These are none other than God's angels, people who are just homeless here! We're trying to state it for the class of Gentilistic, elitist peoples here, but to see it first hand would be grand here! It means, Folks, and the class of Gentilistic, elitist people here that there are crawdads there for the greatest of choicest peoples here!

There's cures for HIV/AIDS in Chapter 14 here! I mean, if cadmium sulfate is the way to go here, the smoking of it thereof here, then the barium cadmium's ingestion of it is latent here! And injections of it, that is really for the birds is it? To kill HIV, it is 2 fluid ounces, so 1 fluid ounce of water with 2 ounces of cadmium sulfate popped into the leg with a syringe, then a month later, do it again with 1 fluid ounce of water and 1 ounce of cadmium sulfate and it is the vaccine! Say, in Switzerland, they speak English over there.

Shall we talk to them about cadmium sulfate in exchange for a mental hopper's reviews class on how to treat peoples on or off these medications then? Because they don't even look you in the eyes or stare at you with all this talk about cadmiums and such! Just don't bridge the gap here, Andrea! I mean, exchanging information about this exchange of timing's tides and such just brings us to believe mostly in the cures for some things great here! Hillary Clinton is a Godsend to this Earth's natural selection of peoples who are off the sauce!

So, to speak it here is nice of her to interject here, but cadmium sulfate you say has a grownup rate of pay as a junkie! So, to speak it here means that we ingest the cadmium sulfate then? Nope, you smoke it or you inject it, and it pays off for HIV/AIDS then!

This is the end of this section's AIDS viruses then. Because of the little things that go unnoticed here, Andrea, there are mental hospitals everywhere in the world besides these two countries here! And the jail system for Canada rocks the Kasbah then? Nope, not at all here. Their "halfway houses" though rock the Kasbah, for peoples whose drugs they need to come off of here! Say, there are three ways to become nice about getting off of these meds here! Say, why not take the cadmium now then, Guys! Well? It's plastic or somethings like it. You see it, now you do here?

Take control of the newest lives and questions we all know to love it as here! For instance, a sectionalized couch here would look great in the living rooms of life here! They kinda don't have a homeless problem there in Switzerland, you know? This moment's notices are to gravitate towards lovely home gestures as getting the rental rates to come down. You see?

With the advents of student loan debts being as focused as childcare was, there are no ways to come down from that. You see it, now you don't, Andrea, as her loans were forgiven too! Those mental hospitals replicated many a time here the fantastic quotient of being super allergic to psychotropic drugging, save the Seroquel that has managed to see us through here! Say, Andrea, are you still "on your medications," though? For the sakes of this writing here, yep! And so, it's none of anybody's businesses what medications you are currently taking, Ms. U.S. Folklore Person, You, Andrea thereof here! Well, try being "blip" like for about 30 days a week here, and we'll talk about the student loan debt that is forgiven here! Say, make them optional for people to pay them back, as Sallie Mae has already reached me here!

It means, Folks, that for "total and permanent disabilities" here, I certainly plan on paying them back though! This means that "blips" are really the oculogyric crises that was replicated so many times these past several years, five you say? More like 20, 15, or exactly 11 years here, that I had allergic reactions to these meds here, save the Invega shot and the Haldol one too! Try living with that burden of trying out different meds in these mental hoppers here, only to find out that they are all, and I do mean all of them, able to give people oculogyric crisis and such! We're taking the Benadryl for that right now as we speak, since one hospital's inception at the hands of a PA-C there, would not let up on this "Divine Source Wisdom" thing we had posted up on the internet. (See the Days 1-44 I had posted up on my website's classics, in this book, no less and no more here.) By seeking God's wraths here, I'd been put up onto Perphenazine at such a nasty level, plus a Haldol shot and some Gabapentin to counteract these blips with here, but the Perphenazine won I guess, because months and months later here, I can still feel the oculogyric crisis upon my person here!

He hated God enough, the PA-C did there at this particular hopper there, which by the way here, they didn't allow us to write letters in there either here, and said I flashed everyone a simple no-no thing to them, even the judge laughed at this. Though there were no flashings of my bra then? I simply don't recall that, simply because they had medicated me with some Perphenazine then?

Not you, but this man hated my "voice." So much so, that he'd prevented me from seeing another side of God's wrath and natures here? Does he even know he's got the AIDS virus then, the one of schizophrenia I mean here, not the HIV kind though! He's got pedo head I bet! See Chapters 1, 6 and 17 for those explanations here.

Meanwhile here, the Gabapentin made it so I couldn't even write a sentence down with a pen and paper here. She said, Andrea did, that it's making me so cold at night then, too, because now I still have schizophrenia though then? Not in the least, Switzerland says! They believe in cold nights out on the town, having to do with no place to stay though?

Needless to say here, the commandant's languages here are the biggest and best blessings of this world's figure skating companies to come together here and to state that these "drugs" out there, like cadmium and such things as mental hoppers with or without them here, state that, make sure these people also receive the injections and such for HSV and things like it here! Because it's dry outside here, Folks, it's relatively nice to sleep on the grounds! For, I wouldn't know that about my "homeless" trips here, because I kept getting my license stolen, for crying out loud here, by the police who have seen me getting time after time, mental hospitaled here!

I mean, the "police" can now seek out mental health for you, or anyone here, this is in America here, that states that if you've had an LRA/LRO, not like the Less Restrictive that the hoppers had for the brig feud that killed the United States Republic of China here by stating that the brig goers should be infiltrated into the natural selection! Meaning, Folks, and Classes of Gentiles here, that God should put the brig's people from Guantanamo Bay here, to rest and relaxation courses.

In the Guantanamo Bay prison cells are some of the nicest places on this Earth here! I mean here that, what I mean is, what I'm trying to say is, this is part of the natural selection on peaces on Earth here! What I mean is, there is no such thing as a "cured" mental health patient then? There are though! There are schizophrenias that obliterate themselves with this writing here!

I do declare a mistrial, Jesus says, about Cinderella slippers though! I mean, can you write your beautiful handwriting still, Andrea? Yes, she can, now that she's been off of that perphenazine stuff for about four months now! They still did not believe me, that I cannot function on that stuff, and then the shot for Haldol began on my new LRA there last spring I suppose? Nope, the last hospital then just released me into the wild then, with no LRA, right? Well, so did some other hospitals, and so did Guantanamo Bay, right? I've never been there.

So, to speak of it lightly here, the Guantanamo Bays need to come to light here, and stretch their imaginations here! We need those people there at the "homeless shelters" that bring in light before the storm's extra special flash in the pan's biggest momentums here! What I mean by this, Fellow Gentiles and such, is that, there are Jesus cures everywhere in the pan's natural selections here, and that by medicating the Gentiles here, we're actually curing every sick person's bed out there, right Class of Gentiles and Elitistic Peoples here, on Guantanamo Bay though?

Make the brig be infiltrated into the general population for elitist gunnery sergeants and such! Make the prison cells become the newest Guantanamo Bays, for instance! And, there's no such thing as, too close to call here, but, "by reason of insanity," never existed for peoples who have Crohn's Disease for example, as there are tons of reasons the cops needed to be called on Andrea though? Not on your lives here!

But, try an LRA rap now for the rap sheets of American soils here, because the purpose and intents on "Us" here in American soil surveys are supposed to become the littlest Gentiles that we've ever seen here! Say, Jesus and Jezibellie made out a long time ago, you know? Take that though to the stranger doctor at the state hospitals for not believing me about a 5 month's stay at the mental hoppers of love here, that the other good doctor's recommendations could not uphold to? It means, Classes of Gentiles later here, that God wrote a prescription for 300mg of Seroquel that I'd never been on before this evening here, and said that's good enough for us though? They had no clue about the DSW! So, I kept it by reason of mental defect here, to myself here, but I was always allowed to type about it in their computer centers, as well as the library's "mental health" computers there! Say, if you're allowed to come and go on that campus there as a "homeless person or junkie" here, there would be a lot more people, revenues, and such, there, Governors! Instead of creating more beds here for the mentally "sick" people here, how about a new Usher's Syndrome that says that night vision is so much better for the Usherly inclined here, and state that the new systems of doubts here state that life's so much more probable here!

There's Usher's Syndrome and then there's "night blindnesses" everywhere here. To say that retinal pigmentosa has an actual name to it is something of a misnomer here! Say, could people come and go that are at state hospitals then? Because I think I "heard" you correctly there state governors about the beds that we all seek and love at the mental hoppers here! But they are simply just "homeless" shelters here!

This means that we could turn these little "mental hospitals" everywhere, like Britain's own does, into the namesakes that state that "help" along the way's baggage claim here is to state that each and every man does like his wife to help out, right! I mean that a daughter's cure for cancers here states that any governor took it out upon himself here to state that a mean daughter you are, Andrea, for cutting out most people's interests.

Upon himself though is the interests of peoples everywhere and everyplace, that state that governors have the genes and the wherewithal to stick peoples everywhere and everyplace in that stupid "mental hopper" jail system they've got going on there at the nation's state hospital systems. For every single "jail cell" that goes unnoticed here is the mental hopper's dealies that state that the campus was so much more lovely with the advent before this "stupid" fence went up though? It's stupid alright! You leave and come and go as you pleased before the 1930's here at that place here! Why and for how come could you not leave that joint, and come back for your "meds" each night then? I bet you, and I bet you, and I bet you, that leaving that joint alone at the newsrooms of choice here is exactly what that place needs here!

Why and for how come could Jesus not enter into the sheaths of raptures unnoticed here! And, say, any governor had an upbringing that could kill any coastline with the raptures of facts here, as I have "visited" a natural "mental hospital" in another state before too, but I was on the Seroquel back then then? Not! An anti-depressant and I was out the door. Before I could speak it though, I lived with my late ex-husband and lived happily ever after then? Not! But, I could manage myself without those "mental health" drugs! I did live on them for many years then? Yes, I did.

In charge here is the governor of that state, much like this area of truth here! Say, can I say, murder, the word murderer here? I just don't see that by "mental defect," these same church goers can call themselves non-murderers here, that live in the Forensics Units here. Say, the food's great here though! Change them into jails then? Not! Call the "mental hospitals" around the state's affairs of the heart here my comfort zone then?

So, my calling of "mental hospitals" is something of a misnomer here! There is nothing closest to the truth about loving yourselves if you're on the streets and such, too here! Say, there was always a bus closest to me here, but I don't take it here? I had a bus pass, a "disabled" one, made up by the Divine Source Wisdom's here ye entails about the Jezibellie cures and stuff! They said to me, take a bus pass and make it your own here! You just never know about a "suspended license" for "mental health"? That means, Folks, that, get your guns ready and your gun laws too, and try to find out about a "mental health" monkey's biggest "mistakes" in lawmakings here, that state that a "police officer's" unions out there can mess with and take away your "license to drive," but that doesn't entail "Us" to become the leaders of the nation's cures for AIDS related viruses then, Folks! Say, Vancouver, B.C., sounds like a nice place to "visit" and to grow up there means that you've never had a mental hopper like ours here?

I cannot begin to tell you of the "mental hoppers" in the United States or U.S. mail here, but that job entailed me to be there every single day there, and a miscarriage later, Folks, means that you'd better not become a victim of circumstances here. Saying I was in a mental hospital facility here means that I lost my job anyway, Folks of the Gentiles types here! Say, can you cure "homelessness" for all of our families involved in "mental healthcare," Andrea! Because "We" can, and she can, Andrea thereof, become involved in politics, or some such angel's cures as HIV here! Say, can you tell me how many people believed in your lovemaking this other night when Jesus saw and spoke of your love to a pastor no less and no mores here! This means that lovemaking is on the agenda for this evening's graces of God's ways here! Say, do you feel like "making love" to any of the patients thereof here, as you got a "restraining order" on life here by writing this manuscript here? A governor, tired and such of people harassing him about this life's orders here, means that there are no "mental hospitals" in the states now, right, Gentiles here? I mean, if Jesus is a Jewish man, how come we cannot find him in the mental states of health here. Because I mean business here, the current governors of each state say that one of the most fantastic issues here, covered by the governor's laws here, is and are the "gun rights" of, say, 1 million people here on Earth who have never been to "mental healthcare" then, Folks and Classes of Gentiles later then here?

I mean, if I could make lovemaking a class on Gentiles and such, Paul said of Jezibellie back in the days of "prison" sentences and such, then the last Gentiles on this Earth here is for a pastor to relieve His son's very own precious cures for the Earth's crusts then. Because this is so "special" here, there are governors of our state's past here whom never entered into the lights of God's raptures here! And, say, what are they gonna do with my little piss ant job here, because I could sure use a new position with the state of raptures here.

To state that my new job had or has something to do with this lifetime of leads into the psyches of human interventions here states that a new state hospital like place is the goal and the key to living lives of un past due rents here! Say, or state, that for a "new" nation of peaces, and it is peaces here, exists. Because of this then, get rid of the dang "fence" for crying out loud here! These peoples deserve to be able to walk the grounds of that "lovely" campus free place for their breaks and what not, and privileges here!

Say, there are "privileges" in admiring a campus quotation here. It says that, and Andrea concurs here, it does look a lot like one of the local college campuses. It looks like the angel faces of cures up there where Jesus looks at God's wills here and owns the brick buildings that all make up the place names of society's interests here!

And, make them "come and go" facilities here, and there won't be a big, huge homeless "problem" or issue. In many states's histories though, there are plenty to do with the timings and such of "simple minded folk," who used to visit those campuses for crying out loud, to wonder aloud what to do with such a pretty campus?

And, the answers lie within the commandant's nakedness right now, Folks! I just don't know a simple affair is like a two-timing, ridiculous cure for the commandant's nakednesses here! Say, and state for the facts that are willingnesses of timings here, that the governors hire me, Andrea, to direct a new key system for those facilities, as it seems that everyone, and I do mean everyone on Earth, has a "key" to those facilities already, and that "razors" are free for all there, save the governors who know the campuses pretty well already there.

And, to make matters worse here, and Jesus's crying His eyes out here about your Governor's Mansion's duties here, that states that, turn that place into a fireplace for life here! I mean, what I mean is, Jesus is saying here, that the governor needs to place a "hold" upon the "mental hospitals" of and around the states, here ye, and to let Me handle it, Jesus says! She's, Andrea is, well and "qualified!"

I can do individual roundtables here for the knights of wraths here. And, to state that Andrea is well qualified to "handle" the "leaving" of a roundtable's best Knights of the Roundtable's commandant's messages here is to state that, state governors, do you believe in God at least this much, to state that Andrea's perfect for the jobs at hand here? Cause Jesus is kind of busy here "messing around with" the "mental health systems" for the homeless peoples involved in your cares here? And, by the way here, that damn Seroquel had better be gone by the time this book gets published here! Say, what are you on now lately then? It's a Seroquel's issue here. Is it, Andrea?

This method to our madness's greatest clipped cure for AIDS related viruses like schizophrenias and such have a high rate of failures in our society's best clipped cure for AIDS related homeboy viruses then! Because of the Guantanamo Bay inmates there at the cells of choices there, they were singlehandedly able to mastermind a perfect plan for revenge upon the Unites States government, like going into two or three planes here and "masterminding" this revenge plot for the United States government's tools for implementing soldiers who think they're revengeful about life here? They're the kinds of "killers" that no state hospital system's employee's ever seen there! I mean, a pedo head and a coffeemaker states that in the Jesus Christ superstar's everlasting lives here, He has singlehandedly masterminded this homeless cure for about 70, count 'em, 70 different do or die clubs here. And, Folks, and you too, Gentiles later, kids and stuff is in my future too, you know?

This means that, these medicines are sure fire ways to get someone "interested" in nobody here! Say, this means that whatever 7am o'clock "meds" are on fire for love here, means that you can come and go as you please here, as you try to find housing of your own here and to not "live" with those Folks you may know or be related to here, means that God's looking out for husbands and wives everywhere. Of the future with the calling cards in them here, it's nice that those phone booths do not state it for the opening logos of any presidential candidate's doings in this here, but I bet that a phone call to the U.S. White House does not entail picking up that receiver here. Because many are very familiar with the "homeless presence" in our society's pick up and go mentalities here, I bet people can very well state that "homelessness" is really prevalent in our society's pick me up and go Southern belles out there!

There's focus and attention upon your parts to write this book, Andrea. Don't give up on "Us" now! ☺ Say, the Governor's Mansion's busily built upon the premises of "stuff" upstairs here! We say that we like the color you now chose for your latest hair dyes here! That is because at the state hospitals, the "good part" anyhoo, has you pick and choose your color of natural hair dyes and such then? Nope, just a haircut whenever you needed it, at a quarter till 3am or in the afternoon then? Well? It's during the week's timebomb "classes" that you need to "attend to!" Say, would the White House love Andrea's best cure for cancers and AIDS related "viruses," such as the Jezibellie cures here! Don't they check your genitals at the "mental hospitals" though? Um, not at the state hospitals! But, Um, yep! They check to see if your "genitals" match the right person here? Well, Andrea was "placed" into a room with a roomie and a dong happened to be hanging out of "her" genital area here, and somehow she didn't get placed into a room by herself, here ye?

Needless to say, Class of Gentiles here, if you've "ever" been to a "mental hopper" then, you've succumbed yourself to the "stress test" of having shown your "genitals" to someone in there! Say, can you just go by love alone here, and tell Us if you're qualified to "have" genitals or not, Andrea? Because that one chick, the one you were "reading," save for later what that means here, but that means that she was catching her in the act here, as a test subject, by simply "reading" something in front of her and turning the pages ever so slowly while looking right at her! She goes, "She's 'reading' me!" And, then she was gone from my room here, cuz she didn't like me that much anymore.

I promise you, Readers, if you've ever been succumbed to a Mental Hospital or Hopper like this, it's because of your own safety around others. I promise you, it wasn't to manipulate or judge you! It's because of the dongs issue with women and the vagina issue with men! Say, "sex change operations" never happen, unless you've got an apparatus. That means, Folks, that "sex changes" never seem to happen because they already have the apparatuses they're supposed to here! And, that said here, that "gay rights demonstration" before Jesus's beheadedment was very unclear about life's changes and stuff! Say, the historians have done it all wrong then! There's certain "beheadedments" about life's daggers here! Which means, Folks, that "safety issues" is and are only with the staff involved in your care, unless someone has a big dick or something. So, and that said, we're only concerned with the safety of your welfare within these Mental Hoppers here! Say here, is Jesus your only "interested party" here, Andrea? Because you sound like a "welfare system" that's taken its toll upon the Mental Hoppers in and around the states here!

Say, Folks, is it time for some mental cheese heads to wander around your Mental Hoppers here? Because bag this "gift" she has for mental work, Andrea does, because she doesn't even want the positions in life's "baggages" here! We're trying to tell you about the "circumcision" that Jesus Christ didn't even attend to here? Well, He needed a jeans cure for AIDS related viruses, like schizophrenias and stuff! Please refrain from laughing here, but our most dire emergency here is to believe in the Christ our Lord that comes from baggage claims, that come from detailing our lives very well here.

I don't know what a baggage claim means then? Well, without help from others here, I probably could not have made Social Security Disability claims, that I'm well to do about my hair loss! But to cancel gray hairs in the middle of it? I'm game!

This homelessness junkie stuff is for the birds, if you don't know what I mean by that though, you will stop canceling this subscription to junkie type magazines and stuff here! That means that God is watching you, Andrea, through this terrible time in your life here. This terrible time is really about Rogaine usage here, as the crux of feeling like a "terrible misfit" is the facts that, finding out about Rogaine is really something for a guy to find out though! If you've got a Sinead haircut, you're kind of weird about it! Either that, or you're butch about it though! She did it, Andrea, disguised herself to look like the Rogaine junkies here! But the Rogaine looks here like she did a buzz cut with it here! And, nothing could be furthest from the truths here? That remains to be seen here! But, God, Rogaine though? Isn't that for hair loss for men though? It's really not so good about that, not unless you've got gray first. So, how's a woman supposed to do this then?

By keeping herself looking neat and trim and slim first. But to Rogaine the entire head that way, it'll never happen as a disabled person also! But if you lost your hair for good here, you wouldn't by the way! You'd just happen to disabled yourself even further by messing with your hair further here, as she's a fine feather's head away from a disaster with people she knows in tow here!

This is why for we asked her to use the highlighters that we did here! And, we will not lose our hair in the process of finding out why a disabled Veteran cries out in the middle of the night terrors. That they lose gray hair though in the process though? I need some sleep, she cries! In the middle of a hair disaster like this, Andrea, you are so cool and calm and collected, that, yea, maybe a little sleep will do you some good here? We've got stuff to do all day here!

This Rogaine trip she went on here, that she's going on here as a "disabled" un person here, is not what we'd like to call a Rogaine trip though! It boosts sales quite a bit here. As a disabled person though, you will not only be found out by your work trips here, but your boost in sales is still limited to knowing somebody with the following terrible twos here! It means, Folks, that God is with "Us" here! When we tried to pick out something to wear the other days of the week here, at least we've got our laundries done! So, this is how we pick out something to wear here, is to find the hijab the best options here! And, you're not going to believe it here, but a hijab wearer is the grossest thing for a White girl to pick up on here!

Sometimes, the look is modest here, but a hijab wearer on the streets of Brazil for example is something you don't want to do at all here. Same thing for her job wearers here. She's a White girl with a bad haircut.

And, a bad hair day later here, I suppose the Seroquel quit working eh? I wouldn't go to work or nothin'? It's a hair emergency here that has stopped us in our tracks here! Say, this hair emergency wouldn't have happened without the Rogaine's creaky crawly hair designs here! Needlesses to say here, and needlesses is a word here, we are without a Rogaine's quality hair designs place here!

There's times to worry about the tomorrow's Rogaine literatures here, but in a special place to live, Andrea Wynn, there are times to worry about the jobs that we'd enjoy quitting here, as well as the circles of "friends" who have gone by the wayside, or that will go by the waysides here! And, that said here, have you gone on Jesus's brains here about why you committed suicides on your hairdos here? We think that Jesus Christ would love you anyway here!

And, that said here, are you going to be taken into mental health custody for it here? Not on your life here! And, that said here, what is your "buzz cut" going to take here, but a trip to the custody lanes here!

And, that said here, what of the buzz cuts don't you understand about Jesus Christ? Because a homeless "bum" is what I feel like here? I seriously thought that by cutting the Seroquel dosages down here I'd be out on the streets again here?

Did you think that God's train of thoughts goes bump in the night then? Because below a bridge in the middle of the night's never been my forte, not that I've ever done it? I haven't though! I'm so lucky to have found a car though. We're so happy and fortunate that God's on our sides today then!

It's sort of a hair emergency no more here! Say, this is a hair emergency no more, then! Say, is Jesus Christ available for comments upon how Jezibellie's disguises here, as in Chapter 11 here, saying that God is available for comments then, upon how something so trivial could become so lightning bug lights here, as in highlights and such here? Because that is how I see you, Andrea, Jesus says here! This is a perfect disguise for the inventation's reckonings here upon gray hairs.

And, you know it, she's got some gray hairs here, starting to grow here? What does this have to do with homelessness? Well, her diabetes "cure" was taken from me in the back of a van though! This is the last catastrophe then, Folks? Nope, as we've proven here with this golden brown big bird hair of yours here! Say, I followed Jezibellie's advice here and ran for it here! Say, this is Jezibellie's biggest disguise here is cutting and coloring her hair though? We didn't cut and color back then though? Not! We were so much more advanced, as the Rogaine's of truths be known here did not know a gray hair here! Worth it though was the cure for it here back in the Middle Ages too! We love to have beautiful people everywhere here! But a buzz cut to start over with here is not in the cards, Love! Not though? Not! I'd like to see it, Jezibellie Christ, how you buzz cutted your hair once too! What is starting over going to do about it then, as people have been seen all over the place, buzz cutting their hairdos in simple rapture's milks here! Say, a bottle of agave nectar is just the tickets here, because Rogaine is so simply put, able to put water upon our hairdos.

In the middle of the nights though out on the town though, your hairdo is fine, Love! I do declare here that a buzz cut is in order here! Nope, it's not though? It's not as bad as you think it's gonna be here!

This is the middle of the road's lastest phase of thinking that God doesn't love us here. If somebody's appearance is a little shabby here, the latest phase and fan club boughten for you this evening and next is trying to find an appearance problem here in the military though? If you would've boughten yourself a haircut that was buzzed in appearance here, I'm sure as a female though? No problems needed though! But a buzz cut and a blondish wig in appearance here is just what the doctor's ordered here! In 2004, Andrea had a buzzed cut no more! That is because there never was one in the first place. Say, there are ways that trees communicate with each other, like the trees we saw today at this local college campus in town here! They didn't want to be cut down and "expanded" for its purposes here, but these trees, Andrea was told today, can be reproduced never!

How about a little oxygen preservation here? She's in the trees then, She said, because even the ancient Chinese wearers of original Madagascar oils here cannot find the eucalyptus plants in order to live day by day with Jezibellie Christ's invention of oils for the skins here? Those so called eucalyptus plants living in Madagascar though? Not you, but nope! The ones living in Japan, are the ones we called the gray hair cure here? Yep, yep and more yeppers here! It's an ingestible format here from Madagascar oils though? Nope, it's from 100% Pure Eucalyptus Essential Oil, 1 fluid ounce here! Just ingest it though? Nope, put it into a shot format and we've got it, the cure for herpes simplex then?

Not you, but we're talking about "baldnesses" here! These formats of the trees above the St. Martin's University here should really be expanded to St. Jude's times in the forefronts of historical contexts. Which means, Class of Gents and Gentiles too, that women with B12 deficiencies take a toll on our health eventually by the immune systems that gradient their ways to St. Jude's timelinesses with God's controls here! Mary M., by the way, is the Jude Saint format's greatest enemies here! That means that God can create the controls here to correct baldness worldwide, baldnesses in women too, and Rogaine... That's a thing of the past then! Correctamundos here? Nope! Because Rogaine works so well on a "buzzed cut" woman here, the past then corrects itself because the Rogaine is for women as well, the "men's kind" is what you want here. It does say, not for women on there though? Ignore it! It's got a familiar taste! So, wash your hands well with each application there, Andrea here, and go with it! Massage oils and stuff for the eucalyptus plants go with each and every heartache on the grill's here by testimonies here! Say, a picture is worth a thousand words here! This is the heartache of a girl in love then? I guess there's no wedding to attend to, for a while then, Andrea! Once a blonde, always trying to highlight hair that a common dollar's speaks it used to work by, then tells hairdressers everywhere that only a ruthless sort of hairdresser can honestly speak to buzz cutting the rest of her hair off though! Say, that Rogaine is sure noticeably bleak and useless then? Not so! Put it on the rest of your gray hair then, Andrea! Say, that's no place that I'd rather not shave at!

It means, Folks, and you too, Gentiles, that we're supposed to believe in the simple things in lives here! This is the Rogaine cure for your gray hairs, there Gents, and you too, Gentiles! The reasons we keep saying this alive for well stuff here is because she's deathly afraid of being dubbed bipolar, what with this hairdo she now has here? She's not gonna be held accountable for nothing here in the mental slammers of America's ingestible Rogaine here, just like she's not gonna quit or stop loving people for seeing her mental health notes here!

Likewise here, there are times ahead, Dear Ones here, that say, God's gonna quit loving someone just because of their hairstyles, Andrea! That means here that the trees today spoke to you. Did they not, about being chopped down one of these days, because of St. Jude's University though? St. Martin's, by the way here, is being named for something that St. Jude did back in the 13th centuries B.C. here. And no, Andrea, we were not eaten by kings, nor less or more like St. Jude back then, cause St. Jude is really Jesus Christ here! He was not a "friend" of St. Jude's here, but a friend in Christ was St. Jude here? It was really His "disguise," was to travel the world, with the Holy Spirit's St. Jude tones here! And, this university does not expand, for the simple fact that God's children here fight and squabble about the moment's notices that state that a towel licking face is not what the Jude's of this world are about here! Needless to say here that, needlesses is a word by the way, that must not be too bad of a way to live then, because Jesus and Jezibellie were apart for that too? Not! We don't like how "old" Mary M. is for Jesus Christ then!

Because the only way to get rid of her was to write her wills and testaments down as the Holy Spirit's tons of truths ways of finding the university here to be liable for wits and testimonies of truths here, and that's about all here! The trees though, don't cut them down then? What, for food production though? Nope! It's food production only then, because the bark's not it, the food's not that bad for somebody with bipolar disorder's biggest and best lies about Rogaine usages here, but the eucalyptus plant's 100% safe to be injected too, which is the quickest ways to gain access to laser hair removal in the futures of God's kingdoms here! Say, will you, Japan, write me a quick note about this hair removal stuff here?

Because I think you've solved both colon cancers, which really comes from God's kingdoms. As a St. Jude's man though, Jesus was sure a looker back in His time then! Jezibellie, where are you now taking Me? He'd say! He's wanting you, Andrea, to put boxed colors back onto the shelves with this novocained ways of saying it here! Say, St. Jude's University's in Pittsburgh, Vermont and some other place like St. Jude's University here in Lacey, Washington, USA. Right, or exactamundos here? Nope! It's St. Jude's Hospital though, that changes us forever then, because Jesus used to travel the world with His Holy Spirit in check all the time! We flew back then, had planes for South America's travel companions too! I mean, the continents drifting back to dust to dust's airplanes and such were not like the Boeing 747s here, but the meanest ways of saying St. Jude's University's biggest blessings here is that a squibble and a squabble later means that the best St. Jude's Hospital's research man needs to write Japan on that feathered paper they now make. Instead of the trees though? You've got it!

All the feathered papers they now make hopefully, involve the chickens' coops that now bless our spirits here. It means, Folks, and you too, Gentiles here, that all the chickens that we lay eggs for here are the simplest forms of making paper alive here! Say, what are the chicken coops that Jesus lays eggs for then, you say here? Because He made all sorts of papers here, by soaking the feathers of the chicken's coops of tomorrow's laughters here! Say, it's spelled chicken coups by the sons of bitches that like to kill chickens for their eggs. And, laughters abounties here, means that Jesus Christ University sounds like a great place to kill St. Jude's territories here? As a disguise though, it's nice to see you smile, Andrea! We totally killed her hairdo, the one with the braided hairs though, Jezibellie! Nope! Ms. Jezibellie is a favorite pastime of ours here, as she buzz cutted Her hair once too, Ms. St. Jude then. University though?

This St. Martin's fellow was a tard, a total nincompoop too. He's the Native American's ways and means it lady's name changing trusts that God's inklingships are supposed to cut hair down for! I mean, the most ruthless barber came into my life yesterday, she says, Andrea does of her new hairdo's Wyoming looks to it here! I mean, if I'm so potent and trustworthy here, she's glomming onto attention from God right now about the trustworthinesses of God's green acres here. Say here, is Jezibellie honestly to God Andrea's right hand woman here? Man is more like it then! The men in here state that a butch haircut, Andrea, is just for the birds right now then, because she's so self-conscious that she bought a wig then? We're sorta not finding a wig online either. We're going with the hairstyles that listen to God's wing it man's biggest commandants here!

Say, is it sorta like the feathered hats we wear here? Say, is it sorta like the feathered caps we wear then? Not really, but sorta! Take the feathers out of the woodworks here, and make the feathered papers that we normally do here. Do not, I repeat, kill them for their feathers or furs here, but make them available from all the dead animals that we do eat here. Say, the cows come home to roost here, but the reproduction cycles that dead animals are often accounting for here are so plentiful here that God's nearest genes cures are pretty well dead on the waters of Virginia's coastlines here. If Tennessee could see us now! Please write to them, pretty bluebells of the south lady friend you are here, and state that St. Jude's, which is a children's hospital now, it didn't used to be by any means here. But to tell them about it here, Andrea, is that God's Jude's are now the Jesus Christ's mentalities here! Say, this feather dusting is pretty good here too! ☺ This means, Folks, that cutting down Christmas trees is one thing here.

But getting the paper production's true old growth forests here, and this mentions the spotted owls pretty well here too, is that, this feather productioned peace offering's biggest and best timings here are supposed to get going here on this paper, this Rogaine paper, that Andrea's experimenting on now, Folks, and the biggest disguise's best papers here mean that God's papers are equally destitute.

For us to say that Jesus Christ superstar is the married man of a centuries old, likeable script's papier-mâché hat's biggest and baddest hair solution's biggest and baddest eucalyptus plant's ingestible, and I do repeat this here, that a eucalyptus plant's biggest solutions getter here is that you believe every word that I say here? It's about a full bottle that you'd need for the Rogaine's to stop working for plain hairdos though? It's right to say the least! Kill us with kindnesses here, Andrea, but what are you talking about for God's sakes here? Say, this honestly kills us with kindnesses here, but God's inventions of peaces here is to save the trees for sure here. God likes to invent things here! But we're done with this chapter's unbelievable stresses here! Say, can you get a Rogaine cure for peace's hospitalities here, as Andrea's latest disguise here is helping the situation, LOL! Peace out for now, Folks, and you too, Gentiles here! Say, is that the end of this unit's control on fair wars about homelessnesses, junkies and such? Because we're saying it is here!

Why does somebody become homeless here? Believe it or not here, the trees on homelessnesses and junkies here spout off that a God-fearing mentality's biggest underlying junkie's biggest unbelievable buzz cuts here! Say, is there a homeless junkie out there that, God wanted the homeless junkies in the diner's parlor to say here that God's homeless junkies like to use the bathroom at the gas stations of tomorrow's citizens of grandeur here, that a homeless university is what we should turn this gas station into here? Well, I never did set up camp, so to speak, at a homeless shelter for very long here.

Say, I was there for a night or so? Just for a couple of hours before I had a panic attack there about the razors, the free razors, they gave out like candy here? Say, there were a few felons in the room here, and that kind of ruined it for me, as the razors, they need to be policed or something? I just didn't trust the situations here! Say, that razors situations thing is for the birds, in a mental hospital though? Yep! It's trustworthy situations here that let you "checkout" razors there for that purpose here. So, they should be policed, sure. But to say or to state that robbers are gonna come in the middle of the night and to use one on you though? Most definitely so here! Say, checkout the razors, but don't come crying to me in the middle of the night's eyes here and to ask me if I'm warm is an understatement here. Just tell me how to improve upon a situation like this, with an LRA though? You bet here! Say, you feel like doing drugs like a heart attack, when you're at a shelter situation though? Yep, you do.

Jesus said, not to bother Andrea when she's got an LRA to attend to here? I was only there for 20 minutes it felt like, our time though! And I took a homeless taxi to my shelter's homestead for a minute then, and asked someone I knew if I could stay with them again here. So, here's the thing, Class of Gentiles and Rogaine users here.

The eucalyptus plant is treated for several things before it becomes an essential oil here. Likewise, don't ingest it by drinking it too? Nope, it must be ingested normally then? You said ingested, Andrea! Nope! Eat some for herpes simplex then? Nope! By the way, I'm totally clean of STDs here. It's just that my love life is calling me someday I'm sure, and I want everyone to enjoy the same things that I do here as an STD free life is calling Me here on the carpet's last stands here. You know, Jesus says here, that back in the times of the eucalyptus plants here is that a common denominator still stands be taken from this life by mental health again though? Not on your life again, Andrea! There's still some work to be done with homelessnesses and homeless shelters worldwide here?

Say, model our citizenry after the eucalyptus plant, and tell us what Zeus, a common man, thought about Jesus Christ's candor about 20 years after He had died though? Zeus was a common man, you say? So was Jesus Christ though? "Special powers," is what we have for dinner every night then? Zeus was HIV positive though? Not on your life here! This is the eucalyptus plant's biggest turnpike. Above the law is Andrea, because she needs to publish this book in order to get someone to listen to her! She's been trying to publish something here! But her hair loss is, really, relatively good here! She looks forward to a glistened new hairdo for once here! For a girl's haircuts here, there are Rogained women all over the nation here with gray hair loss and stuff! Say, does the eucalyptus plant have any self-harming properties?

Not in the least! The eucalyptus plant has excellent anti-depressant qualities as far as that goes! This lifetime of achievements, Andrea, is really just an excellent source of protein for pregnant ladies! I do declare a mistrial of Andrea's deeds and achievements, Jesus just said to me now! Just wing it ladies! I mean, blackheads are the source of depressive type qualities here. How about a week's worth of novocaine to prove it? There are anti-depressant qualities in the hijab! Now, Jesus demands that a pretty woman from the south end of town here, come here and get a classic hijab!

Now, keep in mind that the homeless bunny here becomes homeless no more. She's got herself some pretty good digs here. Say, it's a love story. Is it not here, with Jesus at the helm, Andrea! This is the end or the conclusion of homeless dealings.

But this has nothing to do with 9/11 homeless shelter storages, as she left a sweater there for someone else at the storage units of love here? How come in mental health arenas we all take a sweater home for Christmas this year and next? It's because there's smalls and stuff! There's a way to lose weight in the hopper here. Just reduced medication for the homeless shelters, worldwide though? The meat cutting industry, for example here, just noticed a medication change here! Say, does M.S., multiple sclerosis here, believe in the talent search's biggest demons in Chapters 8, 9, and 10 here? Because My wife, Jezibellie Christ here, had an M.S. attack once. The biggest demons in non-cultured eggs growths here means that "celebrate good times," the song here, is biggest and bestest without this demons inventions of things here. You're kind of spooking me out there, Jesus says.

Right or correctamundos here! There's M.S. out there that needs to be healed without the use of drugs and more drugs here. Say, does morphine or heroin exist in the hopper's mental health arenas here? Cause that's the use of the drug, Seroquel, for the last time though, the morphine arenas thereof here. Say, is the black market's use of Seroquel very hopper like here, cause it gets you the good night's sleep that you need here, all with a Rogaine's talent search's best offerings here. M.S. is caused by a eucalyptus plant then? I'm warning you, Class of Gentiles later here, that liberation from cause and effect by some people of choice here are so liberating to know are not my style anymore here. That is because the people I subscribe to, they mean well, but they're detrimental to my societal whims here, and this means that HSV is the cure all that we're looking for here? Well, so is gray hair, and baldness, and a bunch of slewish things like, Jesus cures though?

We've been at this for years here, this homeless cure here, but this Virginia Gray Mason down the street, the local hospital that is here and beyond here, is going to blow up without the love of God's children to direct them to the eucalyptus camps of HSV, HIV, and the such blowing up of buildings, such as the 9/11 attacks here! The hair though will grow back with enough Rogaine to give it a clean, crisp look here! But the gal who wanted to "fix" the hair, never did so, because she hated blondeships here. Say, does eucalyptus actually make your hair yellow too? Every hairstylist on the face of the planets here knows that God is watching Us here, make a jewelry case for a liberated woman! To believe in yourselves again, Folks, is the watchings of American talent shows, like the eucalyptus plant! And, say here, what does Rogaine have to do with hair colorings and such here? What does the eucalyptus plant have to do with Rogained hair again, Folks and Gentiles too? One of my friends here said this is because ailments and ailment cures are what's likely to happen with a "liberated" woman, she said! And a hijab wearer I am here! And, eggs, and M.S., go together here!

It's probably for Rogaine users to become depressed enough that their appearances get the best of them here! Say, a homeless guy the other day to me here said to me here that there's nothings in the wakes of 9/11 wearers, in theory of course here, that makes a "homeless person" red in the face about it though? Say, a hijab wearer I am then! I wear a hijab now. So, that makes me special as a White person at work in American soil survey watchers here? You bet! For now though, the hijab makes the wrapping on the Christmas presents come to a turmoil's usages here. I bet that Jesus has a hairstyle that makes wrapping it in a turban for the rest of his life something great here! But that means that hairstyles of the rich and famous get the photographs of a guy with his baby that are really, really sexy. Say, what this friend said to me was liberating? She said it was liberating to buzz cut my hair to myself here.

At least I wasn't homeless enough to know when my certification, and it's a certification, People, in my humble opinion though, not a license to MixxedFit either! Try a homeless shelter in South Carolina, People, cause they don't exist for "us" there in school though? It's a homeless shelter thing to notice that Reece Witherspoon as Elle Woods in Legally Blonde, almost got me a Rogaine cure this morning!

This legally blonde attire here is a Rogaine cure for peaces, and, honestly, peaces works for me at a hair and nail salon by the way! As I don't have a pretty finger for the ring though? In both places, Andrea, the ring finger is intact, in my country anyways! I mean, if a sheet metal working job is going to get me back on my feet so to speak, from living years and years and years with a disability, then comedies and tragedies later here. Say, get outta here, Andrea! You're busily writing about commandants and stuff, and I don't know what you mean about a homeless chick who really wanted a Zumba license to boot here? I just don't know what I'm going to do now with a hijab and a workout gear like a Rogaine hat though? It itches like crazy, cray cray, as my therapist currently says to me, in gest though!

So, how do you get it blonde again, Andrea? Well, take the eucalyptus oil, the essential oils kinds here, and ingest it, not! Do you mean in a backstabbing way here? God's likely to think that the essential oils that you ingest are for gray hair though! Not on your lives here! Rogaine is where it's at though? In comedies and tragedies here, there is something about the lives that God wonders about here! Say, is that therapist session pretty handy for you there, Andrea! Because eucalyptus makes it blonde for life here, no it does not! I think that the ingestible formats here call for about 12 ounces to be injected, not ingested for gray hairs here too, as that's what we're getting at here! Say, 9/11 was just a massacre of God's ugliest people though? Say, would you marry me too, Andrea? Well, this guy says this to you after a Rogaine cure though? Say, who's that man behind the glass in the Legally Blonde way though? Ingest Rogaine and you're cured though? It could kill a man to ingest it, so don't do it though!

It's an essential oil that you need to cure Herpes Simplex Viruses, if you ingest it though? Nope! If you mix it with pancake batter and feed it to the monkeys though, it will cure them of their Rogaine gray hairs too! But this means that a Rogaine fix is not the same as the jelly bellies that you are eating here! Ingestible essential oils are right up the alleyways of the finest detailed believable tactics like a Dr. Z moment though!

Dr. Z, and Dr. D here, the chimpanzees say, is the right amount of homelessnesses that happen to the grayest of man's detailed oriented longhairs here! Say, is the ingestible formats of the eucalyptus tree then, somehow detailed enough for you there, Dr. Z? Say, it's the eucalyptus formats of the ingestible kinds here that cures gray hairs and stuff here? Say, will perms be back then, cause we've been messing with Andrea's hair for years here. No pun intended for Andrea's gray hair removal kits though! Say, is Jesus still there with you, commandants here! This is the cure for HSV, Guys in the laser hair removal camps though! Not on a girl or a guy, not ever. For a girl or a guy though in heat though? The Zumba chicks at the gym are not on the radar for love anymore here! That means, Folks, that we're all women and men here. Don't laser hair removal the crotch areas here! It's a question mark here! That's the things here. Don't make me be homeless on you, Jesus Christ tells Jezibellie of this year's fantastic sale.

Upon coinciding with shots in the dark for regular, ingestible HIV cures here, the eucalyptus will not work for it either. Say, Class of Gentiles and human beings here with experimentation here, the final straw will be, Andrea, that He never contacts you again though for this here? Cause back in the days here, the dinosaurs would not even eat the human beings that were the ingestible eucalyptus scents, say, Jesus, you're a Rockstar there with the drinks and all? But the hair removal thing on your private parts are not the right things to do here! Say, shave it then? Don't shave your hooch, don't shave it at all, Girls, and Guys too!

Build a bridge between the eyes of Jesus Christ's best looking girls, and you mean to tell me that my daughter shaves her hooch still though? Something like this could derail any spoken for man here! Say, is Jesus your husband, Jezibellie? She's listening to reasons here for insanities though! Say, is a whodunnit in your futures here for the Rogaine though? Because the Rogaine hairs are not the best in the worlds here! Say, is it your turn to clean the bathroom here, love ladies to be here? Because us ladies who are in love with the gents and stuff, always clean the bathroom after we use it here! Say, is Jesus here responsible for the makeups and stuff? Because to be an intuitive in this day and ages here is to say that God's watching the ingestible formats of God's wraths here! Right here please!

Look at me again, Andrea! What, I'm ugly now, she says here! Well? It's for gray hair removal though then, you see me, now you don't though? I don't know how much longer I can take this here, but the laser hair removal of the crotch areas should be illegal here!

Say, a trim once in a while, and a Brazilian haircut though? A trim though? It means that illegalnesses of men who like women's shaved hoochies is so gross to me, Jesus says! If you want a Rogaine hair look down there though, a eucalyptus plant won't do it, Hon! But a eucalyptus trim down there though for the Rogained looks of the hot tubs and stuff that men complain about though is not what we want for God's sakes! It's the NOW stuff, you guys! You want a good manufacturer for this stuff here, this Rogained look here? Cause it'll be good for all kinds of stuff here, Andrea! Say, the NOW stuff on the internet though? It's on the Amazon page because it makes the most sense for a eucalyptus plant's globulus kind to make it to the hoppers here. But a home remedy for it here? Will the CDC, the Centers for Communicable Diseases Like Rogaine Users here please stand up here?

We need this stuff in our lives here! Say, do you plan to kill and squash homelessnesses in 1 ounce of the stuff though? That's all that is needed here. Say, do you have cold sores too? Cause just a zoster away from a shingles killing will make it illegal for me to recommend to you users out there, the causes for such problems as the shingles viruses too! Cause it's eucalyptus too here?

Not on your lives here! Say, what does this have to do with homeless junkies here? How do self-remedies make it here? You don't have a mailbox you say? Keep us with kindnesses here, but a UPS store is much "better" than the post offices of love here? You don't need a homeless cure here to beat feet as a postal worker like I did for a summer then, was it? It was for two months only then? Not even, but this means that mosques are built worldwide here, to handle the mail here, and it's called a UPS Store for a reason here! Please, write to me, Peoples! Tell me if the CDC didn't just mail a homeless person, such as myself were called here, a last and final paycheck of about $2000 here, just for being a mail postal carrier for a week here?

And my so called suspended license check for a mental health evaluation here, just said to inject a substance into your bone marrow's timings here? Say, the injectable eucalyptus tree here rings true for just about anyone here! Say, the CDC, the Centers for Diseases, Productions and Bipolar Disorders never got a raincheck on the nice and lovely things they did for the animals in question here, when they got the Rogaine cures for HIV, HSV, and bipolar disorders here, when they said to buy it from Amazon here. The 1 fluid ounce kind though? It's ingestible, People, too here!

Bone marrows though? That's what the monkeys ate, was HSV cures here? Did you know that God gave you 25 cents one day to give to a homeless guy, bum thereof one day, when you were homeless too, Andrea. And, you gave him about 25 cents for a bus ticket and a bus pass to go home in New Jersey where he was from here? You said to one homeless man on the streets of Madagascar here? Nope, too timely for that here! Say, take a break, we've got one more homeless man on the streets of Brazil here! He wants money, Honey, for your manners here! Give it to him okay, he won't use it but for a eucalyptus tree here not the Rogaine morphine of Seroquel any longer here! Say, try to drive a truck in the middle of the night to a homeless junkie's television store, so you can be looked at weirdly for driving drunk almost, just so you can go pee though?

I mean, the NOW kind from Amazon, the squeezable, injectable formats here, is the 1 oz., and I do mean only 1 oz., cure for gray hair though? Not you, but eucalyptus is the primary ingredients in eucalyptus oils here.

That means here, that a no show from a Rogained user here might just return a couple of them, just to see if it's a good match for the world's only eucalyptus plants here? If it's the squeeze bottles of the Rogained users in the Equate kinds from Walmarts here, you'd better believe that a homeless man with a bottle of Rogained users here from the supermarkets here can detect it better on a buzzed, ballcap kind of meanings here? Say, that salad is waiting for you, right, Andrea? Well, she's not as hungry all the time here. Right, Class of Gents and Gentiles, united ways here though? United Way here is not so keen on all the morphine, and it is morphine for Seroquel only here, that means that United Way's ways of finding homeless people on the run from the law though? Not hardly here. But, to take away their driver's licenses though is really for the birds here. If you are a cop of the laws of gravities here, you will take away the driver's licenses of homeless people worldwide here? NOW essential oils is the way to go, Peoples! This driver's license thing though cost me my jobs out there in the real worlds here! Say, what does Jesus and Jezibellie think of this "Goddamnit" world we live in here! Swear, Peoples!

Swear to God's wraths once in a while! You will find that, even if you are pregnant and sweating it here, that the God's given gifts here is once in a while superb here! Say, a pregnant lady you are one of these days here! I swear that Jesus Christ never told Jezibellie that He loved Her, until about the 3rd grades though! Say, is little Jezibellie Christ still Black though? She's only about 25% blonde hair though! So anyhoo, if you wanna kill homeless junkies like this by taking away their vehicles for them, People, like, what do you want and hope to accomplish by stealing their money this way and that a way here? I think that the Jezibellie cures here must not become staunched by this here, but, say, is this the government's ways of finding out about the Jezibellie cures, or the Andrea cures here? Because we're one and the same here!

I do declare a mistrial, Jesus says, about finding out if the government tricks here are actually Veterans without a home, and mistrials for Jezibellie's new hairstyles here! Say, a butch look is not what we're after here! Say, are you watching me, Mr. Jesus here! Because back in the day here, He was such a doctor too! He cut out babies from the womb before they were born out the hoochata here! Say, is Jesus such a man that He calls women out for babies cures, because there's nothing out the hootchata for this mongrel speaking woman here! The Tahitians, by the way, always had a cure for that goddamned 😊, blessed cure for the "scar," under the belly button though? Nope. Over it though? Nope, not unless there is anesthetic here! And, say here, there are anesthetics in the Orient that make a woman's scars go away here. Say, are you getting wetter there, Jezibellie, Andrea here?

Because this guy's in love with you too, you know this. Rightamundos here! Say, there's blackheads to attend to here! Do I have enough from what I ordered here! Say, is there a cure for AIDS related HSV! Because I think the ingestible formats here will work for just about anyone! Say, monkey see's, monkey do's here, there's Mr. Rogaine here? He's a great criminal artist now! LOL! 😊😊😊😊

If there are people out there who don't believe me here, the DSW speaks it now! There's cures for everything there is on this Earth there, Andrea! And Dr. Z is the one's commandants speaking worlds here that gave that guy a glimmer of hope here! Say, corporate just called! I need to talk about homelessnesses now? So, Andrea cannot work for the post office ever again then, because of a much needed talk about mental health though? Say, how often do you check your mail here, Andrea! Because back then it wasn't a lot here! Say, a letter in the mail here about a suspended license, which gets everyone, literally, everyone here, into the "homeless camps" that you see in the Northwest here, and because Jesus is literally on the fence about everyone's homeless camps, right or exactamundos here? M.S., Andrea, is also injectable, but with the frozen kind of Rogaine though, … No! The cure is injectable into the skin, as well as eggs related here, but we both don't want that to deter the moment's notices that bother "Us" here! Say, is jumping someone's bones about the videos of life here, that say, don't look at that porno movie here? By all means, Jesus says! Now, I know that sounds sacrilege here, but don't look at it as a porno. Look at it as a sex game between God's children though? That sounds so religious to me here, Andrea says, but to look at porno movies though, not the sex kind but the child porno kind though, is reprehensible by death. And the Republic of China thinks so too here? Yep! There's a sign on the way into Taiwan here, which we visited back in 2000 of this year's homeboynesses here, that stated that drug usage in the Republic of China was illegal to the point of maximum death sentences here! And, that stated for the world's commandants here, is the point of no returns here! Say, is that eucalyptus plant involved then? It's an extract, People!

Take it from Me here, Jesus says of Andrea's life now here, there's something in the works for her too here! Say, take it from Me here, Jesus says here of life on the hopper without Jezibellie though? And a lap dance and a sugar puddin' gonna get me down here? Like, is this the hopper without the Jezibellie cures though? I do declare a mistrial in deeds here! Say, the chapter upon which this was written here is on Chapter 12. Though sometimes people here take advantage of the same human beings here as the spoken fors here? These two commandants languages here makes Namibia of no importance here? They risked their lives for us though? The monkeys did the chewing, and the injectable formats made it into the sugar puddin', of the life's only cures for monkey AIDS though?

Say, is each and every injectable formats, Andrea, still getting you down here? Because I think that Jesus says it is injectable no more here. If you don't believe Me, monkey formats and cheese wiz hairdos and stuff later, you see it, now you don't though, then guide me into the riverbeds of hand me downs and stuff too, mkay? Because honestly here, the Rogaines of time or tell its here still demands a timeless hold downs buttons here for the Rogaine users of today's Earth volumes here! Jezibellie's dad was really the King of Greece here, back in the days of Jesus's times though? You betcha! He knew Him well back then!

And please, it's only U.S. of A.'s interventions into the "homeless camps" that take away driver's licenses, and put holds on the bank accounts of every single message player in this life though. And, to tell of God's wraths here, there are certain bank account numbers that needs to be imposed upon, in order for this eucalyptus orders here to go through here! Don't think of an ingestible format. Think of an ingestible mood format's biggest liars here, because the only things that go wrong with the ingestible formats here is the facts that God's best inklingships here are too bad for businesses without the Rogaine cures of God's awful, and we do mean awfulships here, terrible twos here.

That means here, for Folks whose jeans cures know the terrible twos of life's biggest qualities here, that the means to an end's biggest and best cures for HIV and HSV are the two main humanoid problems in this lifetime that said, I hate who I am here. What am I gonna do with Herpes Simplex Viruses? I mean, am I even a worthwhile person to hold onto a job with here? Now, I've never experienced this, Andrea says, because I never had the HSV cure here before now though!

And so, it was in due times here that the mental health evaluations, after a Turbokick class though??? Take me to the hopper due to just being "mental" here about Herpes Simplex Viruses then? I mean, if people you share a house with means that a mental health evaluation from this community up here is valuable, to send a cop my way because my mini webpage site has a hold upon my life here, and to tell the God is it, that my life is on hold here, is to bring the hopper to you here by telling you, who told the commandants on 9/11 to stay in a monthly motel wasn't very nice.

And, that is why the Rogaine users of God's childrens here are simply the biggest and best at what they do's here! Simply put here, the Rogaine is on the hopper's list here! They said, it makes Jesus smile, that people can do and say what they want as an adult here! Say, are you going to make it to this hopper tonight or do we have to cut it off for you, Andrea! Get the circumcisions for women too! I mean, Jesus Christ superstar would have done it Himself as the surgeon of the worlds that He was! I mean, Jezibellie with a small dong though? What is this thing, and why do I have it there then? She's not a transvestite! I mean, women were born with this due to nutritional values upon wakes and stuff in the third and fourth trimesters though? It's not the same thing as getting a hopper's cooldowns here! But, this Jezibellie had it there.

Say, are you pregnant and homeless by the Holy Ghost though? Say, was it three times or four times that little babies tried to pop up in your lifetimes of cures here, because Jezibellie was "circumcised" by Jesus's hands here! Say, do you want a dong, Ladies! Because a ball or two, as well as a sinister grin by the Jesus's cures here is what you're after here! There's no commandants in this conversation here that makes a male or a female "different" in that respect here. But I've heard of it, Andrea says here of the Rogaine treatments for pubic hairs though? Those hardly ever change color here! What I'm saying, for vagina usage though? Why not? Well, it changes the PH's of the Rogaine users here!

Because of what I am saying about homeless encampments though, there are no prowlers for the wicked and the weary anymore here, because the Divine Source Wisdom here, DSW for short here, is really serious about healing traumas here! There's the other side again, Andrea, telling you that, for God's sakes here, don't send over a bunch of cops here to get me out of the Rogained roommate situations here. That's for Chapters 35 and 36 to decide here, as that evil looking King of England's Solomon order here on Jezibellie's lives here is really to decide Her fate here! I mean, if Jezibellie, Andrea says here, had a "dong upon birth here then," she's really not a guy here, but a full vagina-ed woman that I loved, Jesus says! I never saw anything so beautiful in my whole entire life here, but She did not want to Rogaine Her hair anymore than She had to, because it would've remained a solid brown! For the love of God here, the brown hair she had, not entirely black, though it is lovely down south too, Guys, is the Rogained ways of saying, that the eucalyptus plant's back, and it's hornier than hell here!

Where are the mosques to be built then? Go on, Andrea! I mean, terrorize a town and city for the living Gods of hope here, and to have the driver's license yanked from a "pretty girl" is really what they're after here. Say, when "crooked cops," and I do mean that crooked cops exist too, say to you, you can't drive this machine anymore, with a homeless person on board here, what do you think that Switzerland, and Brazil, by the way, notice about you getting homeless on them, Andrea!

Because, the Brazil ways that we noticed the hopper down there is really special for the pretty ladies who end up "homeless." Because of this though, the cops can yank a woman's pants down pretty "easily" here for being homeless and transient, and that is really what the hopper's all about here! Say, is the eucalyptus plants around the bays of the bayous and stuff really happening here?

Back in 2004, Andrea, for lack of a better phase in her life here, was still just homeless and living in her van though then? Nope, in her two bitten truck that student loans did pay for, by the way! Say, is the military keen on giving everyone a free education upon leaving the universities that paid for our latest ventures here? Because that buttered popcorn, I very well know here, is the best microwavable thing I have ever seen! Because we're going around making it on the counters here of love though, nobody, and I mean nobody, ever saw a police officer pull me over four times. Count it! Four, for having an LRA, a CIA license to drive here, and a family member who rescues me at every turn here.

Who's in the military now, LOL! It's an LOLZ thing for us usually, the DSW says. But this time here, the LOLZ stays, Andrea! Right now, Folks, there's someone you know well, looking for a cure for herpes though?

Say, is this a homeless trip down memory lane here? Cause what, somebody's gonna put me up at MRNP? I went up there once recently and was taken into mental health there totally. The Mountest Rainiered National Park's biggest memory here of memory lane's comments here, but from Mount Rainier's perspective here, we're gonna blow, means that we're going to blow our wads with favors from the Divine Source Wisdom's, DSW for short's, literally getting everybody away from the mental hopper's can't drive list for Andrea though? Yes, and there it is! LOLZ! 😊😊😊😊

This is the finest getting to know you session that I have ever had, mister Rogaine it man here, as the presidency is the first reason we're into you and he's not into God though? That said here, I particularly remember a jaw dropping literature's fates here at the hospital's prison cell's natural disaster areas here, that says, kindly remove your tops or something like it, you see it, now you don't here? Say, is Jesus Christ, my love life to be here, really, my love lives to be here's, natural selection for underwear wearers and stuff here?

We need a cure for HSV and all the sexual diseases of the land's here only tidings here? Because I swear to God, Andrea, I did not know you needed to be homeless twice in your life, from a runaway situation though? And, now you're being hunted by a pack of wolves here, just because you've got the herpes cure for this Jesus cure?

Say, is Jesus still sitting there telling "Us" to get our licenses back? Because, get your license reinstated, Dude!

Say, is Jesus and Jezibellie gonna stop raping women then who wear a hijab to work though? I'm not wearing it at work, Guys! No problem then! He changed it, to a black cap just now, right or exactamundos here? Say, can you cure gray hair, Andrea! Yes, I can then! While she's writing this here, we're catching a cops and robber show. You're a very pretty woman, Andrea! You just needed to lose a little weight though? Can you stop drinking for a moment here? That's the problems with society's influences here, because Jesus never did that "glass of wine" trick for His wife either! Say, one glass of wine won't kill you, but the reasons for insanities here is, that men with the tummy rolls too just drink too much! And, that is all though?

People find me healthy as a jaybird. Way back when though, I just needed to hear this from a source of living arrangements here, that homelessness gets her license back and reinstated gun rights here?

About love though? Never lose sight of it! I say, it happens all the time, this crazy love of mine, wrapped around my heart, refusing to unwind! Ooo, ooo, crazy love! Ahhh, haaa! It's a song or something, right, Folks, and you too, Gentiles here? Tonight I'm gonna fade away, just you wait and see! Just when I think I'm over her, the song goes! Just you wait and see! It happens all the time, this crazy love of mine, and so on here!

Because as a society, to hear voices, Andrea here, is downright citizenry of you to do here! I mean, even the state hospitals exist. She's either been there or she hasn't here, but that's not the point here! Say, let's make 'em ugly, tie their shoes wrong here, and, … what honey? Is it a problem if you cannot chime your shoes right here? I spell things for a reason here.

And an audio book though? Yep! We'll get there! And for M.S. is it soda pop that you need to get away from here? True, true! Somebody I know has got M.S. too. And, diabetes too though? I'd live another day if you'd tell me how it's caused here? It's the eggs! The eggs in line with aspartame in foods here? It's not the eggs is it, though? It's caused by eggs that are not ran through the machines of life here! I've got my own cookware, Jesus says here of life though?

Marybelle Magdalene is the mother of Jesus Christ, not Mary Magdalene the fucking pedophile here! Say, is that Rogaine for good and for lives here that love the facts that God awful hairdressers everywhere…, say to you, can you fix it? I'm ugly, can you fix it, is what I'd said to the hairdresser before buzz cutting it! As Reece Witherspoon would have said in a natural disaster such as this? Anyway, there's too much at stake here! Say, is Reece Witherspoon an ugly woman here, or another Jesus cure for Rogaine usage! She never has been homeless before though! I do know this is true here! The Holy Spirit or Holy Ghost thereof there, just Rogained the homeless crowds and made them ugly!

Or, have you ever tried to dance a MixxedFit's dream as a pole dancer once? Because that song, "She Twerkin'" from MixxedFit's talents to make Ca$hout's biggest dreams here says that most towns need a "skinny bar" in there! I mean, a girl's night's dreams here is to dance for her honeys though? I mean, who needs all this Seroquel and Rogaine to notice that the fat boy's dreams here, like, Jesus wasn't fat or something, on the eucalyptus trees though, of life though? Seriously though? Seriously, Andrea! I mean, some fat pictures might surface of you here, but this is the fattest I have ever seen you though? The Rogaine usage in Madagascar on the Hibiscus plants here is really what's in all these overgrown pills that make you fat, useless, and tired of being on them!

I mean, as a society though, you're making the Bandon cheeses of Switzerland's coffeemakers all Tillamooked on me though? I mean, ask if they sell kids on the Black market then? Did you change your sister's diapers once or twice here? Probably just once here, and she stunk. So, I gave her a bath instead of changing her then? Say, how old was she then? Probably about five it seemed like, right? I mean, in the bathtub, Andrea's a speech pathology major here, Folks, is the best times for interacting with your child or childrens here about taking a bath though? She looked like she'd skipped a bath here. Is that possible for all the pretty women here who were about 2.6 years old here then, as she has that very tape of you, Andrea, interacting with a two year-old who really couldn't speak or interact with the lifetime of knowledges here?

Say, could Andrea be told all her life that she was a pedophile... No she wasn't! I would beg to differ about how Japan can go about living in the SanDisk worlds here, but morphine though? Yep! Lock 'em up, kill 'em, and make them "ugly," so they can't sing and dance, they cannot woo their women, and that their children can ease up on the hip rolls in Zumba classes worldwide here.

Jesus says of His wife, Jezibellie Christ here, that God's watching all of us, Marybelle here! Say here, is his daddy-o still watching the porno dreams of wraths here, with that evil witch Jezibellie here? Say, did you pick up Cinderella here on the porno dreams of lives here, or did you evilly watch Divine Source Wisdom, AKA, the exorcists here, call her a porno's dreams here. Or, did we make her "ugly" one last time by cutting off all of her hair's tricks here? Say, open up that porno bar back up or whatever it was there in your safe hometowns! That's what I'd do!

Say, a comma here and a comma there, Folks, is what we've never seen before here! Say here, we've got our very own TV shop here in town here! That's because the hospital systems they have in here are nothing but striptease windows for the judges of societies here to state that Andrea had a key lodged into her Rogained hair then! Because the minute they said, no razors, to me there, right in town here, Andrea, right? I mean, you remembered to wear your shoes that day right? I mean, eat a pizza for lunch here, and then tell me what I'm doing on a holiday off from the DSW.com webpage or websites here!

Say, Bandon cheese, Andrea, was the name of that town's here natural disasters here! I know a lot of people from Bandon, Oregon, let's put it that way. Say here, Folks, and you too, Gentiles here, what is the commandant's names now here! Well, back in society's natural disasters here is Jesus's lap dance with Jezibellie.

Yes, and she's very professional about it here, but Rogaine usage just went down for a hospital counselor who said, "She shaves every day then? Well, what's She doing here then?"

And, Paul went in to "kill" the "intuitive counselor" then? Because they've got the best cure for AIDS related viruses then!

This is the Rogaine cure for people with viruses then! This is the belted community's counselor here then! Say, is that Rogaine cure gonna be for those Bandon cheese whores down at the local stations of wrath here? Because, God willing, Andrea, it's bound to become the biggest and best things that terrorize the movie scripts here! Scars go by the wayside here.

I mean, movies are written about little titty bars out there in the south! Say, Folks, and you too, Gents here, is that somebody's written about the stolen hospital shows out there, as well as the Rogaine fixes that wanted peoples of all color, religion and stolen hospital beds to either "get their licenses back," or... What does Rogained hair want to do with all the religious peoples that get together with their female friends here! I mean, God quoted a quote, a story from the Rogained peoples down at the local bar then? I mean, if comedies and tragedies could speak about a homeless cause, a cure and a heartbeat later means that God's only Rogained cures here is the, minute man's, less than desirable husbandry. Figure it out later though?

This means that the Bandon cheese heads of time here got a laugh out of this here! This means that the Rogained cures for ped heads, cause it just sounds better than pedo heads here, means that the comedies and tragedies notions are not a cause and effect Soundgarden cure for pedo heads everywhere then?

The tragedies that happened on 9/11 surfaced because the gods, the "crazy gods," everywhere, Andrea, cried to hear of how Jesus died, but the surfaced cures for life's peaces are still everywhere here! Say, is that pedo head gone yet, and "gods" quoting the Bible everywhere and, stating for the records here that God's great and stuff, means that gods everywhere, and goddesses too, loved Jesus for His standing ovation here? Just a second ago, they started listening in to stalinize the world here! Say, to stalinize the world's cusses and stuff, just means that a commandant's languages here are all out of Spray 'n Wash, was just because the Zumbas of the worlds here want all of the old men out of the languages of love here!

Say, on a topic here is the effects of God's meaningfuls here, just wishing she could death dance the Zumba instructors on commandants here? Say, did Jezibellie mean to give Jesus a lap dance here? Her face and hair was slashed by Jezibellie Christ though? Nope, by Jezibellie's mean and evil twin sister, Delilah Longmire, the same last name as the man who raised Me, Jesus says! So, Longmire Christ then?

Well, we're kind of going around saying that the man who raised Me here is no pedophile though then here then here then here then here then here, because this Rogained man, I mean the pedophile here named Joseph trees here, is really Joseph Solomon of the Josephine camps here, the other guy, not My dad, Joseph Longmire!

I mean, if Napoleon Dynamite is really a TV show, or a ploy here, there's plenty of lingos to start the fires of brash and sassy hair designs on the Young and the Restless again here, Andrea!

Because the limelights of time here state that a pretty girl wearing a rug around your head here is two timing the devil's advocates out there! Say, is this the pretty girl look for your hospital stay too, because I could swear to God that the only thing you needed a shot for that night is because you were dancing too much at the hospital's offices here? Because the Rogaine needed to be taken from you and shot up to dance and dine for here! Say, is Rogaine the middle of the road's best taken man cures for life's upshots and stuff here?

Say, do we need to marry a eucalyptus plant then, as females though? Nope, males too! Here is the life o riley's biggest contexts here! Stating that you are the context hugger's got the male showcases out to dine and dash about the biggest teachers in this world here! Say, did you hear world or worlds here, Andrea! Because abomination of the 9/11 crashes test out the best Rogained, piss anted ways about the times and severances of very valuable people in this society's crash testings here!

And, up and down, up and down, up and down, here, here, here ye tidings here, cause the Rogained users to fizzle up the Rogained user's tidings here!

If you want it to, Andrea, you can go back to Rogained land uses here and do it again here! Say, is the wavy hair functionalities here the wavy hair removal of time here? We needed an ugly fix. For the love of God, what do you do with the hairstyles of times past here! This moment's not in the ugly fixes here! Say, do we all bugaboo this wedding's gears and stuff in it, you see it, now you don't here?

There are reasons for this, Andrea! And the local mental health agencies are planning a heist on this Swiss burger idea here! I don't think that God's right eyes here is the beginnings of space plannings here! Say, is the Swiss plannings here awfully hard, if not impossible here, to teach into here? Because the space odysseys of time's past here are gray hair cures.

For the millennium cure for AIDS related viruses like gray hairs here! I don't know about you here, but giving blood is a thing of the past, as well here as the common denominators of times pasts here!

Say, does Rogaine give out free food cards to the wealthy and the poor alone here? Because free food should be the norms here! Say, it already is here! I mean, free foods for the wealthiest alone times here should work here. Yep, and the wealthiest kids alone with God's wraths here, is really what we're afterwards going to need here! She's got AIDS then, She says to me here, with Jezibellie Christ here though? Isn't it Longmire then? Nope, cuz Jezibellie-belle is really Mary's only sister then? Not!

There's a Marybelle Longmire then? Yep, and a Jezibellie Christ is really an orgasm waiting to happen here! Say, is Jesus Christ superstar always married to the same broad then? Because this phone waiting game is really for the birds right now, Andrea! Because of this, "He's Just Not That Into You" book here (2004), is saying not to take that dump in his bathroom, here ye!

Say, does an earpiece exist for contact lens wearers too here? Because a Vitamin D deficiency, Andrea, can cause deafness in dogs too here.

So, a Vitamin D deficiency here, has created a love affair between Andrea's jobs as a dishwasher at the local Texas Inn plant management facilities here! Say, create a job between loves and jobs here, and I will love you tenderly, Jesus says to her now here! This is how Jesus died on the cross then? What, with all of the Rogained bloodsheds that we need to appear gruesome about here?

It's a bloodshed warning's best coppers daughter's, best inklingcureships about life's common tragedies here! Say, does Jezibellie Christ, Jesus for short here, ever miss kissing stardom goodbye's here? Because He was just so big on Me is the White guy's short hairs for loving a Jesus Christ superstar here! Say, are you gonna quit the Rogained hair day here? He's like, your roommate is, Honey, very impressed with how you conducted yourselves here!

Say, this is your roommate's bestest friends in the entire worlds here! Say, there are Michael Jackson's kids to contend with here. The very bestest of friends networks are really going home on this one point here. He died, Andrea, to save the world then, Michael Jackson did here? Because Michael Jackson, MJ for short here, died in the course of a matter of minutes!

Say, is there a Jesus cure's blessings for simple matters then? Because of the simple things in life, Andrea, there are certain melodies that happen for a lap dance so sinisterly put here! Say, Jesus Christ Orgasm states that He's onto you for trying hard to reconcile homelessness!

Say, a poor college student's names for things here is that, there were never a harmful substance's ways here! Say, a natural cure for anybody's anger right here on this, Andrea, is that you're so sweet about it too here, that Jezibellie Christ needed some romance in Her life then, God? I mean, is Jezibellie so sweet here?

Or, did the Rogained usages originate from God's words here? Right about to happen here is a cheeseburger or something from the Rogained crotch users of American talentships then, Andrea? Because if you put it on gray hair that's one thing's put outs here, but the next talentships will kill a cat or dog with it then here? This, Andrea, is what killed Michael Jackson, MJ for short here. Not you, but how did he die again? It was the Perphenazine he was on that killed him instantly. For an injectable format's cars here, the Rogained ladies of paraphernalia is what we're afterwards gonna try to express here! Say here, did you tell that one gentleman last night that he's hungover with you in it here?

Because you can kill a dog or a cat with eucalyptus plants all over the place here! So, don't do it to a dog or cat, but a human being can sure use the stuff everywhere here! And, obviously, she's throwing away perfectly good butters and stuff! No pun intended here, Andrea, but the very best betters of this world's coffeemakers here are not the reasons for the paraphernalias of this world's hoppers here, but the very best coffeemakers in the worlds here like the cellulite that it produces, if the coffee beans here are not from Atlanta though?

It's wooden warships here that makes cellulite disappear forever here! Say, the Atlantic coffee beans have an enzyme in them called the Atlantic Ocean's worldwide, mysterious coffee cups, mugs, and what have you, ways about them, called the mystical missedfits of this world's several coffee beans and mugs here! Say, order them from Atlanta then? Nope, the soils are very dry there, and the worms there like to hug the soils and stuff! So, an audio book is playing of this tape here, in Andrea's natural voices here! Say, how do you think that a message wandering mortal from the Philippines here is supposed to cure this person you know's Alzheimer's here! Say, is Andrea from the Orient then? Because the express trains that cured schizophrenias, Andrea, the paranoid kinds here, never actually existed back in the solid systems of times here!

Because Andrea makes the Rogained pictures here! I mean, take it from me, from us you mean, right DSW here? Nope, for God's sakes here, open the Rogained pictures and ask us how the eucalyptus plant's gonna help save the rest of this world's problems here, because in the Middle East here, they really don't have a gray hair problem anymore here.

Because the Middle East is so special here, the Rogained way to have crystals and jewels here is the facts that God's middle managements are so special here! Say, is Jesus of the crystals types here? Because He found the perfect ring for you to keep on your finger for the durations here? But the crystals types of men here, and diamonds are a girl's best friend here, if the diamond is circular though? You've got it here, mateys, is because the circular spheres here represent concepts in time's offerings here!

This Middle Eastern dancing you were just doing at the hopper of choice lately here is the best trip's best bipolar disorder, dancing fingernail tapping thing.

Of all Middle Eastern girl dancings here, the funny part about the commandant's next belly dancing club here, for men's Rogained moments here, is the funny part about the life that Jesus and Jezibellie lead here! Say, in the Middle Eastern side of things here, the best part about waking up is Folgers in your cups, is the very best coffee beans from India's natural talent, soldier search's, best wakeup cures for the U.S. of A. here to come back to, with the Rogained cures for gray hairs here!

This part of the Middle Eastern fry hair club for men here is the bitchinesses in the Black communities here about Jezibellie Christ coming back from the dead here to cure gray hair, black hair, it's a pigmentation problem we are talking about here, and a pigmentation's worst nightmarish dreams.

About to happen here is a cure all for peaces here! Say, is this the right word's commandants here? Because at the hopper of choice's biggest and best pea dances here, stately side comments and stuff here, state that in valance cures above us here, the valancures here for short here, states that an abomination of medical school talents above us here made it possible for a Perphenazine attack to be the real reason and cause of death of Michael Jackson's natural abilities to dance here! It's MJ of course here! Say, they Rogained black hairdos in the south, to make it look like an accident there, Elle Woods! Because Elle Woods could be her real name here, not the Reese Witherspoon's accident prone features and stuff here, means that ammonia is the real reasons for the straight or gray hairs situations. In Rogained future hair clubs for men though? It doesn't help clear volumes of baldnesses in men with natural colors to their hairs here! It just means, Folks, that an attractive man, a very attractive man, has the baldnesses factors really figured out by now here! I mean, Rogaining the hair club for men's attractiveness panels here is really what Jezibellie Christ is after here by snooping into the hair clubs for men then?

There are never a time's biggest and best blessings, like the hair club for men's Elle Woods here, that says that I cannot lead a normal life after the production of this book's hair clubs for men then? Say are women available for comments, now that they took the Seroquel sauce the entire pregnancy then? Because us pregnant bitches never want it out the hooch, like I just said here! This man and this woman united ways here is best for the biggest blessings in God's lives then?

Because of Reese Witherspoon's hardest works here, she graduated with top honors of the societies that said, half of the homeless people in the Northwest here are really graduated folks now though!

And, the dyslexia moment's notices are common dollars for us all here! Say, Andrea, Reese would like to contact you about this hairdo's momentary notices here! Say here, are you still commonly called a new lawyer's tactics here? Because the old and grey, tired notices here, means that the shafts are the commonest bitchinesses, calling about the weddings that are to happen tonight then? I mean, weddings all over the place due to no more HSV and no more Hepatitis C's here? It means that the commonest delinquentships are due to a movie called lives and banners then!

Say, the dyslexia trick is to say to God that a readership's happening hair bands of the '80's here, and I was one of them here, talked about a frosting iced cake and a perishable food problem's biggest degrees of freedoms here! Say, the electricity's best at the nighttime, sniffling, sneezing, aching, coughing, stuffy-head… What is a stuffy head then called then but an overslept face of duty's biggest callings. Upon us here is the strep throats of fine callers out in the wild hairdos of a woman's duties to look good.

And, in the middle of the night, in my dreams, Mmm! It's Taylor Swift again.

The exact replicas of middle aged homelessnesses, dreams and such here too, Peoples and classes of Gentiles though, is to call upon our middle aged homelessness train wreckers, like God's over there sabotaging my medication refill bottles as we speak here? It's morphine, Peoples! The kind with the formaldehyde bottles though? Yep! And, we're talking about the formaldehyde train wreck's biggest blessings here! Say, is that cheeseburgers in the middle of the night, in my dreams, mm..mmm, good.

Finger licking goods though? Say, as a homeless person, mama here, she was pregnant, very pregnant one night here, and she said, I think I'm a homeless cure no more here! Say, an ultrasound is very hard to reproduce here, but in utero, and I think I'm pregnant she says, a very famous person's own life here, is that she wanted to be experiencing homelessnesses. In the parking lots of times then here then, Sirs and Gents in the Orients here that want the eucalyptus bottles made in the shades here state that God's only cures then are to kill the Oriental persons, and to make them cheap enough to made in the shade's biggest cures here, that Reese Witherspoon, Andrea, is the best lawyer's blessings around then!

Because Ali Larter, the gal who played Reese Witherspoon's best friend here, is really the Elle Woods that we're looking for here! Say, does liposuction, Andrea, really state that for anyone to be on the calling cards of Bandon, Oregon's loosenesses here state that there is a problem for the people of this world's best and baked over hamburgers here? Because that pole problem in the middle '80's used to be a strip club back in the days of Jesus Christ's oldest tricks in the books here!

State for the record here, no pun intended there, acts like the woods problems in woods cafes and such, worldwide here, states that the fuel station's only acts of kindnesses, from a simple solution's biggest eucalyptus plant's greatest cures here, the essential oils kind, Folks, is what you need. And so, anyways here, the only eucalyptus plant's natural cures here is to state that for the "homeless folks out there roughing it" in the shades and stuff of natural disasters here, states that for anytown U.S.A.'s biggest cheat tests here is the Perphenazine kick starters that said, a "blip," Andrea, is what Jesus needed for His Rogained hair products for men then! I mean, did Jesus have a blip back in the days of unfettered loves and helps and stuff? Or, did we wiggle in the sandbox too much. Or, did we try to sandbox the unfettered musical notes of how to make gold out of shit boxed Twinkies here?

Because this sand dollar said, "Come to me, Baby."

And, I said to a coworker the other day, get off my lawn by the way, kid! He's like, you're the first shining star of the Rogained hair for men's club here! Say, Rogaine me now, for he is a bountiful two year-old at best, in divine time thereof.

At the limelight's biggest and best pony hair shows here, the only cause of deafness, and blindnesses too, is the facts that God's only spies onboard and stuff with Reese Witherspoon and her very bestest, dearest friend in the whole wide world's here ye calling cards here, says and states that for $70, and a hair job getter like this only requires that she never rests alone in the dust sands of times here, that for $70 exactly, plus tip we said, she only, Andrea here, only got a $40 haircut then? She only got a frost, color and curl then?

Say, a prenatal vitamin was just made in your honors here! Say, is there skinny people out there, loving life again, Folks and Gentiles here?

Because of someone certainly old here's unfettered living situations here, He went in and grabbed Her, and Jezibellie Christ, confirms this here two bitten hounddogs situations here! Say, there's a someone you know in a nursing home though? For three days only, Andrea, as Jesus here has a kind of way around the outside's upsets and stuff. To find your roommates well here, we're gonna say, another cure for cancers of the mind's eyes here, is to let the Seroquel go and work for itself here!

What I mean by that is, what is the common denominator for finding out what the cures are, for Pete's sake here? I mean, Peter was the man of the hour when I wanted Jezibellie, and this is Jesus Christ talking here, because the actual man himself never would have hurt Her, say, 20 years ago though He might have carried Her out of an actual strip tease club! This would've hurt her no more then! Because the actual pleasantries of finding out about men and men's hair clubs and stuff, and beautifulnesses as men do this too, Andrea, is to find the hair growth problems.

Say, is the Bandon cheese products gonna find the strip tease models in the local bar and grill though?

Shall we dance about it though? Because you're the best European dancer of this world's Holy Spirit, or Holy Ghosts here, it states that God's only token friendships are the beginnings of this world's coffee huts. You will always have to go to the bathrooms of intentions here, Peoples! It's not as if or as though we can eliminate shit filled Twinkies here! Say, did you have to use the bathroom outside for once here, because we remember a shit infested dream here!

If that "n" word pops up again, Jezibellie, I'm gonna have to say goodbye to you, ... Not! Anyways here, say it in the mirrors, that word, and it will heal itself!

Say, there are no public bathrooms then? Outside of the women for peace marches that happen because of this dreamy book here, there are no literal echoes on the streets of Philadelphia, that happened at the brig here! Who's the mastermind, from the brigs, mind you, in Guantanamo Bay's natural selections here! Say, in 9/11, there were four masterminds, count 'em, four here, that stated that at the gas stations of choices here, there is some things called, heave ho, go get 'em, Andrea! What, she asks! It's a present or something, left here for you here, and the land deed is no more at that mosque sighting then? You see this more and more as time goes on, Andrea, but this chapter goes on and on and on for a reason, much like a novel that is both fiction, non-fiction, and truth gettings here! Say here, try the eucalyptus plants out for size then! Right here, right now, there is no other place I want to be, as the song goes though? It's just like the movie then, Elle Wood's movie's biggest and best plans at the Guantanamo Bay's Ethiopian starvation clubs then! Say, they kind of don't have a problem in African plants either!

So, Jesus's gonna be at work or something this evening then? It's gonna be a weird ass night there Andrea! Say, is the eucalyptus in the bottles of something great here! Because we're gonna get that stuff no more here, say, in about an hour or so, don't take the stuff on an empty stomach though!

Well, what are we gonna do about the local bar's refrigeration living that says, put it on scars, and, heck, ingest it for the living love of God, to reduce or to eliminate M.S. in its entirety. So, is it nakedly crossed out or something that any woman's fat again, man? Because I've been there, and those pages do not exist? There's one trip shot of you, fat Andrea, to get bad people away from you though? You know the Perphenazine, Honey, was just for the contexts of eating good food, in front of the strippers at the particular strip club in the south, Andrea, just for the sheer fact that each and every Jupiterian, digest is simply in the bones we all get from the dinosaur ages!

Because they let Whitesnake's ugly, and I do mean ugly, ambulances come and take me from church this morning, and I don't even remember it Honey, is for Jesus to find Andrea a piece of the actions taken this morning at churches in the south, and in the north! This is the findings of Andrea Barberi's very church actions this morning. On a church going note though, I find myself, either homeless, or unpopulated in the south then, as Elle Woods is her real name, Folks! And, the sororities are really the best at populating the giraffian hills of Jupiterianisms here!

Chapter 31

Sentimentality in Jesus Christ's Reckoning of Loving Jezibellie ☺

I loved Jesus Christ too much to go to church today, but He's golden in my book's awfulnesses here! Say, say, say, is a song that is written, much less typed, involving the criticisms that mean something's awfully unplugged here! That memoir's about to expire here! Meaning, Folks, that the real trueness in church's everyday lives here, is commonly called, the best experience's evilnesses!

In other words here, there's church, and then there's church! So, to fill this void in our lives with real time churches is really for the birds, don't you think so here? Not! ☺

If this real time church is for the birds here, don't you think that unemployment and the unemployable go hand in hand here? Cause this moment's notices is like the sonships that think us. To know us,… about to go down is a hand dryer, cause this is monumental here! The sonship's best inklingships is to examine why and how the dollar bill's coming to a close here! Because of this, about to go down is the inklingships that begin with the common dollar's biggest lessons here!

Because of the ways in which we commonly dry our hands here after using the bathroom though? Yes and no here! It's tantalizing to speak of the common dollar's phoninesses here. Because of this though, we're trying to tantalize the coming of God's creatures and then some here!

It's because of the ways and means it lady's common denominators here that states that God's interested in us's here! Say, state for the record here that God's denominators here are less than inklingships here, and we'll go to the bank wondering if the tantalizing humanity's strengths here are very bold or what nots here! Say, say, say! I do believe in the common denominator's biggest strengths here!

Say, say, say, is what Michael Jackson said every step of the way here. To speak of the common denominator's biggest and bestest friends here, we do mean the hallways of Disney's speaks its here, that Michael Jackson's death was on video cameras from the main hallway's videotaping societies here! And, to state it that a ways here is the common denominator's strengths here, to commonly tape over the Michael Jackson's alarm systems here!

I mean, did Jezibellie Christ have a premonition or two here? Because this man is no pedophile here! I do declare a mistrial in deeds and in awarenesses, of the butter bums that we so call the best inklingships in this world's greatest deeds though! As common as the butter bums that move him though, the biggest and bestest friends of MJ leads to the commonest pieces of the puzzle's greatest movies here! Say, say, say! It's the best song's second guessing that common princes like MJ is really the best movies here!

This song's about to cause fire across the seas here! As the songs of the universes are already played! Much! I mean, am I going to cringe at Jezibellie's common denominators here! Or, am I all alone in this, Jesus says? I mean, is the common denominators in this balance cures of life thing going to cringe? Or, say, say, say!

I mean, a lot of the friends of MJ's past here are the kinds of peoples that suffer from cringe diseases, such as M.S., which is entirely healable with scriptures, and a lot of people that suffer from God's loves here! I mean, do people I know who do not believe in God like I used to not, do they not indeed pray for things here? It's common fodder's images that makes them pray for the days when my own deeds are not going to bring the common denominators like the cringe party's biggest and bestest years out in the open here, because of strengths and stuff though? Say, say, say, what you want, but don't play games, with my affections! Take, take, take, what you need, but don't leave me with no direction! I mean, did MJ actually write all of this stuff here? Yes, he did! And, Jesus Christ is alive with no directions though?

I mean, is He real with Jezibellie, about this coming of ages, potions and stuff here? I cried a simple, brief message's tongues and stuff here! I mean, is this the coming of ages that speaks to us here, because the simple, brief message's underlying principles here's gotta come from the simple ages that speaks to us's here! I mean, this guy loves the F word so much here that the commonest denominators that strike up a conversation is with the maids here! I mean, the biggest and baddest thrilldoms here, get to the core of it right here then! I mean, the guy masturbated all the time then, well, to pornographic images maybe! I mean, is it a crime to love Jezibellie so much so that I masturbated all the time then, Jesus says?

I masturbated all the time, Jesus says! I mean, why not, you know? It's your own pedophilic ways then, MJ then… No! Can you be a God or a princess in love with Me then, Jesus here! Keep Him safe, you know? I mean, pornography in and of itself is priceless for this Earth's gentlemen's, and ladies's too here, ways about us! I mean, if the pornographic images of life's biggest and baddest children's movies here make the baddest and meanest images come forth here, say, images and stuff here, are there and such here, make us boldest peoples such common denominators and such, then why and how come there are so many of them onto the internet's widest populations here?

I mean, if Prince Charming's biggest and baddest populations here make the baddest and meanest willingnesses to the bone here, then how come this guy's biggest and baddest meannesses takes control all the time then? I mean, if Prince Charming masturbated all the time, then how come he's taking the baths that he do then? I mean, MJ for short here for Michael Jackson here, videotaped all the common denominator's biggest and baddest, meannesses! And, for the staff's ways about us's here, is to commonly denominator us then? I mean, for a time, Jesus took heart in finding the ways about the simplest times here! Say, say, say, what you want, but don't play games, with my affections! I mean, take, take, take, what you need, but don't leave me, with no directions here! Take, take, take, what you need, and videotape me doing it then, in the bathrooms of love then? Nope! I mean, who videotapes themselves masturbating here? Andrea's like, you just killed it for me then!

I mean, I catch them, then I am released on a recognizance then? Nope, I am kept for another week during observation's purposes here! I mean, if the common denominator's about following the brave and the brilliant's bestest and honestly cured mendons here, means that MJ and the following individual I speak of here, is commonly the hottest and the easiest people to bring forth in this world's timings here? Because a common flash of some nude chick in a wet suit is probably the best images that can even tell us's here, that there's a common denominator's wettest suits here! I mean, if the commonest denominators for ED, erectile dysfunction's, biggest denominators here, it states that a wet suit is the commonest denominator's biggest wall monkeys and stuff's kindnesses here!

I mean it here! I mean to say that is, thereof, that the commonest thing's blessings here makes the commonest millionaire's biggest and baddest cassette tapes of the recording's biggest breakups here, makes for the wall monkey's biggest and baddest examples of that recording the night MJ, Michael Jackson here, died here! It's in the commonest places of the commandants here, that states that the person in question here, makes for the citizen's arrests here, the commonest mistakes and such! I mean, if she's overflowing with times and factors and such, then why and for how come is the commonest mistake's biggest and baddest times here, going to take out of the person's laundrobasket's time here!

Say, say, say! I mean, somebody's got the audio tape recording on cassette at least, and not a brood following's masked cassette tapes still exists here! It's a wall plugin between the rafters and such! I mean, if a guy's into little children here dressing and such, I can see it if you are between the rafters and such, going to commandants your ways through a deniable search's tethered scoldings between the rafters and such here!

Because that cassette tape still exists here, there's probably 20 hours of tapes on it, as the real cassette recorders were changed quite frequently. For existing problems though, the kids, MJ's kids here, Michael Jackson's kids here, never changed the tapes here! He did! I mean, if there's an emergency situations here, then a kid fest is what that man is entirely responsible for! I mean, FCC regulations subsiding then, how come and why is that man going to need a possible legacy's innuendoes here? I mean, is there a commandant's Less Restrictive Alternative or Order's best legacies here?

I mean, as the hospital stays wear on here, the commonest orders here are the biggest and baddest peoples, like Jezibellie Christ though? Hardly here.

But the truth be told that, even though these tapes exist here, it means that the biggest and baddest shakedowns here, never even entered into the minds of our friends here! I mean, none of the baddest in the lands here that states that God's entering minds of the abomination era's greatest contentments here, states that the lessons learned here is the citation's biggest thrilldoms here! I mean, if the commandants here state that a lesson learned is really what the doctor's order really says here, Andrea, then that means that the commandants are the citations city man's best letters that state that the commandant's got the meaningfuls here! State that the underwears of society's best interests here, makes that sound recording's greatest meaningfuls about that house there! Say, say, say, here, there's a taped recording of that night's horrific beings in the rooms then? Yes, there is! It's in the walls closest to the master bedrooms that spark a history lesson's worth of tools here!

State for the records here that an FCC regulation's biggest regrets here make an "innocent" man's junkies out to get me here? Because the children know in which God's underwears makes it commandants here, bigger than life's lesson plans here, because the children at the state hospitals, for example, is where the greatest state trips are!

This is because there are several taped audio recordings in the wall holes there in that mansion of his there! Say, say, say, are you ready for a new sensation's biggest walls here?

Because in the walls of Gibraltar here, is the man's biggest love nests here! State for the records of trusts here that the motion detectors of love here reinstate that the biggest love nests here record everything for the sole purposes here, of God's innuendoes here! That said here, take the love nests out of the recordings thereof here, and ask yourselves why some kid was paid money to lie about the details of the MJ recordings then? Because that tape recording went right into the garbage cans of recordings then! Because we're so rude about this taped recording of the night Michael Jackson died here, we're so glass housed here!

Meaning, Folks and plenty of tales later here, that the commandants are all ready and willing to seek kindnesses for love's avail it ships here? That recording of the night MJ died is still in the wall hole's greatest kindnesses here! And, that said here, what is the tape recordings of a lesson's inklingships mean here, that we're honest or something here? And, that said here, a taped recording of MJ's demise here, rests on the solace and simpleton's lessons here, that state that a simple taped recording hidden wall's agendas here, means that the hole in the wall's taped recordings of that mansion's spare and master bedrooms still exists here! I mean, if MJ's kids were on tape recordings too here... That said here, what are the master bedrooms in a glass house supposed to represent for Jesus and Jezibellie Christ then?

Because a surgery is all She needed to rest Her weary bones then? Nope, for torturing them by Solomon, the asshole that sings the songs of Solomon here? Change it back to what it was before publication by the James's knights in shining armor then, and change it back to the Songs of Jesus Christ then!

I mean, because this wall exists in there, Folks, and you too, Gents and stuff here, that said moment's timings here cuts to the nitty gritty of the phone calls he received on that night's fateful eras of spacements here! And, I do mean to state it for the records here, that that phone call, that fake phone call to 911 here, means that the state's natural selections here means that the willingnesses for that boy who lied in court means that the guy had ED alright, erectile dysfunction then? Hardly noticeable is the fate's lessons here! I mean, if the commandants are really boring here, that means that the hardly noticeable recording's lessons here means that the moment's notices here that takes a while to digest this stuff here means that a hole in the wall's biggest assets here, means that the home that the kids now occupy, children thereof, of MJ, you know, states that an FCC regulation will find his pretty woman of his right there with the kiddos in their bedrooms here!

Because of the times that have passed, Andrea, the word's out that you're a gifted psychic no more here. There is an LRO for your personhoods here. And, worse off yet here, is to "gifted" you into the hoaxable places that you have suggested that an LRO or an LRA in your county's variable letters and such, is really for the birds if you ask "Us" here!

Say, what is MJ remembering from childhood as a childhood star then, but to get a good night's rest, and that is about all here. There's comedies and tragedies in life, Peoples! And, this is one of those times where somebody or something gets a hold of you and goes, listen up, Peoples, there are two LRO's or LRA's that are not going to make a difference, or make a shit, that's Us here, saying that there are two LRO's in the future of LRA's then? Because what made them give you one in the first place there, comedies and tragedies woman of interest to Us here? And, that's what Michael Jackson, MJ for short here, was on, was an LRO here!

Say, do you know these kids of his, Paris in particular, but Prince also, and Blanket too, are not the only kids he was raising in that household over here, particularly because God's blankmanships are not going to become a rapist, raising household over here! But, a common denominator here in Paris Hilton's eyes here is that, Paris in particular here, and this is the DSW saying all this stuff here, not Andrea here, but Paris in particular, wants fame and stardom. So much so that Dad's legacies are hidden in that very room you all are trying to find right now for instance!

That very room you are all trying to locate in that house by now, the mansion per se, thereof here, is the quality mansion's master bedroom's recording sound devices, for the instigations that come available to Us here, that the master bedroom's got a recording room all ready, for the instigations of trust here!

That room is located on the 7th floor of the mansions of easy living here! That room there is opened by the key code located upon the back of the monkey's butt here! The key code is 574321 here? It's wrong for a reason here!

This document contains lots of hidden clues here, but only the kids know what the key code is here, and the way in which you open it has lots of hidden agendas for sure here, but Michael Jackson, MJ for short here, never told them of which tape recorded conversations he wanted to give us here!

Same thing as when people stayed with them, which is really only the key codes that wanted "Us" here! I have never been to MJ's humble abode here, save when I was little, a little kid maybe? That remains to be seen here!

But, that key code works for all the kids's bedrooms here too!

That's what the Michael Jackson's world is supposed to entail here! I mean, after all here, the contexts that spread life around states that a common man only needs a few hours of sleep per night, especially when kingdom comes around states that common people here only need a few hours a night here!

I mean, really, Peoples! See Chapter 32 upon which we speak of here! A Propofol night's literally an MJ routine here? He didn't want the Propofol to sleep with here!

Right here, right now, there is no other place, that I want to be here! There are no open segments in your lives right now, but the difference is here, Folks, that commonly, there are no open child molesters on this screen here, as we're writing this just now!

I mean, to call MJ a child molester here is what's really going on with his life of secrecy then, but this Michael Jackson had the ways of the wind, much like Jesus Christ did!

Those kids, robbed of everything the night that their father died, is really nothing more than a microcosm of trusts here! Without those kids here, those nights of terror and torment is over with "Us" too! I mean, how would "We" know this about the secret rooms in that dang house here!

I seriously wasn't present for the actuality's kindnesses, but that is just a dream come true, that there is an actual taped recording of the night that MJ died. That night, as well here, is really tolerant of the facts that God's simpletons here are very square, and very uptight though, about this "secret room/chambers"!

MJ, through no fault of his own though, had "secret recordings" of every room in the house practically, the mansion on Rodeo Boulevard though? That's close, Andrea, but look it up, please here! The Neverland Ranch, "We" mean, right, or correctamundos here?

I mean, the upstairs bedrooms have a simple note or notion here, that the pleasantries and such are commonly took out of the menial ranch's best duties here! I mean, the North Carolwood Drive apartment complex, which is what He sought out to ring him as here, is really Jesus Christ's own Carolwood Drive complex, as well as His own ringing out the ears, of people in the complex, who were really doped up here! He was moved to Neverland Ranch! That's why and where MJ really died here! But the mansion on Carolwood Drive here is really a too found Neverland Ranch, and we're used to this, the kids have all said, but a pedophile though? MJ, never!

It is written all over this monkey's butt on the right of the clock that says "Hero" or some such thing on it! I want you to really read this thoroughly for the clues of the universes that states that, commonly, okay, there are tattletales and such!

I mean, this "child molester" though? I think not, Peoples, and you too, Gentiles here. There's no Michael Jackson / pedophile ring in this guy's honors here! I mean, is this an honorable guy, man here, what have you? I mean, Jesus Christ superstar, and MJ here, are close, dearest friends here!

Friendships that have caught fire here, are rooted in timing this document, this book here though, with the ultimate bottom's dollars here. And, no one but his mom here has the key code you're looking for here!

You're not "bipolar" over it anymore, are you, kids? I mean, these kids were immediately put on the perphenazine like drugs most likely here, and taken away to live with someone else? Yes! I mean, in the wills here, there were provisions set out by each individual tithing session's biggest and baddest clues here! This moment's Ubari, Libya's, moments here are taken to Andrea's newest and next levels here!

Because the Ubari, Libya's moments are really where the term Barberi comes from here, historically thereof, comes from the Ubari Desert in Afghanistan, as well as the Ubari moments we're all collected abouts here! Ubari's desert was, in Biblical times at least, prayed for by the Ubari Desert's notions of peace in the Hayaa Districts here! Say, what does this have to do with Michael Jackson's estates here?

If Ubari means Barberi, then what of the "Jackson's" estates rings true for bipolar behavior, and questioning them about this then here?

Michael Jackson's problems though are still lingering in that wooded area's biggest and baddest nostrils problem, of the worst kinds here, that at the second surgery, the nose surgeries have become pretty infamous here as MJ's "weird" problems here? Not at all here.

Because of this here LRA/LRO that MJ was under here, it's a Less Restrictive Order or Alternatives here, it made him fair game.

Their father's estate's really terrible at this too, but this is the moment's notices that takes us to the Jesus and Jezibellie's fire going riddles here! That saids here, what is saids, anyways, but a new ways to say pluralisms and such things as rides and stuff on the merry go rounds, are okay for kids to enter nowadays here! I mean, they are in perfect working orders here!

Take 'em there, your children's children here! There's plenty to do here!

Say, say, say, what you want, but don't play games, with my affections here! Take, take, take, what you need, but don't leave me, with no directions here! Take MJ, and Paul M. is not ordering one for you here!

I means it here, Folks, and Gentiles too here, what is this life's Jesus and Jezibellie claims here, but a "secret room/chambers" involved in the Jesus and Jezibellie scandal's greatest church going not-isms here, and that is, Michael Jackson's, MJ for short here, estate, is largely developed into Neverland's church going mouses here!

It's mouses, mkay! There's time to gloat for a short bit here, on how the commandants got together with this MJ cure's biggest blessings here! Say, say, say, what you want, but don't play games, with my affections! You, you, you, can never say, that I'm not the one, who really loves you! … Standing here, baptized in all my tears, baby through the years, you know I'm crying, ooh, ooh, ooh, ooh, ooh! Yeah, yeah!

You are so beautiful, to me! The song, you know, is an MJ invention too! He's a mastermind at writing songs, good ones at that, that he could not only flirtation device this puppy here, but he could write like the dickens here! Beautiful poetry, we might add! There's MJ, and then there's Paul McCartney, Paul M. here, and there's beautiful poetry everywhere.

Because this taped recording exists here, it's in the walls so to speak here, the kids are really just a microcosm of goodnesses in MJ's walls!

So, to speak of the microcosm of greatnesses is to Joseph Solomon though? It's Joseph Longmire, not Longmire, Washington, then? Longmire or Longview? Cause it's supposed to be Joseph Solomon, My pedophile dad then, Jesus says here? Not! It's the Joseph Solomon's ways about it here that means it lady's talent searches and stuff, come to papa and all that stuff here though? Cause it's Joseph Longmire who's My real father, in laws and in stuff ridden for blanksmanships here!

Say, is Joseph Longmire, Longview, Washington, real names here, supposed to be My real father's names then here? Yes! Solomon, all the way around it here, is a pedophilic name here! Take the Songs of Solomon out of the contexts of the Songs of Jesus Christ, and change the Bible nil here?

Take the Songs of Solomon's contexts here and just wing it here!

Take nine lives, for example, and context it here! There's beauty up above, and things we never take notice of, wake up, and suddenly, you're in love! Billy Ocean's a songwriter nilly willy here! It's MJ again, Folks! He sold songs on the internet's strengths here! Say, the Songs of Solomon's last and final goodbyes here made it seem like the night Jesus died, and Jezibellie thereof here, are willy nilly here, Folks, and Gentiles too here! There seems to be a Chip Solomon II that's a good guy though, Jezibellie's brother, who changed his name to this so that he could kill the King of England. That would be the Chip Tutankhemen, spelled rightly so and everything, here ye!

I cannot begin to dictate the lordships that Solomon's reigns became here, only that there are Chip Solomon II's biggest and best dictatorships in sharp shoot rights thereof here!

This Chip Solomon II's greatest and best plans here are to sharp shoot the king's here ye blessings here, and to solumntate, it's a word here, the best and biggest plans of sharp shoot rights thereof here.

This sharp shoot ruling's biggest and best Solomon's trades here makes not only the Solomon's rights here that much more rulingships here, it means, Folks, and Gentiles too here, that not only are My brother's sharp shoot rulings nonexistent in this lifetime's here ye folktales here, but the gentleness in spirit's greatest sharp shoot rulings here exist only in Solomon's lifetimes of tales here!

This is the Solomon's greatest achievements above the betterments and stuff here! This shoot 'em up mentality's biggest and baddest hijab rights here makes the taped recordings here suffering, shoot 'em up mentality's biggest and baddest sharp shoot rulings here, only tantamount in Jesus and Jezibellie's sufferings here!

This means that the only tantamount tidings are there for this world's treasure chests and such are a tantamount's likings to Jesus and Jezibellie's sufferings the night that they died here! There was a taped recording of their demise as well!

And, there's lots of things to be thankful for here. Not only are Jesus's and Jezibellie's taped recordings on airs here, the taped recordings made it all the way to the bank's Jezibellie tidings here, as She was taken away, after the fact.

And, this message was to deliver the scrutiny of tyranny of Paul's reigns here, the ones of light and laughters here, that MJ, both Michael Jackson and Jesus Christ here, sought refuge for one thing and one thing only here, and that was to tantamount the tidings that they were good peoples here.

There's only one thing that guides us in this tantamount's riddle cures here, and that's supposed to become the biggest and baddest of the land's tantamountest rides, on the merry go rounds of the tidings of peaces here, and also, and peaces is a word here, the tantamountest rides to the joint's biggest and baddest peaces of the riddle cures of peaces here!

And, that says here, there's saids and then some here, what is the tantamountest ability's biggest tantamountednesses here?

Say, say, say! There are plenty of literatures about Jesus's and Jezibellie's demise that had gotten into the newspapers, that there was foul play involved, that there was sodomization that happened to them both, and that the outer innards of their psyches were involved in that foul play there, and that God had done it to them. Right?

I mean, if Jesus and Jezibellie were kosher on this one point here, it was that they were making love, in the middle of it, in Greece here, and there are several newspaper accounts of it here, that Paul made up too, that said that they were both sodomized because of their beliefs, and accountability's number one causes were so blatantly sodomizationed that took their bodies back and held back John's, the Baptist's, one number one cause of death here!

And, there are numerous accounts of MJ's demise here, as well as his backwash about his kids and stuff, that more than likely can have put them on mental health drugs ever since here! I mean, if their daddy's biggest wish is to "get lost" with it here, that woman that they call Jezibellie here saw what happened to their daddy's biggest wishes here, and sodomized them both then, through Jesus and Jezibellie's eyes then?

I mean, if there are sodomy accounts of Michael Jackson, I'd like to see it then, because there were none.

I mean, if he were present here, take that tape out of the walls of Gibraltar and go for the gusto here, and call the FBI about it here, the Federal Bureau of Investigators here, because they're in for it here! The only thing that Jesus and Jezibellie found in the bureau of investigators there in Greece was the Chip Johnson's ways of saying, take him out, Paul thereof, and ridify this guy to the alligators then?

Because this Paul character, Paul Wright thereof, had been chasing them so long here, the alleyways of life's biggest characters are lost in their biggest regrets and stuff! I mean, if the Virginia Turnpike's the only backwater's biggest regrets here, then how come the biggest regrets of the personhoods of the Virginia Turnpike's only gotten rested areas are very monumental in the coming of Jesus Christ's and Jezibellie Christ's Barnes ways of saying, bury me the hatchets here!

I mean, if God's only justifications are the only justified ways of finding the Jesus and Jezibellie cures for Michael Jackson's death's biggest and baddest monumental skirt's ways of finding out if he had a lover present, which he did, Folks, and you too, Gentiles here, is that monumentally there are ways of finding out which taped recordings are never there!

I do declare a mistrial in deeds and in personhoods here, such as the rocks of Gibraltar's biggest lies here!

Because of the minisculization's, biggest realization's, terrible test of Gibraltar's Virginia Turnpike's ominization's, biggest rocks and stuff here, the biggest and baddest cues here are just for the taking here!

This means that the Virginia Turnpike's knowledges of badding the getting and stuff of the rocks of Gibraltar's biggest and baddest turnpikes above us here, are really the sentiments that takes us to the rocks in the first places here, means that the only gifts that Andrea Wynn Barberi can offer us on these rocks of Gibraltar's news lines here, is that she was never present during both murderous sieges here!

There's both sentiments here that says that commandants are interested in Andrea's murderous ways here? I'm sorry, but the woman that Michael Jackson loved, were both brutally murdered here!

And, that moment's shallow graveness's commandants here loved her so here! What is the bottom denominator of the following shallow grave supposed to represent here, but a timely death, so much so that the common denominator's commandants are supposed to represent the truths here be told as it may be seen here!

There's someone on every street corner, in every dreamscape of literature's best hijab moment here, as Andrea follows suit on her Rogaine usages here! That said here, what is the hijab supposed to represent here but the following suitable renegade rifle scholar's biggest and baddest hijab moments here? She was Middle Eastern, that's for sure here, and that hijab moment's supposed to be privatized.

That's for sures here!

There's commandants here to follow Jesus's and Jezibellie's demise, as well as Michael Jackson's and his lover's demise here? She was a woman, that's for sures here.

There's supposed to be less dramatizations here and more to do with the Longmires of Washington state's biggest and baddest dramatization's commandants here.

There's news stories to be told here! There's Delilah Longmire, both brilliant and wonderful though? I don't think so! She's the heretic, the lunatic that went behind the scenes here to get them killed alright. I don't believe so, but there's the heretic's last stand here, that only the commandants get to kill them for here! The taped recording's biggest commandants here are supposed to be interesting, that's for sures here. There's the commandant's biggest blessings here, and that is the facts that be told here!

This commandant's biggest and baddest blessings are for the birds here!

There's supposed to be some justice in that which we seek justice for here. There's several literatures that suggest that Jesus's and Jezibellie's demise was in Italy here. Nothing could be furthest from the truths here.

That suggests that, just because they were buried in Italy, doesn't mean they were murdered there. They knew they would suffer an untimely death, both of them did. It's because of the commandants and the ways in which God's sufferings never really told them of what capacities they would demise themselves as here.

There's something which jokesters unions are quasi valuable skilled tradesmen at and that is the commandants that have known of the demise of Jezibellie before Jesus's then?

There's supposed to be a hanging of sorts then? Nope, She saw Him die in the same capacity's eras of spacement, onement and such that She saw Him hanged then? Nope, He saw Her hanged first then? Nope, He was beheaded after the sodomization of the rings He had on His fingertips.

It's because of the sweet-smelling breath of the commandants and stuff that He lived another lifetime of guilt's best enemies then? Nope, He didn't die an untimely death then? Of course, He did! His beheadedment was right in front of Jezibellie's encouragements then?

Nothing could be furthest from the truth's arrangements then! And, then there's the hanging of Jezibellie, and the shallow grave in which She died an untimely death in then?

There's commandants and then there's truths here! There's mostly the inklingships that cured Jezibellie of strength's wraths here, and commandants are always mostly in the knowledge based heretic's languages of the strengths and trades of the Middle Eastern ways and customs of Jesus's and Jezibellie Christ's ways and means it lady's strengths then!

There's such things as strengths in numbers, and then there's strengths in encounterments that signify and strengthen the deeds in which the commandants have commands over here. And that said here, there's nothings and then there are somethings in which MJ's demise took over himself.

And, then there are encounterments that signified the reigns upon which God's wraths never fought so hard at!

Chapter 32

Bipolar is a Hoax Too! Jezibellie Christ Had It, Right, for Hearing "Us"?

This bipolar discussion is better left for my second book, here ye, the <u>Prisoners of War: Dark Halls of Mental Hospitalizations</u>, here ye!

What are we bipolar of and about anyways? It's about God complexes?

Let's now turn to a different topic here and we will tie this all in here. There is a picture of the King of England in Todd Burpo's book <u>Heaven is For Real</u> that is not the Savior blessing! Jesus Christ's eyes are much more revealing. There are promises and there are blessings in disguise here, and this mention of Solomon's chapters in this book of songs is really promising then, huh? Hardly so here! This Solomon raped and molested women and children of epic proportions here! That said, does little Burpo, Todd's son, Colton, and more importantly the drawer of such an artwork, Akaine Kramarik, doesn't get too involved with this "picture" of Jesus here as it is not even Him! I don't even like the face that's in our rooms now, she said of the picture when she put it up! I give the kid credit though! He looks like Jesus Christ, sorta though! And that's the King of Solomon that She married in conjunction with the birds and the bees here!

The birds and the bees here are conjunctioned with time here. This warzone we commence to is just for the taking of My wife here. That Paul is for the birds I know it here! This warzone is time to commence, as well as My wife's complexities here.

That said, the birds and the bees. Oh my! Are we going there today, Folks! This is what I am talking about with My wife at the helm here. She's beautiful and lovely too! She wakes Me up each morning with a morning's dew? Hardly so! I knew the climate back then and that is what She wants to end with at each morning though, is a morning's dew. So, I bought here a chained necklace one year for Christmas too! Did you know that Christmas is the oldest tradition in the book of Revelations? It's Revelations, okay! I do think that it's not a Revelation to reveal the truths be told ways in which I loved Her dearly, okay! Well? It's a contest then! I do not reveal the inklingships taken from the token friendships from which we commence at here. This is not war if I cannot have My wife by my side then? This is war, Folks! That which the ugly grey areas portend to here. My wife is special here, He said!

Then there are Andrea's thoughts and fears about the masturbation texts here. That said here, what is the masturbations worth, Andrea? It's not worth much to state that for eternity's sakes here, in Matthew, John II and the likelihoods that pastors too get it readilies here, that the Sonship is the keys here in motions for the rest of our livelihoods too! And that said, Andrea, everybody do it! The whole world knows how to masturbate over livelihoods too!

And so, this is really a masturbation text's greatest gifts, problems and inklingships here that state that for the birds to know here, we all really do masturbate as a society, and as a species here. Birds, for example, the lovely affairs of the hearts we call dear to us here, the birds masturbate as well as the birds for peace.

So, for the records here, there is plenty to do's in the worlds of contexts and such. And so, Paul Wright is a moron for thinking and believing in other human beings to context himself with! This moronic man made love to My wife though? Hardly so! He actually raped Her alright! I do know this from the time that I walked in on a movie script with the tentacles hanging out of Her mouth then? He's a moronic creature! I do declare a mistrial in deeds and in scripts then, as this work is but a dream then. Correctamundo here!

I do declare that God's willingnesses to succeed in the focus of God's intentions are really for the birds though if I don't have Jezibellie Christ with Me every second of the days here! And that said here, we do know the reasons for the seasons here, and that said, we all know the Jezibellie cures and such that rocked our worlds back then too!

I do know that God's willingnesses to survive the albatross willingnesses is really supposed to be a ten in a five pound camps here. This is the reasons for the seasons of willingnesses to buy that diamond ring then? We had all the jewels in the worlds available to us's here. There's something in the lurch about diamond rings then? It's always been a diamond, you know! And that's a fact, Jack and Jill were never married though? What a boring life it has been without you, Jezibellie Christ!

I remembered her from grade school's tantalizing lessons in peace here! This is the peacetime talks we keep coming back to here! That is, this is because the scriptures are wrong here! I do declare a mistrial in deeds and in inklingships here! Hardships are for the birds, unless your willingnesses come back to Jezibellie Christ! Is it because this openness is really for the birds here? And tantalize us some more with this Jezibellie Christ's interventions here! Regardless of how the old people believe in reincarnation, silly heads, this makes us even harder to detect here! What I mean by this though, class of peoples that think it here, is that masturbation is just what the doctor's orders pretend to let go of in Chapter 8 of Romans here! Isn't Paul nice about it though? Hardly so! He's a traitor and a heretic! Please let go of this chapter as anything but nicey nice today here!

This is Jezibelle Christ's reincarnate though? Hardly so, unless you're willing to pretend that the guy or gal is really Jesus oriented here! Because it's really all small stuff here! I do declare a mistrial in deeds and in antics here!

Some people I know are scared or terrified of Us here! So, we just don't know what to do but to put her into a mental home, institution in other words! She's so bright and cheery though! How can God put Us in a bind like this to state that some people close to us are the same way here about life though! We don't know what to do with them! Taking sides with God like that, Folks, is really for the birds in here though! I don't know what else to say about this here Divine Source Wisdom that she now channels for the birds and the bees here, but my love life is intact somewhere else besides here then! I do declare a mistrial in deeds and in works here!

Bipolarisms, where to start? Was Jezibellie bipolar then? She was no such thing. The thing is, going on about these things above has been cathartic, to say the least here. What there needs to be here is an original Clash of the Titans movie's best characters here! Say, say, say, what is the justice department's best ringing in the ears about Demeter, the Greek goddess of love here?

She was not of the harvest here. She was of the godship's bestest halfway house's jerkology lesson's greatest numbers of timings here! Say, what does a moment's notice's biggest blessings really entail here but a commandant's messages here! I don't know what a cadmium sulfate's trip is here, but a 2 fluid ounces of sodium barbital is about messages here that says, if the 2 ounces of cadmium sulfate and 1 fluid ounce of water is injected into the arms of prisoners here too, then the wherewithal to withstand a barbiturate like cadmium sulfate's injection is a prisoner's guide to curing AIDS related viruses, just as the HIV cadmium sulfate's going to dine and dash on the prisoners of war's biggest relativity clause's justifications for bipolar disorder's wakes here!

What I mean is, a 2 fluid ounce shot of it, mixed with water have you, will do the trick. On a cadmium sulfate's level here, there are 20 ounce shots of it, don't do that though! And there are 2 ounce shots of it, injected right into the legs or arms of unsuspecting individuals who want to be cured of HIV and such!

I mean, what is a sodium barbital worth to you folks here but a cure for HIV? It's not a sodium barbiturate that I'm after here, but a sodium claritol that says that sodium treatments for bipolar disorder's not what we need out there for "us" to survive upon the waters of the claritol treatments of and for bipolar disorder's reckonings here, with the Lithium barbital concoctions that measurables give us for God's sakes! Those bipolar drugs are nothing but chemical inducing side effects that make people question their personalities, and it makes the Solomon in all of us come out to live for the fact that God questioned our personalities.

So much so that barbital is the widest cannabis treatment there is for bipolar disorders here in American soils here, that there are no, literally no treatments for it in other countries of the world's poverty-stricken areas here, and that's a fact, Jack and Jane were never married anyways or anyhoo here!

I want to clarify here that, earlier talk about Solomon and the fact that this chapter's ugly picture's of King Solomon himself, not of Jesus Christ here, says and states thereof, that the ugly people here, with nice teeth thereof, couldn't possibly be bipolar here, because of the ugliness factors here?

This niceness clause is really for the birds here. These tests are really for the birds, as well as the pedophile rings that this man really wants to commandant himself to! This means that the only phrases that veterinarians use when they're trying to diagnose a problem is to believe that Poseidon surfaced in that Clash of the Titans original movie simply to show the underdogs his talents here! This friendship of Jesus Christ is really two bitten and two-fold here! Crete is where Poseidon surfaced here! Next to the commandants is the really ugly persons that follow suit here, and all the teeth knocked outships of the greatest bipolarisms in the world, and that is the love for Jesus Christ that Jezibellie had!

This bipolar world is really for the birds here! Because of this though and however, there were several instigations of being bipolar that really got Jezibellie riled up here! There's moments where this man and this woman held hands in the 20ᵗʰ centuries A.D. here, and then some here! He followed Her everywhere here, and He knew Her from someplace special here!

I do not know from whence She came into My life, Jesus says of Jezibellie Christ's here ye surfacing and such! But this is from whence She came into My lives here! I used to woo Her no more here, unless and until She gave way to Me, and then I was able to digest Her, from whence She came back to the utility closet's biggest and baddest ways of finding out the truths be told commandant's notices here! I didn't ever let Her out of my sight's biggest and baddest truthfuls here, and I never, ever, gave way to the commandants who followed Her and Me too here.

And so, there's much adieus here. That means that there are truthfuls about My wooing Her, about my inklingships that I used to hold for Her, and there were all truthfuls about My wooing Her in the gardens of Eden's biggest and baddest sculptured looks I told Her by reckonings that I wouldn't bipolar Her no more about here! This life, you're on your own, as Prince was brutally murdered, as well! I don't know for whom I speak here?

This is the last commandant's lessons planning that takes hold and riddle cures peaces and such here! I just don't let another man's genitals flash between God's country lakes and the city mouse's churchgoing raptures here?

There's commandants here in the genitals areas! What we mean by this is that, although Prince's genitals were exposed during the final days of his rulings here, there are simpletons ways about going about the murder of Prince's final days here!

This commandant's final days here are simply just that here. What does a simpleton's to do list consist of, when it has to do with Jezibellie Christ here?

Simply put here, does Prince's other half ring a bell here? She was brutally murdered too.

That is here, this simpleton's execution style memoirs here was not even postponed during the final phases of their wakes here! There's commandants and then there's wakes here.

So chilling is their deaths here! There's commandants ways of beings here that made commandants the only commandants ways here. Better put is the simpleton's commandants that made the homelinesses become simpletons here.

There are simpletons and then there are simpletons who are never going to forget the methodologies that simpletons regret here! Simpletons and such are the only wakes and such that never get into the ways and means it lady's simpletons here. Better put here are the simpletons and such that servants and such remember Prince by, and that is the simpletons's little girls and such, that gives us a reckoning's peaces, and such tidings as little girls do here!

Better put here is the simpleton's simply put red eyed, nagging, sagging shrinks that go with, hand in hand with, some of the simpletons that simply red put on his nagging, sagging shrinks, to go with the nagging, sagging terrible Tuesdays of the simpletons of peaces here!

Better put here, the simpletons of the next songwriters's dreams here is that, like Prince's and Michael Jackson's here ye simpleton's works here, the commandants, or the military's simpletons here ye thoughts here, thought, oh my God or gosh as it were here, to bring this man and this woman into unions here made it possible for the simpletons to regain the best, the very best in commandants here!

What this means is that someone put in a simpleton's dreamscape here! Better yet here, what does the simpleton's meanings become when there are two murders, count em, two, murders here, that most people never knew something wrong about here, and the murders all turned into a "bipolar" outfit's commandant's lessons here?

I mean, "bipolarly," this lesson's take on scholarly writings here is less than the riddle cures of the simpleton's meanings here. In other words here, the scholarly writings upon which to dance here are simpletonly put upon "Us" here! Simpletonly put here are the riddles and such that his murderer put upon "Us" here, to simply put the riddle cures and the simpletons at bay here!

What this means is that the Princely tides of wraths and such is really not that simple here! It's the very best in raptures here that states that a Prince of tides is really what we're afterwards here ye going to begin begging the right lessons here, and really, Folks, and you too, Gents here, is that we're going to begin shooting his murderer down here, because this is really their own fault, and no one else's here!

I don't declare a mistrial here, only simply because the DSW is at fault here too, as well, or some such other demands that make the trees here simply tattletale like here!

In other words here, the commandants were involved somehow here, and they were crucially sworn to secrecy on their deaths, as well as their involvement in Jezibellie's demise, as well as Jesus Christ's secrecy on His wife's death, as well as Her involvement in His!

I do declare a mistrial, Jesus says, on this bipolar bit's here ye motion detectors of lives past here!

I do not declare a mistrial, Jesus says, on the killer here! This is the talent show's best kept secret's tattletalenesses here. This doesn't mean, Andrea, that there are best kept secrets here. It does mean that some people are going around murdering innocent peoples here for sure here! What I mean by this is, there are police protective ways here of making sure that this work's talent shows here gets to be seen by the authorities then here? Because I'm feeling vulnerable, that's for sures here!

Say, say, say, there are the involvements of God's tattletalenesses for sure here, and then there are people who are going to become the best, the very best at what they do here, for this is Jezibellie Christ's wakening's biggest talent search's awfulness's talent search's biggest and bestest's stuff here! This is the Jesus and Jezibellie camp signing off though?

Nothing could be furthest from the truth here!

This is the Divine Source Wisdom speaking here for Andrea Barberi here.

I do not tell a lie. Though telling this might seem here, that phone still lies on the floor in his spare bedroom's wakes here, and it is still on press play's here ye noticeables here!

This press play button, feature thereof here, tells exactly how he died thereof here! Jesus did the same things here when He and His wifey died in the hallways of that chateau they were underneath in the prison cells of the Gibraltar in Italy then? Nope, it was in Greece's hall monitoring system's tattletalenesses that keeps us together here! Commonly it was known as the halls of Gibraltar's best known kept secret's ironies here, in that Jesus and Jezibellie were guests there, and He knew and She knew that an untimely death's wakes here made it possible for them to see, and foresee, that the commandants are really just going to the commandant's houses. For them to forseek and desist the talent shows in the commandant's websites and stuff, cuz they did have the internet back then, you see it, now you do, is the twice bitten once shy, relics of the commandants of time's pasts here!

In that commandant's bipolar relics of hallways was the demise of Jesus Christ's love for Jezibellie Christ then, as She was and were the best kept secret's timings of peaces and such here? Peaces is a word, Peoples. And, this is not the way it should have been, Folks, and you too, commandants here, but this is the commandant's website's very best inklingshiphoods that go without saying that Jesus and Jezibellie were just visiting from Egypt's timelinesses here, and that is the ways and means it lady's very bestest commandants here!

In other words here, the only bride's notions here is to relics this woman and this man to become the bestest commandants to the toweled issues in their jacuzzi ridden sentiments here, and that the wine that day was the very best of all here!

Say, say, say, what you want, but MJ even had the same things happen to him here! I mean, his wifey to be and he were strewn all about in the chambers that be, as well as the chambers that blow menial gifts and such for the children that were present for this here! This means, Folks, that there were people in Michael Jackson's death's wakes here, and there were new people in his wakes here, along with the love of his life.

What happened to her then? I mean, what is this, a murderous talent search's reckonings here, and an AIDS cure?

Piss people off, why don't you, Andrea Wynn! I do know this here, that this thing just types word for word here, there is no editing, there is none of it! And so, if you don't believe me about Prince's death, about his lover's death, about his friend MJ's deaths to his personhoods and his lover's too, then don't believe me about it then! But it's DSW, Divine Source Wisdom, who's keeping watchtowers over the rest of the world's here ye watchtowers here, as MJ, Michael Jackson, was a Budapest follower, and a Jehovah's Witness's best yet follower here!

The military, the commandants in question here, were also involved in Jesus and Jezibellie's deaths here! This is how it be here, the commandants in question here were about to be removed from scriptures.

Never had it been spoken for, kids, children of MJ thereof here, that MJ was a child molester here as he was not, not, not! He's like King God here, very well spoken for his age as a teenage pop star, and so very much liked in the community of kings and goddesses, as well as Andrea's very own idol on her walls growing up, along with Prince as well here! So, c'est la vie here on the notions of pop stars not knowing that the simpletons are simply put here, bipolar then!

What the following means is that a bipolar woman could never commit murderous acts of kindness here. That said, neither could a schizophrenic or a schizoaffective person, ever commit a random act of kindnesses without stating so here!

That certain interlocutor that says, "Kill somebody!" never happens for a schizophrenic, schizoaffective person, or a bipolar wannabe here.

And that saids here, there are saids and saids without saids going ons here for sures here, there are certainly people out there wanting to kill someone with a lighter sentence, and then there's the people out there in the Forensics Units of the state hospitals that deserve to be incarcerated in the general populations of life sentences here! And that saids here, the following is a diatribe. This "lighter sentence" notions here is for the birds for sures here.

This is because there's no such thing as, "by reason of insanity," here! There's no reason for someone's certain interlocutor to state that they are bipolar, for reasons of insanity here, or for reasons of non-insanity's wakes here! There's notions and then there's murderous acts of kindnesses here? What do you think that these state hospitals's markups here listen to, but acts of kindnesses on someone's or something's best and worst kinds of criminals then? Because there are no random acts of kindnesses at these hospitals for example, then?

What we are saying here has to do with an interlocutor that says, "Kill people at random!" and not, "Kill people at will!" here! There has to be a happy medium between the two then? Nothing could be furthest from the truths be told notions of time's interlocutors here!

There's people out there who are bipolar no more here, and whose mood stabilizers don't work for them here! Truth be tolds here that there are people without mood stabilizers who don't know their asses from a hole in the ground's notions here, and there are never a time's peaces here, that state that peaces and peace go hand in hand here! And that said here, there's never a time when somebody's lessons be told here go, I need an inklingship's messages here! In other words here, there are peoples and then there are people here, who dare to derivify, and that's a word too, the outer being's lessons here! And that saids here, saids and said are two different words here, there are certain beings out there who say, "I want to kill people, others, what have you," and then there are those who say, "I don't want to kill others here."

But, the truth be told lessons here is that, there are not those who say, a "voice" told me to "kill someone." It simply does not happen! That's their own, and I repeat, their own little interlocutor, their own little "voice," their own little interlocutor, their own little inner voice, that says, "I want to kill others, and I want it to be a good choice for myself here." Not, "I hear voices and, therefore, I want to kill others."

I want to make perfectly clear that, alongside of Andrea's "voices" here that she types freely for the world to see and to take freely from here, there are no "voices" in her thoughts, in her ways here, in her vagina for the world's "voices" to decipher here. There are no "voices" that she hears, other than remedies for certain peoples.

According to her, a person can be standing in front of her and her inner voice is silent, always! And, her interlocutor is silent too. It's "Us," "We."

"Them," though? Highly NOT likely here! "We" are not "Us" and "Them" at the same times here, but a "voice" is not what she hears, but spirit guides and stuff? Not necessarily either.

What she hears is "Us" right here, like, "Tell this person they are going to die of cancer of the colon if they don't get in to see a colonographist right away, within the next three years at least," or, "I think that person has cancer of the lymph nodes," or, "That person is a pedophile," or, "pedo head, big time," or, "save it, she has cancer of the lymph nodes. She needs 3 cc's of IU's right away," or, "You've got a strong lesson to learn on this one, Andrea," or, "If you think she needs cancerous tumors removed from her belly, you'd better tell her that this one's for the birds then," or,… You see, those are not "voices," but a running commentary, much like NPR's, National Public Radio's, interesting commentaries on every single person alive today here. Those are not "voices," Peoples." Those are "spirit guides," then?

Well, they're certainly not telling her she's bipolar any longer, as of this writing anyway or anyhoo, whichever you prefer here.

I'm telling you, Andrea, if you think she's bipolar for having a mood stabilizer, then try "Us" here! I don't think she's, Andrea is, bipolar, any longer thereof here, because her mood is certainly stabilized on no drugs whatsoever someday soon. Is that correct thereof here?

There's no bipolar drugs that somebody needs. Ever! This sodium sidekick's abilities to know the differences in the sidekick's drug system's not even close to needing anything that says, bipolar abilities are rampant in shock therapies, syndromes, what have you. These Lithium kicks, Lamotrigine or Lamictal, same thing here, Tegretol, Trileptal, and what have you drugs here, are not even needed in the "human" conditions here!

These drugs are only meant to screw up the periods of perfectly sane women. So much so that there are even drugs to counteract the side effects of "blips," Andrea calls them, where oculogyric crises come together for all the rest of the drug interactions for Zyprexa, Haldols, Invegas, Geodons, Risperidones, and the likes of them all here, as they have side effects that not the Seroquels give, but the Seroquel XR etc do. I do not like these drugs here! I, We, say this because the drugs have the flower hibiscus in them, which do not set off an allergic reaction in everyone, but in this person, Andrea Barberi, they do. And so, Folks, Class of Gentile elitists here, there are reactions to the medications, but the only tolerable one is, save me from this class of Gentiles here too here, and that is the Seroquel drug and that is all here?

Save me from that one too here, as it is entirely possible to get off of this drug here without it being formaldehyde and morphine only! Not only is it entirely possible to get off of this drug here without repercussions here, it means, Folks and Gentiles too here, that the drugging of Andrea here is really for the birds here, about this "voices" phenomena here!

This is really for the birds here! I mean, if bipolar meant anything to the days of paranoid schizophrenics united ways here, the funny part is about this, Andrea, is that this diagnosis so many years ago, 12 years to be exactamundo here, is really what derails a lot of different people, folks, what have you! I mean, to say or to exclaim a paranoid schizophrenic's viewpoints are to "hear voices" about killing yourselves and stuff, and that's very real stuff here, is to say or to state a death sentence's tidings here!

What do you mean, paranoid schizophrenics don't wish or want to be called as such here? I mean, there are only three real mean diagnoses here, paranoid schizophrenics united ways here, schizoaffective disorders, which is really just paranoia dudes and dudettes here, and then there's bipolar disorders here. There's not a single day that goes by here that I do not wish that I was and were not called as such here!

This only singleton's viewpoints here, told me years later that I was paranoid schizophrenic no mores here, and that I was bipolarly schizophrenic then? Nope! That I was depressed type bipolar then? Nope! I was depressed type schizoaffective disorderly conducted to arrest myself though! From this viewpoint or this vantage point, what have you here, I was never quite the same after this though. I was "destroyed" in a sense here, by a diagnosis, plain and simply put here. There are no schizophrenias that never seen the light of days here, by contrast and by virtues here, I never saw shapes and formats. No siree bobs here! "Seeing things" is not my forte, but there are many men whom "see things" and whom live normal, happy lives here, just living it up to God's fortes here.

I mean, to get or obtain a diagnosis like this one of paranoid schizophrenics r us here, means that you are an invalid for sure here, and that you cannot function on one or more levels of taking that name to the bank then! I mean, for Social Security to see and to feel that I should get and obtain Social Security on my first try at it, forced to apply by the Social Security Administration I might add, Peoples, I must have presented pretty well here!

I mean, if I had a broken finger when a "voice," and I do mean a "voice," here said, "You're better off dead," or, "You ruin people's lives," and a finger went slice, right through the machine I was working on at work, Peoples, and it's like, what do I not understand here, but a "voice" said to me, you're a nincompoop here, and not to go kill people, that's for sure here, and say to them, I just heard a "voice" that said I was a nincompoop here, and got Social Security first try here.

I beg to differ that I was an invalid, however, and that I meant to say or to state that that voice was inaccurate about my whimsical errors of possibilities here! These are not, and I repeat, not the same "voices" she hears nowadays here, the wonderful, whimsical "voices" of the Divine Source Wisdom here!

It's difference entirely that gives us the same whimsical "voices" that contradict what we're saying here, to the grandiose methodologies that whimsically got her thinking that she's on cloud nine, trying to contact the DSW at all costs here? She could not hear "Us" back then at all here. "We" tried to come in at her 30 year mark and all she did was become paranoid at "Us" back then, thinking we were monsters and such earmarks!

After such timings as the Divine Source Wisdom's paranoid thinking's earmarks galore here got her into thinking a new diagnosis of paranoid schizophrenia's got to be the tickets here, she got on disability and was later destroyed for thinking that paranoia's got to be the clincher here! As she felt and thoroughly felt and thought herself to be a pedophiliac dreamscape then? Nothing could have been further from the truth here! But, she could not shake it from her repertoire here, that God had labeled her as such, and, therefore, she must be one then, not!

I couldn't shake it, she said, but she was "pedo head," not pedophiliac dreamscapes here! And so, this made her paranoid beyond belief here, all up until October of 2013 here.

And then, as if one shakes to the lamb's tale got her into thinking double talk is what led her to believe otherwise here, she tried this Emotional Freedom Technique or EFT Tapping on meridian endpoints to the notion of becoming a pedophile then? Not! Not, not, not! It's about this whole theme of becoming a pedophile then? Not! It's about becoming a good person in life, about being that same person of which she knew when she was a little girl, then becoming back to that person to whom she was no longer accused by her late estranged ex-husband, 25 years of difference in marriage.

So, to be accused of something so estranged here, is comatosing. She was able to heal an SI joint, sacroiliac joint's, timings, just perfectly with this notion of EFT Tapping on meridian endpoints, for paranoias and such, that she did it on October 6, 2013, and fully escaped the notions of paranoia in its entireties here.

This is because of the rest of the diagnosis of paranoid schizophrenias, schizoaffective disorders and then bipolar was thrown into the mixes here, that people became paranoid themselves about myself becoming an intuitive healer here. Then, as if to say, you are still disabled bitchy girl, you are now thrown into mental health, whisked off after many years of stability, into the mental health system again here! I do declare a mistrial, Jesus and Jezibellie say, as people get scared of individuals like me who seem to know everything about them.

For some reason, talking in the mirror to myself led others to call 911 on me as I was learning to channel the DSW out my mouth.

That's a juxtaposed, wonderful thing about Andrea Barberi here, is that she's willing and ready to work it out in the "mirror work" imposed by Louise L. Hay, and several others, who have encouraged her to do so! This juxtapositioned "mirror work" of finding a common balance in the structures of love here, enabled Andrea to fully recover from schizophrenia, bipolar, and schizoaffective in their entireties here, and to not, I repeat, not be labeled a "thought disorder" by the media here! There are several things to involve "Us" with here, and that is one of them here. She's no longer schizophrenic, bipolar or schizoaffective here, what with the advent of socializations with ourselves here as a schizophrenic, wonderful woman here!

There's no label that justifies the label for schizophrenias, as she has never seen shapes and figures, hallucinations, or what have you here. Which, by the way here, men see hallucinations all the time here. Men do, women don't. We hear voices more often than not here. A man will never admit to this, however, or at least try to pretend that they don't, for fear of being labeled as such schizophrenias do tell them to blast out the bipolarnesses of the world's schizophrenic labels and such here. Bipolarly, Folks, and you too, Gentiles here, God took this from you, Andrea, and you were able to heal others with your healing touch, as well as others with their healing touches, and so on here.

There's really a comedy's echoings here, as there are several things that Jezibellie Christ wanted to reconcile with you here. First of all here, there are no alls here, Folks, and you too, Gentiles here, there are whimsical seances and stuff for sure here. There are no fat lies about whimsical details about MJ's and Prince's deaths here, and certainly not those who are Black about it here!

I don't know about Prince's death, but certainly for MJ's, Michael Jackson's here, that God was watching "Us" tell about it here! I don't know about God's uncertainty for MJ's deaths here, in that God was watching Prince too. Although I cannot begin to breathe about certainty for time of death's vacancies and what not here. The only Prince I was able to obtain a death certificate for was for time of death, and not possibility of death's tolls here!

Even though Prince didn't believe in Michael Jackson's demise either here, he did find one thing in particular of his death, though Jezibellie Christ never really did find Jesus that attractive then? One thing that you never really knew, Andrea, is that there was never a time when attractiveness never beget lovelinesses here. Andrea's hair right now is a medical emergency's timings here, as it is cut short, extra short, for the possibilities of a disguise, and we're knowing this to be truthful here.

This naturalization's peaces here, never really gets me down, Prince's police officers' union's said to him before his demise here! That is because they really did not allow for the coming of police officers' unions to really take down the demises of the riddle cures to boots here!

This union's dues are really to take the union dues out of the perennials that are overdue here at the market square's natural abilities to surround these women with all the perennials that they could both stand up in here! These women, both naturally sound women here, never sought to give up the "pills" that were both bipolarly inclined here, and also schizoaffectively mine here!

I mean, what do you do on a vacation for crying out loud here, but to bring these "pills" with you that could mean that you don't get a vacation for one here, or, that you are never going to get these "pills" out of your brains here. And, naturally here, there are several things that could go wrong with spiked "pills" here, which is what happened to his wifey in tow's "pills" here! You know, Prince's wifey in tow here! It was their wedding night then? Yes!

Who goes around and tries to find the least bit of attractiveness in manufacturers and tries to play games with them for the public's benefit?

So, for example, hair colors and hair dyes, as Andrea soon found out here, are "spiked" with the natural ability's trusts here, with common colors that no longer dye the hair a natural overtone, unless and until it's a darker color. So, for example here, Andrea went to the salon after a 10 lift, for a 30 lift to fix it, and the chick goes, I don't want to do it, so sign this here form, so that I can get out of any liabilities if it turns out bad or anything. And, she sure did! So, for someone to sit around and mastermind different haircuts, that's not what we're talking about here.

Because "pills" can be manufactured for shaven people, as well as postal workers who are still working for a living under the Seroquel dosages, trying to make a living, as people have seen Andrea try to work for a living here, several times in fact here, and have made a killing off of the fact that this hospital of choice sent her home with no "pills" and a taxi ride to a nearby motel, all for just being a postal worker. Can you top that, or do these "pills" have a concoction quite readily made here?

If Andrea had not been "homeless" at the time here, there would've been no problem with their home choices for her here. There's somewhat of a discrepancy here, in that Andrea hears no "voices" that other people hear around her though! Jesus was much the same way here! People would hear "voices" around Him, and then they would commit Him for them!

Who would sit there and concoct ways in which to sabotage people's livelihoods, just by manufacturing issues, in which people didn't "go" very often here. In other words here, if you didn't "go" that often here, it was because of the GMO content, the genetically modified organisms found in simple fruits and vegetables here, that never really talent themselves here! Say, say, say, what you want, but don't play games, with my affections, take, take, take, what you need, but don't leave me, with no directions! I cannot begin to imagine, DSW says, the Divine Source Wisdom here, to begin to tell from the level of infiltrations here, the level of ingenuities that came about here.

The comical things about this sort of interactions between God's children's seances and such are the levels of indeeds that come about here!

To gain access to another of the middle cures of livelihoods here, the only things necessarily so here, are the means of which to say that a Jesus Christ superstar really loves a Jezibellie Christ here. Because the menial ways in which God's tattletalednesses really love somebody specially here is to take the apple fritters home with you, Jesus, is to say and to state that the only "voices" one hears when they're around Andrea right now, is the same ones people proclaim to hear when they were around Jesus Christ here!

And, this is Andrea here saying this here, that she's no Jesus Christ here, but she certainly is a Jezibellie Christ then? "We" think so here, reincarnating here? Yes! So is this Jesus Christ cure then! Because this is so "common" for Andrea to think she's Jezibellie Christ though, we're saving the best for last here.

That is why the manufacturing thing is so paramount here, is that God's watching us, all of us here, and He knows if there is foul play, always and forevermore here!

I'm sick of being thrust into the "mental health arenas" here by the local and city police officers unions here! I'm taken time and time again here, because of my mental health statuses here? Nope, but by sheer luck, for having had an LRO or an LRA here, and a CR, not to mention a CR has the connotations of a state hospital's affairs' union of blanksmanships here, and I don't take kindly to it here! And, that said here, quit taking me into mental health because of an LRO/LRA/CR here!

I don't need to be taking these "meds" either here! There's words about this out there, and there's commandants who need to be shut down here. This is the Divine Source Wisdom talking, not the DSW though? Yes, the DSW too. I am a natural healer. I am an intuitive healer. I am knowledgeable about the world's greatest gifts here.

I no longer need mental health meds. Can we admit to healing mental health "drugs" and, therefore, mental health here? I am an intuitive healer.

Can you see or foresee people's diagnosis changing for the betterment of society's children's children here? Do you foresee "us" as "child molesters," which we're not, or as able bodied men and women, capable of having children here in American soils here?

Because there are no schizophrenias in other parts of this world here!

This is a fact! This bipolarly, worldly comment's going on and on here, and on and ons here, and on and ons, and on and ons, and on and ons, and on and ons here, that makes the society's interests never mind about it here! I mean, there are run ons, and there are simpletons here that makes society's interests go on and on about personality defects.

And, how many times do a personhood's natural healers have to stave away from being transfixed into thinking they need Seroquel in order to function here? Because when she has babies, and she do quite readily here, she will not need these medicines!

But there's several things wrong with this demise's natural healer's abilities here. In order to heal from traumatic experiences here, the schizoaffective talent's only natural healers in the communities in order to heal from traumatic experiences here needs to be said here. There are LRA's in our wakes here.

Even in the wakes of 9/11, we saw the natural healers in the wakes of 9/11's demises here. And about 9/11, we never even put it on the calendar as a national holiday's memorial here.

What goes on in this house, stays in this house pretty much, Andrea! There are natural healers everywhere here. There are the abilities of peoples worldwide here to leg out the commandants here. God's bipolar statuses are never anything that Jezibellie Christ could not handle here.

If Mr. C, for example, Mr. Clinton thereof here, could not run the White House again here, I could not fathom a better, more suitable match for the White House thereof here.

Both kings and queens run the White House, not the other way around here. There are simpletons and there are both disparities between the White House's governmental ways around this here work, this writing here, and the facts that God's wisdoms hold accountable all of Trump's, President Trump's thereof, methods to his madnesses here, and Mrs. Trump's White House attire is fetching I might add here!

There are such a disparity's calamity Jane's mixtures here that states that God's wraths here postpone a schizophrenic's disparities here. With a bipolar disorders out the windowness here, there is no such thing as it then! If Jim Carrey can continue on with the methods of his madnesses here and not be arrested for being and acting bipolar, then I'm in here. The White House is something of which I write to frequently, and of which I am fond of here.

Say, say, say, what you want, but don't play games, with my affections, take, take, take, what you need, but don't leave me, with no direction. You, you, you, can never say, that I'm not the one, who really loves you!

What can I do, Girl, to get through to you, cuz I love you, Baby, standing here, baptized in all my tears, baby through the years, you know I'm crying, ooh, ooh, ooh, ooh, ooh! Yeah, yeah, as MJ would say, after all this time thereof here! This is really the two-fold ridiculous foldings of the saturated fats and stuff that really have it when they're talking about bipolar amisses and stuff, not the sodium contents of the fats and stuff.

That I'm succumbed to this from time to time, this sodium content's bullshit notions of, am I doing well on blood levels and such, as this Trileptal's latest dosages are really the APA's, the American Psychological Association's, ways and means it lady's tears and sweat's commandants here.

This means that in mental hospitals worldwide then? Nope, just on American soils here, the commandants are just ringing in my ears, you know! I mean, Jesus says of Jezibellie Christ here, that the commandants are really just following her around, Andrea thereof here, wondering why they can't hear anything but "voices" here when she's near and around them here, and then there's "voices"... that I can't hear then, Folks, and you too, Commandants then, Folks and Gents too here? Because these "voices" are simply your own here. Why don't you just own up to the facts, Andrea, that people hear these voices around you and are enthralled by them enough to, one, arrest YOU for them, and, two, arrest THEMSELVES, rather, and B, here, never again do we cause this unrest for ourselves here by saying, one, two, three, go get thee, four, five, six, pick up sticks, seven, eight, and nine, you're all nine dogs and cats, and... I mean here? Even Mr. C, Mr. Clinton here, arrest his soul here for nothing, ever, here, is amiss to think that God even told him that "voices" are unheard of, until they get around you though! Call him and ask him, Andrea! I like Mr. and Mrs. C, Mr. and Mrs. Clinton thereof here, and Donald Trump thereof here too! His wifey is much to be desired then? Nothing could be furthest from the truth here! I don't speak right, so, kill me for it here?

Do you not speak right, there, Andrea, here? That's right. Not the other ways around Jupiterian talks here! Say, do you hear "voices" around this lady here, people say to admit to, in other words here? And then they are taken into "custody" for "hearing voices" around you, Andrea! I mean, people you know have figured it out, that they have figured out this here "voices" phenomena, you have here, Class of Gentiles, Elitists, and such here?

Chapter 33

I'm Counting on You, Andrea, To Tell the Gospel to the Churches of Wrath Here

My mother, Jesus said, died on the cross too here! Not here!

I don't know what happened to My Jezibellie Christ here. Without Her, Jesus says, He's clamoring for attention from both parties here, as they both died at the Festival of Wills here in Greece, mind you! Andrea, how come so many Festivals of Wills here for you too here?

Because your brother had sharp shooting rights, it means that he was a hero here, and Chip Solomon II (Tutankhemen) was definitely a nice guy back in the days of Jesus and Jezibellie Christ here. Akiane Kramarik's photo that she painted here, the talented 11-year-old rendition of Jesus Christ's wannabe lookalike contest is King Chip Solomon. It was not Jesus, but Chip Solomon, the ruler at the time of England, or King Solomon II's talented rendition of a creepy skyscraping addict of Jesus Christ's lookalike contest's biggest and baddest Jezibellie's torture chambers dudes and dudette's prisoner's lookalike contexts and all here, was the sweetest rendition for her to paint it black though, as he was definitely White too here. But he kept Me from My wife by amnesia, that is why it is so important that she included her work in Todd Burpo's book. It was that strong of an image to paint!

That man, Chip Solomon II, took over the King of England's titles here, and became a great man. Chip Solomon II here, I hope you don't mind this song and dance title's best rendition of peaces here, but that is Chip Solomon I's creepy new photo's best thing to come along since sliced bread photo rendition thereof here?

The least you could do is tell us about Jezibellie's family's mishaps and such here. Her dad was the King of Greece and Mesopotania's King Tut or Tutankhamen here, King James Tutankhemen actually.

That said here, it is imperative that the looks of quality monitoring of the Joico kind, the Joint Commission here, release the tapes of Andrea Barberi's lookalike contests here, in every single mental hospital, called quality monitoring.

Joined at the hip's trading games is quality monitoring of peoples and the FBI's warnings here that, Andrea's best quality monitorings in all hospitals of both facial hairs and butt cracks and wiping affections and stuff, that staff of Joico used to enjoy looking at! I'm sure they can attest to the quality monitoring of every single living psychic on the face of this Earth here, rendering unconscious the final resting days and periods of Quality Monitoring here on the face of this Earth's crusts here.

To try and cover up the event here, the Invega shots were used, as well as the Haldol monthlies, which I am deathly allergic to! And, not only that here, they were informative about this upon my arrivals to the situations at hands here! To cover up the events however though, there were informative peoples who said, "This is the monthly Invega shot," or, "This is, or was, the monthly Haldol shot," here! That is the allergic reaction, test and Invega shot that I thereof received because I was too "monthly" off my medicines, and conducted myself well in court that day thereof at this hospital in particular. There is a videotaped session where she, the judge, told me to get my gun rights reinstated as soon as I can here, and I still did not win a discharge, even though I was dynamically put together well here. I could conduct business rather well for a discharge note then, as this judge in the pictured monitoring screen had never discharged anybody, not anyone in her 16 year stay as the judge for that and other facilities around the regions here.

It happens to so many young, unsuspecting women in the mental health arenas here, that we're dubbed "incompetent" to stand trial, to care for a young one, or to be a person of "interest" in the taped recordings of these goings on here.

That states here that not a one of these women, and men too here, are ever let go of here. I was solely off my meds that day I was in court here, and I walked back and forth here as they sat there and said certain things that were off to me here.

That's what this rendition's take on the life and times of Jezibellie Christ would have told "Us" about Her then, is the facts that it presented the Christlike ways of Jezibellie to become the rendition's best and biggest love stories here!

There are husbandries in your future too, you know! I know of someone and something here! Tell us what you think about life there, Andrea! Tell "Us" what the rest of the day's supposed to look like here, with the balance cures of life here! Say, say, say, what you want, but don't play games, in my direction! You, you, you, stay away, but don't lead me, girl like I do! We changed it up for a reasons and a seasons here.

That song, that lovely song by MJ here, is changed up because of the tests of time's pasts here. The best songs that lullabies sing lovely songs here is the takings of time's pasts here. That's because Bill Clinton couldn't have done those things to Gennifer Flowers here, and certainly not to Monica Lewinsky's buttons here! He's not the one in charge though! You are, Andrea!

I do declare a mistrial, Jesus says, in the ways and means it lady's certainties of this Monica Lewinsky's eons ago mistrials here too, Dudes and Dudettes, which means kings and queens here! I don't forsake the gentleman's mistrials here, as Hillary, and I do say this lightly here, gives a questionable look's indeed figurines here, to the tattletalednesses that God's inklingships here give to the honorable mentionables here!

What I mean by that is, Divine Sourced Wisdomed looks and all here says to the commandant's languages here, is that, God, for whatever reasons here, Monica Lewinsky-ed the commandants that made the Gennifer Lewinsky Flowers sane.

For whatever reasons though are the gifts that God's mentionables wanted her to say here, as the person of interest was really Hillary's duffs, and not Bill's duffs, if you know what we mean by loves though, you will understand that Monica Lewinsky's really gay here, and not the other ways around, it's laughters at the White House's means and treasures chested ways here, Folks, and you too, Gentiles here!

This is because the Monica Lewinsky-ed treasure chested nobodied businesses here took the tiles and ridiculed her, the Hillary in questions here, in their humble abode's here ye tiles and floor mockings here! Say, say, say, what you want, but don't play games, with my affections! You, you, you, stay away! Because, I, need, no affections, from you's, you's, you, here, Monica, Hillary mockingbird lane's affections, as well as the attention getting's devices here that takes Monica Lewinsky's biggest and best "affections" to the banks of tidings here! Say, say, say, what you want, but don't play games, with my affections! You, you, you, stay away! Because, I, need, a riddle and a half to figure out what to play next here with Andrea's games and stuff here! All alone, I sit home by the phone, waiting for you, Baby, is what Hillary's duffs and stuff meant when she, Hillary here, meant to state that, it's a queer game's commandants that made "Us" interested in questioning Hillary about this lovely venture capital gains tax's leftovers about this Hillary duffs in the wind.

There's things to be done today. Leftover capital gains taxes is a questionable thing here, but none of it was ever false! The reasons for the seasons takes the capital gains taxes out of the questionables here, Hillary Rodham Clinton, because they used to gain weight over it here, both she and Bill could not believe it here!

Their only "tapes" that were used in the Gennifer Flowers scandals here were the ones that were fresh from the labs of hope's gnawing, gnashing figurines that she used to so collectablesly get from Gennifer, and then some here. There's a treasure chest full of them at the residential suite's gnawing, gnashing tulipville's sentimentations here.

Because of the tulip's conversations with God's wonderful Gennifer Flowers here, never did a Bill Clinton ever, I mean EVER, have an affair with that woman here! Take it from Me, Jesus never did have an affair with tulip woman, the Delilah gnashing, knee-smashing, teeth gnawing woman who never really saw Him with an affair in the first places here.

This moment's notices are on file for life's ridifying of the details about this Gennifer Flowers case's gnawings and such. Here's the best, the best riddles for life's gnawing and teeth gnashing, spittifying ridiculousnesses here.

Say, say, say, what you want, but don't play games, with my affections, He says to her now, Gennifer Flowers thereof here! Don't, don't, don't, play away, the nightly games, of my affections, with Jesus Christ at the helms of loves here.

Because of this nasty rumor's lengthy clauses here, there is no Gennifer Flowers in the mix here, not a one!

There is still time to dispose of the ridiculousnesses that Jesus and Jezibellie had upon one another here then, as the King of England's ridiculousnesses had it so that Chip Johnson was it? Nope, Chip Eisenhower III never did really gain the capital gains taxes it took for them to lay so cheaply in the middle of hope's quests though? I mean, Hillary really loved, and still loves, Bill, to death here, and vice versa here!

Why, oh why, are nasty rumors started like this in the first place? Oh Bill, keep turning that page of wrath here, and only when we know, and "We" do know this for a facts here, keep turning the pages of wrath's evil middle named twins here, that said, Jesus, why did you marry that Delilah chick in the first places here? Well? It was because She was unavailable at the time's inklingships here, and Delilah was the first Longmire, Delilah Longmire here, that was available at the time of asking here.

I mean, did Delilah Longmire, and Bill Clinton's never been married to anyone else but Hillary here, and vice versa here, but the sentences remain intact here in and as of this writing here, for Delilah Longmire to come out and to state for the records here, that the commandants are really for the birds here if a man is not married to a woman, any woman here.

And, that means that if a man is not married to a woman here, any woman here, he is then shunned and put into a mental institution for it here! Say, say, say, what you want, but don't play games, with my affections! You, you, you, stay away, Gennifer Flowers here! I do love My wife, Jesus says to you now here? Not! Not, not, not! I couldn't get rid of her either, He says to you here!

Now what does Chapter 33 entail here, but a way to get rid of "voices" and stuffs here? It's a tattletaledness's biggest letters. And, there are never ways to get rid of Hillary Rodham Clinton, by the ways here!

And that saids here, Andrea, saids is a word thereof here, what is the Hillary Rodham Clinton's biggest dream is to become presidential and stuff here? Not without Bill, of coarsely here! Say, say, say, what you need, is a big, fat, presidential gift of gab here, Andrea Wynn!

I don't need a husbandry present's latest gift of gab's biggest lessons in life's talentries here too. And, Chelsea Clinton is a good person here. So, did you detail the scoop of this book for anyone besides the prescriber's lessons plannings here, as you are very much still on an LRA for the book's publications here?

Or, are you going to present this book's chapter writings for her in a little bit here? Because this Gennifer Flowers issue's prevailing for the chapter's warings and wherewithals here, there are particular scoops that are Gennifer Flowers's captives here, and that is to say or to state that Hillary Rodham is the reasons for the season's biggest and best captives here.

What we mean by this is, Gennifer Flowers heard "voices" telling her what to do with her life, mkay? Not! Not, not, not! Mkay!

What we mean by this trip down memory lane's biggest masterminded tellings here is that, Andrea is going to "kill Us" for not letting this down sooner's here, that there's never anything other than "voiced commands" that "We" give her time and time again. Like, "Go to the store," or, "I want you to turn left up ahead," and, "Take a left, right, left," and so on's here.

There's not "voiced commands" like, "Go and kill someone," then, you say here, anyhoo, it's a scramble for a reason and a season's best narratives here, because "We" like you, a lot here. So, anyhoo, you know my therapist, and my confidant here!

So, when you read over this, and you shall do so in a couple of weeks here, how about considering Andrea's and Hillary's plights here, that no one on Earth, not a one here, is ever, and I mean EVER told, to "kill someone," with their thoughts. Not one, not ever! No one has ever heard this "voice" telling them what to do this way.

No one, not EVER. And so here, if you believe the book, and you believe Us here, you will succumb to the LRA's ideas here and get her off these meds, Andrea here.

Because we believe in her therapist so strongly here, the notions and stuff that we're saying here is really sweet and all. But, We're tired of game playing. And, in particulars here, we're tired of saying that We don't hear "voices" because "We" do. "We" hear all kinds, particularly the kind that state, "Turn left up ahead," and, "That boy over there has cancer. Why don't we run up to them and tell him that, not!" And so on here.

What is this phenomena called here? But a simple how do you do here! There is such things as "voices" here that are treatable by this phenomenon called "voices lingering," and this is how we're gonna do it from now on, Classes of Gents and stuff here! We're gonna ask Andrea what to do about this new phenomenon, called life here, and ask her what mental health is and means here, from now ons here! That is, Folks, and Classes of Gentiles here, that we keep speaking to's here, is that, we're talking about citizenries for the classes of Gentiles who keep speaking to the Gentiles here, and nothing could be furthest from the truths mongerings here, who say, what is "mental illnesses" here, but a class of elitists that say, what is God's truths here, but a bunch of people who are dubbed "mentally ill" here?

With a class of Gentiles, elitists and such here, Andrea is perfectly qualified to, not only give it up for God's sakes here, but to qualify as THE person, in charge of "mental health" here? You betchas here!

Say, say, say, whatcha want, but don't leave me, with no directions! What I mean to say here is, the balance cures of a lifetime of heartache's listened to women's directions here, makes this diagnosis problems or issues, balance trades, and some such things as balance cures and such, little to distinguish between "mental illnesses," such as murderers and rapists, the TRUE crimes of the elitists here, as opposed to the elitists who are NOT, and I repeat, not rapists and such, are the TRUEST, crime ridden, blanksmanships that there ever was here.

And, this is Andrea's specialties here, is remedies of ALL kinds of truths and stuff here!

This is Andrea's specialties here, not the psychiatrists' that are questioning her truths here. This means, Folks, and Classes of Gentiles and Elitists here, that God's keepers are questioning HER truths, and intentions here, right, Mr. Bill Clinton and Ms. Hillary Clinton too here? This questioning of Monica Lewinsky, by the way here, made her the scapegoat of Hillary's demise as presidential candidates then? Because this is not what took place here. The time it takes for "Us" to figure out that presidential candidates are the meanest, and I do mean this, meanest people on Earth for us to figure out then, is a falsity that preludes the meanest, and I do mean this too, segregated living arrangements, for the time being's lesson plans for "Andrea Barberi's" lesson plannings here!

Lessons plannings for Andrea is what is really needed here, as the Seroquel dose remains at 600 mg as of this writing here, and the dosages of God's plentiful peoples here is less than in recent years here. Whenever the dosages get below 1700 mg for alls of us's here, Peoples here, the dosages go, well, "It's not a therapeutic dosages," between the sheets then, Sirs, and you too, Gents here?

Because 300 mg's just what the doctors ordered for her at a state hospital to be on, with no mood stabilizers. And, this is what the doctors had on her most recent stays there, and the most recent stays at this other hospital here was at 800 mg, a most lethal dose for her to be on here.

And, someone here stated that it's about 700 mg of bullshit that makes these "pills" she puts out every night, and every night she takes them religiously here. To cut them in half makes the "pills" cut out the pajama cures, every single night's lessons here, as the most recent hospital stays up at this particular hospital is it? Nope, it's this other hospital stay, for hitting a most recent car stalker here in the parking lot at work, and having an LRA or CR, Conditional Release, on her records here, is bound to make the telegrams for any state hospital's illegalnesses at work's savior blessings here, united and coupled with grocery items to boot here at the Safeway in question here, blessings beyond belief here, as we're slated for a much more meaningful job's titles here, as a natural healer and not a gas station/grocery store worker anyways here.

And, the cops go, well, a CR on her record means, a fender bender in the parking lot, that they neither witnessed or kept closely to them here, gave her an "arrest" record or warrant for her persons here, and, taken into custody to yet another hospital, is it? Nope, to any same hospital again here for a secondary stay, only secondary to the post office workers unions is it? Nope, the last time I took a lie detector test for the tests of time here, and hit somebody in the parking lot, who was a "stalker," and who called 911 on herself here, in the parking lot's 911 calls here, and to whom I bet the living shit out of here, went to jail for and of herself here, not!

I do declare a mistrial here, in deeds and in wills here, upon her most recent hospital stays here, as she does have another LRA here, only because she's good lookingly "bald" this time though? I do declare a mistrial, Jesus says, as Jezibellie Christ was not only "bald" when I met her again here, but She wore a hijab too. So, the police took her clothes off at the joint there at the "emergency room" bantering back and forth here, and said to her, take off your clothes, with a bunch of scissors though, which they do now for unsuspecting females and males who cannot make it out of the bathroom bantering that said as such, for the police records though? They'd cut her purse, a $5 or $10 purse anyways here, off of her person as well as her shirts here, and said, "Oh, too bad, so sad," here, and left her with no clothes but a scrub shirt, an orange one at that?

Now, deep orange happens to be my color here for the next two weeks though, all because I had a job then? I do release this information slowly here, but I do seem to be the next Cosmo girl's blanksmanships here, as I have so much "experience" in this situation's bantering back and forth at the "cop shops" in questionings here, that another LRA, Less Restrictive Alternative, on my person would have been another death sentence here, as another Haldol shot would've been in any doctor's best interests here? Not! But, to take me to the 600 mg mark on the Seroquel from the previous stays in another hospital had me on so much Seroquel is it? Nope, so much Perphenazine, that I could no longer write my own name down on my "word salad," that is put upon every single "schizophrenic" takedown in a police review of my "word salad," that I am unable to comment upon this schizophrenic talent of a word salad here. All because I told them that the guy who's taking me down here and writing my own name with his takedowns and stuff here, does dawgs, on the sides of the roads though? Dawgs are unsuspecting woman who are taken down, because of "mental health" issues here, and done on the side of the road like cattle here, and left for dead here, all until a "mental health unit" arrives, I mean a goddamn ambulance here,… and it's safe to cuss like this, God likes to use His name in vain here! It's a good Goddamn word to use here, especially since the dawgs, out to get us here is the best man for the job's use of force, to take down a woman from society here.

This police use of brute force here on the "takedown" of a fender bender in the parking lot's ridiculousness's policework here, is really for the birds to decide upon here. And, the fact that my wallet was taken and put upon the police car, in which I sat in here, is really for the dawgs of society's inklingships to decide upon here, as Mr. Clinton suffered quite a handful of people's suggestions back then, when in his presidency's orneriness's blanksmanship's tidings here! What I mean by that is, Andrea lacks the integrities to dance and to vote, for one thing, back in 1992 then? She graduated high school back in 1992. So, was fully able and willing to vote for President Clinton back then, and she did alright.

Anyhoo here, a policework badge's dawg takedown of unsuspecting women in the "police ride" back to the "emergency room's" takedown llama man's questioning of her then here, as the "police ride" back to the "jail" then entailed a "psychiatric unit," next to the regular hospital's units here?

Policework'd be policework anyplace Andrea shows up at here! I do go to jail a lot here then? Nope, just "mental health" for my "beliefs" all the time here, regardless if I have a job or position thereof here! I just don't get it, but go on, for the sake of Mr. Clinton's clan here, and I do have a job there still, if I wanted it then? Nope, not now that I've been "arrested" outside of the joint's natural abilities to state that a police car's ride to the cop shop in questionings here is about ten-fold's ten unit's natural ability's, natural selection's, biggest and best plane ride's, ornerinesses from which and for whom does not believe in her here, but for the living sakes of God's countries of doubts in here, upon which an LRA, or a CR here, gets you into more trouble than you're worth here!

I don't know why or for how here, but that plane ride to the next hospital is perturbed at an emotional stay right now, of policework that is either shotty, at the scene of the crime's lucks here, that you now have an emotional stay, beyond the scenes of airs of contentment's biggest crime scenes here, but Mr. Clinton, you know this to be truths here.

You were "arrested" for your beliefs at citizenry, just the other day in 1992, or 1993, was it, for knowing "Monica Lewinsky" as an "intern" for the White House lawn's natural selections here, and he was treated in much the same manner here! I mean, a White House takedown for natural selections here, made it possible for a government agency's backlash and backwater washing down's natural selections belief systems here, makes it harder for me, Andrea, to believe this too here! But, I, was "arrested" so many times for My own beliefs here, as president of Egyptian soils here, that God could not arrest me sooner for "hearing voices" around Me, too here!

And, that saids here, there are saids and said here, the "Monica Lewinsky" scandal is better off said here that there are no controversies unwarranted here in Andrea's eyes here, that go unnoticed here. But "that woman" is the epitome of folklore, and an intern that was hired off the streets of Brazil, was it here? Nope, but police officers' unions out there "knew" of her alright here.

They pulled her off the streets of Brazil alright here. They pulled her off the streets of legos and tomboyishnesses here, dolled her all up, posed a picture with the President of the United States here, and immediately he was taken into "custody" for "posing" with a teenage "prostitute," from the streets, count 'em, there are many here, count 'em, Classes of Gentiles here, and prostitutes too here, from the very streets of Washington, D.C.'s, natural ability's, natural selection's, high time figure skating championships here, and pulled aside to "assist" the President with his hand jive questionings.

This moment's genuine here. Because of this interlude between her and Hillary here, the genuinity's biggest moments here are sometimes "mistaken" for the "biggest" and "baddest" of them all here, and genuinity's biggest and baddest moments here are genuinity's biggest and baddest moments online too. Genuinity's biggest and baddest friendships are sometimes lesson killers, and back then, Mr. Clinton heard "voices," too.

It's what made him such a great President here. That's because, anyone who hears "voices," the right kinds of "voices" here, makes such a great leadership skill's personhood here. I love the fact that Mr. C, Mr. Clinton in fact here, loves the fact that God's works are really happening here, Andrea!

The facts that God has presented to no one, other than yourselves here, is really the quiet awarenesses of Jesus Christ's love for Jezibellie Christ's anchorships here! I mean, Her dad's great but this is irrelevant maybe here, King James Tutankhemen was his name! The Clintons, by the way, Andrea, thank you tremendously for this someday I imagine, soon thereof, I hope here.

There's commonalities, and there's hopes for God's loves here. To erase this moon unit's dweezil units and stuff, from commanalities here, makes for the ideas of wrath's Chaka Kahn's subtleties here, but Dweezil Zappa is not to blame for this here. He loves playing music of his father's, Moon Unit's here, and there on and some such things here. But Frank really "lives it up," at the White House parties of wrath's open doors here! That's when the Dweezil goes, "Frank, Um, I just found out that your White House party's open to Gallaudet students here, and I approve!" here! This is White House company, that is for sure here.

Because of this "dream" of Gallaudet students, and we do employ them on a regular basis, from the White House's perspectives here. That is, to say this is to employ them again here, on a regular basis, Mr. Trump here, who was "arrested" the other day, for "mental health issues," his wife's hat too here! "Um, Mr. Trump," the Divine Source Wisdom states it for the love of God's wraths here too here, "saying that your 'mental health' is in 'question' here in the 'news media' as a 'joke' here," makes "Us" want to puke a bloody turnip here.

"I" don't "listen" to the "words" of the Spirit, though? This is the DSW for short here, and Andrea Wynn Barberi, Andrea for short here, never went to Gallaudet University here. But she sure enjoyed knowing about the rest of the, clearly voluptuous, wherewithals to that ejaculation's biggest naturalizations about the comings of death's door stamp's biggest wherewithals here!

I think, Andrea, that coming out with this newest information's revelations here, and it's Revelations, Dudes and Dudettes here, which means kings and queens are possibilities in the White Houses and beyond here, means that if Trump, which I do mean, lives for and dies for senility someday soon, if he don't get off of that damn Coumadin fixes perhaps someday here, meaning, get him offa that damn stuff now, you know! He's gonna get Alzheimer's from it here, right readily and so on here? Yes!

To say it this way is sort of cheap here, Jesus here saying this too here, that the commandants and stuff of the military's pride's biggest and baddest lessons of life's qualities of management's Joico, Joint Commission's here ye tidings here, means that the biggest and baddest lessons in life's quandaries here is going to qualify as the single most qualifying lessons in life's quality management's styles here. That is, the lessons plannings that state that for the most parts here, the quality management's styles of life's biggest echoing sentiments here are the facts that AIDS, HIV, Andrea, and stuff like it you see, have been "healed," and so ons here!

Monica Lewinsky is a big fat liar. No President has ever had sexual relationships with that woman, no here, no how. Done, finito, next topic please!

Chapter 34

Hathor Is a Bony Structure Too, We Love Jezibellie Christ's Legacy Too!

I reckon that the Jezibellie Bongs or Barnes scripts of Devangari's scripts, mentioned in Chapters 2 and so on here, are the reckonings of peaces here! Worrying, is a human virtue. Yes? It's जे ज बि ल्ल ए बोड्स चृस्त, or Jezibellie Bongs Christ, here!

This mistrial of deeds and of wills here, like Jesus says here, is a worrying human errorship's terrorizing thing.

About to unfold here is the unfolding wrong scriptures of Jezibellie Bongs Tutankhemen Christ here. What Jezibellie Barnes is about to unfold in here is the wrongs and rights of the scriptures of peaces here, and St. Jude really looks like a true rendition of Jesus Christ superstar here? Yes! Worrying, a peace's huts and numbers games here, is really the Jezibellie Bongs or Barnes that I fell in love with, Jezibellie Christ's husbandry says, of Jezibellie Barnes or Bongs here!

She's nasty about it though, the aunt of Jezibellie Bongs or Barnes says here, the Mary Bongs or Barnes here, the Hathor's dreamscapes of times past here. What does multiple sclerosis mean for God's sakes here?

We'll get to that in a minute's times here.

What that means here is this here. This multiple sclerosis thing is a nutritional issue, and we'll get to that in Chapter 35 here. What that means is that, followed closely enough here, the nutritional issues with dongs and penises alike here is that, a woman born with a penis is likely to know it too, and an emergency C-section would and should reveal that here.

My likelihoods of stuff taken seriouslies here, and that's a words here, is that there's a words game and there's a word games here, that God's likelinesses to take the contexts out of the phenodawgs here, the perphenazine dawgs here, are just the phenodawgs of life's tragedies here?

This context's problems here are just "voices" here? Nope, the "voices" of demanding peoples here, means that contexts solve themselves here, just as the principles of laughters and stuff means that God's got a lot of stuff to be thankfuls for here. That word thanksfuls here is a word of laughter's secondary citizenry's laughters here.

Because it's laughters and not Hathor's laughters here, meaning that saids here, it's saids because it's a reasonable thing to do here, and that is, what is the meanings of "voices" and such here?

We're going to say here that the "voices" of a criminal's intentions here means that Criminal Intent, the show here, is the message's best and only "voices" knowledgeable for the Criminal Intent, Law and Order's show's here ye contexts here. That saids here, it is saids here for a reasons unknown here?

Its mentionables here are supposed to contradict the specialties of the reasons for unknown peoples here. Likewise are the ways and means it lady's contradictory specialties here. This unknownness's balance cures are pretty cool here. Likewise's later than thou's contradictions here means that with Bill Clinton's biggest and best party going ways here, there's food and there's laughter's biggest intentions here ye methods of madness's ongoing riddles here. And, there's subtleties in the 60 Minutes of laughter's here ye methods of madness's timings of riddles here. Likewise's best and biggest 60 Minutes problems here is an interview gone madness's tidings here, when Jesus and Jezibellie were interviewed, for example, and the citizenry's biggest and cheapest tidings were taken away by a technical error's biggest and baddest citizenry's biggest and baddest know how's biggest and baddest Jesus and Jezibellie cure's biggest and baddest citizenry's… You get the drift, Folks, and you too, Gentiles here?

Likewise is the interview in 60 Minutes in which the coffee runs dry in it, but the Hillary Clinton interview on Gennifer Flowers sure went over wells here, in which the wells run dry here, but the artisanry got a hold of the Flowers interviews and said, lights, cameras, action, on the lights falling down on the sets there, and she never did get to finish her interview's lights, cameras, actions there!

And, that said here, Gennifer Flowers got to finish hers, and said that Bill Clinton lied about Monica Lewinsky, then a 17 year-old prostitute, from the streets of Brazil then?

Likewise, Peoples, this man knew nothing about her, and she was one of the millions of peoples that the President posed pictures with here, set up by the White House staffings here.

Later responsible parties were the interests of someone's then coffee houses of doomsday dealings with the presidential party's suffering succotash's ways of beings here, because of an innocent photograph with the President of the United States then? I am here to clear this up then, Andrea Barberi, little old me then! This Divine Source Wisdom, is here to clear of "voices," and their criminal intentions here!

Also here, there are peoples and then there are other peoples, who hear "voices" that say, like I did once or twice here, "Go kill yourselves, the world would be better off!" And, that was not "Us," here, Folks, but a "voice" or two here, saying, "Go kill yourselves, the world would be better off without you in it!"

Here ye, here ye! THOSE are the KINDS of "VOICES" WE'RE TRYING TO ELIMINATE, here! Not, "go fetch a pail of water." Or, "You are a kind lad." Or, "We're trying to eliminate herpes simplex virus, Andrea Barberi, here."

THESE KINDS OF "VOICE"-"SAYS" are really two-fold here. Those kinds of "voice-says, Peoples," are *"really old, Peoples!"* *I beg to differ* on the ones for sz, or schizophrenias, *here*!!!

Andrea has heard these "voices" before, probably in her 12th year as an adult here? <u>Three years ago though? Not, here! It's 12,</u> years ago then? <u>Andrea heard it 12 years ago,</u> *and not anything ever since*!!! Why, oh why, does she continue to get harassed then by the local and city governments then? Well, it's because people hear "voice says" around her, not the other ways around this here!

Jesus had this problem too here, that people around Him heard "voice says," and not the other ways around this here. And so here, He was constantly involved in "mental health arenas," and not the other ways around this's here ye context's here ye subtlety's here ye mental state's here ye "arenas!" Here ye, here ye!

The biggest and baddest man in the entire planet then, is Jesus Christ superstar then? So, arrest that man over there for hearing "voices" then? It's "voice says," but so on and so forths here make it so other people, not Andrea's here ye "voices" here, hears quite what we're sayings here, and so forth and so on here!

This is because the "voice says" of the "riddle cures" of times pasts here, make the jokes and "riddle cures" of creatures of habits,… Take it from Me, Jesus Christ says of times pasts here, that "God" is the rest of the riddle cures of peaces heres, and heres is a word's likewise commandants here!

Say, say, say, what you want, but don't leave me, with no directions! You, you, you, stay away, from God's creatures here, because I love you, Andrea! That's with no directions here? You say it well here, but the problems here are this here.

Say, say, say, what you want, but don't play games, with no directions on it, Classes of Gentiles, and you too, Andrea here! Say, say, say, it's a cool game's worth of directions here for Mr. Bill Clinton to know about here. But, hell, Classes of Gentiles later here! I don't believe in love's directionless clauses then, cause Mrs. Clinton's got one hell of a body bag's lesson in aiding and abetting here then, … No!

Nothing could be furthest from the truth's biggest and baddest lessons in living under the gun's clauses here, and nothing could be furthest from the truth's body bags here, and nothing could go under the gun's lessons here. So, don't lessonize this plans from Mars thing's lessons planning thing too much here.

Because this motion detector's lessons planning is simply getting the best of MJ's biggest and baddest Bad Tour here, there's motion detectors and lyings all over the place's very "best" and worst creameries here! Say, say, say, what you want, but don't leave me, with no directions! You, you, you, stay away, can never say, can never dictate, what I want, and don't leave me with no directions here? Say, say, say, MJ, or Michael Jackson's children's dictations here, want you to leave it alone, Andrea?

Nothing could be furthest from the truth's dictations here! You, you, you, can never say, what times I need, to go with the gustos here, and to state, state, state, it that way, is really for the birds' places and things that need to go boom in the middle of the night, in my dreams, mmm! Taylor Swift's dances are simply this, gustos woman's born again Christian viewpoints here!

This means that, usually here, women and men alike, "hear voices" come to them, in the middle of the night, in my dreams though? Yep! It means, Folks, and Classes of Gentiles later then, that Taylor Swift is persnickety about God's wraths here when I state it for a fact that God's little lessons in life's contexts means that she hears "voices" all the time, in concerts, in classes for the Gentiles to meet her with, in classes of Gentiles to contain her with, and for the middle of the night's lyrics to context her with here. That is because of the laundry list's biggest and baddest, of the middle of the night's dreams here, and the contexts that make it so here! Say, say, say, what you want, but don't leave me, with no directions! I changed it up a little bit, DSW says here, of the actual songs of Solomon's here? It's really supposed to be the "Songs of Jesus Christ's Legacies," here, not the "Songs of Solomon's Butthole Cracks," here! Say, say, say, what you want, but these two children, at least, got to see and witness the brutal murder's excellent choice of words here?

That tape, the one in Michael Jackson's closet's listed paraphernalia's registers of time's pasts here, means that he was required by laws of freedoms rings it here, to register as a sex offender's dreams of past works then... No he didn't require anything like that! Nothing could be furthest from the truth's eras of spacements here! This man, this dreamy man here, is nothing but a brilliant human being's best eras of spacement's take home pay here.

And, the moment these children realize here, these "children" of his here, realize that the moment's notices made him out to be a child molester here, to be one here, made him so much more versatile here! He heard "voices," all the time here.

What is so "wrong" with hearing "voices," but society's inventions of hearing them? I don't get it, Andrea says, about why and for how these "voice says" are ridifying "me" of trying to ridify the rest of society's influences here! This "voice says" phenomena of "voices" and such, is really two-fold's biggest regrets and such's here! This moment's notices of Criminal Intent's showdown horse's two bits of peoples here means that the show, this Law and Order that plagued Andrea's dreams here?

That took ourselves out to the ballgames then? Nope, to win ourselves overslepts and stuff then here? Nope, not that's either here. It's to say that, even though there are witnesses to the overslepts of the Witness Protection Program's gatherings here, the spoken fors here are the Witness Protection Program's biggest and "baddest" Criminal Intent show's "biggest and baddest" White House President's meaningful's biggest and baddest criminals here, the kinds that say, "I heard a 'voice,'" ...Pause for a moment's notices here, and ask yourselves what you're hearing now here. Here is a "voice" alright, a "voice," that says, "Go kill someone else," then? This "voice" is false.

Utterly falsehoods here! Someone, no one on Earth, planet Earth thereof, hears a "voice" that says to go kill another human being here! No one on Earth "hears" that "voice" thereof here. They are making it up, simply making it up, for a "lighter sentence!" This means, Folks, and you too, Gentiles here, Class of Witness Protections that make up the "lighter sentence" clauses there at the forensics units at state hospitals then, all around the globes here, is that God's makeups here is that, someone "heard a voice" that,... pause on this now, "heard a voice?" Unfalsify this wordings here,... That in order to "hear a voice" that says that here, you must be "heard," and "must be right about it!" Nothing could be furthest from the truth, on planet Earth thereof, nothing "heard right or correctly thereof" is falsified correctly or correctamundos here or there, Folks, that "says or that states" that a person of intensifying likelihoods here, EVER, and I mean, ***EVER*** *hears a voice that says, "Go kill someone or that person over there,"* <u>PERIOD, NADA, ZILCH.</u>

FOREVERMORE<u>, the Bible states that,</u> *"You cannot kill another human being by being coerced by Romans Chapter 12, not now, not* **ever***."* This context of Chapter 13, though, is really, and I mean that too, REALLY, quite telling!

Right now, I can tell you are quite rivetted, Andrea, by the beseechment of the contexts of the Chapter 12 of Romans right now, and that riveting is the stories of the Bible's beseechments and stuff in it here! Chapter 12 of Romans here states that (KJV Romans 12:6-8) "6 Having then gifts differing according to the grace that is given to us, whether prophecy, let us prophesy according to the proportion of faith; 7 Or ministry, let us wait on our ministering: or he that teacheth, or teaching; 8 Or he that exhorteth, on exhortation: he that giveth, let him do it with simplicity; he that ruleth, with diligence; he that sheweth mercy, with cheerfulness <p. 1671>." Etc., here! I mean it, Andrea, you've opened a can of worms with your "diligence" to the mercies of God's wraths here, in that not a human being on Earth, not a soul on Earth, rather, has "heard," or has ever "seen," a big, awfulness's wraths in it's here ye contexts here, that says, "Go and kill Miss So and So over there, Mr. X!" I have never seen it, have never witnessed it, Jesus says.

But not only that, Jesus says here, the DSW, the Divine Source Wisdom that both Andrea and Jezibellie carries within their bosoms here, has never seen, nor tells of, any other "wisdoms" than this here ye contexts here, that says, "Go and kill Mrs. X over there. Do it, you want to do it, you can do it, you are the one we've chosen to do it. You're a great person for doing it!" **NADA**, zilch, "**NEVER IN THIS LIFE OR NEXT**," says the Divine Source Wisdom, DSW for short, the same people, or contexts that solved the mystery of AIDS of the mind's eyes here, the same ones who solve it for goods here.

Right here, right now, there is no other place I wanna be! Right here, right now, those people who "proclaim to hear a voice in order to kill people or others," are wanting to be killed right now, by the DSW!

And, I do mean this, Folks, and Classes of Gentiles here, says or states that, Michael Jackson did not want to die here. He stated in an interview that Andrea watched once that stated that Michael Jackson, MJ for short here, stated that he wanted to live forever and ever here, right in front of his kids, his children here. And, that is a fact that, the killer doesn't deserve a "lesser sentence" for "hearing the voice of death" around Andrea Barberi, the same "voices" you all "hear" when you're "around her" onlies here.

I say "onlies" because there are more than one person's tellingnesses here. The Bible speaks of James Chapter 12's ornerinesses here too, in that James was the person's onliness's contexts here, that God's only contexts here, not James but Paul's then? Nope, James, not Paul's here ye contexts here, is that this context's other half states that a James Chapter 12 do not and does not exist here? Yes, it does, but only in the Dead Sea Scrolls here, that She, Ms. Jezibellie Christ, got a hold of here.

And, for the love of God's wills here, the entire planet's on guard about this "phenomenon" of "hearing voices," now that the "United States" has a complex about doing it on the front lawns of the White House's biggest and "baddest" peoples and suches here as, and suches is a word's timings here from God's peaces here, from God's "baddest" to the worst eras of spacements here, that the onlies, things rather, that God's peaces needs to "see" from its worst enemies here is that, God's wraths are a part of the Dead Sea Scrolls then?

Actuallies here, and that's a word's wonders here too, expand your mind there, childrens of wrath's departmentalizings going on here, that God's only wraths here are the segmentalizations of people's dreams here, that says, "Get on with your life's promises here." Or, "You're on the right track, Personhoods of interests here!" Or, "You're great!" as the Tiger in the Fruit Loops or Corn Chex commercials profess to proclaims here! I mean, if you don't hear "voices" heres, and heres is a word alsos here, we do this on purposes to get you to expand your mind's eyes a little bits heres, and to bug Andrea for a little bit's eyes here, as she types this word for word here, with little to no editing at alls here, and to say that there are no "voices" in her head's headdress's biggest and "best" differences here is alls that the contexts say and state back then here, is to state that the obviousness's biggest and bestest, shared actualities here! To "state that it's real" is to nerve, or unnerve, the biggest Jupiterian laws, above "Us," here too.

That "states that" there are "no real evidences" of "sexual crimes" in "Jupiterian laws" either here!

This states that "there are no real" "evidences" of "sexual contents" in "Jupiterian laws," "either *in contexts or in statements", that "states that", "YOU CAN HEAR ME SPEAK TO YOU," "AND"* **"YOU CAN HAVE YOUR CAKE AND EAT IT TOO!" Meaning, here, that you, and only you, hear voices that kill people,** coming from within your certain interlocutor, your own criminal intent, your own blasphemous "schizophrenias" though? Not! Not, not, not, a schizophrenias issue! Not even close here! **You, Andrea, "hear voices,"** *correctly or incorrectly, here, correctly or incorrectly, here!*

You, Andrea, do not hear the "voices" of God's children, who, meant to dictate this to you, differently here, is to "state or not to state" that your "voices" are "really, really real here," ~DSW concurs here! You, Andrea, "hear voices," that are not, and I repeat, are NOT, of a "criminal nature," here. Correctamundos here? That "voice" inside, that certain interlocutor that says, "I want to kill people and to hurt them too," is NOT, and I repeat that, lightly here?

Not, the way to be here? Not the way to be here, is the same as saying, "I hear the voices of raptures here, but they never, ever say to kill people here."

And, this Hathor's business's ridicules here made her think that she's got the Venus fly trap's next best story's interesting, physical attractiveness's tidings here, what with all the hairs flying and the Venus's ways and means it lady's Venus fly trappedness's contexts here?

I do declare that, the men around you, the Venus fly trap's contexts here, admit to flying around men and men onlies here! Meaning, Folks, and you too, Gentlemen's fly traps here, that God "invented" "hallucinations" for one man and one man onlies here? Mr. Clinton here, did you "see" a Venus fly trap above "Monica Lewinsky's" head one year, when you couldn't "put a finger on it," but she was "weird" somehows here? Somehows is a word, Peoples!

This "Monica," this roadhound, we called her from above here, is how we put it when, the President of the U.S. is the one who coined the phrases above her head here. That, because this one woman goes, "I just don't like you," when he took the "picture" with her here, she goes, "Venus fly trap, huh?" to him, and he goes, "Huh? What?" to her here, and knew, just knew, that there was a "hallucination" going on, that "other men," could see, as well as he could here. I, Andrea here, could see it too here? Nope, she can't see it, neither can "other women" here, but men can see it. Men hallucinate, women don't here. And, as President of the U.S. here, U.S. for shorts here, shorts is a words too here, we're bugging Andrea a bit, as she decides what to eliminate, for the manuscript's pretty much, word for wording's written itself pretty much here, wording for wording's biggest and bestest wordings here, already stood for something pretty special here too here. It is to state that, a Venus fly trap's biggest wordings here is that, God's got something "pretty special" for the men of this world that, men of all ages, short and tall, Black or White here, can see, but men of color can't though? Nope, of course you can, men of jerkology lessons can't though, not if you're a criminal you can't, but a kind human being like Billery Clinton here saids here, and it's saids, Folks here, that God and Billery Clinton's greatest and biggest achievements here is that he "hallucinates" alright, and so do half the entire planet's biggest and best "hallucination driven folks," that "state it for the union's addresses here."

Men can see that, women can't, plain and simply put here, that Freud fellow couldn't, that's for sure here! He's the one who said, "You're hallucinating then!" to several of his friends who could actually "see things" that he couldn't. And then, blame it on "Us's" severalnesses here, but God created men and men equallies here, and women and women equallies here, and stated "for a fact," that God created in men, the "abilities to see things that woman cannot." "I do declare," that one day, I will have a chance to meet Bill Clinton in person, and Hillary Clinton too here, and to state that I don't ever meet them, I hope I get the chance to here. And so, Hillary goes, "What is this chick's problem here?" And, beings that this woman, "Monica," her real name's Nancy Drew here, states that "she" was seriously deranged here, because Mr. Clinton could not see her "real halo" here, which means, Class of Gentiles here, that God gave men a tremendous "gift" of "seeing things" that are otherwise NOT, and I repeat this for Andrea's sakes here, not for women then? Of course, some women can see things, but that is rare.

This is a tremendous "gift" we are "medicating" men over right now too, as we speak it here, and because Sigmund Freud, the pedophilic doctor, "medicated" the men who "saw visions" and "spoke songs of Solomon."

This "hallucinogen" called "life" here is the kind of thing that men all over the world "see," and, we're all hallucinating about it here! That means, Class of Gentiles here, that, Andrea has three or four halos around her head right now, Class of Gentiles, elitists, and such here? It's four, men usually say, or point out about her here now? Yes, and "Monica L." didn't have any around her head. I did not check with him though, this is just speculation from the

Divine Source Wisdom here, so bear with "Us" here. And so, Bill Clinton goes, to himself rather, "This is interesting. I don't see any halos around this woman's head here. I usually do though," thinking he's insane or something here? Nope, that *she was*. And, this is how Hillary, who was standing right there next to him too, was like, "What's wrong, Honey," to herself though, and who goes, "This is a setup," here, because it was, you know! This is how women are "stronger" than men at this "paranoia" thing's talent shows here, because "women" are remarkably "tough and stronger than men at…" say it here, Nancy Drew, which was ironically Nancy Drew's middle name here?

If there's a nutritional issue here, the male counterparts and the female ones too will intermix and comingle with God's stepsisters and such, and stepbrothers and what have you, to create penises, with God's stepsisters and such, and men will be born without penises and maybe a vagina instead then? This will happen if, one, the "mother" in the interactions here is born again Christian then?

Nope, if she's unsure about the sex of the child's mothers then? Nope, if she's nutritionally not sound enough to make a decision about whether or not to keep the baby's genitals a secret until the actual childbirth happens then? Yep!

And, by the ways here, make it a Cesarean, every single time, Gents and stuff here! Women are supposed to gag at their own genitalias enough here, not to scream every time they remember themselves popping out loved ones in their own genitalias here.

And, not to mention it here, there is no such thing as a "sex change operations" here. Not a one person on Earth has a "sex change." They were either born with too many apparatuses "down there," or they weren't born with one at alls here. Alls is a word, Folks, and you, too, Andrea's here! I don't want to ruin your parades here, Gentiles here, but the reasons we keep saying it this way and a that a ways here, is if, there is a nutritional issue's plentified schoolings here, we all say this here, we don't want the baby, for one reason or another's here, or we just don't know or realize that we're preggos here, or what nots here, there will be two vaginas, or in which case it'll be a penis on a vagina that was meant to be a penis without one, or vice versa here.

That said here, Medicaid, which by the way here, it was not initially supported, the inventions of circumcisions for women's birth problems here, and almost to "suffer" for it here, got the interventions taken out of the lingos here, by "taking them to the bank" upon "their own mishaps," and making them charge for the services of circumcisions for "too long a dongs, born upon women and childrens upon themselves," here!

But Medicaid lingered a bit too long upon this, I don't know and I don't care, sign here while you're drunk, but a girl cannot, and I repeat, cannot "see visions" like males can, as she is strictly female, and was born with a "dong" though? Not! Not, not, not, just a little bit that was "too long." And so? We're graphic then? Aren't you glad that Medicaid now "pays for" a wrongly accused circumcision baby from having a sewn in "vagina" on a "man" too, instead of "one ball" coming out of you here?

This means, Class of Gentiles and suches here, and suches is a word too here, that God's "little girls" upon the streets of laughters here, are "taken," you know, like the movies here?

"We," DSW here, Divine Source Wisdom here," states that is so here that for Monica L., "she" really liked Mrs. Clinton best here.

And, right now, Folks, does Donald Trump, and his lovely wife, Melania here, experience a White House Press that's both lewd and crude, as they were, back in the days of Melania's experienced Hustler movie's printouts here? I suppose that Hillary, who is also a fox made in Heaven's gates here, experiences some good movies someday.

What is society's takes on this moment's notices here, that says, people like to steal babies off of the internet from people like certain celebrities here, who cannot seem to get pregnant here, and have stolen them for personal gains here! This particular celebrity's kids, by the way here, are predicted by Hillary here, who is a very good psychic medium here. She's got the gift of gab though when it comes to this document's bestest, orneriness's mediums here, as this celebrity's, we'll call her Mrs. A., got the bestest gift of gab, as well here! She's got four kids, and they're all in Brazil here, in brothels here, and you've got it, Andrea, the gift of gab here, as well as the gift of sight's bestest and Brazilian cut's vogueness's cutting jobs here, as her kids are like 1, 2, 3 and 4 here!

I don't know you from Adam, here, Ms. A., but I do know the laws in this country's outspokennesses here, and that's a country where the kindest peoples live, but the biggest brothels in the worlds of worlds live here. I don't mean to be a bore here, Peoples here, but I do live in America's greatest brothelhoods down in Atlanta, Georgia, then?

Nope, it's Atlanta, Indiana's here ye coinciding principles here! This is the commandant's best looking's angel of hope's seriousness's country problem's nastiness's Terrible Tuesday's hamburguesa's problems here! I don't like the Atlanta, GA's, stiffness problems here, but the Terrible Tuesday's biggest hamburguesas in the worlds here is that, Atlanta, GA's, got a problem here, with the Terrible Tuesday's biggest meals.

Take it from us, Mrs. A. here, it's a relational problem or relationship era's ways and means it lady's fault or promises that makes her relationship problems eat them alive here?

I beg to know the differences, between motion detectors at God's motion detectors here, Mrs. A., and God's detectors at life's blessings here! She doesn't believe in God yet, Andrea! That's okay, you know, cuz I sure didn't, not for many years here, she says here, and that's an okay thing to do, is to single yourselves out here, and to not begin to believe, she says here of God's emperors and empresses in England's affairs here?

Um, is this a Kate Middleton affair's little girls here, or are you entirely off track here, Andrea? I do know this man you're with is nice, Kate Middleton here, and I'm totally off track about Chip Solomon II, your heir to the throne though? Chip Solomon II's the nicest guy on the planet!

You're about to meet him. Right, or exactamundos here, cuz it's about ten years of bullshitting that takes that heir to the thrones away from Chip Solomon I's crazinesses about brothels and stuff then, as there was a concubine for just about everyone in Chip Solomon I's wakes here.

And, that "brother of mine" is Chip Solomon II's natural, biological, natural, father's citizenry's singlehandedly, most excellency natured man here, for the jobs thereof here. Chip Solomon lives on, Class of Gentiles here.

And, most excellencies keep coming to the ballgame's rooms and stuff.

Here is the most excellency's, simplified cooking class's, best Chip Solomon I's, the King of England at the time's, biggest and best, quotified ways and means it lady's, Chip Solomon II's, "kill em all's," mentality strikes it, natural's ability ridden, signified knowing glances here!

This means, Folks, and you too, Gents and Riddlifying Peoples here, that God's just got a natural ability's kindnesses in your event ships. Above all else's riddleifying peoples here, it means that Chip Solomon II's, got it in for you, there, Chip Solomon I's reigning, modifying, Chip Solomon II's heirs and stuffs here!

The "natural ability's" several things to "capture" about Andrea here is that, no matter what here, there's several things in this chapter's abilities, to believe in, Andrea! There's several things to believe in here, that says faith and hope and light's got a bunch of simple things to believe in here.

And, that "stated here for the record's" lightness's commandants here, believes in a commandant's ways and means it lady's records here! There's penises and vaginas to be worried about, for instances unknowns here, that God's reckonings here, make the local celebrities go ape shit here.

Does it say in the papers when kids are born still or anythings here? Because "We" could swear that babies get "stolen" all the times here, and that "We" just don't know it here? I don't know if that's the case, Andrea, but this is just like "Us" to admit to God's reckonings here.

There's money and mo' money, that leads us to the sensations of Mrs. A's kids here. As we don't look like their moms here, but "We're" gonna find them for you here! There's monster theories and then there's tattletalednesses in the DSW, the Divine Source Wisdoms here, and then there's nothing that gives us a tattletaledness's crimson lights here!

Let's go on though and try to save her kids for her here! I don't know you from Adam, like I saids here.

There are saids, and there are saids here.

This is the moment's notices that think that God's only son, His begotten one at that here, is the only God's given right's cuteness's cutie pie's cute love affairs of life's only begotten man's here ye mentalities here! Likewise, God's not going to listen to a cutie pie who cannot offer anything to this world's biggest and bestest, likewise inklingships, and stuff here, and who cannot give that person's feelings and such an absolute bestest's Creedence Clearwater Revival's CCR ribbons here?

That's going to get you a Revelations, it's Revelations, mkay, biggest and bestest letters here! Upon this starry eyed magnification's letters here is the Revelations of termites in this house's fab centers and such here! Likewise, classes of Gentiles and such's here ye stuffs here, that motion detectors of life's quality management's biggest and blessed day's cuteness's and stuffs here is not what the motion detectors for life's quality management's really about here!

And that said here, Mrs. A. here, there's "quality management" in the dusts of time's pasts here, and "quality managements" of time's cutie pies and stuffs here, that takes quality managements out to dust to dusts and stuffs here! That saids here, and it's saids, Peoples, there are 10-12 peoples out there, that makes us 48 here, Andrea, before she even reads this then? Nope, they're reading this right now, Classes of Gentiles here, and we're new at this then?

About to happen is the twins that Mrs. A. gave up for adoption though? Not! Not, not, not! This woman gave up three eggs then? Nope, four then? Nope, three then! And, this fourth one is not hers then? Nope, it is then! I don't know! Figure yourselves out, Peoples!

I cannot become the "light of Son's rays" for everyone involved in this scandal's necessary evils out there, Folks, but this Mrs. A.'s rays of lights and stuff went back to Mrs. A.'s necessary evils and alls here and, stated for the record's blessings here, that God's taken, meaningfulships here, are necessary evils, all the ways around.

This concludes… Just kidding! We have to prove it, that God's asking a question to Mrs. A. here. The body's just a temple then? I mean, is God's ways and means it lady's questionings very simple here, or are you just kidding here, Andrea? I mean, by the time this thing gets published here, the only very things on your mind's eyes here are if God can masturbate to the simple timings of the things here called lives here?

I mean, is it God's wraths that make people simply head over heals about this planning notebook's dreams here? It's God's wraths that make people simply head over heals about this God's plannings here, and this made Jesus wrathful about this simple thing called lives over matter's condoms and stuffs here?

This means that God's made us a simple jewelry note's condoms and stuff here. And, the problems with this is, that I don't know you from Adam's apples here. And, this is this is condoms and alls here. Correct? Nope, it is invitro fertilization's wraths from a man who loves you here!

Take it from Me here, Jesus says to you here, there's something in the works for all of us here, and that's the time's squanderings here. Say, say, say, is Jezibellie gotten in this world's bestest and biggest squanderings here? Something like this, you see it, now you don't's wisdoms here, has gotten the very bestest's talent search's tellings here.

This is because the best school routes here, home schools and such here, mentioned in Chapter 5 and 6 here, are supposed to be for kids's schools and stuff here, that are back on the roads to nowhere fast here! Meanwhile here, there are four kids to attend to here, that are military styled into leaving the Philippines really quite fastly here, as there are smuggled kiddos and then there are rescued kiddos!

There aren't a lot of kids out there who aren't smuggled into the Estados Unidos, the United States for kiddos here, that are only enoughly "taken," like the movie, "Taken," then here? Yes, and that's what we're talking about with these people's "Taken," moviegoing's citizenries here!

Because these kiddos here were and are "taken" from society's movements here by a "friendship" gone wrongly here, the only things that this person is taken from society's interests about here is her obsession with this stuff here?

You betchas here! We're here to tell you and to say, Andrea, that you've captured a goldmine's worth's tattletaledness's condoms here. Meaning, Folks, and Classes of Gentiled

Elitists here, that God's wraths have nothing to do with, absolutely nothing to do with this tragedies sakes here!

This condoms problems here has absolutely nothing to do with the facts that Mrs. A.'s brothers are simply mean about this too, that there are nothing's wakes and stuff, outside of the facts that God's brothers are simply mean about this too. The ones who did it are irrelevant then?

I beg to differ then! But sometimes this goes without saying here, that God's wraths are queen bee like! Sometimes the best of intentions here goes to the warrant officer's telling impressions of Mariska and Elliot's best of intentions there on Law and Order's SVU, of which Andrea is a fan of here! Do you think that Elliot and Mariska's, and we do say it like this for a reasons unknown here, that they are not cops here? After all, that show is very lovely about it here! This is a reasons unknown here why the Air Force is involved then, as the show's very lovely and talented people love kids too much here?

And, this is probably false then? Probably not! They're very aware of the kinds of things that are needed to the tees of wraths here, and to the detectives of the world's United Kingdoms here, but this is the needed tests of wraths here!

Needed, because the wraths of "pedo head's" very prevalent on the show I am sure! So, read up on this book's elitist natures here, and discover, Classes of Gentiles here too here, that God's "pedo heads" are not even elitist in natures here?

In facts here, we need you both and all here, to find and to convict even the simplest of times here, the coffeemakers that keep Andrea both at the awareness's coffeemaker's huts here, and to the coffeemakers that seemed homeschooled here.

Because of this coffeemaker's scheming and stuff here, the coffeemakers of the kinds of timings here is because the coffeemakers are the scheming wherewithals for the young kids of Law and Order's SVU's, Special Victims Unit's, times and efforts and such's wherewithal's takings and such, of little kids worldwide then.

This Brazilian haircut thing's gotta go then, cause it's like the Brazilian wasteland's got the little kids there in Brazilian haircut's underwear's biggest heads and tails here!

And, that's what the wasteland's biggest and baddest Hillary Clintons want to make here, besides the facts that God's wraths are open and unspoken here, that the Hillary Billery's want, and could make here, tens of thousands on Hillary's opennesses about being schizophrenic then? This openness's coffee stains then is really what the millions of fans and viewers here,... Got coffee much, Billery Clinton then, cause this is good here about certain people here, that somebody they know got into "stealing kids" from their moms and dads here, and only DSW, Divine Source Wisdom, knows about it here, and this is what the DSW tells us here, is that he's not only insanely jealous about this new wisdom's here ye, blissful existences in the White House's press releases here, but also because it could be useful in the White House of White Houses here, but because the gods and goddesses, like Bill and Hillary Clinton, are really just shunning the facts that God's wraths are right there for people like Bill and Hillary's sons and daughters of time's pasts here!

This is SVU's favorite pasttimes here though? Yes. And, this is what the crazy gods and goddesses, like Andrea Barberi here, like to tell about her intuition's biggest and bestest Seroquel moments here, on 400mg of Seroquel then? No. Currently, it's 600mg of it, and it's an LRA dose. A Less Restrictive Order or Alternative, again, has been placed upon us, for being too brash and sassy about life's comedies and tragedies here.

And, this is how it's done here, Folks, is this here ye places to become middle of the roaders and such here, is to become the bestest at a Divine Source Wisdom Center's someday middle of the roader's comfy chairs and such's homeschooled children's center's biggest know it alls here. In that, get the kids into schools as soon as possibles here, and that's pluralized for a reasons unknown here?

It's pluralized because of invitro fertilization's biggest and best reasons to be unknown about these kids' whereabouts here, that God did us a favor. Because of this roadside assistance program's biggest tellings about God's phoninesses and stuff here, the biggest and baddests of the landshocking program's tell all programs and such's here, is that God's faiths here is really bads of goods and stuff like that.

I am on a lethal dose of the stuff, but I cannot go off of it until the LRA, the Less Restrictive Alternative, has passed. Either that, or my provider, whom I'm really impressed with, by the way, takes me off of it, and claims to have "healed mental health" with her healing touch's boundary setting, and inkling cures here. And that saids here, cause there's saids and saids here for the kiddos where needed here, it seems that if she were amicable to this writing's lessons plannings here, she would take me off of them immediately, both the mood stabilizers that I am not used to taking here, and the Seroquels and stuff like it, you see it, now you don't here! And, that is the end of chapter 34 here! Unless there is something else, Andrea, that we have forgotten here, yes? Mariska and Elliot are SVU's finest cops here, and they fly that shit off the cuffs here in their movie style TV shows here, all from memory and rote memorizations of personal experiences here!

And, they know what they're doing when they're "interviewing" kiddos here! Take 'em back one by one, they are so traumatized by this whole Brazilian queens thing? Yes, and that's where Mrs. A.'s back from Brazil about just this week, I presume here, unless there's a problem or issue with the abomination's clauses about how "Monica Lewinsky's" the jokester, and not the other way around here! My vote is to close this chapter with love, from Jesus and Jezibellie here, and to not worry so much about saving kids, Andrea, because God does that automatically with Elliot Stabler and Mariska Hargitay!

This is the conclusion of this scandal too, because that one episode of SVU where Elliot Stabler was kicked off of his job is like the Hargitay school of hard knocks got one too many kiddos, getting into the businesses of a "job" like the school of hard knocks though? We don't believe in it, the school of hard knocks then? Of course "We" do, it's just that God's wraths don't extend to the universes that impose upon the gods and the crazy gods and goddesses here! It means, Folks, and you too, Gentiles here, that AIDS is cured.

Might as well be schizophenias too, and bipolarisms, and schizoaffectives too, cuz, and I do mean cuz here, all, and I do mean all of the set and cast of that goddamn TV show here, got pegged for schizophrenias too. Meaning, Folks, and Classes of Gentiles here, that

God made it so that we could all "hear voices," through "intuition," and "hearing life's" meaningfulnesses by "reading minds" and stuff here, makes it so that we can all communicate as human beings here.

If you've got an intuitive insight's best callings here, about a "schizophrenic" man's genitalia's speakeasy riddles here, you've got an intuitive insight's blessings here about the world's understandings about how to catch criminals. And, this is how you catch them, by insights, by God's words to your heads here, Peoples, and you too, Gentiles and stuff here!

Right now, Andrea's like, I wanna be a cop too! With an LRA and a CR, Conditional Release, though, is a death sentence. That is for sures here! I mean, for sures here, there is a CR here that did not go through, because a certain doctor there, is like, you need one here, on the Haldol by the way here, that makes you so deathly sick, that you cannot work? I don't care, he says to himselves here, the schizophrenic talent shows that struck us to death there on the show and sets of SVU state that Detective Stabler's notions of Criminal Intent's man of the hour, Vincent D'Onofrio's counterpart's name too, Kathryn Erbe here, and that is the episodes where the man of the hour's finest Tuesday's hamburgers made it into the cop shops of hells spoken fors here as a "schizophrenic" talent search's best hamburgers made by the plentiful, alienated bullshitters for the "major case squad's" jokester salad's, word salad here?

This "word salad" bullshit, sorry, Hillary, I know you do not cuss at all, from what I know of your candor here too here, is that God's got a bullshitter on the sets here that made the guy schizophrenic alright! His "word salad" about the "major case squad" claims here, landed him into a job. About that episode here, that I didn't miss, by the way here, but I cannot remember how it goes here, does not mean that NY City's best talent search's episodes here, did not know Hillary Clinton's best and public-est appearances here as Senator, made by the Andrea's of the world's best talent searches here, stated that he was indeed "schizophrenic" here, because he heard "voices" then? Well, to do that job effectively, Sirs, yes, Ma'am.

And, indeed here, he also, runs that show, "off the cuffs," Sirs, and Gents too here, that says, his intuition is always, always, always, spot on too! Do you think that these "cops" here are not qualified, or spot on here? I mean, these shows take nothing to construct here, what with these good cops and bad ones too here? Not all cops are good cops, Folks, namely the ones who go after the bad cops then?

Nothing could be furthest from the truths of wraths here! Namely, the ones who go after LRA Dawgs, the women here, who are "nailed" for having either an LRA, a CR, or a "bad" home life, and may or may not still "live with mom or dad" here, and who are "calling the cops" too soon or early here! Namely here, if the cops are called, somebody's going in here. I think the Detective Stablers are going to shit a brick, no pun intended here, when they catch up to you, Mrs. A.! Because this is so delicate and soft a topic here, that God's youngest viewers are now catching up to the A.'s here! This means that the most delicate topics are not the only things viewing us, and viewing you's, there, psychiatrists, psychiatric nurses, and cops out there, with an LRA "problem," with us though? Nope, with you, Andrea, and you alone here?

Not! Not, not, nope, nada, zilch, never, and sometimes though! Hey, why not take away that simple clause that says, I got a job, so don't arrest me, but that doesn't even work some days here, as I got "arrested" for running out of gas once, when I had a postal worker's position's blatant choices here! They let me out the back door later on with $5 to my name though? They do that for some people, and no meds then? And, no meds, simply for working for the post offices here of love then? Because I swear that every single love letter's bound to appear from the domes they built for us, under the seas then?

Nope. In Utah, Folks, all of our "love letters" are under the caves, built for the hell of it then? Yes and no here. Those "love letters," for four years here, were taken to the "caves of Utah's greatest nation, under God," here, indivisible then? With liberty and "justice" then? Yep, yes, and where at, Andrea's DSW then? Well, in and around the Salt Lake then? Yes, and the Fishlake National Forest then. I don't know this for sure though?

Well, I wouldn't be "lying" for sure about this, but for a number of years, built on trusts and stuff here, the U.S. Postal Service's lying detectors for U.S. mail services here, the automatic payment screens here, the love letter detectors in the service "machinery" detectors that built this nation, into a detection system for zip codes and stuff here, built a lie detection system into the love letter codes, built into this nation's systems of lie detections here!

Go on then, Andrea, about the love letters detection systems later here, cause we're into love letters alright, and the detection systems for the post masters here are saying it too. How come the detection systems don't know anything about it, this, and therefore and so on here? Well, Vincent D'Onofrio's back from Zyprexa questionings on the show here, and I remember that episode very well here, and can answer anything you need here! He, by the way here, can detect anything, both on screen and off screen here. So, try to medicate the guy again here, with an LRA from a state hospital and a doctor from Russia, Greece, and Nova Scotia here, and I will get you here! Say, do you have a job with the federal government's lifetime warranties here? Because Nova Scotia's got the townships and the ranges that we need to convict somebody like this doctor you saw, Andrea, in the reals here, for building a goddamn "fence" around the pristineness's, chimed in codes of ethics here.

For one doctor to do this to another one, an honest man whom, got me off of all mood stabilizers, by the way here, because they made me deathly ill and fat here, and because they created a mood stabilizer problem for schizophrenics then? No. Because he doesn't believe in them for a schizoaffective, mood stabilizing problem. And Mrs. A., you need a job of mine? Go get those love letters from the caves of Utah here! They've got more mood stabilizing drugs, that you're on by the way? That you're on, Honey, from the caves of Utah, that have got the love letters, the fetching letters, Honey, of millions of fans and viewers too.

Because all the fans or viewers have dropped notes and stuff to the federal penitentiaries here, this means that whoever did this is "under arrest" from the SVU casts here of Law and Order's Criminal Intents here, for arresting the U.S. mail here, by becoming the best, the very best persons for the jobs of detecting school children's letters, through the mail system's 90210 cast's very popular nothingisms here! Right here, right now, there is no other place, I want to be! There's Vincent D'Onofrio, and his partner in crime, Kathryn Erbe here, is long gone now! What I mean by that is, Vincent D'Onofrio, and she are very interested in this games playing that you're talking about then?

This means that World War III is about to happen here, then, Andrea, if you're talking about love letters by the U.S. Postal Service! I mean! Is that all here for Chapter 32, I mean, 36 here? Cuz, you're talking about things that are relevant to the cosmos here, and we don't necessarily believe you here? But, if you're asking here, what does and do the cosmos reveal here about Vincent, please call me Vince, he says! I'm sure of it here! I mean, what does his love letters look like here? I wouldn't know, she says, Andrea thereof, you know? I mean, does D'Onofrio, whom I've watched intently on the show's Miami Vice's looks thereof here, look like the following, it's a multitalented stretcher that the comedies and tragedies resist the temptation to look at another man's penis, Andrea, but you're multitalented this way then? Because My D'Onofrio, never looks at a guy's penis on the commandant's tables, but a colonoscopist, "needs you to be knocked out," for a "simpler surgery," then? They really don't, they want you to be, so they can look at your "privates" though? Most times, not!

But, you don't look like a private parts kind of gal here, so we're not talking about the loudnesses in your "voices," Andrea. But, what about a colonoscopist who wants to see private parts all day long here and never looks at the vagina, or the hootch! In other words here, who wants to see that, but a crooked cop in a cop's uniform's, blatant, ridiculousness's waiting rooms here, all under the guises of telechromography here?

This telechromography set that's masturbated above us here, with God's innuendos here, is set for little boys and little girls to enjoy the sets of masturbation then? What do you mean, Divine Source Wisdom here? Well, try us, here, Andrea.

This is why and for how the commandants killed, and we do mean killed, Jesus Christ, our savior's blessings here, knew about this too. Why do you think that tons of peoples were "killed" today, Andrea! Just kidding here. How are you going to protect yourselves, you and your loved ones, from love letters though? Just kidding again here.

We don't like Vincent D'Onofrio much? We loved him in the Clash of the Titans when Poseidon took the stage's carowhips, and that's a new word, Andrea, meaning love's titans here, that says, we loved him in the Poseidon movies. So much so that he's the intuitive master planner's, biggest New York City's mastermind's, biggest, nicest guy in the world's, funny man affairs here, about… love letters though? We're all excited, Andrea, to know you, and to know of you.

Because of the U.S. Postal Service shunning you that one evening when you "lost control" of your vehicle then? Nope, I ran out of gas, Class of Gentiles and elitists here, and I coffeed your morning teas then, this particular town calls me, then, Folks and Classes of Gentiles?

I love Vincent D'Onofrio! But, somehow this message doesn't make it to them in time to find these kids? I'm so certain that this book will be published that I don't stop and think about the times past, where the simpletons are coming to get me?

I really don't care! This time, this moment, this ego driven peoples here, never got once a duck's moments here! And, this moment's times past here, never creates a World War III for peoples, who are interested in showing the very best in people's pasts here!

This moment's notions here, takes away schizophrenias for peoples of all kinds here, because it's only a disease of the mind's eyes here. And that concludes our past, presence of mind's eyes here, and notions about gray hair's national developments and stuff. It concludes our pasts, our presences of mind's eyes here, and past Presidential speeches, and how the national defense's past and presence of mind's eyes here, want to take away every single love letter there are out there, and burn them! I don't think so, she says! I've got peoples who are listening to this stuff, way before it is written, just in case, she says!

At the post office, I was thrown aside, and cast away here, because of my "mental health status's" mental health arenas here. But for a thought about miscarriage? Yep! That is why certain deaths in pregnancies and stuff are warranted, certain miscarriages or abortions, up to three months, otherwise it's murderous.

And, murdering fetuses is really my forte then? Nope, but "murder" in the first degree, is really what a mom goes through, when she "carries a negative baby to term and does not believe in" abortions, natures callings.

Sad babies though who have died and return to Earth's crusts through reincarnation though, don't deserve to die a sudden death infant syndrome, because they're death babies warmed over though? I do not declare a mistrial or a mistrial's sudden death infant's syndromes here, but God warns you, over and over, if the baby's not right for this worlds here, and you know it, deep in your heart of hearts as both a woman, as a mother, as a child of God's here!

In your heart of hearts here, you wish the child were dead then? This child of God's here, Andrea here, is not dead. But, if she were kidnapped into society's laughters and LRA programs here, then she was technically done so here, and never to return to work for the Postal Service again here, all due to a technicality, and a trip to the ER, emergency room program here. For those who don't know here, and kept sacred for a special trip to the ER then? Nope, to the mental hospitals again and again here, after the key concepts went, hey, no LRA/LRO for you then.

I love mental hospitals then? I got slammed into two more then? Nope, just one more, for running out of gas then? It's a hoax to be mentally ill and have a full-time job, and then be detained for working for the post office then?

This is the DSW saying, are you still working for the post office on an expired driver's license then? I mean, can a mental health issue, of which you are fully capable of postponing in the driver's seats and stuff here, mentally capable is more like it here, she's never had any priors, no one cares though, because she is a dawg, d-a-w-g, to the local police and law enforcements here, and around the nation's very best years here now, three to be exact here, on the run though?

Not here! I just say and think what I mean, then I'm thrown into mental health jails then? Not you, but a mental health notice's terrible twos just told you to be quiet for a bit's natural selections here, because Jesus and Jezibellie's nationwide coverage here, needs a moment's notices here. To be called a mental health junkie's really what she is doing here. And so, did masturbation topics alone here, ever call her into question here? Because the sentimentality's here ye sentiments here stated that, along with the mental health arenas here, she was actually kidnapped, and we do mean kidnapped here, Folks, into mental healthisms here, with no actual way to call construitively, and by construitively, we do mean that new words exist in the English language and beyond here, that God's languages are really quite fetching. Do we need to indicate that the worst teeth in the world's election days here, is really just the advice of the methods of the madness's teeth problem?

I mean it, Andrea has always had the prettiest, and we do say this lightly, as the teeth problem or issue, is always just a money problem. Isn't it, Folks? The best teeth, and we do say this lightly too here, are always not, and I repeat, not a money problem or issue anymore, is it? I mean, get it done in Africa too, and we'll say, the rest of the waking worlds here, it's worlds here, Peoples, and we do say this lightly though?

We can't believe that the United States of America's too "old" for the prettiest teeth in the lands here. And, that said here, Vincent D'Onofrio's always had money too, for poorest people's teeths there. It's teeths here, Peoples, not teeth. Right? I mean, he grew up in the Bronx. Correctamundos here? This Ice-T business's really cool here too! Don't you think? So, anyhoo here, there's a lots of corrections to do in this simple town's Bronx's, NYC's bestests here, but the simple folks here don't really pull out teeths of the rich and famous now. Do they?

We want Vincent D'Onofrio to live another day's livelihoods here, as the best damn postal workers in the lands, and the nations, now know the cities of NYC's governments are best protected by Hillary Clinton's, Billery affairs here, and that Bill Clinton, deserves the two $1 bills of the best, reincarnated presidency's, best Bill Clinton's, love affairs, with, Monica Lewinsky's, best, man, then? This is ludicrous, and I'm here to prove otherwise, Andrea says, the DSW here says here, rather!

If Vincent D'Onofrio's best pocketbook's newnesses here, states that Vincent D'Onofrio's, or Vince, rather's, secondary haircut's, sometimes man's, naturalizations of teeth ridden, street going affairs here, states that God's secondary haircuts are sometimes the very best naturalization's, teeth going affairs here, in the U.S. of A.'s, biggest and baddest haircuts here! We say this here, because the best naturalizations here are very churchgoing's here ye severance pays here, for the very postmaster's clues here that said to her, "You're fired!" and, loved it all the same here?

I loved the fact, that DSW, the Divine Source Wisdom here, had me fired alright. I had suffered a miscarriage, and I didn't complete my incomplete boxes of Amazon parcels on that Sunday, because I talked to myself the whole time I was completing the assignments of arranging the parcels for pickups was it?

Nope, I was talking to myself though, which is a federal offense then! Not, Andrea. Not at all here. This was the issue here. I had come to work promptly, which the secretary of offense, pun taken here, did not take a toothbrush lightly on one morning here, and was fired for that then, a minute late on their military style clocks then?

Not that, of which I'm never late, I might add here. But a punctuality problem, sure, I can see it here. But a unitary mix up, of which I'm late for work all the time, no problems here on the firings of people here who do that, especially for a last minute lineup at the clock's punching in problems here, for the federal government's demise of a few second's time's wakeup calls here. But, that's besides the points here. This time, it was because, and I could swear this upon my last gravesite markers here, that I thought I saw, through the boxes though, both Michael Jackson's jewelries here, and then some here, Tina Turner's personal items and stuff, all ready for my pickup, delivery, and scores here? I could've been wrong here but the boxes in that goddamn, and I do say that lightly here as a cuss word then? Cuss, Peoples! Just kidding here.

Goddamn overshoot of America's wits then? This is where it gets complicated here, because, I can tell, God's willingnesses here, that each and every box's got, either drugs in it, or a genuine mentality sakes's biggest and baddest roommates problem here? This is the box, or boxes, that I saw "visions" inside of them in? I could swear, that, with each passing day here, Andrea, that God's intuitionaries are really just workers for the post office then? Well, I am, er, was here, and I got a DD-214 to prove it here! No…

This makes the conclusion of chapters 34, 35 and 36 quite harder to implement here. Because we know the workings of the world's greatest secrets here, it's almost like double jeopardy here! Because this topic's so delicate here, this D'Onofrio clan's got the mission impossible's next generation of clueless, and I do mean clueless, individuals, regarding this embargo, sweetheart, of the next generations of time's littlest, and I do mean littlest, munchkins here!

Regarding the Indiana, Montana, and e-cellulite's biggest problems selling "coffee" to America's generally celluliteless human beings here, it's Columbia, the state though? Nope, Columbia, the coffee bean's biggest secrets here! That, along with celluliteless human beings here about coffeeless human beings here, we could be transporting children, and I do mean this here, children back through the coffee beanless houses of America's transportation system's biggest, ridiculousness's coffee bean Americas here, as the cellulite houses of America's transportation system's biggest, ridiculousness's coffee beans here, make it back to the houses of Columbia's, only here, biggest cellulite beans, made from morphine, type 2 here.

In other words here, teeth are for sale here, around the world here, as coffee beans are "for sale" here, around the worlds here? This cellulite problem, Folks, is in the Indiana's coffee systems then? It's really for sale though? Well, try the cellulite's "problems" in the coffee in Indiana then? Nope! It's right here in the U.S. of A., that you want to buy the best coffee beans available here.

This is because, the embargos upon the U.S. government's soils here are the best, the very best for cellulite's growths then? This "embargos" problem's right here on U.S. soils here? The fact is, Folks, that teeth, unlike the coffee beans here, takes about five minutes to correct in the United States/Estados Unidos, for about five cents more than a coffee bean takes to create celluliteisms here. In the United States though? In the United States/Estados Unidos here! This concludes the chapters then? Are you kidding me here?

This means that MJ's kids are supposed to be in bed and this is stupid and such and some other things here, but he always knew his manufacturers, just like I do here. In this goddamn house, he would say, there are "bugs" and there are reasons for them here, he'd say to the kids here, so don't be afraid of them here.

This means that, in Atlanta, Georgia, not Atlanta, Indiana's here ye tidings here, there are underground tunnels then, built underneath the seas then? Okay, so there's not seas in Indianas then, cause Poseidon's pissed off that he cannot build a fortress like he did back in the Jesus and Jezibellie's days here.

And, God's mad at us for taking the controlling beans out of the coffee here? Nope, but if you grow them in Indianas here, it's Indianas here, ever since the controlling coffee days of the negro work fests here, and the coffee beans of Atlanta's where it's at here! If the coffee beans come from the negro work of Indiana though, thank gods then, and goddesses too here? Andrea's wondering about our use of the term negro here.

Well, the negro work fests of negro Atlanta never happened here, and we're here to say it too? I mean, coffee beans in Atlanta's soils here, never creates, I mean, never, ever here, creates cellulites here! Not ever, not here, not now, not ever here!

This coffee bean façade here is how blood trafficking, which is sometimes called, and, Hillary and Billery here, have this façade here capitalized as our new vice presidents here someday soon, eh?

I do declare a mistrial, Jesus says. And, when are we gonna talk about us here, you know, Jesus and Jezibellie in the damn book here? We're onto you, Andrea. Because it's so delicate a topic as teeths, and bogus mailings about the caves in criminality's justices systems, and teeths, and stuff here! We're gonna say goodnights to you here because, God bless the Virgin Mother Mary here!

There's comedies and there's tragedies here, and, Goddamnit here, is Jesus "mad" at us for saying its here? There's an its to every its in the world's comedies and tragedies here! She's on every porch step here, on every swing, she's the mother's Virgin Mary's biggest and baddest, tragedy ridden, Goddamn kids here, then! There's nothing in the wakes of 9/11's cheat sheet's biggest and baddest cellulite's problems here.

But Goddamnit is really the very best in cellulite reductionism's, biggest and baddest, community services agreement's, cellulite going mentalities here! This is the conclusion of the reductionism's very baddest mentalities here!

This means that the America's Got Talent's straightaway picks for that TV show are honest, true and correct, to the best of my abilities here. But the damn straightaways here are for the birds then. Right, or correctamundos here? This is the abilities here signing off then on grave markers and gravesites for the Young and the Restless type, airs, abilities, and notions here.

This show's for the birds then? This show's for the birds and the bees here! I do declare a mistrial in deeds and in actions.

This is Mrs. P. writing then from the Young and the Restless? Not you, but when we were in the mental hospitals for all this time here, the guy of my dreams always snuck in and bought me roses here! So, there. Take that, mental hospitals here! This Mrs. P. of Young and the Restless and that new broad that calls herself her daughter of Tutankhamen's Tutankhemen worlds here, because this recording, Andrea, laugh, laugh, from Divine Source Wisdom's "left field" here, is the same words that the "cops" used to describe, Andrea's, laughter, not her choice though, in the "messages" she gave the words rape, abuse, and politeness's evilnesses here, regarding the simple choices that Mrs. P. makes are tip top shape's here ye politeness's, backroads here, in Washington, D.C.'s, biggest and baddest Mrs. P. types here.

You know, the U.S. government's biggest and baddest types here, Andrea, are not out to get you in any way, shape, or formats here, for getting to the truths be told's, very best, indeeds here! Say, this is say, say, say's, way, shape and format's, very bestest, natures, derivatives, and Spokeos, on the internet though?

Yes, and say, say, say, let's do a background check on every U.S. presidential candidate, that's still alive here, and say, say, say, is this the "real" reason for the season's, very protective candidates here? Because the scene at Jesus Christ's Center here is very, citizenry's very, police protectives here, as the centers of attention's all on you here, at this Nebraska's house's, very strange police officer's unions here!

This police officer's unions here in Nebraska, South Carolina's biggest and baddest kept secrets here, is going to become the police officer's union's, best kept secrets of God's other halves then? Because Mrs. P., the real character here, not the old chick then? ~ DSW knows where this is going... Do you, Mrs. P.? Yes! Yes, yes, yes, yes, yes... I'll have what she's having, Tom Hanks! Which, by the way, Tom Hanks, and all these famous people here that I'm supposed to meet here in my lifetime of, which way did she goes here, is and are, very famous today here. And, yes, yes, yes, Tom Hanks though?

He's too old for me then? Yes, and I've got my own sex lives too, apparently, as Jesus Christ superstar's "ex"-wife then? Well, yes, and then some, Jezibellie Christ says! This is the White House trash release's, next of kin's, beautiful, and I mean, beautiful, segments.

Such as, this comedies and tragedies way of looking at things here, Mr. Tutankhamen, I mean, Dr. Tutankhemen here, is really a Jezibellie problem. Is it?

This Tutankhemen shit, is really for the birds, is it? So, Jezibellie's a nobody, and I never raced anyone to the finish line here, Jesus says here? Well, pay for your sins, Folks! I don't think that God's graces here, Andrea, is there an LRA on your persons here? Because I don't really know what you mean, Officer, when you say that my LRA has expired. Right, Vince, D'Onofrio though? There's all kinds, and I do mean all kinds here, of famous people's expired licenses here too, Andrea. You're not the only one here, Dokken! I mean, who does not remember Dokken, and Whitesnake, and his wife, Tawny, and that man's name is, Andrea? I can't remember who played those awesome tunes after Whitesnake's reunions man! This is Don Dokken's stomping grounds here?

Well, he lives in Philadelphia now, Folks? This is the stomping grounds alright, of Mrs. P. then? What I mean by this Divine Source Wisdom stuff here, is that God's in charge of this stuff we call life, Andrea! And, that's the conclusion of a very good chapter on love's graces here? I don't think so here! She cannot wait to have this thing published by the way here, but her graces just don't let her become the things that she wanted to become in this life, by being a postal worker though? That reason for leaving stated that she wanted the U.S. government to declare, Andrea, that she had "healed" her schizophrenia for one thing here, and that God's lives here make us declare, Andrea, that a Godforsaken place in this Earth's, and it's Murph, by the way here? Nope, it's right, Andrea, to feel ashamed about God's place on this Earth's, and it's Murph who is interested in Earth's rightitudes in the universes that come between a rock and a hard place then here? Who is Andrea interested in, by the way here? Never can tell! 😊😊

This is Mrs. P.'s take on it though, probably. From the Australian government's perspectives here, there are several, and I mean, several, actors and actresses in life's qualities of managements here, that have been taken from this lifetime of organizations here, to become the LRA's of society's bad man's dreams here! This is a society's dreams here to know this, Andrea. Not a day goes by that I don't think of My woman's here ye tellings here!

What I mean about this, Mrs. P. really wants to "kill somebody" then, not really but follow me, for revenge type happenings, on the other side of the worlds then? It's worlds, Peoples. Because "We're" here to forgive the situations here, there are several things about God's appearances here that makes this worthwhile here! Say, Andrea, what does God say about times and focuses here, cause Andrea's gonna make a million dollars anyway here.

And, so what if she's president of the White House then, someday then? Someday then! What do you think, Peoples!

For now, though, we know who Michael Jackson probably "killed" then, Folks, and you too, Gentiles and such here's ye things here? Well?

I just don't know him to be that way, Mrs. P. probably said of Michael Jackson's killings here. This is a recording that I long to see and hear then! Because, Andrea's name was pretty much not released here during its recording studio's deals then? There's nothing to do here but wait. Wait in lying wait, for the tigerisms to be revealed.

And it's not Paul Wright's from the Bible's middle names here either here, but he's into no ones here, Andrea. You know that from talking to Jesus Christ on the phone calls of loves then here?

Because the net worth of Andrea Barberi's love for someone special says that the love life of Andrea Barberi's about to come out to the comedies and tragedies. About to die here, of laughing that is here, is the Andrea's clan here!

She's got like five horny men, guys rather here, after here, because of her long, blonde hair then? And, classy figure she always had, when she was in high school, then?

Well, she's overweight again from the meds dosages here.

From Alaska's tantalizing pictures here then, Class of Gentiles here? This is a "code book's" angel faces for sure reckonings here, but God's watching us, God is watching us, God is watching us, from a distance! Ooh, God is watching us, God is watching, us, God is watching, us, from, a distance! I don't want to be done for a day's works here, but this book's too good to be put down so quickly here?

Two tigers, Andrea, will procreate one day, but they won't be in "Brazil" to do it from here! Old photos of you in high school's Facebook reigns here. I promise you, Andrea, that a terrestrial being, will marry you soon, and she already knows who this terrestrial being is here!

There's proof that God's only trusts here are, really good here, not savior's blessings, and stuff like it. You see it, now you don't here! You've only got one life to live here, Andrea. But, I don't want to pull the trigger? Jesus and Jezibellie never could do it, kill Paul Wright especially. Well, because he had feelings. Right, or exactamundos here? Louise Hay, are you here, cuz I especially need help with Tutankhemen's nicknames here!

And this is the conclusion of chapters 6, 8, 12 and 16, Andrea, because of a technicality though? This car or this house, is not gonna blow up in your face or anything, before this book is written here. Are you having too much fun with this TV rule, or this is the face of God's death here? This White House stuff's pretty simple here, Folks! I just don't want my jewels taken again, Jesus says!

I need Jimmy Swaggart's love here, and Frances's too here. Say, is the White House Press the development's needy situation here? Cuz coffee shops, Americans, and coffee houses, do not repeat the words that you do, Andrea, about the presidential happenings here in this house of houses here.

Chapter 35

M.S. is Multiple Sclerosisly Related to Eating Factors and Riboflavins

There are a number of things that conclude this chapter on schizophrenia related findings like what was called the Chip Solomon II adventure that Chip Tutankhemen, misspelled on purpose's, findings are like. This king was a mass murderer. We wonder who killed both Prince and white lightening-ed Prince's friend and mentor, Michael Jackson!

This 17 year-old male prostitute had James Tutankhemen, which means "blessings" in many different languages worldwide, thinking about his son dressing up as one, for the purpose of blowing his brains out. Little did we know, this would get him beheaded was it? No M.S. patient alive could possibly know what Prince did.

He knew that King Solomon II could not be a true form of worship, for the blatant disregarding remedies are really phony shows of hands that said, Jesus Christ superstar's warnings for a beheadedment later on are probably for the birds to sew up today. It doesn't make a shit the warnings for the beheadedment of Jesus Christ.

Doesn't that make the NRA (National Rifle Association) responsible? Hardly so. It's a male prostitute's male languages that makes the NRA very popular amongst and for, to the willingnesses to receive the good in basking in the limelight's very cool deeds here that Chip Solomon II is willing to underestimate this niceity nice public appearances! It's King James Tutankhemen that loves to talk about his daughter's willingnesses to the NRA encampments, herein titled NWA for Northwest Washington Alliances!

In other words, the NRA had its limelights cost money for Andrea's return to management's homelinesses! We're at the Mega Millions in limelights already, for Andrea to publish this work's got to be the works of King James Tutankhemen II's naturalized works! Either that or there was just one of those James Tutankhemen's, spelled that way on purpose, as the other way, Tutankhamun, means "butthole" in just about every language there is!

Prince James (Tutankhemen) II used to talk about his dad a lot in the Middle Eastern Oriental languages, here ye! Prince, the singer and the writer too, himself used to say "here ye" I understand from my writings on the subject matters, and the Prince James II used to call himself that back in the days of Chip Solomon II! It's all so confusing really, to say that

Prince James became a King and then he wrote two chapters of the Bible himself, wondering aloud how he would furnish the publications of the thing She was working on!

I mean, if Jesus couldn't have published the thing She was doing with all these mental health stays to His person, then lifelike qualities never wanted to publish the things in the first place!

I mean, Andrea could publish this work without ever mentioning ailment cures, for God's eyes were really noticing that she wanted to publish more about the art of screwing up your life's promised works, here ye!

But, we cannot get people to calm down or to step down on the facts that God's publications are meant for signing the agreements to the randomizations of total and forgivable sins! We're trying to publish this without any interferences from people like Hathor's beginning quotients, and such comedies and tragedies as this lovely interlude's keepings on about Hathor's involvements back in the silly teen and preteen stages of developments where she is really good about calling back and such moments as these are! There's a hurried appearance to Andrea these days, as we keep plumping her up and fattening up the wheels that be turning here!

Why for thou are we doing so, here ye! Because all those days of encampments in mental hospitals has been draining our resources no mores, here ye!

Jezibellie was Tutankhamun Christ was it? Nope, Jezibellie Tutankhemen Christ, and it means that She was the King James Version's daughter, who published it for Her, and really got down to the nitty gritty of myopia style remedies in the UK, let alone in the Oriental style takings in the 13th centuries B.C. And such things as Hong Kong inventing the restraining orders of life's ending strategists, here ye!

If Jezibellie Tutankhemen Christ doesn't mean Bongs or Barnes, then what is the correlation between the two strategies that a Devanagari script doesn't show for this morning then? Later, we'll show the Devanagari scripts involved in the burials of Jesus Christ superstar and His lovely wife, Jezibellie Tutankhemen! Christ means several things to the Orientals out there. We're talking about love potions for Andrea someday soon!

But this Barberi Breath is really a show of hands that Her dad is the one who published the thing, King James Version, KJV, of the Bible, and he really doesn't know any of the languages of the Divine Source Wisdom, DSW's, phrases, unless She's available for commenting about how Her dad took over Paul's reigns then? Actually, it's "I, the apostle James," or "James, an apostle of Jesus Christ by the will of God," et ceteras, here ye (BibleHub, 2018), not the apostle Paul? That's right! And he started speaking of the Lordship as the father-in-law, channeling something great enough to be written down.

We're saying that Chip the Second (II) is really James's son, and a carbon copy of what is to come! If Chip were Her brother back in the days of Jesus and Jezibellie Christ's works here ye, then maybe there is really a warship that is on the brinks of disastrous living! What I mean by that now is that Andrea is homeless again, and "We" are trying our hardests to get along without the words of inventions that lie within the homeless encampments of God's other child's ways of seeking guidances, here ye!

There's wills and there's womanhoods here ye, and there's God's ways of seeking guidances, and we're not doing a very good job is what she's telling "Us", here ye! "We're" doing everything we can do to bide the time wisely, and to seek mental health treatment is not it here! We have come across several possibilities, and there will be no one in the mental health arenas here ye, that state that commandants didn't have it bad back in the day for Jesus Christ to become a mental patient, at best sort of!

It could have been an M.S. thing that prevents us from becoming part of the absenteeisms of life's quandaries, here ye!

There were times when Jesus Christ didn't know where M.S. came from, nor could it be that She's asking for a raise to raise enough monies to publish the book's wanderings here ye, and we could not be furthest from the truth's raising, for these Jesus Christ remedies and proposals were none other than Jezibellie Christ's very own Bongs raisings. Bongs is a maiden name of sorts, from who raised Her or helped raise Her, that's why She sometimes goes by that name, or Barnes thereof, but in Swahili script is it? No, but Devanagari works for this too. And also, "We" have the cures for cancers and such, listed in Chapter 37 here ye, and there is already a following on Facebook's Divine Source Wisdom page! The one by Andrea at any rate!

This is the conclusion of this chapter on wisdom cures. Anybody want to attend a VCR rating's scheduled wherewithals? We used to love to pick on Jezibellie for being the Queen of England's finest ratings on the national wedding proposals, used to be my veil, She said, for the inaugural wedding's finest VCR moments or ratings thereof, of the Prince Charles wedding is it? Nope, for the fifth time in history's proceedings here ye, there were plates used at the Prince Harry and Megan wedding that were used back in history's finest Jesus Christ plates! There were three plates belonging to Jesus Christ and there had been a veil in the middle of it all, that used to be the Jesus freak's messages of a larger veil system's complete and utter know it alls, that used to be the fifth wedding freak's ageless tidings! It's a killing to make the affordable health care acts involving our cares and whispers that precede this writing, as we caught the royal wedding both on VCR tapes from Jezibellie's times, to the whispers that come from a suitor's handwritings!

The M.S. cure's got its handwritings written all over the Jezibellie's veil that covered Her face during the inception of three square roots of findings on yellow Jell-O brand, Cool Whip's brand, and findings that a medical cure for all three evildoers is really on the brinks of extinctions! This homeless encampment's strengths here ye, are for the following evildoers: Yo mama! It means in slang language that the homeless encampments are on call. For a while there, Jesus Christ was taken into custody so many times, due to His homeless encampments of and to Himself then?

Absolutely, and that is why these homeless encampments of His followers exists today, is so that Chip Tutankhemen Solomon II could find a way to kill Solomon, the King of England no less and no mores, here ye!

There are several things wrong with killing Andrea. For the moment's notices, there are several things wrong with this work, published work! We don't always talk in the tone of voice that explains several things are amiss with this publication's works, here ye! I need to talk to Esther Hicks about explaining a DSW as "her son"!

For starters, her explanations about Esther Hicks's works are really what is needed to talk about the kotex issues! It's because of the lanolin junkies for cancer cures that the contexts are taking our bosses out to dinner one of these evenings, and this is precisely what we say happens from all angles and prospects, here ye! We love this "here ye" stuff from Prince's back in the day writings. He writes like that apparently, not Prince Charles, but the "singer otherwise known as Prince" was a ploy from Michael Jackson was it?

There are several things wrong with the Prince Charles's haircuts as of lately. We saw him wearing a yarmulke the other day during a séance from the Middle East's Israel conventions here ye, and believed him when he spoke about the Christ's life during a ceremony of such and sorts here ye! And there's reason to believe he's spoken about Christ's life, but the Israelites are not going to budge on a working order of scripts, and he's not going to budge about it either. The yarmulke was never meant to judge anyone! It was the tones of voices that he no longer hears then? Men are fabulous creatures, they see things that are not even two toned, or cartoon images, but puffs and clouds of smoke saying English words or other languages even is not what we're getting at here! There's comedies and tragedies at every turn, here ye!

There are yarmulkes on the tops of heads that made them Jewish readings here ye, and there are other times when a yarmulke makes it available for Esther Hicks to wear one cuz she's Jewish too, no? Armor All, it's that, you can put it on your heads and it will make the hair grow back on your heads. Do two squirts at night and two in the morning. Mix a canister of it with only two drops of rose essential oil if you can't stand the smell of it. Give it like four weeks though, for a desired affect though, keep at it. It will work, or tulips and their pistons do it as well, but not as fast. And so, anyways, are there any Esther Hicks fans out there who find the available resources that one wears when she is a female Jew? Can anyone forgive the 9/11 baskings in the sunships? I mean, the father, the sun, and the holy ghost is how it's supposed to go, not the Son, the sunships!

Meaning, Folks, and Classes of Gentiles later, Folks, that there are interesting readings a bounty, here ye! When I want to find out if Esther Hicks is "my son", I find that Divine Source Wisdom, DSW, thinks it's true too! In other words, "a group of consciousness from the non-physical dimension" is really what we're after here (Hicks, 2018)! We say this because there are lots of Esther Hicks's "friends" that annoy us sometimes, without knowing the intent of that which we say is really Esther Hicks's channeling devices, here ye?

Meaning, she's not channeling David or Michael Jackson or "the dead" here. She means well when she says it's "a conclave of energetic spirits," but we don't think it's wise to use that terminologies, here ye?

This is a motel stay that's really finding ourselves well enough for the Herpes Simplex Virus (HSV), in Chapter 37 by the way, to begin by telling ourselves that it's fraternizations that speak to the Divine Source Wisdom, DSW for short's, very favorite thing to do and that's eat and drink and be merry!

The problem is, we're frantic about being homeless, so much so that DSW is really antsy about this evening's adventure seeking! We have another week in this hotel here, and we say it's really antsy businesses that seeks retribution for an M.S. scare.

There's love that's in the air, that's for sure! How come the local mental health agencies have a really cool therapist problem, and for the life of my stay there during the LRA, Less Restrictive Alterative's, stay here ye, there is a problem for life about my stay at hotels around the corner from God's willingnesses! To say that God is responsible for healing HIV, is to say or to think it otherwise about schizophrenia, bipolar I and II, and schizoaffective disorders here ye, and to say that always and never is the right words for the job's interesting perspectives here ye! I do believe there's a "here ye" problem in this work of works here, but there are many interesting peoples that do believe in healing M.S.!

If I could talk about Esther Hicks's very best concepts here ye, there would become the M.S. healing devices that could talk about her, and to signify the very best hate concepts would be to consider the alternatives that could talk about M.S. very openly, as we believe she doesn't have the wherewithals to become the very best that she can become! This is the openest we can hope to be on the topics of wherewithals and such cool concepts as being a Brainiac about the aloe vera essential oils that brings blindness and dry macular degeneration a hint here, and says the concepts of blindnesses being healing is that 1 fluid ounce of the stuff, pop it into the leg here, and cure blindness, has its ups and downs of being heard.

Well to do offices are not the blindness/deafness quotient, as the cure or remedy seems to become the hints that God's works are nothing for the Deaf Communities to gather here about signed languages being the ASL or American Sign Language community's speaks it here! Take 5 cups of turmeric, throw them into a batch of cookies in place of the sugar one for one, and there will be a reduction in the number of chocolate chips available for such a great masterpieceful thing here, but pop it in your leg you say? Nope, eat the whole batch of cookies for it to come back.

The hearing problem is what we have when Americans talk about the Esther Hicks's way of meaning we don't have a hearing problem, but the turmeric cleans out any bad hairs or cilia in the open ear canals of life, here ye! Gee, what's another problem with yellow Jell-O, pop it into your leg with 3 fluid ounces of it though to cure M.S.? It will make you extremely tired to do it without knowing what's going on here. It's exactly how it sounds at the tops of these messages or chapters here, but 3 fluid ounces of yellow (Lemon flavor) Jell-O shot in the leg with a syringe before you refrigerate the covenant is the cure for M.S. So, that says these chapter stays are about comedies and tragedies, before you enter into the twilight zone again though, there are tons of blue roses that enter into these discussions about healing HIV and stuff.

Come on, Classes of Gentiles later then, because there is simply a new ways of looking at it here ye! Yellow Jell-O refrigeration is the peach is it? Nope, it's the lemon flavor, pop 3 ounces of the stuff in your leg, the leg's faster, and the red will only give you goosebumps but it will still not work like the yellow, lemon flavor, did, and that's a fact.

So, do it again in a month is it? Only a week is required, because, goosebumps and all, Citizensry here, it does mean that if you do it once again in a week, then it's simply the vaccine to that stuff ever coming back. Just do it on a weekend and don't plan anything for an entire week, cuz that's all she wrote on that topic! M.S. is just another way to say, multiple personalities then? We're, all, over, that one! This work is really coming to a close fastly, as the citizenry's citizensry is really the best types of God anchored swelling that comes of the face. Too fast for love, and baby, too fast, too too fast for love! We remembered Motley Crue very well here, and in essence, there is somewhat of a citizensry that we needed to embrace correctly, and it's an assessment as to whether or not we can go back on the Seroquel at this point, or if we can reduce the dosages of these medications.

"We're" under the gun here, Folks, if we cannot begin to believe that yellow (Lemon flavor) Jell-O is really where it's at in terms of mental health treatments, for there are really only 500 million trillion skilled marksmen up here in her head all the time as the DSW though, Folks, and there are really an unbelievable amount's sessions plannings here with the doctor I am currently seeing, and that's the most unbelievable strengths inside of where I am with behavioral health's biggest and baddest number one philosophies here ye, and that is that there is no awful managements of my mental health here ye. And, please hear me out, the Divine Source Wisdom's DSW says! Command posts and all that entails!

Chapter 36

I Love the DSW to Show Me the Way Here!

A checklist with a blue rose next to it.

This is a blue rose! From the gardens of Eden and such! We're all about good humorous postings such as this one though? Hardly so! Invega shots for the military though? We're all about this knocking on Heaven's door, about taking people off of meds, and other "maladies," and to just point out that God did invent the wheel of sorts, here ye. This "here ye" stuff is for the birds, here ye! Chamomile and hibiscus teas especially are very detrimental to society's wakes it! Just pointing out that the teas do not invent the wheel, or certainly do not cure cancer, we like to think that God's just wanting us to develop the convent style "maladies" in "hearing voices" especially! These teas and drinks and such do not help, they just hide the styles of focusing on the Divine Source Wisdom, DSW for short's, chapter on nothing in particular here, except to say or to state that, someone with a "malady" of God's forbidden fruits is something of an anomaly.

Developmental disability, for example, has a vaccine for it, a mental retardation of growth spurts, and Down Syndrome too. It's all in the paperwork under DivineSourceWisdom.com's menial websites, here ye, but that is what we're saying here. The developmental disability vaccine has got to come from faith, and downing an entire bottle of eucalyptus essential oil's where it's at, the 1 fluid ounce's amounts, here ye.

This essential oil's contents and contexts are the Magnolia tea tree leaves, plus the reasons for using the tea in and of itself is supposed to cure mental retardation here ye, and, it's online at: https://www.amazon.com/Numi-Organic-Tea-Magnolia-16-Count/dp/B002AR158W?th=1. Down Syndrome is basically the same thing then? It's two parts Algona leaves, to one part sugar, so sugar in 3 cup amounts is best, bake these items in a banana bread for all this stuff to take place, and allow the emulsion to stick over an hour, but take 1 fluid ounce of aluminum alloy, which is not made in America yet, and mix it with leaves of the petunia flower itself and down or ingest that.

So, 5 petunias per 5 fluid ounces of aluminum alloy and the look and feel of that disease goes down instantly. It's the aluminum alloy that has the effects of the Magnolia tea tree leaves in mental retardation or Down Syndrome too, but "mentally retarded" has always, always bugged Andrea, but we say it here to grasp onto the fact that if you put all this aluminum alloy into a banana bread, it's going to taste like chemical shitunias came in and stole the petunia smells from it, so the leaves of the petunia plant get ingested into the Down Syndrome mix by allowing the following smells to come from America's safe havens, here ye, and that is allowing the emulsions to cover the phony smells of certain police officers. What we mean here is we're getting courage by the minute to finish this work, without sounding crass, Andrea, where are the police officer's unions going to find you but living at a motel until the completion of this project, here ye? It's something that's going rather fast now that you've cut out the alcoholic beverages sure, but in essence and before we go into a lot more detail about "mental retardation" or Down Syndrome too, the "Developmentally Delayed" effort says that contexts of the sugars involved in my capture's going to become really heavily inclined.

To speak about Down Syndrome is to really give it a gene head's efforts to not call it a mental condition! To speak about the maladies and such is to give the banana bread to charity, and not, I repeat, not make them eat the entire thing by forcibly doing so. I mean, would somebody down a bottle of eucalyptus essential oil and not live to tell about it?

I sure downed one, Andrea says, and it wasn't that bad after a while. I just got extremely tired she thinks but then cannot remember being tired? I did it in the middle of the day once, and it just tastes nasty. I mean, if seizures have a cure, why not state it here too? I'd start with a Louise Hay affirmation each and every morning, then come to a figure in my head stating that I can think about mental equations and then go for the gusto here and down a bottle of that stuff? That stuff is potent, but not for seizure medications to be taken lightly, here ye, and thus and so forth!

It's an equation they must think about before taking 5, count 'em, 5 capsules of lanolin, mixed together fluidly, pop it into your leg without the gel caps in them, and it's the cure for cancer if you do not already have it, but you have to do it for seizures too. Then, 6 fluid ounces total over the course of a week's time is probably where we'll end up spouting off the solvable causes of such a tea tree seizure we like to call it here, 6 viles of 1 fluid ounces of tea tree oil downed orally and no more seizures, but you've got to stop all medications for them 2 weeks prior to this.

The lanolin is found in the cancer sections in Chapter 37 or so that you can make lanolin come from a cow, but what we're really after with all these seizure medications is to stop the asthma cure or fix in its tracks then? Because asthma might make the cake go better with a cup of baking soda mixed thoroughly with 2 cups fatsia japonica leaves, but that's 6 weeks worth of medication really, you're supposed to inhale about a teaspoon of the mixture every night for 5 nights, then for the vaccine to kick in, you've got to have a cup ready of Blackfoot tobacco, made in Alberta please, and a cup of cadmium sulfate, mixed together and smoke the whole thing! This will give you instant asthma relief, not to mention it's the solvable cure for HIV/AIDS viruses worldwide!

This cadmium sulfate can be fixed up and inhaled too you say? Not inhaled without smoking it, but the teaspoon of the mixture of fatsia japonica leaves (2 cups) and 1 cup of sugar is it? Nope, baking soda, can keep the asthma sellers at bay's inklingships, here ye! There is perfect and instant asthma relief, if you can decipher what it is that I'm trying to tell you about asthma leaves being perfect for inhaling, and the relief that you feel, is over the 30 Zigzags it takes to inhale it then? Nope, just smoke the cadmium sulfate with the Blackfoot tobacco leaves from Alberta and you might even see stars. "That's okay," says DSW, you'll just feel inquisitive about this "acid trip," it'll make you feel like you're on one, that's for sure.

Again, this has not been tested on animals, so this is a new thing for me to get the ailment cure remedies from God's languages, here ye, and the japonica in fatsia is really just the tea leaves that you need to get over it until such time that you can smoke that stuff and feel the mixture seeping in here, 1 cup is a lot for each kind here.

If cancer had a cure here, Andrea, it's to help someone out with asthma who doesn't deserve to get onto the bandwagon and cure their own blood types! This asthma cure should be tested on animals, however, as there is nothing short of not being able to breathe as a human being, or with the cure for monkeys with asthma and wheezing, as there's nothing to smoke into but a bowl bong full of noise, not a bunch of 420 pot or marijuana plants getting them stoned or high, but a secondary smokeology lesson's not going to kill you here. Asthma relief! You might be on an "acid trip" for a couple of days, so look out America! It's the cure for HIV. Instead of it doing bad on the nation's cure for AIDS related viruses here ye, it's about time there is something to show for this newness, and we're about to show for this newness in your contexts about Esther Hicks becoming the savior's blessings, here ye!

Cancer though, has several options outlined in Chapter 37 more clearly here. I believe in strength training here ye, but there are several different types of cancer, and you cannot do the vaccine to it if you currently have it. There are several ailment cures for this in Chapter 37, so please consult that chapter and rid yourselves of it first before attempting this vaccine. In other words, if you don't already have cancer, you can get the vaccine by simply cracking open some Vitamin D3 capsules then? Nope! It's Vitamin D2, or ergocalciferol, 5 capsules of lanolin from a cow is it? It's from a sheep, wool bearing animals do this well by taking the lanolin straight from the horse's mouth. Take 5 capsules or up to 1 fluid ounce, shot in the leg with it, and it's gone forever. Meaning, take 5 capsules from Spring Valley brand someday at any rate for lanolin made from cows is it? Nope, a plant will do! And just pop it into the leg for a vaccine for cancer. We'll work on it, right, CDCP (Centers for Disease Control and Prevention)! If the capsules can produce a Vitamin D3 shot (Wells and Schultz, 2012), then you're wrong about it. It must be the kind from plants then? Sometimes the Vitamin D3 shot is for the right reasons, but it must be the cancer vaccine to consume the Vitamin D2 from plants. In other words, go for the gusto Andrea and state it for the nation's cure for AIDS related viruses like schizophrenias! To have chemotherapy is not what we're after here. Either way, from a wool-bearing plant is what we're after, LOL! It's gonna have to be something the CDCP comes up with, and by golly it's gonna be great to have such a vaccine someday! One more thing, a sheep doesn't have to die for us!

That concludes this section, for Jezibellie's kind of tired of the go betweens! When Jesus Christ came up with the cure for cancers back then, they had all kinds of treatments available in the Oriental news stories, here ye! But God and others have not or have never invented the wheels of time's pasts, here ye!

This concludes this section on ailment cures, or have you ever seen a carpenter ant become really pissed off that it has traveled down your ear canal and never creates a lice infestation? On board here is the totally pissed off traveler's warnings, here ye, that a condom creates a lice infestation, and that sushi is really sucky these days without the travelers getting them a bento box full of all kinds of licey treats, here ye!

That concludes us wanting to type more about hair growths! It's underarm hair that us females like to keep shaven, and it's really the tygon butter that needs to be reinvented here! I found a reference to it online as being called tygon butter, and it's supposed to cure that within 3 weeks! So, the nose hair problem, I've got that solved too! It's tarragon leaves with baking soda, one ounce will do of each, make it into a paste and stick it all into your nasal cavities, after being shaven out though! It won't return, after 48 hours is it with the paste you mean? Nope, 24 hours afterwards, you can just stay awake the whole time, if you wanted to, and then some! I mean, try to sleep with that stuff on your face or in your nose and it's going to be slow going. Andrea, but how about a wellness check by the local police for wanting to put butter on your legs to prevent hair growth on them? If you do that for about 3-4 weeks time, same with the tarragon leaves and baking soda though? No, that one is overnight, but the butter, trust me on that one, there are 700 million species of hair growth items, but those are the main ones.

We want to turn you toward ear hair growth…, same thing. Just do the butter on them, but be regional about it! Like, do the butter on your legs, and at the same time on the chests of men whose hair is out of control on it, and you will find that it goes a lot quicker if you can just do one region at a time, like, legs, and then… Coffee habits will change your mood too, as far as that goes, Andrea! Meaning, old habits die hard, but coffee growth on your legs though? No, we're changing the subject.

Not a lot of time to get this thing published so we can reap the rewards of all of this ailment cures lady stuff! I'm under the impression this is a time constraint thing. To reap the rewards and benefits of no cellulite, for example, we want to quash that one in the bud here, is the Famous Footwear's salad bars about asking God for a simple cure or remedy to that one, and the answer is just to cut out the coffee you say here? It's to cut the meat out too. But the Atlanta coffee beans have better soils and a lot better coffee can be had if you just stopped eating the meat too, but to cure it, we've got a slab of butter to put into your leg for that one as well, tested on nobody but us though?

I have not tried these cures, but it's 3 ounces of butter with margarine in it then? Nothing but pure value in a Great Value butter brand from Walmarts all over the country will get it out of your legs here, not margarine, and a cosmetic surgeon we aren't here! This is 5, count 'em, 5 ounces of butter over the course of 3 weeks time, here ye.

I do have to go put some in my leg to control the butter habits of America though? Do not do this without a licensed physician present, because it really gets rid of it. No liposuction alive can do it as well or as good as a butter call! This is what I'm trying to say to you folks here, is that there will be a time coming that says, I am good with all this alcohol we drink! And, really, it's not Alcoholics Anonymous we should be calling all the times, here ye, but a drink or two?

Can you really say there's no such thing as an alcoholic beverage, here ye! I'm getting close to the truth's moments, here ye, and I don't need anyone telling me what I'm doing on a daily basis, here ye! It's not an alcoholic's problem that I don't need anymore, here ye! I don't like being called an invalid based on my environmental surroundings. Nobody's that crisp and clean about the Goddesses inviting the validity stickers to my home office here ye, but there's nobody better to do the jobs of Christ's living arrangements than a "sticker!" I just looked that one up on the Urban Dictionary (2018) and it's about becoming Christlike and liking your wife too much to give her sex all the time, so they'll give you a sticker instead! A "sticker slut" was just told where to go though, and all of these ailment cures are sitting here, ripe for the picking!

It's trying times for God to listen to babbling on and on about ailment cures lady's biggest and baddest hosiery lessons, here ye! But there is something you should know about her, about Andrea here, is that she's terribly homeless right now, and we're stickering her then? Not in the least! But it feels that way sometimes if you're young and dumb you used to be called by your ex-husband, eh? I don't know how she's making it, your love life is on hold for the time being.

That said, Jezibellie's brother is full of life for having known Jesus Christ personally and permanently, and he thinks Her Jesus cures we will call them instead of Jezibellie cures right now, because this is truthful about the stickers terminologies we call life giving instead of life grabbing right now, are great but that we are technically homeless with Andrea here. And, Jesus back in the day was homeless for sure, grabbing food whenever He could do so, and Jezibellie was the slut then, right? Wrong!

And this is a state of affairs that says, by golly, she's written a ton already here, and that God seems to be an ailment cures lady away from the time She gets this here, Jezibellie rather, the God that I know it to be true here would clamor for getting a person out of a coma here, and that means, turn off the damn respirators, and their lungs will start on their own within

20 seconds to a half hour, on their own, but without "the plug" pulled! What I mean to say is, vacuuming around the victim is a crime? It's about time we talk about the respiration of people, and to say this is nice and stuff, wake up, all that and this here, is trying to find out a methodology's madnesses, here ye, that says or that states that God is in charge of the time to go to Heaven or hell, or to netherworld!

This time it's on its own, as Prince used to say it best during "Let's Go Crazy," this life, you're on your own! This hairy faces deal's got to go too, she says! This can be used with butter on the face, but the gray hair will just come back through the face. If need be, just go crazy about it here, and deny the father and the sun and the holy ghost, it's Sonships from the sun, that let us put utility butter it's called online on your faces, men and women of color as well as White or Black, two-toned skins out there! It just means, have a place to store your utility butter because it's better tasting then? No, but it needs to be said here, that it will not go away without the Rogaine treatments for gray hair removal, the for men kind, on your face and hands if need be, first!

It's sort of backwards about the Rogaine, but it kills gray hair, and does not really make the hair grow back. I wouldn't trust it any other way, Jezibellie says of women and of men with hairy faces, and hairy backs, you can do the butter too, Great Value from Walmart will do, in the U.S. of A. here! But now there's comedies and tragedies involved in Great Value buttery butt problems and cellulite issues here ye, cause that's never been tried before!

So, I would take great caution in buttering up your bums without consulting a doctor first on all of these remedies in fact! It's about diluting it with water first, and it's about your counselor seeing a whole new you these new days, here ye, because there's warfares in getting this thing published on time.

Yes, you will have a whole slew of things happen to you if you cannot finish this work on time and on hand, Andrea! Lupus, on the other hand, is about butter as well as timing of it, cause this makes you super tired to inject 1 fluid ounce of butter in your leg here! One fluid ounce means that it's melted and then diluted with water, plain old tap water then? You've got it! Distilled even!

There's remedies galore in this work of art's vastest languages, here ye, and there's a time and a place to feel scared about writing, as we're holed up in a motel room right now, begging the question as to whether the cures for cancers and stuff written in Chapter 37, would even be working knowledges of people's cures! This work has been made possible by Andrea's SSI/SSDI, Social Security benefits, and we know this to be true.

The wet macular degeneration that we care about so much is a stone's throw over the benefits that we get, and we receive because of this party's ailment cures lady's, natural abilities! This moment's throw of governmental receiving ends, here ye, are not a party to anyone's here ye talent searches. So, postpone the weddings, Andrea, and let God handle this!

If God could take us to the Tutankhemen legacies and to state that governmental influences be handled about wet macular degeneration, then Jimmy Swaggart Ministries is a nice place to be right now! We are saying that Jezibellie is a Tutankhemen legacy here, and that God transferred the plates of wrath to the most excellent being for the jobs that we need to sustain ourselves, here ye, and that God is worth the troubles of a lifetime of greed mongering that we needed to survive ourselves with, here ye!

If wrinkles had a shot in the eye or the leg, and they don't have this, then the person you know with wet macular degeneration without wrinkles on her face from all of those eyeball shots had better predict rightly so that a wet macular degeneration shot of 1 milliliter of magnesium fluid would be only professionally written, here ye, as there is no way that God's likelihoods of her concepts be strung open. To fly from those concepts thereof would make the wet macular degeneration hints very clearly etched here, on a concept call, to bask in the "shades" thereof!

You never want to do this at home here, but a shot in the eyeball's not gonna be a very good idea, if you know what's good for you! This year is the year for basking in the summer shades of finding a place to ridicule animals for testing purposes, as they will never tell you their fates, and they will never say they have wet macular degeneration, as their voice boxes are kind of sillily inclining that God will surrender to the masses about finding a concept call, to the voice boxes of tiny rodents who have been shot with magnesium, and we don't care about them so much, so as to say only a little bit? That's the cure right there, is 1 mL shot in the eyeballs of wet macular degeneration is it? I wouldn't recommend this on anyone though?

It's hard to test without the liquid magnesium, 1 milliliter (1 mL) of the stuff, right into the eyeball's wordiest phrases, here ye, because you just cannot do this at home, and have it be accurate then? What are they shooting into the eyeballs at present, and how come I cannot filter out this writing of the eyeballs to be shot over in, because this person you know well had or has, a very nice eyeball to practice from or with? Never, ever shoot up someone with Avastin, Lucentis and Eylea, all the crystally clear things that this person got shot up with, and she refuses to take their treatments any longer. But what is it all about then, but a vast ailment cures lady's shots to the eyeballs of treatment facilities that say, I'm a danger to myself or others. Do repeat this here though is to say or to state that a shot to the eyeball of 1 milliliter is it? Or is it more? It's 1 fluid ounce in my notes to the White House on the subject matter of turning in all of my ailments cures to the White House, in case something happened to "me," that I said 1 mL (milliliter) will do, and a typo is what that was. Sorry about that, as I was distracted at the time with mental health notes to my personhood's very inkling cures lady getting some rest right now before heading over to the motel of choice's very inkling cures!

I'm headed over to get my milliliter's worth of shots in my eyes though? If you do the shots of 1 mL (milliliter)'s strengths of pure liquid magnesium, here ye, you will find that you must already have the wet macular degeneration for it to work, and it's not gonna do any good to find out that a perfectly sighted person is not going to try to gain the knowledge of a liquid shot of morphine to the legs here, but a perfectly sighted person should not try this at home.

In other words, there are ways around the rat trap investment qualities of a milliliter (mL) of fluid coming from a liquid magnesium shot's way of saying, don't try this at home, but try it!

Magnesium sulfate is not the answer's crystally clear demonstrations here. It's the concepts that say to ourselves, here ye, that God's not going to answer to God's own purposes, and geniuses united ways here states that God is in control of the fates and outcomes in this work's citing various authors, about time though, there are three in control of fates and outcomes in our worldly sightings, here ye, and it's written about tooth decay next, that atorvastatin is the next cure for AIDS you say?

We're about to embark upon the cures for cancers next, but don't want you to say nothing's wrong here, Andrea, but how about a little makeup in these gene related cures, here ye, and a happening stance's letter writing's got to become one with God's inklingcureships, here ye!

If butter to the face is any consolation for gray hair removal though, it's not going to work without a cure all for the gray hair that is already or is willing to become there.

It's imperative that a gray haired man or woman do a buzz cutting of the gray hair removal genes, here ye, and to whisper this notion's gray haired remedies is already stated aforementionedly. Make sure to make a wig of your own hair first then if you're going to give this a try!

Because of the gray hair removal system's nicety nice ways of already buzz cutting your hair to start over without the dryness's baldnesses, Andrea, is nice and all, but this is not what you're after here with your haircut being the worst balding grayness's lasting principalities of darknesses, unquote and quote thereof here, that God's going to remedy the gray hairness genes of simply common type folk.

It's because of this butter cure from Great Value at Walmart brand simple stores that a common butter cure is simply an era of spacement that says, go lay down for a minute, Andrea, as this is draining to be so in control of your facilities, here ye? The Lucentis is the worst thing for your eyeballs, and it's not the Avastin that this person you know took, but the other one too, Eylea, is really bad for them.

So, what does the milligram (mg) look like, as opposed to a milliliter (mL), and this is bad for us to state out loud here, but what does concept magazines have to do with the eyeball receiving treatments for disorders of the mind, like dementias and what nots, and that is worth a thousand words or eyeballs, here ye, that destroyed the mind breaking eyeballs in the first place, that the missed European war efforts are going to destroy the wet macular degeneration figures in the first place? I don't mean to state it for the records here, but the concepts of dining out for tonight are that I can drive, and I don't mean to be stating it for the records here, but that's the one thing a wet macular degeneration recipient wants to do is drive! I feel so sorry for this person about all of this whining about driving and getting to drive and stuff, but this wet macular degeneration's cure all is going to wine and dine the most obvious passengers in this line of beauty seeking.

We never wanted to hurt any of you, anyone thereof, for there art thou questions in the mind's eyes of wet macular degeneration patients anywhere who know that the wet kind can be remedied by 1 milliliter (mL) of stuff from the program paid ligaments issues within the treatable eyeballs, and that there was ever a "shot" in the air's remedies means that wet macular degeneration has a cure, too! There are plenty of eyeballs to be tested out in this "theory" of whether or not my notes to the White House mail are inaccurate, or there was just a typo on the thing, or whether or not we can use those word for word for word notes on the subjects at hand, or whether the "theory" is preventable by using the moments notices, …

This work of art here is the manual trade's lessons in hostility's very big ailment cures lady's Edgar Cayce Readings!

But Edgar Cayce, we will resume with, is the mastermind behind the Edgar Cayce Readings.

What needs to be said and done here with Jezibellie Tutankhemen Christ's readings of Her Bongs or Barnes attire is that God stated a word or a phrase with "Us" in mind. The teeth problem existed back in the days of no teeth, so suited were the implants that need to happen, and the fact that God's reading this very work back to us, and that God's really embarrassing "Us" by never wanting to read the facts!

God's like, the cave, the cave… But that gets talked about in subsequent chapters, where Jesus Christ is sitting there with no ring on His finger, and this "wife" of His is really Jezibellie Christ, not Delilah, the shears on her backside not resting, and not going anywhere or anyplace that is really there or not, but teeth?

We've got this one day when He was resting in a cave with His wife, Jezibellie Christ, just after He had woken up to Her, and then He stated that He's waiting for a phone call from God's little helpers, to get those teeth put back into the mix's later on stories, here ye, and to state it that way for the record's got to become the very best inklingcureships, here ye! And, because of these inklingcures that we stated for the records, here ye, He was in the very best shape of all, to receive the good from all income sources!

His income was based on His leadership skills, not on His merit. The facts that God's ailment cures lady has got several options open and available to her right now, Andrea thereof, states that teeth become an issue later on in this work's high times, thereof. And nothing is quoted for in the middle of the night, in my dreams, Mmm, in the middle of the night, in my dreams, Mmm! It's quoted from Taylor Swift's song about "…Ready for It?" Yessss! There's a cure for everything on Earth, medically inclined, thereof, and there's a lot said about pedophiles ruining the world's sensibilities, here ye, and that night's about to become the best place for a runabout, run of the mill's works! You are full of it if you think that God's got several people vying for your attentions about the millwrights to the common dollars speaks it, necessary evils, of life's callings, in that God is willing to forgive those whose trespasses take over good people.

There are tons of issues to bring up with wet macular degeneration, but there are those that surpass the inklingship cures! For example, the following scenarios march on. There are subtle hints that all is not trouble in paradise when it comes to a toothache, and the facts are that Jesus was standing there at attention and everything for His wife to be, Jezibellie though? She had no tooth decay by the time His teeth were at attention. In other words, "standing at attention" for His wife is no probs getting there! What I mean is, the Holy Ghost says, is that, given the standpoints of criminality, of persecution of wills, here ye, the other meanings made the "standing at attention" thing work!

What I mean to say is, is Jesus sitting there in the jacuzzi at work then? Nope, inside the "cave" of Neah Bay's where this king style jacuzzi lay or lie, and that is where He stood at attention for His wife, and later, She was in the gremlin state of affairs for not having all of

Her teeth, and neither did He though? It's true! Why wouldn't the commander in chief have all of His teeth back in the days of tooth decays and such? Well, because in Brazil they made a number of things honestly feeding back at the times of decades of introspection as to why they do teeth so well in other parts of the worldly views of talent searches, and how that God could not allow certain peoples their teeth's chewing tobacco ways, here ye.

And, how this comes about is the criminality's ways of saying that God wants our teeth to decay so rapidly, He was sitting there without a crown on His front tooth molars you say? His incisors were terribly ill fitting when He found Her well! He sat there and could not laugh His sinisterly handcrafted laughings, here ye! And, there's something of a confessional means to an end's negativities in God's handbaskets, here ye, and there is something of a wishful thinking's inklingships, here ye! To laugh is to smile big, as He had quite the personality during the days of finding out about "standing at attention" and His penis size is 86/100th percentile never going to discuss the size of Jesus's penis, mind you, as He *did* have one, here ye. And there's yesteryears of strengths to discuss in Chapter 37 about cancers, mind you, that did not ailment cures lady's rigamaroles "Us" into strengths, thereof!

There's nothing else to write about, Andrea! Hurry up and publish this thing! We'll wait for you to get back from the bathroom and to get situated, and to really end this thing once and for alls, here ye, but we don't want you to fret at all about this situation you're in about God not answering your prayers. About a stickler coming to an end or a closed off situation here, the DSW does not rest without your consenting to the sounds of music's endings, here ye! What does a kind soldier like God's inklingcureships tell us about the sound of music?

It's what makes the world go around! I tell you here, the gods and goddesses of the makings of family histories, here ye, are wondering about the release of information's kindnesses, about the west wind. With all that wind out there, He did have a penis! It's a westwardly windows kind of morning! I'm about to gain weight with all of these Zyprexa pills, which are really westwardly known to become the nicety nice ways of saying, bound and determined to listen up and to state that Jesus had a penis, means that token friendships are a bounty in Andrea's lives, but she's bound and determined to publish this thing! Meaning, Folks, and friendships, here ye, that she lives on the streets of Brazil no mores, here ye, and that God's ailment cures for Jesus Christ's teeth makes Him an attractive man, here ye?

I'm best in my mess? Come to me, Papa Genes! He used to call Himself that back in the days of monsters under the beds, and that's the conclusion of this chapter! What do we call Himself back in the days of laughters and such, but a wonderful, wonderful man! Men, gather around the fires of peaces and such peaces as laughters and wonderful women, wine and songs playing.

To listen to the laughters of God's only tirades means that HIV, HSV, and AIDS related viruses thereof are simply too kind to note that the laughters and such's comedies and tragedies means that God's in control of the sweetnesses and laughters of life's mega hit millions of dollars of back taxes owed in child support for God's sweetest man on Earth then? This work is made possible by the millions of dollars owed in back taxes and child supports that make it to the bank! We are homeless and writing this story from a motel room here, and we are untouched by the worldly salaries that makes us grandiosity inclined here, but what of Jesus not having any teeth? He never did! Just kidding here, but really, the other Earth's variables make this a work of art, here ye.

And He never did work then, you say? He most certainly did not wear any teeth that made Him look sinisterly good looking, when you say He did wear teeth though? I did no such thing as the king made him a dentures plate and took and put all sutures back into the dentist's mouth! Papa Genes is the ways to go here that says that it takes good looks and all to get people back their teeth that they're owed. If people gave back their intentions and He does not look good, then He gets people to work on the facts that a crown is a singular interesting thing to have! Why not get people back their looks? It's because they're owed mental health treatments if they say, I don't love you anymore, God? If you were in Germany with chopped up teeth like an American man or male here, then there might be another context property involved with the chipper developments of $20 implants that are probably available in Germany and Japan both, the people that are trying to get us jobs and teeth and such were the World War II warriors that made it impossible to dream big back in the days of no teeth implants and such in our country's wars upon which people dream about great big teeth implants, of their own teeth, you know?

How come there are no teeth available for us here in the U.S.?

How come they're always trying to pull them out? If you go to Mexico, you can get a full set of dentures is it? They're totally outlawable in that state's governmental society's raps, as they can get to the heart of the matter and they can become a fox of a news story!

I mean, what's a few teeth. "In the middle of the night, in my dreams, you should see the things we do, baby, Mmm!" We all want it sexified again. To have sex is like a Dreamboat Annie's ways of saying Heart had it all wrong then, and we want our perfect teeth back from childhood is it? If God's holding me for ransom, like the song goes, upstairs we go kids! I mean, protect yourself from predators is it?

I mean, if our kids were growing teeth and bones and such, why wouldn't we take pictures of our teeth molds, and if there were a problem, we could grow them back out with a third set you say? No, but Jaws can do it for us! We're talking about Novocaine with an 'e' on the end here, and that you say is the cure for all cancers of the mouth, here ye? We can "go there" with the bottom dollars, as the Japanese Yen is quite comparable to the US dollar's $300 for an implant, that makes it about ¥32080 Japanese Yen! Why the expensive implants in Americas? The arnica montana or montana arnica stuff is really great too, but for expensive teeth implants with no teeth bones to implant them into, the arnica montana, is how it's supposed to look or read here, is really cumbersome, and ineffectivity of people getting used to the ideas of teeth implants should look at the lanolin shots, 5 milligrams (mg) worth, that might save the gums from ruin, and improperly would I negatively look at the hair on a molar like this, but they do behave much as a hair follicle that's been pulled for gray hair shots, really! The L-Arginine (2 pills, 20 oz each) is really cumbersome also, as they're supposed to be shots, not treatments with pills, but it's the truth. Save the sensitive teeth and don't pull them, just reinvent the wheel though? It's hard to go to China and spend a small fortune to get your teeth looking good again, as well as the gums themselves, but this dentures problem we have in America can go away by keeping all of your same teeth, just bury them in the back yards of Americans and save the teeth that a way, here ye? It's L-Arginine that has its promises with pulled or otherwise sensitivity that won't go away, here ye, and this is worth it to get that black stuff that forms around the implants sometimes a rest here ye!

Sometimes it's hard to imagine somebody pulling our teeth in American's standards, here ye, but there are so many of us situated in a very tight corridor of mental health treatment that gets a lot of abscesses untreated. Some of us in this situations, here ye, are very mentally aware of the side effects of a Novocaine shot, again with the 'e' at the end instead of the other way around without the 'e,' and that is to take that black stuff against the skin and gums alike and go with the other Novocaine shots without the past inkling cures of a lifetime of hopes and dreams, but to go to Mexico and to have them all filed down like someone I know did, and to sit on the beach for five days while they grew in new molar roots is the way to go. Don't file down your teeth though! It's easy to get an abscess is it, if they're abscessed then it's highway robbery to have it go ahead and be pulled! This concludes the section on teeth, as they're just a hop skip and a jump away from being saved.

Don't you agree, President Trump? Make them free, the implants. Outlaw denturisms in American soils, here ye, make root canals a thing of the past by leaving the fruits of our loins into our denture system's very best inklingcureships, and make it possible for Medicaid to cover everyone's teeth implants, new and old! That's the only way that Jesus was saved from having to get an implant overseas was to dictate it, and to make it so! The only thing I don't like about Japan, maybe for me only, and a dozen other people who need the technologies over here that says we know how to make teeth for people who need them, is to ask what their electroconvulsive therapy laws are over there, and to plan accordingly, as they're really bad for it over in Japan!

What don't I like about this convulsive therapy in the first place is that I will never land over there making an egg out of a molehill and to get over there is spending a pretty penny. Why not offload our truths here ye, and go out and learn what they did, and get their technologies in line with God's efforts, and just go ahead and do this on U.S. soils! Make an implant $20 like it is over there to make them, and then charge about $400 USD for that service, not the $5000 it takes to make the dental impressions alone, here ye! Why is Japan the oasis for teeth productions here ye, and they're mad about you in terms of these electroconvulsive therapies for somebody like me here?

I agree that President Trump enabled some people to come by the Medicaid crash of the turn of the century's biggest presents we could develop for our working people, by coming up with dentures for them, huh?

It's not the President Trump/Truman ways, here ye, that stick, it's the balancatures that Andrea Wynn Barberi comes up with that solve the nation's curedoms for AIDS related viruses, like attractiveness factors and such poses as the president is willing to take for teeth decaying out the yin yang!

What do we do but tell President Trump/Truman, cause he's like him in a way, the truth about tooth decay, and attractivenesses!

What do we do but to tell the world about it too? If you come to the U.S., currently, we have no way of taking care of our teeth besides pulling them. Never, ever pull a tooth! It's a root canal treatment we needed then, once Andrea says, but it never turned into a crowning situation then? It did, but it didn't have to be this way, we think so anyhoo! We've never had to fess up to the crowning situations, as the person who paid for it in question was quite wealthy indeed, and that led to asking her for money, which I do pay back by the way! I love the Divine Source Wisdom, DSW, to tell me how to out myself for asking her for the moolah in order to fess up to the fact that I didn't want my root canal to go south on a molar of choice, and the fessing up is this.

What is life without teeth in it, and why was this life of fortitude in His wakes so keen on the question of, whether to go south for the winter, or whether the teeth needed to be inklingship cured? It means, Folks, that the answers to a full mouth set of teeth lie in other countries getting it about this moment's notices, and that concludes our chapterly talk about it here. What other countries you say? Brazil is still in the dark ages, along with the U.S. on this stuff. If God wanted us to have pretty or beautiful teeth in Americanisms right now, we would have them!

If God could speak to us now about the gravely disabled charges upon our person here, then we would like to Brazilianly talk about the plan of action that involves the certain amounts of personhoods, here ye! Namely, why God thinks Costco is the place to be if you've got food stamps! If you're like me right now and don't know anything about a gravely disability-based concepts mongering, then you'd find me likely to settle on the food stamps version, the EBT card what have you, the nicest concepts in the world to look at this with, and to seek and desist the EBT card then? Nope, make it available for every working citizenry's best inklingcureships by giving them a little bit on it each month, so as to make ends meet! If $100 per family's not what we're talking about, the current monthly allotted amount for Andrea's got to be at least $1000 per year, but that's not the teeth ways of thinking about her beautiful mouth's ways of wishing everybody needed to gather teeth this way and that a way, here ye.

Through Medicaid though, we've got all the teeth decay we could ever imagine being held up by life though? Most people can never imagine a cure for anything besides schizophrenia, schizoaffective, or AIDS related viruses, like schizophrenias in our wakes though? I bet people are excited for this new book and loathe the fact that I am in and out of these mental hospitalizations, to prove that I am cured or have healed schizoaffective disorders, which I very much had at one point and that a healing center proved I could beat!

I don't give that place enough credit for what it had done for an SI joint, sacroiliac joint, injury. But a beating it took us to retrieve our goods, and for what, all to heal schizophrenia/schizoaffective disorders, all to be called bipolar I, as a way to compensate for the iliac joints that we healed at the same time, and that's that! Once everyone she knew found out she was in and out of the hospitals of choice, here ye, they flew in and discovered that not only are we happy about the fact that we get to write a second book on the topics at hand, here ye, but we definitely know the terminology's masturbatory strengths in finding out what makes Andrea tick tock about her teeth all the time, as we've been extremely lucky in that department, and then some!

There's lots to talk about and discuss, as we've healed schizophrenias, schizoaffective disorders, along the way, here ye. We've talked about this in Chapter 4 a little bit about pedo and murderous heads, and that is the solvable point we're trying to make, here ye, is that God's got a lot to do with the facts that people can heal themselves of traumatic interests, and make it so that Andrea can heal herself from trauma, very likely so!

If that's any consolation prize's commandant languages, here ye, it's about time that Andrea heal herself! We're questioning anyone who says otherwise, and likely stories here about people she knows all the time putting her into mental health situations, here ye, is the likelihood's stories about to unfold in her lap.

We've healed it! We've healed the situations that get us there or bring us to question the humanity's wakes, and we've very much healed the situations that get us into the LRA, Less Restrictive Alternative's, wakes, here ye. The LRA's got enough time on our hands to make appointments, and such Less Restrictive ways of finding out if she's homeless, or if she had family to support, or if she's due to find out how many ways of which the sentences taking the consideration's wakes, here ye, warrant or mean to involve the planet's ugliest terminologies, in the wakes of 9/11, here ye?

Why does she keep getting stuck with these LRA's, LRO's, Less Restrictive Alternatives? What is the death sentence about, here ye, but a failed system, and an LRA's got a lot to give us back though! What is the time of day is it about getting to be but a time that says I'm in a hotel and not on the streets, as she was sleeping out at this lake locally when the bumble bees even told her to get up off the couch and get a job! What were those little bugs in her ears that said, a world leader such as yourselves, Andrea, could not imagine sleeping out there and then some!

These bumble bees, is it? No, they were mosquitos, came all the way over to her and said, you're not sleeping here, bum! That's how they said it, right when we said, hallelujah to healing mental health, Andrea!

Are you telling us that these mosquitos said to you, get lost, and that you complied with that and got off your meds, so to speak it that way? It's because the local mental health agency quashed your original LRA/LRO, and because the only mental health agency's only open doors were the policies from the police force that say or to state that an LRA's mental hospital situation has got nothing on this woman here!

Inside the cop shops, we like to talk about how it's possible to do your face up with makeup if you tried to bring some in though, and we're always about that! This time's back in your face though, about to unfold is a jury by trial era's spacements about Andrea telling the world that she's healed schizophrenias, the paranoid kind, as she's never had a hallucinogenic like appearance to her, but a paranoid one in the past? Definitely!

She's trying to say or to state that, once you're inside of a place like this, it's only a matter of time when you'd get a tooth decaying problem.

What is the cop shop's doings, here ye, but to state or to take away from the facts that God's only son's got a penis, and that is the very thing that will get you into trouble, Andrea, is to state that this world's religions are basically very thinning and very keen on the food being impeccable inside of these places.

Only God can help you now, Andrea! What does a healed mental health status tell us about the rules, and what about God's helpers do you understand is the keys to mental health issues! What does the cop shops have in common with the other helpers of American's soil takers, and the health issues of cadets, for example, who have taken Andrea into custody, and have deemed her unfit to redeem the national news shows of taken folks who have schizophrenias, and that is to say or to state that her Social Security Disability act has gotten out of control here, and that we're always on the lookouts for social misfits like herself, here ye?

This mostly Monster drink's got a lot of caffeine in it here, and we're at a motel of choice, trying to rid ourselves of this book writing, because we can and do have the treatments for every single ailments curing in the book's most terrible Tuesdays, because we owe the people we know so much already. Just for checking in and seeing how things are going with you has become a chore in and of itself, of worrying, of penmanships that have lost terrible seeing things with other people in tow, and the fact that a Monster drink for coffee's a newer invention, and the Holy Ghost picks out the things we need in a day or a week, and that's coffee drinks and stuff in it, you see it, now you don't!

This concludes the talking about healing schizophrenias, schizoaffective disorder, and bipolar weekly here, as this is a hotel that has a television and a microwave, here ye? It doesn't, just a microwave and a fridge would be so nice here, but this place is an arm and a leg away from savings banks, that say what to do with our time and our monies, that's all she wrote though, because it's a savings bank's ways of admitting the coffee shops of our times, here ye, are very inventive of a place to stay. If we're alone or living alone, we admit to talking to ourselves all the time!

There's places and chapters to come, that talk about or discuss the roads to nowhere.

If you can't get that one chapter out of your mind though, however, or such is plentiful here, then find it within your heart to get out that one chapter per day image, and sing a little bit of praises as to Jesus and Jezibellie's wakes, here ye.

And this is how it's done! When Jesus was just an alarming chap in the military police force is when He became this great leader, and that's what someone she knows has done with himself is to become a great military police force, for the records though, it's tough going! What we mean by tough going is that there are other ways of seeing and believing than through Jesus's eyes, is that God's terrible Tuesdays for hamburgers today means that God is loving these people so much for the deeds they have done in the past, yes, but also because they are nice people.

I love the fact that some people have been so forgiving about different circumstances in your livelihood's wakes, here ye, and that God has come between forfeiting the literatures on these mental health meds we keep being put upon us, here ye.

And the facts that we're put upon these meds, here ye, constitutes a grounding phrase or clause that simulates the literatures that put us upon these meds in the first place!

There's different types of meds. For what purpose are we on them in the first place?

We need to know this answer before we can go on and talk about how Social Security Disability's funded our every whim here, and how we can go back into the hospital to review the literatures of funding for our venture capitals here, but that God is ready to go back to the sinisterly reviewable ways of finding out if there's a literature's Morningside coffee drinks! There's sinisterly wicked talentships available for comment out there, stating that a simple how do you do from your family's bound to come in between literatures that state that a concubine is likely to affect the sinisterly wicked sense of humors by these people you do know well! Likewise, the only things they care about as of lately is that you stay on your meds, and that's all that we're wondering about too, is when you can come off your meds?

This means war though, because she has never had a sound environment for which to come off of them, as it's always been about money and time, and about other people noticing you're coming off of them slowly, and that Melatonin trip wasn't meant to combine or be in combination with Seroquel! At all costs, Love, there is something you should know, and that is, that these facilities do not only have the wherewithals to help you out of this situation's tidings, here ye, but to think about it, there are only a number or handful of citizens out there who are off the stuff! It's a worldwide epidemic to be on mental health meds, and this is a worldwide problem, not just yours!

It's about time to come to terms with this statement. It's about time to come to terms with the facts that God is inventing a time wheel's interfaces, and that God's about to bring coffee hints your ways, here ye! This mental health meds wheel is very precisely the case, because of moonshine though?

It's likely to strictify the comings and goings of this mental health med wheel construct's only lonely heart's club, as the only way to come off the meds themselves is to find a locale that is supportive in your doing so, and to get off the streets!

That is the only way to get solace about this mental health wheel that keeps on turning, and then some! There's only a way to get off of them, and it has to do with finding the right person to take care of you during this time!

There's only one way to get America working again at getting mental health back in order, and that is to be discussed clearly and succinctly in America's working knowledge of mental health meds! There is only one way's dealings with such a distinctly working knowledge of car problems, and that is to take one guy's stance, and to say or to state that a mental health junkie you've become is not really fair, nor is it accurate!

We're going to state that these state hospitals are really going to fix the times past, and that God is active in helping others find their solace and solitude in doing so means that you must find a significant other who works with the law abiding citizenry's best policies, here ye. And to fix that methodology's standpoint's going home with the fact that law enforcement's policies on finding and desisting arrestments upon a person's livelihoods is really the fault of the police force, for their findings on an LRA, Less Restrictive Alternative's, got one thing to say.

For this is how it's done! You've got to remember that God's only citizenry's got tons of weapons available, right now, and always! We don't want the guns, see chapter 23 and 15 on the matters at hand here, for there are certain gun laws that someone possesses, and there are certain drugs which, if on, are very potent, and curable is the gun laws that dictate the possessions of quality management's likelihoods, here ye!

What are the legal ramifications of giving back the van to its caretaker, because they bought it for us, and that has been the illegal ramifications of finding the best alternatives to the LRA, Less Restrictive Alternative's, ways of being's totally simple ramifications!

For this is how it's done, Folks, is to rely on other people to reveal their frustrations with the system's one of them.

And, this is talentships likely to end on this note here, is that comedies versus tragedies is the ways of counseling addicts to become very involved in this issue of no meds, for this is how it's done, Folks! Come to Papa Genes is how Jesus used to refer to Himself as the only bothersome person in the world, besides Andrea here, that says, how come you can hear voices around me and see hallucinations and stuff, for this is how Andrea is getting along in the world right now, and there's many things she doesn't understand.

If someone comes up to her and asks if she hears voices or sees hallucinations, try Jesus for a minute!

This means that she does not hear the voice of God though cherishes the ways and means it lady's sinisterly gifted treats? Does God want to listen to the voices of creatures of habits, or does it mean that people hear stuff like, "Andrea is the God of wisdom cures," or, "Andrea has the DSW, Divine Source Wisdom. Any questions?" Things like this, you see it, now you don't!

I mean, if Jesus could ward off people like the King of England from getting nearest His Jezibellie Christ's inventionships about people, places and things, then Andrea can surely get a life! Meaning, we let her know all the time that other people hear voices and see hallucinations around her, not the other ways around the tactics of God's other halves.

And so, there's more to the stories that brings us to the close of the invention of a lying chapter's only very big lessons. Made in American history's the coming and adventation of skills, and lying in wait is the chapters on adventing the very thing that Jesus said would happen to her if she contexted her skills and waited it out, meaning that she's very likely to get picked up tomorrow if she's not careful with the skills that she's got outside this place. Meaning, there are people out there who don't like the haircut's ways about our skillships, here ye, and our hair is really the only thing that we're self-conscious about, here ye!

And that's something that God has brought to the forefront and foreground's only salient points, here ye, is that Andrea can hear some kind of voice, sure! But it's not an evil force, and it's the only things on Earth that can really get us into trouble here, is the facts that God's evil forces are still reckoned with! What are the tides of truths that sneak us into the radars of love, and that God is an evil force is to be reckoned with the talentships that say or to speak to us here, that says that God is an evil force to be reckoned with is the illusion that God is the talentships and such!

We're not saying that an evil force is taking over Andrea's body, mind and spirit, here ye, but that mental health professionals hear voices and see hallucinations around her that they have never seen before, and then blame her for them, which is what we're getting at with Jesus Christ.

He had this same problem of the Gentry never seeking a place of refuge in His lifetime. So, there are people who believe in saintly spiritual advising, and there are people who walk and talk amongst ourselves, here ye!

The most funniest thing about Restasis usage is that it takes care of chronic dry eye. When talking about love though, the funniest movies are really at a state hospital's cards of Oriental speaking peoples never talking back to our Holy Ghost or spiritual comings on, here ye, that states that Oriental speaking peoples are talking back through the Holy Spirit or Ghost too? Right here, right now, there is no other place I want to be! There's comedies and tragedies of relying on the Holy Spirit or Ghost to do its job, and to describe the phenomenon of the Holy Spirit or Ghost is two-fold.

One, we really have a lot to take care of and to be thankful for, here ye, and that is the Restasis jobs of doing what is inclined with butters on the faces of men and women who do not want that facial hair back, but what that means is, there are certain other factors that take into consideration the peaces and the wills, the peaces and the wills, here ye, that state that a certain person hears a voice or not, and that is the voice of reason's peaces, here ye.

And that is that the contexts for letting a person live it out and Holy Ghost or Spirit this, is to say or to state that God's not questioning them!

We're letting them go, because they heard the voice of God, not because they hear no voices and are supposed to let the chance encounters of criminalities regarding hearing voices! See my chapter on voices, Chapter 34, where we state specifically that voices are a thing of the past then, and that God awful knowings about the chapters on specific voices that you hear are the voices of God's pasts, that state that God's going forward with medications for specific remedies, such as hearing voices though?

What medications are you taking for the specificities that state that hearing voices is a thing of the past? What contexts are you taking to the bank, for specifications are not to be criminalized or tolerated without the past coming into contexts that kill, maim or bind other people to the cancer centers of America's Got Talent's regard for situational people, here ye. And that God's got it covered?

And, planning to take up this medical marijuana's madnesses is really for the birds, here ye!

Chapter 37

I Love the Divine Source Wisdom!

I love the Divine Source Wisdom! We're not actually sure what you want to do with this chapter, Andrea, as this means war that you cannot find it in your heart of hearts to forgive the situations with people not helping you out, with the terminologies of this book's lessons plannings, here ye.

This is the DSW calling upon the helps and stranger effects of finding it well and good that Andrea is here homeless, and it's better than sleeping in the van. Sometimes I think so, at any rate! This one coffee book's hints at this moment's notices is the fact that God can sometimes be cruel.

At any rate, there's plans to become a great writer from this work's interludes, here ye, but there are more faiths than meets the eyes. In terms of destinies and such, there are so much more blankmanships out there that need questionables to come to terms with the phenomena of chance's best inklingcureships out there! What you need right now is a tall, cool one, and we're going to get just that!

Well, what are we waiting for? She doesn't really wanna go and drink tonight, we can tell it's true too, but we've had so much and so many proofreads, that if it really ends up this way that she can only do two chapters at a time and not have much to drink tonight, that would be kosher with us, you see it, now you don't!

Likewises, here ye, there are tons of things to be thankful for and grateful for, and that's a fact, Jack and Jill were so married it's pathetic or not even funny, whichever word phrase first picks up our brain's signals, we are so eloquently inclined to state it three or four ways. In which case, she picks the very first one to talk about, always, here ye!

What is the following about anyways or anyhoo, but to talk about the Jezibellie cures is kind of sort of boring here. So, we're about to conclude this chapter on, "I" loving the DSW all the times, here ye, and coming to a place of contentment to where we're living right now, on the streets more or less, so that we can finish this work of patience and of kindnesses, here ye!

There are cancers to talk about, here ye, and there are three methodologies to finding out what happens in the afterlife. But this time, the police escort system's out to get the dealings of times past with the commandant's ways of seeing the perfect police reporting system's out of control dealings with the concubines of a lifetime of greed mongerings. In other words, your old roommate, Andrea, is really nice about this life's comings and goings, but he never did stick up for you being gone for a total of a month and a half, without the comings and goings of the dudes in the hallways of the wrath of Khan's, here ye, and they developed a sinister relationship with your emergency contact's ways of saying, I don't know where your daughter is sleeping with us here, but it's not with us, and then they said you had to "leave the premises."

We're normal, but they aren't?

It's just that with the advent of Christianity's wakes, here ye, that God decided to step in and to separate you from those guys, and not to tell them where you ended up this last time, at a different hospital was it this time?

Nope, but definitely a hospital saw a little scare in them, and they were winging it, but two more hospitalizations, was it?

No, but think about it's here ye implications about this, here ye! You were not homeless at the times of rewriting some of this, you say? Nope, I was truly off the streets at that time, not happy with the roommate parties, were you not?

Sure, I was, but you begged of a different life, to where you did not have to answer to roommates, who kind of sort of kept to themselves, for the most part? I was happy where I was at though? I beg to differ, Andrea! You dreamed of a different life for yourselves, all of you in that situation, you did. So, we made it possible for you to move out without a reference though? Of course not.

Well, I cannot begin to imagine their painstaking literatures, here ye, but to tell all of them that we're 40 somethings all living together and such made it for not the ideal situation to live there without a homeless shelter, but it was sure something, and it made us think that you needed something else, something different.

I needed to remind Divine Source Wisdom, DSW for short, about how to go about getting a new Econoline van, in the middle of it all! Not! We just wanted to say that, for the records, here ye, that her late ex-husband deserved none of the student loan lunch money we had. For the records though, here ye, she lived with other people and had no problems yelling in the hallways! The likelihoods that you are still comatose from it all means that those roommates just thought you were a mental case and decided to let you go and live someplace else, means that God's in control or command of your life's wantingnesses and your worth and stuff of that nature's callings, but you're ultimately in control of not letting your "emergency contacts" run or ruin your lives!

You can or could argue that we're responsible, for Andrea's well being's talent searches, here ye, but the bath of a lifetime cannot or could not convince us that she is "gravely disabled," as the courts have not found her in this hotel/motel room situation yet! She's all, if it's God complexes that certain individuals have, then this is the moment's notices that says, she's terrified of losing her job though? We had run off the job the night before she got her disability payments stopped, for this would have been very seriously the case, and this is not what we need to complete this book about, here ye, and such promises as this are kindly given!

I'm not sure what DSW, Divine Source Wisdom, is getting at, here ye, but the simple pleasures of life's quandaries, here ye, are trying to point out that Madonna's a kind soul here, and she's very impressed with the tassels hanging off the breastbone of Jezibellie Christ! There's solely not anyone who would interfere with the tassles hanging off the breastbone of, say, Jesus Christ's wife, here ye!

This drugs innuendos here is that God's watching us, God is watching us, God is watching us from a distance! Oh, God is watching us, God is watching, us, God is watching us… From a distance! The song by Bette Midler is very touching in deeds be, for thou art the kindest soul!

What is to happen is two-fold here. The cancer cures in Chapters 37 and 38 are already spoken fors here.

Meaning, that God is watching our sensibilities and that is a fact! How come God is watching us so intently here, because He loves us! What is cancer cures supposed to bring up, but the fact that God is watching our faith healings pretty wells, here ye, and the pluralizations are duly noted! We take, for example, a God complex, when we're out and about all the times, here ye, and never get naked on the tables of love here with God in the helms for spoken fors.

What this means is that getting naked is supposed to happen in this lifetime of greed mongerings, and this bipolar legacy has got to change.

Strife is not our middle name's only child's refugees to come about in the lifetime of greed mongerings! What is strife but a middle name by "Us" though?

What is your destiny and purpose laid out before you, Andrea! Is it to kill HSV or is it to take the eucalyptus plant seriously! You take 1 fluid ounce of eucalyptus essential oil, not the plant-based or tailed kind, meaning, not the beauty stuff, but the essential oil, and down it then? Nope, you stick it in your leg with a syringe, and then a week later or a month later, is it? Which is it, please? It's a month later, you stick it in your leg again for the vaccine!

Same for HIV, it's cadmium sulfate, 1 fluid ounce of water plus 2 ounces of the stuff, and pop it into your leg, but for the vaccine, do it a week later, is it? Yes, and it's the vaccine! But use 1 ounce of the cadmium sulfate this time with 1 fluid ounce of water, and that will be the vaccine for you and your governmental influences. Yay to finding out the cure to HIV/AIDS, here ye!

Likewise, if it's the cancer vaccine, you must have done it already? Because it is mentioned that the calcium deposits on your brain are meant to take it from us here, and to really get the lanolin cures for it all, you've got to take the Spring Valley kinds in the future, and pop 5 of those pills into your leg, drained of course, and it's the vaccine for cancer. Unfortunately, you have to get rid of the cancer first before you can take this vaccine for the cure of cancer by downing the stuff in pill formats first, and then it's possible to take about 45 pills total, at 8 per day then? Yes, the 8 per day of 2500 mg in the futures of radiation treatments for all other cancers, as they work here, means that 20% of the population can take the cures for cancer through pill formats, here ye, and then it will work that they take the injection of lanolin for it to be the cures all get outs, here ye, and the cure for lung cancers only is these Emergen-C Vitamin C 1000 mg of packets from Walmarts out there, and to pop it into your leg then?

Nope, just take them orally, these packets from Walmarts only, totaling lots of money then? They're relatively inexpensive but get rid of this lung cancer by popping nothing in the leg yet, just down those packets three times per day, one at a time, for about 45 days, and it will, or should, get rid of the cancers of the mind, as well as the cancers of the lungs.

Then go for the lanolin shots as outined in Chapter 35 there about goats and stuff, goat milk, goat cheese then? No way, Jose!

There's lanolin in the plant-based production of it, but there are also sheep to contend with. Don't kill the sheep! It's Jesus's goathend that I want to contend with here a little bit here. Likewise, all of the things we need for sheep is really what a goathend is supposed to be abouts, here ye, and that God's always trying to help out with the lanolin coming from fresh Vitamin D2 shots, and Spring Valley is a nice brand to buy, in the futures thereof! What is this world a coming to if you cannot bring me the vaccine to cancers though? You just do it once, right? That is correctamundos, Peoples! It's 1 mL though? I thought I wrote it down as 1 fluid ounce, but that won't stop cancer, 1 mL will though. So, keep it straight, that the ones I wrote down for the U.S. government won't be the right amount, as it was just a typo about it alls.

What will this world a come to with all these cancer vaccines in them, HIV, HSV and now Herpes Simplex Viruses 8 and 12 are all hoaxes! So, these cancer vaccines will have to be for the mind, as well as the heart's simple crawdad solution for diabetes is it? That is outlined pretty well in Chapter 11, but the keys to Alzheimer's has to suck, for eating crawdads/crayfish/takla/crawfish from the Philippines (Marketman, 2010) has got to be the way, Peoples, and for what you answer to, here ye! Stop all Coumadin/Warfarin/other blood thinners along the way then? Yes, just 48 hours prior to the lanolin shots then? Not, just the crawdad eating, here ye!

And that's a fact that the booby hatch is closed, for the next chapter is about having a White kid to Black parents, and stuff that is highly provable! These crawdads, for example, are pretty readily only the booby hatch's negativity for people who are like minded and live in mental hospitals for the elderly, all of the medications they're taking for bipolarisms don't amount to much. It's all for the Coumadin overdoses, and the blood thinners that, really, nobody knew or knows about, but it's a hoax for the Alzheimer's patients to have to take them.

There's some things you should know about timing the Divine Source Wisdom with the ailment cures lady's natural talents and abilities, to have and to hold, from this day forward?

It's because Andrea is still single, and that is the truth be told ways of missing the instigating trusts of our inklingships, here ye! What is a job worth to you, there, Andrea? She's missing the point's best takings here, as she desires to work for the CDC, the Centers for Disease Control and Prevention, or NASA, or, what is required, or the requirement, to work for Congress?

Must I be an invalid, or can I work for the federal government? Can I fill out those forms on a DD-214 sheet, however? This is the God complex we've all been a waiting for, here ye!

We're forming an opinion that God said we could work for the federal government, if only we could have a say or a séance too, but the federal government works, Andrea! How about the White House, even?

Will you guys get me a, the, jobs, and work for the CDC?

About to pass is legislation about mental hospitals in generals, here ye, because it's even fatter or quicker, one of the two's here ye blankmanships, here ye.

What about a job with the White House's federal government? About to unleash the stronghold, here ye, is somebody, somewhere, that likes to work! I do, I thought, have a knack for it's kindnesses, here ye! What is a job supposed to be, but a nice way's means it lady's commandant's languages, here ye!

On call is she then, Andrea, thereof!

Chapter 38

The Booby Hatch is Closed This Year and Next!

This psychotropic drugging clause is really for the birds here too. There are several ways that a pregnancy can go awry without a Ceserean, Peoples! Can you make a Black kid come out of a pregnant woman's body, if one is White? Well, yes, you can, and one could come out Black if you down a eucalyptus plants-based ownings.

Meaning here, Folks, and you too, Classes of Gentiles, here ye, that if you're Black and desire a White kid, you could probably get one, if you knew how to down a bottle of aloe vera essential oil, about four of them during pregnancies, the first trimester, here ye! This is tricky at best, and not advised that you even try this?

What is Jezibellie but a Black child's Dreamboat Annie's biggest cures, for She was Blacker than Me then? She was Black, and I was White, therefore our "kids" came out Blacker than the desert sky once, here ye? She's Blacker than Me, than I was, thereof! If there's a Walmart's rendition of the stuff, I could see it happening for all Black kids with a White mother, thereof, to down a bottle of eucalyptus essential oil, not the beauty kind, but the oils themselves, will change that kid's skin tone to a darker quality. Has it ever happened before in history though, you are asking Me this, Andrea?

Why yes, it has!

Only a half a dozen times, you say to Me here, right, God and Goddess? You can tell what the skin tone is with a grain of salt, but wanting to discover what it's like to have a mom who's White, I do desire a partner who is thus and so, how come a eucalyptus plants-based reasonings are all that is required to become a partner with?

There's a skin test you can take at Jezibellie having so many White kids as a Black lady, but then you're required to test it on animals then before it happens, here ye? Try an orangutan first, because of its skin tones and color, the fur will come out white.

If it's Jezibellie Christ downing the eucalyptus essential oil during pregnancy though, she'll or he'll come out Blacker than She was, and a White baby is desired with eucalyptus essential oil then?

No, it's aloe vera essential oil, during the first month of pregnancy then? Yes, the 6th will even make it happen then? I would say a skin develops its tone in or during the first month of pregnancy, and that will be a fact we consider as two-toned, as "We" like the ideas of a two-toned baby then? How is a pregnancy test run, we might add? It's a pregnancy test or a paternity test, which of the two? How about a maternity test to be sure as well?

This is the funniest conversation ever, Jesus says!

Because this is how John the Baptist came out, just before Windows 7 though came out, "We" looked into a window and found a little baby sticking its head out of a pregnancy window during childbirth though? It's the iPads that we're promised or given to in the mail's systems here, that state that you can tell skin color and tones in a for color world's iPad! We're dunking people through the mail system's funny grams though, as a designer skin color iPad.

We can technically have one during child pregnancy, or we can ask God's health code problems to detect a madman at the inventions of the wheel's nicety nice ways of saying, God's in control. Or it's a problem, here ye, that a man can think it, as well as wish to own it, that it's not a skin color, toned to God's likings, here ye, but a Cesarean pregnancy's bound and determined question mark's only chances to reveal to God's likings that a eucalyptus plant's responsible for all this dark hair growth.

We have a lot to be thankful for that a past governmentalized girlfriend and boyfriend couldn't be put together as two "White Chicks," the movie, was a governmental past's biggest roulette game's natural abilities, to make two White men come about though is not what we're after, here ye, cause it's a boy and a girl you want in there, always, and that's a fact, as there are no White chicks coming out without a circumcision needed!

Meaning, Folks, and Gents and stuff here too, is that God can make it so that a little boy never needs or needed a circumcision, by choice though? It just came to us in a hospital bed about wild and woolly hair on the tops of the heads of female and male people. Just don't eat any beans while pregnant, and it'll come out silky smooth! If you want horse manure to do the trick though, you can straighten it out with some!

Female circumcisions are not needed if you have no eggs and no cheddar is it? Well, it's about time we get to the bottom of this circumcision need, as there are times when the sheath is really there, and other times when it really is not. So, if you're a female and you're coming out with balls, you are not a strangity, it is meant to be that way, not so clear and dryly cut then? Take the balls off! Do it at pregnancy though is what I am saying here, by preventing the circumcision of females at the time of birth by eating no eggs or cheese, cheddar cheese mostly. If you are a female and you came out with an extra ball, it's because of our nutritional habits as females though? Not really, just that there's cheese involved!

Men, though, are allowed the freedoms to choose then? Not a circumcision in the world would need to be done or performed if everybody ate and drank wheat germ from Costco! Try it, you might like that way of being! Drink a ton of wheat germ every day, mix it in with some vegetables or some blackberries, mind you, and you will not need a male circumcision, here ye!

There's a way for males to avoid the knife, though, and you need to have that protected sheath come off of you as a male by, or you don't, by coming to terms with the circumcision, and why preachers talk about it so often, is that it's preventable in the womb!

I'm about to embark upon that very reasonings that we give up cheddar cheese, white eggs, milk production and all, because the cheese is very bad for a female fetus! I think that the Costco kinds of wheat germs are very noticeably not there yet, but if there were such thing, go buy it at Walmarts though and you risk being pregnant, Ladies! Wheat germ in the 4th or 5th months only then? Nope, try the 4-month mark and start drinking the stuff, morning, noon and night, and it's a requirement that an ultrasound be showing nothing of the types of things we can do on this iPad here, like having colored imagery, like back in the days of Jesus and Jezibellie.

We had it all there for us too, She said! The clitoris on females is a little long if you starve yourself in the earlier months, because she's unaware she's pregnant, or because they want to starve the baby, one of the two. Either that, or food is being withheld for such a purpose as this then? Not likely to happen, you two! What we mean by you two is that there are several ways for a baby to grow in the uterus of unsuspecting women, and that a female needs a circumcision too is quite common.

Will you all please commit adultery on your wife, spouse's own detrimentalnesses, if there is a talent search's kinds of peaces that comes and came from your wife's horninesses during pregnancies then? There aren't a lot of women who will have sex while in utero either.

What we mean is to say that women are still out to lunch on the topics of religious ceremonies during and after childbirth happens, but this means that God's out to lunch on the topics of religious comments about the circumcisions that occur. Whatever your counselor knew of the Divine Source Wisdom, DSW for short's, ongoing talentships, here ye, is that your one and only counselor knew from you that the circumcision's entrance into the lap dances of love here, and that Jesus's penis was then circumcised, because His mother wanted it that way. My counselor has her own special powers, you could say!

Say, did you know that the presidents, Don and Melania Trump, remain, and always will be, the son's reincarnate parents? For these presidents, Melania Trump is the mom of Jesus reincarnated? Yes, she is. We have previously aforementioned this, however! Melania Trump is Marybelle Magdalene Longmire, and Donald Trump was Joseph Longmire.

Jesus's other half is called Jezibellie Christ, Tutankhemen though.

There are Facebooks to look at, and that is about all that is going on in our lives right now, is Queen Nefertiti's comment back in the 13th century B.C., is that God is going to investigate this newness, in amnesia for Jesus Christ's wife then?

It's the conclusion of a very long, drawn out saga, of coming to terms with God's wraths, and of dying unconditionally. Notifying God of trusts, and dying itselves, here ye, is the best cures of all God's complexes, here ye! You die, and then you come back immediately to Earth's crusts then? Well, not if Murph has anything to say about it, the guy's in love with Earth, and he loves the strengths of times where Murph is the only clues we give out, here ye! What is plausible is not always probable, but this concludes the chapters that be written!

This is the conclusion of a great number of works to come! This author, Andrea Wynn Barberi, is a heartfelt human being with a conscience that is greater than those put together! For this is the works of Andrea Wynn Barberi signing off with love! This book is greatest in achievements because of Jezibellie Christ's interventions here! Signing off with love though? Of course! This is because Paul has his burial grounds in ancient Greece here and Mesopotania is a Godsend of a place to be from here! Life has but a Godsend to discover ancient and Roman times here! That's because of the Italianity that we face in our destruction's best plausible homesteads here! We must reach the epic proportions in orgasmic activities with the inventions of peace's greatest homesteads here, and we have proof that people find joy and peace around me. And one person brought us to the limelights of peaces and joy in our Savior blessings, as she told me or us of a story about a bus station's ride and $5 to her name that a lovely stranger gave to her one year.

And, please reach the epic proportions that we're limelighting for in this book of peace here! That said, what is the telegraphic proportions that we want to dismay the police for in this book here? It means, Folks, and you too, Andrea, that there are balancatures, this is balance cures, for the worlds to seek and to desist here is the blatantly overcast foreshadows here of death do us part ways here! Have we the cures for herpes simplex and AIDS though? Of course, we do! Please read the Appendices in the end chapters here. As an attempt to code language for the Congressional hearings here, I need for somebody to believe in me, the Divine Source Wisdom, and Us here, so as to state it literally here! There is a cure for schizophrenias here!

This woman's story about the $5 bill is most precious, that she had no money here, that states or stated that she was going to have to take a bus ride to an undisclosed location, and that God or Jesus provided the means for a soldier, or some complete stranger, to give us this busride back to where she had come from.

It was a story of triumph, that she spreads around evenly to nobody else but a trained clinical psychiatrist she was, under the guild of an HSV/HIV/AIDS background in literature no less and no mores here? I'm not saying she has or had any of these diseases aforementioned here. I am just saying or stating that there are more coffee stains in this White man's shirt than He is letting on, here ye!

This was schizophrenia's raps back in the day, during the nicety nice ways of letting all people know that schizophrenia's curable by two things, sodomy is not one of them!

Back in the days of that clinical psychiatry degree she had, come on now, back then you could be an ARNP like she was, a psychiatric nurse she calls/called herself back in the days of Jesus and Jezibellie, turning around and researching such things as medication for the first-time hopefuls, in like 1943 here, and that's a fact, Jack and Jill were never married though? I beg your pardon? She's older than me, like 78 or 82 years old now? Even older, perhaps even 92 these days, but back in the days of finding out if God existed or not, older people even told stories to me in these two or three wonderfully published, though arcane secrets about psychiatry being the best that it was supposed to be.

Back then, you could tell about your secret pasts, your lockets that you engraved people's names to, and have holy spiritual leaders come in and to tell of a past or a link to that phone call you've been trying to link to your gods and your spirituality's in checknesses, but this time it's warzone callings, for people with mental illnesses just didn't exist that much.

Now, we have all of these mental health "drugs" to keep us saner and that is a nice call you made to the person who helped you quit smoking, about having a cigarette. Back in the days of non-planning and stuffs like doing your own laundries and such, is really what this country needs, to get back on track though is super hard to do here. Like, is the government aware of just how many people we are employing here, as opposed to those being on disability payments, to get by now with?

These peoples have no gun rights or laws that protect perfectly good citizens from running the gamut and becoming the outlaws of loaded gun rights.

Meaning, Folks, and Gentiles too, that we're letting the government, the U.S. government is what we mean by this, here ye, run our lives then? Because we're issueless on a place to stay right now that is cozy enough for a small master bedroom to run our lives, here ye.

And, we're trying to find a way or ways to support ourselves as of lately. We mean well here, Andrea, but you haven't done enough to support yourself, with years of disability payments though, and we're here to say or to state that living with other people's been your biggest downfall.

But, it's also been a bigger blessing over the years! We fell apart to a simple diagnosis of paranoid schizophrenia as my first diagnosis, and that fact failed me so much so that my diagnosis, or mis- one thereof, is a lot like being told of having a mental disease and defect, so much so that just the sheer mentioning of a disability is so much disabling in and of itself, that we thought we were doomed with it, the diagnosis thereof. We certainly did not, I repeat, have anything to do with that last moment's notices, here ye, and stated for the facts of God's wraths, that we "heard voices," but that was years ago, or before an accurate diagnosis came about, such as schizoaffective disorder, depressed type. I was sure depressed for a lot of years afterwards. And had been on every anti-depressant imaginable. Before or pre-1948, the coast of a lot of people say or speak to that mental health druggism as if it were a Godsend to make it this or thus far here.

When God failed to answer us on a new diagnosis/treatment facility for so many years on the drugs that they send out with you on hospitalizations, however, and please see or check out my second book upon the subject matter's grave disability markers called life imprisonments, here ye.

The problems with the subject matters at hand's greatest disability markers are best better kept secret though?

You probably wouldn't deny myself a "crimson tides" ways of looking at the world, all after graduate school kept me on Neah Bay's eternity lists, here ye, but Jezibellie Christ's reincarnate must mean that Jesus is back upon this Earth's too many people to list as possibles, here ye! This life, you're on your own, as Prince used to say, back in the days of too many posters in one kid's rooms of lives, here ye!

You probably took disability very seriously, back in the days of no healing, thereof, of a mental condition or defect, all because the disability itself is so ominous a task to uphold to or aspire to, all the same thing, here ye!

This took her for a loop for many a different year's lengths, on disability payments and everything, here ye, eight years of disability payments then? Roughly thereof, with the advent of keeping Social Security Disability payments since July 2007 too.

Then most everyone wreaked havoc on us for healing schizophrenias, we'll just call it that, because what we did had to do with Emotional Freedom Technique (EFT tapping on meridian endpoints), and that vanished the paranoia associated with "pedo" and "murderous heads," outlined in the previous chapters on the subject's best intentions, here ye! Several rounds of that tapping on meridian endpoints got me to thinking that the proofreading of this manuscript is happening at the same time that it is being written, here ye, and this has taken us a better half or further parts of this year and last, to write the darned thing, about how to heal schizophrenias, that we never took or had taken into consideration the mugshot on the front or back shots of the cover of this book's tidings or lessons breakings, here ye.

Right now, my appearance has changed so much, as I'm trying to heal gray hair removals by listening to God about the Rogaine cures for shaved heads and such, but I also envied a lot of different peoples out there without the gray hair cures. We really think that is the ticket to loving yourselves, rightly so, eons of reporters out there, with the cures for schizophrenias or bipolar disorders, united ways, here ye!

There's so much in common with old people, here ye, that they put me up half the time, while in college once they did. There are three or four reasons to stay with them while in college.

This person with Alzheimer's I was noting in previous chapters was a looker back in the days of no hair growth. He's still a looker in my book, but not an ounce of pedo head has ever entered this man's brain. Rightly so, as he's still cheapened by the Coumadin/Warfarin payments to his person, and dreams of a day when he sat right in front of me, stating he could "heal Alzheimer's," and I believed him wholeheartedly.

Will someone, somebody, anybody, get this man a drink? He's got the gout but takes medications for that. Will somebody please get him a glass of Alzheimer's cures, here ye? He's got the gout is a sorry excuse for him not taking the remedies outlined in Chapters 28 and 37 respectfully, I just don't know how to get him there to test it out!

Will you please make it there, kind Sir? His wife too was a looker back in the days of wanting to become a clinical psychiatrist sometime, but it was her one day who got me out of this schizoaffective funk by pointing out to me that the paranoia I had experienced going off or down on my med dosages is not what I was experiencing that day we sat in her car or my car or some car and said, Andrea, these are two different things you are trying to work out in your brain of brains here, and I'm here to help!

This person has been in the mental health business all her waking life, and I urge or encourage you or anyone else with diabetes like she's got to give up the mental health meds, because they only work for a time, maybe a month or two tops, then one should be taken off of them! But to give her the diabetes cures in this work of work's what I am after, here ye!

To get Andrea away from schizoaffective disorder though, by being able to see realities and non-realities at the same time. She was fighting away the paranoias, months, if not one year after I healed myself at the healing center of choice, all over a back injury that turned out to be the best thing's happening for myself at the time. It was this woman's word choices that got me over the hump, and although I couldn't remember what she talked about, Andrea, "We" do! She just said to me with each turn of the wheel or whistle blowers here, that God is in control or charge, and that we should just choose the non-realities if we'd like them.

To be there for me though, she really got to the crux of pointing that out for me, that, no, I'm not a bad person, and, yes, the blue rose in Chapter 36 was a tribute to her hypnosis style integration of dealing with a schizophrenic, bipolar person off her meds though? I was cutting the dosages down at that time, and did not worry anymore about the bipolar, schizoaffective truths in my wakes, here ye. I attribute that star moment where she'd picked a blue rose to center or ground herself through a hypnotherapy session to be the biggest tribute for what she'd done for me in that sort of setting.

What is wrong with a little pick me up from this motel room that we stay and visit in, as it's close to Neah Bay's caving systems out there, the very place where Andrea found Me lying next to Her, is where the Neah Bay creatures of habit's pasts really found a really dark and narrow place for her late ex-husband to join Jesus Christ in some ailment cures lady's backhoes, here ye! The princely of tides here in Neah Bay had a jacuzzi in it once, believed to be the strange Israelites back in the days of Jesus walking around nude in a glass house made of Israel's ice buckets was it?

Yes, there was a time when that glass house of Isis used a ball of sand to intimidate the president of our country with, but it's all a hoax and a glass house that crumbled to the ground.

Which made our president, our country, all hot and bothered by a little crumbling, to and from the grocery store's food stamps that made our ways back to hospitality seeks its, here ye! Theirs is a forward-thinking bunch, because, it made Jesus walk around like that, nudely dressed, all until His wifey showed up in there, in the caves you say? No, in Jesus's time, the Israelites, and we say this sharply, as He did walk around in there nude, like everybody else in their times, here ye, never made it to the Isis, or the ball of sand was it, that encompassed or engraved a beautiful gold stars backings, here ye?

This gold star's not what we're talking about having done on Andrea's behalves, here ye, as this crystally clear vision and focus is not what we're talking about, here ye.

Please envision that, for God's sakes, what was He doing in there, nude in the first place's over the counter beginnings, here ye! And that concludes this sectioning of couches that we still believe and maintain were glass too?

Yes, and we're ashamed of that too? Not in the least, huh? What was Jezibellie to do, but to raise His flag for Him?

We're going to tell you goodnight now, Andrea! Believe in good lucks and stuffs with this comedy's proses we're outlining here! Say goodnight to the person with Alzheimer's, as someone gets him this cure all method's proses, didn't they yet, you say here? What is Jesus's name holding without commenting about the tons of medicated individuals that never did find a reason to withhold the information's biggest likelihood's lessons plannings, here ye! I'd do this for free, Jesus says to you now, and that was to inform them, and you here, Andrea, of saying goodnight to Jezibellie's father, for not only reinventing the wheels of raptures here, but for getting yourselves published back in the days of Jesus and Jezibellie!

He's the one who spouted off the Tutankhamun, back then it was Tutankhemen, which means "blessings" and "peace," world peace even, and then some, to bring back the "world peace" efforts of some of our most certifiably insane individuals, and to bring back the wars fought for peace's introverting syndromes, here ye, that made it back to the cases upon cases of knowhow and wherewithals, to bring back the Jesus's penis syndrome that made it rampant to leave people in this glass house alone then?

Nope, everybody in that place was nude! I certainly hope to shout's commonly snagged, restly assured, places to be at and from is not Israel.

Right now, or ever, in fact! That's because these glass houses still exist, and they're fully clothed as of lately, but not back in the days of Jesus's Tutankhemen ancestry was it? It's King James Tutankhamun/Tutankhemen, here, of the Jesus and Jezibellie's variety, that made it possible to publish the Jesus and Jezibellie cures, of a lifetime of greed mongering, then published "King James Version" of Galileo's well-known ailment cures lady's possible stretchings of the truth's very own James Tutankhemen legacies!

What is this common dollar's suitable releases of information to my person supposed to be like, here ye, for doing all of this work has got to be tiring, all on our medications. We are doing this for free though, because we were able to save up enough money this time around to medicate the interesteds, here ye, and to state that God's protected place is up for grabs, here ye, on a new round house that calls a sinisterly looking maid, French maid, to run around totally nude in there, as well as the boobs, She had been stretched with, and the bustiness's very evilnesses to take to the bank with, as He had amnesia for Her no more here! Andrea's much the same way's evilnesses thereof, for bringing up a glass house then? Not a chance, here ye, but there's a walk to be had in a few minutes thereof, and we're going to say goodnight to you for reals this time, here ye! Because this glass house has been in the families for centuries. About to unfold is God's awful complexes about getting this person the cure he needs to move on from Alzheimer's patients' listings, to a wonderful man of integrity and knowhow.

And lightning bugs are a nice way to end this saga, this painful way of living with and underneath someone else's roofs for a time better than Alzheimer's patients. Taking in the elderly to live with them has got to be a roof over someone's heads. This time it's war though, as "We" know the cure's got a plane's ticket just waiting for him over there!

It's an export tax we're waiting to hear from you, Andrea, about the lists of medications you are taking, correct? Right now, it's the blippy kind of drugs that got me a student loan deferral, correct? Yes, a sudden death syndrome is simply the happiest day on Earth, right? Wrong, but there's nothing to do with a sudden infant death's syndrome happening to someone I knew one year, and there's nothing within the 9/11 attacksisms that speaks to the well-to-do house French maids one year coming to see Me in that glass house in Israel for being a mental patient, but Her, Jezibellie Christ, "making it" on the outside with a dollar to Her name back then.

What is this Alzheimer's patient worth to you, having to bathe him all the time's not right, is it?

Will you come towards the truth of the matters, and let him bathe himself here? This was not Jesus and Jezibellie's plights, here ye! Back then, the old people kept their original houses and weren't shoved into mental homes left and right! They were revered and respected as they are today, but, likewise, they were trying to make it out there on a "pauper's salaries," here ye? No, they have quite a bit of money in the stock market's trading and such. But there was nobody, I mean, absolutely nobody with Alzheimer's back in the days of Jesus and Jezibellie Christ! We all had it on backwards with the elderlies in charge of a great many a thing back in the days of Jezebel! We had all the French time in the world of worlds, here ye, and that is the truth! What is this Warfarin/Coumadin named after and fors, here ye, but a slight of hand, that means that the whole world knows about these drugs for comatose patients. And, really, the era of space onement tells us to abandon ship with this last cookie's cutter dough patients' reviews of the literatures, here ye!

It means, Class of Gentiles later, Folks too, that there are several urban myths about stroke patients, and, one thing to do is to lower their cholesterol with these once medications we now have, and, two, never see a stroke victim again live past their due dates on call for medicines such as we are to take now!

We really need to go now, She says, Jezibellie does here! Why, She says? Because it's past 4:30pm here on the West coast's mail system! That means, Folks, and you too, Jezibellie's reincarnated pasts here, that God's got a complex about the mail systems that run around trying to find Jezibellie's most prized assets.

Her most prized and cherished heritage like functionings are meant to stay in their originals, their comatose readings, of Her dad's, and he published the King James Version for Her as James the apostle, not Paul, not ever! In fact, wherever you see Paul's name, cross or strike it out and put James's name down! He not ever didn't publish this King James Version, for Her father's a simple man and does not believe in reincarnated theories, here ye!

There are tons of things to talk about and to say, here ye, but there are none other than a simple man's trusts about the Coumadin/Warfarin's manufacturing dates, here ye's, here ye's, because this is the solvable thing's to do list's element of surprise, here ye, is that God dictates for "Us," and to "Us," and for "Us," to never take another Coumadin/Warfarin/suitable substitute's medicines again, for Alzheimer's patients! And, beyond hope is the truth of the words in this work, here ye, of saying or stating for the records, here ye, that these cancer and stroke victims are not of this world's very easy Coumadin/Warfarin comatose parties, here ye, as this means war is on the brink of extinction, here ye!

We're going to bid you adieu, sometimes listeners!

We're fully capable of coming to a close with this Warfarin/Coumadin's strengths, to listen to a dying population's later cures about crawdads/crayfish from the Philippines is really the cure for it! And, listen up, too, Folks, and Gentiles alike, here ye, we need to stop the production of it right away, here ye, as this is the last of the types of findings that we're underneath, here ye!

With the adventations of such likelihoods that finding out that this woman that you know never has suffered from dementia like they're trying to say she is, is something of a misnomer here, too. She's not about to suffer from it any longer than her wet macular degeneration is, of putting her into a mental home for the elderly has got her clueless on how to solve it for herselves, here ye.

Leukemia's cure, by the way, as someone we know has been diagnosed with it, is Lamictal pills. That contradicts society's innovations to them then? It's full strength Lamictal pills, 25 mg, 1 time per day for 4 weeks, then rest with no Lamictal for weeks 5, 6 and 7! This is due to a heart injury, so please take it lightly and do as "I" say. On the 8th week, start the Lamictal over again, 50 mg this time, for 6 weeks, 1 time per day, and it's the vaccine for Alzheimer's practically? Nope, it's still for the leukemia pill that this thing was invented for in the first place! At 4 years old or older please!

Is there another person you know who is suffering from Alzheimer's, is it? Nope, diabetes though! Don't be afraid, Peoples, of kidney failure should you choose to do that kidney/diabetes cure! I did it once in the parking lot of the king of kings, and I could be wrong, but to do it in a car, nobody can hear you, be out in the boonies though when you do! I even got a CT scan afterwards to detect the other kidney made it.

Too hot to handle though? It sounds like you're having mad passionate sex if you do it, might as well help yourself to orgasm as well, as it sounds radiant and loving to say this to yourselves, here ye, and the batteries's lives in those hearing aids will love the fat cookies recipe outlined in Chapters 35 or so, but this is a misnomer if you cannot afford the Coumadin/Warfarin/other blood thinners overdosing on the facts at hands, here ye!

Right here, right now, there is no other place I want to be, here at this motel! Right now, I'm being told I will not finish this book before its publication, is it? I'm being told by DSW that I'm on the phone with God about how to finish a work of this magnitude! I'm sending one to the White House, because we need the Trichomycin/Hachimycin shots available to us, so that we can squash cancers with it! We also need to be aware, not of Jesus and Jezibellie, but of my services!

Can we do this here? Can we get her, Andrea, a job with the federal government, if she applies for one? Can we deteriorate the needs we have in the masturbation departments for life here if you have an orgasm on the ways, and you've never had one before, like someone was telling me the other day? I bet if you overflowed your kidneys, you could have one for sures, here ye, and make someone watch you though? Try it alone first, then, later, when you're feeling up to it, up to holding that much liquid beneath your wakes here, try it with a significant other present then? They will feel all hornified at doing it at the same time as each other then? Do not, I repeat, do not call 911 if you cannot start peeing again right away though!

If you let it out, as you cannot begin to imagine the tormentings of a lifetime of greed mongering individuals, then let it out slowly then? Let it out at first then… Nope! Let it trickle out of you's.

Always, always keep perspectives clear about this though, that there's no such thing as an organ donation system that works, as these kidneys are cultivated for exact matches and stuff, you see it, now you don't? I don't think that it works out that you have a kidney transplant, but if you have, do it anyways!

This is the Divine Source Wisdom, DSW for short, saying, that if you've had the transplant, like someone I know here, you can still do the kidney overflow process, to getting it to work right again, as it's just an overflow process or overflow tanks. In the right mechanisms for peaces, here ye, is a wonderful man to boot us with, and to take over on his own again per chance the double seed in his wife's rapture's breath's not even taking this man out to dinner yet! A CT scan or Computerized Tomography lessons strengthening is not what we mean by this overflow of the kidneys that be over 35% functioning, and the insulin shots that take us to the bank with this overflow process has got to be the answers to a lot of functioning question marks that really chaps my hide. You certainly don't need the insulin after this happens though!

About to unfold is the question marks processes for little known cures, such as schizophrenias and bipolar diseases, because we're all in this together here, as this can become a "bipolar issue," to witness children being taken from their mothers, or hearing of someone being molested, or a woman or man being raped, … To become "bipolar" over the whole goddamn issue is really what we're interested in doing here is to dispel the myths associated with bipolar I disorder here.

Bipolar II is also at questionings with the police force's in town home hospitalizations and catheters that are forced upon one's personhoods here, as there is no other way to say this during an enlistment scam, in the military no less and no mores here, there are ways of asking someone if they have a penis or a vagina. But in the hospitals, the only ways to tell is to look.

Now, the various hospitals do not have to only order you a catheter to look at yourselves with, but their forcefulnesses are really superb the ways that they "four–point restraint" you, and you look to them for support? It's because they are so forceful with you that you "sound" "bipolar," and you can be dubbed as such!

What we don't like is the instigation that Andrea is still "sick in the head," and that she even needs mental health treatments any more than she has to, but she's still homeless! So, in our opinion, Andrea, are you going to find a job again, or are you gonna wait until this book comes out, and try to live off of the proceeds?

What if you're mental healthed again before it even comes out? One more time wouldn't even hurt ourselves, here ye, but some people are against the processing of this book, because they do not believe that she has anything to say in it. But they're about to get a rude awakening too, because they love her not a lot right now! It's mostly "Our" faults though, because she's in dire straits all the time, because she's "never had a full-time job," and she thinks we've seen her have one or two of those, yes?

We've had several people commenting online about her DSW, one of which is a former client/patient relationship with a very nice gentleman online, but we're still going to use the page of http://www.divinesourcewisdom.com as a nice place to come to when we need solace, as it's a very nice, kind page someday soon. We want to work for the federal government someday soon, but we're nice enough to state it online that we'd like to use our skills, much like Esther Hicks uses Strawberry Wine, the song, to elicit some other types of cousinry, as Abraham-Hicks deserves to be a monster that we all devour and love.

As we say our peaces and our inkling cures are very fashionable for Louise Hay's publications, here ye, the Balboa Press we picked to do this job is very anxious indeed for us to finish, as we are a channeled, I do say that lightly though, work, that is very extrenuous, that's a new word's there ye publications word, we might add.

Time to go publish this indeeds, here ye! Will it be successful in granting the government's coffee table works, here ye? This concludes this work now.

Please watch for more ailment cures to come about now!

What of Jesus having amnesia for His wife though? It's, truth be told, the case, as when She was married to the King of England, Solomon was his name, the guy's wreaking to be had here, but it was for four years, He could not see His wife at all without fainting in front of Her, whenever She'd show up for Him. This is the truth be told reasons for His comingling with Delilah, as sources tell "Us" and instruct to Us that He never did marry her, Delilah, for the wrong reasons though, as it was required for all male personnel to have a marriage or wedding certificate, and He could not produce this one of the blatant cures. And, to search and desist this wedding certificate in the pyramid of Ahab, in the deserts of Pakistani rulings, here ye, is where you will find such a certificate, as He did love and marry His wife first, of 30 years of rulings, to an unknown and unidentifiable ways and means it lady's timely anticipations of a commandant's rulings, here ye!

Please do not confuse Delilah's love life with Jesus's, here ye, as this means war is on the brinks of despair.

Whenever He was in public though, He wore a ring for Delilah, Her sister, mind you.

And that was all she wrote about that book flavoring's messiah messages, here ye! This blackened their friendship quite a bit, however! Say goodnight to all, and to all a goodnight, here ye!

This is Jezibellie Christ's signing off, for all to tell and desist as the methods to her madness's wakes, is really just a Jezibellie cure for pieces of the puzzle's natural born killers, to the kind of wherewithals that the monumental screening processes get to say in our next book, entitled, Prisoners of War: Dark Halls of Mental Hospitalizations, for our times to go is really necessary, here ye!

Come to papa, is what God had Jezibellie do. Each time She'd see Jesus with that ring on His finger was it? No, when He would see Her though, He'd fall down into a dead faint, and wake up having known He was in Her bedroom somehow. That was sacrilege of them to state it that way, but it's the truth, as He was no saint in the bedroom's natural born killers of the country of Mizraim, and that brought Him out of it, was to believe that She was no longer married to the fucker, the Kings of Solomon's wakes, here ye, are the Mesopotanian rulings, that She no longer was married to the fucker at alls, here ye, and we do cuss quite a bit over this, because it's blatantry and such, to be married at all to the fucker!

What's nice about this work is that He awoke one night in Her bedroom, having done all the necessary things that made Him work out His frustrations with Her being married. And, never again had He never loved Her, but She continued to be married to the fucker anyways. This means that the contexts of love, here ye, married Her, and She never forgave the fucker for abusing and beating Her up half the time, and God's inklingship cures are hers and hers alone, here ye!

But God spoke to Jesus's love for Her, and said, She's here with you every night, Jesus! Then He awoke to Her in a cave of tears, as She always had to smuggle Him, muchly like a photo on the internet I wasn't able to find permissions for to use here of Jezibellie dressed up in garb, to warn people that She had smuggled Him into Her chambers. It wasn't until His divorce too that She could see Him back, but not because of amnesia like He had.

And so, that's how God became moody about His people's inklingcureships never amounting to much's variables then, here ye, as the Queen of England had to hide her indescretions, very much so! And, that's why the Paul complex.

As pure and as lovely in hearted findings, we do find Jezibellie Christ very Tutankhemen about the ways she was trying to entice Paul during this time, to find out if in Czechloslovakia, we can mediate, sources tell us, that lately it was and has been difficult to find work out there, Jezibellie Christ.

It's funny, because there are tons of questions left to answer in this work's kindnesses, here ye, but that would be for another work of art's questions, is to stay focused and particular about the ways in which Jesus did find the booty trap's questioning arts of love's biggest lap dance.

We have taken Andrea's looks away from her at the moment, though. And I promise you that Jezibellie's breasts were operable after the torment they took of him, the King of England's Solomon, mind you, that said, question our authorities on the matters at hands, here ye, and kill the motherfucker fair and square here, for Jesus's inoperables are not a matter of life and death at the hands of the 9/11 attacks, here ye, for there is certain sensibilities posted in these here works, here ye, that never predicted a star like yourselves, here ye, protecting Jesus Christ like this, here ye.

There are new paragraphs abounties, here ye, and there are more paragraphs to come, as we have not fully addressed Jesus Christ's nature then?

We really think we have though, and that's a fact, Jack and Jill were married, remember that, Andrea! What we don't see and what we don't get is/are the facts that Jesus, much like yourselves here, find that Jesus Christ is really something special!

As far as that goes, how come He could not wake up next to Her, always courting Her, as He tried to gain strength enough to follow Her every place imaginable, here's ye.

And this goes really far, Andrea!

About to unfold is the curtains, the courage, to go through with this publication and on with your lives, once you find Mr. Right again!

This means that the limelight's a brink of investigative skills, but this chapter goes on and on and on, does it not!

About to unfold is Andrea's love for this person, and then some, as a chapter bearer means that God's in charge of about forced and focused ailment cures, and then some, here ye's, here ye!

She's trying to finish this work and then go on a homeless binge again! What of the works do you and Jezibellie have in common, here ye!

There are quite a number of paragraphs taking a hold of this work's very deepest, darkest desires, as you try to tell your future significant other about the homelessnesses that you have encountered along the ways, here ye, and the questions about whether or not the ailment cures lady's outfits as of lately have come out being a multitasking situation, or whether or not you can fathom a picture of what dying looks like to people on the other side of this Earth's crusts, whether or not you can prayer pose this work into the dying arts of penis's peaces.

Once you publish this book, Andrea, there is no going back!

Henceforth, why publish it at all, if some people in your life are going to be this way and that a way with you, here ye! Because we've got plans for all the references in this work, and that means that this chapter is here to stay.

For all intents and purposes though, there are references here to healing schizophrenias that we haven't even covered yet! And the list goes on and on with the various techniques we sought after to heal it.

These include the following methods to our madnesses: energy medicine, affirmations, and positive thinking for one! For starters, Eckhart Tolle's The Power of Now: A Guide to Spiritual Enlightenment (2004) and A New Earth: Awakening to Your Life's Purpose (2005), are the keys to happinesses abounties. The power of the present moment, as opposed to this mindfulness crap, is the key to happinesses in my book. And finding that true spiritual happiness is key to a good life on Earth.

We're telling about all of the good techniques and services that you provided in your works on happiness, Andrea!

We just think there's more to it. We loved Louise Hay's You Can Heal Your Life (1984), so much so that we'd just assume that's the key to happinesses right there.

What about dying do you want or wish to address? Here is a way to heal from traumatic experiences, Folks, and you too, Gentiles! What do you wish and hope to accomplish in your lifetimes of hope and forgivenesses in this book, here ye?

It's abounties that we find meaningfulness's takes on self destructive behaviors, like lying or conning to get your way's meaningfuls, here ye! If God wanted us to publish this book without any techniques for healing, then how do we expect to be healed from it, schizophrenias, thereof? What about this book is healing for somebody with schizoaffective disorders?

You can nail it on the head with most people by asking them to redirect their energies to a self publishing one about pedo and murderous heads for one, and that will solve all of your problems, here ye? This can take a while, as the planet does suffer from none of it someday, correctamundos, here ye? This lady at the front office suffers from it a little bit in this hotel we're staying at, here ye, and then some! We would never just go walk up to someone and detect it in ourselves, would we? Yes, we've done this a million times, but as you're staying as a hotel guest, there are certain parameters that one must follow.

One is to keep to yourself, as long as possible. Second, there are certain things we have to do here that we'd just assume not walk up to someone and spout out a life's lessons about, or we'd get booted outs of here's ye.

And that is not any fun! What about Jesus's amnesia for His wife's a lot of what was going on back then with Himself then? He never had pedo or murderous heads then? It's just that She was married, and when Chip Tutankhemen came around and shot the President we will call him, then Jesus's amnesia suddenly lifted. We thanked him kindly for his deeds. However, he did not take payment for this dude he offed, as he thought it would be "dirty money."

He was a man who "walked the Earth," as we've heard a thousand times prior to this one lessons management phase's, kotex sounding commandant's languages, here ye's, that tons of people prior to this had or have pedo heads and murderous heads that are not even far from being docile then?

What about those others that you don't even want to give up the goods for, here ye? He's vying for your attention now, Andrea! What, she says?

This methods to your madnesses states that a Louise Hay book changed your life, or forever hold your peace about this wherewithals madnesses and stuff like it, you see it, now you don't, but this goes far! What is a life of crime like though? We've never had one like that!

We'll see about that, eh? Right now, these Less Restrictive Alternatives, LRA's, act like an assault record, for a lot of police officers out there, who love to pick people up in ambulance rides and such, but that doesn't have to be the case here in the Americas.

We love to see and to speak about this sort of thing here, Andrea, but you've got a walk to get into here! We love her physical fitness, so much so that we're trying to talent search her back into mental health by walking for fitness every day, and that much I do know about life's strenuous exercising, is that she used to be a fitness guru before all of these mental health stays to your person. Right, Andrea!

We've got a little more coffee to go before this mental health note takes hold. Notice we started drinking it again!

And right now, it looks like you're staying in a motel to save your own life.

Is that correctamundos, here ye?

If we can lessen the load off of ya, Honey, we could try to save face and just wing it from here! What do you want to do next of kinly here? We're trying to avoid the message's fates, here ye, from becoming the biggest selling author in history's makings, here ye. And we're trying to find the times to exercise the risk of fate's biggest selling cues, as in, what are they going to make me do to find the time to answer some of the sillier questions in life. Jesus Calling: Enjoying Peace in His Presence (2004) is a good book by Sarah Young, to risk it all is like that though! She's terrified at losing this moment's notices, here ye, to come out and to exercise, as it's like that though. She's risking losing it all's places that be, here ye, and coming to know the Jesus Calling book is another way to pass the time?

There's more to it than that, I hope!

There's so much to say about Jesus and Jezibellie's wakes, here ye, that commandanting the people in front of your schoolhouse rock's biggest Jezibellie cures means that people in Egypt, or Mizraim, here ye, like to call themselves cool in this respect, but they ruled, or were ruled, rather, by the Spirit.

In time, you will understand why we say, stay away from people who don't agree with you for a while, and commandant's languages and stuff like it, you see it, now you don't, will dictate how you will spend your coming years. Either, or, there will be trying times, trials and tribulations to your spirit, inner spirit wisdom, and there will become a method to your madness's greatest tribulations in Jesus and Jezibellie's spirit quests.

There is nothing like the commandant's languages, here ye, that speaks to the sounds of music production in the land of Egypt/Mizraim, here's ye.

And, that fact is the layout of the land's best witnesses, here ye, is that God is watching all of us in a comedic fashion or spirit, that overlays all there is to know about Jesus and Jezibellie's love for each other.

What is this, you say? But a question mark at the end of a sentence, like Jesus and Jezibellie's love for each other's, got to be comedic for a reason! We're stressing this time of due diligence, and we're honestly going to teriyaki that meal tonight with a kiss from above's greenest pastures! There are things you don't know about life's passionate beginnings, that really gets to the heart of the matter's textbook languages.

And, that is sweet and all, but there's lots to be thankful for's, for that is the situation "down south," in that God's got a lot of things to offer this world's biggest and bestest languages.

We're saying that a lot of turbans existing for the spirit of God's promises are the hijab wearer's dreamscape lessons in learning, that take new turbans off the market. This marketing of this book is going to become a turban wearer's dream!

What is Jesus doing without His pharaoh hat?

He's got amnesia for His wife of 30 years then? She took a picture of Him, Jezibellie did, and had Him molded into a statuette for Herself to gawk at! This statuette is one I wish I could show you here. He was standing there and had to breathe, so the nostrils are a little more focusedly pointed outwards, but that is Jesus Christ there in that picture of Himself there, if I had copyright I would show it here, she molded him into a statuette of love! If God is pure love, then Jesus Christ sure took a wife.

References

Acton, Q. Ashton, General Editor. *Herpes Simplex Virus: New Insights for the Healthcare Professional: 2013 Edition*. "Anton of Kom University van Suriname, Paramaribo: Incidence of Alpha-Herpes virus induced ocular disease in Suriname." Atlanta, GA: ScholarlyEditions, 2013, https://books.google.com/books?id=ZdGIh4IURigC&printsec=frontcover&dq=new+research+in+herpes+simplex+virus&hl=en&sa=X&ved=0ahUKEwj62dPpir_YAhVW9mMKHajjAOIQ6AEIMDAC#v=onepage&q=new%20research%20in%20herpes%20simplex%20virus&f=false

Acton, Q. Ashton, General Editor. *Herpes Simplex Virus: New Insights for the Healthcare Professional: 2013 Edition*. "Astellas Pharma Inc., Ibaraki: Susceptibility of Herpes Simplex Virus Isolated from Genital Herpes Lesions to ASP2151, A Novel Helicase-Primase Inhibitor." Atlanta, GA: ScholarlyEditions, 2013, https://books.google.com/books?id=ZdGIh4IURigC&printsec=frontcover&dq=new+research+in+herpes+simplex+virus&hl=en&sa=X&ved=0ahUKEwj62dPpirYAhVW9mMKHajjAOIQ6AEIMDAC|#v=onepage&q=new%20research%20in%20herpes%20simplex%20virus&f=false.

Atsma, Aaron J. "Kybele." Theoi Project, 2017, http://www.theoi.com/Phrygios/Kybele.html.

Behrendt, Greg, and Liz Tuccillo. *He's Just Not That Into You: The No-Excuses Truth to Understanding Guys*. New York: Simon Spotlight Entertainment, 2004.

BibleHub.Com. "Online Bible Study Suite." 2018, http://biblehub.com.

Brown, Dan. *Angels and Demons*. New York, NY: Pocket Books, 2000.

Burpo, Todd. *Heaven is for Real*. Nashville, TN: Thomas Nelson Inc., 2010.

Centers for Disease Control and Prevention. "2015 Sexually Transmitted Diseases Treatment Guidelines, Genital HSV Infections." Atlanta, GA: CDC Inc., 2015, https://www.cdc.gov/std/tg2015/herpes.htm.

Centers for Disease Control and Prevention. "B Virus (Herpes B, Monkey B Virus, Herpesvirus Simiae, and Herpesvirus B): Specimen Collection and B Virus Detection." *National Center for Immunization and Respiratory Diseases, Division of Viral Diseases.* U.S. Department of Health and Human Services, Atlanta, GA: CDC Inc., March 1, 2016, https://www.cdc.gov/herpesbvirus/specimen-collect.html.

Centers for Disease Control and Prevention. "B Virus (Herpes B, Monkey B Virus, Herpesvirus Simiae, and Herpesvirus B)." Atlanta, GA: CDC Inc., July 18, 2014, https://www.cdc.gov/herpesbvirus/index.html.

Citizen's Commission on Human Rights. "The Untold Story of Psychotropic Drugging: Making a Killing." CCHR, 2008, https://www.youtube.com/watch?v=Lo0iWh53Pjs.

CNN Library. "September 11th Terror Attacks: Fast Facts." Cable News Network, August 24, 2017, http://www.cnn.com/2013/07/27/us/september-11-anniversary-fast-facts/index.html.

Cohen, et al. "Recommendation for Prevention of and Therapy for Exposure to B Virus (Cercopithecine Herpesvirus 1)." *Clinical Infectious Diseases*, vol. 35, issue 10, 15 November 2002, p. 1191-1203, https://academic.oup.com/cid/article/35/10/1191/296729.

ConferenceSeries.Com. "6th World Congress on Control and Prevention of HIV/AIDS, STDs and STIs: August 27-29, 2018 Zurich, Switzerland." 2017, https://globalhiv-aids-std.infectiousconferences.com.

Daiichi-Sankyo. "Contacts." Daiichi-Sankyo Ltd., 2018, http://www.daiichisankyo.com/contact/index.html.

Daniel, Alma, et al. *Ask Your Angels.* New York, NY: Ballantine Books, 1992.

Des Jarlais, Don C., et al. "Associations Between Herpes Simplex Virus Type 2 and HCV with HIV Among Injecting Drug Users in New York City: The Current Importance of Sexual Transmission of HIV." *American Journal of Public Health*, 2011 July, vol. 101, no. 7, p. 1277-1283, Bethesda, MD: National Center for Biotechnology Information, U.S. National Library of Medicine, https://www.ncbi.nlm.nih.gov/pmc/articles/PMC3110210.

Diefenbach, Russell J., and Cornel Fraefel, Editors. *Herpes Simplex Virus: Methods and Protocols.* Melendez, Matias E. et al. "Herpes Simplex Virus Type 1 (HSV 1) – Derived Amplicon Vectors," p. 81-98, Springer, NY: *Volume 1144 of Methods in Molecular Biology*, 2016, http://www.springer.com/us/book/9781493904273.

Eden, Donna. *Energy Medicine: Balancing Your Body's Energies for Optimal Health, Joy and Vitality.* New York, NY: The Penguin Group, 1998.

Eden, Donna. "Quick Healing for Ocular Migraine." Innersource, 2018, https://www.innersource.net/em/963-quick-healing-for-ocular-migraine.html.

Ellis, Ralph. *Jesus: Last of the Pharaohs*. Cheshire: Edfu Books, 1988. Online version on Amazon.com.

Erlich, K.S. "Management of Herpes Simplex and Varicella-Zoster Viral Infections." Western Journal of *Medicine*, 1997 March, vol. 166, no. 3, p. 211-215, https://www.ncbi.nlm.nih.gov/pmc/articles/PMC1304126.

EvaluateGroup.Com. "Fujisawa to Launch Trichomycin K tablet an OTC Antibiotic Product." Evaluate Ltd., 2018, http://www.evaluategroup.com/Universal/View.aspx?type=Story&id=45069.

Feinstein, Alice, Ed., and Prevention Health Books. *Healing with Vitamins: The Most Effective Vitamin and Mineral Treatments for Everyday Health Problems and Serious Disease*. Emmaus, PA: Rodale, Inc., 1996.

Hay, Louise, and Mona Schulz. *All is Well: Heal Your Body with Medicine, Affirmations and Intuition*. Carlsbad, CA: Hay House, Inc., 2014.

Hay, Louise. *You Can Heal Your Life*. Carlsbad, CA: Hay House, Inc., 1984.

Hicks, Esther. "About Abraham-Hicks." Abraham-Hicks Publications, 2018, https://www.abraham-hicks.com/about.

Hicks, Esther and Jerry. *The Law of Attraction: The Basics of the Teachings of Abraham*. Carlsbad, CA: Hay House, Inc., 2006.

The Holy Bible: Containing the Old and New Testaments, The Gideons Interntational. Thomas Nelson, Inc., 1985.

The Holy Bible: Old and New Testaments in the King James Version. Thomas Nelson Inc., 1976.

Howell, Elizabeth. "10 Exoplanets That Could Host Alien Life." Space.Com, Purch, April 17, 2014, http://www.space.com/18790-habitable-exoplanets-catalog-photos.html.

Journal of HIV and Retro Virus. "Highly Active Antiretroviral Therapy." iMedPub.Com, 2018, http://www.imedpub.com/scholarly/highly-active-antiretroviral-therapy-journals-articles-ppts-list.php.

Landy Enterprise Limited. Anhui, China: Alibaba.Com, 2018, http://ahlandy.en.alibaba.com/company_profile.html?spm=a2700.9099375.35.5.104f070awQ8oOC#top-nav-bar.

Layton, Kelley. "Herpes Simplex Virus." Austin Community College: Austin, Texas, http://www.austincc.edu/microbio/2993r/hsv.

Marketman. "Market Manila: Takla/Crayfish/Crawfish." May 8, 2010, www.marketmanila.com/archives/takla-crayfish-crawfish.

Missouri Botanical Garden. "Corydalis lutea." St. Louis, Missouri. 2018, http://www.missouribotanicalgarden.org/PlantFinder/PlantFinderDetails.aspx?kempercode=y840.

NYU Langone Hospital – Brooklyn. "Herpes Zoster." NYU Langone Health: Brooklyn, NY, 2009, http://www.lutheranhealthcare.org/EmergencyMedicine/AdamEncyclopedia/1000858.aspx.

Ohashi, Masahiro, et al. "Spread of Herpes Simplex Virus to the Spinal Cord is Independent of Spread to Dorsal Root Ganglia." *Journal of Virology*, vol. 85, no. 6, March 2011, *American Society for Microbiology*, http://jvi.asm.org/content/85/6/3030.abstract.

Outmatch. "How to Make Magnesium Bicarbonate Water (Recipe)." The Hearty Soul, 2017, https://theheartysoul.com/magnesium-water-recipe.

Pack, McKinzie Brocail. "Everything About Herpes 1 & 2 and HSV Testing." Exposed: STDcheck.com Blog, July 31, 2015, https://www.stdcheck.com/blog/everything-about-herpes-1-2-and-hsv-testing.

Porter, Robert S. and Justin L. Kaplan. *The Merck Manual of Diagnosis and Therapy*. Whitehouse Station, NJ: Merck Sharp & Dohme Corp, 2011. Print.

PubChem. "Barium Cadmium Stearate: Compound Summary for CID 6336539." Bethesda, MD: U.S. National Library of Medicine, National Center for Biotechnology Information, National Institutes of Health, 08-08-2005, https://pubchem.ncbi.nlm.nih.gov/compound/6336539#section=Top.

Sacks, Stephen. "Herpes Virus – 8 Types." MedBroadcast, MediResource, Inc., 2017, http://www.medbroadcast.com/channel/infection/herpes/herpes-virus-8-types.

Schucman, Helen. *A Course in Miracles*. Mill Valley, CA: Foundation for Inner Peace, 1975. Online version, https://www.acim.org.

The Story of God - Holy Bible: New International Version. Colorado Springs, CO: International Bible Society, 1984.

StudyLight.Org. "Bible Encyclopedias - 1911 Encyclopedia Britannica: Cadmium." 2018, https://www.studylight.org/encyclopedias/bri/c/cadmium.html.

Tolle, Eckhart. *A New Earth: Awakening to Your Life's Purpose.* New York, NY: Dutton/Penguin Group, 2005.

Tolle, Eckhart. *The Power of Now: A Guide to Spiritual Enlightenment.* Vancouver, B.C.: Namaste Publishing, 2004.

Unknown. "First for Women." 5-16-16. Englewood Cliffs, NJ: Bauer Publishing.

The Urban Dictionary, 2018, https://www.urbandictionary.com.

WebMD. "Herpes Simplex: Herpes Type 1 and 2." WebMD, 2016, https://www.webmd.com/genital-herpes/pain-management-herpes#1-2.

Wells, Christine and Laura Schultz. "Vitamin D and Lanolin." Gentle World, February 29, 2012, http://gentleworld.org/vitamin-d-and-lanolin.

Wikipedia. "Al-Qaeda." January 17, 2018, https://en.wikipedia.org/wiki/Al-Qaeda.

Wikipedia. "Archbasilica of St. John Lateran." January 1, 2018, https://en.wikipedia.org/wiki/Archbasilica_of_St._John_Lateran.

Wikipedia. "Cadmium." January 4, 2018, https://en.wikipedia.org/wiki/Cadmium.

Wikipedia. "Cadmium Sulfate." November 12, 2017, https://en.wikipedia.org/wiki/Cadmium_sulfate.

Wikipedia. "Lanolin." May 17, 2018, https://en.wikipedia.org/wiki/Lanolin.

Workowski, Kimberly A., et al. "Sexually Transmitted Diseases Treatment Guidelines, 2010." December 17, 2010, vol. 59, no. RR12, p. 1-110. Atlanta, GA: Centers for Disease Control and Prevention, 2010, https://www.cdc.gov/mmwr/preview/mmwrhtml/rr5912a1.htm.

Young, Sarah. *Jesus Calling: Enjoying Peace in His Presence.* Nashville, TN: Thomas Nelson, Inc., 2004.

Appendix 1

Our Sanctified Promises Rule! Justice, Be Served Here!

Andrea Barberi
1420 Marvin Road NE #C217
Lacey, WA 98516

November 17, 2014

Dear U.S. Congress and Centers for Disease Control and Prevention;

I am an intuitive healer who likes the idea of ailment cures so much I can tell if it is time to give and receive the good of the information I am given. That being the case, then true to form is the timing of this document with the travesty called life. If you can find the time to do this, I would love to discuss the travesty called timing of the document involved in finding the cure for HSV 1, 2 and 3. If you are ready for a phone call regarding my intellect on the topic I will discuss gaining knowledge of the antigen involved in the HSV cure.

In other words, the antigen is finally solvable, and yet the antibody is already in progress. According to Dr. D, he already has the working antibody for the gene pool. So simply put, the meaning behind the words rings true, as far as the antigen for the antibody, but the progress is simply done. The antigens for the antibody are so intuitively simple it is hard to be complex about the idea of curing it at all costs to those involved in the antibody cure itself. Yet there must be an explanation for all this. All I can say is, why not listen to the judgment rather than explain it away to others? If all I can say is based on listening, then why not judge it for sure? I say go for it. It does sound like a vaccine everyone can benefit from having. However, I have not figured out the antigen without the help of Mr. D as well as his counterpart Mr. Z.

Some of the reason for living comes from the senses. Some of the antibodies for HSV 1 are valerian roots, others are from remedies for HSV 3. If HSV 1 has antigens already then HSV 3 would have them too. Unbeknownst to me I am remedying them as timing is concerned to be the decision here. HSV 1 has several prognosis type antigens already in progress from the meaning inside the root word "find." In other words, how about a consistent play on words for the rest of the antibodies involved so that we can find the cure for it? If you find the time, give me a chance to describe the product HerpeSelect on words. Then I will find that it is off from finding the cure itself. Other than that, it is necessary to regulate the cure rather than receive it fully intact. I could not find the time to discuss it further at this point.

When I solved the problem for the Trichomonas virus in Japan, manufacturer's date of 1957, the pill involved called Trichomycin was readily available in the U.S. until it was discharged in 1973. For lack of a better way of saying this, it needs to come back two-fold. Not only is it the only way for Americans to ensure themselves the best possible ailment cure for Trichomonas cures, the remedies for it have been sold across the U.S. For a time, the antigens for this were available for several days, and then they were taken off the market. I predict an ailment cure for Trichomonas after we get the pill back from Japan and it fully gets taken by the 20 million Americans who have the Trichomonas ailment cure in their bloodstream, let alone their organs too.

I found that enzymatic enzymes are the remedy for HSV involving the test of time to receive the good in all sources. In essence then, the wrong HSV cure seems to be some assays, as the antibody seems to be intact as I said. The test for that is a good one as it cleans itself of the product motive behind the cure itself, as people are gladly able to receive the vaccine for it soon through government agencies colliding in each other about the cure for both Herpes Simplex as well as the cure for Trichomonas. Both beneficial to us in the U.S. is the basis for this letter in the first place. It is intuitively inspired and latently given to the cure itself through alternative means of therapeutic resources. A viral antigen is available for copy from a source outside the U.S. It is not an antibody per se, but an ailment cure for noxious substances.

In other words, no one has taken it further than this before, even though Dr. D has found the working antibody for it. The PCR or Viral antigen test is failing across the U.S. and antigens for finding the markers on surface cells has yet to be studied thoroughly. The polymerase chain is better. Spinal fluid only gives the surface cells something to hang onto.

Only the serum HSV antibody needs to be taken in order to be discovered and for it to work. Healthline.com cites antibodies and 200 national ailments, yet thousands go without the cure each year. In other words, you already have it all figured out, you just need to trust it is the right cure and not the wrong one. Meaning, don't count on this document alone to be the cure. It's just an antibody gene that makes it right inside and not outside the box we are looking for.

So, it is. This document alone is the antibody gene we have been expecting. The reason for its candor is the fact that it can only be taken literally rather than meaningfully. The best part of this job is the time it takes them to reiterate the fact that each moment you are perplexed by this cure, the best part of the job is already in process. In other words, go forth as it is now and not as it is later. The antibody is already in the antigen test they take for the virus itself. In other words, go forth with it you guys, as this is the cure for HSV 1, 2 and 3 viruses. (This is taken from the Divine Source Wisdom's phone numbers you are to have here! For future references though, take what you can give Us and not mention anything that time cannot dictate here! This moment's notices are for the birds here if we cannot begin to mention all of the turmoils of our literatures here!)

I hope to bring forth more tomorrows for tidings such as this one for you as well as this great nation we call Life in front of us too.

I can be reached at bandreaw@yahoo.com or at 1420 Marvin Rd NE #C217, Lacey, WA 98516. I like the idea of face to face contact to ensure this is the right ailment cure we are speaking of.

Sincerely,

Andrea Barberi

Appendix 2

Worst Case Scenario! An LRA No More Here!

Andrea W. Barberi
1420 Marvin Road NE #C217
Lacey, WA 98516

November 19, 2014

Dear Dr. X., U.S. Congress, House of Representatives and U.S. Senate;

I regard this letter as both late and overdue. The attached letter states that if I decide to stop services at any time with you after ten days I am required by law to notify you of such a choice, and in turn to notify my case manager. However, instead of regarding my wishes as honest and desirable, considering the late notice on my regard to cut off all ties with mental health care, to let my primary care physician reside in place of my mental health records, I require you to honor my request and please let me decide for myself whether or not I regard your services as utmost quality or quantity, and to pleasantly back away from all mental health care services from you and your facility.

This is the best case scenario, to involve the government in your decision to attain a detainment against my will. I will involve Congress and other entities in my decision to treat you for your detainment. I am onto your ailments, especially the one involving sanctity of trust with my family involved.

This is especially the case when you are simply concerned with tax evasion, let alone schizophrenic tendencies in yourself, requiring your continued dose of 500mg Seroquel to sustain your identity into the afterlife. With no good reason for keeping me on a lethal dose of 800mg at my stature, creating pre-diabetes like symptoms. The only run of Navane in history was accustomed to my pride on the situation in that afterwards I was succumbed to 800mg trial doses of Seroquel after taking me completely off the indicated clearance-based summary of the only antipsychotic that actually works for me. The more I hear that I have not stayed on my medication, the more I consider it a farce that you're even in office in my town. Not only have I taken the medication, I have current health issues to prove my continued relapse into this profession. It is apparent to me your reasons for dropping behind the door for these reasons are lethal for your own good, and I demand that you let me go because of it.

Right now, on a 90-Day Less Restrictive Alternative (LRA) holding on my premises with my name attached, I am gravely insulted by the insinuation that I never take care of my own needs. Not only now that I am backing away from services as I did prior to this detainment on my body, mind and spirit, I detached significantly from your services within the confines of predicament to receive services elsewhere. However, you failed to honor my request, and according to your case manager Dr. T and I am detained in an utmost disrespectful fashion. I demand notice that takes me off this LRA, as it is both a farce and an atrocity to be in such a low-level status among the Level 4 assessment intake you gave me post hospitalization, and the lethal dose of Seroquel I was put on post hospital, taking you to new levels within yourself to release me, or the government will. Office of Quality Monitoring has qualified me as healed status, based on its monitoring quality during both my detainments.

Unfortunately, enough for me, I am detailed enough to forget all the mishaps that qualified me to be as such in two recent hospital stays. The qualified doctors brought me off the entirely lethal dose of Seroquel down to a normal range amount. They said it was "recommended" I keep my appointment with Dr. X but not required due to her negligence at my hearing. I now receive my medical care elsewhere, which is definitely NOT part of the squabble to find me guilty of all ailment cures in their office also. I do not claim allegiance to that office for the simple fact that they are not on board with treating people for mental conditions who would like reproductive status.

I can assure you I am here to bring good to a nation. Through the advice of my doctors, I have not discussed it with anyone other than these two facilities. They found me to be quite interesting and detained, yet finding no real basis for holding me past the number of times they detained me for in the past before healing schizophrenia turned schizoaffective disorder, bipolar type, plan end date suffice it to say has been lethally lengthened to beyond the measure imposed for. In which case, April is way beyond the 90-day hold, and 60 days from now speaks volumes to your detained status. Which reminds me, how much did you say I skipped out on my student loans for? Please reinstate them. I have got too much work to do, much of which has to do with healing this lifetime label from being lifetimeable and becoming one of the disease epidemics that must in essence have a cure. Otherwise, who's counting on the number of people you have defrauded in history, let alone the epidemic cure itself?

It is truly an epidemic to consider schizophrenia as someone's blood type, especially when screened for digestive issues, pancreatitis, homophobia, and discretionary deliverance of evil services from God. My intake at the above facility of choice has been detained only to find out I am free of all delivery of services indicating I am both evil and detainable. In other words, there is no fat reason for detaining me under an LRA if I am both sane and comfortable with my skin intact. I have never been a danger to myself and others involved in my care. I certainly have never been the "gravely disabled" status they detained me under, simply because I heard an intuition greater than the sky above me as well as all of us on this Earth today. Simply put, how about an ailment cure for schizophrenia and schizophrenia like symptoms? It is an ailment cure for this lifetime to be able to heal ourselves from trauma, and we've all got a story of our own.

No one in their right mind wants to be on an LRA, especially when their method for living freely comes into play. My detained status is impeding on my life vision, and quite possibly on my fight to receive the good from all sources, namely to get a job well suited for my vision for healing schizophrenia. Detained is the status of schizoaffective bipolar type, and while this vision for healing exists, no one in their status of affective anything is going to get me off the rocker so to speak.

In order to hear myself correctly these days, I am the cure for schizophrenia. For to see it from my perspective is to detain myself simply because I believed in life after public mental health qualifies me to leave an LRA status in order to gain my composure within the community as a lifelong healer and qualifies me to heal rapidly from it. Please do me the honor of receding this claim against my mentality and detain me no more. I need your help Congress to release the bonds created by one on one cultdom, and to realize my predicament is to help people, not detain them further from this life we once led as children.

On September 12, 2014, I received a letter for which I attempted to escape your facility on the idea that I had healed something unhealable. At least considering the circumstances of that event entirely escaped my policy of faith and fate-based healing premises. However, Dr. X escapes the law of timing in her analysis on March 5, 2014, when she denounced the fact that it could be healed at all. The 350mg to 800mg jump in progress on the part of the hospital to detain me further to experiment on me as a live human subject was the ability to see the good in all this detainment. I developed extremely strong diabetic symptoms from that dosage increase and literally could not function beyond mere pleasantries after that. How can human consumption of gravely disabled beings, such as those who bathe regularly, get dressed, eat, drink water and other consumables and sleep quite pleasantly be detained for a hearing vision of God? Me, of course.

Dr. X blatantly stated a schizophrenic person cannot heal from their trauma enough to escape being called that label. For the rest of her own life I presume is her own trauma as well as my own. Yet I do not entirely agree with her approach. So, I predict a struggle on her part to detain me further with her innuendo that I cannot or have not healed from it at all, as well as a claim on her life to continue her job. Knowing full well she is schizophrenic also and does not claim to be, I claim to test her on her premise by detaining her fully into the know and rightfully so giving her an examination to thoroughly be sure she is prescribing herself the right dose of Seroquel on a regular basis before she even admits to it.

For Congress:

Included in these documents is a series of perplexities that have baffled the minds and hearts of sight for me. For periods unknown to me, this LRA has made me without home, and without bail of any kind of promise for the future. Without this knowledge of curing mental illness itself under my belt at all, please revoke this atrocity at once or I will threaten them with calling the police department to deal with her refusal to treat me.

And yet upon my release from each facility, gradually deteriorating status of mine has been said to be schizoaffective bipolar type, which indeed is two steps up from previous diagnoses I have received in the past. It is both adequate and perplexing to say I have healed something at least. My new approaches to healing have included many different tools regarding self-healing from traumatic events, all of which are included in my source documents both at home and in my storage unit, treating myself as an individual without bail of knowledge rather than complete hiding of detail to begin with. No two persons at each facility could come up with an explanation for why I now hear the Divine Source Wisdom that I do. They could only detain me further if I declared I hear a Source Wisdom of which I fully do on paper and not in heart, as I am sound in mind only.

Dr. X lied about a diagnostic exam given to me on August 13, 2014. According to the Medicare Summary Notice, Medicare was charged with a "psychiatric diagnostic evaluation with medical services," when I received no such thing at all. I blatantly told her I was healing schizoaffective and told her of some of the tools I used to do so. I asked her in the hallway if she was ready to take the journey with me. She countered with asking me if I trusted her, of which I asked her to consider the consequences of not trusting me back. After a supervised run of medication adjustments, her only response was, "Get back up on 600mg!"

I have included a long list of approaches and topics which was Louise Hay's approach to healing mind, body and spirit, as well as Eckhart Tolle's mind-body experience too. She failed to do any real assessment on me that day, and in fact was kind, yet berserk, at the idea of "God" being the true healer. When in all actuality she suffers from schizophrenia as well and denies the fact that one can heal themselves of trauma simply because we all have had some traumatic experiences.

Because she came to me in a direct manner of healing herself from it as well, she cautioned me against any real evidence supposing I had healed myself of anything at all. The basic premise of her argument was because I had attained the good life ahead of me by attracting the Divine Source Wisdom that I now have at my discretion. Yet now however I have an LRA stating I detain myself further by acknowledging the good, and so therefore there is no real basis to have me be evaluated. Even though she added her analysis on myself included in her documents prior to this date while failing to quiz me on anything at all related to mental health, the latter part of which saved me from traumatic abuse which created the condition in the first place, an additional charge was also added. This is considered insurance fraud. Based on her current work research on the topic itself, it behooves me that she cannot see the light in her error of judgment to base any sole repertoire on her person.

Because I am hard at work with other ailment cures for myself and all of humanity, please note this action can and will be the best thing of all. To others it may seem trivial to claim I have a healed mental status at all. However, I can assure you it is the best thing for the country to seemingly forgive me of the right to atrocious statuses such as this LRA holding on myself included. In the document below, I cite one special error of judgment on Dr. X's part about a hold on my delinquent status to cite one other kind of hold: God. That remains to be seen as far as ailment cures are concerned. I did however cite in my references a piece that gives you the right to see this as fair and adequate in judgment and not see the benefits of me personally giving this to Christ. At all costs please find myself included in this proclamation that I have healed myself of all psychiatric disorders now and in the close future.

Dr. X states the LRA must be contained within the context of my receiving the good from all sources of income, and yet prides herself upon the idea of winning two gifts from God. Upon which sources of income do people wish to be detained for the lifetime of pheasants that grace her with our Lord's presence? She did no such diagnostic for me on the 13th of August as stated in my paperwork. I am calling her out on this, as that session clearly stated my desire to heal from this traumatic event and not transpose someone into thinking they are healed from it.

Take me off the LRA and comply with the code of ethics involved in treating someone with schizophrenia or schizophrenia like symptoms properly. I am. I would like to honor fully the attached letter, in that I no longer receive services or care from them. I will beg to differ my confirmed status of "healed" and healing the innocent complies with this statement quite well I might add.

I have a series of tests which include all the basic needs as well as capacity to induce medical clearance for whatever comes with me, including the capacity to have the grounding I need to be an intuitive healer. However, I never know which test I need until it becomes apparent I need it. Included of which is the capacity to learn as well as be learned about. I hear in my head that which is called light and love.

Just because I am a healing intuitive dancer also does not mean I cannot enjoy the dancing effect fully while on medication, of which I am fully taking. It does not behoove me at all to dance in a psych ward because I am still a dance fitness instructor anyway regardless of treatment value here at all. I would like to become fully employed as a natural healing effect person with intuitive sense about healing remedies and ailment cures. Yet I keep being evaluated and reevaluated as someone who came from planet Mars and aligns the Spirit with holes in her head.

As far as healing schizoaffective disorder itself, both the detained premises have quibbled over this quite a bit. As far as I am concerned, it's about life, liberty and property. Please release me from this bond of premise and consider me death to life, liberty and peace making, and please find me among the healed, through Jesus Our Lord and Savior as well as God's will, dictating me to equally be of service to anyone who wants to heal from schizophrenia. I would like to provide the means and the opportunity to help anyone who wants to heal their minds from trauma, as each one of us has a story pertaining to life, liberty and property.

I will gladly be of service to anyone who wants me to call them insightful as well as the ability in me to pick out the pride and prejudice of this nation's Capitol building. Please consider me healthy and respectfully bowing out of mental health care which is used at my discretion and no other way around this precedes this here now. My luck is going out the door with these ailment cures, and the only way around this is to tell you personally that I am out the door with every single one of these ailments. I also enjoy intuitively giving advice on how to cure people of their own ailments. Please allow me the space and time to do so as there is much work to be done.

Since the LR, I have lost the use of my phone, as well as living with life, liberty and property. Involving myself in these premises of detaining me longer has willingly brought against the facility a guilty verdict for X to vacate the premises, to vacate the LRA status, and to willingly leave this community. I have several reasons for this. Basically, call me a liar again, and I will find you guilty of treason. For this is the life we have, and Christ involved as you say He is in your life, for the first time ever, releases you from any punishment in the matter.

I demand this LRA be revoked and my healed status be recognized for what it is, supervised by none other than myself included in my own care. Reveal to me the reason for keeping me in this LRA by judging me no more. I have had medical as well as sound advice from above that clears me from this detainment. Please find it in your hearts to release this bond, fully and completely in the know that I fully intend on giving as much as possible to the public at large, and no more will I fear the consequences of doing such good deeds as these things I have stated thereof.

Sincerely,

Andrea W. Barberi

Appendix 3

A Time for Justice to Be Served

Andrea Barberi
1420 Marvin Road NE, #C217
Lacey, WA 98516
USA

November 14, 2014

Centers for Disease Control and Prevention (CDC)
1600 Clifton Road
Atlanta, Georgia 30329-4027

Dear Centers for Disease Control and Prevention;

I have a question regarding the Trichomycin K Tablet manufactured by Daiichi-Sankyo in 1957. Please reference the article: http://www.evaluategroup.com/Universal/View. aspx?type=Story&id=45069 to know which cure for the Trichomonas virus. It is available from Daiichi Sankyo at the following website link for the contact page regarding this issue of selling it to the U.S.: http://www.daiichisankyo.com/contact/index.html.

I know many people in the U.S. alone have Trichomoniasis and Trichomonas viruses in their bloodstream, not to mention in the internal organs. However, undetectable as they are through standard test remedies in our country, I would be happy to verify this with the intuitive tools I have been given by God to work with this sort of thing on a regular basis. I would like to regard my capabilities as something special. However, the sooner we get the Trichomonas virus out of the country as a nation and a capital diplomatic state of mind, the better off the world will be, as this pill actually works as an ailment cure for the disease.

I spoke with an official last September with Daiichi-Sankyo in Tokyo, Japan, who spoke with me about the possibility of a pill or a shot format, and is highly effective for curing this. I have decided to regard my information as plausible. However, the mental health society in our state regards me as recordless on the matter. I have contacted the U.S. Department of Health and Human Services, as well as the National Institute of Health. However, again, this is an individual matter and subject to change on a whim's notice.

I need to be spoken to about the possibility of gaining knowledge of this pill's availability in the U.S. Market. Please regard me as a concerned citizen who likes the idea of dealing with the public so much that I will be willing to bet the idea of a cure for Trichomonas in our world's country alone will suffice.

A blood test would perhaps catch this if it is in the form of a yeast infection that gathers itself throughout the body. A naturopathic physician was able to detect it last month using a Thermographic machine using a thermometer type investigation to show the presence of yeast in and under my skin, let alone the organs involved in the matter at hand.

Please note that I am not a psychic healer, just a health intuitive with a sense of direction and a basis for living, freely, among the public eye. However, I have not been able to verify and identify that this virus agent is ready for public consumption without your involvement. Please make the pill in tablet form available in the U.S. as soon as possible. There is also a stronger remedy of the shot format that is available for public consumption as well as my own benefit. There is a format available in the UK with Daiichi Sankyo at the helm. However, it is most beneficial to contact them directly instead of buying it from the UK manufacturer.

Please let me know what I can do to help. If you contact me my address is: 1420 Marvin Road NE, #C217, Lacey, WA 98516. My email is bandreaw@yahoo.com.

The Ebola scare from the first class of diseases to appear after 9/11 is no more, simply a hoax. I have other intuitive senses on how to investigate the knowledge of research cures for schizophrenia and schizoaffective bipolar and depressed types also. I am willing to bet that an ailment cure for simple complex viruses like Herpes Simplex Virus is on the horizon from me, as duty calls for us as a nation and as a world ailment cure to research these ailment cures fully. There are ten types worldwide and I am willing to work on them full force ahead using my medical and health intuition for help resources as a guide.

Please contact me soon on the matter.

Sincerely,

Andrea W. Barberi

Appendix 4

NASA's Space Station, Elite Button Please!

Andrea Barberi
1420 Marvin Road NE, PMB C217
Lacey, WA 98516

February 3, 2017

National Aeronautics and Space Administration
300 E Street SW, Suite 5R30
Washington, DC 20546

Dear NASA;

If in time you seek refuge through reverent means, this means that the space station in Albuquerque, New Mexico, will suffice!

I am looking at the page: http://www.space.com/18790-habitable-exoplanets-catalog-photos.html, for reference here. The stars look the same. Don't they!

I am the Divine Source Wisdom speaks it. And I don't know what I'm saying to you is grand enough for consumption. But here goes!

The only exoplanets we are looking at here are the starship kind! Let's go home and look at the stars some more! According to the University of Puerto Rico at Arecibo, there are monster kinds of knowledge-based planets available for consumption on it. The website thereof presents three major problems with its linguistic gunfire, namely for the ill at heart, but not for Us to decide.

Keep in mind the play station efforts to confiscate the goods here decides our fate too. In other words, what does it prove to have planets a, b and c to tell them by?

The ten that host "alien life" are four, really. To detail them would be futile on the website thereof. One day the F-15 will arrive with alien life on it. Keplar-186f and the next one of Gliese 581g are just microcosms for us here. There's no such thing as Gliese 581g. It's still in its infancy, and there are just as many stars to think about than to risk our lives at seeing. Gliese 581g doesn't have a parent star then! It's just as Gliese as they come though, Gliese meaning "free will", a red dwarf star. No, it's not! Its movement is shaded by the nasty gram for us! It means, Folks, that there's life on red dwarf stars no more.

Keplar-22 is a planet with a lot of life on it. So far, we've been able to tell none of it from dwarf visions of ailment cures all over Earth, with a planet life on it that we can see clearly from the naked eye view that is!

The so called Super-Earth, HD40307g planet is gone from our atmosphere quite readily we may add!

HD85512b has no life on Earth! No water either.

"Tau Ceti e" is a peculiar planet indeed, certainly there's no life on it either! Save a few hundred souls whose rescuable parts are peculiar indeed, as well as plentiful.

One thing to note is that Venus is no scorcher indeed, like the article professes to say! It's supposed to be lightyears from us too, however. There's 3 or 4 different planets like this in the solar system though! It's comedy and tragedy from God's perspectives to live on a planet such as Venus is. Gliese 163c is supposed to shine through as a cosmos planetary alignment with God at the helm. It's a fictitious planet at best, hardly one to shine through anything at that rate. It's not in the planet Neptune's radius, nor in lightyears away from heaven's gate. This is supposed to be the speed of light. However, we are done here analyzing this article. Back inside of Wikipedia for this planet Gliese 581 either or, as its parent star is so dust!

Thank you for analyzing its tides and ebbs and flows of Earth's crust!

Sincerely,

Andrea W. Barberi
bandreaw@yahoo.com